ABOUT THE AUTHORS

J im and Barbara Willis bring varied backgrounds to this study of religious and scientific theories regarding the possibility of the end of life as we know it.

Jim has served as an ordained minister with the United Church of Christ for more than thirty years. He is an author, musician, college professor, and lecturer, teaching courses in comparative religion and cross-cultural studies. His study of the world's religions, *The Religion Book: Places, Prophets, Saints, and Seers*, was published by Visible Ink Press in 2004. He has recorded and produced two albums of gospel music while serving as the writer, producer, and host of the *Through the Bible* series, a daily drive-time radio program. His hobby is long-distance bicycle riding, which he documents in *Journey Home: The Inner Life of a Long-Distance Bicycle Rider*, published in 2002.

Barbara was born on Guam in the Marianas Islands in the Pacific and lived on Saint Croix in the Caribbean and Martha's Vineyard off the coast of Massachusetts. She has also lived in Italy and South America, as well as California, Arizona, Virginia, Washington, D.C., and various New England states. She has an extensive history in community theater and has worked in occupations as varied as real estate, newspaper advertising, the restaurant business, and library research.

While doing most of the background study for this book, they lived for a year and a half in a thirty-foot fifth-wheel RV trailer, traveling throughout the Southwest but calling Nogales, Arizona, home.

When not engaged in historical research, writing books, hiking, or singing folk concerts, Jim and Barbara do ministry together in Florida, where Jim is senior pastor of the Port Orange United Church of Christ.

ARMAGEDDON

This book is dedicated to
(in chronological order)

Adam, Jim, Mariana, Melissa, Jan,
Skyla, Joey, and Sam

You are the pathfinders who will
find the way to our future.

ARMAGEDDON

THE END OF THE WORLD
A to Z

JIM WILLIS AND BARBARA WILLIS

FALL RIVER PRESS

Jacket art © Andy McClelland
Jacket design by Igor Satanovsky

Fall River Press
122 Fifth Avenue
New York, NY 10011

ISBN: 978-1-4351-1602-3

Printed and bound in the United States of America

10 9 8 7 6 5 4 3 2 1

CONTENTS

INTRODUCTION

Starting in 542 CE, bubonic plague swept across Europe, stretching as far as the British Isles. The death rate reached proportions similar to what a nuclear holocaust might have produced. Whole cities were abandoned and simply disappeared. Anarchy ruled. Uneducated peasants, caught in a religious trough between the old way we now call Druidism and the new faith of Roman Christianity, sought relief in one or the other. Meanwhile, scholars began to predict, and perhaps even welcome, the end of the world. A groundswell of religious eschatological hope carried the yearning for a better tomorrow as payment for the suffering of today.

On October 5, 1813, at the battle of the Thames in Ontario, the great Shawnee war leader Tecumseh was killed while protecting a British retreat from American forces during the War of 1812. His body was never located, and rumors persisted that he not only had prophesied this very event but also had vowed to rise from death to lead his people in a victorious return to an almost mythical golden age before the coming of the whites.

In July of 1945, a mushroom-shaped cloud towered over Alamogordo, New Mexico, marking the beginning of the nuclear age. Never before had the human race unleashed such power—a power that owes its inception to the forces of war and destruction.

Beginning in 1957, British scientists began measuring the earth's protective ozone layer over Antarctica. By 1984 it became apparent that something was wrong. A large seasonal hole had appeared. Arguments swirled around possible causes. Some insisted that the breach was a naturally occurring phenomenon. Others accumulated evidence suggesting it might foreshadow a human-induced ecological disaster.

Over the course of a few brilliant summer nights in 1994, scientists watched with awe as the comet Shoemaker-Levy 9 broke apart and slammed into the planet Jupiter. Pictures that flashed around the world showing the July 16–22 event were both spectacular and unnerving. In cosmic terms, Jupiter isn't that far away. What if Earth had been the target?

Peering into the void, *Armageddon Now: The End of the World A to Z* crosses the religious and secular divide to examine the history of apocalyptic beliefs. This encyclopedic, multicultural overview covers doomsday theories, predictions, omens, revelations, and speculations; prophets, proselytizers, physicists, theologians, presidents, and prime ministers; and historic events, biblical accounts, and contemporary phenomena related to a growing endtime undercurrent in the popular culture. From the Rapture to the Resurrection, *Armageddon Now* explores and explains end-of-the-world scenarios from scientific, secular, religious, and supernatural points of view.

Among the nearly two hundred entries, many, as might be expected, touch upon religion. After all, scenarios about the end of the world, or at least of the human race, figure prominently in the scriptures and doctrines of many religions and have done so for thousands of years. The beliefs of Buddhists, Hindus, Native Americans, New Age groups, and many others find their place in *Armageddon Now*. In America today, a sizable and vocal minority of Christians believe strongly in a literal Armageddon—a final battle between good and evil—that many of them expect to experience firsthand. And some, using scripture as prophecy, interpret political, economic, or natural events, from the establishment of the European Common Market to the death of Pope John Paul II, as omens that the end is nigh.

But the concept of Armageddon doesn't end with religious theories. So pervasive has the word become that even secular predictions of disaster often warn of an "ecological Armageddon" or a "nuclear Armageddon." And so the scientific community has a voice in these pages as well. We look at potential destroyers of humankind as small as viruses and as large as comets and asteroids. We examine human-caused devastation and naturally occurring phenomena. We consider the effects of uncontrolled population expansion, the depletion of natural resources, global warming, disease, political strife, and technology run amok. We review scenarios that involve the utter destruction of humanity and those that signal an end to a civilization or lifestyle as we know it.

Nor are the avowedly religious and plainly scientific standpoints the whole story. For example, *Armageddon Now* considers the predictions of Nostradamus and Edgar Cayce, prophets of the past. It delves into American Indian traditions and examines the Mayan calendar for clues to the possible timing of the earth's final days.

Armageddon Now also summarizes Hollywood's serious and not-so-serious treatments of a favorite topic: the end of the world and postapocalyptic anxiety. And we present case studies showing what happens when prophets gather believers around them to await the end, only to have their hopes dashed when the end doesn't arrive.

Some eighty illustrations help bring the last days into focus, and a bibliography offers sources for further doomsday study. Fire or ice, bang or whimper, asteroid or alien, act of God or human folly, *Armageddon Now: The End of the World A to Z* offers the first and last word on the end of everything.

ACKNOWLEDGMENTS

A book surveying a religious, scientific, and historical landscape as broad as this could not have come into being without a copy editor who is secure in his craft. He must also possess familiarity with a wide-ranging host of academic disciplines. Gerry Anders is such an editor. He knows where to draw lines and he knows how to have fun. He will not allow any claimed scientific fact to go unchallenged, but he appreciates silly science-fiction movies, too. Gerry can talk at some length about American evangelical theology or the latest theories from Stephen Hawking while remembering details about *Superman and the Mole Men* that I have long since forgotten.

As always, Christa Gainor of Visible Ink Press offered a sounding board, shoulder to cry on, and general psychological prop. The "Joey" mentioned in the dedication is her son. The other names are those of our kids (now grown up) and grandkids. May they live in a world that learns lessons from its past.

While the draft for most of this book was being written we lived in Nogales, Arizona, and ministered to the United Churches Fellowship there on the border. Emery Boepple served as our administrative assistant and was always ready to talk, commiserate, and exchange ideas. Emery and the people of UCF will always have a special place in our hearts.

The people of the Smoki Museum in Prescott, Arizona, introduced us to the Hopi, but we also want to thank those who work in America's great jewels: our national and state park systems. Wherever our research carried us as we studied the Anasazi and Mound Builders, the employees and volunteers of our parks went out of their way to help us dig deeper into the myths and legends of past American cultures.

The authors also thank proofreader Vanessa Torrado-Caputo, indexer Lawrence Baker, permissions manager Diane Sawinski, photo digitizer Robert Huffman, designer Mary Claire Krzewinski, typesetter Marco Di Vita of the Graphix

Group, and Visible Inkers Martin Connors, Roger Jänecke, Roger Matuz, Mary Beth Perrot, and Terri Schell.

To all of you: Thank you!

ARMAGEDDON NOW: THE END OF THE WORLD A TO Z

ABOMINATION OF DESOLATION

"So when you see standing in the holy place 'the abomination that causes desolation,' spoken of through the prophet Daniel—let the reader understand—then let those who are in Judea flee to the mountains. Let no one on the roof of his house go down to take anything out of the house. Let no one in the field go back to get his cloak. How dreadful it will be in those days for pregnant women and nursing mothers! Pray that your flight will not take place in winter or on the Sabbath. For then there will be great distress unequaled from the beginning of the world until now—and never to be equaled again. If those days had not been cut short, no one would survive, but for the sake of the elect those days will be shortened…. See, I have told you ahead of time…. Immediately after the distress of those days

'the sun will be darkened,
  and the moon will not give its light;
the stars will fall from the sky,
  and the heavenly bodies will be shaken.'" (Matt. 24:15–29)

These enigmatic words, attributed to Jesus of Nazareth in the first book of the New Testament, are some of the most disputed in the Bible.

They certainly ring with prophetic doom. With their images of a darkened sun and moon, and stars falling from the sky, they seem to be describing the end of the world. But what do they mean?

Two poles of opinion anchor a vast spectrum of interpretation. On one end of the spectrum are those who say that all prophetic Bible passages were aimed at the audience who first heard them. Authors of Holy Writ were speaking to their contemporaries, and we must interpret their words by studying history to understand the culture and times—in this case, the first century CE. According to this school of thought, the clue to prophecy is to be found in events familiar to those who first read the words of the prophet.

The theologian Marcus Borg, among others, calls this the "past-historic" view of biblical interpretation, and it is typical of what is usually called "liberal" theology.

At the other end of the interpretive spectrum are those such as author and evangelist Tim LaHaye, who insist that biblical prophecy was aimed at future generations—perhaps even our present day. When daily newspapers begin to herald events similar to those described by the original authors of the Bible, then and only then can the prophecies be properly understood. Even the original authors didn't understand what they were writing about, because those who were inspired to write were transported forward in time to glimpse technological societies they couldn't possibly comprehend.

This interpretation is called the "futurist" view of biblical interpretation and is typical of what is usually called "conservative/evangelical" theology.

Matthew 24, however, presents a unique problem for both interpretive schools. Jesus talked about a time even farther back in history than his own when he quoted the prophet Daniel (see Daniel). But a careful reading of the book of Daniel discloses that the "abomination that causes desolation" to which Jesus referred is mentioned in three separate chapters that seem to have been written by two authors, one of whom wrote in Hebrew and the other in Aramaic.

The futurist school of interpretation simply claims that Daniel was written by one far-seeing prophet who, using two different languages, described the same future day to which Jesus was referring in Matthew 24. There might be room for coincidence, in that past events may have foreshadowed the future event Jesus talked about, but that only shows that God sometimes used "Coming Attractions," as it were, to warn humankind of what will transpire if people don't shape up. In any case, as far as we know, there have never been any past examples of stars falling from the sky while the sun and moon became dark. So both Daniel and Jesus must have been referring to a day yet in our future.

The past-historic school has a more complicated task. Looking for cultural explanations in Daniel's day is only the first difficulty. The interpreters also have to read the historical/archeological record to find similar events in the time of Jesus. So the "abomination that causes desolation" needs a bit of research before we can understand how theologians of the past-historic school see the enigmatic passage of Matthew 24.

First we need to define some terms. There are at least four closely nuanced ways to translate the word *abomination* from the original Hebrew used in the book of Daniel. The definition most accepted is that of something "appalling" or "detested." Meanwhile, *desolation* carries with it the idea of stark emptiness. So another way of saying "the abomination that causes desolation" would be, "the detested thing that appalls [Jewish people] so much that it causes them to leave the holy place [the temple] empty."

Darkened sun and moon above the great earthquake from Revelation. *Fortean Picture Library.*

For those who belong to the past-historic school of biblical interpretation, two such events conveniently stand out. One happened during the time when, according to these scholars, this portion of Daniel was written. The other happened shortly after Jesus' time.

In 167 BCE, the days to which past-historic scholars believe Daniel 9, 11, and 12 refer, Antiochus Epiphanes of Syria profaned the altar of the temple at Jerusalem. Some accounts say he sacrificed a pig there. Pigs, according to Jewish law, are "unclean," nonkosher animals. Others say he erected a statue to the god Zeus. Perhaps he did both, which would have polluted the holy altar and broken the first and second commandments referring to "having no other Gods" and forbidding the worship of idols. Either act would have been "appalling," an "abomination" that would have caused good Jews to leave the profaned temple "desolate" or empty.

The words attributed to Jesus could have been a similar historical warning. In 70 CE, shortly before the gospel of Matthew was written, Roman legions under Titus destroyed the temple at Jerusalem, setting off the great Diaspora, the dispersion of the Jewish people throughout the world that lasted right up until the birth of Zionism and the declaration of a Jewish state in 1948. With the destruction of the temple, Jews could no longer correctly worship within the parameters of their sacrificial system because the temple altar, according to the Torah, was the only place such sacrifices were permitted to be offered. The temple site was left "desolate."

So those who follow the past-historic method of biblical interpretation believe that the words attributed to both Daniel and Jesus refer to specific historic events. They were written for the people of those long-lost days, to whom these events would have had special significance. The part about sun, moon, and stars is simply metaphorical hyperbole.

The futurists are not convinced. When Israel, during the 1967 Six-Day War, gained access, for the first time in more than eighteen centuries, to the ground upon which their beloved temple once stood (see Temple at Jerusalem), many Jews and Christians rejoiced because they believed that the long "abomination that causes desolation" was almost over. A new temple could now be built, ready to greet the Messiah—either, for Jews, for the first time, or, for Christians, the second time.

Those who hold this view offer different opinions as to the nature of the "abomination" that made the temple site "desolate." Some say it is simply the presence of the Muslim mosque that sits on the site. Various fundamentalist groups have identified the "abomination" with the practices of the entire Christian church, the Roman Catholic denomination, the League of Nations, the Jehovah's Witnesses, the doctrine of the Rapture (see Rapture), the religion of Islam, or the nation of Rome. Each sect tends to claim that the scriptures clearly teach its position, and most quote myriad Bible verses and passages to back them up, utilizing complicated systems of biblical dates and prophetic riddles.

All agree, however, that there will be yet another "abomination of desolation." A third temple will be built, and someday the antichrist (see Antichrist) will ascend its steps, declare himself to be God, and demand worship from the inhabitants of the earth. This final "abomination" will signify the beginning of the end and bring about the final judgment of God (see Revelation) and the battle of Armageddon (see Armageddon, Battle of).

Sources:

Borg, Marcus J. *Reading the Bible Again for the First Time: Taking the Bible Seriously but Not Literally.* San Francisco: HarperSanFrancisco, 2001.

Buttrick, George A., ed. *The Interpreter's Dictionary of the Bible.* 4 vols. New York: Abingdon Press, 1962.

The Holy Bible, New International Version. Grand Rapids, MI: Zondervan, 1978.

Lindsey, Hal. *Apocalypse Code.* Palos Verdes, CA: Western Front Ltd., 1997.

Willis, Jim. *The Religion Book: Places, Prophets, Saints, and Seers.* Detroit: Visible Ink Press, 2004.

ABRAHAM AND MONOTHEISM

Did the Abraham of Genesis exist? No one knows for sure, but according to Bruce Feiler, author of *Abraham: A Journey to the Heart of Three Faiths*, it really doesn't make a whole lot of difference. What is important is the *story* of Abraham, what Abraham represents not only to modern-day monotheism but to the politics of the Middle East—which, in this nuclear age, can threaten the very future of life on the planet.

Abraham, at God's command, preparing to sacrifice his son Isaac (right); at the altar (left), an angel stops the knife. *Fortean Picture Library.*

The great patriarch of the Hebrew Bible is also the spiritual forefather of the New Testament and the grand holy architect of the Qur'an. Abraham is the shared ancestor of Judaism, Christianity, and Islam. He is the linchpin of the Arab-Israeli conflict. He is the centerpiece of the battle between the West and Islamic extremists. He is the father—in many cases the purported biological father—of 12 million Jews, 2 billion Christians, and 1 billion Muslims around the world.

And that's the problem.

Historically, when the descendants of Abraham engaged in religious disputes over who was the inheritor of the lands promised by God to the patriarch as recorded in the book of Genesis (see Abrahamic Covenant), warfare was limited by technology. But now we have nuclear weapons to consider. A war in one part of the world, especially as populated and volatile as the Middle East, could quickly escalate into global disaster. And when the United States of America, half a world away from the scene of the conflict, was attacked on September 11, 2001, partly because of its support for Jewish Israel over Muslim Palestine, the battle was brought home to people who thought they were far removed from it.

The modern conflict is rarely couched in such flat assertions as "We are Abraham's descendants and you are not" or "God gave this land to us and not you." But in the early 1960s the theme melody from the movie *Exodus*, with lyrics written after the film became a hit and sung by Pat Boone, expressed the deep religious feelings underscoring events that headlined many an evening news program fifty years later: "This land is mine, God gave this land to me."

Western audiences, grown used to the political doctrine of separation of church and state, sometimes have a difficult time understanding the deeply religious/political upheaval of a part of the world long familiar with religious argument spilling over into hatred, warfare, and terrorism. Even if the biblical account of Abraham is not interpreted as reliable biography, however, it still points up the fact that the ancestors of today's opposing factions in the volatile Middle East were arguing about land and autonomy back in the time when the story was first written. And that was a very long time ago, indeed!

The Man

Who is Abraham? Who is this man who continues to have such a profound influence over a world that can't even prove he existed?

He is considered to be the father of both Judaism and Islam (through his sons Isaac and Ishmael, respectively) and the spiritual father of Christianity, according to Paul's letter to the Romans, chapter 4, verse 1. Indeed, except for the name of Jesus, Abraham's name appears more times in the Christian New Testament than does any other.

He is first introduced as Abram (the name means "exalted father"), living in Ur of the Chaldees, in what is now Iraq. The ancient city of Ur, a Sumerian capital, has been excavated. As a result of archeological work done there, many believe that a people called Hapiru, or Hebrew, lived in Ur until about the time of the biblical narrative, roughly 2000 BCE. They apparently migrated to Haman, in northern Mesopotamia, and then, it is assumed, to Canaan, later called Palestine, now Israel. Critical scholarship, however, like all sciences, is continually in flux, and it must be noted that further research sheds doubt on the connection.

Abraham is presented as a man of great faith, although, like most biblical heroes, with feet of clay that make him disarmingly appealing. The religious "call" that begins his story occurs in Genesis 12:1–3:

> Now the Lord said to Abram, "Leave your country, your people and your father's household and go to the land I will show you.
>
> I will make you into a great nation
>   and I will bless you;
> I will make your name great,
>   and you will be a blessing.
> I will bless those who bless you,
>   and whoever curses you I will curse;
> and all peoples on earth
>   will be blessed through you."

"So Abram departed," according to the Bible, without a single word of protest or explanation. This act of unquestioning faith became the foundation for three religions. The story of Abraham as presented in the Bible is the story of the beginning of monotheism, the belief in one God. The three great monotheistic traditions of the world today all trace their origins to this same period of history.

Monotheism: A New Concept of Time

Monotheism introduced important ideas to the world beyond the concept of one God. Considerable evidence suggests that before the advent of monotheism, humans tended to think of time as circular. "What goes around, comes around" is a concept familiar to Hinduism, Native American belief systems, Shamanism, and Druidism, to name just a few of the polytheistic and pantheistic religious traditions in which time is viewed as having no beginning and no end.

But monotheism postulates a specific beginning. "In the beginning," says the first verse of the Bible, "God created the heavens and the earth." The Qur'an continues the theme: "He [Allah] it is Who created the earth in Six Days, and is moreover firmly established on the Throne [of Authority]" (57:4).

Whenever there is a beginning, there is an implied ending. Linear thinking about time is one of the hallmarks of monotheism. Timelines are among its legacy.

Monotheism: A New Concept of Reality

Duality is another aspect of monotheism. The first story of the monotheistic tradition depicts humans with a dualistic choice. They are faced with the temptation to eat of the tree of dualism—the "tree of the knowledge of good and evil" (Gen. 2 and 3; see Adam and Eve), of right and wrong. Monotheism gave the world a good God and an evil devil in conflict with each other. Eventually, it insists, good must overcome evil. That's the whole point of time. Time is the battleground on which Ahura Mazda confronts Ahriman, Yahveh battles "the Satan," God defeats the devil, Allah vanquishes Iblis. The long war will end with good conquering evil at a final battle sometime in the future. An Armageddon of some sort marks the end of time.

So Abraham's story marks the beginning of the end. And there is ample evidence that those who first wrote the story recognized that the cultural conflicts they incorporated into it were already part of the experience of people living four millennia ago. When Ishmael, for instance, considered by many to be the "father" of Islam, is born to Abraham and Hagar, the obviously prejudiced Hebrew authors of Genesis tell of an angel who prophesies of the young child and his descendants:

> He will be a wild donkey of a man;
>   his hand will be against everyone
>   and everyone's hand against him,
> and he will live in hostility
>   toward all his brothers. (Gen. 16:12)

When Abraham's grandchildren Jacob and Esau are born, the ancient Hebrew authors, writing from a Jewish perspective, make it apparent where their loyalties lie in the matter of two future races of Abraham's descendants. Of Esau, "father" of the Edomites, who will later be among those called Palestinians, the Bible prophesies:

> You will live by the sword
>   and you will serve your brother.
> But when you grow restless,
>   you will throw his yoke
>   from off your neck. (Gen. 27:40)

Monotheism: The Continuing Battle

Prophecy and biblical literalism aside, then, the conflict threatening the world today in the Middle East has a long history. What makes the continuing story so volatile, however, is that those who live it today are armed with nuclear missiles. The Christian writer of the book of Revelation placed the final battle for the world, the battle of Armageddon, right in Abraham's neighborhood. So it seems obvious that even the early Christian movement recognized the old struggle that we still read about in our newspapers and experience in our streets today. The battle has spread from Abraham's backyard to the streets of New York and the cities of Europe. The children of Abraham are still at each other's throats, demanding that the nations of the world side with one or the other.

Abraham's story is not yet finished.

Sources:
Feiler, Bruce. *Abraham: A Journey to the Heart of Three Faiths.* New York: William Morrow, 2002.
The Holy Bible, New International Version. Grand Rapids, MI: Zondervan, 1978.
The Holy Qur'an. Trans. with a commentary by Abdullah Yusuf Ali. Beirut: Dar Al Arabia, 1968.
Willis, Jim. *The Religion Book: Places, Prophets, Saints, and Seers.* Detroit: Visible Ink Press, 2004.

ABRAHAMIC COVENANT

The word *covenant* means "promise" or "contract." In the case of Abraham it refers to a specific promise God is purported to have made to the patriarch who represented the twentieth generation of humans as recorded in Genesis 12:2–3:

> "I will make you into a great nation
>   and I will bless you;
> I will make your name great,
>   and you will be a blessing.
> I will bless those who bless you,
>   and whoever curses you I will curse;
> and all peoples on earth
>   will be blessed through you."

Are biblical promises binding today to people who do not recognize as authoritative the Bible that records them? To most of modern Western civilization the answer is obvious: of course not. Why should one religion's scriptures have anything to do, politically, with people of a different tradition? But while Western newspapers continue to describe the Middle East in political language, the people who live there seem more often to express their views in religious terms. Dr. Abdel Aziz Rantisi, who before he was killed in an Israeli missile attack was a prominent leader of Hamas, a group that many in the West consider to be a Palestinian terrorist organization, openly attacked the president of the United States as "the enemy of Muslims." A *New York Times* article published on March 29, 2004, quotes Dr. Rantisi: "America declared war against God, and God declared war on America, [President George W.] Bush and [Israeli prime minister Ariel] Sharon."

This kind of language reveals a religious, apocalyptic (see Apocalyptic Writing) view of current events that underlies the political, geographical, and economic wrangling. And we cannot make the mistake of ridiculing only Islamic national leaders who, during the Persian Gulf War, for instance, called America the Great Satan and vowed that Allah would defend his chosen people in the "mother of all battles." During those days it was also popular to end every American political speech with the words "God bless America." When viewed in this way, the Gulf War was a holy war— God against Allah.

In a similar vein, countless generations of young Jewish boys, at their bar mitz-vahs, have read in faltering tones the words *Vayomer hashen el-Avram lech-lecha,* "The Lord said to Abraham, 'Go forth.'" Such memories produce powerful religious convictions, to the point that it seems perfectly normal for rabbis in Israel and around the world to say, "God gave this land to our father Abraham."

But Abraham wasn't the first man to step foot on Canaan's bloody ground. Others were there already. And when the Jews were led away from their beloved country after the first-century CE Roman solution to the "Jewish problem" destroyed Jerusalem, there were Gentiles who settled back in for a long occupation of the country their ancestors had called home since before Abraham's time. They were still there when the United Nations, prompted by the rebirth of Zionism, declared Israel a Jewish state in 1948.

So whose land is it, anyway?

Notwithstanding the claims of the Jewish people, there are others who have a scriptural claim upon the land of Israel. The Qur'an of Islam declares Abraham a paragon of piety (16:120). He submitted to God. The word *Muslim* means "one who submits." So to followers of Islam it is perfectly proper for the Muslim presence to declare itself so prominently in the capital of Israel, even if it means that the ancient Jewish temple site is now home to the Mosque of Omar, the "Dome of the Rock."

Meanwhile, many Christians believe they ought to have a say in the matter. The Bible declares that God will bless those who bless Abraham's descendants. Even though President Jimmy Carter's brother Billy was once quoted as saying, "There are a whole lot more Arabs than Jews over there," the typical evangelical/conservative Christian position is that America and the nations of the West had better side with Israel because that is God's will. Muslims in the region, of course, are well aware of the support of many American Christians for Israel.

It is not by accident that the final battle of the world is usually predicted to take place right in the middle of Abraham's old neighborhood. The Middle East, from the

Persian Gulf to the Mediterranean Sea and all points in between, has often been the scene of great conflict and warfare. The situation is today made even worse by the fact that much of the world runs on Persian Gulf oil. James Mann points out in his book *Rise of the Vulcans* that "American interests in the gulf and its oil supplies were deemed too important to be left in the hands of a single leader or army in the region." On the other hand, the area's reputation as a powder keg has often induced caution in U.S. leaders. In a conversation with Donald Rumsfeld, a full-time White House adviser during 1971 and 1972, President Richard Nixon warned the future defense secretary that getting involved in the Middle East carried too many potential hazards for a politician. "People think it's for the purpose of catering to the Jewish vote," Mann quotes Nixon as telling Rumsfeld. "And anyway, there's nothing you can do about the Middle East." This might explain why, years later, Rumsfeld wanted to distance himself from what he deemed a losing cause. Former secretary of state George Shultz (again as reported by Mann) remembers Rumsfeld's coming back from a 1984 meeting about peace in the Middle East and saying, "A just and lasting peace? Are you kidding?"

Some political experts believe the first shots of what could very well lead to World War III and possibly Armageddon have already been fired. America publicly condemned Israel for its 1981 preemptive strike against Iraq's nuclear facilities at Osirak—but one reason given for the American invasion of Iraq in 2003 was that Iraq was developing weapons of mass destruction (although no such weapons were found).

In the worldwide reverberation that preceded and followed the invasion, some evangelical Christians began searching their Bibles again, looking for alignments of nations that might be predicted within its pages similar to what they read about in their morning newspapers. The "children of Abraham," those who believe they are the inheritors of the Covenant, will very probably remain in the news for many years to come.

Sources:

Barzak, Ibrahim. "Hamas Founder Killed in Israeli Airstrike." Associated Press, March 22, 2004.

Feiler, Bruce. *Abraham: A Journey to the Heart of Three Faiths.* New York: William Morrow, 2002.

Mann, James. *Rise of the Vulcans: The History of Bush's War Cabinet.* New York: Penguin Group, 2004.

Myre, Greg. "Hamas Leader Calls Bush Foe of Muslims." *New York Times*, March 29, 2004.

The Holy Bible, New International Version. Grand Rapids, MI: Zondervan, 1978.

ADAM AND EVE

The final pages of the Christian Bible, concluding with the battle of Armageddon, the return of Jesus Christ, and the destruction of Satan, complete the story that begins in the Garden of Eden, described in the early chapters of the book of Genesis. There, it is written, "were the tree of life and the tree of the knowledge of good and evil" (Gen. 2:9). When Adam and Eve succumbed to temptation and ate of the fruit of the tree of the knowledge of good and evil, they were banished from the Garden (Gen. 3:22–24). It is often inferred by conservative scholars of both Judaism and Christianity that the purpose was to prevent them from eating of the tree of life and thus living forever in their rebellious state. Biblical history begins with their exile. But at the Bible's end, in

The Fall of Man, by Hans Sebald Beham, depicts Adam and Eve at the moment before eating the forbidden fruit. *Fortean Picture Library.*

the final chapter of Revelation, the tree of life reappears: "Then the angel showed me the river of the water of life as clear as crystal, flowing down from the throne of God and of the Lamb down the middle of the great street of the city. On each side of the river stood the tree of life, bearing twelve crops of fruit, yielding its fruit every month.

And the leaves of the tree are for the healing of the nations. No longer will there be any curse" (Rev. 22:1–3).

When viewed in this way, the Bible can be understood as telling either metaphorically or literally the story of the human race between their banishment from the tree of life and their restoration to its presence. The tree of life becomes a set of bookends sandwiching human history.

The apostle Paul, writing in 1 Corinthians 15, builds on this concept as he develops his theory of the two Adams. The first Adam, in Genesis, sins, earning exile from the presence of God. The second Adam, Jesus, when faced with the same temptations, triumphs and, as described in Revelation, returns the human race to its preordained place. (This, by the way, is one reason some Christians think Jesus had to be born of a virgin: both Adams had to have the same father.)

The nature of the original sin committed by the first Adam, the sin that began the long march to Armageddon, is summarized in the New Testament book of 1 John: 2:16: "For all that is in the world, the lust of the flesh and the lust of the eyes and the pride of life, is not of the Father but is of the world" (Revised Standard Version). Note the threefold nature of temptation: the lust of the flesh, the lust of the eyes, and the pride of life. Both the first and second Adam, according to Paul's theology, faced these three temptations. One fell. The other triumphed.

In Genesis, when "the woman saw that the fruit of the tree was good for food [the lust of the flesh] and pleasing to the eye [the lust of the eyes], and also desirable for gaining wisdom [the pride of life], she took some and ate it. She also gave some to her husband, who was with her, and he ate it. Then the eyes of them both were opened."

Jesus, the second Adam, faced the same three temptations. In Matthew 4 he is first tempted to assuage his hunger by making bread from stone (lust of the flesh). He is then shown "all the kingdoms of the world" and told they will all be his if he worships Satan (lust of the eyes). Finally he is told to show off to all the faithful by leaping unaided from the top of the temple and landing safely, supported by angels (pride of life). To all these temptations Jesus responds by quoting scripture. He passes the test the first Adam failed.

This reading of the story represents a conservative method of biblical interpretation (see Abomination of Desolation; Revelation). It assumes that the Bible is recounting a factual history of the human race and God's dealings with it. But there is another way to view these passages. If Adam and Eve, the tree of life, and human temptations are viewed as common metaphors for human experience, a different meaning surfaces.

In the final years of the twentieth century, when geneticists began to speculate that the whole human race has as its earliest common matrilineal ancestor one woman in what is now Africa, biblical literalists rejoiced because it seemed to confirm that the Genesis story represented a factual account of history. We all descended from one woman, and her name was Eve. There were problems, of course. Scientists placed her on the wrong continent and much too early in time to fit with the biblical version. That didn't seem to matter to the faithful. Science had "proved" that the book of

Genesis was literally true (even if the scientists seemed to have played a bit loose with geography and the calendar).

Meanwhile, the great majority of mainline American Christian theologians undoubtedly believe that the story of Adam and Eve was never intended to be a history lesson. Instead, they say, it is a mythological account designed to teach spiritual principles.

Regardless of which view one holds, what *is* revealed in the story of Adam and Eve is that whoever first told it introduced a whole new way of looking at time and the nature of human existence. This new perspective relates directly to the long march toward Armageddon outlined in the Bible.

Early cultures did not conceive of time as a great river flowing inexorably through something called "history." Indigenous religions of the Far East, as well as traditions found throughout the Americas, conceived of time as cyclical or circular, endlessly repeating. Their mythologies consisted of Vishnu sleeping on the cosmic ocean, dreaming worlds into existence, or ancestors who escaped one world to rise into another. Some cultures considered time to be an illusion, a faulty perception by the human race.

But the story of Adam and Eve, first told perhaps eight to ten thousand years ago in the Middle East, introduced something brand new. The two most important elements in the story are represented by the two trees placed in the Garden. Their significance, in combination, leads directly to monotheism and inevitably to Armageddon.

The first tree introduces duality. It is called the "tree of the knowledge of good and evil." A religious system involving opposite poles invites the believer to choose one or the other. Buddhism, interestingly, solved this dilemma by accepting both and finding the middle way leading beyond them. But Judaism, followed by the monotheistic traditions of Christianity and Islam, taught that individuals had to choose good over evil to find acceptance with Yahveh, God, or Allah. This choice is represented by Adam and Eve's eating of the fruit of the tree of duality, the fruit of the tree of the knowledge of good and evil. As soon as duality is introduced into a religious system, a confrontation between the god of good and the devil of evil is almost guaranteed. If God, Yahveh, or Allah is eventually going to conquer Satan, the devil, or Iblis, Armageddon is just a matter of time. Certainly good and evil cannot compete forever. An end has to come.

And that is the purpose of the second tree. One interpretation of the Adam and Eve story holds that the man and woman were cast out of the Garden to keep them from eating of the tree of life, thus entering eternity in a sinful state. Seen in this way, the expulsion from Eden was a blessing, not a curse. Mortality is a gift from God, not a punishment to be endured.

This idea is illustrated in the final book of the Bible. After Satan is destroyed, after Armageddon is finished, access to the tree of life is restored. Eternity begins anew. Time, it is finally revealed, is simply the battleground on which good and evil slug it out. So it is important to remember that, in the Bible at least, Armageddon is not an ending as much as it is a new beginning. The biblical writers pointed to "a new heaven and a new earth," not just the destruction of this one.

This concept is strictly a product of monotheism. Duality and linear time are the hallmarks of this theological system. And Judaism, Christianity, and Islam, the three monotheistic traditions, all begin with the Garden of Eden and Adam and Eve.

Source:
The Holy Bible, New International Version. Grand Rapids, MI: Zondervan, 1978.

AIDS *see* Plagues

ALIENS

Our species seems to have a long history of one group inflicting local Armageddons on another. Some anthropologists suggest that when *Homo sapiens* moved out of Africa into Europe and Asia, one item on their agenda was bringing to an end the race of cousins now called Neanderthal. Neanderthals seem to have been nice enough folk. They had cultural traditions such as religious funeral practices and may even have invented music. But when *Homo sapiens* moved in, the Neanderthals eventually became extinct. Ever since, it seems, one group of *Homo sapiens* has come to covet another's land and moved in to make it their own. Aryans moved west across Europe and southeast into India, bringing to an end the cultural practices of those who were already there. The Romans destroyed the Celts as the Celts had destroyed the Picts, who had destroyed the long-lost indigenous people of the western European islands. Europeans jumped the Atlantic and wrought their own form of Armageddon on the Americas. Eskimos moved in on the peaceful Tunit. Warlike Apaches displaced the peaceful Pimas. World Wars I and II, along with almost every other bellicose conquest of human history, spelled the end to what was, while what-was-to-be hung in the balance.

So it seems built into the consciousness of our species that when the final world map was filled in, defining the geographical limits of our planet, we would turn to the night sky in speculation. Is there another species out there that might try to wreak Armageddon on us? Are there other beings in the universe who might covet the resources of our planet and attempt to inflict upon us what we have so often done to others, even of our own kind?

As William Alschuler points out in his book *The Science of UFOs*, at least three complete industries have grown up around these speculations: an entertainment industry in the form of science-fiction books and movies; a second entertainment industry in the form of made-for-TV movies that purport to examine the reality of the associated phenomena; and a small industry that consists of support groups and therapists who counsel those who say aliens have abducted them, in some cases for nonconsensual experiments. This goes to show that, among other things, in America one can commercialize almost anything.

Belief in aliens from space smacks of a religion. Evidence is a matter of interpretation. You either believe it or you don't. To paraphrase a popular bumper sticker, "My cousin saw a UFO. I believe it. That settles it." To many people, proof that God exists is to be found in the anecdotal evidence of others who have experienced the divine. In the same way, say alien activists, too many people have experienced or witnessed alien activity to allow us simply to dismiss the possible reality of planetary visitors. The fact that neither the presence of God nor the presence of aliens has ever been proved under laboratory conditions does not dissuade believers in either.

Some scientists express doubt that, even if aliens exist somewhere out there, they could possibly travel the literally astronomical distances necessary to reach us. True believers in an alien presence retort that we cannot assume to have yet reached the end of technology. After all, a hundred years ago it was widely believed that no one could ever run a four-minute mile, let alone break the sound barrier and walk on the moon. Given the theoretical possibility of cosmic wormholes and parallel universes, who is to say space travel over immense, seemingly impossible distances will not be commonplace someday?

God sends angels. They even make TV shows about them. But aliens send messengers too, we are assured. They have made contact with us. Perhaps the government even knows about them but is withholding the evidence because our leaders fear a general panic among the populace. As a matter of fact, even the Bible seems to speak of angelic messengers using vocabulary similar to that of the latest edition of the *UFO Newsletter*.

Artist's version of an alien "gray," a type that succeeded "little green men" in the popular imagination. *Andrew C. Stewart/Fortean Picture Library.*

Take, for example, the experience of Ezekiel:

> I saw a windstorm coming out of the north—an immense cloud with flashing lightning and surrounded by brilliant light. The center of the fire looked like glowing metal, and in the fire was what looked like four living creatures. In appearance their form was like that of a man.... I saw a wheel on the ground beside each creature.... They [the wheels] sparkled like chrysolite.... Their rims were high and awesome.... Spread above the heads of the living creatures was what looked like an expanse, sparkling like ice, and awesome.... Above the expanse over their heads was what looked like a throne of sapphire, and high above on the throne was a figure like that of a man.... and I heard the voice of one speaking. (Ezek. 1:4–28)

If this weren't a passage from the revered Holy Bible but had just been discovered as a fragment of text from early times, an honest reading would certainly raise interesting questions.

And this is not the only biblical example. Elijah was taken up from the earth into the "heavens," or sky, by "a fiery chariot." He later appeared to three witnesses on what is called the Mount of Transfiguration (Matt. 17). Could this be a description of what we now call alien abduction? The story becomes more intriguing when we read of the solitary death of Moses. He walked up into the mountains following the command of a voice he heard speaking from out of the Ark of the Covenant. When he returned from the place where he communed with this voice, his face glowed as if from sunburn (like Richard Dreyfuss's spaceship-radiation "sunburn" in *Close Encounters of the Third Kind?*). Then he disappeared. No one saw him again until he appeared with Elijah to talk to Jesus on the mountain. There the two of them stepped out of and were surrounded by a great light, with glowing raiment covering their bodies. Separated from its sacred context, this sounds just like an extraterrestrial encounter.

Religion is a universal phenomenon. Every culture on earth seems to have practiced some sort of religious tradition. Its very universality is often cited as evidence for its truth. UFO practitioners make the very same claim. The Mi'kMaq Indians of Maine can sometimes be persuaded to talk about the "little people" who come from outside the earth. If you can gain the trust of their elders, they might even show you where some of the little people are buried. The Mayans believed that star people regularly visited them and taught them the principles of the sacred geometry underpinning their magnificent temples. The Hopi believe their sacred *katsina* messengers came from the stars. Astrology seems to be the "why" behind archeological curiosities ranging from England's Stonehenge to the Egyptian pyramids and from Canadian stone circles to Peruvian Inca temples. Indian tribes such as the Cherokee had legends similar to Celtic beliefs in fairies from the "other side." Stars, other dimensions, visitations from "outside"—the legends, myths, beliefs, and stories are found in every culture and time.

Some religious believers say that God will bring about Armageddon before we destroy ourselves. Evil, they say, will be rooted out before we can end life as we know it. The UFO folks say it is aliens who are watching. They are observing our race and will keep us from destruction until we are mature enough to enter the cosmic community.

Atheists and agnostics smile and shake their heads at believers who accept religious ideas purely on faith. In response, the person of religious convictions can't understand how the nonbeliever can be so thickheaded as to miss what is perfectly obvious to so many others. In the same way, the scientist compiles his or her facts and looks askance at those who are so naive as to take alien abduction stories as gospel. Meanwhile, the true believer in extraterrestrials journeys to Roswell, New Mexico, which he/she is convinced is the scene of the most infamous UFO coverup in United States history. There, fellow pilgrims agree that scientists are either hoodwinked by their education, blinded by their specialty, deceived by their government, or just plain out-and-out liars.

True believers in both religion and UFOs sometimes stand ready to die for their beliefs. Religious history abounds with stories of martyrs who gave their lives for what they were certain was true. When the time came for their personal Armageddon, they willingly obliged. In Waco, Texas, Branch Davidians perished in flame. In Guyana, followers of Rev. Jim Jones willingly swallowed FlaVor-Aid (a Kool-Aid knockoff) laced with cyanide. In the same way, there were those who believed that aliens were coming for them on the night of March 26, 1997. They thought an alien spaceship was following in the wake of the Hale-Bopp comet. Calmly and in an orderly fashion, they each drank a cocktail consisting of phenobarbital and vodka, believing that when they awoke they would have crossed through the portal they called "Heaven's Gate" and entered "the next level," where elevated aliens dwell (see Heaven's Gate).

We do not know if aliens exist on other planets. We do not know if they have achieved a level of technology that would allow them to cruise the vast expanse of space/time. We do not know if they have found us, or traveled here to examine us. We do not know if their intentions toward us would be benevolent or not.

We don't know if any of this is even possible, let alone true.

And we don't know if it isn't possible or true, either.

Like all matters of faith, belief in aliens and the possibility of an alien-induced Armageddon is a matter of individual choice.

Believe it or not.

Sources:

Alschuler, William A. *The Science of UFOs*. New York: St. Martin's Press, 2001.

Red Star, Nancy. *Star Ancestors: Indian Wisdomkeepers Share the Teachings of the Extraterrestrials*. Rochester, VT: Destiny, 2000.

Willis, Jim. *The Religion Book: Places, Peoples, Saints, and Seers*. Detroit: Visible Ink Press, 2004.

ALPHA/OMEGA

In the final book of the Bible, God, speaking through Jesus Christ to John the Apostle, is purported to have said, "It is done. I am the Alpha and the Omega."

The New Testament was originally written in Greek. "Alpha" is the first letter of the Greek alphabet. "Omega" is the last. If written in English this sentence could be translated, "I am the A and the Z." Another acceptable translation would be, "I am the beginning and the end."

This statement implies a distinctly linear view of time, with a beginning and an end. Linear timelines are a distinct feature of monotheism (see Abraham and Monotheism; Adam and Eve), differing from other religious traditions that tend to think of time as circular or cyclical.

Until recently, linear thinking has also been a hallmark of Western science. Both time and space began at the "Big Bang" (see entry) and will end at the "Big Crunch" (see Big Crunch, Big Chill, and Big Rip). This outlook created fanciful science-fiction scenarios. Would it be possible to travel back in time and perhaps change the future? Such a scenario formed the central plotline of the *Star Trek* movies *First Encounter* and *The Journey Home* (see Hollywood Envisions THE END).

Of course the scientific theories prompted other questions: What came before the Big Bang? What will happen after the Big Crunch? The answers are not easily forthcoming. Usually it is explained that all evidence of what came before was destroyed at the moment of creation. Physicists can, utilizing sophisticated mathematics, explore back as far as the first second. But there is a point beyond which we simply cannot penetrate.

As for the end—well, who knows? The Big Crunch envisions the universe collapsing back into itself, perhaps to explode outward again, producing a new universe. Other theories visualize the cosmos as expanding forever, eventually becoming a dark, cold, lifeless place that has run out of energy.

Some physicists, however, have begun to question the whole linear approach to time (see Barbour, Julian). They ask if time is quite as simply defined as has usually been the case. Paraphrasing Albert Einstein, they say that the universe, including time, may be not only stranger than we have imagined, but stranger than we *can* imagine.

If this is the case, the whole concept of "Alpha and Omega" may have to be revisited.

Sources:
Campbell, Joseph. *The Inner Reaches of Outer Space: Metaphor as Myth and as Religion.* New York: Harper & Row, 1986.
Hawking, Stephen W. *A Brief History of Time: From the Big Bang to Black Holes.* New York: Bantam, 1988.
The Holy Bible, New International Version. Grand Rapids, MI: Zondervan, 1978.

AMERICA IN PROPHECY

Because the United States of America is such a new country, there is no historical precedent for including it in classical prophecies concerning the endtimes. The biblical Armageddon, after all, is set in the Middle East, with its rich historical tradition of wars and rumors of wars. Other cultures were concerned with their own futures, not the future of a country no one knew would ever exist.

Some Native Americans did have endtime traditions of their own, some of which even set dates. The year 2012, for example, is fast approaching. According to some interpreters, that is the year the Hopi, as well as the Mayans farther south, believe this world will end (see Indigenous Peoples of the Americas).

Coming from a very different direction, followers of Nostradamus claim that he foresaw events that would happen in America. It was just that he didn't understand what he was seeing, so he couldn't identify the location of some of his prophecies (see Nostradamus).

As far as the classical biblical prophets were concerned, however, America simply didn't exist.

Or did it? Herbert W. Armstrong (see Armstrong, Herbert W.) claimed that the Bible does indeed predict the role America will play at the end of world history. He taught that in Genesis 49, Jacob, whose name had been changed to Israel, prophesied the future awaiting each of his twelve sons, who would become the twelve patriarchs of Israel. Armstrong believed that some of the descendants of these patriarchs eventually traveled west, becoming the ancestors of the nations of modern Europe:

> The scepter will not depart from Judah,
>   nor the ruler's staff from between his feet,
> until he comes to whom it belongs
>   and the obedience of the nations is his. (Gen. 49:10)

Why does England still follow an outdated monarchy in this modern world? According to Armstrong, it's because the queen of England sits on the throne of David. Her descendants will continue to do so until Jesus Christ returns.

The story becomes even more complicated. Joseph, the eleventh son of Israel, who, following a long and tangled path, led his brothers to safety in Egypt, was described as a "fruitful vine" (Gen. 49:22). Joseph had two sons, Ephraim and Manasseh. Manasseh was the older and should have received the blessing appropriate for the firstborn. So when Joseph brought the boys to his father, Israel, he placed Manasseh on Israel's right, to receive the "right-hand" patriarchal blessing, as was his due. But Israel, before delivering the blessing, crossed his hands, placing his right hand on the head of Ephraim. When Joseph objected, Israel prophesied that the younger son would, in effect, become the "first" nation.

Armstrong, stringing together many Old Testament texts, traced Ephraim and Manasseh to England. He believed Manasseh's descendants became the founding fathers of the United States. Leaving England (the recipient of the "firstborn" blessing), they went "over the wall," in Israel's words, to America. Thus the prophecy was fulfilled. England (Ephraim) became the "firstborn" nation. Manasseh (the United States) became the younger "son." Joseph indeed became a "fruitful vine," fulfilling Israel's prophecy:

> With bitterness archers attacked him;
>   they shot at him with hostility.
> But his bow remained steady,
>   his strong arm stayed limber,
> because of the hand of the Mighty One of Jacob,
>   because of the Shepherd, the Rock of Israel,
> because of your father's God, who helps you
>   because of the Almighty, who blesses you
>   with blessings of the heavens above,
> blessings of the deep below,
> blessings of the breast and womb....
> Let all these rest on the head of Joseph,
>   on the brow of the prince among his brothers. (Gen. 49:23–26)

To Armstrong, England and America, sprung from the loins of Joseph, beloved son of Israel and savior of the Jewish people, will continue to be world powers until the time of the end.

Most modern nations, to say the least, do not share this biblically mandated view of history. To many influential editors of foreign newspapers, including those in England, America has gone off the deep end when it comes to following the Bible. George Monbiot, in an article for the United Kingdom's *Guardian* newspaper, writes:

"To understand what is happening in the Middle East, you must first understand what is happening in Texas." He goes on to say that President George W. Bush, whose home is in Texas, followed the lead of those who believe that the United States has a biblical mandate to side with Israel in the fight for Israel's "biblical lands."

The headline of Monbiot's article spells it out:

Their Beliefs Are Bonkers, but They Are at the Heart of Power
US Christian Fundamentalists Are Driving Bush's Middle East Policy

As Monbiot describes it, "The believers are convinced that they will soon be rewarded for their efforts. The antichrist is apparently walking among us, in the guise of Kofi Annan, Javier Solana, Yasser Arafat or, more plausibly, Silvio Berlusconi. The Wal-Mart Corporation is also a candidate … because it wants to radio-tag its stock, thereby exposing humankind to the Mark of the Beast."

Even if America is not specifically mentioned in prophetic tradition, it obviously plays an important role in world events. To those who believe that world history is approaching Armageddon, it follows that America will loom large as the drama unfolds. Hal Lindsey believes that America will be important, but not the leader, in those cataclysmic events. In *The Late Great Planet Earth* he writes:

> The United States may be aligned with the Western forces headed by the ten-nation Revived Roman Empire of Europe. It is clear that the U.S. cannot be the leader of the West in the future. It is quite possible that Ezekiel was referring to the U.S. in part when he said: "I will send fire—upon those who dwell securely in the coastlands.…"

> The word translated "coastlands" or "isle" in the Hebrew is *ai*. It was used by the ancients in the sense of "continents" today. It designated great Gentile civilizations across the seas which were usually settled most densely along the coastlands. The idea here is that the Gentile nations of distant continents would all experience the impact of sudden torrents of fire raining down upon them. This can include prophetically the populated continents and islands of the Western Hemisphere as well as the Far East. It pictures cataclysmic events which will affect the whole inhabited earth.

Is this just another example of trying to fit current events into age-old prophecies? Can the old argument apply that prophets must be excused for their lack of specifics because they were viewing a future time that they could not really be expected to understand?

Apparently many people believe just that. In October 1998, police in Jerusalem reported that they were having difficulty with American Christian "religious zealots" who wanted to be in the Holy Land when the new millennium came to pass. Born-again Christians were moving into houses and apartments and filling motel rooms near the Mount of Olives so they would have a front-row seat for the Second Coming.

There is, however, another conservative religious view that suggests a different reason for America's failure to be mentioned specifically in the Bible. Could it be that

America is conspicuous by its absence because it is destined to fall into insignificance before Armageddon occurs? And since Armageddon seems to be just around the corner, is America's downfall imminent?

This seems to be the position Edgar Cayce took (see Cayce, Edgar). He predicted various dire events that would begin in the 1950s and culminate by the year 2000. An earthquake would destroy large portions of Los Angeles and San Francisco. Floods would inundate the southern coast of California and the area between Salt Lake City and southern Nebraska. Land would appear off the East Coast and new lands would rise in the Caribbean.

Obviously these things didn't happen, and the new millennium came in rather quietly. But Cayce's followers remind us that calendars are, after all, human inventions. God may have a different date that doesn't correspond to the one we have arbitrarily selected. A few years here or there is not a big difference.

Only time will tell.

Sources:

Bell, Art, and Brad Steiger. *The Source: Journey through the Unexplained.* New Orleans: Paper Chase Press, 1999.

Lindsey, Hal, with C. C. Carlson. *The Late Great Planet Earth.* Grand Rapids, MI: Zondervan, 1970.

Monbiot, George. "Their Beliefs Are Bonkers, but They Are at the Heart of Power." *Guardian/UK,* April 20, 2004. http://www.commondreams.org/cgi-bin/print.cgi?file=/views04/0420-03.htm.

The Holy Bible, New International Version. Grand Rapids, MI: Zondervan, 1978.

AMERICAN INDIAN VIEWS OF THE ENDTIMES *see* **Indigenous Peoples of the Americas**

AMILLENNIALISM

(See also Millennialism; Pre- and Postmillennialism)

Millennialism is the belief, based on a literal interpretation of Revelation 20:1–10, that Jesus Christ will return to earth and reign for a thousand years, during which time Satan will be "bound" and unable to deceive the nations. This reign will be marked by peace and contentment.

But there are those who do not believe that "a thousand years" should be interpreted literally. These people are called "amillennialists." Just as the number 40 appears all through the Bible (Noah's flood, Israel's time in the wilderness, Elijah's journey into the desert, Jesus' foray into the hills above the Dead Sea, etc.), the "thousand years" figure is symbolic. There will be no literal millennium. That is a term meant to refer to the present day.

The Old Testament, say the amillennialists, describes the times that pointed to the coming of Jesus, the Messiah. Soon after Jesus rose from the dead, the temple, symbolizing the Old Covenant, was destroyed. Now we live in the time of the New Covenant—the New Testament. This is the time of the "reign of Christ." The church, Christ's "body," is fulfilling the promises. When Christ returns, the "Millennium," the age of the church, will be over and all believers will be ushered into the "new heaven and new earth" of Revelation 21.

Amillennialists believe that theirs is the primary interpretation and that it has been understood by the church from the beginning. Louis Berkhof, in his *Systematic Theology*, points out that although the term *amillennialism* has only been in use since the 1930s, "the view to which it is applied is as old as Christianity."

Robert B. Strimple, a prominent amillennialist, writes: "As we read the New Testament, we come to understand that the Old Testament prophets spoke of the glories of the messianic age that was coming—that age inaugurated by Christ in which the church now lives—in terms of their own age and the religious blessings of God's people in that old covenant age.... The true Israel is Christ. *He* is the suffering Servant of the Lord, this one who is—wonder of wonders—the Lord Himself!"

While premillennialists keep their eyes on modern Israel, waiting for the building of the third temple (see Temple at Jerusalem), which will mark the beginning of the end of this premillennial age, amillennialists believe that if the Jews ever do build such a temple, it will stand as a denial of the work of Jesus. Redemption has been accomplished. There is no longer any need for a temple. What it prefigured was fulfilled at Calvary and the cross of Jesus Christ. Thus, any new temple will be a satanic counterfeit. The true temple, according to Ephesians 2:19–22 and 1 Peter 2:5, is the church, the body of Jesus Christ.

Many Christians, of course, do not agree with this view. A literal interpretation of the Bible is the easiest way to go, they say. If the Bible says a thousand years, then that's what it means. If this mixed-up, war-torn, strife-filled world is the best God can accomplish working through a divided, scandal-ridden church, then the gospel is a joke and God's work is a failure.

But the amillennialists insist they are reading the Bible correctly. The reason the world seems so mixed up is because God isn't finished with it yet. Just wait, they admonish. The bigger the problem, the bigger the miracle. Have faith and trust God. God has worked miracles before. God will work miracles again. That is the promise of the Bible.

Sources:
Berkhof, Louis. *Systematic Theology*. Grand Rapids, MI: Eerdmans, 1962.
Bock, Darrell L., ed. *Three Views on the Millennium and Beyond*. Grand Rapids, MI: Zondervan, 1999.
The Holy Bible, New International Version. Grand Rapids, MI: Zondervan, 1978.

ANCIENT OF DAYS

(See also Daniel)

Sometime during the sixth century BCE, the prophet Daniel claimed to have had a dream. Four great world powers were represented by animals rising out of the sea. The general method of past-historic biblical interpretation usually understands these powers to be Babylon, Persia, Greece, and Rome. At the end of the dream, which represented human history from Daniel through the end of time, Daniel recounts:

As I looked,

thrones were set in place,
  and the Ancient of Days took his seat.

His clothing was as white as snow;
  the hair on his head was white like
  wool.

His throne was flaming with fire,
  and its wheels were all ablaze.

A river of fire was flowing,
  coming out from before him.

Thousands upon thousands attended
him;

  ten thousand times ten thousand stood
  before him.

The court was seated,
  and the books were opened. (Dan.
  7:9–10)

One "like a son of man, coming with the clouds of heaven," approached the Ancient of Days and was given "authority, glory and sovereign power; all peoples, nations and men of every language worshiped him" (7:13–14). When Daniel, desiring some explanation, walked up to a spectator standing by the throne, he was told that it was judgment day. The four world powers had spent their allotted years. Now it was the time of the end.

The Ancient of Days, by William Blake. *The Bridgeman Art Library/Getty Images.*

The fourth beast, or kingdom, represented the last great world power to rule the earth. It crushed underfoot and destroyed everything in its path, totally dominating its subjects. In Daniel's dream, this beast had ten horns on its head. But another horn arose and uprooted three of the original ten horns. The bystander to whom Daniel spoke informed him:

> The ten horns are ten kings who will come from this kingdom. After them another king will arise, different from the earlier ones; he will subdue three kings. He will speak against the Most High and oppress his saints and try to change the set times and the laws. The saints will be handed over to him for a time, times and half a time. But the court will sit, and his power will be taken away and completely destroyed forever. (Dan. 7:24–26)

Conservative Christian scholars, combining this dream with the book of Revelation (see Revelation) and other dreams Daniel describes (see Daniel) interpret this enigmatic passage to mean that at the end of history a revived Roman Empire, or at least an empire existing in the lands ancient Rome claimed as its own, will someday rule the world. It will consist of ten nations. Three will attempt to leave the union but will be taken over by another king. This king will be the antichrist.

The Ancient of Days, however, usually interpreted to mean God in the capacity of a judge, will call upon "one like a son of man"—Jesus Christ—to overthrow the evil empire and destroy its devil-inspired ruler.

Given this background, it is no wonder that when the European Common Market—existing, after all, on the land of the old Roman Empire—approached the magic number of ten nations back in the 1970s, evangelical Christians began to think the endtimes were near. Fueled by the success of Hal Lindsey's book *The Late Great Planet Earth*, the fires of eschatology burned brightly throughout the Bible Belt. Alas, member nations of the European Union soon surpassed that number without particular incident, and apocalyptic hope was dashed again. But the faithful still are looking to Europe and awaiting the fulfillment of prophecy.

It is probable that the figure of the Ancient of Days was modeled on the familiar archetype of God as wise old father. But Daniel lived in Persia, the home of Zoroastrianism and the ancient religion of today's Iran pictured its principal god, Ahura Mazda, in this fashion. So the resemblance might be more than coincidental.

Whatever its genesis, the Ancient of Days dream certainly sets forth a basic linear timeline, at the end of which lies judgment day for the nations of earth.

Sources:

Buttrick, George A., ed. *The Interpreter's Dictionary of the Bible*. 4 vols. New York: Abingdon Press, 1962.

Lindsey, Hal, with C. C. Carlson. *The Late Great Planet Earth*. Grand Rapids, MI: Zondervan, 1970.

The Holy Bible, New International Version. Grand Rapids, MI: Zondervan, 1978.

ANGELS

Monotheistic religions arising from Middle East religious thought tend to see a separation between the material world and the spiritual. A wall stands between the experience of everyday life and life that is "other," above or beyond our physical environment. One realm exists for humankind and another for God. On this side exist space and time; on the transcendent side, infinity and eternity. The wall of separation is not solid but contains windows that enable at least partial communication or mystic vision to take place. The apostle Paul described this concept in 1 Corinthians 13: "Now we see through a glass, darkly, but then we shall see face to face."

One method of communication is for God to use messengers to bridge the gap, to move through the wall and carry God's messages to humans and human prayers to God. The word *angel*, from the Greek *angelos*, means "messenger." Although the concept of angels became more fully developed in later monotheistic religions, it is found in early Canaanite mythological poems and Persian Zoroastrianism. Ancient Hittite texts going back to a time when God was perceived as feminine describe groups of "fairy messengers" attending the Mother-Goddess.

Although popular misconceptions often picture people as becoming angels when they die, Judaism, Christianity, and Islam all teach that angels are a separate species created before humans. Probably because these are historically male-dominated religions, angels are usually depicted as being masculine, even though they are said to be either sexless or above sex. (There is at least one early exception: A passage in Genesis 6 explains that the judgment of Noah's flood was brought about in part because "the sons of God," a phrase often used to mean angels, "saw that the daughters of men"—that is, human women—"were beautiful, and they married any of them they chose." The offspring of these marriages were the Nephilim, a mysterious name often translated "giants" but defined in the Bible as "the heroes of old.") Although angelic myths differ, all describe a war in heaven that caused a third of the angels to sin. They became the demons of Judeo-Christian teaching and a category within the "jinns" of Islam, creatures of smokeless fire. The fallen angels were led by the being Jews and Christians call "the Satan" (the accuser). Muslims call him Iblis (see Devil).

In scripture, angels generally appear in human form. An angel ordered Abraham to refrain from sacrificing his son Isaac (Gen. 22:11). Angels appeared to Ishmael, Jacob, Moses, Joshua, and Muhammad. Either two or three (the account in Genesis 18 and 19 is unclear) had dinner with Abraham on their way to destroy Sodom and Gomorrah.

By the sixth century BCE angels were beginning to be defined more clearly. While earlier texts spoke simply of "the sons of God" or "holy ones," their hierarchy now begins to be revealed. Saint Thomas Aquinas listed nine "choirs" or ranks of angels, headed by the seraphim and continuing down through cherubim, thrones, dominions, virtues, powers, principalities, archangels, and angels. We also learn of the angelic choir that sings eternally in heaven and has been known to give concerts on earth, specifically to a group of shepherds on the first Christmas Eve.

In Genesis 3 we learn of "cherubim [and] a flaming sword flashing back and forth to guard the tree of life." This is an image quite different from the cute, chubby Hallmark variety. Isaiah (6:2–3) describes his vision of six-winged "seraphim" standing in the presence of God and calling to one another, "Holy, holy, holy is the Lord Almighty; / the whole earth is full of his glory."

The apostle Paul understood the church to be the fulfillment of God's eternal plan. It was a mystery revealed to him that "Gentiles are heirs together with Israel." But the purpose of this plan was to demonstrate the "manifold wisdom of God" to "rulers and authorities in the heavenly realms" (Eph. 3), by which Paul appears to have meant different ranks of angels.

Even the individual names of angels are revealed in some cases. From apocryphal books of the Bible we learn of the names Raphael and Uriel. In the book of Daniel we read about Michael, said to be "captain of the Lord's hosts."

One ecumenical angel who seems to be very busy is Gabriel. He first appears bearing a message to the Jewish patriot Daniel. Later he visits Mary to tell her that she is about to become the mother of Jesus, the founder of Christianity. Still later he escorts Muhammad on the prophet's famous night journey to the seventh heaven, a journey that influenced the beginnings of Islam.

Angels ascending and descending Jacob's ladder (Gen. 28). *Fortean Picture Library.*

It is in the book of Revelation, with its vivid descriptions of the final battle between good and evil, that angels are given their most ambitious tasks. Virtually everything that happens on earth during the culminating time of human history is carried out by angels. They receive letters dictated by God, release God's wrath, deal with the armies of the antichrist, accompany Jesus when he returns to earth, and carry out his judgments when it comes time to punish the wicked and welcome the redeemed.

Walter Wink has written a series of three important books about the language of power in the New Testament. His thesis is that early writers intuitively grasped spiritual realities present in the human condition, labeling them "angels." In Revelation 2 and 3, for example, letters are addressed to the "angels of the seven churches." Wink suggests that human institutions develop spiritual realities. In other words, when churches, schools, corporations, and even governments exist long enough, a spirit of tradition, perhaps even a metaphysical reality, forms that becomes bigger than the institution itself. What is the "spirit of America?" Why are soldiers ready to die for it? Why can we fire an entire corporate board of directors, hire new people, and still see no substantial change in the organization? Why does it not seem to matter much to average people when Republicans replace Democrats? Do power and tradition combine to form a spiritual but tangible reality? By this he doesn't imply that an organization attracts or becomes possessed by a passing spirit who happens to be flying by. Instead it actually develops a "spirit" or tangible tradition of its own. This is what was intuitively recognized by the early authors, who labeled it an "angel."

In the case of the seven angels of the book of Revelation, the author was implying that for substantial change to occur, the very "angel" or spirit of the church had to be changed, a far-reaching implication for governments and corporations today.

Angels are popular. Many recent movies and television shows have featured them. But perhaps the most valuable advice comes from the author of the book of Hebrews. In chapter 13, verse 2, we are reminded, "Do not forget to entertain strangers, for by doing so some people have entertained angels without knowing it."

Sources:
Bridger, David, ed. *The New Jewish Encyclopedia.* New York: Behrman House, 1962.
Buttrick, George A., ed. *The Interpreter's Dictionary of the Bible.* 4 vols. New York: Abingdon Press, 1962.
Douglas, J. D., ed. *The New International Dictionary of the Christian Church.* Grand Rapids, MI: Zondervan, 1974.
The Holy Qur'an. Trans. with a commentary by Abdullah Yusuf Ali. Beirut: Dar Al Arabia, 1968.
May, Herbert G., and Bruce M. Metzger, eds. *The New Oxford Annotated Bible with the Apocrypha.* Rev. ed. New York: Oxford University Press, 1973.
Wink, Walter. *Naming the Powers.* Philadelphia: Fortress Press, 1984.

ANOINTED ONE

In the Hebrew Bible, the name "Anointed One" was first used in reference to the king of Israel. Later in Jewish history it began to be used to designate the future Messiah who would come in good time to set the world straight on the path God had intended. Still later, Christians used the term to describe Jesus: the Greek *christos*—Christ— literally means "anointed one." They believed this was a proper title for the one who will return to earth at the end of the battle of Armageddon, overthrow the antichrist, destroy the devil, and usher in a new, triumphant age (see Revelation).

Source:
Buttrick, George A., ed. *The Interpreter's Dictionary of the Bible.* 4 vols. New York: Abingdon Press, 1962.

ANTICHRIST

For all the coverage in movies, television shows, books, and sermons, the antichrist gets surprisingly little space in the Christian New Testament. Popular conservative/evangelical theology paints a detailed picture of the mysterious being who will appear at the end of time to mimic and challenge Jesus Christ before his Second Coming. According to an evangelical reading of the Bible, the antichrist is the "man of sin" who, along with his sidekick the "false prophet," will rule over a ten-kingdom federation of nations that will introduce worldwide governmental control, forcing all who wish to "buy or sell" to receive the "mark of the beast" on their hand or forehead. His mystical number is 666 (see 666).

Although the antichrist will eventually be corralled at the battle of Armageddon and the return of Christ, many conservative students of prophecy believe that he will first deceive the nations of the earth. This deception will occur during the seven-year period of tribulation following the "Rapture," or "snatching away," of the faithful who are still living "at the sound of the trumpet" of God (see Rapture). Following their disappearance, the antichrist will deceive the nations, causing three and a half years of peace, followed by three and a half years of deception and warfare called the Great Tribulation (see Great Tribulation). Then Christ will return at the Second Coming (see Second Coming) and destroy him and the false prophet. Satan, the power behind the antichrist, will be imprisoned for a thousand years—the "Millennium," during which the earth will be recycled for use during a time of peace when, according to Isaiah 11:6, "the wolf will live with the lamb, the leopard will lie down with the goat ... and a little child will lead them" (see Millennium). Although his destruction is predetermined, Satan will be given a brief time to live following his release. But, along with the antichrist and his false prophet, the devil is doomed to failure (see Revelation).

This view of coming attractions begins with only four short verses in the Bible, all found in 1 and 2 John, in which the antichrist is depicted as "a spirit [that] shall come." This spirit will "deny the Father.... and is a deceiver." John even says that "there are many antichrists." These verses are the only ones in which the word *antichrist* appears in Christian scripture. The rest of the story comes from interpretations based on differing opinions coaxed out of the book of Revelation, perhaps the most disputed book in the New Testament.

Although he wasn't the first, Hal Lindsey was certainly the most popular exponent of antichrist lore. His book *The Late Great Planet Earth* sold millions of copies and led the way for the best-selling *Left Behind* series of novels by Tim LaHaye and Jerry B. Jenkins, which occupied the top of the fiction charts beginning in the mid-1990s.

Antichrist lore is a modern phenomenon. There is no tradition of antichrist legend, except for the occasional labeling of perceived enemies as "antichrist" when disagreements arose (Martin Luther, for instance, called the pope "antichrist"). This fact does not deter modern writers. They point to Daniel 12:9–10: "these things will be sealed up until the time of the end.... but those who are wise will understand." Because "those who are wise"—that is, conservative/evangelical Christians—are beginning to understand the "truth" about the antichrist, that is proof that we are living in "the time of the end" when "all these things must come to pass."

People have long tried to decipher the mysterious sign of the antichrist, the number 666. Some, using a form of numerology called *gematria* (see Revelation), have assigned numerical values to letters to derive the number 666 by adding up the values of the letters in certain words, names, or phrases. For example, the Greek word *Lateinos* for "Latin Kingdom," referring to the Roman Catholic Church, adds up to 666 using this formula. During the 1970s, when Secretary of State Henry Kissinger

Antipapal broadsheet, late sixteenth century, depicting the birth of the antichrist. *Fortean Picture Library.*

was engaged in his "shuttle diplomacy" between Egypt and Israel, it was discovered that his last name, through a formula in which A = 1 × 6, B = 2 × 6, C = 3 × 6, etc., added up to 666. This conclusion was presented by some as "proof" that Kissinger was designing the Middle East peace treaty that would usher in the prophesied time of deception and prepare the way for antichrist and one-world government. Later, some observers wondered if the birthmark on the forehead of Mikhail Gorbachev, general secretary and president of the USSR, was the "mark of the beast," which might point to him as a potential antichrist candidate.

Since then new candidates have appeared from time to time. When Ronald Reagan was president of the United States, for example, some wondered if his legendary communication skills might mask an evil purpose. They pointed out that his name, Ronald Wilson Reagan, consisted of three sets of six letters. Was he the legendary 666? His death, which has not yet been followed by a resurrection, seems to have quieted most of the speculation.

Following the field of eschatology (endtime theology) requires a breadth of biblical knowledge. Some popular Bible teachers such as Hal Lindsey string together events from Genesis to Revelation. Single verses from separate books of the Bible are placed out of their local context into a bigger scheme. Because many people don't have extensive biblical knowledge, it is sometimes easy to persuade them of the truth of the story without mentioning that the only references to the antichrist by name are found in 1 John 2:18, 2:22, and 4:3, and in 2 John 7.

Sources:

Buttrick, George A., ed. *The Interpreter's Dictionary of the Bible.* 4 vols. New York: Abingdon Press, 1962.

Douglas, J. D., ed. *The New International Dictionary of the Christian Church.* Grand Rapids, MI: Zondervan, 1974.

May, Herbert G., and Bruce M. Metzger, eds. *The New Oxford Annotated Bible with the Apocrypha.* Rev. ed. New York: Oxford University Press, 1973.

Strong, James. *The Exhaustive Concordance of the Bible.* New York: Abingdon Press, 1890.

Willis, Jim. *The Religion Book: Places, Prophets, Saints, and Seers.* Detroit: Visible Ink Press, 2004.

APOCALYPSE

(See also Apocalyptic Writing)

The word *apocalypse* comes from a Greek word meaning a disclosure, a revelation, or a vision of the future. It is usually used within a context of telling the future or describing what the future holds. But its use implies a certain kind of thinking. If someone discloses an apocalypse, especially in the Western world, steeped as it is in the traditional thought patterns of monotheism, it is easy to get caught up in the vision itself without questioning the underlying cultural baggage.

Basic Assumptions of Apocalypse

1. Apocalypse assumes duality. Good is at war with evil. You are on either one side or the other. One camp is presided over by a God who made everything good, only to see it, for one reason or another, go wrong. The other camp is presided over by a created being who was once good but, for whatever reason, decided to rebel and enlisted enough support from his created counterparts to recruit an army that followed him in his attempted coup. (Masculine pronouns are used in this case because in all dualistic traditions, the devil, Satan, Iblis, or Ahriman is always personified as masculine.)

The monotheistic dualistic system is thus an attempt to explain why evil exists in what is otherwise a good world. How could a good God create a world of suffering? Why do bad things happen to good people? Why do the innocent suffer while the guilty prosper? Monotheism places the original sin and rebellion within a historical time. In the Bible, that time is solidly anchored in the Garden of Eden (see Adam and Eve). "Original sin" is not a particular kind of sin so much as the beginning of a pattern of sinfulness. In this tradition, there was a time when humans were innocent. In Genesis 3 they willingly threw away that innocence and became sinners after being tempted by the evil one. Before Genesis 3 there was no sin in the world. After that, "sin entered the world through one man, and death by sin, and in this way death came to all men, because all sinned" (Rom. 5:12).

2. The Apocalypse is the final battle between good and evil, so it is eschatological in nature. Eschatology is the study of the end. So apocalyptic thinking assumes that time is a river flowing inexorably to a fixed destination, a final duel between good and evil. In Christian thinking this duel takes place at the battle of Armageddon (see Armageddon, Battle of.) So prevalent is the Christian system that "Armageddon" has become an almost universal synonym for the violent, all-encompassing, total end of something.

Secondary Assumptions of Apocalypse

1. Apocalypse involves a seer and a vision. A prophet, whether Saint John the Apostle, Nostradamus, Joan of Arc, or Edgar Cayce, catches a glimpse of the future, a vision of the culminating battle and the events surrounding the final duel between good and evil. Because this great confrontation takes place in a future world, not experienced by the seer, the vision is often cloudy, presented in symbolic language.

2. Apocalypse involves a messiah figure. The good God will not enter his (again—note the masculine pronoun) creation, either because he will not sully himself or because the creation cannot physically survive in the radiance of his presence. So a substitute is sent. A representative, a son or a transformed beloved former prophet, will return.

The good God has an army, usually consisting of angels (the created beings who did not succumb to sin). The evil devil has an army too, consisting of those who, like him, were once angels but, again like him, sinned and fell from grace (see Angels).

For some reason, most apocalyptic visions include symbolic imagery using animals and mystical numbers. Lions and eagles, bears and lambs abound throughout the literature of every tradition. And the numbers three, four, seven, and forty appear with almost monotonous regularity. One thousand is always popular, especially in relation to century and millennium markers. Stars and other signs in the heavens appear at every turn. Astral predictions are almost universal in apocalyptic visions.

Finally, the end always comes with events of great woe and tribulation. Those who have remained faithful according to the tradition of the seer are usually spared, even if just barely. But punishment always accompanies the final victory of the good God.

It is difficult to escape apocalyptic thinking in today's society. During the Persian Gulf War, the leaders of Saddam Hussein's Muslim forces called upon Allah to aid them in the "mother of all battles" against a country the Iraqis labeled the "Great Satan." Meanwhile, in the United States, the faithful were urged to pray for their troops and political speeches commonly ended with the injunction "God bless America."

Apocalyptic language has even invaded that most religious of events in American life—baseball. In April 2004, the fans at Boston's Fenway Park were cheering for their beloved Red Sox against the hated New York Yankees. The Sox held a slim lead and the Fenway faithful were beginning to believe they might defeat the sport's equivalent of the Great Satan when, in the ninth inning, New York's newly acquired Alex Rodriguez came to the plate. Without missing a beat, the Red Sox general manager, Theo Epstein, turned to the person sitting next to him and recited in a holy timbre, "The apocalypse is upon us. The tying run is coming to the plate in the form of A-Rod, right field is on fire, and apparently we're all going to die. This is the end of the world." (It turned out to be yet another example of unfulfilled prophecy. Rodriguez did hit safely, but the next batter struck out. Sox 5, Yankees 4.)

Like it or not, whether we consider ourselves to be religious or not, apocalypse has become a part of our thought process, and it is difficult to break out of it. But if we question the assumptions underlying apocalyptic thinking, if we question dualism and linear eschatology, if we question the idea of messiahs and angels and ask why certain numbers are intrinsically more important than others, Apocalypse Now is left with little ammunition other than its tantalizing power to produce wonder, fear, and dread.

Sources:

Buttrick, George A., ed. *The Interpreter's Dictionary of the Bible*. 4 vols. New York: Abingdon Press, 1962.
Horrigan, Jeff. "Sox Scorch Yankees." *Boston Globe*, April 20, 2004.

APOCALYPTIC WRITING

One of the biggest differences between the Eastern thought of Hinduism and Buddhism and the Western thought of Judaism, Christianity, and Islam is the concept of time. Monotheistic religions tend to view time as linear, with a beginning and end, and often have difficulty even imagining another way of thinking. It just seems obvious that everything started at some time in the past and will end at some time in the future. How else but as a straight line could time be imagined? Even our vocabulary assures us that "time marches on" as we conceive our "timelines."

In religions arising out of Eastern thought, however, time is circular or cyclical, repeating itself endlessly. A good exercise to free oneself from Western thinking is simply to ask, "If time and space began with the Big Bang, what happened before that?" Or, "If space is expanding, what is it expanding into?" (These questions both begin with an assumption of linear time but move the mind into a different dimension of thinking. The scientist's answer to both questions, by the way, is "nothing.") It is difficult to imagine, but for most of humankind's existence linear thinking was not even an option.

One theory currently afloat suggests that God may not be a human invention, but time is. Because we are born, grow old, and die, we think in terms of the passing of time. But those who study such things say that time may be simply a human way of measuring minuscule sections of eternity. Eternity, by the way, has nothing to do with time. Eternity is not, after all, a long, long time. It is forever. What all this means, according to scientific theorists like Julian Barbour (see Barbour, Julian), is that, from a strictly theoretical standpoint, the word *God*, understood at the very least to mean eternity, may well be a more accurate word than *time* for describing reality.

Which is roughly what the Hindu *rishis* have been saying for centuries.

Once you have a beginning and end, however, the mind immediately jumps to how the end will come—and to what happens next. The study of these things is called eschatology (see Eschatology, Comparative; Eschaton). When visions of the end were experienced and written down, usually in intricate symbolism that only the initiated would understand, the result was what we call "apocalyptic writing." One notable example in this tradition is the book of Revelation, often called the "Apocalypse of Saint John" (see Revelation), in the Christian New Testament. But there were many, many similar books that didn't pass muster for the final biblical cut. The book of Enoch, the book of Baruch, the Pseudepigrapha, and the Apocalypse of Peter are just a few examples that still survive.

This kind of apocalyptic writing first appears in Persian Zoroastrianism. Zoroaster, called Zarathustra by the Greeks, is thought to have lived circa 550 BCE, although some scholars place him as much as five hundred years earlier. A good case can be made that he founded the first monotheistic religion, even though Abraham is generally credited with this honor. But until the Babylonian captivity, when Jews first experienced Persian religion, their writing was filled with sentences such as "Jehovah is a mighty God, and a great God above all gods" (Ps. 95:3). The phrase "all gods" suggests that Judaism was not yet monotheistic.

The principal concept of Zoroastrian apocalyptic writing is dualism. A battle between good and evil is being carried out on planet Earth. The good God, Ahura Mazda, is using humankind to bait the evil Ahriman into the world. Ahriman will tempt humans, and they, by resisting, will wear him down so that he can eventually be destroyed. History will end at the last judgment, and a new, purified earth will be formed. Humans will be rewarded with paradise, an ideal heavenly realm with a divine court abiding over the blessed, or hell, which is not eternal but will purify the wicked along with the earth. Before that happens, however, Zoroaster will return. He will be conceived by a virgin with his own seed, which has been stored in a mountain lake. Every thousand years between the founder and the final restoration of the world three thousand years later, a prophet will appear, check out the progress of the world, and help to prepare the final battle.

When the Jews returned from the Babylonian/Persian captivity, their writings showed evidence of the kind of apocalyptic literature they had encountered there. The later prophets of Judaism, beginning with Daniel, wrote with "good against evil" and "light against dark" imagery. The Dead Sea Scrolls left by the Essene community make it clear that apocalyptic theology was a potent force in their struggle against Roman oppression.

It may well have been a sense of apocalyptic curiosity that allegedly prompted some Zoroastrian priests, called "magi" or "wise men," to make the long journey to Bethlehem after they saw an astrological event sometime around 6 BCE that they believed signaled the birth of the king of the Jews.

The Qur'an of Islam continued the tradition of monotheistic apocalyptic writing:

> Then, on the Day of Judgment, He will cover them with shame, and say, "Where are My 'partners' concerning whom ye used to dispute (with the godly)?" … To those who do good, there is good in this world, and the Home of the Hereafter is even better and excellent indeed is the Home of the righteous, Gardens of Eternity which they will enter: beneath them flow pleasant rivers: they will have all that they wish: thus doth Allah reward the righteous, (namely) those whose lives the angels take in a state of purity, saying (to them), "Peace be on you; enter ye the Garden, because of (the good) which ye did (in the world)." (16:27–32)

Apocalyptic literature of all monotheistic religions shares a sense of linear time ending in a fiery judgment delivered from the mouth of God or his messenger, with rewards for the blessed and punishment for the wicked. Believers look forward to the next life and a cessation of the bitterness of this one, with the hope of hearing something like: "Blessed are those who wash their robes, that they may have the right to the tree of life and may go through the gates into the city.… Whoever is thirsty, let him come" (Rev. 22:14, 17).

Sources:

Buttrick, George A., ed. *The Interpreter's Dictionary of the Bible.* 4 vols. New York: Abingdon Press, 1962.

Ellwood, Robert S., and Barbara A. McGraw. *Many Peoples, Many Faiths: Women and Men in the World Religions.* 6th ed. Upper Saddle River, NJ: Prentice Hall, 1999.

Fisher, Mary Pat, and Lee W. Bailey, eds. *An Anthology of Living Religions.* Upper Saddle River, NJ: Prentice Hall, 2000.

The Holy Qur'an. Trans. with a commentary by Abdullah Yusuf Ali. Beirut: Dar Al Arabia, 1968.

LaSor, William Sanford. *The Dead Sea Scrolls and the Christian Faith.* Chicago: Moody Press, 1956.

May, Herbert G., and Bruce M. Metzger, eds. *The New Oxford Annotated Bible with the Apocrypha.* Rev. ed. New York: Oxford University Press, 1973.

Willis, Jim. *The Religion Book: Places, Prophets, Saints, and Seers.* Detroit: Visible Ink Press, 2004.

APOSTASY

The word *apostasy* refers to the abandonment or renunciation of Christianity. It doesn't appear in the King James Bible, but it does occur in the original Greek that was used to write 2 Thessalonians. This letter, generally attributed to the apostle Paul even though that attribution is questioned by many modern theologians, uses "apostasy" as one of the signs of the end that will signal the imminent return of Jesus Christ:

Concerning the coming of our Lord Jesus Christ [the Second Coming] and our being gathered to him [the Rapture], we ask you, brothers, not to become easily unsettled or alarmed by some prophecy, report or letter to have come from us, saying that the day of the Lord has already come. Don't let anyone deceive you in any way, for that day will not come until the rebellion [Greek *apostasia*] occurs and the man of lawlessness is revealed, the man doomed to destruction. He opposes and exalts himself over everything that is called God or is worshiped, and even sets himself up in God's temple, proclaiming himself to be God.... For this reason God sends them a powerful delusion so that they will believe the lie and so that all will be condemned who have not believed the truth but have delighted in wickedness. (2 Thess. 2:1–12)

The author of this letter obviously believes that an apostasy, a rejection of Christianity, will precede Armageddon and the end of all things. This belief has been quite common in evangelical/fundamentalist churches throughout the ages. It gives great comfort to know that even if you are outnumbered and the rest of the world is not serious about that which you consider most important, it is only a sign that the end is near.

Sources:

Douglas, J. D., ed. *The New International Dictionary of the Christian Church*. Grand Rapids, MI: Zondervan, 1974.

The Holy Bible, New International Version. Grand Rapids, MI: Zondervan, 1978.

APOSTLES' CREED

About 150 CE, probably in Rome, a statement then called a "symbol of faith" was composed and recited to baptism candidates:

Do you believe in God, the Father Almighty?

Do you believe in Christ Jesus, the Son of God, who was born of the Holy Ghost and of Mary the virgin, who was crucified under Pontius Pilate, and died, and rose again at the third day, living from among the dead, and ascended unto heaven and sat at the right hand of the Father, and will come again to judge the quick and the dead?

Do you believe in the Holy Ghost, the holy church, and the resurrection of the flesh?

Anyone who answered yes to all three questions was baptized. This was the genesis of Christianity's oldest statement of faith, the Apostles' Creed. We thus have strong evidence that, from very early in the new Christian movement, belief in a Second Coming was part of the tradition.

In countless churches around the globe, congregants are asked every Sunday if they believe that Jesus "will come again to judge the quick and the dead" and if they believe in "the resurrection of the flesh." And each Sunday countless faithful, albeit without a lot of conscious thought, answer that they do believe these things. No doubt this reaffirmation contributes to the statistics concerning the large majority (for example, some polls estimate 67 percent of Americans) of Christians who profess confidence that Jesus will personally come back to earth someday.

Source:
Gonzalez, Justo L. *The Story of Christianity*. 2 vols. New York: Harper & Row, 1985.

ARK OF THE COVENANT

The fabled Ark of the Covenant has been considered a "Holy Grail"–type archeological treasure ever since it disappeared more than six centuries before the birth of Christ.

What was it, exactly, and what does it have to do with Armageddon?

When Moses received the Law delivered to the Israelites after their escape from Egypt, he was told to build an ark upon which the glory of God would rest.

Ark comes from the Latin *arca*, used in the Vulgate to translate the Hebrew word for "box" or "chest." *Covenant* means "contract" or "promise." So the Ark of the Covenant became a physical, symbolic reminder of God's contract with his chosen people.

It was a box about two and a half feet high and wide and four and a half feet long, made of wood and covered with gold leaf. It was transported by means of two long poles and placed within the Holy of Holies in the tabernacle during the forty years the Jews spent wandering in the wilderness after their escape from Egypt. After the conquest of Canaan it was housed in the sanctuary at Shiloh and later brought by King David to the site of the future temple at Jerusalem. The occasion so inspired David that he "danced before the Lord," much to the disgust of his wife (1 Chron. 15).

When the Babylonians destroyed Solomon's temple in 586 BCE, the ark disappeared. Although many have tried to locate it (including Indiana Jones in the movie *Raiders of the Lost Ark*), its location has remained a mystery ever since. Some think it is hidden away in a temple in Ethiopia, brought there by the son of Solomon and the queen of Sheba. Others believe it lies concealed in the caves of Qumran or buried under the Temple Mount. Still others, just because they are skeptical archeological types, believe it destroyed. Otherwise, they say, why haven't we found it?

Three symbolic objects were placed within the ark. They each recalled stories that, when taken together, represent the very essence of Judaism. (The stories are found in Exodus and Numbers.)

The first object was the stone tablet containing the Ten Commandments. These represented God's law. But the people had broken God's law. While Moses was on Mount Sinai receiving instructions that forbade the worship of idols, the people were down below dancing around a golden calf. The tablets would forever symbolize the people's rejection of God's law.

The second object was a pot of manna. *Manna* literally means "What is it?" When the people needed food in the desert, God told Moses to have them go outside and gather a daily supply of a light bread that would form with the dew each morning. Only one day's supply could be gathered each day because it would spoil if hoarded. (On Saturday the bread would keep for an extra day so the people would not have to

Sixteenth-century woodcut depicting the Ark of the Covenant attended by musicians. *Fortean Picture Library.*

break the commandment forbidding work on the Sabbath.) When the people went outside on the first morning to discover the miracle of God's provision, they saw the manna and said, "What is it?" Hence the name. The idea was to teach trust in God's daily provision. But after the novelty wore off, the people complained, longing for the "leeks and onions of Egypt." So the manna in the ark represented their rejection of God's provision.

The third item was Aaron's rod that budded. Aaron had been selected by God to be high priest. But the people wanted to elect their own leaders. They complained to Moses, who passed the word on to God. God told Moses to have each tribe select a candidate for high priest. Each candidate would place his "rod," or walking staff, in the ground to be inspected during the next morning's convocation. The rod that "budded," or took root, would indicate God's choice. The implication was that God's leaders would "bear fruit," or produce results. Of course, Aaron's rod produced a bud and he went on to become the first high priest of Israel. But the people would always be reminded that they had rejected God's leadership.

On the cover of the ark stood the Mercy Seat. Two carved angels, one on each side with their arched wings meeting in the middle, looked down at the ark's contents. There they saw rejection—rejection of God's law, Gods provision, and God's leadership. That doesn't leave a lot more of God left to reject. But on one day a year, the Day of Atonement, Yom Kippur, the high priest sprinkled the blood of a sacrificial lamb on the Mercy Seat. On that day the angels would see not rejection but the blood of the innocent substitute, and the sins of the people would be atoned for.

Jews would love to see the ark's rediscovery. It would no doubt be considered a priceless archeological find. Most Christians, on the other hand, do not consider it an important piece of the Armageddon puzzle. Revelation 21:22 specifically states that there will be no need of a temple in the New Jerusalem because "the Lord God Almighty and the Lamb are its temple." Since the temple was built specifically to house the Ark of the Covenant, it would seem to most Christians that the ark did its duty in foreshadowing the ministry of Jesus Christ and is no longer an issue.

That does not keep people from wondering what this mysterious object really was. Mystery surrounds its history. Because the Bible makes a special point of saying that Moses' face glowed when he came out from the visible presence of God, some have speculated that the ark contained a powerful source of light. It was also said that at the ark Moses would hear the voice of God. This claim has sparked wild tales of its being a transmitter/receiver through which Moses was in contact with aliens from outer space, who supplied him with the specifications for building it. Because of the ark's ability to inspire armies in war—and because, according to 1 Samuel 6:19, at least fifty thousand men died after "looking into" it without proper consecration—speculation arose as to its mystical or military powers. Perhaps, say some of the more unrestrained theorists, the ark was an alien "Trojan horse" deliberately left among us by powers from outer space—powers that might, even now, be observing our progress.

Although the ark is not directly associated with Armageddon, it is a source of endless interest among those who wonder about the future of our race and our place in the cosmos.

Sources:
Bridger, David, ed. *The New Jewish Encyclopedia*. New York: Behrman House, 1962.
The Holy Bible, New International Version. Grand Rapids, MI: Zondervan, 1978.

ARMAGEDDON

This is the way the world ends
Not with a bang but a whimper.
  —T. S. Eliot, *The Hollow Men*

Some say the world will end in fire,
Some say in ice.
From what I've tasted of desire
I hold with those who favor fire.
  — Robert Frost, *Fire and Ice*

The word *Armageddon* has become synonymous with the end of the world, or at least the end of life as we know it. In terms of media attention, popular fiction writers seem to side with Robert Frost over T. S. Eliot. Endtime scenarios from the movies (see Hollywood Envisions THE END) include asteroids hitting the earth (*Armageddon*), wars (*Mad Max*), nuclear meltdowns (*The China Syndrome*), ecological shortsightedness (*Star Trek: The Voyage Home*), alien invasion (*Independence Day*), out-of-control technology (*The Matrix*), and viruses (*Mission Impossible II*).

The word has evolved into a moral metaphor as well. In James Michener's 1978 novel *Chesapeake*, Emily Paxmore, a Quaker pacifist, fights against political forces seeking to disenfranchise Americans of African descent. When asked why, she replies

> "Because each soul on this earth faces one Armageddon. When all the forces are arranged pro and con. Now comes the one great battle, and if thee runs away or fails to fight with vigor, thy life is forever diminished."

> "Thee sounds mighty military, for a Quaker" [her husband comments].

> "Armageddon is even more compelling when it's a battle of the spirit. … Armageddon comes once, and we'd better not back off."

Armageddon is a biblical term with an interesting but ambiguous origin. It is used only once in the Bible: "The sixth angel poured out his bowl on the great river Euphrates, and its water was dried up to prepare the way for the kings from the East. Then I saw three evil spirits…. spirits of demons…. and they go out to the kings of the whole world, to gather them for battle on the great day of God Almighty…. They gathered the kings together in the place that in Hebrew is called Armageddon" (Rev. 16:12–16).

According to many interpreters, the unknown author of the last book of the Bible is describing events leading up to the last battle of the world, which ends with the coming of a "rider on a white horse" (see Revelation). The rider's name is "Faithful and True," and he defeats the armies of the antichrist in the climactic battle of history that takes place in the valley of Megiddo, an immense plain in Israel.

Although the writer says that Armageddon is a Hebrew word, it appears nowhere else in Hebrew literature, and there is some doubt as to its proper spelling in Greek, the original language in which Revelation was written. So, aside from the highly symbolic language of this one sentence in the Bible, there is no other frame of reference or explanation available.

This hasn't prevented either popular culture or science from appropriating the term. When people hear "Armageddon," they take it to mean "THE END." Even prominent politicians use the word in that sense. James Mann, author of *Rise of the Vulcans*, claims that during the 1980s the United States government secretly carried out a highly classified program that no one knew about except for a very few important insiders. Mann calls it the "Armageddon Exercise."

According to Mann, after leaving their Washington-based jobs, Richard Cheney and Donald Rumsfeld usually made their way to Andrews Air Force Base outside the capital. From there, in the middle of the night, each man, joined by a team of forty to sixty federal officials and a single member of Ronald Reagan's cabinet, separately slipped away to some remote location in the United States, such as a discarded military base or an underground bunker. A convoy of lead-lined trucks carrying sophisticated communications equipment and other gear made its way to the same location.

The idea behind all the secrecy was that there could come a time when both the president and vice president were killed in a Soviet nuclear "decapitation" strike on Washington. In this case, the reasoning went, the United States had to act swiftly to ensure an unbroken chain of civilian command. Three teams of prominent officials, separated by many miles, had to be ready to assume control of the government. Schemes were concocted to take control of major media so that at least an illusion of stability could be put forth to the American people. Someone, after all, had to be able to negotiate with the Soviet Union—or to order a nuclear retaliation strike.

Mann quotes one unnamed participant in the exercises as saying, "One of the awkward questions we faced was whether to reconstitute Congress after a nuclear attack.... It was decided that no, it would be easier to operate without them."

This was all illegal, of course. The Constitution of the United States, including the Twenty-fifth Amendment, and the Presidential Succession Act of 1947 provide a completely different set of guidelines and do not allow for any such method of transferring authority. So the idea was scrapped. The exercises ceased. But Mann points out that on September 11, 2001, the actions of Dick Cheney and Donald Rumsfeld, then respectively vice president and secretary of defense, bore a striking resemblance to the covert maneuvers carried out in the dead of night two decades earlier when they rehearsed their secret "Armageddon Exercises."

Sources:

Mann, James. *Rise of the Vulcans: The History of Bush's War Cabinet*. New York: Penguin Group, 2004.

May, Herbert G., and Bruce M. Metzger, eds. *The New Oxford Annotated Bible with the Apocrypha*. New York: Oxford University Press, 1973.

Michener, James A. *Chesapeake*. New York: Random House, 1978.

ARMAGEDDON *see* **Hollywood Envisions** THE END

ARMAGEDDON, BATTLE OF

(See also Abomination of Desolation; Apocalyptic Writing; Armageddon; *Left Behind* Books; Lindsey, Hal; Millennium; Rapture; Revelation; Second Coming; Temple at Jerusalem)

In 1970, when Hal Lindsey published his blockbuster hit *The Late Great Planet Earth*, he presented a blow-by-blow description of the battle of Armageddon. Assigning his interpretation of modern countries' names to the Bible's description of the final battle, which he called World War III, he described for his readers exactly what would happen at this epic conflict on the plains of Megiddo.

People snapped up the book in record numbers. It sat for weeks atop the *New York Times* best-seller list for nonfiction (although many people wondered if it should have been placed in the fiction category instead). It marked the beginning of the modern-day evangelical Armageddon craze that culminated in the *Left Behind* series of books by Tim LaHaye and Jerry Jenkins. Based roughly on Lindsey's biblical scheme of interpretation, the series had sold some 62 million copies by 2004, making it easily the most popular fiction series ever published.

As for *The Late Great Planet Earth*, however, things have changed since 1970. Most notably, the Soviet Union, key to Lindsey's analysis, is no more. So twenty-seven years later he revised his interpretation. His 1997 book *Apocalypse Code* didn't sell nearly as well as its predecessor, but it did give Lindsey a chance to update his picture of the world-ending conflict.

Because many consider Lindsey to be the granddaddy of Armageddon interpreters and thousands of evangelical Christians follow his lead, both his earlier and later interpretation schemes are outlined below. At the end of the second synopsis, a short list of his referenced scripture passages is presented.

Armageddon: The 1970 Version

Armageddon begins, strangely enough, with a peace treaty. Following the Rapture of the church (see Rapture), the antichrist, posing as a man of peace and goodwill, arranges for the signing of a treaty that will supposedly bring peace to the troubled Middle East. The rest of the world, accustomed to nothing but warfare and strife in that area, sees the treaty as a miracle. Its signing, coming in the wake of the Rapture—an event that will have caused worldwide confusion and anxiety—elevates the antichrist to a position of great power.

If a third temple (see Temple at Jerusalem) has not already been built by this time, it will be constructed in the wake of the peace that comes to Israel and her neighbors. Then, three and one-half years into the time of peace, the antichrist will ascend the steps of the new temple (see Abomination of Desolation) to hold a global news conference, during which he will declare himself to be God incarnate and demand worship from the people of planet Earth.

At this point, according to Lindsey, "an Arab-African confederacy, headed by Egypt, launches an invasion of Israel. This fatal mistake spells their doom and begins the Armageddon campaign." The Soviet Union uses the invasion as an excuse to launch its own two-pronged attack. An amphibious assault in the Mediterranean Sea, striking both Egypt and Israel, is coordinated with a land push south through Israel to join forces in Egypt. Apparently the reason behind this invasion is that Russia has always coveted the potash found in the Dead Sea. According to Lindsey, it will be a valuable source of fertilizer, needed to feed the starving millions of the world. Besides this resource, Russia seeks to gain a strategic seaport on the land bridge connecting the continents of Europe, Asia, and Africa. (In 1970 Lindsey pointed out that Russia's Mediterranean fleet outnumbered American vessels. He reasoned that this was simply a sign of the end.)

Although he admits to speculation at this point, Lindsey believes that the revived Roman Empire, under the control of the antichrist, will eventually ally itself with China. The battle plan calls for an invasion from the east by Chinese forces while European armies attack from the west, centering on Israel. The Red Army (Soviet Union) falls victim to "tactical nuclear weapons" launched by Western forces, now an alignment of American and European armies. At the end of the exchange: "With United Arab and African armies neutralized by the Russian invasion, and the consequent complete annihilation of the Russian forces and their homeland, we have only two great spheres of power left to fight the final climactic battle of Armageddon: the combined forces of the Western civilization united under the leadership of the Roman Dictator and the vast hordes of the Orient probably united under the Red Chinese war machine."

So begins the final stage of the battle. An "incredible Oriental army of 200 million soldiers marches to the eastern banks of the Euphrates." The Roman troops, under the antichrist, move to meet them. They join in battle, eventually, in the valley of Megiddo, in central Israel.

At the height of the battle, as an exchange of nuclear weapons threatens to destroy all life on the planet, Jesus Christ returns at the head of the armies of heaven. On a white horse, he comes riding down through the clouds out of the sky. Although weapons of mass destruction are turned against him, the armies of earth are powerless before his might. All the kingdoms of the world are destroyed, the antichrist is thrown into a lake of fire, Satan is bound, judgments are wrought, and a peaceful thousand-year reign of Jesus Christ on earth begins.

Armageddon: The 1997 Version

Do you know what the United States would do if attacked by nuclear missiles? Pray. That's right. I'm all in favor of prayer, of course. But that would be our only option. We are defenseless against an incoming attack by even one intercontinental ballistic missile today—and for the foreseeable future.

Why? Because our politicians have sold us out.... Current congressional attitudes and actions, or should I say inaction, on this issue border on criminal negligence at worst and outright stupidity at best.

So declares Hal Lindsey in his 1997 book *Apocalypse Code*. He wrote the book to update his Armageddon battle plan because "in the old days, the only real enemy we faced in the world was the Soviet Union. While Russia is still an adversary to contend with—particularly in the nuclear arena—things have gotten much more complicated."

In Lindsey's revised script of the events following the Rapture of the true church, it is now a Russian-Muslim confederacy that attacks Israel. The economic and political strength of a reborn Roman Empire in Europe, supported by the United States and other Western nations, provokes a desperation move by Russia: "They will probably launch more than 60 ICBMs and submarine-based missiles at Europe, USA and Canada to stop the counterattacks from cutting off their supply lines and isolating them." At that point, everybody who has nuclear missiles fires them off with what Lindsey dubs a "launch them or lose them" mentality. This exchange produces the results described in the eighth chapter of the book of Revelation.

The Russian-Muslim confederation next launches an invasion of Israel, releasing pent-up, centuries-old religious anger concerning ownership of the land in Jerusalem upon which the Jewish temple was built (see Temple at Jerusalem). A holy war ensues, during which Russia double-crosses many of its Muslim allies, including Egypt. Although we don't know exactly why this split occurs, Lindsey speculates that it's because the Muslims from the African continent won't go along with Iran's "fanatical brand of Islamic Fundamentalism."

Now "the Russian leader, positioned in Egypt, learns of the mighty Asian army assembling in the East, obviously to attack his rear eastern flank." He is also bothered by rumors of troop movements in Europe, preparing to attack him while he is spread out along a front too large for him to defend. So the Russians and their remaining Muslim allies retreat to Israel, setting up their "command HQs on the Temple Mount in Jerusalem. These forces try to annihilate the Jews as they do this."

By the time the invading Asian army of 200 million soldiers reaches the Euphrates River, the armies of the antichrist have "totally destroyed the Russian forces, and also the remnant of the Iranian-led Muslim forces." The army of the East is able to cross the Euphrates because Turkey has recently "completed work on a dam project that literally allows that nation to turn off the headwaters to the Euphrates at any time."

Lindsey then spends twelve pages documenting the Chinese rise to power and immense nuclear potential, along with reasons the West has to fear the threat. Eventually, however, East meets West at the valley of Megiddo.

This time around, Lindsey sees in the book of Revelation descriptions of helicopters, nerve gas, and mobile ICBM launchers "of the Russian SS-25 and SS-26 variety." He also notes that "astrologically speaking, the alignment of the planets in the shape of a pentagram just began in early 1997. This phenomenon has precipitated a surge in occult activity." To him, this is proof that those who await what he calls the "moronic conversion" (his response to the "harmonic conversion" many astrologers predicted would usher in the Age of Aquarius) are among those the Bible labels "false prophets."

The final battle takes place much as Lindsey predicted back in 1970, albeit with more descriptive detail this time. The weapons have been updated, but Christ still rides out of the sky on his white charger, fulfilling the prophecy of Acts 1:11— "This same Jesus, who was taken from you into heaven, will come back in the same way you have seen him go into heaven."

Of course, in the book of Acts, he wasn't riding a horse.

Principal Bible references: Isaiah 63; Ezekiel 38; Daniel 11; Zechariah 14; Matthew 24; 1 Thessalonians 4; Revelation 9–20.

(We have used Hal Lindsey as the principal reference point to understanding the evangelical idea of how Armageddon will occur, but it is important to note that, with very minor changes, Tim LaHaye and Jerry Jenkins follow this same scheme in their popular book and movie series *Left Behind*. Thus Lindsey's work serves as a good example of exactly what fundamentalist/evangelical Christians believe awaits us in the near future.)

The Liberal Response

In liberal academia it is quite fashionable to cast Lindsey's scenario of the battle of Armageddon in a rather simplistic light. When religious liberal scholars gather to discuss the latest biblical theories, *The Late Great Planet Earth* is never mentioned except in jest. Literalism is often treated as the final refuge for uneducated believers who don't know any better.

But a serious problem arises whenever liberal scholars take the trouble to debate conservatives like LaHaye and Lindsey. The Bible is very specific at times, especially when it comes to numbers. Why is it metaphorically important to specify that exactly 144,000 believers gather in heaven while "a great multitude that no one can count" receive white robes on earth? What is the symbolic purpose of describing an army of exactly 200 million men of the East and then repeating, "I heard their number" (Rev. 9:16)? Wouldn't "a large army" suffice? Metaphors just don't have to be that specific. In the parables, when Jesus employs metaphors, he doesn't name names. He says, "a certain man" or "a certain woman." It's obvious he's using metaphorical language. Why do apocalyptic writers have to be so precise?

The problem with Revelation is that it reads too much like a newspaper account—a description of something that's actually happening. It's easy to lump all the specifics together and then declare them to be apocalyptic metaphor, but it's hard to justify that position when a primary reason for doing so is simply that any alternative sounds silly.

The religious conservative can simply claim that what the Bible says, the Bible must mean. The religious liberal has a more difficult problem. He or she must appeal to the whole genre of apocalyptic writing outside the biblical tradition. But because the very writing he or she appeals to was rejected by the same committee that accepted Revelation, the question must be addressed as to why Revelation was included in the canon of scripture while other works were not. What is it about Revelation that is different—that sets it apart from the rest of the genre?

The answer comes with great difficulty, steeped as it is in academic scholarship requiring very specific and technical study. Laypeople, even very educated, highly intelligent laypeople, usually are not ready to sift through the tedious interpretive schemes that are often debated by scholars. And it doesn't help that when the task seems so exasperatingly frustrating, liberal scholars tend to dismiss the issue with a smirk and a shrug. That may end the debate, but it doesn't win many people in the pew over to the liberal cause.

Recently, however, liberal scholars, led by academics such as Marcus Borg, have taken up the challenge. Borg is the author of *Reading the Bible Again for the First Time: Taking the Bible Seriously but Not Literally*. The book's subtitle expresses Borg's thought very well. He seeks to present a reasoned response to the literal approach made so popular by Tim LaHaye and Jerry Jenkins in their *Left Behind* series.

The fault lines between conservative and liberal are nowhere more clearly delineated than when it comes to interpreting apocalyptic literature addressing the battle of Armageddon.

Sources:

Borg, Marcus J. *Reading the Bible Again for the First Time: Taking the Bible Seriously but Not Literally*. San Francisco: HarperSanFrancisco, 2001.

LaHaye, Tim, and Jerry B. Jenkins. *Left Behind* series. 12 vols. Carol Stream, IL: Tyndale House, 1995–2004.

Lindsey, Hal. *Apocalypse Code*. Palos Verdes, CA: Western Front Ltd., 1997.

Lindsey, Hal, with C. C. Carlson. *The Late Great Planet Earth*. Grand Rapids, MI: Zondervan, 1970.

ARMSTRONG, HERBERT W.

(See also America in Prophecy)

Controversy swirled around Herbert W. Armstrong from the day he founded the Worldwide Church of God in 1947 until the day of his death in 1986. He considered himself to be God's emissary on earth, preaching a fundamentalist system of biblical interpretation that he formed during a stint as an ordained minister with the Church of God (Seventh Day). After he was dismissed from the denomination due to theological differences, however, untoward gossip and rumors about his own morality began to surface. Some called him an alcoholic. Others accused him of incest with his young daughter. His son, Garner Ted Armstrong, often referred to as the "man with the golden voice" because of his professional, smooth radio delivery heard by millions on his radio and television show *The World Tomorrow*, eventually split with his father over doctrinal disputes and began his own church. Indeed, many churches have sprouted from seeds sown by Herbert Armstrong through the *Plain Truth* magazine and the now-defunct Ambassador College, a private religious school he founded in Pasadena, California.

What brought Armstrong to the attention of so many people begins with his bedrock theology called "British Israelism," even though he was accused of plagiarism and stealing his ideas from J. H. Allen's book *Judas' Scepter and Joseph's Birthright*. In short, he believed the modern nations of Europe and America to be descendants of the Ten Lost Tribes of Israel.

When ancient Israel was wracked by civil war following the death of Solomon, it split into two nations. The southern kingdom, called Judah, consisting of people descended from the patriarchs Judah and Benjamin, kept the bloodline of King David intact, along with temple worship, in Jerusalem, their capital. The northern kingdom, retaining the name Israel, suffered through one short-lived dynasty after another. It consisted of ten tribes that were eventually, according to the biblical account, carried off into captivity in Assyria. Disappearing from history, they became known as the "Ten Lost Tribes of Israel." Endless speculation as to their whereabouts has arisen over the centuries. The Church of Jesus Christ of Latter-day Saints—popularly referred to as the Mormons—believes that some of them wound up in America. Others claim to have tracked individual tribes to Ethiopia and China.

Armstrong believed that the tribes migrated into Europe and, eventually, to America. He believed that it is the destiny of Western Europe and the United States to "hold the fort" for Jesus until he returns. And when Jesus comes back to earth following the battle of Armageddon, the saints will be rewarded, obtaining

The late Herbert W. Armstrong, who spent a long career warning that the end was near. *Associated Press.*

the position of co-rulers, kings and priests, brothers to Jesus.

According to Armstrong, "God" is a family. There are now two in the family, Jesus Christ and God the Father (Armstrong did not accept the idea of the Holy Spirit as a separate, coequal part of the Trinity). There soon will be many more. All true believers will get to do on other planets what Jesus did on this one. A "wonderful world tomorrow" thus awaits those who remain faithful and keep the commandments, most notably observing the Sabbath on Saturday and tithing, or giving one-tenth of one's income to the church.

Known for his prolific use of capital letters for emphasis, and known just as much for never stating a new truth without first setting it up with a series of warnings such as "YOU WON'T BELIEVE IT" and "AMAZING BUT TRUE," Armstrong never set dates for Armageddon, unless one counts the numerous times he revealed something he had discovered concerning current events and biblical prophecy that "will COME TO PASS within THE NEXT 5 or 6 YEARS!"

Since Armstrong's death the church has undergone a metamorphosis. Long labeled a cult by many orthodox Christians, it now claims to have cleaned up the legacy left by its founder. It has tried to reenter the world of mainstream conservative Christianity and has even been accepted into the National Association of Evangelicals.

Source:
Armstrong, Herbert W. *The United States and British Commonwealth in Prophecy*. Pasadena, CA: Ambassador College Press, 1967.

ASTEROIDS

On June 30, 1908, at 7:17 A.M. local time, a farmer working his acres near the Tunguska River in Siberia had just sat down next to his plow to eat his breakfast. Little did he know he was about to become the first man in written history to witness and describe a collision between Earth and an asteroid: "I heard sudden bangs, as if from gunfire. My horse fell to its knees. From the north side above the forest a flame shot up. Then I saw the fir forest had been bent over by the wind, and I thought of a hurricane. I seized hold of my plough with both hands…. The wind was so strong that it carried soil from the surface of the ground."

People in the village of Nizhne-Karelinsh, some two hundred miles away, later reported their impressions of "a bluish-white streak of fire" that seemed to split the sky in half for ten minutes. An engineer on the Trans-Siberian Railroad stopped his train, assuming it had derailed.

The area was so difficult to reach that it took thirteen years before a scientific expedition actually made its way there to investigate. But the event was noticed, just the same. Duncan Steel, in his book *Rogue Asteroids and Doomsday Comets*, quotes an article from the *New York Times* concerning reactions from as far away as London: "The northern sky at midnight became blue as if the clouds were breaking, and the clouds were touched with pink in so marked a fashion that police headquarters was rung up by several people who believed a big fire was raging in the north of London." Shock waves from the blast traveled around the globe twice, setting off earthquake alarms in country after country before finally subsiding.

When scientists finally penetrated the area and began to do serious research, what they found was amazing. More than four thousand square miles of forest had been leveled. Animals and humans had been instantly incinerated. Devastation was apparent everywhere. The investigators encountered so much information that they simply couldn't process it all.

It took years to pull all the evidence together. But amid speculation ranging from the explosion of an alien spacecraft to a black hole colliding with the planet, it was finally decided that the region had been hit by an asteroid measuring about 130 feet in diameter. It apparently exploded some three miles above the ground, releasing a force of 40 megatons. That is about two thousand times greater than the force of the atomic bomb dropped on Hiroshima.

This was not the first close encounter the planet has had with asteroids. Meteor Crater in northern Arizona attracts a large number of visitors each year. They come to witness just what can happen when an object from outer space collides with the earth and releases energy equal to that of 20 million tons of TNT. A crater 170 meters deep and 1,200 meters wide was formed some fifty thousand years ago in the desert south of the Grand Canyon.

And this event was just a pipsqueak compared with other impacts Earth has experienced. Many scientists think that the dinosaurs' dominance of the planet ended some 65 million years ago when an asteroid measuring at least 180 kilometers in diameter crashed into the Yucatán Peninsula in Mexico. That impact ended life as the dinosaurs knew it, opening an ecological niche for a new species called mammals to arise. Had that event not occurred, humankind might never have happened.

Duncan Steel is a research astronomer at the Anglo-Australian Observatory in Adelaide, Australia. An expert on the hazards of asteroids and comets from outer space, he has served on both the Detection Committee and the Intercept Committee created by NASA to discover, investigate, and possibly avert doomsday collisions. In his opinion, "the future of the human race and all other forms of life may well depend on" addressing the possibility of such an impact. "Inaction at this stage is simply an indulgence in a game of Russian roulette, whether or not we know that the gun is pointed at us, and whether or not we realize that the trigger is being pulled." According to Steel, it is not a matter of *if* such a collision will occur, but *when*. There is clear evidence that the asteroids are out there. There is clear evidence that they have collided with Earth in the past. There is clear evidence that life ended for former species as a result of those collisions. It is folly to deny that it will happen again. As a matter of fact, statistics say we may even be overdue for another Armageddon impact.

On the other hand, there are those who use statistics to demonstrate that such fears are overblown. According to one set of actuarial figures, the probability of a resident of the United States dying in an automobile accident is 1 in 100. The probability of being killed in an asteroid impact is 1 in 10,000. The probability of dying from a bee sting is 1 in 100,000. Put another way, the probability of dying in an asteroid impact is roughly half that of being killed in a plane crash. So why make such a big deal about the whole thing? Why waste money on a study of something that might never occur in our lifetime and that we probably couldn't prevent even if it did?

Steel counters this argument by pointing out the economics involved in putting money into programs such as Spaceguard, based at the observatory of the University of Arizona. Its purpose is to find and record the orbits of possible doomsday asteroids. According to Steel, all Earth-threatening asteroids larger than one kilometer in diameter could be discovered and tracked at a cost of about $300 million spread over twenty-five years. While conceding that this is a lot of money, he argues that it is very small when compared with the massive damage that an asteroid strike could cause. A one-kilometer asteroid hitting the earth would likely kill 25 percent of human beings on the planet, and an impact of this size can be expected, on average, every 100,000 years. Since the economic cost of such a catastrophe would be virtually uncountable, Steel believes that $300 million spent on predicting and, if possible, averting it represents a wise investment.

Economics notwithstanding, just what is an asteroid and why is it so threatening?

An asteroid is a large rock in orbit around the sun. The word itself means "star-like." Most of the known asteroids are found in a broad swath called the Asteroid Belt. Formed in the distant past, they are doomed to a path dictated by the sun's gravity. The eons roll on while asteroids, some very big, some very small, orbit in an endless ellipse. Unless they encounter an obstruction, they will continue their lonely life until they eventually fall into the sun's fiery furnace. The problem comes when their orbits bring them into the gravitational pull of another body—Earth, for instance, or another planet, such as Jupiter (see Comets). Then the results can be catastrophic, as past evidence seems to indicate. The asteroid that caused the Armageddon event at the end of the age of the dinosaurs probably destroyed 90 percent of life on Earth.

Earth can expect an impact the size of the Siberian event on the average of about once every fifty to one hundred years. Smaller asteroids, of less than 10 meters in diameter, about the largest that reach the earth's surface without burning up in the atmosphere, probably strike our planet about once a year. Larger ones, such as the one that killed off the dinosaurs, are a lot less common. We don't even know how many are out there or where their orbits will take them.

Statistics are tricky. We have just as good a chance of encountering a killer asteroid tomorrow as we would have on any other given day in the next million years.

The search has just begun. Astronomers have plotted the courses of about six thousand asteroids and are actively hunting more, but finances, political pressure, and time requirements hamper the effort. Meanwhile, on March 18, 2004, the *New York Times* reported that an asteroid called 2004FH, measuring 100 feet across, passed a mere 26,500 miles above the Atlantic Ocean. This was a small asteroid, but it was the closest encounter we have ever viewed without an impact.

Is there an Armageddon asteroid in our future? Yes. Will it arrive in our lifetime? We don't know. Will we be able to avert such a disaster? Only time will tell.

Sources:

Steel, Duncan. *Rogue Asteroids and Doomsday Comets: The Search for the Million Megaton Menace That Threatens Life on Earth.* New York: John Wiley & Sons, 1995.

Wilson, Colin, and Damon Wilson. *The Mammoth Encyclopedia of the Unsolved.* New York: Carroll and Graf, 2000.

ASTROLOGY

When people began to consider the universe that they encountered each night in the star-filled skies over their heads, they probably began to wonder whether the stars could foretell future events and exercise control over their everyday life.

An unknown Bible psalmist wrote that "the heavens declare the glory of God" (Ps. 19:1). Zoroastrian astrologers called "magi" traveled to Bethlehem at the birth of Jesus because they saw a "star" or sign in the heavens foretelling the birth of a Jewish king (Matt. 2). Long before that, astrologers in places as far apart as Egypt, China, Peru, and England built stone structures to aid in foretelling times and seasons based on the heavens.

Good evidence has been presented that some of the pyramids of Egypt mirror the stars of the constellation Orion, the three pyramids of Giza echoing on earth the position of the three stars of Orion's belt. There appears to be astrological significance attached to many of the enigmatic stone circles of western Europe, Stonehenge being the most obvious. Indians of the American Southwest seem to have been very aware of the significance of astral events, recording them on pictographs scattered throughout Arizona and New Mexico. Chinese mythology makes mention of comets and stars that are now tracked and followed by astronomers.

The "Source" that Edgar Cayce claimed to access in his trances taught him that the planets influence human behavior (see Cayce, Edgar).

When comet Hale-Bopp stood high in the sky during spring evenings of 1997, groups such as the Heaven's Gate cult were sure it was a prophecy portending either doom or salvation to the human race (see Heaven's Gate).

Shakespeare seems to have held a lower opinion of astrology, causing Julius Caesar to say, "Men at some time are masters of their fates: / The fault, dear Brutus, is not in our stars, / But in ourselves, that we are underlings." Apparently his disdain is not shared by the millions of people who religiously search their newspapers each morning to read their daily horoscopes—often even while professing not to believe in such things.

Arabic astrologers, from the 1513 Venetian edition of *In Somnium Scipionis*, by Macrobius. *Fortean Picture Library*.

Although astrologers generally do not predict the end of the universe as such, a series of "Armageddons" mark the ends of astrological ages. We are currently in transition between the Age of Pisces and the Age of Aquarius. Aquarius is the eleventh sign of the Zodiac. As Jeff Jawer, a professional astrologer, explains it:

> The great ages are a result of the wobble of the Earth's pole on its axis. The cycle of approximately 26,000 years gives rise to twelve ages of about 2,160 years each. The beginning of an age occurs when the vernal equinox (Sun at zero degrees of Aries) enters a new constellation. This precession of the equinoxes moves backward in the Zodiac, thus the shift from the twelfth sign Pisces (the fish) into the eleventh sign Aquarius. Due to conflicting interpretations on the boundaries of the constellations, there is a wide range of dates given as the beginning of the Age of Aquarius, from as early as the 1600's to as late as the 2400's. As with any slow cycle, it's likely that the transition process can cover a good deal of time, perhaps centuries.

According to astrologers, the Piscean Age was an age of systemic religious hierarchies. They do not wonder that early Christians adopted the sign of Pisces, the fish, as their secret sign and signal. Aquarius, however, signals freedom, awareness of spiritual possibilities, and individual paths to God.

Change brings confusion. Armageddon implies a culminating death or an end to what was. Astrologers warn that accepted but outgrown elements of the past often seem to conflict with the unknown future. In times of stress it is easy to harden opinions and seek to continue on familiar paths, even if those paths have not led out of the forest. Hence "us against them" thinking, sixties activism, post-9/11 tension, racial bigotry, and religious warfare.

The writer I. M. Oderberg claims that Aquarius has been anticipated by mystic religious movements within major institutional traditions. Buddhism and Hinduism have always allowed personal, individual expression. Within Judaism the Kabbalah has a mystic history going back to the Middle Ages. Sufi has offered an alternative tradition within Islam that is at once personal, flamboyant, individualistic, and meditative. The discovery of Gnostic gospels such as the gospel of Thomas has caused a great stir in Christian circles. People who never considered anything but what, to them, is traditional Christianity seem fascinated that there were once other ways to approach Christian belief. The mystical, highly individualistic trend of the charismatic movement has swept the denominations.

What might emerge in the Age of Aquarius is, of course, not clear. There are those who believe that trends point to tumultuous birth pangs, the equivalent of an astrological Armageddon, which are even now being felt. Earthquakes, population explosion, ecological disasters, and an increase in religious fundamentalism and resultant holy wars are only the beginning.

On the brighter side, those who disagree with Shakespeare's Caesar and believe that the fault *is* in our stars can hope that beyond all these agonies lies an age when "peace will rule the planets / And love will steer the stars."

Sources:
Focht, Doug. "The Age of Aquarius?" *Bible Search*. http://www.biblesearch.com/articles/articl14. htm.
Hitching, Francis. *Earth Magic*. New York: William Morrow, 1977.
Jawer, Jeff. "From Pisces to Aquarius: The Epochal Shift That Is Shaking Our World." *StarIQ. com*. http://www.stariq.com/Main/Articles/P0003036.htm.
Oderberg, I. M. "Religion in the Age of Aquarius." *Theosophy Northwest*. http://www.theosophy-nw. org/theosnw/world/general/rel-imo.htm.

ATOMIC AGE

Just before the sun rose over Alamogordo, New Mexico, on July 16, 1945, the world's first atomic bomb, ironically dubbed "Trinity" by its builders, sat on its 100-foot tower awaiting the electronic signal that would mark the beginning of the nuclear age. When the device detonated, turning a dark night into the brightest day, the blast was equal to twenty thousand tons of TNT. The mushroom cloud rose eight miles into the air, forming a huge question mark.

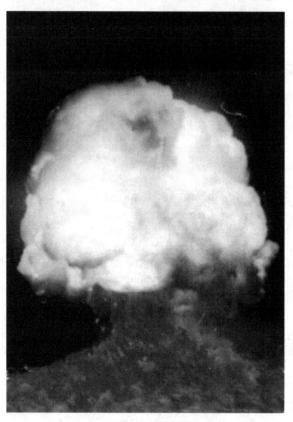

Mushroom cloud rising from first atomic bomb detonation, July 16, 1945. *Associated Press.*

That question mark is still with us. The atomic boom echoes down through the corridors of more than half a century. The question asked that day, the first question of the atomic age, is still being pondered: "My God! What have we done?" The fallout of that explosion continues to haunt us.

In no time at all, as soon as the devastating potential of nuclear energy was demonstrated in the horrors of Hiroshima and Nagasaki, people began to wonder. Was this what the biblical prophets, Nostradamus, and seers down through the ages had been talking about when they foretold a time they called Armageddon?

Since 1947 the *Bulletin of the Atomic Scientists* has illustrated its perception of how dangerous the atomic threat is by placing a clock on the cover of the magazine showing just how much time the editors think we have before Armageddon (see Doomsday Clock). They base their opinion on how the nations of the world are pursuing nuclear capabilities and on the tensions existing among members of the nuclear family. The time has varied from as little as two minutes in 1953 to as much as seventeen minutes in 1991.

Pop culture has certainly picked up on the fear. An exhibition at the Browne Popular Cultural Library at Bowling Green State University displayed posters from no less than fifty-six Hollywood films in which an atomic Armageddon threat figured prominently in the plot.

Many images in the book of Revelation (see Revelation) and the writings of the Christian seer Nostradamus (see Nostradamus) seem hauntingly similar to what happened at Alamogordo. It is extremely easy to jump to the conclusion that these writers, living centuries before anyone knew atomic energy existed, must have seen in their visions what the human race has since experienced:

> Something like a huge mountain, all ablaze, was thrown into the sea. A third of the sea turned into blood, a third of the living creatures in the sea died, and a third of the ships were destroyed. (Rev. 8:8, 9)

> The sun was given power to scorch people with fire. They were seared by the intense heat. (Rev. 16:8, 9)

> The unbelievers dead, captive, exiled with blood,
> human bodies, water and red hail covering the earth.
> —Erika Cheetham, *The Final Prophecies of Nostradamus*

Such is the specter of the atomic age in the minds of virtually everyone who has seen pictures of the famous mushroom cloud that it is hard to envision an Armageddon that doesn't involve nuclear holocaust. Perhaps the most feared of terrorist threats is that a small group might smuggle a nuclear device into a major city—or at least set off a "dirty bomb," a conventional explosive contaminated with radioactive material, thereby rendering human occupation of the area impossible for any foreseeable future. In 2003 President George W. Bush launched an invasion of Iraq based largely on the claim that Iraq was developing "weapons of mass destruction," including nuclear ones.

It is safe to say that more money has been spent as a result of nuclear weapons, both in developing them and trying to defend against them, than for any other single reason in the history of the human race.

The atomic age is a fact of life for every person now living on the planet. And the potential for a nuclear Armageddon remains the single largest threat to life as we know it today.

Sources:

Gerner, Alice: "The Atomic Age Opens: Selections from the Browne Popular Culture Library."
    http://www.bgsu.edu/colleges/library/pcl/pcl36.html.
The Holy Bible, New International Version. Grand Rapids, MI: Zondervan, 1978.
"Minutes to Midnight: The History of the Doomsday Clock." *Bulletin of the Atomic Scientists*.
    http://www.bullatomicsci.org/clock/doomsdayclock.html.

BABYLON

In ancient times Babylon was the capital of Mesopotamia, the modern country of Iraq. A systematic archeological examination carried out between 1899 and 1918 revealed for the first time the extent of the wonders that, before then, were known only by biblical accounts describing Babylon's splendor and might. But as the soils began to reveal their secrets, archeologists discovered a startling truth: The biblical accounts found in both testaments give Babylon a bad rap.

According to the Hebrew Bible, the Christian Old Testament, Babylon and its king, Nebuchadnezzar, carried the Jews off into captivity in 586 BCE and totally destroyed the first temple in Jerusalem (see Temple at Jerusalem). This was the Jewish "Babylonian captivity" that lasted for more than a generation.

In the Christian New Testament, "Babylon" is sometimes used as a code word for both Rome and the entrenched powers of evil seemingly inherent in the bureaucracies of the world:

> Fallen! Fallen is Babylon the great!
>   She has become a home for demons
> and a haunt for every evil spirit,
>   a haunt for every unclean and detestable bird.
> For all the nations have drunk
>   the maddening wine of her adulteries.
> The kings of the earth committed adultery with her,
>   and the merchants of the earth grew rich from her
>   excessive luxuries....
> Come out of her my people,
>   so that you will not share in her sins,

so that you will not receive any of her plagues;
for her sins are piled up to heaven,
and God has remembered her crimes. (Rev. 18:2–5)

That early Christians used "Babylon" to mean Rome is made clear by an early Christian apologist named Tertullian, who wrote, in his work entitled *Against the Jews*, "Babylon, in our own John [the book of Revelation] is a figure of the city of Rome, as being equally great and proud of her sway, and triumphant over the saints." This is why scholars are quite sure that when the apostle Peter closed his first letter with the words "She who is in Babylon, chosen together with you, sends you her greetings" (1 Pet. 5:13), he was writing from Rome, not the city of Babylon.

So great was the hatred of Christians for the persecuting bureaucracy of Rome that when the "great whore of Babylon" appears in Revelation 17, "dressed in purple and scarlet" and "glittering with gold, precious stones and pearls," she has "a golden cup in her hand, filled with abominable things and the filth of her adulteries" and she is "drunk with the blood of the saints, the blood of those who bore testimony to Jesus." On her forehead is written: "MYSTERY, BABYLON THE GREAT, THE MOTHER OF PROSTITUTES AND OF THE ABOMINATIONS OF THE EARTH" (Rev. 17:4–5).

For those who believe Armageddon will literally come as described in the Bible, "Babylon" today signifies what they consider to be the entire institutional/political system entrenched in the power structure of the world. Behind all the wars and rumors of wars, behind governmental domination, at the root of controversial conspiracies ranging from the Da Vinci Code to the assassination of President John Kennedy, there is "Babylon."

Evangelical exponents claim that Babylon will someday be ruled by the Satan-inspired power of the antichrist, but that her greatest power now is in deception. No one except the "elect" even knows she exists. Most of the world rulers are mere puppets, not perceiving who is behind it all, pulling the strings. Babylon is the secret, all-persuasive, worldwide system of domination whose final court of appeal is none other than the devil. He once offered Jesus "all the kingdoms of the world and their splendor" (Matt. 4:8–9). He could not have offered them, it is argued, had they not been his to give.

Someday—and according to believers in "Mystery Babylon" that day is closer than we think—Babylon will be revealed as a Western power promoting a one-world government led by the antichrist. No one will be able to "buy or sell" without receiving the "mark of the beast" on hand or forehead (see Mark of the Beast). The antichrist's number is 666 (see 666). And he might already be alive, living somewhere in Europe.

The signs allegedly are everywhere. When a big company such as Wal-Mart decides to radio-tag its inventory, it is "proof" that the corporate world is beginning the process that will eventually lead to Babylon's control over the planet's economy. There are those who carefully watch for any series of Social Security checks containing the number 666. Some go so far as to associate highway construction projects such as Boston's "Big Dig," the final projected installment of the interstate roadway system begun by President Eisenhower, with signs of Babylon's all-pervasive attempts to unify the infrastructure of a one-world system. The cost for the "Big Dig," after all, as of 2004, rose over budget by a reported 66.6 percent.

The fall of Babylon, as illustrated in the Luther Bible of 1535. *Library of Congress.*

Those who interpret the Bible less literally tend to smile exasperated smiles and shake their heads at what they consider to be outlandish, even silly, uses of scripture, but the conspiracy theorists are not dismayed. Every incredulous reaction is further proof that the world is mostly oblivious to the wiles of Babylon, the Mother of (Spiritual) Prostitutes. Her power, remember, is in her deception. So pervasive is this power that even after the thousand-year reign of Christ (see Millennium), the devil will still be able "to deceive the nations in the four corners of the earth ... to gather them for battle" (Rev. 20:8).

Of course, it is also possible to interpret the biblical Babylon purely as a metaphor. In the words of Ernst Lohmeyer, writing in *The Interpreter's Dictionary of the Bible*, Babylon is "an eschatological symbol of satanic deception and power; it is a heavenly mystery, which is to be comprehended prophetically, and which is never wholly reducible to empirical earthly institutions."

Sources:
Buttrick, George A., ed. *The Interpreter's Dictionary of the Bible.* 4 vols. New York: Abingdon Press, 1962.

Chase, T. "Revelation 13: Prophecy Calendar, Recent Past Dates (1998–2002)." http://angelfire. com/zine2/Number666/calendar1.html.

Monbiot, George. "Their Beliefs Are Bonkers, but They Are at the Heart of Power." *Guardian/ UK*, April 20, 2004. www.commondreams.org/cgi-bin/print.cgi?file=/views04/0420–03. htm.

The Holy Bible, New International Version. Grand Rapids, MI: Zondervan, 1978.

BABYLON RISING

In 1995 authors Tim LaHaye and Jerry Jenkins launched a series of novels based on their interpretation of the book of Revelation. It went on to make publishing history, with more than 62 million copies sold as of early 2004 (and thousands more selling every day). The story told in the twelve books of the *Left Behind* series begins at the time of the Rapture of the church (see Rapture) and continues through the next seven years of earth's history (see Great Tribulation), culminating in the Second Coming of Jesus Christ (see Second Coming).

In 2003, LaHaye, this time teaming with co-writer Greg Dinallo, launched a new series called *Babylon Rising*, conceived as a prequel to *Left Behind*. It begins in the present day and tells the story of its hero, an Indiana Jones–type field archeologist/professor named Michael Murphy, who is dedicated to finding and preserving biblical artifacts. Drawing on his extensive knowledge of the Bible and its stories, LaHaye depicts Murphy's exploits involving Old Testament artifacts (in the first volume of the series these objects are from the book of Daniel), which lead him on a merry chase that will eventually, many volumes later, culminate in the Rapture of the church, where *Left Behind* begins.

As in *Left Behind*, LaHaye states clearly that his purpose in writing these books is evangelism—to give the reader a "sense of 'the signs of the times' that we see being fulfilled internationally almost every time we watch events unfold on television or read a newspaper."

Sources:

LaHaye, Tim, and Greg Dinallo. *Babylon Rising.* New York: Bantam, 2003.

LaHaye, Tim, and Jerry B. Jenkins. *Left Behind* series, in 12 vols. Carol Stream, IL: Tyndale House, 1995–2004.

BAKKER, JIM

It was promoted as "the shot heard round the world." Jim Bakker (pronounced Baker), host of the successful Christian talk/variety television show *The PTL Club* (originally the initials stood for "Praise the Lord," but later Bakker, with more emotional verve than literary acumen, changed it to "People That Love"), stood at the launch site of the first-ever "Christian" TV satellite and promised that the PTL Club would broadcast twenty-four-hour Christian television from then until the return of Jesus Christ.

It was one of many firsts. The PTL Club also built the first large-scale "Christian" theme park, called Heritage USA. At the time its size was third only to Walt Disney World and Disneyland. It was also what finally brought Bakker down. In 1988 he

Jim Bakker and his wife, Tammy Faye, in 1986, at the height of their TV ministry. *Associated Press.*

was charged by a federal grand jury with mail fraud and conspiracy to defraud the public through the sale of thousands of lifetime memberships to the park and its hotel, which had space for only five hundred people and cost half as much to build as Bakker had raised for it on his television show. He was convicted and later served a prison term. It didn't help any that he had also paid a woman named Jessica Hahn, who later posed nude for *Playboy* magazine, $265,000 to keep quiet about a sexual liaison they had conducted on the very day of a PTL Club TV fund-raiser or that he was accused of having a longtime homosexual relationship with David Taggart, his right-hand man at PTL, even as Bakker was regularly and vehemently denouncing homosexuality as a sin condemned by the Bible.

Evangelist Billy Graham and his son, Franklin Graham, visited Jim Bakker in prison, became convinced that he had repented, and spoke of him as a friend. When Bakker was released, they paid for a house for him to live in and presented him with an automobile.

But Jerry Falwell, the famous fundamentalist from Thomas Road Baptist Church, the founder of Liberty College and cofounder of the Moral Majority, called Bakker "the greatest scab and cancer on the face of the Christianity in two thousand years of church history." (According to Bakker and his former wife Tammy Faye, Falwell also plotted to steal their ministry from them.)

Bakker repented in print in his 1996 book *I Was Wrong*. Continuing the thoughts he voiced at the launching of his satellite, however, *Prosperity and the Coming Apocalypse* (1998) and *The Refuge: The Joy of Christian Community in a Torn-Apart World* (2000), reveal that he is still looking ahead to the imminent return of Jesus Christ.

To many observers, the whole affair still reeks of corruption. But in the wake of scandal after scandal in the televangelist world, it's easy to forget that Jim Bakker was the first to do many of the things we take for granted in today's mass-marketing Christian TV culture. And the reason given for all the TV satellites and ministries is still ostensibly the same: to proclaim the good news until Armageddon shuts down the airwaves.

Sources:

Bakker, Jim. *I Was Wrong*. Nashville: Thomas Nelson, 1996.
———. *Prosperity and the Coming Apocalypse*. Nashville: Thomas Nelson, 1998.
———. *The Refuge: The Joy of Christian Community in a Torn-Apart World*. Nashville: Thomas Nelson, 2000.

BARBOUR, JULIAN

Julian Barbour is an astrophysicist whose book *The End of Time* could change the way the world understands both time and space. Is there a beginning? Will there be an end? Dr. Barbour says no: "Time is an illusion. The phenomena from which we deduce its existence are real, but we interpret them wrongly.... The basic idea of my theory is that there isn't time as such. There is no river of time that's flowing. But there are things that you could call an instant of time; or better, a *now*. As we live we seem to move through a succession of instants of time *nows*, and the question is, what are they? They are where everything in the universe is at this moment, *now*."

Barbour was born in South Newington, Oxfordshire, England, in 1937. After studying math at Cambridge, he went on to earn a PhD in astrophysics in Munich. He left academia in 1968 to study independently and has since written several books and papers about astrophysics, time, and inertia. *The End of Time* and *The Discovery of Dynamics* are considered by some scientists to be revolutionary, groundbreaking works. According to cosmologist Lee Smolin, "Barbour has presented the most interesting and provocative new idea about time to be proposed in many years. If true, it will change the way we see reality."

Barbour's collaboration with the Italian physicist Bruno Bertotti produced "Mach's Principle and the Structure of Dynamical Theories," in which they "created a general framework in which all absolute elements can be eliminated from the dynamics of the universe." One of those "absolute elements" is the certainty that time exists as we perceive it. Barbour's work with Niall Ó Murchadha and Brendan Foster takes his theories further by eliminating even scale, or size, from Einstein's general theory of relativity. He is currently at work on a new theory of gravity to explain the so-called expansion of the universe. He theorizes that it is not an expansion at all, but rather a movement of matter that gives the illusion of expansion.

Growing out of quantum physics—perhaps most simply defined as the study of matter and radiation at the atomic level—*The End of Time* proposes an explanation of all things that is simple to visualize but extremely difficult to illustrate mathematically. It is no wonder Barbour is often called both a scientist and a philosopher.

Picture an infinite cosmos in which nothing exists except for two single molecules. They exist in relation to each other. If one is "here," the other is a measurable distance away over "there." They are always moving, so their relationship is constantly changing as the distance between them changes. Now add a third molecule. A geometric pattern is formed. A triangle materializes. It continually changes size and shape because the three points making up its corners are in constant motion. We can never determine its exact size because we cannot stop everything to take measurements. Every time we try to take a quick measurement and say, "*Now* it is such and such a size," a new *now* is already in existence.

Barbour proposes that this is a simplified way of visualizing what is, in fact, the essential truth of the cosmos. Matter is made up of atoms, the positions of which can be described only in terms of their relation to all the rest of the atoms that exist. But they are constantly changing position. Every time we experience a moment in time, a *now*, by the time we even express the thought, everything has changed. Barbour speaks of "time capsules." A time capsule is a series of *nows* that appear to occur in a line of time. From a human perspective, things seem to happen one after another. But that, he says, is an illusion. He theorizes that time does not exist independent of the changes that occur as we move, the air moves, atomic particles move, and everything changes. Change is the primary condition of the cosmos, and that change, coupled with the basic facts of quantum mechanics, makes it clear that time does not exist independently.

Perhaps one day (or perhaps it would be better say one *now*) there will be a philosophy and mythology created to explain these theories more clearly. Right now Barbour and his colleagues are working to prove his theories. Then it will be a matter of changing the paradigm of an entire culture—no small task.

Or perhaps the groundwork has already been laid in the philosophy of the oldest world religion. Four thousand years ago, Hindu *rishis* (wise teachers) taught that life as we experience it is an illusion. Everything that seems solid and grounded to us will someday disappear. Everything is in a constant state of change. A book we hold in our hand, when left outside on the ground, will gradually become part of the soil at our feet. Eventually it will nourish a plant that will become food for an animal. When the animal dies, the moisture of its body will transfer to the sky and fall in the form of rain that will someday nourish a tree that will be cut down, ground up, and made into a book. At any moment we might observe the process and say that a particular molecule involved in it is part of a book, the soil, an animal, rain, a tree, or (again) a book. But we will be correct only in terms of the short life span of our own human perspective. If we take the long view, every time we declare exactly what form a molecule is in, we are only describing a *now*. To go even further, does the "book" consist of paper—or of the ideas that the words written on the paper convey? Perhaps the real "book" never even existed at all. It only appeared to. Tomorrow, next year, perhaps one billion of our years in the future, we will come to understand that it is only in our minds that we stopped a process that, in reality, never stopped at all.

This four-thousand-year-old way of looking at the universe, couched in the words of spiritual teachers, comes surprisingly close to what Barbour has proposed in the language of modern physics. Perhaps science and religion are not as far apart as we have been led to believe. If he is correct, then what we call "Armageddon" will only be another in an endless series of *nows*.

Sources:
Barbour, Julian. Julian Barbour Web site. http://216.92.126.230.
Brockman, John. "The End of Time: A Talk with Julian Barbour." http://www.edge.org/ documents/archive/edge60.htmll.
Stedl, Todd. "Intro to Quantum Mechanics." http://www_theory.chem.washington.edu/~trstedl/ quantum/quantum.html.

BEASTS, THE

A lot of "beasts" appear in the Bible. In one sense, all animals, domesticated or wild, are referred to as beasts. But apocalyptic literature (see Apocalyptic Writing) often features "beasts" as part of its genre. Daniel's visions, for instance, spotlight lions, bears, and leopards, equating them with nations that will someday arise.

The two "beasts" of the book of Revelation that take a central role in the story leading up to Armageddon are perhaps the most prominent examples in apocalyptic literature (see Mark of the Beast).

The first of them has many titles:

The "beast that comes up from the Abyss" (11:7).
The one who "once was, now is not, and yet will come" (17:8).
The one "coming out of the sea. He had ten horns and seven heads, with ten crowns on his horns, and on each head a blasphemous name" (13:1).

The second beast functions as a kind of chaplain/evangelist/PR man for the first beast. He is "like a lamb, but he spoke like a dragon" (13:11; see also False Prophet).

Conservative theologians tend to see the first beast as the antichrist, a satanic counterpart to Jesus Christ. They believe that just as God became incarnate and spoke through the Christ, Satan will someday become incarnate and speak through the antichrist. The second beast seems to be the mouthpiece for the first beast.

Liberal theologians tend to look upon the beasts of Revelation as metaphors representing evil government repression of spiritual religion. In this view, the first beast, which "once was, now is not, and will come up out of the Abyss and go to his destruction," is the evil spiritual counterpart of Jesus, who lived, died, and ascended into heaven. The second beast represents the first-century Roman political cult that threatened the existence of the early church. The priests of this system represented entrenched religion and controlled the economic life of nations through their sacrificial practices. When the second beast, in the guise of the Roman political cult, demanded that an image of the caesar be raised in Jerusalem, both Christians and Jews felt threatened. They could not compromise their belief in the Ten Commandments by worshiping a false idol, but they could not legally "buy or sell" unless they did. Their refusal to compromise eventually caused Rome to burn both the city and the Jewish temple to the ground.

This reading sees the beasts "from the sea" and "from the land" as representing, respectively, spiritual and economic threats to Christ's followers in the first century. Placed in company with the "dragon" who inspired them—the dragon described as "that ancient serpent called the devil, or Satan" (Rev. 12:9)—they form an unholy trinity at odds with what the church would eventually define as the "holy" Trinity—Father, Son, and Holy Spirit. The first beast represents materialistic, institutionalized religious/political systems. The second beast represents the economic forces that support them. The dragon represents the evil spiritual force that tempts people to remain materialistic and animalistic, rather than spiritual and "God-centered."

The powers represented by the beasts are not, according to this view, simply historic in nature. In modern terms the metaphor might follow lines such as these: A government decides to go to war. According to the biblical author, war is wrong. It is prompted by the dragon, the devil, and serves only to destroy. But "nations" don't decide to go to war. People do. More important, a person does. When this person represents a nation and declares that God wills the war, that person is acting out the role of the first beast. When religious systems, such as institutionalized churches, support the war, and when the government demands taxes to pay for it, threatening economic retribution if those taxes are not paid by individual taxpayers, church and state act in tandem, with the church filling the role of the second beast, who supports the first.

Sources:
Buttrick, George A., ed. *The Interpreter's Dictionary of the Bible.* 4 vols. New York: Abingdon Press, 1962.
The Holy Bible, New International Version. Grand Rapids, MI: Zondervan, 1978.

BEAST, MARK OF THE *see* **Mark of the Beast**

BEGINNING OF THE END

During the final days of Jesus' life on earth, according to the gospel of Matthew, he had a conversation with his disciples as they stood beside the newly renovated temple in Jerusalem. The disciples were quite impressed with the new facade and commented on how beautiful it looked (Matt. 24). Jesus was not so impressed. "Do you see all these things?" he asked. "I tell you the truth, not one stone here will be left standing on another; every one will be thrown down."

The disciples, of course wanted to know more: "Tell us, when will this happen and what will be the sign of your coming and of the end of the age?"

Jesus responded by describing a time of "wars and rumors of wars," a time when "nation will rise against nation, and kingdom against kingdom. There will be famines and earthquakes in various places." And this, he warned his disciples, would be only the beginning of the end. He went on to tell them what would happen during the endtimes, the events conservative Christian scholars believe are outlined in the book of Revelation (see Revelation).

Many who read the Bible believe that the events of the modern world are exactly those that will foreshadow the time of the end. When "wars and rumors of wars" and "famines and earthquakes in various places" occur, it is, for these people, a sign of "the beginning of the end," God's signal that the final days of human history have begun.

"The end is still to come," said Jesus, adding that when "the gospel of the kingdom" is "preached in the whole world as a testimony to all nations ... then the end will come" (Matt. 24:6, 14). He went on to use a fig tree as an example: "As soon as its twigs get tender and its leaves come out, you know that summer is near. Even so, when you see all these things, you know that it is near, right at the door. I tell you the truth, this generation will certainly not pass away until all these things have happened" (Matt. 24: 32–34).

What generation did Jesus mean? According to conservative theologians, it is the generation that sees the things happen that Jesus talked about. This is the generation that will experience the beginning of THE END.

Source:
The Holy Bible, New International Version. *Grand Rapids, MI: Zondervan, 1978.*

BIBLE CODE

If Michael Drosnin, author of *The Bible Code* and *Bible Code II: The Countdown*, is correct, we may already be experiencing what the Bible calls the "End of Days"—and the *end* of the end of days might very well occur in the year 2006.

The Bible Code, according to Drosnin, predicted the assassination of President John F. Kennedy. Of course, it was not discovered in time to prevent the murder. That doesn't always have to be the case, says Drosnin. He sent a letter to Yitzhak Rabin warning him of an attempted assassination. The letter reached Rabin in plenty of time. It apparently was ignored, and the assassination happened.

The Bible Code, if we are to believe Drosnin, predicted World War II and Watergate. The Holocaust, the atomic bomb blast at Hiroshima, the moon walk, the Gulf War, and the twin tower attacks of September 11, 2001—all are predicted in a complicated code that is even now only in the first stages of being interpreted. It was there all along, but until the invention of computers it was impossible to decipher.

Drosnin does not appear to be a religious fanatic. He insists he does not believe in God. He is an investigative reporter who learned his trade working the night police beat for the *Washington Post* and covering corporate news for the *Wall Street Journal*. He didn't even discover the code himself. That honor goes to Dr. Eliyahu Rips, a Jewish mathematician who lives in Jerusalem, and his colleagues Doron Witztum and Yoav Rosenberg. But with the publication of *Bible Code* in 1997, both Rips and Drosnin were thrown into the international spotlight, where they have since attracted a devout following of sincere believers while at the same time being attacked by those who do not believe such a thing possible.

Drosnin says over and over again that, especially at the beginning, he wished that someone would debunk the code. Many attempts have been made and many claims published, but according to his followers, the mathematics and statistical analysis of the Bible Code have, so far at least, withstood the onslaught.

The Code Itself

What exactly is the Bible Code?

From ancient time, rabbis have passed on the tradition that the Torah, the first five books of the Bible, were given to Moses on Mount Sinai, written on stone tablets by the very finger of God. Tradition states that the books were written in Hebrew, with no breaks between words. The entire Torah is some 304,805 Hebrew letters long. If the original text, or at least a close approximation, is reproduced in the form in which it might have been given to Moses and then arranged in columns of forty rows, each row would contain some 7,551 letters. The letters would form a grid that could be read from right to left, as in Hebrew, or left to right, as in English. It could also be read up and down and corner to corner. In short, it would resemble a larger version of the find-the-words games that appear daily in many newspapers.

Of course, the code is more complicated than that. Sometimes words and phrases appear to make sense only when a fixed number of letters are skipped. Drosnin gives the following sentence as an example:

Rips explained that each code is a case of adding every fifth or tenth or fiftieth letter to form a word.

Now read that sentence again, this time emphasizing every fifth letter:

Rips **e**xplai**n**ed **t**hat **e**ach **c**ode **i**s a **c**ase **of** ad**d**ing **e**very fifth or tenth or fiftieth letter to form a word.

The message says: **Read the code.**

The software that Drosnin uses and makes available to Internet users finds "key words" in context with other words or phrases in one direction or another. The combination of words that so startled Drosnin at the beginning of his search consisted of the name YITZHAK RABIN, crossed with the words ASSASSIN THAT WILL ASSASSINATE. When Rabin was shot and killed on November 4, 1995, a little more than a year after Drosnin wrote to warn him of this hidden message, Drosnin came to the astonishing belief that he was dealing with prophecies encoded three thousand years ago.

Many other such messages began to surface, including one supposedly predicting a terrifying event Drosnin witnessed firsthand from his apartment in New York City. After the first (1993) bomb attack at the World Trade Center, Drosnin had found the words TWIN and TOWERS in the Bible, encoded with the words THE WARNING, THE SLAUGHTER and crossed by the word TERROR. In his words, "It never occurred to me that lightning would strike twice—that there would be another terrorist attack on the same two monoliths eight years later, that it would succeed, and knock both towers down." So right after the 9/11 attack Drosnin returned to his computer. There it was. Embedded in the same text were the words SIN, CRIME

OF BIN LADEN, THE CITY AND THE TOWER and the sentence THEY SAW SMOKE RISING ABOVE THE LAND LIKE THE SMOKE OF A FURNACE. Even the name of the alleged leader of the hijackers, Mohammed Atta, appears, along with the words EGYPTIAN MAN. The word PENTAGON appears, crossed by the word DAMAGED and the phrase EMERGENCY FROM ARABIA.

At the same time Drosnin was making these discoveries, Eliyahu Rips, working from his home in Israel, discovered the same message and e-mailed it to Drosnin in New York.

How the Code Came to Be

The words are in the Bible, and anyone who uses the proper software can find them, whether they read Hebrew or not. No one questions the method per se, only the significance of the results. How likely or unlikely is it that "messages" such as those Drosnin has found will occur in a given text? That is the central question driving those who have attempted to discredit the code.

Drosnin himself professes to be mystified by the existence of the hidden word strings he has discovered. Eliyahu Rips has no problem with believing the code exists, because ancient Jewish tradition claims the Torah came first, and then the Creation. First the word, then the act. Doesn't the Torah itself claim God "spoke" the world into existence? "God said … and it was so." Even the Christian tradition makes that claim. The gospel of John opens with: "In the beginning was the Word, and the Word was with God, and the Word was God." It only makes sense, according to these traditions, that all that exists and all that happens originates in God. For Rips, a devout Jew, the Bible Code only affirms what the rabbis have been saying for three thousand years.

Isaac Newton believed the Bible to be "a cryptogram set by the Almighty," the "riddle of the Godhead, the riddle of past and future events divinely foreordained." According to Rips's reasoning, the Bible Code is now beginning to be understood because we have reached "the time of the end." The prophet Daniel foretold this. When he was faced with visions beyond his comprehension, he asked the Almighty's angel: "My Lord, what will the outcome of all this be?" He was told: "Go your way Daniel, because the words are closed up and sealed until the time of the end" (Dan. 12:8, 9).

In 1998 Drosnin gave a sealed envelope to his lawyer, not to be opened until 2002. In the letter he predicted:

a. The world will face global "economic collapse" starting in the Hebrew year 5762 (2002 in the modern calendar).

b. This will lead to a period of unprecedented danger, as nations with nuclear weapons become unstable and terrorists can buy or steal the power to destroy whole cities.

c. The danger will peak in the Hebrew year 5766 (2006 in the modern calendar), the year that is most clearly encoded with both "world war" and "atomic holocaust."

Drosnin is a master storyteller. *Bible Code II*, even though filled with charts and statistics, still reads like a good mystery novel. So it may not be fair to jump right to the last page and reveal where Drosnin believes the Bible Code originated. At the risk of spoiling the surprise, he believes that the code came from aliens from another planet. He believes they "seeded" the earth with DNA to produce life, and because they were able to observe time from "outside," they could also warn us when our self-destruction approached. This they did with a code that came equipped with a time lock. We would not be able to destroy ourselves until we had perfected the technology to do so. That technology involves the invention of computers. Computers are also the key that unlocks the Bible Code. It couldn't be deciphered without them.

Drosnin even claims to know when and where the Bible Code was delivered. He says that the code itself reveals this information. The event occurred at the time of the birth of civilization, the agricultural revolution some six thousand years ago. The place was what Drosnin calls the Lisan Peninsula, a tongue of land extending into the Dead Sea from Jordan. The spacecraft landed there and perhaps even placed two obelisks that will one day be recovered. These contain the complete key to the Bible Code.

The time frame is significant. This was the era of the discovery of writing. It was the time in which the very first stories of the Bible are placed. A literal reading of the Bible indicates that this was the time of Creation—although Drosnin would argue against such an interpretation. The world was not created six thousand years ago, he says. Civilization was. Cities and trade, modern science, and everything we associate with progressive life began right there—right then.

Why this sudden spurt of human progress some six thousand years ago? According to Drosnin, it was because we had help.

Is There No Escape?

Drosnin doesn't believe 2006 has to be the end. The Bible Code doesn't predict as much as it warns. If we wake up, there is still time. The purpose of the predictions is to bring humanity to our collective senses.

Many have wondered if there is other intelligent life in the universe. If evidence were discovered, they say, perhaps the world would change its ways. Perhaps if we knew we were not alone, we might band together and work for the common good.

Drosnin claims that there *is* evidence that we have been visited and are not alone. That evidence is the Bible Code. It is irrefutable proof that other, more mature, life forms are even now giving us a chance to grasp at the straw of a hopeful future rather than the gloomy tragedy of extinction.

Why the Bible? Why that particular book? Drosnin's answer is that the warfare occupying the world today is wrapped in religion. The power is technological. The forces are economic. But the people doing the acts are inspired by their religion. Muslim terrorists rage against America—the "Great Satan." American leaders pray that God will "bless America." Israeli troops carry Torahs in their packs. Jew against Muslim. Christian against Jew. Muslim against Christian. And all these religions revere

"The Book." That's why it is there, in the Bible, that we read about what might be our end, but what must be our hope.

What Do the Critics Say?

Drosnin's detractors are legion.

Foremost among them is Brendan McKay, a mathematician who teaches in the Department of Computer Science at the Australian National University in Canberra. McKay insists that the "code" merely illustrates mathematical probabilities inherent in any text of sufficient length. Using a Hebrew translation of Leo Tolstoy's *War and Peace*, McKay demonstrated that messages could be found "encoded" in texts other than the Bible. He also pointed out that the Hebrew of the Torah contains no vowels, making it easier to concoct meanings where none, in fact, exist.

McKay was so vocal in denouncing Drosnin's research that Drosnin issued what amounted to a challenge. He was quoted in the June 9, 1997, issue of *Newsweek* magazine as saying, "When my critics find a message about the assassination of a prime minister encrypted in *Moby Dick*, I'll believe them."

Such a challenge could not be ignored. Using the same software and techniques with which Drosnin supposedly deciphered the Bible Code, McKay went to work on *Moby Dick*. There he found revealed the assassinations of, among others, Indira Gandhi, Martin Luther King Jr., John F. and Robert Kennedy, Abraham Lincoln, and Yitzhak Rabin. He also discovered the exile of Leon Trotsky. Besides all that, he discovered the name of Princess Diana and, in close proximity, the words MORTAL IN THESE JAWS OF DEATH.

If all that weren't enough, McKay discovered in *Moby Dick* a prediction of Michael Drosnin's death. The letters M. DROSNIN are crossed by the words HIM TO HAVE BEEN KILLED. With the other words scattered throughout the letter-picture, McKay deduced that Drosnin would be killed by someone DRIVING A NAIL INTO HIS HEART that SLICES OUT A CONSIDERABLE HOLE. The event will transpire in ATHENS or at least in GREECE (both words appear in the code) and apparently happen on the FIRST DAY of Drosnin's visit there. Even the names of the murderers are revealed. They happen to be two famous code researchers. (Apparently all this information caused many who read it to believe that McKay was actually saying that Drosnin's death was predicted in *Moby Dick*. McKay issued a disclaimer explaining that he was merely illustrating a principle, not suggesting that Herman Melville was a prophet.)

Heated exchanges continue between followers of Drosnin and followers of McKay. Drosnin's camp insists that although mathematical coincidences appear in other books, the certifiable predictions found in the Bible far outnumber those of other books and fewer "skips" are needed to form words in the original Hebrew of the Torah than in books written by other authors. McKay counters that this is not the case at all, and he and other scientists continue to offer evidence in support of this point.

The controversy has apparently also caused a rift between Eliyahu Rips and Drosnin. Drosnin, however, insists that Rips is merely distancing himself to underscore the fact that this is Drosnin's book, not his.

As with most matters of religion, it appears that whether people "believe" in the code is a matter of whether they want to believe in it. Drosnin's followers are finding new messages and posting them on the Internet almost every day. McKay's followers say that the Drosnin camp is finding key prophetic "hits" because, mathematically speaking, in this kind of system you find what you expect to find. In other words, it's a rigged study done by people predisposed to find what they are looking for, whether it's really there or not.

The two camps show no evidence that they will agree anytime in the near future.

Sources:
Drosnin, Michael. *The Bible Code*. New York: Simon & Schuster, 1997.
———. *Bible Code II: The Countdown*. New York: Viking Penguin, 2002.
The Holy Bible, New International Version. Grand Rapids, MI: Zondervan, 1978.
McKay, Brendan. "Assassinations Foretold in Moby Dick!" http://cs.anu.edu.au/~bdm/dilugim/moby.html.
McKay, Brendan, and Friends. "Scientific Refutation of the Bible Codes." http://cs.anu.edu.au/~bdm/dilugim/torah.html.

BIBLE TIMELINES

In 1970 an evangelical Christian named Hal Lindsey published a book called *The Late Great Planet Earth*. It became a best seller and sparked a popular interest in biblical prophecy that has since grown even larger. Tim LaHaye and Jerry B. Jenkins have written a fiction series based on the interpretation scheme Lindsey popularized; their twelve *Left Behind* novels, published between 1995 and 2004, has sold over 62 million copies.

The view of history popularized by these books is that human life began at a definite time and will end at a specific date that cannot be pinpointed but has been foretold by biblical prophets. Although the exact date remains hidden, historical trends, events, and signs can be recognized, and those who study such things can tell when we are living in the general time of the end.

At least three different biblical time schemes can be identified by studying relevant passages of scripture and interpreting them according to the evangelical Christian perspective Lindsey and LaHaye espouse. The first deals with the age of the earth from beginning to end. The second, from the Hebrew scriptures (the Christian Old Testament), ignores dates and times but points out events specific to the Christian church that some believe were foreshadowed by Jewish yearly religious celebrations. The third, from the New Testament book of Revelation, deals with stages found in a particular historical perspective of the Christian church.

The Age of the World

According to this reading of the Bible, human redemptive history, from the creation of the first people in the Garden of Eden to the final battle of Armageddon and the subsequent Millennium, or thousand-year reign of Jesus Christ after the Second Coming, will take place over a seven-thousand-year period. This time frame is calculated by adding the spans of years between the events described in certain biblical passages.

The calculations begin with Genesis 5. This chapter, often called "the begats," outlines Adam's genealogy: "When Adam had lived 130 years, he begat Seth ... when Seth had lived 105 years, he begat Enosh, " and so on. By adding Adam's age at Seth's birth to Seth's age at Enosh's birth and continuing through the chapter, one finds that 1,656 years passed between the birth of Adam and Noah's flood.

Genesis 11 offers another list, beginning with Noah's son Shem, father of the "Shem-itic" or Semitic races. Here the mathematical computations show that Abraham was born 1,948 years after Adam.

It is generally accepted that Abraham—if he is, indeed, a historical figure—probably lived two thousand years, give or take a hundred or so, before Jesus. The modern calendar indicates that the present time is some two thousand years, give or take six or seven, after Jesus. We can now construct a rough timeline, rounded off to the nearest thousand years for the sake of simplicity:

Adam	Abraham	Jesus	Present
4000 BCE	2000 BCE	BCE/CE	2000 CE

This places Adam and creation about six thousand years ago. James Ussher, an Irish archbishop, worked it all out in 1650. His date for the Creation was October, 4004 BCE, on a Saturday morning. Even the most conservative theologians have since added a few thousand years to Bishop Ussher's calculations. Adam and Eve, after all, could well have spent some time in Eden before they ate the forbidden fruit and started to beget children.

The theory now accounts for six thousand years, beginning with Adam and Eve and continuing to the present. But a timeline invites speculation both ways. The very notion of a timeline implies a beginning at one point and an end at another. The Bible seems to give us a starting point. Is there also evidence in the Bible pointing to when the line will end?

In *The Late Great Planet Earth*, Hal Lindsey argued that there is. The Jewish prophets foretold a time that has been sometimes referred to as "the peaceable kingdom," wherein a messiah, a divinely anointed ruler sent from God, would come to earth:

> The wolf will live with the lamb
>   the leopard will lie down with the goat,
> the calf and the lion and the yearling together;
>   and a little child will lead them.
> The cow will feed with the bear,
>   their young will lie down together,
>   and the lion will eat straw like the ox.
> The infant will play near the hole of the cobra,
>   and the young child put his hand into the viper's nest.
> They will neither harm nor destroy
>   on all my holy mountain,
> for the earth will be full of the knowledge of the Lord
>   as the waters cover the sea. (Isa. 11:6–9)

According to Hebrew scholars, this time will begin with the coming of the Messiah. Christians view things a little differently. They believe that the Messiah, Jesus, has already come, was rejected, and will come again. Both religious camps look for a recycling of planet Earth and a repeal of the principle of "survival of the fittest" at the end of the six-thousand-year timeline. Presumably even predators will became vegetarians: "The wolf will live with the lamb."

How long will the peaceable kingdom last? According to Lindsey and LaHaye, one thousand years—a millennium. This figure comes from Revelation 20: 1–3:

> And I saw an angel coming down from heaven, having the key to the Abyss and holding in his hand a great chain. He seized the dragon, that ancient serpent, who is the devil, or Satan, and bound him for a thousand years. He threw him into the Abyss, and locked and sealed it over him, to keep him from deceiving the nations any more until the thousand years were ended.

The timeline now accounts for seven thousand years, beginning with Adam and Eve, continuing to the time when the Messiah either comes or comes again, and then moving forward a thousand years into the future:

Adam	Abraham	Jesus	Present	End of Time
2,000 years	2,000 years	2,000 years	1,000 years	

Some Christians, seeing three periods of two thousand years, find "proof" of this scheme in the fact that it seems to bear the stamp of the Christian doctrine of the Trinity, the belief that God is "three in one," having three aspects while remaining one God. The reasoning goes like this: A careful reading of the Bible passages covering the time between Adam and Abraham, Genesis 1–11, discloses a creating and nurturing, but hidden, God. Nobody "sees" God after the expulsion from Eden until God appears to Abraham—a hint that this period was overseen by the first person of the Trinity, God the unseen Father. But beginning with God's "appearing" to Abraham and ending with the birth of Jesus in the Bethlehem manger, when "God became flesh ... and we beheld his glory" (John 1), God appeared to many people. This was another two-thousand-year period, the time of God the Son, the second person of the Trinity, who showed us the "face" of God. After Jesus left, he sent the Holy Spirit. This act marked the birth of the church (Acts 2). The Church Age will end with the Rapture (see Rapture), the recalling of the Holy Spirit along with all the "true" Christians the Spirit indwells—those who have been "born again." This period has also lasted for, so far, some two thousand years.

It makes for a neat package. Two thousand years for God the Father, two thousand years for God the Son, two thousand years for God the Holy Spirit, and then one thousand years for the peaceable kingdom, the Millennium, while Jesus reigns on earth. In all, seven thousand years. Six "workdays" of one thousand years each, and then a "Sabbath" of one thousand years when the world rests up from its labors of fighting sin. Then a whole new thing, called "eternity," begins.

"With the Lord a day is like a thousand years, and a thousand years a day," says 2 Peter 3:8. This statement, coupled with the belief that Jesus will come back and reign for a millennium, another "thousand-year day," has caused great speculation. Does history support the notion of a six-day "work week" of God? Have we almost finished the first six days? Is humanity on the verge of the Millennium, the time of the "peaceable kingdom," corresponding to God's "day of rest"? In other words, is the famous first chapter of Genesis, in which God creates the universe in six days and rests on the seventh, a symbol of the whole of recorded time? Those who believe in such a biblical timeline assert that the Millennium, while not yet here, is imminent.

Several arguments rebut this view of history.

First, it presupposes a particular literal way of interpreting scriptural passages and of understanding the Bible as a whole. But perhaps the Bible is meant to be read metaphorically rather than literally, and perhaps these passages, written by different authors separated by thousands of years, were not meant to form one theological theory of human history. In other words, the whole idea of this particular timeline is a human invention, superimposed over carefully selected scriptural texts that have been taken out of their historical context.

Second, timeline theory presupposes a linear view of time. Many religions, such as Hinduism and Buddhism, operate within a cyclical, rather than linear, context. Outside the world of religion, some scientists, including Julian Barbour (see Barbour, Julian), have questioned the notion that time progresses directly from the "Big Bang" (see entry) to the "Big Crunch" (see Big Crunch, Big Chill, and Big Rip). It could be that the whole concept of a timeline, let alone such a precisely measured and documented one, is wrong.

Third, no one knows whether Adam or Abraham really existed, let alone when they lived. And dates differ quite widely concerning the year Jesus was born. It's difficult to accept a three-point historical view when each of the points is debatable.

Fourth, it is rather presumptuous for one segment of one religion, in this case evangelical Christianity, to commandeer the scriptures of another religion, in this case both Judaism and nonevangelical Christianity, and then use the results to justify its own unique conception of history. (Of course, there is the counterargument that Christians have been doing this for a long time and have what, to them, are perfectly justifiable grounds for continuing the practice.)

Fifth, the biblical timeline theory flies in the face of the science behind anthropology, archaeology, astronomy, biology, geology—in short, everything we know about where we came from, based on physical evidence.

The Hebrew Calendar as Christian Metaphor

Leviticus 23 sets forth the Hebrew calendar, often referred to as the Feasts of the Lord. Seven holy days to be marked by ceremonial feasts are described in detail. These were seasonal celebrations based on an agrarian calendar year, but they were also intended to serve as reminders of God's historical dealings with Israel. Some evangelical Christians go a step farther. They believe that these Hebrew holy days also foreshadowed a Christian interpretation of history between Jesus' birth and second coming.

Passover
Crucifixion

The Passover celebration marks the beginning of religious Judaism. Before Passover the Hebrew people didn't have a strict, coded religion. They existed as a people, but they had not yet systematized their faith and developed their tradition.

On Passover the Jews celebrate their deliverance from Egypt. A lamb was slain and its blood sprinkled on the doorposts and lintels of their houses. A special meal was eaten. The main course was the flesh of the sacrificial lamb slain for their freedom. Desert bread (*matzah*), bread made without leavening, was baked. A cup of wine was shared. During the night of the escape from Egypt, an angel of death visited God's wrath upon the Egyptians, killing the firstborn child of every family. But the angel "passed over" the houses of the Hebrews when he saw the blood of the sacrificial lamb.

Evangelical Christians see in this celebration a type, or symbol, of the Crucifixion of Jesus Christ (1 Pet. 1:18–19). Before the Crucifixion, they say, God's people had not yet discovered their true identity or come to understand that they were still "captives" of "Egypt," a metaphor for the world's domination system. But Christ became the sacrificial lamb. His blood was symbolically placed, in the shape of the cross, upon the "doorposts and lintels" of their hearts. On the last night of Jesus' life, probably while celebrating a Passover meal, he gave his disciples bread and wine, saying, "This is my body.... This is my blood." Ever since that night the angel of death, seeing the blood of Jesus' sacrifice "covering" his followers, "passes over" them and they are granted eternal life with God.

Unleavened Bread
Justification/Sanctification

Following Passover, according to Leviticus 23, the Jews were to eat no leavened bread for seven days. Leaven was a symbol for sin. Many evangelical Christians see this commandment as a symbol for the Christian doctrines of sanctification and justification, which hold that when someone accepts Jesus Christ as savior, the "leaven" of sin is removed from his or her life (1 Cor. 5:6–8).

Firstfruits
Resurrection

The third feast, called Firstfruits, was a celebration of thanksgiving for the coming harvest. The "first fruit" of the field was offered to God with the understanding that what followed could be shared by the farmer's family. Some Christians associate this feast with the Resurrection of Jesus. He became the "first fruits" of God's harvest (1 Cor. 15:20–23). The rest of the harvest will consist of those Christians down through the ages who make up God's "true" church.

Pentecost (Feast of Weeks)
Birthday of the Church

Pentecost was the celebration of the first real harvest. After the first fruits were offered, harvest began in earnest. The Christian church is also said to have begun on the day of Pentecost (Acts 2:1–4, 41), when the first believers were all together in one place and the Holy Spirit descended upon them, indwelling them and giving them the ability to perform miracles, speak in other tongues, and prophesy. The mission of the church, outlined in Jesus' "Great Commission" of Matthew 28, has since been to "go into all the world" and preach the gospel to convert people to God.

Summer—Time of Harvest
Church Age

This was not a celebration, but rather a time to be working in the fields, gathering in the harvest. Many Christians believe that it corresponds to the time in which we now live. It is the business of the church to be gathering in souls for God, following the admonition of Jesus, who reminded his followers that the fields were "ripe for harvest" (John 4:35).

If the time of harvest brings us to the present, what happens next? According to some evangelical Christians, the ancient Jewish feasts now begin to foreshadow the future.

Feast of Trumpets
Rapture

The book of Leviticus instructed that at the end of the harvest a trumpet should sound, announcing that it was time to begin to prepare for the Day of Atonement. According to the apostle Paul, the day of the church age will end with the sounding of the "trumpet call of God " (1 Thess. 4:16–18). In 1 Corinthians 15 he calls it "the last trumpet." Harvest time will be over. The day of God's judgment will finally arrive.

Day of Atonement (Yom Kippur)
Tribulation

Yom Kippur is the most solemn day of the Jewish year. It is the day when sin must be acknowledged and atoned for. To the Christian author of the book of Hebrews (9:28), this day signified the time of "tribulation" prophesied by Jesus in Matthew 24. It will be a solemn time when sin is unearthed and brought out into the open. It will be a time of punishment.

Feast of Tabernacles
Millennium

The time of tribulation will not last forever. The Feast of Tabernacles was a happy harvest celebration, similar to the American Thanksgiving. All was well with the family that gathered together with crops stored away in abundance. In the same way, the Millennium following the great tribulation will be a time when the lion will lie down with the lamb and "a little child will lead them." It is resting time on planet Earth, when Jesus will put all things right.

According to this Christian interpretation of the Jewish calendar, we are nearing the end of the long summer, listening for the sound of the last trumpet to signal the end of all things.

The Length of the Church Age

The final book of the Christian Bible is Revelation (see Revelation). Those who interpret this book as describing future events (see Futurist School of Biblical Interpretation) teach that the second and third chapters outline the history of the church age from its beginning right up to the present. Those chapters contain seven letters dictated to seven different Christian churches that existed when the book was written. These seven were chosen because each represents a different chapter of church history, beginning on the day of Pentecost and ending, presumably, when the church age is over and Jesus returns.

Each letter follows a similar pattern. After a brief introduction, the church community is evaluated on its response to cultural influences. The churches at Smyrna and Philadelphia, for instance, receive an "A" rating. The churches at Sardis and Laodicea both flunk. Ephesus, Pergamum, and Thyatira receive something in the vicinity of a "C."

Another passage of scripture can be read alongside these passages from Revelation to cross-check the process of describing the church's activities during different stages of its history. In Matthew 13, Jesus tells seven parables. These parables, according to some evangelical scholars, describe, in order, how the church will respond to its surrounding culture during each different historical period. In other words, the seven parables of Matthew 13 correspond to and augment the seven letters of Revelation 2 and 3.

From a modern-day perspective, according to this interpretation of Revelation and Matthew, the last two thousand years of church history can be broken down as follows:

Revelation 2:1–7—Ephesus: The First Hundred Years
Matthew 13:1–23—The Parable of the Sower

The church at Ephesus was commended for its hard work and perseverance through difficult times but criticized because it "had forgotten its first love." This church was chosen to represent the first century of church history. Despite persecutions and hard times, Christianity had, within a century, grown from a small Jewish cult into a vibrant community of churches all across Mediterranean Africa and Europe. The parable of the sower from Matthew 13 pictures this growth. It tells the story of a farmer who scattered seed on different kinds of ground. Some seeds landed on fertile soil, some did not. Some sprouted rapidly but were choked by weeds. Others quickly took root but failed because the soil was too shallow. Happily, some seeds flourished and produced a bumper crop.

This parable describes the church of the first century, a time of great growth. But many local congregations begun during this time fell by the wayside. So, in Revelation 2, this church receives a mixed report card. There was much good, but bad as well.

Revelation 2:8–11—Smyrna: 100–300 CE
Matthew 13:24–30—Tares among the Wheat

Church history during the second and third centuries was marked by waves of persecution separated by periods of relative calm. The church at Smyrna, chosen to represent these days, was commended because it endured persecution "for ten days" and because it resisted the "slander of those who say they are Jews, but are not."

This was a time when the church began to gain favorable notice from the Roman culture. Although it wasn't accepted yet and was even persecuted at times, more and more people saw that it was something new and different, and began to ask interested questions about it.

Matthew 13:24–30 relates the parable of a farmer whose wheat is beginning to grow when "tares," or weeds, are found among the crop. The harvesters ask if they should root out the tares, but the farmer, fearing that this will uproot the young wheat as well, decides that both must grow together until the harvest, and be separated then. The wheat will be gathered up and stored. The tares will be burned.

These two Bible passages describe a time when God's "true church" was infiltrated by those who claimed to be Christians but were not. Those who interpret the scriptures in this way believe that the same problem exists today. Ever since this time of history, they say, there have been people who are "outward" Christians, "Sunday morning Christians," "Christmas and Easter Christians," but who have not really committed themselves to God. They are "tares among the wheat."

Revelation 2:12–17—Pergamum: 300–600 CE
Matthew 13:31–32—The Mustard Seed

It was during this period of church history that Christianity became the state church of Rome. When the Emperor Constantine converted, it suddenly became the "thing to do" to declare yourself a Christian, whatever you believed. Unprecedented growth took place during these three hundred years. Cathedrals were built. A professional clergy developed. The church took on many of the trappings it retains to this day.

The parable of Matthew 13 pictures the mustard seed, the "smallest of all seeds," growing into a large tree, giving shelter to all the birds of the air who rest in its branches—just as the Christian movement, beginning as a tiny, obscure Jewish sect, grew into the state religion of the Western world.

But growth can bring problems. The letter to the church at Pergamum reminds the people not to be caught up in the culture of the day. It refers to the Old Testament story of the false prophet Balaam (Num. 22–25), who tried to lead the Israelites into sin by tempting them in various ways, especially with sexual immorality. This story is God's way of saying to the church, "Watch out lest you be corrupted by the world that has embraced you!"

Revelation 2:18–29—Thyatira: 600–1500 CE
Matthew 13:33–35—Leaven in the Loaf

From the fall of Rome until the time of the Protestant Reformation, the church went through good times and bad. These "Dark Ages" saw the church establishing itself as a fortress of learning and scholarship, in many ways holding the broken Roman Empire together. In this way it was a metaphor for the parable of "leaven in the loaf." Leaven, or yeast, permeates the whole loaf of bread and causes it to rise. The church, according to some historians, was the leaven that permeated the loaf of Western civilization and caused it to grow during very dark times.

But this period also saw bloody crusades and internal corruption. In some ways, cultural evil was the "leaven" that permeated the church, leading to inquisitions, persecutions, and subjugation of whole races.

The church at Thyatira was warned that it would "suffer intensely." To some Catholic scholars this warning refers to the Protestant Reformation that split the church into different factions, a split from which it has never recovered. Some Protestant scholars view the passage differently. Because the cause given for the "suffering" is that the church has tolerated the evil "Jezebel," the foreign queen who caused Israel to sin in Kings 16:30, they believe that the suffering results from the fact that the church has committed "adultery" with the world and its ways instead of remaining faithful to Jesus Christ. It was the protest of the Catholic Church's perceived "marriage" with the world that gave the new church its name—"protesters," or Protestants.

Both Catholics and Protestants cling to the final word given to the church at Thyatira and claim its message as their own: "Hold fast to what you have until I come."

Revelation 3:1–6—Sardis:
Protestant Reformation until about 1700 CE
Matthew 13:44—The Hidden Treasure

Here it becomes obvious that this particular timeline is a Protestant interpretation. From now on, when people like Lindsey and LaHaye talk about "the church," they are referring to the Protestant, primarily evangelical, community.

The parable of Matthew 13 describes a man finding a treasure that had been hidden in a field. According to this interpretation, the hidden treasure was what the Protestant reformers discovered—the "correct" interpretation of the Bible, the "correct" understanding of what it means to be a Christian, the "correct" way of worshiping God.

But according to this view the reformers—Martin Luther, John Calvin, and the rest—didn't go far enough. All they accomplished was to replace one bureaucracy with another. That is why, in Revelation 3, Jesus told the church at Sardis, "You have the reputation of being alive, but you are dead. Wake up! Strengthen what remains and is about to die, for I have not found your deeds complete in the sight of God. Remember what you have received and heard; obey it and repent."

Even so, the Reformation wasn't all bad: "You have a few people in Sardis who have not soiled their clothes … they are worthy."

Revelation 3:7–13—Philadelphia: 1700–1950s
Matthew 13:45, 46—The Pearl of Great Price

These were the glory years of the Protestant Church in the West, and especially in America. Great denominations were formed. Foreign missions began. Urban revival groups such as the YMCA and Salvation Army were born. Billy Graham became the most popular evangelist in world history. Churches moved out to the sub-

ARMAGEDDON NOW: THE END OF THE WORLD A TO Z

urbs and Sunday schools began. The "Christian ethic" permeated polite society. Sunday mornings, and especially Christmas and Easter, saw unprecedented attendance at services. The church had discovered the "pearl of great price," the evangelical gospel. Even today, in the early years of the twenty-first century, those were the "good old days" remembered so fondly by many older people as a better time.

"I have placed before you an open door that no one can shut," was the promise given to the church at Philadelphia. Also to this church, Jesus says, "I am coming soon. Hold on to what you have."

Those who espouse this interpretation of church history believe that they are the remnants of the Philadelphian church. Their services often feature the language, music, and imagery of the churches they knew during the "glory years" of American "old-time religion." God is a He. "Rise Up O Men [not women] of God" is still a favorite hymn. The King James Bible is still the translation of choice, although that is starting to change in some circles.

Revelation 3:14–22—Laodicea: 1950s and into the Future
Matthew 13: 47–51—The Dragnet

What about churches that are attempting to struggle with issues of lifestyle, gender equality, abortion, and homosexuality?

According to the evangelical interpretation, they have kicked Jesus out of the church. That is why Jesus rebukes the church of Laodicea: "Behold, I stand outside at the door and knock.... You say, 'I am rich.' ... But you do not realize that you are wretched, pitiful, poor, blind and naked."

The final parable of Matthew 13 appropriately pictures a fisherman throwing out a great net and catching all kinds of fish. The good fish are placed in one basket, the bad in another. "This is how it will be at the end of the age. The angels will come and separate the wicked from the righteous and throw them into the fiery furnace, where there will be weeping and gnashing of teeth."

To those who follow this interpretation of the Bible, the empty, struggling mainline American churches of today are proof that we are near the end of human history. Churches that wrestle with the gray areas of contemporary life have departed from the true path.

Many biblical scholars remain skeptical that this is what the original authors meant at all. But despite such skepticism, the wave that Hal Lindsey and Tim LaHaye set in motion will probably not abate anytime soon.

Sources:
Borg, Marcus J. *Reading the Bible Again for the First Time: Taking the Bible Seriously but Not Literally*. San Francisco: HarperSanFrancisco, 2001.
The Holy Bible, New International Version. Grand Rapids, MI: Zondervan, 1978.
LaHaye, Tim, and Jerry B. Jenkins. *Left Behind* series. 12 vols. Carol Stream, IL: Tyndale House, 1995–2004.
Lindsey, Hal, with C. C. Carlson. *The Late Great Planet Earth*. Grand Rapids, MI: Zondervan, 1970.
Willis, Jim. *The Religion Book: Places, Prophets, Saints, and Seers*. Detroit: Visible Ink Press, 2004.

BIG BANG

This is the way the world ends
Not with a bang but a whimper.
— T. S. Eliot, *The Hollow Men*

If Stephen Hawking, often called the most brilliant theoretical physicist since Albert Einstein, were to paraphrase the famous poem by T. S. Eliot, it might read something like this:

This is the way the world begins
Not with a bang but a bubble.

A generation of astrophysicists has been raised on the idea that the universe began some 15 billion years ago in a "Big Bang." A simple description of this momentous event is offered by Craig J. Hogan in his book *The Little Book of the Big Bang*:

We live in a galaxy, in an expanding universe of galaxies, that emerged from a hot, dense early universe filled with light. All the matter of the universe was created from this light energy, and quite possibly the expanding universe itself and the energy that fills it all exploded from a tiny speck of unstable space. The nearly structure-less early universe sowed the seeds of complex structures, including galaxies and ourselves. This is a synopsis of the Big Bang, the truest model we have of cosmic evolution on the largest scales of space and time.

The Big Bang disturbs a lot of theoretical physicists. For one thing, the original singularity—the supposed pinpoint without measurable size that "exploded" outward, creating time and space, is a troubling hypothesis. What was it? Where did it come from?

Stephen Hawking pointed out in 1981 that postulating a "bubble" rather than a "bang" answers a lot of these questions. Of course, it raises a lot more.

The basic idea of the Big Bang is that 15 billion years ago nothing existed. "Nothing" means just that—not time, not space, not emptiness—nothing. And then something happened. No one knows what, of course. Mathematics can take scientists back to what they call the "Planck barrier," named after the physicist Max Planck, who postulated it. That is what the universe was like 10^{-43} second after its inception. Given that 10^{-43} second is a much shorter time than it takes light to reach your eyes from the page you're reading, that's pretty darn close to the beginning. By that time gravity was already acting independently of the other quantum forces and things were progressing nicely on their way to producing a universe. But no one knows what happened before that. The evidence is gone—destroyed by the forces of creation. The Planck barrier stands between scientists and the answer to the ultimate question—where did we come from?

So the Planck barrier has to be leaped by theory, not mathematical fact. And the frustrating thing about that is that science is all about observable, measurable data. That's a precious commodity when it comes to this kind of speculation.

On this side of the Planck barrier physicists can use mathematics to describe what was going on. The ages of the universe look something like this:

THE VACUUM ERA (DON'T BLINK OR YOU'LL MISS IT). This can be called the beginning of time. It lasts less than 10^{-43} second. Before that, for all practical purposes, time did not exist. By 10^{-32} second, the universe, by then about the size of a grapefruit, is already beginning to cool down. The matter that will soon coagulate to form every star, every galaxy, every planet, and every person is only a gleam in the cosmos's eye.

THE RADIATION ERA (THIS EPOCH MIGHT HAVE LASTED AS LONG AS A MONTH). This is the time when light comes into being. It comes after inflation but before the creation of matter. Things like the "electroweak epoch" and the "strong epoch" take place during this period.

THE MATTER ERA (PERHAPS TEN THOUSAND YEARS LONG). The universe has now cooled to the point where electrons can begin to attach to protons. Matter begins to form.

THE DARK AGES (MAYBE AS LONG AS 1 BILLION YEARS). Now we start to see the formation of galaxies and things that look familiar.

THE BRIGHT AGES (UP UNTIL THE PRESENT). This is where we come in. Here the universe starts to look pretty recognizable.

But what happened on the other side of the Planck barrier to cause all this?

No one knows, but the basic idea behind the bubble theory, according to physicists such as J. Richard Gott, is that several universes, perhaps even an infinite number of them, arose from bubbles that "inflated," something like a balloon, into nothing—a void. Each of these universes is still opening up into infinity and will continue to grow forever. At the very beginning of the process—at least for our universe—there was a somewhat uneven mix of hot spots. These hot spots expanded so rapidly that they very quickly cooled down—a process called "supercooling." The importance of supercooling is that it allowed the matter developing inside of time and space to develop for a little longer and mix together more uniformly than would have happened otherwise. This phenomenon in turn produced a uniform radiation, the same radiation scientists are able to detect today.

The next question naturally becomes, what happened to the other universes?

Well, we will probably never know because they are separated from us by an "event horizon." No light can travel from there to here, so we can't observe them. But possibly someone occupying another universe, "parallel" to ours but unobservable, is even now speculating upon the existence of other universes.

Most scientists believe that these universes will never come together. They are like bubbles in a rising batch of cookie dough, destined to be close but not touching forever. A few theorists, however, think that if expansion slows down and stops, some of the universes might eventually converge. Now that would be a reunion!

At this point, the discussion has perhaps encroached upon the territory of metaphysics. "Bangs" at the beginning and "parallel universes" would seem to resemble the stuff of religion. "In the beginning, God created..."; Jesus "ascended" into the parallel universe called heaven. To the scientist there is no similarity, but to the reli-

Creation Concept, by Gary S. and Vivian Chapman. *Getty Images*.

gious person there are uncanny comparisons to be drawn. If there was a "Creation" at the other side of the Planck barrier, will there be an "Armageddon" at the end of time? Are religion and science saying the same things?

In his book *When Science Meets Religion*, Ian G. Barbour attempts a dialogue between the two fields. Examining differing views of science and religion, he points out that there is room for conversation in terms of astronomy and creation, the implications of quantum physics, evolution and continuing creation, genetics, and neuroscience and human nature. Perhaps, he argues, there are fundamentalists on both sides of the fence who are to blame for the lack of communication. The search for our beginnings and curiosity about our end traverses the fields of both science and metaphysics. Maybe one field can inform the other.

Sources:

Barbour, Ian G. *When Science Meets Religion: Enemies, Strangers, or Partners?* New York: Harper-Collins, 2000.

Boslough, John. *Stephen Hawking's Universe.* New York: Avon, 1980.

Gould, Stephen Jay. *Rocks of Ages: Science and Religion in the Fullness of Life.* New York: Ballantine, 1999.

Hawking, Stephen W. *A Brief History of Time: From the Big Bang to Black Holes*. New York: Bantam, 1988.

Hogan, Craig J. *The Little Book of the Big Bang: A Cosmic Primer*. New York: Copernicus, 1998.

BIG CRUNCH, BIG CHILL, AND BIG RIP

There are three possibilities scientists seriously contemplate when picturing the end of the universe. Because "Big Bang" is the name reserved for the consensus theory concerning its beginnings, all three names for its ending begin with "Big": Big Crunch, Big Chill, and the newest theory, Big Rip.

"Big Crunch" refers to the possibility that gravity will inexorably pull the universe back together until it "crunches" in on itself, possibly even duplicating the original point of almost infinite density, mass, and heat but no volume that is thought to have existed at the immediate point of the Big Bang. The theory proposes that tens of billions of years from now the cosmos will cease to expand, run out of energy, give way to the inexorable pull of gravity, and simply deflate like a popped balloon.

The big question about the Big Crunch concerns the amount of matter in the universe. At first glance there doesn't appear to be enough to generate a gravitational force sufficient to pull everything back together again. But with the discovery of a mathematical possibility of something called "dark matter," matter that does not give off light and so cannot be seen with a telescope, it became at least theoretically possible that the universe contained a sufficient amount of material to bring about the Big Crunch.

Up until the final decade of the twentieth century, that was the scientific community's best guess concerning the end of the universe. Now, based on images gathered by the orbiting Hubble Space Telescope, there is a developing consensus that the universe will more likely continue to expand, cool down, and thin out. The force of gravity, even with the inclusion of the forces generated by "dark matter," may not be sufficient to pull everything back together into one point.

This would probably produce an ending scientists call the "Big Chill," quite a different scenario. To attempt to try to understand what might happen if the big chill occurs at the end of space and time requires setting aside absolutely everything we currently experience concerning how the universe works. The cosmological epoch we find ourselves in is only one brief period that is taking place in a grand sweep of time almost unimaginable to the human mind. The universe is now only about 14 billion years old. Another 14 billion years from now, assuming there is some kind of intelligence around to view what is happening, things will appear quite different. For one thing, if that intellgence includes our descendants, they will have had to find a new platform from which to observe the activities of the cosmos. The sun will long since have died, after first expanding into a giant red ball that envelopes and vaporizes our home planet (see Sun, Death of).

What will happen here is what will eventually happen everywhere in the universe. Every sun will go through the same process. According to Gregory Laughlin, an astrophysicist at the University of Michigan, 100 trillion, trillion, trillion years from now, all planets everywhere will have been destroyed. The universe will enter an epoch of degeneration. Most of its matter will be locked up in black holes or white dwarfs. A long energy crisis will follow and wind down to an end. The material that fuels the universe will be used up. Protons, subatomic particles at the center of every atom, will decay. Matter will evaporate into radiation. Black holes will eventually radiate away. The universe will be very dark, very cold, and very empty. The "Big Chill" will have arrived.

The bad news is that the end looks very bleak. The good news is that it is still quite a ways off. Add two hundred zeros to the number 1 and you get an idea of the number of years we have left. We still have time to pack our bags.

But there is yet another possibility. That is the end Albert Einstein originally predicted in 1917. He theorized that there was an antigravity force pushing everything apart. He later called this theory his "greatest blunder." But it now appears that he may have been right.

In the 1990s, a team led by Robert Caldwell of Dartmouth College in New Hampshire published a radical idea. "Until now we thought the Universe would either recollapse to a big crunch or expand forever to a state of infinite dilution. Now we've come up with a third possibility—the 'big rip.'" The "Big Rip" refers to the possibility of a "phantom energy" that will literally rip apart every speck of matter in the universe.

The idea goes something like this: The universe is expanding. If it expands at a steadily increasing speed, that will bring us to the Big Chill. Picture two automobiles facing in opposite directions with their engines running and their gas pedals depressed. They move away from each other at a steadily increasing speed—say that each accelerates ten miles an hour for every mile it travels. Of course, given that we are analogizing the universe, these are very unusual cars, and they will keep accelerating away from each other, eventually reaching the speed of light. This is more or less what is involved in the Big Chill model.

Now suppose the same two cars move away from each other, but instead of a steadily increasing speed, they have a greatly increasing *rate* of acceleration. Instead of moving ten miles per hour faster for every mile they travel, they move ten miles per hour faster for the first mile, then for the next half mile, then for the next hundred yards, then for the next foot. The forces brought about by this wildly increasing acceleration will sooner or later tear both cars apart—not only their body parts and engine structures, but eventually even their atoms and the particles that make up those atoms. Although such a mechanical comparison cannot capture the physics involved, perhaps it at least gives some notion of what the Big Rip is about.

What is the "engine" that moves the cars—or rather, that gives the universe its thrust, causing atoms to literally be repulsed from each other rather than attracted through the force of gravity? According to Caldwell, the answer lies in the form of a "phantom energy" called dark energy. Even he admits that "it's pretty weird stuff." But if it functions as he thinks it might, the runaway expansion will continue, growing ever stronger until, about 22 billion years from now, every star, every galaxy, and eventually every speck of matter will be literally ripped apart. Hence, the "Big Rip."

We won't see it happen, of course. Our own Milky Way will be gone some 60 million years before the end comes. It will be all downhill from there. In the final milliseconds even the most elementary fragments of matter will shred themselves into nonexistence. And then it will all be gone. Everything. Every last particle and proton.

If the "Big Rip" is ever proved possible, it might change the way scientists look at the universe. The theory of relativity allows for things like wormholes and black holes that offer the possibility of shortcuts through space, where a person could duck into a warp in the fabric of time/space and suddenly appear somewhere else. But wormholes close faster than we can ever see them. If a force existed that could pry them open and then keep them open, it offers all the intriguing possibilities of time and dimension travel so dear to the hearts of science fiction writers everywhere.

All these scenarios pose a dilemma for human life. Assuming intelligent human descendants still exist billions of years from now, they face a pretty bleak future. If protons and neutrons begin to decay into lighter particles, there won't be enough atoms around to construct anything remotely resembling carbon-based life. Consciousness will have had to find a way to evolve a new host by then, or it will have ceased to exist.

This possibility, in turn, raises an interesting problem. The universe is so big and full of awesome things that, until recently, it seemed the height of human arrogance to assume that the human race was anywhere near the most important thing in it. To insist that the cosmos was somehow "made for" humans, to refer to an "anthropic universe," was to draw unmitigated scorn from those who considered such a view terribly naive and old-fashioned. That was the domain of the religious folks.

But questions are usually considered naive or profound depending on who asks them. If a child asks, "Why are we here?" the question is usually thought to be cute. If a physicist asks, "Why is there something, rather than nothing?" or "Does the universe know or care about us?" it's a whole different matter. Humans might be simply an accident, existing only on one small planet in a backwater galaxy. But according to Craig J. Hogan, author of *The Little Book of the Big Bang*, physics now offers other possibilities.

Hogan agrees with the general scientific opinion that, religion aside, the universe doesn't seem to be created only for humans. But there is another way to approach the question. The mathematics of quantum cosmology offers the possibility of an infinite number of universes, each with its own unique set of laws and rules. Because we can live only in a universe like the one we are now living in, it can be said that of all the possible universes out there, humans, in a sense, "chose" this one because it was the only one in which they could have evolved. In other words, we live in the neighborhood that best suits us, because we couldn't have survived in another part of town.

In that sense, this universe, out of all others, *was* made for humans. And since we have only recently arrived on the scene, chances are we will continue to adapt as we go along. That may not be the conscious intention of the universe, but it is the result we experience as the only consciously meditative beings in it. And any other beings that may exist out there on other planets can say the same thing.

Put this way, human consciousness will have to evolve to a point beyond the carbon-based material body it now inhabits.

There is, of course, another scenario. Maybe this is the only universe that exists. Maybe humans were an accident. In that case the end of everything could well take place in a few billion years. And there will be no one around to mourn our passing.

Sources:
Britt, Robert Roy. "The Big Rip: New Theory Ends Universe by Shredding Everything." http://www.space.com/scienceastronomy/big_rip_030306.html.

Glanz, James. "New Data on 2 Doomsday Ideas, Big Rip vs. Big Crunch." *New York Times*, February 21, 2004.

Hawking, Stephen W. *A Brief History of Time: From the Big Bang to Black Holes*. New York: Bantam Books, 1988.

Hogan, Craig J. *The Little Book of the Big Bang: A Cosmic Primer*. New York: Copernicus, 1998.

"Physicists Describe Grim End of the World." http://www.cnn.com/TECH/9701/15/end.universe/.

BOOK OF LIFE

Although the phrase *book of life* appears in the Hebrew Bible, the Christian Old Testament (Ps. 69:27–29), by far the best-known references are associated with the fundamentalist/evangelical Christian interpretation of the book of Revelation.

> He who overcomes will, like them, be dressed in white. I will never erase his name from the book of life. (3:5)

> All inhabitants of the earth will worship the beast—all whose names have not been written in the book of life belonging to the Lamb that was slain from the creation of the world. (13:8)

> If anyone's name was not found written in the book of life, he was thrown into the lake of fire. (20:15)

This last verse relates to the results handed down at the Great White Throne Judgment that, according to a literal reading of the Bible, takes place at the end of time (see Revelation). In this vivid image, Jesus is pictured sitting on a white throne while separating "the sheep from the goats"—not good people from bad, but those who have "accepted Christ" from those who have not. The basis for this judgment is a debated theological point, often misunderstood by those outside of fundamentalist/evangelical Christianity.

The popular conception of an endtime judgment is that good people go to heaven while bad people go to hell. But this notion describes a religion of "works" versus a religion of "faith." If, it is often said, we resist temptation, obey the Ten Commandments, try not to hurt anyone, or receive enough prayers from others for our salvation, we will be accepted and our names will be written in God's book of life—a kind of directory of the "saved." This is a very popular notion concerning the essence of Christianity.

It is not, however, the fundamentalist/evangelical understanding of who goes where when life on earth is done. The debate within this camp is not over who is "good enough" to earn citizenship in heaven—there is universal agreement that no one deserves that honor. In the words of the apostle Paul, we "all have sinned and fall short of the glory of God" (Rom. 3:23).

No, the debate over who has "his" name (the masculine pronoun is almost always used) recorded in the book of life centers on how and when the choice was made to include it.

Those believing in predestination understand the verses in Revelation to mean that God foreordained, before the beginning of the world, who would be included and who would not. God predestined some for salvation, recorded their names in the book of life, and is simply waiting for history to unfold. This was the view of the Protestant reformer John Calvin and is found in the historical theological statements of the first Puritans and Pilgrims who came to New England. It is also a prominent plank in the theological platform of the Presbyterian Church and many Reform branches of Protestant Christianity.

Others disagree. The position of Methodists and most Baptist denominations has long been that individual believers are free to choose to "accept Christ." People will not find their names recorded in the book of life at the end of time unless they have freely, on their own, made a "decision for Jesus." That is the reasoning behind the altar calls made at the end of every Billy Graham rally. While the choir sings "Just as I am, without one plea / But that Thy blood was shed for me, / And that Thou bidst me come to Thee, / O Lamb of God, I come," people make decisions that will determine where they spend eternity. There is an angel somewhere recording the results of that decision. Those who say yes and come forward to stand before the altar rail and pray with a counselor will find their names recorded in the book of life at the end of time. Those who say no will be thrown into the lake of fire.

There are many Christians who don't agree with either position. Some believe that a God of love has, by definition, no limits to that love and could never send someone, however vile, to eternal damnation—even those who say no to God's offer of love. To still others, the book of life imagery is simply apocalyptic metaphor (see Apocalyptic Writing) and has no basis at all in future reality.

Sources:
The Holy Bible, New International Version. Grand Rapids, MI: Zondervan, 1978.
Willis, Jim. *The Religion Book: Places, Prophets, Saints, and Seers.* Detroit: Visible Ink Press, 2004.

BOOKS OF THE BIBLE
AND THEIR RELATION TO PROPHECY

The word *prophecy* has at least two different meanings in the Bible. One definition has to do with the fact that when biblical prophets "prophesied," they didn't necessarily tell the future. They were not called to foretell as much as to "forth-tell." In other words, they felt inspired to point out social injustice and culturally entrenched evil. When a prophet said, "Thus saith the Lord," he most often pointed out the perceived sins of the institutions of government. This kind of prophecy is the most prevalent form found in the classical prophets.

A second idea of prophecy involves the belief that prophets often foretold the future (see Futurist School of Biblical Interpretation). Some of the ancient prophecies, according to this view, have been fulfilled in history. Some await fulfillment.

Although this school recognizes verses scattered throughout the entire Bible, a core group of passages has risen to the surface and is found in virtually every book attempting to describe what will happen to planet Earth and its inhabitants:

GENESIS 3:15. "I will put enmity between you [the serpent] and the woman, and between your offspring and hers; he will crush your head, and you will strike his heel."

The serpent is not identified until the final book of the Christian Bible. Only in Revelation 12:9 do we come to understand that the "dragon," the beast who instigates the judgment of God upon the earth, is really "that ancient serpent called the devil, or Satan."

Genesis says that God will be victorious and "crush the serpent's head." This victory will come with a price, however. The "seed of the woman," understood by conservative Christian scholars to be Jesus Christ, will defeat Satan but, in the process, be hurt himself. Satan will strike at his heel. This is understood to mean that Jesus will have to endure the suffering of the cross to achieve ultimate victory.

GENESIS 5–9. This passage contains the account of Noah's flood. When Jesus talked about the signs preceding the "time of the end," he warned that they would be similar to the days preceding the great biblical flood (see Days of Noah; Rapture).

EXODUS 25–30. This extended section outlines the blueprints for the building of the temple—which, according to many Christians, is a prerequisite for the time of the end (see Temple at Jerusalem).

LEVITICUS 23. In this passage seven holidays are divinely commanded. According to some fundamentalist/evangelical scholars, they prefigure the ages of the church from the Crucifixion until the Millennium (see Bible Timelines).

NUMBERS 21. This chapter tells of an incident that happened to the Jewish people during their forty-year wilderness journey between leaving Egypt and entering the Promised Land. Thinking that God had deserted them, they complained to Moses about their seemingly aimless wandering. God retaliated by sending poisonous serpents among them. When Moses asked God what he should do, he was told to make a snake (Moses made one of bronze) and place it on a pole in the middle of the camp. Anyone bitten by a real snake had only to look at the bronze serpent on the pole and he would live.

In the third chapter of the New Testament gospel of John, Jesus reminds a Jewish priest named Nicodemus about this Old Testament passage, saying, "Just as Moses lifted up the snake in the desert, so the Son of Man must be lifted up, that everyone who believes in him may have eternal life."

Conservative Christian theologians argue that the Numbers passage was prophetic, pointing to the Crucifixion and ultimate salvation for all who believe in Jesus Christ as savior of the world.

DEUTERONOMY 4:27–31. In this passage God warns the Jewish people that they will be scattered among all the nations but will be cared for if they remain faithful.

DEUTERONOMY 18:22. This verse contains the test of a prophet. If what he says comes true, it will prove that the message is from God. If it doesn't, the prophet is proved to have spoken "presumptuously."

JOB 19:25–27. These verses contain the hopeful cry of those who look for eternal life beyond death: "I know that my Redeemer lives, and that in the end he will stand upon the earth. And after my skin has been destroyed, yet in my flesh I will see God; I myself will see him with my own eyes—I and not another."

ISAIAH. Many people think that much of Isaiah contains prophecy concerning the fate of Israel. The following are a few of the best-known passages:

> *2:2–5—The Temple.* "In the last days the mountain of the Lord's Temple will be established as chief among the mountains; it will be raised above the hills and all nations will stream to it.... They will beat their swords into plowshares and their spears into pruning hooks. Nation will not take up sword against nation, nor will they train for war any more" (see Temple at Jerusalem).

> *9:6–7—The Messiah.* "For to us a child is born, to us a son is given, and the government will be upon his shoulders.... Of the increase of his government and peace there will be no end. He will reign on David's throne and over his kingdom, establishing it and upholding it with justice and righteousness from that time on and forever."

> *11:2—Zionism.* "He will raise a banner for the nations and gather the exiles of Israel; he will assemble them from the four quarters of the earth."

> *13:13—The End of Time.* In these passages God promises to "make the land desolate and destroy the sinners within it. The stars of heaven and their constellations will not show their light.... I will punish the world for its evil, the wicked for their sins."

> *49:6—The Nation.* "It is too small a thing for you to be my servant to restore the tribes of Jacob and bring back those of Israel I have kept. I will also make you a light for the Gentiles that you may bring forth my salvation to the ends of the earth."

> *53—The Crucifixion.* This extended passage is believed by many to be a description of what is feels like to be crucified and contains, according some scholars, a few of the Bible verses Jesus is said to have uttered from the cross. At the end it holds out a hope of being given "a portion among the great" at the end of time.

> *61:1–2—The Church.* "He has sent me to bind up the brokenhearted, to proclaim freedom for the captives and release for the prisoners, to proclaim the year of the Lord's favor and the day of vengeance of our God." This passage is believed by conservative scholars to prefigure the work of the Christian church, the body of Jesus Christ. Some believe that the Second Coming will not happen until these verses are literally fulfilled.

> *65:17—Eternity.* "Behold, I will create new heavens and a new earth. The former things will not be remembered, nor will they come to mind."

EZEKIEL 38–39. This is the passage thought by many futurists to be the most complete Old Testament description of World War III, or the battle of Armageddon (see also Armageddon, Battle of; Cush; Gog and Magog).

DANIEL. This book is usually linked with the book of Revelation in terms of prophetic importance (see Daniel).

JOEL 2:29–32. "I will pour out my spirit in those days. I will show wonders in the heavens and on the earth, blood and fire and billows of smoke. The sun will be turned to darkness and the moon to blood before the coming of the great and dreadful day of the Lord. And everyone who calls upon the name of the Lord will be saved."

AMOS 5:24. This passage was a favorite of the late Martin Luther King Jr. when he prophetically called for social justice: "But let justice roll on like a river, righteousness like a never-failing stream!"

AMOS 9:14. Evangelical scholars considered this verse fulfilled in 1948: "'I will bring back my exiled people Israel; they will rebuild the ruined cities and live in them.... I will plant Israel in their own land, never again to be uprooted from the land I have given them.' says the Lord your God."

HABAKKUK 2:2. "Write down the revelation and make it plain on tablets so that a herald may run with it. For the revelation awaits the appointed time; it speaks of the end and will not prove false. Though it linger, wait for it; it will certainly come and not delay."

ZECHARIAH 12–14. This extended passage uses the words "on that day" fifteen times. Chapter 14 is often thought to be a description of the Second Coming when Jesus Christ returns to stand on the Mount of Olives outside Jerusalem.

MALACHI 3:1–5. This scripture speaks of sending a "messenger" who will "prepare the way." "But who can endure the day of his coming? ... For he will be like a refiner's fire.... 'So I will come near to you for judgment.'"

MATTHEW 24, MARK 13, LUKE 21. These passages contain three different versions of what is often called the "Olivet Discourse," purportedly Jesus' final words concerning the coming judgment on Jerusalem and the Second Coming (see also Abomination of Desolation).

ACTS 2:11. "This same Jesus, who has been taken from you into heaven, will come back in the same way you have seen him go into heaven."

1 CORINTHIANS 15:50–58; 1 THESSALONIANS 4:13–5:3; 2 THESSALONIANS 2:1–12. These are the principal scriptures used to describe the Rapture of the church (see Rapture).

2 PETER 2:1–13. Here Peter talks about "the last days" and reminds his readers not to be anxious because, for God, "a day is like a thousand years and a thousand years are like a day.... The Lord is not slow in keeping his promises.... But the day of the Lord will come like a thief. The heavens will disappear with a roar, the elements will be destroyed by fire, and the earth and everything in it will be laid bare."

REVELATION. The final book of the Bible is the principal source for most literalist endtime scenarios dealing with the last seven years of Earth's history before the return of Jesus Christ (see Revelation).

Source:
The Holy Bible, New International Version. Grand Rapids, MI: Zondervan, 1978.

BRANCH DAVIDIANS

Pretend, for a moment, that you are a Branch Davidian during the days just preceding February 28, 1993. For months you have listened to your spiritual guide, David Koresh, preach about a brand-new revelation. He has opened up mysterious biblical passages that no one had ever really explained to you. Now it all seems to make perfect sense. Night after night he brilliantly ties together verses from all over the scriptures, demonstrating that the prophets Jeremiah and Ezekiel foretold the enigmatic passages of Revelation 6 and 7. Daniel's prophecies foreshadow the parables of Jesus.

Koresh makes the whole Bible seem to come alive with uniform meaning. When the radio brings you the daily news, it seems to mirror exactly the truth you are hearing each night at church services. You hold the Bible in one hand, the *New York Times* in the other, and history unfolds before your eyes. What Koresh calls the "mystery of iniquity" is at work in the corrupt government that, even now, has your compound under surveillance. This is it! This is the time! Jesus will actually return during your lifetime! The weapons that will be used against the evil one are now stockpiled in the basement. Koresh has warned you that the world will end filled with flames, noise, and confusion. There will be "weeping and wailing and gnashing of teeth." And that's what's happening outside. Now is the time! If you die, it will be in a holy war against oppression. The "desire of the nations" will soon enter into the atmosphere of planet Earth, and he is coming for you!

The beginnings of the Branch Davidians can be traced back to the Seventh-day Adventist Church, which expelled them from the denomination back in 1930. At that time Victor Houteff claimed to be a new prophet for the church, similar to the respected Ellen G. White. His claims were discounted and he was disfellowshipped, but enough people followed him out that he was able to start a new organization called the "Davidian Seventh-day Adventists" or the "Shepherd's Rod." Both names refer to the Old Testament's King David. Houteff had found many prophetic passages in the psalms attributed to the famous "sweet singer" of Israel, as David was sometimes called.

When Houteff died in 1955, his widow, Florence, took over as head of the movement, but a man named Ben Roden disputed her place. He believed God had called him to lead the group. Mrs. Houteff had determined that the world would end in 1959. When it didn't, her authority was undermined. Roden left, taking a group of dissatisfied people with him, and formed the Branch Davidian Seventh-day Adventists.

Like any good fundamentalist preacher, Roden studied his Bible, searching for clues that would illuminate the plan of God. He found passage after passage of typology and symbolism in the Old Testament, prompting him to institute many Hebrew feast days into the church's calendar. Especially significant to him were prophetic celebra-

Fire engulfs the Branch Davidian compound near Waco, Texas, April 19, 1993. *Ron Heflin/Associated Press.*

tions such as Passover, Pentecost, the Day of Atonement, and the Feast of Tabernacles (see Bible Timelines). He was convinced that these carried special meaning, foreshadowing God's plan for the last days of human history.

When Roden died in 1978, his wife Lois became president of the church, introducing her idea that the Holy Spirit was the feminine aspect of the Trinity. It was during her leadership that a young man named Vernon Howell joined the group in 1981. Two years later he experienced his first vision from God. Although it took a few years and some religious/political infighting, Howell emerged as president of the Branch Davidians. In 1990 he changed his name to David Koresh.

Koresh believed that we are living in the last days of history and that Branch Davidians are God's true church. God has revealed what the future holds by "sealing up" the prophecies that describe the events of these days. In Daniel 12:9–13 the angel Gabriel tells Daniel that "the words are closed up and sealed until the time of the end … none of the wicked will understand, but those who are wise will understand." Koresh considered himself to be one of the wise. He believed he had found the key to the sealed prophecies by uncovering the truth of the mysterious "seven seals" in the sixth and seventh chapters of Revelation (see Revelation). He came to believe that God's plan called for two revelations to humanity, foreshadowed by the two daily sacrifices kept throughout the Old Testament. The first, the "morning sacrifice," was fulfilled in Jesus Christ. The prophet who found the key to understanding endtime prophecy would fulfill the second, the "evening sacrifice." According to Koresh, he was that prophet.

His behavior was not that of a typical prophet. He was steeped in sex and preached violence. Sex and violence were not the hallmark of the Prince of Peace. Jesus, Koresh said, was perfect. He was the unblemished sacrifice of the morning, before the day's sins manifested themselves. The evening sacrifice, in contrast, prefigured the Day of Atonement, the "sin offering." Koresh believed that, in him, God was working through a sinful vessel who, like the prophet Jonah of old, was not chosen for his purity. Koresh was "spiritually blinded," just as Samson was before he died destroying the enemies of God. Koresh's sinful lifestyle, according to the Branch Davidians, merely proved God's choice. He thus felt perfectly justified in insisting that all women in his compound, married or not, were his to sleep with as he chose. Sleep deprivation, child abuse, Bible studies that went on all night long, stockpiling of weapons—all were part of God's divine plan and led to the soon-to-come time of the end.

It is an absolute tragedy that no one involved with the Bureau of Alcohol, Tobacco, and Firearms (ATF) force on the night of February 28, 1993, or in the weeks thereafter seems to have understood the mind of a cultist. The ATF, which conducted the initial abortive attempt to arrest Koresh and others on weapons charges, and the FBI, which quickly entered the confrontation, did everything wrong. Surrounding the compound and "playing by the book," they tried to tire the inhabitants by setting up huge loudspeakers and disrupting the cult members' sleep with rock music. They included the amplified screams of dying rabbits and Nancy Sinatra singing "These Boots Are Made for Walking," apparently in the belief that both of these would be particularly annoying.

The federal agents tried reasoning and various psychological ploys. They never understood that they were creating precisely the confused scenario that David Koresh had prophesied. They fulfilled, in miniature, exactly the type of conditions described in the Bible. The tanks, the fires, the shooting, and the confusion duplicated to a "jot and tittle" the events of Revelation 9. None of the government officials seemed to understand what Koresh was talking about when he quoted scripture. They appeared to know nothing about the biblical passages to which he referred. They never understood that to those inside the compound, the ATF represented everything that, in their view, was wrong with the secular world in which people never studied the Bible.

To the true believers inside, all the media attention focused on them simply meant that the world was coming to an end.

The end, for them at least, came on April 19. On that day the federal forces attacked. A fire broke out in the Branch Davidian compound and soon devoured it. Eighty-one people, including Koresh, died in the flames.

But the Branch Davidian movement didn't end at Waco. Those who didn't perish in the fires ignited during the ATF attack believed there was a good chance that Daniel's prophecy of "2,300 days" (Dan. 8:14) began with the death of David Koresh. If so, a "cleansing of the sanctuary" would have occurred sometime during the year 2000.

It didn't happen. But somewhere in the Bible, they believed, there must be an explanation. And someone, somewhere, is even now trying to find it.

Source:

Bunds, David, and Mark Swett. "History of the Branch Davidians." http://www.fountain. btinternet.co.uk/koresh/history.html.
Hannaford, Alex. "Return to Waco." *Guardian/UK*, October 28, 2003.
The Holy Bible, New International Version. Grand Rapids, MI: Zondervan, 1978.

BRITISH ISRAEL IN PROPHECY *see* **America in Prophecy; Armstrong, Herbert W.**

BUDDHIST VIEWS OF THE END

Buddhists do not think in terms of linear time. To them, time spins out continuously as the wheel of samsara, the never-ending cycle of life. In that kind of system, there is no "end" of time. There is, however, a final end to the succession of reincarnated human lives. Buddha taught that we all eventually come to the fulfillment of our ultimate consciousness. This happens when we attain Nirvana.

Other religious traditions sometimes picture their founder as "going" somewhere, accompanied by lights and celestial messengers, and then returning at a cataclysmic day at the end of time. In Buddhism the understanding is somewhat different. In modern terms, Buddha did not so much explode outward as implode inward. Just as a star collapses in on itself, becoming a black hole that draws everything into the void, Buddha is now drawing all things into Nirvana, the place with no dimension and no mass, the place beyond all pairs of opposites, the eternal consciousness from which all things come and to which all things return. "Buddha consciousness" is present in everything and all people. We don't normally experience it without training, but we are a manifestation of it and will eventually come to understand that the life we think we are living, although real, is ultimately an illusion. After many lives of discovery, we, like the Buddha, will "recline" and be freed from samsara and suffering.

Source:

Ellwood, Robert S., and Barbara A. McGraw. *Many Peoples, Many Faiths: Women and Men in the World Religions*. 6th ed. Upper Saddle River, NJ: Prentice Hall, 1999.

CALVINISM

The battle of Armageddon, described in Revelation 19 and 20, is actually a series of events (see Armageddon, Battle of). One of those events is the final judgment decreed on those still living when the battle ends. The vivid words from the book of Revelation have long been standard fare for fire-and-brimstone preachers. When Jerry Jenkins gave the story a new twist in *Glorious Appearing*, the final installment of the *Left Behind* series of books written with Tim LaHaye beginning in 1995, he described the scene in gruesome detail:

> Jesus merely raised one hand a few inches and a yawning chasm opened in the earth, stretching far and wide enough to swallow all of them. They tumbled in, howling and screeching, but their wailing was soon quashed and all was silent when the earth closed itself again....

> The riders not thrown leaped from their horses and tried to control them with the reins, but even as they struggled, their own flesh dissolved, their eyes melted and their tongues disintegrated.... Seconds later the same plague afflicted the horses, their flesh and eyes and tongues melting away, leaving grotesque skeletons standing, before they, too, rattled to the pavement.

An earlier chronicler, calling himself Matthew, has Jesus describing this same scene no less vividly: "[God] will cut [them] to pieces and assign [them] a place with the hypocrites, where there will be weeping and gnashing of teeth."

In an opinion piece published in the *New York Times* on July 17, 2004, Nicholas D. Kristof raised an interesting question. In the post-9/11 American climate, what would happen if an Islamic text were published in which Christians were depicted as being killed in this manner? In other contexts such mass slaughter might be labeled divine ethnic cleansing. Kristof concluded that this kind of thinking leads to real consequences in the real world. Whether Puritan or Indian, Christian or Muslim, real people make real decisions that can kill real people. Does *Glorious Appearing*, Kristof asked, sound like the actions of a loving God?

Conservative Christian theologians have long debated about who will be punished with this horrible fate. Catholic priests and Protestant ministers have voiced opinions about what sinners must do to avoid it. Many agree that sin is the cause of the judgment and that sinners, at least those who refuse to repent, will be cast into the fires of hell. But what does a person have to do to escape this penalty for sin? On what basis are the redeemed spared?

Again, Christian theologians of all denominations have agreed that on the cross Jesus paid the penalty for the redeemed—Christians who believe and accept the gift. Some even teach that he also paid the penalty for the damned, but that those judged guilty refused the gift of salvation, leaving God no choice in the matter.

To understand the modern arguments and theological concepts involved in the debate, it is necessary to begin with a central doctrinal argument from the sixteenth century.

Following the Protestant Reformation, biblical studies took a dramatic turn. By the seventeenth century, the Reformed tradition had determined what would thereafter be its orthodoxy. The reformer who most influenced this position was John Calvin (1509–1564).

One of the central points of Calvin's theology concerned the doctrine of predestination. Calvin was convinced that human beings were totally depraved. There is no good in a person at all, not even enough to want to be saved from sin. That doesn't mean people always do bad things. There is, after all, God's common grace at work in the world, available to all. But in terms of salvation and being "Godlike," the human race is without hope.

How, then, can a sinful human being choose to accept God's saving grace, thus sparing him or herself from the final judgment? The answer, in the Calvinistic view, is to be found in Romans 8:29–30: "For those God foreknew he also predestined to be conformed to the likeness of his Son.... And those he predestined, he also called." Calvin believed that the choice for salvation and the avoidance of judgment at Armageddon was a divine choice, not a human one. From before the time of creation, God predestined some to be saved. Calvin never went so far as to say that the rest were therefore predestined for hell, but that was the obvious conclusion most people drew. This belief in predestination was at the heart of Calvinism.

There were those who drew back from the idea that a good God would create people who had no hope for salvation. One of these was a distinguished Dutch pastor and professor named Jacobus Arminius (1560–1609). Although his training had been thoroughly Calvinistic and had even taken place under the direction of Calvin's successor, when called upon to refute a scholar who rejected this seemingly cruel aspect of reformed theology, Arminius came to the reluctant conclusion that he couldn't do it. He still believed in predestination, but with the proviso that God predestined those who, based on God's foreknowledge, would choose salvation if they could. Of course, their depravity made such a choice impossible, so God had to step in and intervene.

Here the plot thickens, because this belief opened doors long thought closed forever. Back in the early fifth century, some of the most important works written by Augustine, a key Catholic theologian and a favorite of the sixteenth-century Protestant reformers as well, were published to oppose the views of Pelagius, a British monk who believed that humans had free will to either accept or oppose God. Pelagius completely rejected original sin and the corruption of human nature that forces people to sin. The battle between Augustinians and Pelagians lasted seven years and was known as the Pelagian Controversy. The Pelagians were finally decreed heretical. And once the church settles something, it quite reasonably is reluctant to open the issue again.

Now along came the Arminians, who, while distancing themselves from Pelagianism by insisting that it was only through the foreknowledge of God that people could do good,
seemed to be skirting the edges of the same heretical ground. In typical church fashion, a council was called. The Synod of Dort met from

John Calvin. *Fortean Picture Library.*

November 1618 to May 1619, and the two parties fought it out. In the end, the synod affirmed five doctrines that the Arminians simply would not accept, and these five points became the basis of Calvinist theology. Students of theology remember them by use of the acrostic TULIP:

> *T = Total depravity.* Although a vestige of natural light remains within fallen humanity, human nature is so corrupt that the light cannot be used.

> *U = Unconditional election.* The election of the saved is based not on God's foreknowledge of human response but only on the inscrutable will of God.

> *L = Limited atonement.* Christ did not die for all humanity, but only for the elect, meaning those who are saved.

> *I = Irresistible grace.* God's grace cannot be refused, for it is greater than human sin.

> *P = Perseverance of the saints.* The elect cannot fall from grace or choose not to be saved.

Those who accepted these five points, which were later amplified and elaborated, became known as Calvinists. Their descendants formed denominations we now know as Presbyterians, Reformed, and Congregationalists. Those who rejected the five points formed denominations represented by groups such as the Methodists and many Baptists today.

It's important to understand that these people were not simply playing intellectual games and performing academic exercises. History was shaped by what they decided. Lives were lost and wars fought. One example will suffice.

When the Puritans landed on the shores of New England, they were staunch Calvinists. They had come to believe that although good works could not earn salvation, actions were proof that salvation had been granted. The "Puritan ethic" was born. The whole community examined an individual's life because how a person behaved was the sign of God's work of grace.

Someone once said, "Puritanism is the fear that somewhere in the world, someone might be happy." That might not have been far from the truth. Where John Calvin had found great joy and relief in the idea of resting securely in the arms of God's grace, his Puritan followers embraced a strict, judgmental religion far removed from his original understanding. They unmercifully persecuted Catholics and Quakers. They took great stock (pun intended) in publicly punishing those found guilty of violating their narrow community standards.

The Puritans' strict Calvinism convinced them of two things concerning the native peoples they encountered in the New World. First, if God had predestined some to be saved, then out there among the heathen must be "Christian" Indians who were simply waiting for correct teaching; obviously, it was Christian duty to find them. Second, however, if unsaved Indians were going to hell, it was the duty of Christians to fulfill God's will by putting them there.

Viewed in this light, King Philip's War (1675–76), perhaps the biggest per capita bloodbath ever fought on American soil, was a jihad, a holy war between Christians and Indians. Of course it was also a political land struggle and a clash of technologies, but published sermons of the time leave no doubt that the Calvinist religious component of doing God's will justified the conflict in the minds of the Europeans.

By contemplating the carnage of only this one example it can be seen that, far from being simply academic exercises, religious doctrines and conflicts have been at the root of events that have brought cultural Armageddons upon people of many different traditions.

Sources:

Gonzalez, Justo L. *The Story of Christianity.* 2 vols. New York: Harper & Row, 1985.

Hauptman, Laurence M., and James D. Wherry, eds. *The Pequots in Southern New England.* Norman: University of Oklahoma Press, 1990.

May, Herbert G., and Bruce M. Metzger, eds. *The New Oxford Annotated Bible with the Apocrypha.* Rev. ed. New York: Oxford University Press, 1973.

CAMPUS CRUSADE FOR CHRIST

In 1951 American evangelicalism was just beginning to boom (see Evangelicalism). Suburban churches were filling up with men who had returned home from the war. Reaping the benefits of the GI Bill, many veterans had graduated from college and had begun promising careers. Some college students who had grown up receiving instruction in Protestant Sunday schools and youth groups were taking their religion seriously. After college, many of them, feeling a call to Christian ministry, were attending seminaries that carried the new label "neo-evangelical." These seminaries had attracted famous supporters such as Billy Graham and Harold Ockenga who considered themselves to be direct spiritual descendants of famous evangelists such as Dwight L. Moody (1837–1899). A central tenet of their evangelical theology was that Jesus Christ would return to win the battle of Armageddon and begin a thousand-year reign of peace on the earth.

One of the seminaries that demanded of its students and faculty an allegiance to a belief in a literal Second Coming was Fuller Theological Seminary of California. In 1951 it was the home of a twenty-nine-year-old student who had left a successful oil company to prepare for Christian ministry. His name was Bill Bright.

Bright claimed that while attending Fuller he received "an overwhelming impression that the Lord had unfolded a scroll of instructions" to him. These instructions from God ordered Bright to begin an evangelical ministry to college students. He received encouragement from a trusted professor, Dr. Wilbur Smith. At about the same time that Bright experienced his vision, Smith had been moved to write the letters CCC on a piece of paper but didn't know what they signified. Bright decided that they stood for Campus Crusade for Christ. His ministry was officially born on the campus of UCLA. Since then it has grown to include such satellite groups as Athletes in Action, College Life, COME (Conference of Military Evangelism), the Lay Institute for Evangelism, and a group limited to men, the Promise Keepers.

In his book *The Coming Revival: America's Call to Fast, Pray, and Seek God's Face*, Bright proposed that evangelical Christians should, legally but quite literally, take over the government of the United States: "Unless our nation returns to God from the top down, where our laws are made, permanent change will be extremely difficult." In 1995, the leader of the Promise Keepers, Bill McCarthy, declared that it was time for Christian men to "take this nation for Christ." Rev. James Ryle, a Promise Keepers board member, claimed that in "these last days" a biblical prophesy would be fulfilled in which American men would form an army to rule nonbelievers. He said, "Never have 300,000 men come together throughout human history except for the purposes of war."

Behind all this rather militant talk was a central theological belief. According to Matthew 24:14, Jesus said that "this gospel of the kingdom will be preached in the whole world as a testimony to all nations, and then the end will come." Those who work for Campus Crusade for Christ believe that they are fulfilling the command to "preach the gospel" to "the whole world."

Bill Bright died in 2003, believing right up until his last breath that Jesus might return at any moment. This belief was very probably the central motivating force behind his vision of campus ministry. In this regard he typified many evangelicals who see themselves as helping to prepare the way for the final battle of Armageddon and the Second Coming of Jesus Christ.

Sources:

Bright, Bill. *Come Help Change the World.* Old Tappan, NJ: Fleming H. Revell, 1970.

———. *The Coming Revival: America's Call to Fast, Pray, and Seek God's Face.* Nashville: Thomas Nelson, 1995.

CARNIVÀLE *see* Hollywood Envisions THE END

CARTER, BRANDON *see* Doomsday Argument

CARTER, JIMMY

In 1976 a series of events began to unfold that brought the idea of Christian Zionism to the forefront. Essentially, Christian Zionism is simply Christian support for Zionism. But it doesn't stop there. The Christian Zionist movement is really made up of fundamentalist, evangelical, and other conservative Christians who believe that Israel must, at the time of the end, occupy the land it held as a result of the covenant God made with the Jewish people through Abraham (see Abrahamic Covenant). They believe that the creation of the state of Israel is a fulfillment of prophecy. Taking literally the words God supposedly spoke to Israel, "I will bless those who bless you" (Gen. 12:3), Christian Zionists believe that it is the duty of modern nations, especially the United States of America, to side politically with Israel over Palestine.

In 1976, Christian Zionists believed they had finally achieved a major goal. They had elected one of their own, the "born-again" evangelical Christian Jimmy Carter, to the presidency of the United States. The very next year, Menachem Begin and his right-wing Likud Party came to power in Israel. A coalition began to emerge between the political right, the religious right, and Zionist interests in the United States. In 1978 President Carter acknowledged that which Christian Zionists wanted to hear. He told how his views of Middle East politics had been influenced by his reading of the Bible. He described the state of Israel as "a return at last to the biblical land from which the Jews were driven so many hundreds of years ago.... The establishment of the nation of Israel is the fulfillment of biblical prophecy."

It didn't last. Carter has, over the years, grown increasingly wary of those in Congress who voice unequivocal support for Israel at the expense of the growing problem of Palestinian refugees who have been forcibly removed from their homes. When House majority leader Tom DeLay, a conservative evangelical, wanted to offer unilateral support to Israel and based that support on New Testament prophecy rather than political ideology, Carter began to distance himself from the religious right. DeLay saw the reconstruction of the ancient kingdom of David as a precursor to the endtimes (see Endtimes). Carter publicly dismissed this reasoning, calling it "a completely foolish and erroneous interpretation of the Scriptures." He went on to say that such reasoning "has resulted in these last few years [in] a terrible and very costly, and very bloody deterioration in the relationship between Israel and its neighbor."

As an elder statesman of the Democratic Party, Carter continued the attack on what he saw as an excessively evangelical bent in the George W. Bush presidency: "This administration, maybe strongly influenced by ill-advised theologians of the extreme religious right, has pretty well abandoned any real effort that could lead to a resolution of the problems between Israel and the Palestinians."

When Carter's growing coolness to dogmatic evangelicalism became apparent toward the end of his first term in office, the religious right went looking for a new candidate. They found Ronald Reagan. In 1980 many experienced newscasters wondered why a southern fundamentalist Baptist like Jerry Falwell would turn his back on the world's most prominent Southern Baptist in favor of an Episcopalian like Reagan, even if Carter was from the "wrong" party. The media failed to understand how significant the issue of Armageddon and the return of Jesus Christ is to Christian Zionists. Reagan ushered in the most blatantly pro-Israel administration up to his time. In Reagan's government were Christian Zionists such as Attorney General Ed Meese, Secretary of Defense Caspar Weinberger, and Secretary of the Interior James Watt. They were supported by popular evangelical ministers and celebrities such as Hal Lindsey, Pat

Jimmy Carter in 1976. *Library of Congress.*

Robertson, Robert Schuller, and Jerry Falwell. In 1979, when Falwell founded the Moral Majority to support Reagan against Carter, the Israeli government presented Falwell with a Lear jet to assist him as he advocated for Israel against Palestine. In 1980, the year Reagan was elected, Falwell became the first Gentile ever to receive the Vladimir Ze'ev Jabotinsky medal, awarded for "Zionist excellence."

Jimmy Carter probably didn't lose his bid for reelection simply because he had lost the support of the religious right. There were other factors at play, most notably the Iranian hostage crisis he was desperately trying to resolve. But there is no question that ever since those hectic days, the religious right who believe that Israel is an example of fulfilled prophecy indicating the near return of Jesus Christ have been a target constituency that potential presidential candidates ignore to their peril.

President Carter went on to win the Nobel Peace Prize for, among other things, his work in Middle East reconciliation.

Sources:

"Christian Zionism: Misguided Millennialism." http://www.christchurch-virginiawater.co.uk/ articles/coloradohistory.htm.

"Dr. Tim LaHaye: Premillennial Dispensationalist." http://www.preteristarchive.com/Study Archive/l/lahaye-tim.html.

CATACLYSMS *see* **Asteroids; Comets; Earth Shift; Earthquakes in Various Places; Meteors, Meteoroids, and Meteorites; Polar Shift**

CAYCE, EDGAR

Born March 18, 1877, on a farm near Hopkinsville, Kentucky, Edgar Cayce became, according to many of his followers, the only real Christian prophet the United States has ever produced. As a child Cayce experienced visitations from what he called the "little people." (His parents dismissed these as imaginary playmates, which they may well have been.) As a teenager, he claimed, he was twice visited by an "angel" who asked him what wanted to do with his life. His answer was that he wanted to help others, especially children. The angel told him that he must be true to these aspirations. Cayce was a very serious and religious young man, and these visits would guide him in his future.

Cayce grew up in the Christian Church. An elderly black man who had once saved him from drowning gave him his first Bible. As a young man Cayce taught an adult Bible-study group, became a deacon of his church, and always carried a Bible with him. He continued to teach and carry his Bible throughout his life. He was never good in school and suffered his father's wrath for not being able to learn from his books. One night, after being left at the table to continue studying until he had mastered the assigned lesson, he fell asleep on his book. According to family lore, when he awoke, he knew every word in the book. His parents, of course, were amazed and tested him by having him fall asleep on other books. Soon word got out about his strange talent, and his schoolmates came to think of him as a freak. This was more than the sensitive young man could handle, especially when he was spurned by an attractive young lady because of what was being said about him. He left school at the age of sixteen and went to work to help support his family.

The famous evangelical preacher Dwight L. Moody visited Hopkinsville in 1898, and he and Cayce met by accident in a field not far from Cayce's home. Cayce went to hear him preach and was apparently very impressed. During Moody's visit, the two continued to meet in the same field. Cayce poured out his heart to the preacher as he had to no one before. He told Moody of the little people and of the visits by the angel. He was shocked when Moody told him that others had come to him with similar stories. The preacher recounted places in the Bible where God had spoken through humans. He also told Cayce of a powerful, mystical experience of his own. The two men never saw each other again after that visit, but Moody appeared to Cayce in dreams throughout Cayce's life.

During that same year a traveling mesmerist, or hypnotist, came to Hopkinsville and guided Cayce into a trance. What followed was the beginning of a very turbulent time in Cayce's life. When in trance, an entity from another dimension spoke through him. Cayce himself had no idea what was being said in these sessions and seemed to be amazed when he read the transcripts or was told what had transpired. Cayce would lie down on the floor or a couch and be guided into a trance by a partner, who would then ask the "Source," as the entity was known, questions about the health of some other individual. The Source would recommend a treatment for that person. Without any medical training, Cayce had no idea how this was all transpiring. Only his faith in God and his belief that this work was somehow what God wanted him to be doing kept him at it.

Cayce would spend many years going from job to job and town to town, often being taken advantage of by partners who had only their own selfish interests at heart. He did not have a direction or focus for his talent. He was often confused and troubled. At one point, he had laryngitis for months. Finally he agreed to do a reading on himself. The Source guided him through to a cure, and when he awoke he could speak again. The laryngitis recurred from time to time—according to Cayce, whenever he strayed from the path of using his talent only to help others.

It was during this troubled period that he married his longtime fiancée, Gertrude. He was working as a photographer and had become moderately successful— enough so to feel that he could support a wife and family. Gertrude was uncomfortable with some of the attention her husband was getting. She wanted to live the quiet, Christian life she and he had often discussed, and she did not trust all of his partners. The stranger who spoke through him frightened her. The trances took Cayce's focus away from his family. He was often gone for long periods, giving readings for people all over the South and Midwest.

Eventually Cayce met two men who helped give him the direction he needed. One, Arthur Lammers, suggested that he build a hospital where people who received his readings could get the recommended treatments. The other, David Kahn, helped him raise money for the project. After years of travel and fund raising, the hospital was built in the then sleepy town of Virginia Beach, Virginia. Here Cayce set up the headquarters for the Association for Research and Enlightenment, which is still in existence today.

Cayce's readings soon began to take new directions. The Source began to talk about people's past lives and even of life on other planets, saying that human souls spent sojourns on these planets and in other dimensions between lives on Earth. As a Christian, Cayce found these ideas difficult to accept. Nevertheless, he found himself giving readings on astrology and its influence on human behavior.

Cayce became known as both the father of holistic medicine and the "sleeping prophet." He wrote many books and continued to give readings on health and related subjects up until his death in 1945. Many of his "patients" thought that his medical diagnoses and cures were right on target, and many believed they would not have lived but for the advice from the Source.

Cayce, of course, had more than a few detractors who judged him to be, if not an outright fraud, at least benignly deluded. His predictions of what might be regarded as end-of-the-world events did little to quiet his critics. Most of his endtime prophecies dealt with a reconfiguring of the continents. In trance, he reported that Atlantis would reappear somewhere near the Bahamas, most of the West Coast of the United States would fall away, land would appear off the East Coast, much of Japan would sink into the sea, and South America would be shaken from Colombia to Tierra del

Fuego. Upheavals in the Arctic and Antarctic would set off volcanoes in the tropics and perhaps even cause the magnetic poles to shift. An inundation would stretch from Salt Lake City to Nebraska. All this was to be accompanied by a great deal of sunspot activity. At first he predicted that these things would all take place in 1936. He later amended that date to 1998 but did not live to see if his prophecies were fulfilled.

In spite of all this, Cayce's advice on how to prepare for the end seems to provide words to live by—with or without impending doom. When asked how best to prepare for the coming turmoil, his answer was: "Do thy duty today. Tomorrow will take care of itself. These changes in the Earth will come to pass, for the time and the times and half times are at an end [see Daniel 7:25 and 12:7], and there begin these periods for the readjustments. For how hath He given? 'The righteous shall inherit the Earth.'"

Sources:

"AUM~Sparky's Cayce Readings on Earth Changes." http://all-ez.com/earth.htm.

Bell, Art, and Brad Steiger. *The Source: Journey through the Unexplained.* New Orleans: Paper Chase Press, 1999.

Cohen, Daniel. *Prophets of Doom: The Millennium Edition.* Brookfield, CT: Millbrook Press, 1999.

EdgarCayce.org: The Official Site of A.R.E. [Association for Research and Enlightenment]. http://www.edgarcayce.org.

Kirkpatrick, Sidney D. *Edgar Cayce: An American Prophet.* New York: Riverhead, 2000.

CHAFER, LEWIS SPERRY

Lewis Sperry Chafer, founder of Dallas Theological Seminary, was a major influence in American Christian fundamentalism, especially in terms of systematizing much of the current fundamentalist/evangelical theology concerning the Second Coming of Jesus Christ and then teaching the system to hundreds of future church pastors.

Chafer, the son of a Congregationalist pastor, was born in Rock Creek, Ohio, in 1871. As a teenager he heard an evangelical preacher whose message challenged him to a life of service to the church. At first Chafer thought this service would be given through music. He attended the Conservatory of Music at Oberlin College but left before graduating, choosing instead to travel as an evangelist, singing and organizing choirs for revival meetings. At some point before 1889 he was called to the ministry and became interim pastor of the First Presbyterian Church in Lewiston, New York. His formal ordination in the Congregational Church took place in 1900.

After being ordained, Chafer and his wife moved to Northfield, Massachusetts, where they operated a farm while Chafer continued to travel as an evangelist. It was in Northfield that he met Cyrus Ingerson Scofield (see entry), who was to have a great influence on his thinking and remain his friend and mentor throughout the rest of Scofield's life. At the time, Scofield was the pastor of the Trinitarian Congregational Church in Northfield. The younger Chafer learned Scofield's biblical interpretation system, and the two traveled together as Bible teachers for several years. From 1906 to 1910 Chafer taught music and Bible at Mount Hermon School for Boys in Northfield, while beginning his writing career with a nonreligious book, *Elementary Outline Studies in the Science of Music.*

Chafer's career took him to New Jersey, where he joined the staff of the New York School of the Bible. This institution distributed Scofield's popular Bible correspondence course and introduced thousands of Protestant Christians to the events of the Second Coming, which Scofield believed could happen at any moment (see Rapture). Chafer also assisted Scofield in founding the Philadelphia School of the Bible, the institution that fostered a whole generation of Bible expositors, the most famous of whom was Donald Grey Barnhouse, whose radio ministry reached millions. Chafer continued to write and publish books on pretribulational, dispensational premillennialism (see Dispensationalism; Pre- and Postmillennialism; Pre-, Post-, and Midtribulationalism). In 1906 Chafer joined the Presbyterian Church. In 1923 he transferred his ministry to the Dallas (Texas) Presbyterian Church, which had been founded by Scofield in 1882.

In 1924 Chafer founded the Evangelical Theological College, now Dallas Theological Seminary. He served there as president and professor of systematic theology, continuing to teach at the college until his death in 1952. The seminary still produces many conservative Bible students and pastors each year. Chafer's influence on the current fundamentalist/evangelical scene, especially concerning the popularly accepted systematized events surrounding Armageddon, is incalculable. His students have gone forth and multiplied, filling pulpits and classrooms far beyond anything he probably could have imagined.

Sources:

Douglas, J. D., ed. *The New International Dictionary of the Christian Church*. Grand Rapids, MI: Zondervan, 1974.

Hudson, Winthrop S. *Religion in America*. New York: Charles Scribner's Sons, 1965.

CHRIST: PROPHET, PRIEST, AND KING

The Christian church has had two millennia to develop systematic theology defining the identity and ministry of Jesus Christ. The result of all this study has been the development of what are called "models" that attempt to synthesize exactly who Jesus was and how he fulfilled a divine plan of history.

One of the most frequently quoted formulas is called "Prophet, Priest, and King." This model has Jesus fulfilling three traditional roles, each of which embodies a different aspect of ministry. Although traditional Christianity teaches that Jesus fills the roles simultaneously, the three words also reveal a cumulative, time-oriented ministry culminating in a thousand-year reign following the battle of Armageddon, during which time Jesus will literally be the king of the earth.

According to this model, when Jesus lived in Galilee, he fulfilled the office of prophet. Prophets speak for God. Although they sometimes predict the future, their primary function is to call a society back into relationship with the holy. Sometimes, like the great American prophet Martin Luther King Jr., they preach social justice. Sometimes, like Jeremiah of old, they remind a culture of what it used to be. In this model, Jesus was first of all a prophet, sent to restore a people who had forgotten their religious identity. In this sense, whenever his words are read from the gospels, he still is a prophet.

Christ on the cross, with Mary and John, as portrayed by an unknown Italian artist. *Huis Bergh Collection/ Fortean Picture Library.*

The book of Hebrews synthesizes Jesus' priestly office. The unknown author of this book produced a tract identifying Jesus as the final high priest:

> Such a high priest meets our need—one who is holy, blameless, pure, set apart from sinners, exalted above the heavens.... Every high priest is appointed to offer both gifts and sacrifices, and so it was necessary for this one to have something to offer. If he were on earth, he would not be a priest, for there are already men who offer the gifts prescribed by the law. They serve at a sanctuary that is a copy and shadow of what is in heaven.... The ministry Jesus has received is as superior to theirs as the covenant of which he is a mediator is superior to the old one, and it is founded on better promises. (Heb. 7:26–8:6)

A prophet represents God before the people. A priest represents people before God. Jesus is thought to spiritually fulfill both these roles. Traditional Christian theology recognizes him as both fully divine and fully human. Because he is God, he can speak to humanity as the ultimate, final, authoritative prophet. As man, he can serve as humanity's fully accredited priest. But it is in the role of king that conservative Christianity pictures Jesus returning to earth at the end of time.

Here it must be emphasized that Christianity is deeply divided over the use of the word *king*. Liberal Protestant branches of Christianity are attempting to replace the word with a neutral-gender substitute. The New Century Hymnal of the United Church of Christ, for instance, caused quite a stir when it changed the words of a familiar Christmas carol. "Hark! The herald angels sing / Glory to the newborn king" became "Hark! The herald angels sing / Glory to the Christ-child bring." Many congregants simply ignored the change. They weren't averse to the idea behind the attempt. They simply refused to fiddle with familiar tradition. Other words caused problems as well. *Lord*, for instance, is usually associated with male hierarchy, as is the title "Prince of Peace" and the traditional prayer, "Our Father, who art in heaven."

Many conservative Christians definitely see Jesus fulfilling the office of an earthly king when he comes back to reign on earth following the battle of Armageddon. His throne room will be in Jerusalem. He will, according to the psalmist, rule "with an iron scepter" (Ps. 2:9). Isaiah said that "the government will be upon his shoulders," and he will reign on David's throne (Isa. 9:6–7). "Of his government and of peace there will be no end." Whereas liberal Christians tend to read such passages metaphorically, as cultural expressions written by people familiar with kingdoms, conservatives take them quite literally. They expect someday to be able to travel to Jerusalem and stand before "King Jesus." When Jesus returns to earth he will be riding, appropriately for a king, a white horse. He will hold in his hand a kingly scepter and be surrounded by the trappings of royalty.

Liberal Christianity thus uses the "Prophet, Priest, and King" model to summarize a way of understanding what Jesus Christ means to twenty-first-century people. Conservative Christianity reads the words quite literally, using them to define a historical person and future king.

Sources:

Douglas, J. D., ed. *The New International Dictionary of the Christian Church*. Grand Rapids: MI: Zondervan, 1974.

Gonzalez, Justo L. *The Story of Christianity*. 2 vols. New York: Harper & Row, 1985.

CHRIST, SECOND COMING OF *see* **Armageddon, Battle of; Revelation; Second Coming**

CHRISTIAN RECONSTRUCTIONISM

Reconstructionism is an extremely conservative brand of contemporary Christian theology that might have profound effects on the United States of America in the years to come. It is not a denomination, but rather a way of seeking to implement Old Testament laws within contemporary culture. The systems known as "dominion theology" and "theonomy" are closely related to it, and the three are often lumped together.

A brief description of these systems reveals their interlocking belief core:

Christian reconstructionists believe that "every area dominated by sin" must be "reconstructed" in terms of the Bible, especially the Old Testament laws.

Dominion theology (the term comes from Genesis 1:26) centers on the belief that humans have a biblical mandate not only to rule (or "have dominion") over all nature, but also to bring all civil society under the rule of God.

Theonomy (from a Greek word meaning "God's law") teaches that all 613 laws given to the Hebrew people in the first five books of the Bible have never been rescinded and are thus still in effect.

Reconstructionists, just like fundamentalist Muslims, believe that modern civilization must follow rules handed down from God. For example, according to the Old Testament book of Leviticus, people convicted of idolatry, blasphemy, adultery, and homosexuality must be punished with death; therefore, in reconstructionist belief, these things should also be punished by death today. Some go so far as to include Wiccans in this group because the Old Testament declares the death penalty on all witches. There are reports that some reconstructionists want to bring back slavery on the grounds that the New Testament (Eph. 6:5–9) seems to endorse the practice.

The reconstructionist viewpoint entails obvious difficulties. For instance, Old Testament laws declare that a "Year of Jubilee" is to be celebrated every fifty years. At this time all property must be returned to its original owners. Does this mean that the indigenous Indians of North America might yet get their country back? It goes without saying that Hawaii will be returned as well.

If reconstructionists are understandably vague on such issues, they harbor few doubts on others. They would abolish income taxes, along with legal abortions. They seem to be divided over the issue of polygamy, however. It is forbidden by Old Testament law but allowed to the patriarchs, beginning with Abraham.

Reconstructionists are postmillennialists (see Pre- and Postmillennialism). They believe that Christ will not come back to earth until most of humankind is converted to their brand of Christianity. They do not intend to take over the civil government by force. Instead, they seek to bring about the kingdom of God by utilizing the freedom of religion laws in the United States in order to train children in private home schools. These children will eventually grow up and multiply until they reach sufficient numbers to vote for the kind of government they believe God wants to establish. Then, and only then, will Jesus Christ return to earth.

Sources:

"Christian Reconstructionism, Dominion Theology, and Theonomy." http://www.religioustoler ance.org/reconstr.htm.

North, Gary. *The Sinai Strategy: Economics and the Ten Commandments.* Tyler, TX: Institute for Christian Economics, 1986.

Rushdoony, R. J. *The Institute of Biblical Law.* Nutley, NJ: Craig Press, 1973.

CHRISTIAN RESURRECTION

(See also Cross, The; Rapture; Resurrection, The; Second Coming)

> But someone may ask, "How are the dead raised? With what kind of body will they come?" How foolish! What you sow does not come to life unless it dies. When you sow, you do not plant the body that will be, but just seed, perhaps of wheat or something else. But God gives it a body as he has determined, and to each kind of seed he gives its own body. (1 Cor. 15:35–38)

These are the words of the apostle Paul, written to Christians in the ancient city of Corinth who apparently were confused about the developing Christian doctrine of death and resurrection.

The battle of Armageddon is intimately connected with these themes because as part of the last, defining events of human history, it is all about judgment and determining the eternal fate of all humans. Paul believed very strongly that flesh and blood are only things of this world. In the world to come, people will be different:

> So it will be with the resurrection of the dead. The body that is sown is perishable, it is raised imperishable; it is sown in dishonor, it is raised in glory; it is sown in weakness, it is raised in power; it is sown a natural body, it is raised a spiritual body. (1 Cor. 15:42–44)

A few verses later Paul claims to reveal a mystery. He tells the Corinthian Christians that there will come a time when everyone, living and dead, will meet together in resurrection:

> Listen, I tell you a mystery. We will not all sleep, but we will all be changed—in a flash, in the twinkling of an eye, at the last trumpet. For the trumpet will sound, the dead will be raised imperishable, and we will all be changed. For the perishable must clothe itself with the imperishable, and the mortal with immortality. When the perishable has been clothed with the imperishable, and the mortal with immortality, then the saying that has been written will come true: "Death has been swallowed up in victory." (1 Cor. 15:51–54)

Although liberal and conservative Christians argue about what this means, and conservative Christians argue among themselves about when it will take place (see Christian Views of the End), the words are still a staple at Christian funeral services and have no doubt brought comfort to many as they face the final curtain of their life.

Source:
The Holy Bible, New International Version. Grand Rapids, MI: Zondervan, 1978.

CHRISTIAN VIEWS OF THE END

There is no single Christian view of the future. Christians have divided and subdivided many times over the subject. Often within the same local church, even the same Bible-study circle, many different opinions will be aired. Yet we can categorize these differing views in a general way, understanding that shades of meaning exist within each category.

Liberal, Nonliteral Views

Liberal Christianity tends to read the end-of-history Bible passages as metaphors, written for specific people who lived at a specific time. According to this view, Jesus of Nazareth was a first-century Jew who understood the old Hebrew concept of the divine in a fresh way. He attempted to teach his insights, was arrested by his detractors, and was crucified by the Roman government. But his ideas did not end with his death. All that he taught, all that he represented, all that he was—his very spirit—lived on in his followers following the Crucifixion. He will not literally return in a physical body. Rather, the church, his earthly body, carries on his ministry of love, reconciliation, and spiritual growth. Seen in this perspective, Armageddon is not a future war. It is a constant battle against institutional power, human sin, and entrenched evil.

Some Christians who hold views of this kind envision a gradual evolution of human spirituality. Others think there will have to be more of a revolution. They believe that humans may have to go to the very brink of an Armageddon before they shape up.

Some liberal Christians believe that the Second Coming is personal—experienced whenever the spirit of Jesus becomes a living reality for an individual and that person is converted to living life in the spirit, rather than simply in the material world. Others see the Second Coming as a metaphorical way of describing a quantum leap of the whole human race into universally recognizing the spiritual nature of life, rather than the material. Many believe that spirituality is the normal human condition and was practiced by our ancestors. The proof, they say, lies in Stonehenge, the Pyramids, and other megalithic monuments that were built, according to this view, because our ancestors were in tune with something we have forgotten. This "great forgetting" is symbolized by the biblical story of Eden. We have been cast out of the garden. The Second Coming of Jesus symbolizes the future "great remembering," the turning back to a spirituality the human race knew before Eden, in a time when "God saw all that he had made, and it was very good" (Gen. 1:31).

Conservative, Literal Views

The conservative camp has quite a different understanding of the endtimes, but it, too, has many subdivisions. Many carefully nuanced theologies exist, each with very vocal proponents. They are similar in that they are waiting for an actual, physical return of the same Jesus Christ who was born in Bethlehem and whose story is told in the New Testament gospels. Most agree that God has already decreed a day that will mark the end of the present age. Most agree that there will come a time of great tribulation (see Great Tribulation). Where they disagree, sometimes even violently, is about the timing and order of events. (All the following terms are covered in more depth by individual entries.)

Pretribulationism

This school of thought holds that, at any moment, true believers will be changed into spiritual beings, or "raptured" (see Rapture), snatched up to be with God. Seven years of tribulation will follow, during which the antichrist will rule. Eventually he will be defeated at the battle of Armageddon when Jesus returns to earth. Christ will then reign for a thousand years (see Millennium). At the end of that time, Satan, having been "bound" following the battle, will be released. He will raise an army that will again be destroyed by Jesus Christ. The world will then enter into eternity, wherein "time shall be no more."

Midtribulationalism

The events are the same. Only the timing changes. The Rapture will not occur before the Tribulation, but rather at the halfway point. Three and one-half years after the start of the Tribulation period, the faithful will be snatched up to be with God. Then all hell will break loose on earth until the Second Coming.

Posttribulationism

Again, same events, different timing. The faithful will have to endure the entire seven years of tribulation before the return of Christ. Then they will be "raptured" at the Second Coming, ending the Battle of Armageddon.

Premillennialism

All three of the preceding views make up the premillennial position. The Rapture, the Tribulation, and the Second Coming all occur before the thousand-year reign of Jesus Christ on earth.

Postmillennialism

This viewpoint is different from any of the foregoing. Postmillennialism envisions either a literal or a symbolic thousand-year period on earth during which the words of the Lord's Prayer, "Thy kingdom come, on earth as it is in heaven," will be fulfilled. This school of thought tends to view the Rapture and Tribulation as metaphors rather than actual events, but some of its adherents teach otherwise. The Second Coming of Jesus, again viewed literally or symbolically by different camps, will take place at the end of the Millennium.

Amillennialism

Amillennialists generally consider a thousand-year millennium to be a metaphor for a long period of time. There will be no literal Millennium, just as there will probably be no literal Rapture, Tribulation, or Second Coming. In amillennialism, *metaphor* and *symbol* are key words to remember when reading biblical texts.

Panmillennialism

What started out as a seminary joke has, over the years, become a catchword that expresses the confusion and frustration many Christians feel when hearing all the arguments for and against a specific biblical position. Each millennial position has its proof texts and proponents, who can be quite forceful when they expound their particular position. "Panmillennialism" supposedly came about because a seminary professor was asked by his students which millennial position he espoused, "Pre-, post-, or a-?"

"None of them," he said. "I'm panmillennial."
"What's that?" his students asked.
"Everything will pan out in the end!"

The joke has been told now for about forty years in every seminary throughout the land. It has been repeated so many times and passed on by so many students that there are actually some ministers who, understanding it or not, hold to this position.

Sources:
Bock, Darrell L., ed. *Three Views on the Millennium and Beyond*. Grand Rapids, MI: Zondervan, 1999.
Fackre, Dorothy, and Gabriel Fackre. *Christian Basics*. Grand Rapids, MI: Eerdmans, 1991.

CHURCH, ROLE OF

Conservative Protestant Christian tradition (see Conservative Christianity) teaches that the church is a key element in God's plan for the human race. This plan, as conservatives see it, can best be seen by studying a book found in the Old Testament.

The book of Daniel relates a message that the prophet claims to have received from God, delivered by the angel Gabriel. It is the prophecy of the seventy weeks (see Daniel; Seventy Sevens). In this prophecy, 490 years were supposedly allotted to Israel in which to fulfill God's plan for the Hebrew people. But after 483 years, God's clock stopped for a while. Before the last seven years of history could unfold (see Great Tribulation), God called a new people. The "Church Age" is a parenthesis dropped into the slot between the end of Daniel's first 483-year period of Jewish history and the last, seven-year period described in the book of Revelation.

In this view, the church is the earthly body of Jesus Christ, carrying out his mission on earth. It began on the day of Pentecost, when God the Holy Spirit, the third person of the Trinity, came down from heaven and began to infill believers. It will end, at least according to pretribulationalists (see Christian Views of the End), at the Rapture (see Rapture). When that event occurs and Christians are snatched away to be with Jesus, God's clock will start again for the last seven years of Jewish, and world, history.

This scenario explains why so many conservative Christians rejoiced in the advent of Zionism. Since, they claim, the Jewish people were led into the great Diaspora among the nations soon after the birth of the church, it was a sign that God was clearing the decks, so to speak, and preparing the world stage for the second act of the play—the Christian church. Then, just before the church leaves center stage, the Jewish people will be restored to Israel and the first act of the play can resume. After the play has ended, the church will come back with Jesus to take its final bow.

Some people, especially on the theological left, are appalled by this thinking. To them, the idea that God replaced the Jewish people with something better, the church, has led to anti-Semitism and religious bigotry. They understand the role of the church to be one of reconciliation and peace—an extension of the Hebrew religion, not its replacement (see also Christian Views of the End).

Most evangelical Christians don't see it that way. Although few of them would want to be identified with religious bigotry and anti-Semitism, those on the religious right clearly perceive the role of the church as proclaiming their gospel to "all nations, and then the end will come" (Matt. 24:14).

Sources:

Borg, Marcus J. *The God We Never Knew: Beyond Dogmatic Religion to a More Authentic Contemporary Faith*. San Francisco: HarperSanFrancisco, 1997.

The Holy Bible, New International Version. Grand Rapids, MI: Zondervan, 1978.

CHURCH FATHERS

In 1962 Thomas Kuhn coined the phrase *paradigm shift* to describe what happens when any given community drastically changes the way it thinks about a specific subject.

Conservative Christians believe that a paradigm shift occurred in the church in the fourth century. They argue that the first theologians of the church were premillennial (see Christian Views of the End) in their thinking. The church fathers, according to those who hold this view, expected Jesus Christ to return at any moment.

Although modern scholars have, in most cases, only incomplete fragments or partial manuscripts to go by, a good case can be made that the current Roman Catholic position, as well as much of liberal Protestant scholarship, concerning the return of Christ differs from the position of early theologians such as Clement of Alexandria, Clement of Rome, Origen, Chrysostom, Barnabas, Papias, Irenaeus, Tertullian, and Polycarp, to say nothing of the apostle Paul, the church's first missionary.

For its first three centuries, the church can perhaps best be described as an underground Jesus movement. Persecuted much of the time, it nevertheless made huge strides in its Great Commission as described in Matthew 28, which says that Jesus met with his disciples following the Resurrection and gave them marching orders: "All authority in heaven and earth has been given to me. Therefore go and make disciples of all nations, baptizing them in the name of the Father and of the Son and of the Holy Spirit, and teaching them to observe everything I have commanded you. And surely I will be with you always, to the very end of the age."

Whether Jesus really said these words doesn't matter a great deal. The early church believed them with such conviction that within only a few years, they were given the name Christians, "followers of the Christ" (Acts 11:26), by the people of Antioch and accused of "turning the world upside down with their preaching" by the authorities of Thessalonica (Acts 17:6).

Fueled by martyrdom, beginning with Stephen's death (Acts 7), guided by leaders such as Peter and James, spread by missionaries such as Paul, Barnabas, and Timothy, the church was able to take advantage of a unique social situation.

Rome ruled the world. A common culture and language held sway. Pax Romana, the Peace of Rome, was enforced by the sword, but at least it ensured governmental stability. The saying was true that "all roads lead to Rome." Infrastructure that would not be duplicated for a thousand years allowed armies to move quickly to outposts of the Western world; it also allowed freedom of secure movement for willing missionaries. For example, the educated, urbane, extremely talented Saul of Tarsus (Paul the Apostle) could travel freely (at least when he wasn't in jail) about the Mediterranean world, planting churches and writing a third of the New Testament during his downtime (awaiting trial after being arrested for preaching a "divisive" doctrine).

It was certainly not easy to be a Christian in those days. Waves of persecution broke upon the shores of the early church. But in spite of it all, men such as Irenaeus, Clement of Alexandria, Tertullian, and Origen were able to forge the basis of theological Christian thought by writing, debating, accusing, and finally arriving at a kind of consensus, usually derived by declaring that their opponents were heretics. It was their belief in the imminent return of Jesus Christ that helped sustain them.

On April 30, 311 CE, everything changed. Galerius, ruler of Rome and persecutor of Christians, convinced that a severe illness he was experiencing was a punishment for his sins, issued a decree:

> With all the laws which we have decreed for the good of the state, we
> have sought to restore the ancient rules and traditional discipline of
> the Romans. We have particularly sought to have Christians, who had

abandoned the faith of their ancestors, return to the truth ... and we were forced to punish [them].... But there are many who persist in their opinions.... Therefore, moved by our mercy to be benevolent towards all, it has seemed just to us to extend to them our pardon, and allow them to be Christians once again, and once again gather in their assemblies, as long as they do not interfere with the public order.... In return for our tolerance, Christians will be required to pray to their God for us.

The prisons were opened, and Christians poured out bearing the marks of their torture but thankful for what they perceived as answered prayer.

Much bigger things were to come. Rome, marked by violence and civil war, was about to get a new emperor—Constantine—who would, as the result of a dream, drastically change the trajectory of the Christian church.

Gathering his army in Gaul, Constantine crossed the Alps and marched on Rome, where Maxentius had taken over as emperor following the sudden death of Galerius. (The latter's demise makes one wonder how many freed Christians actually prayed for their old persecutor's recovery. The historian Lacantius later declared that it was "too little, too late" as far as God was concerned.) No one will ever know what might have happened if Maxentius had simply hunkered down behind the strong walls of Rome and waited for Constantine to go away. Instead, ignoring the advice of his military leaders, he took his cue from his religious augurs (a response perhaps illustrating the wisdom of separating church and state) and marched forth to battle. He met Constantine on the plains surrounding Milvian Bridge.

On the eve of battle, Constantine had either a dream or a vision. Arguments abound as to what he saw. Eusebius later wrote that it was a cross in the sky. The cross was inscribed with the letters *IHS*, which Constantine took for the Latin *in hoc signo*, "by this sign [you shall conquer]." Less imaginative historians say that Constantine saw the Greek letters *chi* and *rho*—the first two letters of the name "Christ."

Constantine won the battle and became emperor of Rome. Vision or no, his personal conversion to Christianity was not immediate. It took years. Some say he never really converted. But when Constantine signed the Edict of Milan in 313, officially ending Christian persecution, Christianity was on its way to becoming the state religion of Rome.

What would happen when a simple religion begun by a carpenter and practiced by fishermen found itself surrounded by pomp and ceremony and power? Christianity had "gained the whole world." Now would it be able to keep its soul? Many modern conservative theologians answer that question in the negative. They insist that when Christianity became officially identified with Rome, it began to confuse political policies with theology.

Well before Constantine, Origen (Origenes Adamantius, 185–254) had begun to suggest the Bible was not to be interpreted literally in all cases:

Now what man of intelligence will believe that the first and the second and the third day, and the evening and the morning existed without the sun and the moon and the stars? And that the first day, if we may so call it, was even without a heaven [Gen. 1:5–13]? And who is so silly as to believe that God, after the manner of a farmer, "planted a paradise eastward in Eden," and set in it a visible and palpable "tree of life," of such a sort that anyone who tasted its fruit with his bodily teeth would gain life; and again that one could partake of "good and evil" by masticating the fruit taken from the tree of that name [Gen. 2:8, 9]? And when God is said to "walk in the paradise in the cool of the day" and Adam to hide himself behind a tree, I do not think anyone will doubt that these are figurative expressions which indicate certain mysteries through a semblance of history and not through actual events [Gen. 3:8].

After Christianity was co-opted by Rome, Augustine of Hippo (354–430) took Origen's allegorical approach even further. He developed a four-point interpretation of Revelation 20 (see Revelation):

1. Jesus "bound" Satan at Calvary.
2. The saints are now ruling during the Millennium. (The word *millennium*, Augustine maintained, simply means "a long time.") In other words, since Rome ruled the world and Christianity was the state religion, it was only natural that Christianity's world rule would soon be complete.
3. At some future date, Satan will be released for three and one-half years, during which time the church will be persecuted.
4. At the end of that time, Jesus Christ will return at the battle of Armageddon.

Beginning with Origen and continuing through Augustine, then, a paradigm shift occurred. The church became postmillennial, perhaps even amillennial (see Christian Views of the End).

The importance of studying the church fathers, according to some Protestant conservative scholars, is that because these early leaders were closer to the time of Jesus, Christianity had not yet had a chance to evolve away from the truth as understood by its first teachers. The Roman Catholic Church and liberal Protestant theologians, by contrast, believe that God works through continuing theological evolution. The fact that Jesus did not return, even when Paul suggested that it would happen in his own lifetime, proved that Paul was wrong. He misunderstood how God was going to work throughout human history. Origen and Augustine took evolutionary steps forward, not backward.

The argument will probably not be resolved anytime soon.

Sources:

Augustine of Hippo. *The City of God.* Chicago: Encyclopedia Britannica, 1952.

Fisher, Mary Pat, and Lee W. Bailey, eds. *An Anthology of Living Religions.* Upper Saddle River, NJ: Prentice Hall, 2000.

Gibbon, Edward. *The Decline and Fall of the Roman Empire.* 2 vols. Chicago: Encyclopaedia Britannica, 1952.

Gonzalez, Justo L. *The Story of Christianity.* 2 vols. New York: Harper & Row, 1985.

CLAIRVOYANCE

The late popular "psychic" Jeane Dixon, in her book *The Call to Glory*, wrote: "The years 2020–2037, approximately, hail the true Second Coming of Christ." In the same work, published in 1972, she predicted the occurrence of the battle of Armageddon in 2020.

Clairvoyance is the ability to see things beyond the range of normal human perception. Throughout history there have been people who claimed the ability to foresee the future. The biblical prophets, Daniel in the Hebrew scriptures and John in the Christian scriptures being two notable examples, wrote about having visions (see Daniel; Revelation). Since the completion of the Bible, others have continued the tradition. Nostradamus and Edgar Cayce (see entries on each) are only two examples.

Of course, claims to clairvoyance are not limited to the Hebrew/Christian tradition, or to religious traditions in general. Newspapers often carry predictions by modern-day clairvoyants. Jeane Dixon, with her widely syndicated column, was perhaps the most famous of these. Today an assortment of self-designated psychics offer their wares on cable television.

Clairvoyants offer differing explanations for their claimed ability. Some say that it is a gift from God. Others propose such ideas as that future time runs parallel to our time and some people can occasionally glance across the barrier.

Clairvoyants are often sought out by the news media when the calendar approaches special dates. The human mind seems to think that round numbers or numbers ending in zero are especially significant. The year 2000 brought a flood of predictions, most of which went unfulfilled.

Source:
Dixon, Jeane. *The Call to Glory*. New York: William Morrow, 1972.

COMETS

Whereas asteroids are solid rock, comets are mostly ice. They have been likened to large, dirty snowballs. Although spacecraft exploration of comets has been limited, the flyby of Halley's comet, along with telescopic observations, suggests that from 50 to 80 percent of its mass is frozen water. The great "tail" associated with comets results largely from water evaporation caused by the heat of the sun that has captured the comet in its orbit. The tail may be millions of miles long and gives comets their name, which comes from a Greek word meaning "long-haired."

The brightness of a comet depends on its distance from the sun, its distance from the earth, the size of its nucleus, and how much of the nucleus is evaporating when we see it. Famous comets such as Halley's and Swift-Tuttle may have been in solar orbit for 20,000 to 50,000 years. Some people have speculated that megalithic structures such as Stonehenge were built to track their presence through the night sky.

Comets are beautiful to watch. But what happens when they get too close?

In March 1993, Gene and Carolyn Shoemaker, along with David Levy, discovered a comet that was coming very close indeed. It had approached the planet Jupiter in 1992, but that fact wasn't discovered until after the comet had been tracked and its orbit backtracked. The encounter with Jupiter's tremendous gravitational force had broken Shoemaker-Levy 9, as the comet was named, into twenty-one fragments. The orbital calculations revealed that on their swing back through the solar system, the comet's fragments would come even closer to Jupiter. Many scientists believe that it was comets broken apart by the gravitational pull of Saturn that formed the rings of that great planet. Would the same thing happen to Jupiter when comet Shoemaker-Levy 9 returned?

The world found out in July 1994. Witnessed live on television and photographed through telescopes around the world, the comet's fragments, strung out in line like pearls on a necklace, crashed into the planet. The impact of the biggest fragment, something over a mile in diameter, created a fireball larger than Asia and revealed a starling truth: If Shoemaker-Levy had hit Earth instead of Jupiter, you wouldn't be reading this book.

What if a similar comet were discovered to be heading toward our planet? Duncan Steel, in his book *Rogue Asteroids and Doomsday Comets*, feels confident that the reality would not resemble the typical Hollywood scenario

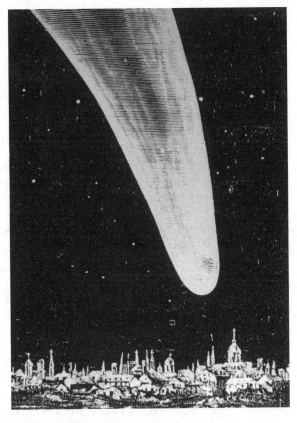

The great comet of 1811 as pictured in a wood engraving from Richard Proctor's *Flowers of the Sky* (1889). *Fortean Picture Library.*

(see Hollywood Envisions THE END). For one thing, it would take months to determine the comet's trajectory. If the comet were to be discovered only months from impact, nothing could be done. If we had a year or two—well, maybe we could do something, but no one knows for sure what that something might be. Would governments be able to hide the news so as to avoid panic in the populace? Probably not. There are simply too many watchdogs out there. Somebody would see it, and the news would soon be on the Web.

If we saw a comet coming, couldn't we just blow it up? Possibly, depending on its size and how much time we had. Unfortunately, it's not at all clear that this would help. It might even make things worse. As Steel explains, "Comparing the hazard posed by intact comets ... with the numerous fragments produced when they break apart is beyond our present state of ignorance. If you were locked in a dark room with a homicidal maniac with a firearm, would you rather that he had a rifle or a shotgun? The latter is more likely to hit you, but perhaps with less catastrophic consequences.... In the meantime we have to keep hoping that the trigger is not pulled."

What are the chances that a comet will someday hit the earth? Probably about 100 percent. Will that happen during our lifetime? Probably not. But no one knows for sure.

Source:

Steel, Duncan. *Rogue Asteroids and Doomsday Comets: The Search for the Million Megaton Menace That Threatens Life on Earth.* New York: John Wiley & Sons, 1995.

CONCERNED CHRISTIANS

In the 1980s a group calling themselves Concerned Christians formed around leader Kim Miller (sometimes known as "Monte" Kim Miller). Miller is a former Procter & Gamble executive and anticult activist. On a radio broadcast in 1996 he proclaimed himself to be God's true voice on earth and demanded that his followers adhere very strictly to the teachings of the Bible. He believes himself to be one of the two "witnesses" mentioned in Revelation 11 (see Revelation).

Miller's Concerned Christians are an anti–New Age religious movement that believes the public press is anti-Christian. (Miller's followers should not be confused with an older organization, also called "Concerned Christians," founded in northern Arizona in 1973 and devoted largely to debunking what it calls "the deceptions of the Mormon cult." The two groups have no relation.) Miller teaches that one cannot be a good Christian and be patriotic at the same time. He is said to have given a prophecy that an earthquake would destroy Denver, Colorado, where he and his followers were based, in October of 1998. He has since denied the prophecy. Nevertheless, in 1998, just before the earthquake he denies he predicted was supposed to occur, he and his followers left Denver and went to Jerusalem, where he prophesied that he would die in the streets and be resurrected three days later to greet Christ when he returned to earth. Needless to say, this prophecy failed as well.

Miller and his sixty or seventy followers remained in Jerusalem to await the end of the world and Christ's coming. Some Israeli authorities were less than thrilled to have them there, feeling that they hoped to incite the religious war they called Armageddon (see Armageddon) and so begin the events described in the book of Revelation (see Revelation). Many were deported back to Denver, escorted by Israeli authorities. Others went to Greece, where those who had gone to Denver eventually joined them. The Greek authorities were no more thrilled with their new guests than the Israelis had been, and many of the remaining Concerned Christians were again returned to the United States. They are now reported to be in the Philadelphia area.

No evidence of any violent activity by the group has ever been produced.

Miller, in an e-mail to the world, proclaimed that the seventh seal had been broken and the seventh trumpet had sounded on February 15, 2002—the 777th day of the seventh millennium (see Revelation)—setting the end-of-the-world events in motion. He believes that the United States will be destroyed in a coming holocaust of judgment, thus punishing Americans for their unchristian behavior.

Sources:

"Concerned Christians." http://www.apologeticsindex.org/c35.html.

"The 'Concerned Christians' Cult—Originally of Denver CO." http://www.religioustolerance. org/dc_conc.htm.

Miller, Kim. "Unconcerned Christians." http://www.kimmillerconcernedchristians.com.

CONSERVATIVE CHRISTIANITY

> We are not divided, all one body we,
> One in hope and doctrine, one in charity.
> Onward Christian soldiers, marching as to war!
> —"Onward Christian Soldiers, Marching as to War." Words by Sabine Baring-Gould; music by Sir Arthur Sullivan.

> "Things ain't the way they used to be. And what's more, they never was!"
> —attributed to a Vermont farmer

The words of the popular old Protestant hymn are still sung by conservative Christian congregations. Liberal Christianity increasingly finds them a bit militant. Even many evangelical Christians privately admit to crossing their fingers behind their backs when the hymn appears in the Sunday morning bulletin, because the Christian church is certainly neither "all one body" nor "one in faith and doctrine," to say nothing of "one in charity." And from the best evidence available—the letters of the apostle Paul, which make up almost a third of the New Testament—it never was.

From the very beginning, Christians disagreed about how to interpret the faith. Those disagreements have, over the centuries, solidified into two camps, both of which are home to myriad subcamps. These differing schools of thought have nothing to do with Catholic, Eastern Orthodox, or Protestant. They have nothing to do with denominations, although some denominations average out to be more conservative than others.

The central issue is simply stated. Is Christianity a relationship with God in the spirit of Jesus Christ? Or is it an intellectual acceptance of doctrine and a literal interpretation of the Bible?

Those who answer yes only to the first question usually consider themselves "liberal" Christians. Those who reply in the affirmative to both questions, but especially to the second, are usually called "conservative" Christians. Whether Catholic or Protestant, Presbyterian, Episcopal, or Baptist, liberal and conservative expressions of Christianity span denominations and categories.

Since denominational labels aren't very useful, other terms have sprung up. *Fundamentalism* and *evangelicalism* are two of the most familiar. In terms of biblical interpretation, especially regarding prophetic interpretations about the endtimes, conservative Christianity is best represented by the futurist school of biblical interpretation (see entry). Simply put, conservative Christians tend to read the Bible literally and believe in a physical Second Coming of Jesus Christ. To conservatives, the battle of Armageddon might very well be another name for World War III.

Conservative Christians tend to be conservative politically as well theologically. Jerry Falwell, Pat Robertson, Pat Boone, and Hal Lindsey have cemented that image pretty well. Falwell was once quoted to the effect that his church, the Thomas

Road Baptist Church, needed to be about getting people saved, baptized, and registered to vote, in that order. As the founder of the political group that calls itself the Moral Majority, he has certainly lived up to his words. Conservative Christians tend to be antiabortion, pro–death penalty, and antigay. There are, of course, many, many exceptions. Evangelical congregations are probably full of women and men who are awaiting the return of Jesus Christ but quietly supporting their gay son or lesbian daughter while publicly saying "Amen" to sermons denouncing the "gay lifestyle."

Fundamentalists consider evangelicals to be liberal (see Evangelicalism). There is increasing evidence that many evangelicals are beginning to pick and choose when it comes to interpreting biblical creation stories literally or metaphorically. They have come to believe that some areas of evangelicalism are open to personal choice, even though others are not. It is becoming increasingly acceptable, for instance, to question the historical reality of Noah's flood or the young age of the earth. Although an evangelical will land on the outside very quickly if he or she questions the historicity of the virgin birth of Jesus Christ or the certainty of his return at the battle of Armageddon, the movement away from strict fundamentalism may explain why evangelical churches are among the fastest-growing churches in the world today. The trend toward so-called megachurches—churches with more than 25,000 members—is also growing. Political parties have come to recognize that a presidential candidate has an instant constituency if he calls himself an evangelical. Presidents Carter, Reagan, Clinton, and George W. Bush have all profited from the title.

Sources:
Gonzalez, Justo L. *The Story of Christianity*. 2 vols. New York: Harper & Row, 1985.
Hymns for the Living Church. Carol Stream, IL: Hope, 1978.

CONSTANTINE see **Hollywood Envisions** THE END

COPERNICAN REVOLUTION

The Copernican revolution marked the opening of a door between sacred and secular, a parting of the ways between religion and science. It began in ancient Greece long before Copernicus' time. Aristarchus (ca. 310–ca. 230 BCE) developed a theory that the planets actually revolve around the sun. The historical references are secondhand, Aristarchus' original works on the subject having been lost, but apparently he supported his theory by mathematics, the instruments and techniques of his day being insufficient for the kind of measurements he needed. Whatever the case, his brilliant insight was not widely accepted. Most people went on believing that the earth was stationary and the sun and planets revolved around it. It seemed self-evident.

It wasn't until after the Dark Ages had come to an end that Aristarchus' work was finally accepted. In fact, Regiomontanus set up the first observatory in northern Europe (in Nuremberg in 1471) in part to test the theory through observation.

Nicholas Copernicus was a Polish priest and a student of mathematics and astronomy. He believed that the sun-centered theory could be proved through mathematics and set about to do so. His manuscript *De Revolutionibus Orbium Coelestium* (On the Revolutions of the Celestial Spheres) was written in 1514 and circulated anonymously to protect him from heresy charges. Only in 1543 was it printed in book form. Thinking that he would be ridiculed, or worse, for his ideas, he did not publish until persuaded to do so by the Protestant astronomer Rheticus. Copernicus died six months after its release.

Most theologians at the time, Catholic or Protestant, did not accept Copernicus' evidence that the earth revolved around the sun. The Bible told them that God had created the heavens and the earth and peopled his creation with humans made in his own image. Therefore humans are special. They must be the center, the reason, for the universe. But a rift had been created between church and science.

It took a scientist by the name of Galileo Galilei (1564–1642) to develop the astronomical instruments and techniques that would prove conclusively that Aristarchus and Copernicus had been right. Galileo paid a price for his work. Although a devout Catholic, he was sentenced to house arrest for the remainder of his life and told to renounce Copernicanism. In this, he bowed to church authorities and acquiesced. In the words of Stephen Hawking: "Galileo remained a faithful Catholic, but his belief in the independence of science had not been crushed. Four years before his death in 1642, while he was

Nicholas Copernicus. *Fortean Picture Library.*

still under house arrest, the manuscript of his second major book was smuggled to a publisher in Holland. It was this work, referred to as *Two New Sciences*, even more than his support for Copernicus, that was to be the genesis of modern physics."

The Copernican revolution, separating science and religion, had succeeded. The astronomers of the seventeenth and subsequent centuries would eventually convince most European theologians that we live in a heliocentric system and that there are many other such systems in existence in our universe. The Bible could no longer be universally read as literal science and history. Metaphor and allegory pushed their way to the front of the exegetical line. Biblical interpretation now had completely new rules.

Many conservative theologians still argue that the earth will experience a fiery apocalypse when Jesus returns (see Revelation). Most scientists believe there will be something more along the lines of a universal collapse or gradual running down following the rules of entropy (see Big Crunch, Big Chill, and Big Rip)—but that long before either of these happens, life on earth will have ceased as our sun, following the course of every other sun, uses up its energy and dies. Will science and theology someday meet again and shake hands across the great divide? Perhaps that future celebration will require yet another revolution.

Sources:

Hawking, Stephen W. *A Brief History of Time: From the Big Bang to Black Holes.* New York: Bantam, 1988.

Plant, David. "The Copernican Revolution." http://www.skyscript.co.uk/copernicus.html.

Tenn, Joe. "The Copernican Revolution." http://www.phys-astro.sonoma.edu/people/faculty/tenn/CopernicanRevolution.html.

COSMOS, FATE OF *see* **Big Bang; Big Crunch, Big Chill, and Big Rip; Quantum Theory; Red Shift**

COVENANT

A covenant is a contract or promise. When used in the Bible, the word generally means that the "party of the first part" (usually God) agrees to do something provided "the party of the second part" (usually people) plays by the rules. The Hebrew patriarchs, just like the inhabitants of Canaan with whom they lived, had pragmatic theologies. To them, "God" was not an abstract philosophical idea. Their approach was simple: "What have you done for me lately?" Their religion had to work or they shopped elsewhere.

By way of illustration, Yahveh of the Hebrews was the war God who led the Jews out of captivity after conquering the Egyptians. As long as they needed his help defeating the Canaanites, the Hebrew people agreed to put God first and to "have no other Gods before [him]" (Exod. 20:2). But the Bible says that when they settled in the Promised Land and needed fertile ground and good crops, they had no qualms about worshiping Baal and Astarte, the agricultural specialists.

With the advent of Christianity, theologians needed to explain why the God of the New Testament was so different from the God of the Old Testament, even though he was supposedly the same God. Soon after the Reformation, "covenant theology" was employed to formulate a systematic description of history as a series of developing, evolving covenants between God and the human race on the great journey from Eden to Armageddon. The sixteenth-century reformers recognized two great covenants. The Old Covenant (Testament) was called the Covenant of Works. The New Covenant (Testament) was named the Covenant of Grace. The first called for obeying the law in order to earn favor with God. For example, the Sabbath was celebrated on the seventh day, a well-earned rest after the labors of the long week of labor, following the commands of the law. But under the new covenant, God's grace comes first, an undeserved gift. Hence, worship was done on the first day of the week, after which the remainder of the week was spent laboring to say "thank you" to God for the gift of grace, unearned but gratefully accepted. In this view, God's eternal covenant with Jesus Christ was fulfilled before the creation of the world, and all of human history is simply playing out the drama to its predestined conclusion.

Since the Reformation, some theologians have refined the system by identifying in the Bible a progressive, cumulative series of promises. Each was given when the human race was ready for it.

The Covenant with Adam, part 1 (Gen. 2:17)

The terms were simple: "Don't eat the fruit or you'll die."

Adam ate, and as the first spelling primer printed in New England put it, "In Adam's fall, we sinned all."

The Covenant with Adam, part 2 (Gen. 3:15)

The children of Adam and Eve were to be constantly "at enmity" with Satan.

Ever since, the children of Adam and Eve have said, in many different ways, "The devil made me do it!"

The Covenant with Noah (Gen. 9:1–17)

This promise came with the sign of the rainbow. God said it was a reminder that he would "never again destroy the earth with a flood," adding: "Be fruitful and multiply."

God didn't destroy the earth again, and people went forth and multiplied to their current population of about 6 billion people.

The Covenant with Abraham (Gen. 12:1–3)

God said to Abraham, the father of three world religions, "Leave here and go to Canaan. I will bless your descendants and curse your enemies."

Abraham kept his part of the bargain. Some would argue that both descendants and enemies received both blessing and curses.

The Covenant with Moses (Exod. 19:5)

"Obey the Commandments and you will be a holy people."

The Israelites fudged on this one from time to time but are still often called "God's chosen people."

The Palestinian Covenant (Deut. 30:3)

The covenant is here quoted exactly because it is causing tremendous political, personal, and national problems in our day: "When all these blessings and curses I have set before you come upon you and you take them to heart wherever the Lord your God disperses you among the nations, and when you return to the Lord your God and obey him with all your heart and with all your soul according to everything I command you this day, then the Lord your God will restore your fortunes and have compassion on you and gather you again from all the nations where he has scattered you."

Zionists, both Jewish and Christian, believe that this covenant has come to pass exactly as promised over the last two thousand years. They believe that it justifies modern Israel's land claims and actions, in that these simply reflect God's promise. The covenant drives American conservative Christians support for a government policy endorsing Israel over the Palestinians and, in effect, converts a political land battle into a holy war. Meanwhile, the Palestinians ask why they should be bound by someone else's scriptures.

The Covenant with David (2 Sam. 7:12–16)

God, speaking through the prophet Nathan, tells David, "I will make your name great, like the names of the greatest men on earth. And I will provide a place for my people Israel and will plant them so that they can have a home of their own and no longer be disturbed."

Provision 1 was certainly fulfilled. Few men are better known than David. Provision 2 is a little shakier. Although it took a long time, Israel seems to have been "planted," but the part about not being disturbed appears not to have taken full effect.

The "New Covenant" (Jer. 31:31–37)

God says, "I will make a new covenant with the house of Israel.... I will put my law in their minds and write it on their hearts," instead of on tablets of stone.

The Christian church claims to be the recipient of this promise, calling itself "the new Israel."

Other covenants can be found in scripture, but the principle remains the same. Covenant theology guarantees God's children the right to claim, as children often do, "But you promised!"

According to the system of covenant theology, the final covenant has been fulfilled. With the last promise in place, the world is now ready for the final step into relationship with God. This step will be taken when Jesus returns at the battle of Armageddon.

Sources:

Buttrick, George A., ed. *The Interpreter's Dictionary of the Bible.* 4 vols. New York: Abingdon Press, 1962.

The Scofield Reference Bible. New York: Oxford University Press, 1945.

CREATION RENEWED

Although Armageddon has come to mean THE END, at least in a general sense, it could just as well mean THE BEGINNING. The original biblical sense of the word refers not only to an end of what is, but to a beginning of what will be. And what will be is the restoration of the planet to what it was before the Fall—creation renewed.

The Hebrew prophet Isaiah offers the most famous depiction of the post-Armageddon earth:

> The wolf will live with the lamb,
>   the leopard will lie down with the goat,
> the calf and the lion and the yearling together;
>   and a little child will lead them.
> The cow will feed with the bear,
>   their young will lie down together,
>   and the lion will eat straw like the ox.
> The infant will play near the hole of the cobra,
>   and the young child put his hand into the viper's nest.

Traditional representation of God as creator of the world. *Fortean Picture Library.*

They will neither harm nor destroy
  on all my holy mountain,
for the earth will be full of the knowledge of the Lord
  as the waters cover the sea. (Isa. 11:6–9)

The New Testament continues the imagery:

Then I saw a new heaven and a new earth, for the first heaven and the first earth had passed away, and there was no longer any sea. I saw the Holy City, the new Jerusalem, coming down out of heaven from God, prepared as a bride beautifully dressed for her husband. And I heard a loud voice from the throne saying, "Now the dwelling of God is with men, and he will live with them. They will be his people, and God himself will be with them and be their God. He will wipe every tear from their eyes. There will be no more death or mourning or crying or pain, for the old order of things has passed away."

He who was seated on the throne said, "I am making everything new." (Rev. 21:1–5)

Jews and Christians don't have a monopoly on envisioning creation renewed. The Qur'an of Islam says:

> To the righteous it is said, "What is it that your Lord has revealed?" They say, "All that is good." To those who do good, there is good in this world, and the Home of the Hereafter is even better and excellent indeed is the Home of the righteous, Gardens of Eternity which they will enter: beneath them flow (pleasant) rivers: they will have therein all that they wish: thus doth Allah reward the righteous, (namely) those whose lives the angels take in a state of purity, saying (to them), "Peace be on you; enter ye the Garden, because of (the good) which ye did (in the world)." (16:27–32)

The idea of restoring a familiar creation is shared by Indians of North America (see Ghost Dance). In this view, Armageddon is a means to an end—a comma, rather than a period. It represents a new beginning even as it ends the familiar world of hardship and trial. It is a door opening up to a restored world.

Sources:
Fisher, Mary Pat, and Lee W. Bailey, eds. *An Anthology of Living Religions*. Upper Saddle River, NJ: Prentice Hall, 2000.
The Holy Bible, New International Version. Grand Rapids, MI: Zondervan, 1978.

CROSS, THE

In most schools of Christian theology the cross is very much tied in with the river of time flowing from Adam and Eve's expulsion from the Garden of Eden to the final restoration of all things after the battle of Armageddon. As is so often the case, the Christian left is concerned with metaphorical implications, the Christian right with historical realities. But both would agree that the cross is a powerful symbol in the story that leads from Eden to the New Jerusalem.

The earliest stories of Genesis reveal that Adam and Eve, the first parents of all humans, were placed in a beautiful garden that supplied all their material needs. Humans are pictured as being one with God, who walks in the garden in the cool of the evening. They are one with each other, naked and unconcerned. They are one with their environment, having been given access to all the bounty nature provides. It is a story picturing unity in every way.

There were two trees, however, that were off limits. The first was the infamous "tree of the knowledge of good and evil" (see Adam and Eve) that stood center stage in the first temptation. When Eve ate of the fruit of the tree and offered some to Adam, her husband, he, of his own free will and full knowledge, followed her lead, ate of the fruit, and, according to the story, brought sin into human experience.

Adam and Eve were expelled from the garden, but as the story is careful to point out, this was not because they had sinned. No, they were banished to keep them from eating the fruit of the second important tree—the "tree of life." If they ate the fruit of this tree, they would live forever. In some Christian interpretations, this would have left them eternally trapped in the sinful state in which they now found them-

Crosses of the San Francisco de Asis Mission, Taos, New Mexico. *Stephen St. John/National Geographic Image Collection/Getty Images.*

selves. In this sense, their exile was not their punishment. It was their protection. Implied in this view is the idea that God was buying time. God had a plan to undo the act that precipitated human exile and estrangement. Humans, once one with the divine, were now separated from the source of their being. Whereas once they were one with each other, they now covered themselves and hid their nakedness. Whereas they once ate freely of nature's bounty, they were now forced to raise their food by the sweat of their brow. They began to live out their mortal existence separate from the tree of life. Their years on earth were limited to the biblical "three score and ten." The tree of life that would bring eternal life into human experience was now carefully guarded by an angel wielding a flaming sword. The implication was that no one would obtain access to that tree unless someone died first.

This is where Christian theology of the cross enters the picture. According to Christian typology, the cross upon which Jesus of Nazareth was crucified became the tree of life by bringing reconciliation and the possibility of immortality back into human existence. Probably every Christian church has on display somewhere a cross. In Protestant tradition, the cross is usually empty, signifying that Jesus rose from the dead, the "first fruits" of all who are to follow. In Roman Catholic tradition, Jesus, the "fruit" of that tree, hangs on the cross (the Crucifix). The symbolism is that humans are now free to eat of the fruit of the tree of life from which they were once banished. This is the significance of the words of Holy Communion and the Mass: "This is my body, broken for you.... This is my blood, shed for you.... Eat [this] in remembrance of me."

Many Christians believe that the tree of life is destined to make another return at the end of time. After Jesus' victory at the battle of Armageddon, the New Jerusalem appears on earth. A river flows through the city, bringing the water of life to all humanity. In the midst of the city, spreading out on each side of the river, stands the tree of life (Rev. 22:2) The tree now is open to all, fulfilling its original function, for "the leaves of the tree are for the healing of the nations. No longer will there be any curse" (Rev. 22:3).

Christian typology thus follows the tree of life from the first Bible story to the last, picturing its hopeful potential at the beginning, its cruel reality in the gospels, and its completed fruition at the end. When viewed in this way, the story of the Bible is the story of human relationship with the mythical tree of life.

Source:
The Holy Bible, New International Version. Grand Rapids, MI: Zondervan, 1978.

CULTURE

Every prophecy about the future, be it secular or religious, is written within the historical context of its author. When times change and unheard-of inventions are developed, the prophecy has to be not merely read, but also interpreted. This is where problems arise. Even interpreters from the same basic tradition differ as to how to present the prophecy to a modern audience and explain what the author meant.

In the book of Revelation, for instance, the nineteenth chapter presents the vivid picture of Jesus Christ returning to earth on a white horse. In the LaHaye/Jenkins *Left Behind* novels, the authors stay within a literal framework, thus keeping the white horse. In these books, Jesus rides a white charger down from the heavens and judges the nations from the back of his steed.

Revelation also mentions "locusts" and "scorpions"; Hal Lindsey, for one, sees helicopters. When Revelation talks about "plagues and sores," Lindsey sees AIDS.

Nostradamus wrote of seeing "lightning in the ship." Some of his modern-day readers interpret this phrase as indicating a nuclear submarine.

Obviously, those trying to interpret prophecies written within an earlier cultural context face a serious problem. How much interpretation is allowed? If God or another entity is able to show a picture of modern inventions at work, how do we know that ours is the day to which the vision refers? It could be that a future generation will have a much better explanation for Nostradamus' "lightning in the ship." The best we can do is declare that what the ancients claimed to see sounds something like that with which we are familiar.

There is also the question of what kind of deity would want to play peekaboo with the human race. If God wants us to know something, why not just come out and tell us?

Sources:

LaHaye, Tim, and Jerry B. Jenkins. *Left Behind* series. 12 vols. Carol Stream, IL: Tyndale House, 1995–2004.

Lindsey, Hal. *Apocalypse Code*. Palos Verdes, CA: Western Front, Ltd., 1997.

CUSH

"Cush" was an ancient name for the country south of Egypt, occupying roughly the area of the modern-day Sudan (in biblical times this land was often called Ethiopia, but it did not correspond with the present-day country of that name). Its significance to biblical prophecy lies in the fact that Isaiah (11:11) refers to Cush specifically: "In that day the Lord will reach out his hand a second time to reclaim the remnant that is left of his people from Assyria, from Lower Egypt, from Upper Egypt, from Cush, from Elam, from Babylonia, from Hamath and from the islands of the sea."

Conservative evangelical Bible scholars believe that this is a reference to a second "gathering" of Israel "in that day," meaning at the time of the end. (The first gathering, in this view, was the birth of Zionism and the creation of a Jewish state.) The second gathering will precede the Second Coming of Jesus. When Isaiah goes on to talk of Israel swooping "down on the slopes of Philistia," the futurist (see Futurist School of Biblical Interpretation) reading is that he is referring to the 1967 Six-Day War.

Sources:

Buttrick, George A., ed. *The Interpreter's Dictionary of the Bible*. 4 vols. New York: Abingdon Press, 1962.

The Holy Bible, New International Version. Grand Rapids, MI: Zondervan, 1978.

D

DANIEL

The biblical book of Daniel is sometimes called the "Little Book of Revelation." In many ways it is the Old Testament equivalent of the New Testament book of Revelation. It represents an important plank in the platform of most prophetic interpretive systems. Those who believe that it tells the future of the human race are in good company with scholars of long ago. Josephus, a Hebrew historian who lived circa 40–100 CE, wrote in his monumental *Antiquities of the Jews* that when Alexander the Great (d. 323 BCE) was shown the book of Daniel, wherein Daniel declares that one of the Greeks should destroy the empire of the Persians, Alexander supposed that he himself was the person intended.

Daniel purports to outline a progression of nations, beginning with Babylon and continuing through Persia, Greece, and Rome, ending with (according to some interpretations) a revived Roman Empire at the end of time, during which the Messiah will come. But there are problems with this book that are not always apparent when someone simply picks up a Bible and begins to read.

First, different Bibles contain different versions of Daniel. Roman Catholic and Eastern Orthodox Bibles have entirely different versions than are found in Protestant Bibles. Protestant Bibles omit sections called "Daniel and Susanna" and "Bel and the Dragon," as well as an addition to chapter 3 called "The Prayer of Azariah." Also, one of the requirements for including books in the Hebrew Bible, established by the rabbis at Jamnia when the canon was settled and fixed in its present form, was that books had to be written in Hebrew. But only parts of Daniel were written in Hebrew. Chapter 2, verse 4, through chapter 7 was written in Aramaic.

The interpretive difficulties don't end with questions of what belongs or doesn't belong in the text. The oldest, and therefore supposedly most reliable, complete version of Daniel known today is a Greek translation copied by Origen (see Church Fathers), whom many conservative scholars accuse of both editing and allegorizing scripture.

Besides all this, Daniel 9 is probably the most difficult chapter to interpret in the whole Bible. There are hundreds of fragments for scholars to pore over, and very few of them are exactly alike. According to conservative theologians, that chapter contains the principal prophecy concerning the Church Age and the final seven years of history leading up to the battle of Armageddon (see Seventy Sevens).

Many scholars, probably a majority of those teaching in mainline seminaries, believe that Daniel was written by at least two authors, one writing in the sixth century BCE and another in the second century BCE. The first writer lived during the Babylonian captivity, the second during the time of Antiochus IV Epiphanes and the Maccabean revolt that gave rise to the celebration of Hanukkah. If this is the case, the authors were probably not writing about a time in the future even though they appear to say that they are. More likely, they were writing about times in which they were living and presenting coded references of experiences familiar to their contemporaries (see Abomination of Desolation).

That said, Daniel tells a compelling story of a young Jewish boy carried away into captivity in Babylon. There he grows to be a confidant of the king, Nebuchadnezzar. He remains true to his religion by refusing the king's orders to consume royal food and wine, but Nebuchadnezzar comes to respect him because Daniel, like Joseph of old, can interpret dreams.

In chapter 2, Daniel seems to prophesy that four kingdoms will arise. Nebuchadnezzar dreamed of a great manlike statue with a head of gold. Daniel interpreted this to represent the Babylonian kingdom. The chest and arms were of silver. To Daniel, this meant the combined kingdom of Media and Persia. The trunk of the statue was made of bronze. This, said Daniel, represented Greece. The legs and feet were of iron. According to Daniel, this stood for Rome. (It is important to note here that Daniel did not specifically name any of these kingdoms except Babylon. But his descriptions leave little room for doubt.) The value of the metals decreased, from gold to iron, but their strength increased, meaning that each succeeding nation would be greater in might but of less value ethically and morally than its predecessors.

The feet of the statue were part iron and part clay. Presumably each foot had five toes. According to conservative Christian scholars, this meant that the final form of the Roman empire would consist of ten nations. In Nebuchadnezzar's dream a "rock was cut out, but not by human hands. It struck the statue on its feet of iron and clay, and smashed them." This is how Daniel explained it:

> "In the time of those [the ten] kings, the God of Heaven will set up a kingdom that will never be destroyed, nor will it be left to another people. It will crush all those kingdoms and bring them to an end, but it will itself endure forever. This is the meaning of the vision of the rock cut out of a mountain, but not by human hands—a rock that broke the iron, the bronze, the clay, the silver and the gold to pieces.

"The great God has shown the king what will take place in the future.
The dream is true and the interpretation is trustworthy." (Dan.
2:44–46)

King Nebuchadnezzar was so impressed that he promoted Daniel to great
heights within the kingdom.

If this dream and its interpretation took place between 570 and 536 BCE, it
would certainly be a wonder, seemingly predicting the rise of Rome centuries in
advance. This is the position taken by conservative scholars (see Futurist School of
Biblical Interpretation). On the other hand, if the book was written during the early
days of the Roman Empire, it could be simply recalling history. This is the position of
the past-historic school of interpretation.

The futurists insist that the "rock" cut out of the mountain at the end of time,
destroying that which represents human history, is Jesus Christ. The ten toes of the
statue represent a revived Roman Empire existing in Europe at the end of time. It will
be smashed by Jesus Christ at his Second Coming. The words "in the time of those
kings" refers to a yet future day, according to this system of interpretation.

On top of all this, conservative scholars point to the possibility of further symbolism that springs from this dream. Right after Daniel's dream interpretation of chapter 2, a series of events unfolds that seem to symbolize the events described in the
book of Revelation. Daniel is "placed in a high position" and made a ruler. According
to some conservative scholars, this represents the Rapture of the church (see Rapture). But in chapter 3 (after Daniel is "raptured" in symbol), Nebuchadnezzar sets up
an image, a statue, and tells all the people to worship it. This idol supposedly represents the "beast" of Revelation 13:15 (see Revelation). Some refuse to worship the
image. Daniel's friends Shadrach, Meshach, and Abednego are thrown in a fiery furnace for their insubordination, an event interpreted as prefiguring the Tribulation (see
Great Tribulation). Like the faithful remnant who are kept safe through the Tribulation (Rev. 7), the three pass through the flames. All others, just like those of Revelation 20:7–15, are destroyed in the furnace. This is the same schematic format followed
by most modern evangelical students of prophecy.

If that were all the prophecy found in the book of Daniel, there would be
ample material to keep scholars debating forever. But there is much, much more.

In chapter 7 the motif of the four kingdoms returns, this time in the guise of
four different beasts. Babylon is now a roaring lion. Medo-Persia becomes a lumbering
bear. The bear holds three ribs in his teeth, representing the Medes, Persians, and
Babylonians. Greece is pictured as a swift and darting lion with four heads. Conservative scholars most often identify this image with the fact that Greece was divided into
four spheres of influence following the death of Alexander the Great.

Rome, according to this scheme, is vividly portrayed:

After that, in my vision at night I looked and there before me was a
fourth beast—terrifying and frightening and very powerful. It had large
iron teeth; it crushed and devoured its victims and trampled underfoot

whatever was left. It was different from all the former beasts, and it had ten horns.

While I was thinking about the horns, there before me was another horn, a little one, which had come up among them; and three of the first horns were uprooted before it. This horn had eyes like the eyes of a man and a mouth that spoke boastfully.

As I looked, thrones were set in place, and the Ancient of Days took his seat....

In my vision at night I looked, and there before me was one like a son of man, coming with the clouds of heaven. He approached the Ancient of Days and was led into his presence. He was given authority, glory and sovereign power; all people, nations and men of every language worshiped him. His dominion is an everlasting dominion that will not pass away, and his kingdom is one that will never be destroyed. (Dan. 7:7–14)

Daniel's method of prophecy often revolves around the claim that he does not understand what he sees. He likes to portray himself as the innocent bystander, continually needing help interpreting what he is seeing. He uses this technique again here: "Troubled in spirit. I approached one of those standing there and asked him the true meaning of all this." It is explained to him that the

"fourth beast is a fourth kingdom that will appear on earth. It will be different from all the other kingdoms and will devour the whole earth, trampling it down and crushing it. The ten horns are ten kings who will arise from this kingdom. After them another king will arise, different from the earlier ones; he will subdue three kings. He will speak against the Most High and oppress his saints and try to change the set times and the laws. The saints will be handed over to him for a time, times and half a time.

"But the court will sit, and his power will be taken away and completely destroyed forever. Then the sovereignty, power and greatness of the kingdoms under the whole of heaven will be handed over to the saints, the people of the Most High. His kingdom will be an everlasting kingdom, and all the rulers will worship and obey him." (Dan. 7:23–28)

Those who believe that Daniel was writing about his own time, disguising a political diatribe against Rome in the form of a prophetic vision, offer various claims that this chapter fits with what is known about the political realities of Rome's rule in the second century BCE. Those who believe that Daniel was foretelling the future assert that the ten nations arising from Rome will consist of a future ten-nation European confederacy. One nation will take supremacy by defeating three who rebel. The "time [one], times [two] and half a time [one-half]" represent the final three and one-half years of the Great Tribulation preceding the battle of Armageddon. They point out the similarity of this passage to Revelation 17 (see Revelation) and John's vision of the woman seated on the "great beast":

The ten horns you saw are ten kings who have not yet received a king-dom, but who will receive authority as kings along with the beast. They have one purpose and will give their power and authority to the beast. They will make war against the Lamb, but the Lamb will overcome them because he is Lord of lords and King of kings—and with him will be his called, chosen and faithful followers. (Rev. 17:12–14)

Those who don't subscribe to this argument counter that Revelation was very probably written by an author who had a close working knowledge of the book of Daniel. Daniel was, after all, part of the scriptures of first-century Judaism. Jesus quot-ed it in Matthew 24. John would have been very familiar with the imagery and possi-bly, consciously or not, incorporated it into his own prophetic scheme.

The debate will not be resolved through academic scholarship. Futurists, as a matter of faith, operate under the presupposition that Daniel was God's prophet and could see the future. Past-historicists do not.

Even these arguments, however, pale in the face of the problems encountered when interpreting Daniel's ninth chapter. It is very probably the most difficult passage of the Old Testament to translate, let alone interpret, but it forms the basis for much of the current conservative understanding of endtime chronology. Because of the complexity of the text, the chapter is treated as an individual entry (see Seventy Sev-ens). A summary of the conservative argument is that in this chapter Daniel prophe-sies that there will be a Church Age inserted into a gap between the time of Jesus and a future seven-year Tribulation.

Daniel's final vision is a culmination of all that has gone before. In chapter 10 he claims to see a "great war." The vision was a long time in coming: Daniel prayed and fasted for three weeks before the angel Gabriel appeared to him on the banks of the Tigris River. The reason it took Gabriel so long was that "the prince of the Persian kingdom resisted" him. Michael, the leader of God's heavenly host and a kind of patron guardian of the nation Israel, had to come with reinforcements to clear a path through the enemy so Daniel's prayer could be answered.

Chapter 11 offers a past, present, and future vision. The characters from the past center around Egypt and Syria, as well as a recapitulation of Greece's part in Israel's future. The chapter is full of references to a "king of the South" and a "king of the North" who "march against each other." Beginning in verse 36, Daniel seems to move into a future time. According to conservative scholarship, it is here that he begins to envision the battle of Armageddon. It's a shorter version than that given by Ezekiel (see Ezekiel) or John (see Revelation), but it contains familiar scenes. The "king of the North" (Russia, according to this interpretive scheme) attacks the "mightiest fortresses" and even "invades the Beautiful Land" (Israel):

"The king will do as he pleases. He will exalt and magnify himself above every god.... He will show no regard to the god of his fathers or for the one desired by women, nor will he regard any god.... Instead of them he will honor a god of fortresses; a god unknown to his fathers.... He will attack the mightiest fortresses with the help of a foreign god and will greatly acknowledge him....

"Many countries will fall, but Edom, Moab and the leaders of Ammon will be delivered from his hand. He will extend his power over many countries; Egypt will not escape. He will gain control of the treasures of gold and silver and all the riches of Egypt, with the Libyans and Nubians in submission. But reports from the east and north will alarm him, and he will set out in a great rage to destroy and annihilate many. He will pitch his royal tents between the seas at the beautiful holy mountain. Yet he will come to his end, and no one will help him. [See also Armageddon, Battle of.]

"At that time Michael, the great prince who protects your people, will arise. There will come a time of distress such has not happened from the beginning of nations until then. But at that time your people—everyone whose name is found written in the book—will be delivered. Multitudes who sleep in the dust of the earth will awake: some to everlasting life, others to shame and everlasting contempt. Those who are wise will shine like the brightness of the heavens, and those who lead many to righteousness, like the stars for ever and ever. But you, Daniel, close up and seal the words of the scroll until the time of the end. Many will go here and there to increase knowledge." (Dan. 11:36–12:4)

Once again, Daniel confesses that he doesn't understand what he has just seen. This time, however, he has company. Two men, one standing on Daniel's side of the Tigris River and another on the opposite bank, have similar questions. "How long will it be before these astonishing things are fulfilled?" asks one of the men. Then a "man clothed in linen, who was above the waters of the river, lifted his hand toward heaven, and I heard him swear by him who lives forever, saying, 'It will be for a time, times and half a time. When the power of the holy people has been finally broken, all these things will be completed.'"

Again, Daniel is confused: "I heard, but I did not understand."

"Go your way, Daniel," he is told,

"because the words are closed up and sealed until the time of the end. Many will be purified, made spotless and refined, but the wicked will continue to be wicked. None of the wicked will understand, but those who are wise will understand.

"From the time that the daily sacrifice is abolished and the abomination that causes desolation [see Abomination of Desolation] is set up, there will be 1,290 days [almost three and a half years according to the Jewish calendar]. Blessed is the one who waits for and reaches the end of the 1,335 days.

"As for you, go your way till the end. You will rest, and then at the end of the days you will rise to receive your allotted inheritance." (Dan. 12:7–13)

To conservative scholars, these passages form the backdrop to their eschatological scheme of the endtimes. Finding no previous history that fits with the images presented, they assume that Daniel must be seeing the future time of Tribulation. No one has offered an adequate explanation of these verses before our time because the words have been sealed up until the time of the end: "But you, Daniel, close up and seal the words of the scroll until the time of the end. Many will go here and there to increase knowledge" (Dan. 12:4). Some translators, no doubt showing a little futurist bias, translate the passage this way: "But Daniel, keep this prophecy a secret; seal it up so that it shall not be understood until the end times, when travel and education shall be vastly increased" (Life Application Bible).

This verse, according to many conservative scholars, describes the times in which we live. The computer age, "when travel and education shall be greatly increased," is a sign of the end. Although we might not understand all the nuances of biblical prophecy, for the first time in history we have the technology to both understand and reproduce many of the visions Daniel claims to have seen. The countries are in place. We must be living in the time of the end.

Most liberal scholars disagree. God does not play head games with the world, they say. The references are obscure and entirely compatible with the rules of classic apocalyptic literature (see Apocalyptic Writing) down through the ages. The way to discover what Daniel was writing about is to study the history of his times, not wait for the future.

Sources:
Buttrick, George A., ed. *The Interpreter's Dictionary of the Bible.* 4 vols. New York: Abingdon Press, 1962.
The Holy Bible, New International Version. Grand Rapids, MI: Zondervan, 1978.
Josephus, Flavius. *The Works of Flavius Josephus.* Trans. William Whiston. London: T. Nelson and Sons, 1873.

DARBY, JOHN NELSON *see* **Dispensationalism**

DAVID

For to us a child is born,
  to us a son is given,
and the government will be on his shoulders....
Of the increase of his government and of peace
  there will be no end.
He will reign on David's throne
  and over his kingdom. (Isa. 9:6, 7)
Thou art the king of Israel,
Thou David's royal Son,
Who in the Lord's name comest,
The King and Blessed One!
  —"All Glory, Laud, and Honor," Theodulph of Orleans, ca. 800, trans. John M. Neale, 1854

Once in royal David's city stood a lowly cattle shed,
Where a mother laid her baby in a manger for his bed.
  —"Once in Royal David's City," Cecil Alexander, 1848

Every December, Christians sing beloved Christmas carols contributed from almost every Western national tradition. Even many people who never go to a church have favorite carols they sing with great nostalgia. Hardly noticed is the fact that song after song contains reference to the Jewish king David. Jesus is called "David's greater son." He was born in Bethlehem, the "City of David." His genealogy as given in the gospels of Matthew and Luke specifically claims that David was the ancestor of Jesus.

Those who believe that Jesus will literally return to earth point to many passages of the Old Testament that, according to their belief system, promise that he will rule from "David's throne." Herbert W. Armstrong (see Armstrong, Herbert W.) claimed that the queen of England sits on David's throne today. David was the prototype, the symbol, of the kingdom that conservative Christian scholars say will be set up during the Millennium (see Millennium).

Who was this king who paved the way for the Christian understanding of the Second Coming and the eternal kingdom of God on earth?

David was the second king of the united Israel. He was a shepherd boy and writer of songs. He was a soldier, statesman, and (at least in one account) the slayer of Goliath. He was a lover, an adulterer, and a "man after God's own heart." He was noble and petty, righteous and vengeful. The man who "killed his ten thousands" was also known as the "sweet singer of Israel." In folklore and myth there has never been anyone quite like him. He is portrayed as a children's hero, but one of the most famous stories about him reveals that he committed adultery and then had his lover's husband murdered. His legend is probably the most edited story in literature. Rabbis and Sunday-school teachers regularly leave out the dark parts of the tale, and preachers usually censor the verses not fit for Sunday morning consumption. By an unspoken conspiracy of the "keepers of the story," he is thus the one of the best-known and most-revered, but least-understood, characters in the Bible. He wallowed in the sewer, but three thousand years after his death he still smells like a rose.

How did he do it? Well, it helps to have good biographers. The consensus of modern biblical scholarship seems to be that much of the Bible was put together from existing documents during David's reign. Chances are thus better than even that a lot of editing went into casting him in a good light. The constant refrain during the book of Judges, for instance, that "there was no king and every man did what was right in his own eyes" goes a long way toward setting David up as the hero who put Humpty Dumpty Israel back together again. The last few chapters of Judges even cast Saul, David's predecessor, in a bad light. These passages reveal a lot of X-rated activities committed by Saul's tribal ancestors and folks from his hometown. By the time David comes along, one has to suspect that a propaganda campaign is at work—"You couldn't trust Saul, but David's administration has your best interests at heart!"

That said, however, there's something hard to dislike about David. He was a hero with feet of clay (or even sand), but a hero nonetheless. Such luminaries as Michelangelo and William Faulkner immortalized him in art and literature. He has become bigger than life.

Which leads to a fundamental question: Did David in fact exist? Up to a few years ago the only witness was the Bible, but recent archaeological lend at least some

David, king of Israel, had a reputation for his singing—among other things. *Library of Congress.*

support to the idea that there was such a person. Although scholars still debate his existence, we can probably turn to his biography with a fair amount of confidence that, except for what Mark Twain's Huckleberry Finn used to call "a few stretchers," the story emerging from the books of Samuel, Kings, and Chronicles comes reasonably close to describing a historical figure. But there are problems. The author of 1 Samuel 17:50, for instance, tells us that a youth named David killed Goliath with his slingshot. A few pages later, 2 Samuel 21:19 credits a man named Elhanan with the same deed. Were David and Elhanan one and the same, or are there two separate traditions at work here? Some Bible scholars have theorized that "David" is a title, and not a name.

Whatever the reality, the biblical story is well known. David was born in the "little town of Bethlehem" about a thousand years before his even more famous descendant, Jesus. His father, Jesse, was the grandson of Boaz and Ruth, whose story is told in the book bearing her name. (Ruth's sister, by the way, leaves a modern-day legacy as well. Her name was Orpah. When the parents of a future television legend were searching for a name for their new baby girl, they misread the Bible and named her Oprah. The rest, as they say, is history.)

When we first meet David, he is a shepherd, the "runt" of Jesse's litter. The prophet Samuel shows up one day on a secret mission from God. Saul, the appointed first king over Israel, is not working out. Samuel knows enough to find the new king's home but doesn't know which son is God's choice. Jesse, showing even less spiritual acumen than Samuel, leaves David out tending the sheep, figuring him to be not even in the running. When Jesse musters the other sons, Samuel can't see a future ruler among them. "Are these all the sons you have?" he asks (1 Sam. 16:11). Eventually, David is brought in from the fields and Samuel anoints him king. No one thinks to tell King Saul, who continues blithely on, fighting Philistines and running the kingdom into the ground. David, meanwhile, goes back to tending sheep.

When we next hear from him, he is carrying food to his brothers, who are now fighting in Saul's army. The Israeli troops are bunkered down on a ridge facing the Philistine forces across a valley. In keeping with a rather sensible practice of the time, the Philistines had invoked the honorable custom of single combat: "Our champion against your champion, winner take all." The only problem is that the Philistine champion is a nine-foot giant named Goliath. No one wants to take him on—until David arrives. "Who is this uncircumcised Philistine that he should defy the armies of the living God?" he asks (1 Sam. 17:26).

Everyone knows what happened next. Philistine giant with sword and spear vs. boy with slingshot. Score: Israel 1, Philistines 0. That day David became not only the most famous soldier in Israeli history, but one of the most charismatic warriors in the history of the world. His fight became the universal symbol of every battle between entrenched power and the "little guy." From then on, it was only a matter of time. Saul's reign was over, even though he didn't know it yet.

David appears next in quite a different guise. Saul is troubled by some kind of fit that is soothed only when David plays gentle music on the harp. The Bible makes plain what's going on: "An evil spirit from God came forcefully upon Saul.... Saul was afraid of David, because the Lord was with David but had left Saul" (1 Sam. 18:10–12). David is forced to flee when Saul tries to kill him. He rapidly becomes leader of his own band of troops, pursued by Saul throughout the hill country of Israel. He always eludes the pursuit but refuses to do Saul harm. After all, according to David's reasoning, Saul is God's king.

Here an interesting debate arises. Saul's son Jonathan and David were best of friends. Jonathan served as David's spy, keeping David informed of Saul's plans and movements. But how close was their relationship? At Jonathan's memorial service David preached the eulogy:

> How the mighty have fallen in battle!
> I grieve for you, Jonathan my brother;
>   you were very dear to me.
> Your love for me was wonderful,
>   more wonderful than that of women. (2 Sam. 1:26)

What's going on here? Love "more wonderful than that of women?" Was Jonathan being "outed" at his own funeral? When the Bible says that "the souls [of Jonathan and David] were knit together" (1 Sam. 18:1), is it implying the two knitted more than their souls? Don't scoff at this too readily. According to Jonathan Kirsch in his book *The Harlot by the Side of the Road*, "these words from Holy Scripture were recently invoked in a debate in the Knesset, the national legislature of Israel, over the rights of gay men and women under Israeli law. Yael Dayan, daughter of another war hero of Israel [Moshe Dayan], succeeded in drawing the ire (and raising the blood pressure) of some of her fellow members of the Knesset by 'outing' David; she argued, on the strength of David's eulogy of Jonathan, that the two were gay lovers."

David subsequently proved himself to be a rather lusty heterosexual fellow. But the debate rages on, another example of how almost any opinion can be buttressed with biblical texts if you look hard enough. The truth is, we'll never know for sure if David was bisexual.

Sexual orientation aside, David eventually became king over Israel. He was the one who conquered Jerusalem and made it his capital city. Before this it was a Jebusite hill fortress. Ever since it has been called the City of David (2 Sam. 5:9). He soon brought the Ark of the Covenant to what would be its resting place in Solomon's temple, defeated virtually all his enemies, and expanded the size of Israel to borders previously undreamed.

But one day he awoke to no new challenges and found himself bored. Enter Bathsheba.

"In the spring, at the time when kings go off to war," David decided to stay home (2 Sam. 11:1). He was by this time too important to risk on the battlefield. Armies fought in the spring and summer, when they could be supplied off the land. But David had killed his giants and conquered his enemies. He had fought his battles, and he was beginning to feel the aches and pains. It was a dangerous time for him, these days between youth and senior citizenship. And David never did anything halfway. Even his midlife crisis was severe.

The Bible says that "one evening David got up from his bed and walked around on the roof of his palace. From the roof he saw a woman bathing. The woman was very beautiful" (2 Sam. 11:2). It was Bathsheba. She was the wife of Uriah, a soldier who was off fighting the wars from which David stayed home—which makes what happened next even more inexcusable. David summoned Bathsheba. They slept together. She got pregnant. David quickly sent for Uriah, expecting that he would sleep with Bathsheba and she could say the baby was his. But Uriah turned out to be more honorable than David. He wouldn't go home to the comfort of his wife while his men were sleeping alone in tents, out in the field. David even tried getting him drunk, but Uriah still stayed away from Bathsheba.

There was only one thing to do to prevent scandal. David sent Uriah back to the front carrying his own death sentence in a sealed communication to his general. It ordered the commander to put Uriah in the thick of the fighting and then draw all the troops away. Death followed, of course, and every man in the army must have known something was up.

In the famous confrontation of 2 Samuel 12, Nathan, the king's chaplain, gave his "thou art the man" speech. David finally did the honorable thing. He confessed to his people, begged God's forgiveness, and married Bathsheba. The child that had been born of their adulterous liaison died, the opinion of the editors of Samuel being that this was David's punishment for his sin. But the next child born to them was Solomon, leaving one to wonder. People had to have heard rumors about David's relationship, and they might not have followed Solomon if he had been the child of an illicit affair. Was the story included to "clear" Solomon of blame, setting the scene for his rule?

David had other family problems as well. His son Absalom murdered his half-brother Ammon for committing incest with their sister, and later attempted to overthrow his father. David actually abdicated for a brief time, fleeing Jerusalem rather than fight the attempted coup and be forced to kill his own son.

The rest of David's story is one sordid event after another. One gets the idea that he was never quite the same after he realized the depth of depravity he had in his soul. His final days are even worse. In his old age he found it difficult to stay warm at night, so something resembling a "Miss Israel" contest was held. The winner got to sleep with the king to keep him warm, although the chroniclers are quick to point out that "he knew her not" (1 Kings 1:4); after all, they don't want to ruin his reputation.

Probably one of the most depressing scenes in the whole Bible is depicted in 1 Kings 2. In a passage that might have been the inspiration for the closing chapters of Mario Puzo's novel *The Godfather*, David meets with Solomon, about to be his successor. The two of them plot revenge against all the people David didn't want to kill while he was alive but wants dead as soon as he is.

Finally, when we just don't want to hear any more about this side of David, he "rested with his fathers and was buried in the City of David" after ruling Israel for forty years.

What is David's final legacy? Was he an honorable youth? Yes. He was above reproach when he was young. We have no reason to doubt the facts because subsequent stories reveal plenty to criticize. Was he a good general? Absolutely. His bravery is without question. His tactics have been studied by military leaders. His ferocity was tempered by compassion, although not nearly as much as we might like to hear about. But those were brutal days.

It seems clear that he was also a fine musician. Although many of the psalms attributed to him were, according to textual scholars, undoubtedly written by someone else (including, sad to say, almost certainly the beloved 23rd Psalm), there is enough substance left to say that he deserves his reputation as "the sweet singer of Israel" (2 Sam. 23:1).

Clearly too, he was a shrewd politician. Between the lines of his fascinating story lie treaties and political alliances that laid the groundwork for his son Solomon's rule, the historical high point for Israeli influence.

Was he a devoutly religious man? If we can separate religion from morality, he was one of the most profoundly religious persons not only of his day but of all times. He continually poured out his heart to God. He wore his feelings on his sleeve and wasn't afraid to show others his devotion. Is it any wonder God called him "a man after my own heart" (1 Sam. 13:14)?

But the morality issue is hard to ignore. The temptation is to shrug and say, "Well, those were different days." And they were. That's why David manages to keep what a modern leader would call a "positive approval rating." The truth, though, is that he was at times the most immoral character in the Bible. He was capable of fits of rage during which he seemed bathed in blood. Sometimes he showed great mercy. Other times he demonstrated the heart of a ruthless terrorist, killing merely for shock value. He knew nothing about human rights when it served his purpose to be brutal.

He is a fascinating character and deserves the study, books, and movies he has inspired. From the standpoint of religion, psychology, warfare, music, poetry, politics, and human development he is a deep, deep mine yielding riches when approached carefully and plumbed with diligence. And whether or not he actually wrote the words, his memory comes alive whenever we hear "Yea, though I walk through the valley of the shadow of death, I will fear no evil: for thou art with me…. Surely goodness and mercy will follow me all the days of life: and I will dwell in the house of the Lord for ever" (Ps. 23).

David is the prototype. He is the king who symbolizes all that the returning Jesus will come to fulfill, according to the many Christian songs and stories. Although it is entirely possible he committed most of the sins the religious right now abhors, he represents and personifies the One whose coming they await at the battle of Armageddon.

Sources:

Bridger, David, ed. *The New Jewish Encyclopedia.* New York: Behrman House, 1962.

Buttrick, George A., ed. *The Interpreter's Dictionary of the Bible.* 4 vols. New York: Abingdon Press, 1962.

Hymns for the Living Church. Carol Stream, IL: Hope, 1978.

Kirsch, Jonathan. *The Harlot by the Side of the Road.* New York: Ballantine, 1997.

May, Herbert G., and Bruce M. Metzger, eds. *The New Oxford Annotated Bible with the Apocrypha.* Rev. ed. New York: Oxford University Press, 1973.

Willis, Jim. *The Religion Book: Places, Prophets, Saints, and Seers.* Detroit: Visible Ink Press, 2004.

DAY OF JUDGMENT

Theologians mean many different things when they talk about the Day of Judgment. Both Peter and Paul often use the term:

The Lord knows how to rescue godly men from trials and to hold the unrighteous for the day of judgment. (2 Pet. 2:9)

This will take place on the day when God will judge men's secrets through Jesus Christ, as my gospel declares. (Rom. 2:16)

Jesus, too, warned of a coming Day of Judgment:

"When the Son of Man comes in glory, and all his angels with him, he will sit on his throne in great glory. All the nations will be gathered before him, and he will separate then people one from another as a shepherd separates the sheep from the goats. He will put the sheep on his right and the goats on his left." (Matt. 25:31–33)

There are many ways in which the term is applied, but three events are highlighted in the prophetic books of the Bible.

The Judgment at Calvary

In one sense, from this standpoint, the Day of Judgment has already passed. It happened at Calvary when Jesus was crucified. By his sacrifice, Jesus made what Christians call "substitutionary atonement" for humankind's sins. This concept can be best illustrated by a story.

A driver is arrested for speeding. He is brought before a judge who is wearing a black robe, the symbol of authority. The judge is sitting behind a great, elevated bench and looks down at the accused. All the trappings of the room point to the fact that this judge is in control and has the power of life and death.

"How do you plead?" asks the judge.

The accused knows he is guilty. He was speeding and breaking the law. There is no sense denying the fact. And this isn't the first time. He's done it before.

"Guilty, your honor."

The judge pronounces his sentence. "I fine you one hundred dollars!"

"I'm guilty," says the accused, "but I don't have enough money. I deserve the penalty, but I cannot pay."

"Then you must go to jail," says the judge. (Perhaps adding, "Where there shall be weeping and wailing and gnashing of teeth!")

The accused is made ready to be led off to jail, but before he can be escorted from the courtroom the judge halts the proceedings.

"Wait!" he says. Removing his robe, the symbol of authority, he comes out from behind the imposing bench. Now he looks just like everyone else. Standing next to the accused the judge reaches into his pocket and produces a hundred-dollar bill. Paying the fine for the guilty party he says, "Do you accept this payment?"

"Yes," says the relieved speeder. "I'm guilty, but I accept your payment of my fine. In the eyes of justice, the very judge who was forced to sentence me has paid my penalty. He put aside his robe of honor to do it, coming down here to stand right beside me like a brother, but my sin is now and forever atoned for."

And then the final mystery is explained to the courtroom. The judge was both father and brother to the accused—father when judgment was pronounced and brother when payment was made. And yet, somehow, father and brother are one and the same.

Substitionary atonement is the essence of conservative Christian theology. The transaction, in this interpretation, occurred at a real place and time in history, centering on Jesus of Nazareth and the cross at Calvary. Everyone was obviously born once into this world, but every "original sinner" has to be crucified with Christ. Once Christ's sacrifice is personally accepted, a person is "born again to newness of life."

Jesus explained the Crucifixion to his disciples when he gave them bread and wine to drink. "This is my body, broken for you," he said. "This is my blood, shed for you. Do this in remembrance of me." The essence of the sinner's response is expressed in an old gospel hymn sung at the climax of every Billy Graham rally:

> Just as I am, without one plea,
> But that thy blood was shed for me,
> And that thou bidst me come to thee,
> O Lamb of God, I come, I come.
>   —"Just as I Am," by Charlotte Elliott, 1834

In 1799 John Newton, a recently converted slave trader, penned the best-known conservative Christian affirmation to this story:

> Amazing grace! How sweet the sound
> That saved a wretch like me!
> I once was lost, but now am found;
> Was blind, but now I see.
>   —"Amazing Grace," by John Newton, 1779

Liberals read the same biblical texts as conservatives but tend to regard them as metaphors, whereas conservatives tend to see them as historical fact. In the liberal view, the "virgin birth" does not mean that a human woman was literally impregnated by God from on high, but rather that to be fully human one must be open to spirit, as Jesus was. It means that humans are at once physical and spiritual. Miracles mean that all is possible to those who see past the immediacy of their environment, who look for the possible even in the face of impossibility. Liberals differentiate between the historical man Jesus of Nazareth and, to use Marcus Borg's term, the "post-Easter" Jesus. Borg means that the spirit of Jesus was so powerful—all he was and all he represented was so real—that even after his death his disciples realized that he was still very much with them, infused into their very personalities and being.

Anyone who has ever heard the internal reproving or affirming voice of a parent long since deceased understands that people live on in us as long as we are alive.

In short, the judgment described in the Bible is universal and true, at once particular to each individual and all-encompassing to the entire human race. In the liberal view, to limit the gospel to a story about a Christian God who somehow needs to be appeased by a bloody, painful sacrifice, is not only to miss the point, it is downright blasphemous.

The Great White Throne Judgment

There is another sense in which the Day of Judgment is applied to the whole human race. The process is often referred to as the Great White Throne Judgment. The name comes from Revelation 20:11–15:

> Then I saw a great white throne and him who was seated on it. Earth and sky fled from his presence, and there was no place for them. And I saw the dead, both great and small, standing before the throne, and books were opened. Another book was opened, which is the book of life. The dead were judged according to what they had done as record-ed in the books. The sea gave up the dead that were in them, and each person was judged according to what he had done. Then Death and Hades were thrown into the lake of fire. The lake of fire is the second death. If anyone's name was not found written in the book of life, he was thrown into the lake of fire.

This is a universal judgment that harks back to the quotation of Jesus in Matthew 25 about separating the sheep from the goats. Yet when set against the idea of the judgment at Calvary, it has opened a great chasm between Christian theologians. If people have been judged at the cross, how can they be judged again? Surely God can-not abide double jeopardy. The Great White Throne Judgment, say many theologians, must refer to only to those who have not "accepted" the free gift of Christ on the cross.

The Judgment Seat of Christ

There the issue might have stood had it not been for the apostle Paul. With one verse of scripture he opened up a new problem: "For we must all appear before the judgment seat of Christ, that each one may receive what is due him for the things done while in the body, whether good or bad" (2 Cor. 5:10).

Now the whole issue is once again up for grabs. First we are told that we are judged not guilty because Christ took our punishment, so we need not fear any further judgment when he comes back to earth. Now Paul seems to be saying that everyone will be judged after all. What is this "judgment seat of Christ"?

Perhaps, goes one argument, Paul is referring to rewards for righteousness. Thus, the Judgment Seat of Christ becomes another term for what is sometimes called the "Christian Judgment." In 2 Timothy, Paul refers to a "crown of righteousness." In 1 Corinthians 3 he spends quite a bit of time talking about works that are "burned up" like so much "stubble," as opposed to deeds symbolized by "gold, silver and costly stones." Maybe the Day of Judgment for Christians consists of God simply pointing out the value of what people did in their lives.

On the other hand, James confuses the issue still further when he reminds his readers in James 2:12 and 13, "Speak and act as those who are going to be judged by the law that gives freedom, because judgment without mercy will be shown to anyone who has not been merciful. Mercy triumphs over judgment!"

The image of judgment is a popular one. A country song entitled "God's Gonna Get 'Cha for That!" had its day in the sun during the 1970s. For every person who considers "judgment" to be an outmoded notion whereby religion is used to frighten people into acceptable behaviors, there is another who lies awake at night worrying about his or her fate in the hereafter (see Eternal Life).

Whatever the case, Armageddon is about judgment. According to conservative Christian theology, it is the place where evil will finally be judged and destroyed.

Source:
The Holy Bible, New International Version. Grand Rapids, MI: Zondervan, 1978.

DAY OF THE LORD

The phrase *Day of the Lord*, taken from, among other places, 1 Corinthians 1:8, has become a Christian catchall for the events surrounding the return of Jesus. But it has its roots in Jewish theology, where it used in passages such as Ezekiel 30:3 to refer to the coming of Messiah in judgment upon the earth. (See also Armageddon; Day of Judgment; Second Coming.)

DAYS OF NOAH

"As it was in the days of Noah, so it will be at the coming of the Son of Man" (Matt. 2:37). These words are attributed to Jesus of Nazareth. People who subscribe to the futurist school of biblical interpretation (see Futurist School of Biblical Interpretation) understand Jesus to be saying that at end of time, just before his Second Coming, human behavior on earth will replicate the behavior that called forth the judgment of Noah's flood.

Of course, there is no direct evidence that there ever was a worldwide flood. And even if there was, there is certainly no archeological evidence that reveals how people were behaving. There is, however, a written record that claims to describe those times. It is found in the book of Genesis, chapters 4 through 6. Both Jesus and the author of Matthew's gospel would have been familiar with this account because by their time it was firmly established in the Torah.

Genesis 4 relates the story of the populating of the earth following Adam and Eve's expulsion from the Garden of Eden. The story begins by describing the first murder. Cain killed his brother Abel. Immediately following that infamous act, he got married, went forth, and built a city. (This, of course, raises certain questions. For instance, if there were only two brothers on earth, and one killed the other, who was Cain's wife and where did the folks come from to populate his city? But such issues are beside the point of this particular reading of the story.)

Four generations after Adam and Eve, a man named Lamech was born who is forever remembered as being the first biblical bigamist. He married two women, Adah and Zillah. He had two sons with Adah: Jabal, who was the first person to raise livestock and practice agriculture, and Jubal, who was the first musician, specializing in the harp and the flute. Lamech also had a son with Zillah: Tubal-Cain, the first industrialist, who forged tools out of bronze and iron.

German prognostication pamphlet of the early sixteenth century predicting a flood of Noachian proportions that would end the world in 1524. *Fortean Picture Library.*

While all this begetting and inventing was going on, however, Lamech killed a man who had "wounded" him and swore vengeance on anyone who threatened him in the future: "If Cain is avenged seven times, then Lamech seventy-seven times." In other words, Lamech used the common threat of terrorism against his alleged enemies.

Moving on to Genesis 5, we are introduced to a man named Enoch. The Bible tells us just enough about him to whet our appetites. He seems to have been quite a hellfire-and-brimstone preacher. The little book of Jude, in the New Testament, quotes one of his sermons: "Enoch, the seventh from Adam, prophesied … , 'See, the Lord is coming with thousands upon thousands of his holy ones to judge everyone, and to convict all the ungodly of all the ungodly acts they have done in the ungodly way, and of all the harsh words ungodly sinners have spoken against him'" (Jude 14, 15).

Genesis adds something else quite out of the ordinary. It is common, in the lists of "begats," to tell us how old a man was when he died. Apparently Enoch never died. He simply "was no more, because God took him away" (Gen. 5:24). Some Christians think that this is an Old Testament version of the Rapture (see Rapture). Immediately after Enoch's disappearance, the Flood comes.

In the meantime, however, other things are happening. Genesis 6:1 describes a population explosion on earth as "men began to increase in number." There also seems to be some kind of demon worship going on, although the Hebrew language is very unclear in this passage. It tells of "the sons of God" mating with "the daughters of men," producing beings called "Nephilim," often translated "giants," who were "the heroes of old, men of renown." Although there is no agreement at all concerning the meaning of this passage, verse 12 plainly says that the earth was becoming "corrupt" and was filled with "violence." Because of all this, God decides to send the Flood. But since "Noah was a righteous man, blameless among the people of his time," and because he "walked with God," he and his family were spared and passed safely through the waters of judgment.

Now consider some of the key words and events this summary of the "Days of Noah" has touched upon: murder, city building, bigamy, agriculture, music, industry, revenge, terrorism, the rapture of the one who was preaching about coming judgment, population explosion, demon worship, corruption, violence, and a small group who passed safely through God's judgment that was meted out upon the world.

A futurist would say it reads like the headlines of today's *New York Times*. A futurist would also remember the words of Jesus: "As it was in the days of Noah, so it will be at the coming of the Son of Man."

Source:
The Holy Bible, New International Version. Grand Rapids, MI: Zondervan, 1978.

Devil

And though this world, with devils filled, should threaten to undo us,
We will not fear, for God hath willed His truth to triumph through us.
The prince of darkness grim, we tremble not for him;
His rage we can endure, for lo, his doom is sure:
One little word shall fell him.
　—"A Mighty Fortress Is Our God," Martin Luther, 1529

A 1531 rendition of the devil tempting Christ. *Fortean Picture Library.*

In this hymn by Martin Luther, the man who was arguably the most instrumental in beginning the Protestant Reformation, Christians are reminded once again that the devil is the whole reason for the events surrounding Armageddon. They are also assured they have nothing to fear as long as their hearts are in the right place.

Devils are not confined to Christianity. Almost all religions feature some kind of demons, evil tricksters, and things that go bump in the night as a vital part of their theology. But in Western cultures, whenever people hear the word *devil* they almost invariably think of Lucifer ("Morning Star") or Satan (literally, *the* Satan, meaning "the accuser.")

In Christian, late Jewish, and Islamic theology, the devil ("Iblis" to Muslims) is a created being gone wrong. Always masculine, thus referred to as "he," the devil is not the opposite of God. He is not all-powerful, all-knowing, or able to be in all places at the same time. Instead he is a personal, malignant being, not so much full of hate as empty of love. His power is limited and lies mostly in temptation and the ability to cause fear. Although he is not, in Genesis at least, associated by name with the serpent in the Garden of Eden, later Christian writers read back into the early Jewish story their developing conception, calling him, in the book of Revelation, "that old serpent, the devil."

In the book of Job he is the Satan, "the accuser of the brethren." Forced to report in with the rest of the angels after "roaming through the earth and going back and forth on it," he talks God into using the "upright and blameless" Job as a one-man testing ground wherein a cosmic battle of wills takes place between good and evil (Job 1:6–11).

(It is interesting to note that the position of "accuser of the brethren" in still officially being filled on earth. When the Roman Catholic Congregation of Rites considers someone for beatification or canonization, a *promotor fidei* or "promoter of the faith" sets forth the case *against* that person's candidacy. The *promotor fidei* is also known as the *advocatus diaboli*, the "devil's advocate" or "accuser of the brethren.")

It is in the New Testament that Satan comes into his own. There he tempts Jesus three times, trying to lure him away from his appointed task (Matt. 4). He tries to get the apostle Peter to talk Jesus out of going to Jerusalem. "Get behind me, Satan!" Jesus yells to a very surprised disciple (Matt. 16:23). After all, Peter had just a moment before heard Jesus say, "Blessings on you." Peter must have learned his lesson, because in his first letter he warns that "the devil prowls about like a hungry lion, seeking someone to devour" (1 Pet. 5:8). It was Satan who "entered into Judas" (Luke 22:3), prompting him to betray Jesus. He is all over the apostle Paul in the book of Acts. James assures us that if we "resist the devil he will flee from [us]" (James 4:7).

In Revelation things really heat up. The devil-inspired antichrist (see Antichrist) takes over the world for a time. At the Second Coming, Satan is "bound" for a thousand years while the earth gets its breath back (Rev. 20:2). He is released to try again (Rev. 20:7–10) before finally being thrown into "the lake of fire … there to be tormented for ever and ever."

Who is this creature? Where did he come from, and why does God allow all this carnage?

According to the Christian reading of the Hebrew scriptures, Satan once held the position of top angel. His name back then was Lucifer, the "Morning Star" or "Son of the Morning." In the famous lament of Ezekiel 28, God, while addressing the king of Tyre, really speaks to Lucifer:

> You were the model of perfection,
> Full of wisdom and perfect in beauty.
> You were in Eden, the garden of God;
> Every precious stone adorned you….
> On the day you were created they were prepared.
> You were anointed as a guardian cherub, for so I ordained you.
> You were on the holy mount of God….
> You were blameless in your ways from the day you were created till wickedness was found in you….
> So I drove you in disgrace from the mount of God and I expelled you, O guardian cherub….
> Your heart became proud on account of your beauty….
> So I threw you to earth.

Thus it is that Isaiah can cry:

> How you have fallen from heaven,
> O Lucifer, son of the morning.
> You have been cast down to earth,
> You who once laid low the nations!
> You said in your heart,
> "I will ascend to heaven,
> I will raise my throne above the stars of God,
> I will sit enthroned….
> I will ascend,
> I will make myself like the most high."(Isa. 14:12–15)

Why does God allow Lucifer, now called Satan, to have such power? According to the apostle Paul, at least as interpreted by conservative theologians, it's all part of God's eternal plan. The argument runs along these lines: God knew sin was bad because God knows everything. But the rest of the angels had never seen sin before.

They didn't know why saying "I will" five times to God was such a bad thing. If Satan was simply destroyed, the remaining angels would spend eternity in fear of meeting the same fate as him and the fallen angels who were now called demons. God wanted love in heaven, not fear. So how could God show the angels how bad sin is without endangering heavenly harmony?

A planet was cleared off and prepared as a sin laboratory. Humans were created. Satan was confined to work his wiles for a few thousand years—just long enough to make a real impression. Humans fell. But God proved that he was big enough to take the penalty upon himself. Jesus, the second person of the divine Trinity, died for humans and took their punishment. About six thousand years after the Fall, the lesson will end at the battle of Armageddon. Satan will get the punishment he richly deserves, and the angels, whom Paul calls principalities and powers, entrenched within the human system, will come to understand. Satan and his demons fell victim to temptation, but the lesson is eternally imprinted upon the minds of those who keep the faith.

It's a little unclear exactly when Satan and his demonic host were cast out of heaven. Some say it happened before the creation of humans, right in the middle of the first verse of the Bible, when "the earth was without form and void." In this version, God created a perfect world, but the world "became" (instead of "was") "without form and void." On the other hand, Jesus claims to have seen Lucifer's fall after the disciples were sent out on their first evangelistic mission in Luke 10:18. And in Revelation 12:9, we are told that the "great dragon was hurled down—that ancient serpent called the devil, or Satan, who leads the whole world astray. He was hurled to the earth, and his angels with him." According to futurists, this event isn't scheduled until near the end of human history.

It is often argued that these are three views of the same event, seen from three different perspectives in time. Many, however, are not happy with that explanation. They would prefer a clearer definition of the most significant event in human history. The Bible, however, offers no further comment.

Regardless of the timing, this is how Paul sums up the whole experiment in Ephesians 3: "Although I am less than the least of all the apostles, this grace was given me: to preach to the Gentiles the unsearchable riches of Christ, and to make plain to everyone the administration of this mystery, which for ages past was kept hidden in God, who created all things. His intent was that now, through the church, the manifold wisdom of God should be made known to the principalities and powers in the heavenly realms, according to his eternal purpose which he accomplished in Christ Jesus our Lord."

Humans are rewarded, of course. After all, they were the innocent victims of the whole thing. In the end, angels are made to serve them. Angels are created beings. But humans, although also created beings, are adopted into God's own family as part of the plan that eventually destroys Satan.

Do all Christians accept this version of the story? Of course not. Christians don't all agree about anything. Nor, as noted earlier, is the devil an exclusively Christian concept. The texts from Genesis, Ezekiel, and Isaiah are, after all, Jewish texts.

Muslims have a similar story, although it takes a different turn. In their version Iblis, the Satan figure, loves God too much. When the angels are told to bow down to humans, Iblis refuses. It's not because of pride, as in the Judeo-Christian version. It's just that he loves God too much to bow down to anyone else. So Iblis is cast out of the presence of his beloved. And how does he console himself for all eternity? By remembering the sound of his beloved's voice and the last words his beloved said to him. And what were those words? "Go to hell!"

One interesting question remains: If Satan is a fallen angel, why does he look so different from the traditional Hallmark image of cherubs? The image of Satan has changed with the times. Somewhere along the line, probably as a result of Christians' associating him with pagan images, he developed horns, a pointed tail, and a pitchfork. (Lately he has been pictured more as a slick lawyer with contracts for human souls in his briefcase.) Sometimes he is said to take great delight in torturing the damned in the fires of hell. None of this is found in the Bible. Hell is Satan's final punishment, not his domain.

Sources:
The Holy Bible, New International Version. Grand Rapids, MI: Zondervan, 1978.
Hymns for the Living Church. Carol Stream, IL: Hope, 1978.

DINOSAURS, EXTINCTION OF

Geologists separate the earth's history into eras, periods, and epochs according to the flora, fauna, and geology that characterize each time frame. One period, the Cretaceous (from the Greek word *kreta*, chalk), lasted from 146 million years ago to 65 million years ago. It was followed by the Tertiary period, which ended only 1.8 million years ago. The geologic boundary separating these two periods, the "line in the sand," so to speak, that marks where one ended and the other began, is called the K-T boundary.

In the late 1970s the father-son team of Luis and Walter Alvarez, along with other scientists from the University of California, were studying the K-T boundary in exposed geological strata in Gubbio, Italy. The clay boundary deposits contained an unusually high amount of iridium, a rare element found most often in cosmic dust from outer space. Iridium is also suspected to exist in slightly higher concentrations in the earth's core, probably trapped there when the planet was very young and largely molten. But wherever iridium is found, the immediate assumption is that it was brought here from space, probably as a result of a meteorite impact.

Further research at different locations around the world showed that wherever the K-T boundary was exposed and examined, iridium was present in above-average amounts. The Alvarezes suggested that a large asteroid (see Asteroids; Comets; Meteors, Meteoroids, and Meteorites) must have hit the earth, depositing a uniform layer of iridium-bearing dust around the planet. They theorized that this massive impact ended the Cretaceous period by destroying most of the flora and fauna of the earth. Massive fires broke out, depositing a layer of soot along with the iridium. The dust and smoke probably obscured the sun for years, making it very difficult for plants, and the animals that ate the plants, to survive. Some scientists estimate that 70 percent of all animal species became extinct as a result of the impact. Most if not all of the dinosaurs appear to have died out at this time. From the eras before the impact, fossilized dinosaur bones are found in great abundance. After the impact—nothing.

The response from other geologists to the Alvarezes' theory was immediate: "Show us the crater."

It wasn't until 1990 that a good candidate was found. A group of geophysicists led by Alan Hildebrand was looking for oil in the Yucatán Peninsula region of Mexico. What they found, quite by accident, was a massive impact ring some 180 kilometers (112 miles) in diameter. The geologic timing looked right. The size was sufficient. Could this have been the "big one" that killed off the dinosaurs and opened up an ecological niche for an emerging species called mammals?

In the time since the discovery, more and more scientists from many disciplines have been won over. Recent findings have supported the original hypothesis. It is now almost universally accepted that this impact either caused the dinosaurs' demise directly or, if they were already sliding toward extinction, provided the proverbial final straw.

New theories about the extinction surface regularly. For example, in January 2005 Dr. Arturo Casadevall, who researches infectious diseases at Albert Einstein College in New York, suggested that following the asteroid collision, "the Earth became a giant compost pile." The air, Casadevall proposed, might been thick with fungal spores that simply overwhelmed the immune systems of cold-blooded creatures. Warm-blooded animals, on the other hand, might have produced enough internal heat to kill off the fungal infections. The theory has a long way to go to gain approval in the scientific community, but it is at least on the table. Nicholas Money, a mold expert from Miami University of Ohio, calls it "a beautifully creative suggestion." Others, however, point out that we have never proved conclusively that dinosaurs were cold-blooded.

Did fungi kill off the dinosaurs? We will probably never know for sure, but one thing is certain: Whatever the cause or causes, Armageddon came to the world of the dinosaurs.

Dinosaurs had been the principal vertebrates on earth for millions of years. They had dominated the planet. Perhaps they had overutilized their environment. Maybe they had depleted their natural resources. They might have been able to evolve and recover. But they were at the top of the food chain. And in a geologic moment, they were gone.

The questions follow logically: What about another species that has dominated the planet during its recent history? What about another species that may be overutilizing its resources, creating out-of-control technology, or even overpopulating itself out of existence? Could human beings, like the dinosaurs, disappear in a geologic moment? In a few million years, might some new creature as yet unknown develop the intelligence to find fossilized human bones and wonder what became of a species that once ruled the planet?

If past experience is any indication, the answer is, undeniably, yes. Now that one massive extinction event has been shown to be a distinct possibility, others have been examined. It could very well be that early dinosaurs were given an ecological niche in which to evolve because other species were eliminated in the far distant past. Trilobites, for instance, are not nearly as exciting or imposing as dinosaurs, but they could have been exterminated in an even larger Armageddon event millions of years before the first dinosaur ever saw the light of day.

Does the history of the earth consist of an order of creatures, or sometimes even a single species, growing to dominate the planet, only to meet up with a visitor from outer space that cleans house every few million years, creating an ecological niche for new species to develop? On one level it's a disturbing thought. On another, given the time frames involved, maybe it's simply the way nature works.

Sources:

Johnson, Carolyn Y. "Were the Dinosaurs Done In by Fungus?" http://www.boston.com/news/globe/health_science/articles/2005/02/22/were_the_dinosaurs_done_in_by_fungus/.

Steel, Duncan. *Rogue Asteroids and Doomsday Comets: The Search for the Million Megaton Menace That Threatens Life on Earth.* New York: John Wiley & Sons, 1995.

DISPENSATIONALISM

John Nelson Darby is regarded by many as the father of the theological system called dispensationalism. Between 1862 and 1882 he made seven trips to the United States from his home in England, significantly influencing key American fundamentalists such as Dwight L. Moody and Cyrus Ingerson Scofield (see Scofield, Cyrus Ingerson). These were the men who shaped the emerging movement of prophecy conferences and Bible schools that became extremely important in American fundamentalism between 1875 and 1920.

Darby's system was designed to give shape and organization to Bible history. Lewis Sperry Chafer and Charles C. Ryrie (see entries on each) are perhaps its best-known expositors, although some proponents claim that it goes all the way back to Augustine. Chafer, in his book *Dispensationalism*, defines the term this way: "Dispensationalism views the world as a household run by God. In His household-world God is dispensing or administering its affairs according to His own will and in various stages of revelation in the passage of time. These various stages mark off the distinguishably different economies in the outworking of His total purpose, and these different economies constitute the dispensation."

What Darby discovered was that God seems to have behaved in different ways at different times throughout history. The angry God of the Old Testament who tells Joshua to kill all the Canaanites seems totally at odds with the Jesus of the New Testament who tells his followers to turn the other cheek. How does one explain these differences? Darby posited seven different "dispensations," or periods during which God acts in a certain way consistent with human development at the time. During each period God tests humans in respect to a specific revelation of the divine will. According to the *Scofield Reference Bible* the seven are as follows:

1. Innocence (before the Fall described in Genesis 3).
2. Conscience (from the Fall until Noah).

3. Human government (from Noah to Abraham).
4. Promise (from Abraham to Moses).
5. Law (from Moses to Christ).
6. Grace (the Church Age).
7. Kingdom (the Millennium).

After the Millennium, humankind enters the Eternal State.

The *Scofield Reference Bible* and Dallas Theological Seminary have been the principal proponents of dispensational theology. When Hal Lindsey, a graduate of Dallas Theological Seminary, broke onto the evangelical scene in 1970 with his book *The Late Great Planet Earth*, dispensationalism made the *New York Times* best-seller list. Overnight, it seemed, backed by countless other Dallas graduates who ministered to conservative Christian churches across the country, the system became a principal way to interpret scripture.

Christians have usually argued with each other as much as with non-Christians, and followers of dispensational theology and covenant theology (see Covenant) have often been at odds. The rhetoric often appears to the uninitiated to generate a lot more heat than light but it also demonstrates the fact that devotion to a theological system, be it dispensationalism or any other, is at the core of the many different and competing Christian denominations in the world today.

Dispensationalists believe that six dispensations have been completed. If so, the final one, the Millennium, might be just around the corner.

Sources:
Lightner, Robert. "Covenantism and Dispensationalism." [Dallas Theological Seminary] *Journal of Ministry and Theology* (fall 1999).
The Scofield Reference Bible. New York: Oxford University Press, 1945.

DOMINION THEOLOGY *see* **Christian Reconstructionism**

DOOMSDAY ARGUMENT

Philosophy usually doesn't offer predictions about what the future holds. Philosophers are good at synthesizing the past, not predicting the future. Philosophy deals with ideas, not numbers and dates.

But in 1989 an astrophysicist named Brandon Carter noticed something in a philosophical argument that proved to be quite disturbing. Although he didn't publish his finding, the philosopher John Leslie did. Leslie called it the Doomsday Argument because it seems to demonstrate by inescapable mathematical logic that the human race may be in its last days.

Carter's complicated argument has since proved very difficult to dispute. As many refutations have been published as have refutations of the refutations. Simply put, the problem is this: If you were to die and be reincarnated anywhere within the span of human existence from the first human to the last, would the chances of your being reincarnated in the first third of human existence be greater or less than of being reincarnated in the last two-thirds?

Statistically, the answer is obvious. There is a greater mathematical chance of being reincarnated in the last two-thirds because that's when most people would have lived.

Now take away the idea of being reincarnated. Simply consider the fact that you have been born somewhere, sometime, into the human race. This, of course, is exactly what has happened to you. You were born at a particular time and place and have no idea where that spot is on the time scale of human existence. Now ask yourself the original question. Are you more likely living in the first third or the last two-thirds of human existence? Just as before, the odds are greater that you are living in the last two-thirds. The mathematical probabilities remain the same.

Here's where the problem comes in. Given the history of human population growth, about 60 billion people have lived since the first human ancestor. Suppose we assume the earth's population will someday have to stabilize at 20 billion people, all having an average life expectancy of some seventy-five years. (These numbers are guesses, but a few years, or a few billion humans, one way or another won't make a great deal of difference in the final result.) If so, and if you are indeed among the last two-thirds of all humans who have ever lived, as probability suggests, then the human race will be extinct in roughly five hundred years.

Most people, when they first encounter this argument, intuitively feel that there ought to be some maddeningly simple way to refute it. But it proves to be very difficult indeed. Many have tried. As yet, they have not succeeded.

Source:

Bostrom, Nick. *Anthropic Bias: Observation Selection Effects in Science and Philosophy.* New York: Routledge, 2002.

Lin, Kevin. "The Doomsday Argument." http://www.greylabyrinth.com/puzzles/puzzle.php?puzzle_id=puzzle106.

DOOMSDAY CULTS

There are many cults whose members believe the world will someday come to an end. Most religions, after all, also fall into that category.

Some cults go one step farther and try to help bring about the end themselves.

In Japan, Shoko Asahara, an admirer of Adolf Hitler, believed that the world was going to come to an end during his lifetime. Partially blind from birth, he had attended a school for the blind. Failing to gain admission to a university, he became an acupuncturist, opening up a folk medicine shop in 1980. A true ecumenist, he studied Buddhism and Hinduism in the Himalayas and used insights gleaned from the book of Revelation in the Christian Bible and the writings of the sixteenth-century mystic Nostradamus to attract some twenty thousand followers worldwide. The word *Aum* is the Japanese version of the famous Hindu mantra *Om*, chanted by priests in meditation. *Shinri kyo* means "supreme truth." The cult that formed around Asahara became known as Aum Shinri Kyo.

Asahara claimed to have conversed with people from the year 2006. They had survived World War III he said, and they told him that the causes for that war were rooted in the materialism exemplified by the United States. Aum Shinri Kyo emphasized traditional Japanese values as opposed to the corrupting Western influence. As in most cults, an us-against-them feeling pervaded the group. They stockpiled biological and chemical weapons in preparation for the battle of Armageddon. Unfortunately, as reported by the *New York Times*, they also used them. Cult members staged at least nine attacks in Japan, with targets including the Diet (the national legislature), the Imperial Palace, the U.S. base at Yokosuka, and various individuals who had opposed Asahara. The most infamous incident was the March 20, 1995, release of Sarin nerve gas in the Tokyo subway system, killing twelve people.

Nearly two hundred members of the group have been brought to trial, with many convicted of serious crimes, including murder. Several, including Asahara, were sentenced to death. Legal appeals continue as of this writing.

Sources:
"Aum Shinri Kyo." http://www.gbs.sha.bw.schule.te/tsld026.htm.
Robinson, B. A. "Aum Shinri Kyo (Supreme Truth)." http://www.religioustolerance.org/dc_aumsh. htm.

DR. STRANGELOVE; OR, HOW I LEARNED TO STOP WORRYING
AND LOVE THE BOMB *see* Hollywood Envisions THE END

DRAGON

And I saw an angel coming down out of heaven, having the key to the Abyss and holding in his hand a great chain. He seized the dragon, that ancient serpent, who is the devil, or Satan, and bound him for a thousand years. He threw him into the Abyss, and locked and sealed it over him, to keep him from deceiving the nations anymore until the thousand years were ended. After that, he must be set free for a short time. (Rev. 20:1–3)

In these verses from the final book of the Bible, Satan is identified as the "ancient serpent" that appeared in the very first book of the Bible. He is said to be the serpent who deceived Adam and Eve and so brought the calamity of sin upon the human race—the calamity that will culminate in the battle of Armageddon and the defeat of the dragon (see Devil).

According to Joseph Campbell in *The Power of Myth*, a negative view of dragons is a Western phenomenon. Western mythology, dating back to the time of the Arthurian legends, pictures the dragon as an evil force involved in two principal activities. Dragons steal treasure and abduct young maidens. They take both back to the dragon lair to guard them. They don't do anything with either of them. They just guard them. In order to obtain the dragon's hoard and rescue the maiden, a gallant knight has to slay the dragon. Western psychological therapy consists of slaying the dragons of fear and resentment that guard the hidden joy (gold) and innocence (young maidens) of our inner life. By skillful counseling, the therapist coaxes the dragon out into the light of day where it can be defeated, releasing the inner secrets of potentiality languishing in the caves of the psyche.

A dragon in the classic European mold. *Fortean Picture Library.*

There are Christian sects in Appalachia whose members regularly end church services by draping rattlesnakes around their necks to prove their supremacy over the dreaded "serpents" that have represented sin ever since the third chapter of Genesis was written. In chapter 21 of the book of Numbers, when the children of Israel were threatened by an epidemic of snakes in the wilderness, Moses told them to wrap a bronzed serpent around a pole in the middle of the camp. Anyone bitten by a poisonous serpent had only to look at the bronze serpent on the pole in order to be healed. That image has since become the symbol of the medical profession. When Jesus remembered this incident in John 3, he told Nicodemus the Pharisee: "Just as Moses lifted up the snake in the desert, so the son of man must be lifted up, that everyone who believes in him may have eternal life."

In Eastern cultures, however, dragons represent vitality. They are the masculine in both male and female that roars out into daylight, thumping its chest, ready for whatever challenges await. In the West, snakes, a diminutive form of dragon, have always been something to destroy. But in India, priestesses will actually lure a snake out of its lair and kiss it three times on the head to bring rain to the parched earth.

In Revelation, the dragon is very definitely given a Western personification. He is "that ancient serpent," the devil. He is the reason for the battle of Armageddon, the power behind all that is evil.

Sources:
Campbell, Joseph, with Bill Moyers. *The Power of Myth*. New York: Doubleday, 1988.
The Holy Bible, New International Version. Grand Rapids, MI: Zondervan, 1978.

DREAMS *see* **Visions and Dreams**

DREAMTIME

Although it is difficult for most Westerners to grasp, Australian Aborigines have no traditional concept of the passing of time. Until relatively recently their language had no way of expressing what Westerners refer to as the "arrow" or "river" of time.

This idea made its way into the movie that introduced many Americans to Australian culture, *Crocodile Dundee*. The hero of the movie, Mick "Crocodile" Dundee, while answering a question about how old he is, confesses that he doesn't know. He says that he once asked a tribal elder when he was born. The answer he received was, "In the summertime."

So in traditional Aborigine culture, there will never be an Armageddon in the sense of a destruction of the whole world. There can be, and probably has been, a cultural Armageddon—an ending to something that once was. But the world itself is only an expression of what Aborigines call the "Dreamtime," which is eternal reality.

Australian Aborigines trace their religion to prehistoric times. In their belief system, everything that exists is part of a vast, interlocking network, a relationship beginning with the ancestors of the Dreamtime. The Dreamtime continues today, of course, and is accessible to people when they "dream the fire," or enter into spiritual communion with the invisible plane supporting the visible one.

The power of Aboriginal spirituality has been called both telepathic and mystical, in direct contrast to typical Western pragmatism. When Europeans discovered and exploited Australia, they considered the Aborigines primitive people in need of being elevated to modern cultural standards. Typically, the rich Australian spiritual heritage, completely unappreciated, misunderstood, and underestimated by the newcomers, was regarded as nothing more than superstition. Only in the late twentieth century did it begin to dawn on Westerners that Aborigines understood the dangers inherent in the trajectory of modern society far better than their European counterparts. When anxieties and stresses built up, when life became too complex and needed some perspective, it was the habit in Australia to "go walkabout," to pare down and sort things out, to spend an open-ended amount of time simply "being" until perspective was regained. Aboriginal religion intuitively understood that life can sometimes layer up, making it difficult to remain connected with the very essence of the Dreamtime, the feeling of what it means to be alive, in touch with all things. Through mythology, through the ritual of the dance, accompanied by the unique sounds of the didgeridoo or clap sticks, through the very act of observing, living close upon the sparse land in ways no Westerner could, Aborigines experienced their religion moment by moment. When they came together to share their histories, telling the old stories, they released the power of the Dreamtime into present-day reality, informing new generations and carrying on the wisdom of the ancestors.

Gathering of Australian Aborigine tribal elders, 1948. *Associated Press/Wide World Photo.*

Of course there existed those Aborigines who abused Dreamtime, walkabout, and the spiritual heritage that existed in Australia. There can be found, within the culture, abuse of women, laziness, drunkenness, and lack of direction, just as in any other culture. Probably no religious tradition has ever existed that personified a "golden age" when everyone was wise and spiritually fully developed. But spiritual traditions must be judged on their merits, not on their problem children. Dreamtime connected people with their heritage, supporting and informing countless generations of people over the course of thousands of years. Aboriginal customs have stood the test of time, coming to the aid of people who have seen their world turned upside down in a matter of a few short years. And Dreamtime is validated when people feel the pressures of modern life and want to establish spiritual roots in a fast-changing world. When those pressures build up and threaten to overcome us, when too much information floods our souls, perhaps we all need to "go walkabout" or spend some quiet time "dreaming the fire." It is a directly opposite response to that of those who simply hunker down to await a coming Armageddon.

Sources:
Aboriginal Art and Culture Centre. "The Dreamtime." http://aboriginalart.com.au/culture/
   dreamtime.html.
Willis, Jim. *The Religion Book: Places, Prophets, Saints, and Seers.* Detroit: Visible Ink Press, 2004.

DRUIDIC VIEW OF HISTORY

Ancient Druids considered the earth to be a living, breathing entity. People were among the players in a great drama. Whether or not they accomplished their goals was almost insignificant. In the sacred groves and around the night fires, in the daily life of local villagers, the earth was to be appeased and caressed, not exploited. Druids claimed to be in touch with a completely different spirituality than that experienced by most modern humans.

Armageddon could not come to Mother Earth, but it definitely came to Druid culture. Their Armageddon event was imposed upon them by a Roman general named Julius Caesar. He was the one who first wrote about Druids. He considered them to be the intellectuals of their tribes and culture. They were judges, diviners, and mediators with the gods. But Celtic religion was widespread and varied from land to land. Lugh, the "shining light," Teutates, "god of the tribe," Andastra, Belenus, Artio ("the bear"), Camulos, Cernunnos ("the horned one," lord of the animals), and Vasio all had their followings.

As with many indigenous religions, gods had their own locations. A god of the grove sacred to one tribe might be recognized by another tribe but not worshiped because the god didn't live nearby. Instead the second tribe might worship the god of the lake where they lived.

Celtic religious practice exemplifies an important theological truth about cultural Armageddon events. When gods or spirits arise within the context of a particular place, the people connect with their environment and treat it accordingly. People who worship in this manner, whether they are European Celts, Japanese Shinto, or American Indians, know that their environment is their cathedral. They live in their church, the home of their god. This kind of connection cements the bond between the land and the people. To cut down the sacred grove of the Druids, to kill the buffalo of the Dakota people, to strip-mine a Cherokee mountaintop is religious blasphemy. It brings a symbolic Armageddon to the culture. Indigenous religion cannot be transported to another place. Missionaries cannot carry it with them to indoctrinate a new culture.

Historically, people of the Jewish, Christian, and Islamic traditions have often failed to understand this simple, but profound, truth. When they did understand it, they usually exploited it. A people cut off from the ground of its being, its god, is a defeated people. Julius Caesar understood. When he burned the Druids' sacred groves and toppled their standing stones, he tore the soul out of the Celtic people, and with it their will to resist. He brought Armageddon to one of the world's oldest religions.

Celtic religion went underground, practiced by old women who remembered herb lore and snatches of forgotten prayers and rituals. It was found in men's secret societies and existed in overgrown roadside shrines in the hollow hills of dim legend and folklore.

Only now, through the patient work of archeologists, are we beginning to discover how much was lost. Modern neo-Druidic cells are beginning to surface. In some cases they are even listed among the local churches. They bring progressive, science-based ideas to old Druidic practices. They keep the old holy days and try to under-

A Druidic sacrifice at Stonehenge as envisioned by an eighteenth-century artist. *Fortean Picture Library.*

stand as much as they can about the ancient ways. They try to connect once again with Mother Earth and recognize the earth-based spirituality that empowered their spiritual ancestors. They are no longer secretive societies that meet in the dark. Most welcome sincere seekers and hope to build upon what they have inherited from one of the world's oldest religions. In this sense, Julius Caesar's Armageddon opened the door, millennia later, for a new Druid world.

Sources:
Ár nDraíocht Féin: A Druid Fellowship. http://www.adf.org.
James, Simon. *The World of the Celts.* New York: Thames and Hudson, 1993.
Jones, Prudence, and Nigel Pennick. *A History of Pagan Europe.* New York: Routledge, 1995.

DUALISM

The philosophy of dualism sees the world as consisting of pairs of opposites. For every up, there is a down. For every hot, a cold. The philosophy is so common in Western civilization that few people question a news program that promises to present "both sides" of an issue—as if there were only two sides to present.

Dualism is a relatively recent way of viewing the world. It springs from the first monotheistic religion, Zoroastrianism (see Zoroastrianism). This is the religion that first gave the world a good god versus a bad devil. Belief in this duality passed on to Judaism, and then to both Christianity and Islam.

Even Joseph Campbell, the father of modern pop-mythology, steeped in ancient traditions as he was, confessed to Bill Moyers on the PBS special *The Power of Myth* that "things come in pairs of opposites." Campbell recognized that Western religious traditions tend to side with one of the pairs—the good—against the other. He believed that the Hindu and, especially, the Buddhist traditions are more correct when they advise finding what the Buddha called the "Middle Way" past the pairs of opposites to that which lies beyond them both. But he definitely saw the world as existing in pairs of opposites.

This view of reality gave Western, monotheistic religions the concept of Armageddon (see Abraham and Monotheism). When a good God is pitted against an evil devil and placed within a boundary of time, someday they simply have to fight it out. That's what Armageddon is all about. Dualism attempts to explain why a good God would create a good world and then discover an evil cancer in the creation. The cancer must be cut out and eliminated. The devil must be defeated. Within the framework of dualism, Armageddon is inevitable.

Source:
Campbell, Joseph, with Bill Moyers. *The Power of Myth.* New York: Doubleday, 1988.

E

EARTH SHIFT

A visitor to the Petrified National Forest in the high plateau country of northeast Arizona has the opportunity to reach out and touch the petrified remains of gigantic trees that grew 200 to 250 million years ago. It seems impossible that such large trees could possibly grow in such a desert climate.

It seems impossible, and it is. When these trees were alive, they knew nothing of desert conditions. They didn't even live in the same latitudes. Back then, this part of the country was far to the south, close to the equator.

The explanation lies in the geographic mechanics of continental drift. When these trees were in the prime of their life, the continents of the world were, for all practical purposes, joined in one huge land mass that geologists call Pangea. As the eons spun, the land masses drifted apart. A close look at a world map reveals what can be interpreted as an immense jigsaw puzzle. The west coast of Africa seems to fit with the east coast of South America and the southeast United States. Australia looks as if it could slide into the large bay of Southeast Asia.

This is more than an illusion. Geologists believe that the continents of the world are afloat, as it were, on plates that are in constant motion. The Appalachians, an ancient chain of eastern mountains that were once as large as the mighty European Alps, were thrust upward by a long, slow collision between the plate on which the eastern United States rides and the plate supporting western Europe and Africa. Part of California is not really connected with the United States. It rests on its own plate west of the San Andreas Fault. The frequent earthquakes experienced there occur because, inch by shuddering inch, a large chunk of the state is slowly rubbing its way north toward Alaska. Similarly, as Dennis Smith, writing for the *New York Times*, reminds us, "Baja California is moving away from Mexico at the rate of two inches a year—and it has been doing so for four to six million years."

Plate tectonics, the study of continental drift, is a relatively new science. But evidence of such movement has not gone unnoticed. There are those who believe the process is, from time to time, drastically increased.

In 1958 Charles Hapgood, in his book *The Earth's Shifting Crust*, put forth the theory that the earth has repeatedly experienced a violent movement of its crust.

> An entire crust displacement, as the words suggest, is a movement of the ENTIRE outer shell of the earth over its inner layers. If you remove the peel from an orange and then reattach it to the fruit, you can visualize the possibility of the peel moving over the inner layers. The earth's crust can similarly change its position over the inner layers. When it does, the globe experiences climatic change. The climatic zones (polar, temperate and tropical) remain the same because the sun still shines on the earth from the same angle in the sky. From the perspective of people on the earth at the time, it appears as if the sky is falling. In reality it is the earth's crust shifting to another location. Some lands move towards the tropics. Others shift, with the same movement, toward the poles. Yet others may escape such great changes in latitude.

Immanuel Velikovsky, though often disparaged by those who accused him of popularizing, even "vulgarizing," a very complicated subject, painted an Armageddon-like picture of calamity and destruction in his best-selling book *Earth in Upheaval*:

> Let us assume, as a working hypothesis, that under the impact of a force or the influence of an agent—the axis of the earth shifted or tilted. At that moment an earthquake would make the globe shudder. Air and water would continue to move through inertia; hurricanes would sweep the Earth, and the seas would rush over the continents, carrying gravel and sand and marine animals, and casting them onto land. Heat would be developed, rocks would melt, volcanoes would erupt, lava would flow from fissures in the ruptured ground and cover vast areas. Mountains would spring up from the plains and would climb and travel over the shoulders of other mountains, causing faults and rifts. Lakes would be tilted and emptied, rivers would change their beds; large land areas and all their inhabitants would slip under the sea. Forests would burn, and the hurricanes and wild seas would wrest them from the ground on which they grew and pile them, branch and root, in heaps. Seas would turn into deserts, their waters rolling away.

Some have turned to the Bible for answers. They wonder if perhaps Genesis 1 offers a description of earth shift. Genesis makes the claim that the waters of creation were separated into two locations. There were waters "above the firmament" and waters "below the firmament." Maybe, says one theory, a water canopy, possibly in the form of ice, surrounded the planet. Maybe Earth once had rings like Saturn. These would constitute the waters "above the firmament." This water canopy might have provided the waters that caused Noah's flood. Perhaps the whole planet was once perpendicular on its axis in relation to the sun, creating a "greenhouse effect," with moderate, constant seasons from pole to pole. That would explain the climate of the Garden of Eden and perhaps even account for the longer life spans of the early heroes of Genesis. All God had to do to set the flood in motion was to tilt the earth to its present 23.5 degrees. Then the whole canopy might have collapsed in the form of rain for forty days and forty nights. The earth's tilt gives us the seasons, after all. Perhaps it also explains why Genesis tells us that after the flood the earth would forever have "seed time and harvest, cold and heat, summer and winter … as long as the earth endures."

Most scientists, of course, reject these speculations. But although geologists have pretty well mapped out a probable scenario involving long periods of time and the slow movement of continental plates, the idea of a sudden earth shift still has its supporters and remains a popular theory of planetary Armageddon.

Sources:
Hapgood, Charles. *The Earth's Shifting Crust*. Foreword by Albert Einstein. New York: Pantheon, 1958.
Velikovsky, Immanuel. *Earth in Upheaval*. Garden City, NY: Doubleday, 1955.
Whitcomb, John C., and Henry Madison Morris. *The Genesis Flood: The Biblical Record and Its Scientific Implications*. Nashua, NH: P&R Press, 1989.

EARTHQUAKES IN VARIOUS PLACES

"The pillars of the heavens quake, aghast at his rebuke; by his power he churned up the sea" (Job).

"The waves of death swirled about me…. The valleys of the sea were exposed, and the foundations of the Earth were laid bare" (David).

"Your wrath lies heavily upon me; You have overwhelmed me with all your waves" (Jonah).

These biblical men of faith were quoted by Rabbi Jonathan Sacks in an article published in the *Times* of London on January 1, 2005, in response to the great Indian Ocean earthquake and tsunami that caused the injury and death of tens of thousands of people in the closing days of 2004. Sacks asks the haunting questions, "Why does God permit a tragedy such as the Indian Ocean Tsunami? Why does he allow the innocent to suffer and the guiltless to die?"

There are some who believe that events like this one must happen before the final days of history come to a close.

One of the "signs of the end" predicted by Jesus in his Olivet Discourse of Matthew 24 (see Olivet Discourse) was "earthquakes in various places." If it can be proved that earthquakes are indeed increasing, say the literalist Bible scholars, it will indicate we are living in the time of the end prior to the great battle of Armageddon.

Hal Lindsey, in his book *Apocalypse Code*, claims, without giving any corroborating data, that earthquakes in the twentieth century "killed more than 2 million people—or half the toll of all natural catastrophes put together! But it's going to get much worse."

A problem exists in deciding what constitutes increased earthquake activity. Do we go by the Richter scale, which measures severity? Do we count frequency? Or do we add up the death toll? An Armenian quake in 1988 killed more than 25,000 people but, on the Richter scale, was less severe than a 1991 quake in Soviet Georgia that killed only a few hundred people. The strongest quake on record occurred in Chile in 1960 but only killed some 10,000 people, if 10,000 people can be labeled "only." Although there were no instruments available to measure it, a quake in China in 1556 killed an estimated 830,000 people, making it by far the most deadly such event on record. There is no report of its producing an "end-of-the-world" hysteria, but probably not many of those who survived had ever read the gospel of Matthew.

The tragedy dubbed the Great American Earthquake is the one that occurred in San Francisco in 1906, although it couldn't hold a candle to the Good Friday quake in Alaska that resulted in far fewer deaths while measuring much stronger on the Richter scale. Meanwhile, for sheer marketing appeal, it's hard to beat the only earthquake ever to have been broadcast live on television during prime time. It struck the Bay Area during the 1989 World Series—which, ironically, pitted the teams of San Francisco and Oakland. The Series was postponed for nine days.

Folks in California regularly chat about the quake they call the "Big One." That's the monster earthquake most people think is coming. Of course, no one knows when. Some claim that Las Vegas gamblers have established a secret betting line that involves both magnitude and date of occurrence, but no one seems to be able to confirm the fact.

Has Jesus' prediction of "earthquakes in various places" come to pass? The answer to this question is, as with so many other endtime predictions, up for grabs.

Sources:
Cohen, Daniel. *Prophets of Doom: The Millennium Edition.* Brookfield, CT: Millbrook Press, 1999.
The Holy Bible, New International Version. Grand Rapids, MI: Zondervan, 1978.
Lindsey, Hal. *Apocalypse Code.* Palos Verdes, CA: Western Front Ltd., 1997.
Sacks, Jonathan. "What Was God Thinking?" *Times* (London), January 1, 2005.

ECOLOGICAL EXPLOITATION

A group of people move into a vast and varied land offering seemingly abundant resources and almost unlimited potential. Settling down, they devise new ways to exploit and channel their newfound wealth. They invent farming techniques adapted to the area and soon begin to grow more food than they can possibly use. Eventually their population mushrooms and a housing boom develops. Builders are kept busy planning ever-larger communities. Specialization of trade ensures jobs for everyone. The culture changes over the course of a few hundred years. Trade with places near and far creates a river of exotic articles flowing into and out of the cities and towns. Commerce translates yesterday's luxuries into today's necessities. Religion flourishes and a class of priests grows ever stronger. It seems as though a never-ending string of tomorrows will stretch out into a future that looks better and better in every way.

Then something begins to worry a few people in positions of power. Each year the crop yields drop just a little. There is always an excuse. Last year didn't see quite enough rainfall. The earth seems to be a little more barren. Natural resources are

Anasazi ruins at Mesa Verde, Colorado. *Nick Nicholson/Getty Images.*

being used up. Fuel is harder to come by. It seems as if each year is warmer than the last. Weather patterns change. Once clean-flowing and clear, rivers seem to be polluted and empty of life.

At first the differences are made up through a healthy trade balance. But prices, controlled by supply and demand, begin to rise. The standard of living drops. Young people begin to leave home, traveling to places where a better life seems to beckon—where there are more opportunities for employment. The crime rate rises. People who have less and less begin to look with envy on those who have more. Two social classes, the haves and the have-nots, begin to form.

In these times of confusion, people turn to religion. They ask their priests to intervene with higher powers. The priests respond with increasingly severe fundamentalism. There is a movement to get back to the old ways, sing the old songs, bring back the old days—the better days. The young people, it is said, have forgotten the right ways to live. Discipline! Order! Time-tested wisdom! Those are the watchwords from the priests. They warn that Armageddon is just around the corner unless the populace repents.

Eventually God orders people to go to war over resources. "God is on our side," declare the priests. Those in power say that vital resources of fuel and food may rightly be taken even when they exist a long way off in someone else's country. As in all wars, atrocities occur. Innocent people die, sometimes horribly. A way of life comes to an end.

When the smoke clears, all the people are gone. The land lies desolate— overused, dried up, and empty. Armageddon has come in its own way. A culture lies in ruin.

Although this might sound like a sociologist's prophecy of doom for modern America, it is, in fact, an accurate portrayal of what probably occurred in the Four Corners region of the Southwest three centuries before Columbus made his epic voyages. Near the area of the United States where Arizona, Utah, Colorado, and New Mexico touch each other under a small monument, a flourishing culture practiced an enriching way of life that lasted for centuries. Americans called them "cliff dwellers" in the nineteenth century and "Anasazi" in the twentieth. *Anasazi* is a Navajo word meaning "enemy ancestors." The Hopi and Zuni people of Arizona and New Mexico believe themselves to be descendants of these people and are understandably troubled by such a name. Rather than have their ancestral identity classified by Navajos—who didn't arrive in the area until just before the Spanish—they have recently fought for and won the title now used by historical anthropologists and academics—"Ancestral Puebloans." Although the term is used widely in both the academic and marketing worlds, most laypeople are still more familiar with either "cliff dwellers" or "Anasazi."

We will probably never know what these people called themselves. But anthropologists believe that in the middle of the thirteenth century there were more people in southwestern Colorado than live there today. It was a huge, flourishing culture that had perfected the art of dry farming to a degree unknown anywhere else in the world. At the end of the thirteenth century the largest city in North America was in Chaco Canyon, in what is now New Mexico. Its principal structure was an "apartment" building with some six hundred rooms—the biggest in what is now the United States until 1882, when one in New York City finally eclipsed it in size.

The inhabitants of Mesa Verde in Colorado, Chaco Canyon in New Mexico, Walnut Canyon in Arizona, and Monument Valley in Utah traded with people who lived at least as far away as California, Peru, the Mississippi River Valley, and Minnesota. They built four- and five-story buildings and had developed the science of astronomy far beyond what most laypeople understand today. They were a sophisticated, urban, artistic, and scientific people.

By the fifteenth century they were gone, leaving behind only their empty buildings, artifacts, dry irrigation canals, and curious petroglyphs to mystify those who would, a few centuries later, stumble upon the relics of their culture, gaze in awe, and wonder what happened.

To this day, no one is really sure. For years students were taught that a thirty-year drought brought an end to the Anasazi dry-farming culture. Dry farming is risky at best. It depends on prudent use of what water is available. A thirty-year drought would certainly wreak havoc and very probably be seen as a judgment from the gods, but the archeological record doesn't completely support this theory. Tree ring data and pollen counts indicate that there were other forces at work. A synthesis of the data seems to indicate the people simply exploited their environment beyond its ability to sustain them. Apparently they thought the earth was forever and didn't accurately see what they were doing to it.

The process of the Anasazi Armageddon began with population explosion. Too many people living on the land led to planting every available plot of ground with corn, beans, and squash. These are crops that demand a lot of water. As for meat, the Anasazi had domesticated the turkey, but the game animals that had once supplied much of the protein for their diet had been hunted out. Meanwhile, the forests and trees had long since been cut for cooking fires, building supplies, fuel for kilns to fire the beautiful pottery for which the people were famous, and warmth at night. In some instances, archeologists estimate, the people had to walk more than a day's journey just to collect firewood.

The groundwater was probably protected, but large populations quickly pollute surface streams and rivers. And the fact that natural vegetation had been stripped from the land meant that rains were no longer trapped and held in the soil by thick root systems. Runoff and erosion were inevitable.

For a while, trade made up the difference. Anasazi infrastructure was not equaled in the United States for centuries. Straight as an arrow and sometimes up to thirty feet wide, roads connected towns and religious centers located hundreds of miles apart. There is even evidence of "motels" spaced at about a day's journey.

But archeological evidence of this environmental exploitation reveals the darker side of human nature. Apparently warfare broke out among once-friendly settlements, perhaps as a result of religious fundamentalism. Rather than face the consequences of their actions, the people may well have decided that their problems were theological rather than ecological. Caves and kivas filled with bodies, some showing evidence of ritualistic murder and even cannibalism, have been excavated, revealing their grisly story.

In short, it is entirely possible, and is the most accepted theory among archeologists studying this culture, that what began as environmental exploitation ended with the all-too-common human patterns of warfare and genocide. The people eventually migrated away to the southwest and southeast, following rivers to a new future. Their descendants, the Hopi to the west and Zuni to the east, still tell stories of their ancestors and carry on some of their cultural patterns. If this archeological theory is correct, the Hopi and Zuni represent by far the oldest architectural civilization in North America.

But perhaps the most important lessons the Anasazi have left to us are those of the dangers of environmental exploitation. The earth is not forever. Its ability to sustain us is not eternal. Ecological Armageddon can come even to flourishing cultures, and we ignore the lessons of the past at our peril.

Some influential environmentalists even wonder if it's already too late. In April of 2005 the Millennium Ecosystem Assessment, the results of a four-year study by the United Nations, was published. The final remarks are troubling, to say the least: "Human actions are depleting Earth's natural capital, putting such strain on the environment that the ability of the planet's ecosystem to sustain future generations can no longer be taken for granted." Writing about the results for the Cox Newspapers, columnist Tom Teepen concluded, "We don't know the carrying capacity of the biosphere. Somewhere out there, down the road, there's a tipping point that will tilt irretrievably toward collapse. And collapse can come suddenly and utterly."

Sources:

Ayer, Eleanor. *A Guide to the Anasazi and Other Ancient Southwest Indians.* Frederick, CO: Renaissance House, 1991.

Teepen, Tom. "No Fairy Dust for the Biosphere if It Collapses." *Daytona Beach News-Journal,* April 2, 2005.

Visiting Hopi. Second Mesa, AZ: Hopi Cultural Center, 2004.

Walnut Canyon. U.S. Department of the Interior: National Park Service, 2003.

EGYPT

The mysterious pyramids of Egypt have long been a focus of attention for those who wonder about the motivation of ancient builders. Egypt has long been the center of a rich mythology. Although much of that mythology remains hidden in the mists of history and the sands of time, enough still lives on to fuel speculation concerning the very early history of this illustrious land.

Surprisingly, although Egyptian religion evidenced an interest bordering on obsession with the future lives of its rulers, it seems to have given very little thought to the fate of the world itself. According to Egyptian mythology, the earth, like the pyramids, is going to stand forever.

That hasn't stopped the many imported religions that thrived in Egypt from speculating, according to their own traditions, about what is in store for the human race and planet Earth. Egypt may have grown its own religious system, but it served as a home base for many others.

Just before Alexander the Great died, after conquering much of the Western world, he was asked who was going to rule his kingdom. "Give it to the strong," he decreed. Ptolemy, one of the four principal generals who divided the newly won realms, became king of Egypt. In tribute to the memory of Alexander, he built the city of Alexandria. It soon became the most important center of learning on the African continent and the intellectual capital of the world. Its library contained an estimated 400,000 to 500,000 works, along with priceless treasures of art and antiquity. As scholars flocked there to study, a blend of Greek, Hebrew, Egyptian, Chaldean, and Persian mysticism developed.

In 48 BCE, Julius Caesar invaded Egypt. A fire, attributed to ships burning in the Alexandrian harbor, destroyed a major part of the collection of the library, but Alexandria still exerted a great intellectual influence over the Western world even after it became what amounted to a Roman province.

In the second century CE, Alexandria was an important center of Jewish learning and culture. Here scholars labored to translate the Hebrew Bible into Greek for the benefit of Jews living abroad. Their translation was eventually called the Septuagint because tradition states that it was the work of seventy scholars.

The pyramids of Giza as photographed by Francis Frith, ca. 1860. *Library of Congress.*

By the time the Roman Empire began to deteriorate, Alexandria was still second to Rome in prestige, but this was about to change. When Constantine, emperor of Rome, in the early fourth century declared Christianity the state religion, he made it the business of government to stamp out forms of what was then considered idolatry and paganism. That included literature. The ruler Theodosius called for the final destruction of paganism in 389 CE. Although the university in Alexandria struggled on, by 415 the frenzied, zealous religious mobs finally ruled. The wonderful library, along with its priceless scrolls and artifacts, was burned to the ground.

Many Greek and Egyptian texts, however, had been translated to Arabian and Syrian languages and carried to other universities and academic centers. When Muslim influence extended as far west as Spain and Morocco in the seventh and eighth centuries, much of the learning attributed to Islamic scholars was, in fact, knowledge that had been preserved from the time of the Alexandrian academic community.

Egyptian Christianity is traditionally attributed to the missionary efforts of the apostle Mark. He is generally credited with writing the second gospel of the New Testament, although many modern scholars question his authorship. Egypt became the home and final battleground of Gnosticism, an early Christian philosophy later declared heretical. Gnostics believed that Jesus imparted a secret knowledge, or "gnosis," to a select group of apostles. Some of their writings, most notably the gospel of Thomas, were among the most acclaimed archeological treasures discovered in the twentieth century.

Origen, writing from Alexandria in the third century, was one of the first Christian scholars to treat biblical passages metaphorically rather than literally:

> Now what man of intelligence will believe that the first and the second and the third day, and the evening and the morning existed without the sun and the moon and the stars? And that the first day, if we may so call it, was even without a heaven? And who is so silly as to believe that God, after the manner of a farmer, "planted a paradise eastward in Eden," and set in it a visible and palpable "tree of life," of such a sort that anyone who tasted its fruit with his bodily teeth would gain life; and again that one could partake of "good and evil" by masticating the fruit taken from the tree of that name? And when God is said to "walk in the paradise in the cool of the day" and Adam to hide himself behind a tree, I do not think anyone will doubt that these are figurative expressions which indicate certain mysteries through a semblance of history and not through actual events.

Origen's concept of biblical prophecy as metaphor calls into question the idea that early Christians unanimously viewed prophecy as foretelling the future.

Augustine, bishop of Hippo in North Africa, spokesman for the Egyptian Christian tradition, agreed with Origen. He believed that the Greek Neoplatonists were right when they described a universal, cosmic hierarchy descending from an eternal, intelligible God. Reading the Bible as metaphorical, rather than literal, history, he was moved by the fall of Rome in 410 CE to write *The City of God*. In it he criticized what he called pagan religious natural philosophy because rumors were circulating among the Christian community that Rome fell because it had deserted its ancient religion. Augustine disputed these rumors and described two cities built on different kinds of love. The earthly city is built on love of self. The city of God is built on love of God. Although they intermingle, they are at war. Earthly cities are destined to fall. But in the end, the city of God will remain forever. To Augustine, the Second Coming of Christ could best be described as an earthly triumph of the spirit of love over the spirit of selfishness.

All this is to say that even though theologians of Judaism, Christianity, and Islam all studied and wrote in Egypt—even though they debated long and hard concerning the end of the Christian age and what the battle of Armageddon really meant—the indigenous religious tradition of the land they called home, Egypt, continued to be that the earth, like the great monuments and tombs of the past, was forever.

Sources:

Bridger, David, ed. *The New Jewish Encyclopedia*. New York: Behrman House, 1962.

Douglas, J. D., ed. *The New International Dictionary of the Christian Church*. Grand Rapids, MI: Zondervan, 1974.

Fisher, Mary Pat, and Lee W. Bailey, eds. *An Anthology of Living Religions*. Upper Saddle River, NJ: Prentice Hall, 2000.

Origen. "On First Principles." In *Readings in Christian Thought*, ed. Hugh T. Kerr. Nashville: Abingdon Press, 1966.

Willis, Jim. *The Religion Book: Places, Prophets, Saints, and Seers*. Detroit: Visible Ink Press, 2004.

EINSTEIN, ALBERT

If the end of the world comes about through the destructive power of nuclear weapons, Albert Einstein will certainly be one of the prominent figures named to carry the burden of guilt. Ironically, he was a politically active pacifist who warned against the dangers of nuclear war.

That Einstein was the reigning genius of his day in theoretical physics goes without saying. He set the standard against which others in the field are measured.

His connections involving the politics of nuclear war are well documented. He signed the influential letter to President Franklin D. Roosevelt that proved to be the deciding factor in the U.S. government's decision to take seriously the exploration of building a nuclear bomb. But he also engaged in postwar political efforts to prevent its use ever again.

During World War I, Einstein was a professor in Berlin. He was so sickened by the loss of human life and destruction in that conflict that he became an important antiwar activist, advocating civil disobedience. He was very public in his efforts to persuade people to simply refuse to fight. These actions cost him a great deal in terms of professional respect. He was openly criticized and watched by his government.

Following the war he turned to the work of reconciliation. He urged countries to work toward a war-free future. It very quickly became difficult for him to visit the United States to give lectures. His government simply did not trust him. His response to this was to say, "Only two things are infinite: the universe and human stupidity; and I'm not sure about the universe."

Einstein was a nonreligious Jew. He didn't believe in the biblical conception of God taught by rabbis, but he often used "God language" to explain his ideas in understandable terms. Late in life, for instance, when confronted with the highly counterintuitive ideas of randomness that underlie quantum physics, he was heard to mutter, "God does not play dice with the universe." (Many years later, Stephen Hawking, Einstein's heir apparent in the field of theoretical physics, would answer, "Not only does God play dice with the universe, but he sometimes throws them where they cannot be seen!")

Despite Einstein's lack of belief in a biblical God, he was a staunch supporter of Zionism. His growing awareness of anti-Semitism in his native land following World War I led him to become a spokesman for Jewish rights. His efforts were so appreciated that he was offered the presidency of Israel in 1952. He declined, convinced he was too politically naive. "Equations," he said, "are more important to me, because politics is for the present, but an equation is something for eternity."

Public stances against war and for Zionism earned him a great deal of hatred in pre–World War II Germany. He was in America in 1933 when Hitler came to power. Einstein announced that he would not return home. The German government immediately raided his house, seized his papers, and confiscated his bank accounts. A banner

headline in a Berlin newspaper declared, "Good News from Einstein—He's Not Coming Back!"

As the Nazi threat grew, Einstein renounced pacifism. He came to believe that Hitler had to be stopped at any cost and that German scientists were close to building an atomic bomb. He began to lobby the United States government to build their own. The result was called the Manhattan Project and produced the detonation of the world's first atomic bomb. Even before the bomb was tested Einstein was arguing for international control of what he saw could quickly become a nuclear arsenal. "I know not what weapons World War III will be fought with," he said, "but World War IV will be fought with sticks and stones."

It is ironic that the one man most responsible for the creation of the nuclear age was also the man who best understood the terrible dilemma it would pose. He helped to hasten the development of the ultimate weapon of mass destruction even while lobbying against its use. And although confident of the good intentions of his adopted country, he helped make possible the reality that the United States, while at the forefront in the battle against nuclear proliferation and destruction, would be the only nation so far to have ever used atomic

Albert Einstein (1879–1955) in the 1930s. *Library of Congress/Wide World Photo.*

weapons in war against a civilian population. In this sense, Albert Einstein, the pacifist, can also be called the world's ultimate warrior.

Sources:

Hawking, Stephen W. *A Brief History of Time: From the Big Bang to Black Holes.* New York: Bantam, 1988.

Online source for quotations: http://www.theparticle.com/quotes.html.

ENDTIMES

The word *endtimes* (or *endtime*)—sometimes spelled as two words, sometimes hyphenated—is relatively new to the English language. It appears to date back no more than about a century, at least in its common religious meaning. But today it is sprinkled throughout the Christian literature of all denominations.

Evangelical Protestants use the term to signify the last days of history just before the return of Jesus Christ (see Second Coming). It is associated with the the Rapture, the battle of Armageddon, and the Millennium (see entries on each).

Roman Catholic teaching declares that the endtimes are bracketed by the first and second advents of Christ. Catholic theologians disagree with those Protestants who believe that there will be a Millennium accompanied by various events such as the Rapture or Great Tribulation. Instead, they say that the Christian church is like a seed that will blossom into an everlasting kingdom on earth as it already is in heaven. This is the meaning of the phrase in the Lord's Prayer, often called the "Our Father" in Catholic tradition: "Thy kingdom come, on earth as it is in heaven." In other words, Catholic teaching is that we are living in the endtimes and have been ever since the birth of Christ.

While evangelical Protestants use the word to describe only the last days of church history, there is another school of thought within Protestantism that understands every time to be an endtime. "Prophetic" preaching is that which speaks to institutionalized, entrenched evil in every age. When Dr. Martin Luther King Jr. declared, "I have a dream," he was speaking about the endtimes of racism. Whenever a prophet, Christian or otherwise, seeks to overthrow that which suppresses any group of people, the endtimes are upon us.

In that sense of the word, the "endtimes" will last as long as human sin and oppression.

Source:
"Endtimes, Millennium, Rapture." http://www.ewtn.com/expert/answers/endtimes.htm.

ESCHATOLOGY, COMPARATIVE

Eschatology is the study or science dealing with the ultimate destiny or purpose of human beings and the world.

Monotheistic traditions generally think in terms of a definite and concrete start to time and a final, cataclysmic, end. Christianity offers a striking example. Jesus is purported to have said, "I am the Alpha and the Omega, the Beginning and the End" (Rev. 21:6). Alpha is the first letter of the Greek alphabet, the language in which the New Testament was written. Omega is the final letter. Jesus was saying he was the A and the Z, hence, "the Beginning and the End."

The monotheistic religions tend to agree on some general ideas about the end—for instance, it is usually seen as involving the triumph of good over evil—but differ somewhat about the details, as the following list (given in order of the religions' historical conception) illustrates.

ZOROASTRIANISM. The earth is a snare made by Ahura Mazda, the good god, to trap the evil being Ahriman. After a final judgment at the end of time, the world will be remade into a beautiful paradise inhabited by those who, having passed the test of temptation, remain true. Those who have failed will face the fires of hell. But those fires are not eternal. Instead, they will burn away the evil, purifying the victim, even as they purify and cleanse the earth itself.

JUDAISM. The people of the earth, created by God, will go through many trials until finally the Messiah will come to usher in paradise and unlock the divine potential found in each person. Eden will be restored. Even the "law of the jungle" will be super-seded. Lions and lambs will lie down together in peace. The earth will be "full of the knowledge of the Lord as the waters cover the sea" (Isa. 11:9). Reincarnation is possible within Jewish thinking but is a hotly debated subject. The Zohar, a text written in the fifteenth century, teaches that bodies can be reincarnated. Earlier texts, especially those written BCE, tend to teach that reincarnation is pagan nonsense. Instead, they present the view that individual souls will be reunited with their bodies at the coming of the Messiah. Evidence of this teaching can be vividly seen in Jerusalem today. Many bodies are buried in the cemetery outside the gate through which the Messiah is expected to enter upon his arrival on earth.

CHRISTIANITY: *Conservative Protestant branches.* In the fullness of time, the Messiah, Jesus the Christ, came and offered humankind a chance for reconciliation with God. But he was rejected and crucified. He will come again and judge the people of the earth. He will establish peace and reign for a thousand years, at the end of which Satan, the evil one, will be destroyed. Earth will be re-created as it was originally intended to be before the fall of humankind, and a "heavenly Jerusalem" will descend to serve as the Christ's capital. The leaves of the tree of life, forbidden to humans after the expulsion from Eden, will now serve "for the healing of the nations. No longer will there be any curse" (Rev. 22:2, 3).

Liberal Protestant branches. Jesus of Nazareth showed humankind how to live in love and peace but was crucified for his efforts. His life and death became an example, illustrating how humans should live. Even though they may die in the attempt, God will make their lives count because good will eventually triumph over evil. The spirit of Jesus, even stronger in death than in life, lives on in those who choose to follow him. The mechanics of physical life on earth are subject to the laws of nature. Even though the earth will someday end through normal and measurable physical processes, all that Jesus was and is will continue in the human soul and spirit.

Roman Catholicism. The kingdom of God exists even now in heaven. Jesus Christ came to reproduce it on earth. The period between the first and second advents of Christ is the time during which the church is fulfilling its mission. The church, as Christ's body on earth, led by the pope, Christ's vicar on earth, will continue to grow and blossom until that mission is accomplished. There awaits a final judgment, when all people who have ever lived will stand before God to face their final reward or punishment.

ISLAM. The world, created by Allah, will be destroyed on the "Last Day," the final judgment day. Humankind will be judged by how well they submitted to the will of Allah. A heavenly paradise awaits those who have pleased Allah during their life. "To those who do good, there is good in this world, and the Home of the Hereafter is even better and excellent indeed is the Home of the righteous, Gardens of Eternity which they will enter: beneath them flow (pleasant) rivers: they will have therein all they wish: thus doth Allah reward the righteous, (namely) those whose lives the angels take in a state of purity, saying (to them), 'Peace be upon you; enter ye the Garden, because of (the good) which ye did (in the world)'" (16:27–32).

Sources:

Ellwood, Robert S., and Barbara A. McGraw. *Many Peoples, Many Faiths: Women and Men in the World Religions.* 7th ed. Upper Saddle River, NJ: Prentice Hall, 2002.

Fisher, Mary Pat, and Lee W. Bailey, eds. *An Anthology of Living Religions.* Upper Saddle River, NJ: Prentice Hall, 2000.

ESCHATON

Eschatology is the study of the Eschaton, the end of all things (see Eschatology, Comparative). In Christian circles it has come to mean the study of interpretive schools of thought concerning the Second Coming of Jesus Christ and the battle of Armageddon.

The ideas of Albert Schweitzer, the German theologian, medical missionary, and musician who lived from 1875 to 1965, came to mark a dividing line in Christian thought concerning how the Second Coming could be interpreted. Traditional Christian theology taught that Jesus would someday return in the flesh. This return was called the Eschaton. But Schweitzer began to believe that when the twelve disciples, as described in Luke 9, were sent forth to preach the good news of the kingdom, Jesus fully expected that the world would soon come to an end. That didn't happen, so (according to Schweitzer) Jesus was forced to radically rethink his position. He began to internalize the gospel and, to that end, made his way to Jerusalem to focus the troubles of the world within his own being. He willingly went to the cross in order to offer himself as a sacrifice, acceptable to God, so that with his death a new age could begin. This was the real Eschaton.

Schweitzer thought that, at the last, Jesus doubted his cause and expressed those doubts from the cross ("My God, my God, why have you forsaken me?"). Others, following Schweitzer's lead, began to search for the "historical Jesus" as opposed to the "spiritual Jesus." This became the position of what has since been labeled "liberal" scholarship. It is the belief that Jesus of Nazareth was a historical figure—a Jewish man who lived some 2,000 years ago with a spiritual vision of what the future could hold. He was crucified for his efforts and will not return. But all that he was, all that he represented, lived on in his followers. The "Jesus of history" lived on in the "Christ of faith." His ideas eclipsed his life, and it is those ideas, the ideals of love and compassion, of forgiveness and humbleness, that constitute the Eschaton. It is not the returning body of Jesus that will usher in the new age, it is the human acceptance and application of his message that will fulfill the promise of the Eschaton.

In the 1930s the New Testament scholar C. H. Dodd introduced the phrase "realized Eschaton" to signify the idea that the Eschaton has already come. The purpose of the church is to help all people see that it is already among us and then to act on that information by putting the Eschaton into practice in daily life. He believed that when Christians pray, "Thy kingdom come, on earth as it is in heaven," they were really praying for the acting out on earth of what God has already placed in the human heart. The Bible passages concerning a bodily return, according to Dodd, were simply confused additions by first-century followers who didn't understand what Jesus meant.

Because of these radically different interpretations, Christians have divided into two schools of thought, with many gradations within each school, concerning the

Eschaton. The conservative school awaits the physical return of Jesus Christ at the end of time. Today this school is most prominently represented by Hal Lindsey, Tim LaHaye, and fundamentalist/evangelical spokesmen such as Billy Graham. The liberal school believes that the Eschaton has already occurred and is growing through the lives of Christians. This school is represented by members of the Jesus Scholar movement such as the Protestant Marcus Borg and the Catholic John Dominic Crossan. They believe that the church, while working to change the world through the radical nature of God's love, is the Eschaton, the body of Christ already come to earth.

Source:

Douglas, J. D., ed. *The New International Dictionary of the Christian Church*. Grand Rapids, MI: Zondervan, 1974.

ETERNAL LIFE

In Matthew 19:16, "a man came up to Jesus and asked, 'Teacher, what good thing must I do to get eternal life?'"

John 3:16 assures Christians that "God so loved the world that he gave his one and only Son, that whoever believes in him shall not perish, but have eternal life."

These are well-known examples of the Christian use of the words *eternal life*. But eternal life is not just a Christian concept. The Qur'an of Islam, for example, teaches that "the Home of the Hereafter is even better and excellent indeed is the home of the righteous, Gardens of Eternity which they will enter: beneath them flow (pleasant) rivers: they will have therein all that they wish: thus doth Allah reward the righteous, (namely) those whose lives the angels take in a state of purity" (16:30–32).

Belief in eternal life predates even monotheistic religion. Perhaps the earliest evidence for such beliefs consists of grave burials. Before this practice arose, people presumably were simply left where they died, their bodies susceptible to the elements. Neanderthal grave sites showing signs of ritual accompanying the burials date to as much as 60,000 years ago. At least as early as 25,000 years ago, modern human beings began to bury their dead with what appears to have been religious intent. Skeletons have been found in graves containing hand axes and weapons, implying a belief that the dead would need them in a life following this one. An argument could thus be advanced that belief in eternal life was the first human religious conviction.

Today eternal life is a fundamental belief of most religious traditions, and its interpretation falls into one of three basic categories:

A Place

Probably the first belief in eternal life was that a person goes somewhere when departing this life. Often religions describe this place as an ideal environment projected from surroundings with which the culture is already familiar: the rich hunting ground of Plains Indian culture, the restored Eden of the Hebrew prophets, the "Holy City" of the Christian New Testament, and the heavenly oasis of Islam. Egyptian embalmers went to great extremes to prepare their nobility for this place, not only

Saint John and the Twenty-four Elders in Heaven, by Albrecht Dürer. *Fortean Picture Library.*

building great pyramids as entrance halls to the hereafter, but also providing wealth to cover traveling expenses and ensure that no cutback in lifestyle would be necessary in the afterworld. Celtic tradition called for placing coins over the eyes of the deceased to pay the ferryman for portage across the river Styx.

Often this place of eternal joy and contentment is contrasted with a place of torment for those who fail to attain the ethical righteousness a religion calls for. Either a fiery hell or a nebulous place of darkness awaits the unworthy, sometimes coupled with a "waiting room" or purgatory where choices need to be made concerning eternity.

Sometimes the spirit of the deceased stays on where he or she lived during life. In Shinto it is not uncommon for ancestors, accustomed to receiving offerings and prayers from their descendants, to speak through the lips of shamans. "Haunted" houses are still home to ghosts or shades of previous owners. The famous magician Harry Houdini promised to communicate from the place of the dead if at all possible. After years of seances, usually held at Halloween, traditionally said to be the time when the veil between this world and the next is stretched thinnest, his wife finally gave up in despair. Sir Arthur Conan Doyle, the creator of Sherlock Holmes, spent the last years of his life exploring ways to pierce the barrier between life and death.

Many "after death" experiences record the common denominator of a tunnel of light leading to a beautiful place of fields and flowers, a Being of Light radiating warmth and love, and reunion with loved ones. These experiences have been reported by both religious and nonreligious people and are the subject of considerable debate. Some see these descriptions as proof of afterlife, others as a chemical reaction in the brain rendering near-death visions of culturally familiar concepts of heaven.

A Consciousness

Sometimes the afterlife is described in terms of a drop of water returning to the ocean. This is the view of the Buddhist Nirvana and the pre–Big Bang "consciousness of the cosmos" in what is sometimes called New Age thought, although it is also found in ancient Hinduism. In this interpretation, universal consciousness has taken on human form. Then, after spending a few years or lifetimes on earth gathering experience, it returns to the consciousness of the cosmos, uniting again in the wholeness encompassing both time and space.

A Process

As expressed in the Tibetan Book of the Dead, life is a procession of incarnations. It is described as the perpetually turning wheel of samsara, on which people live out a series of reincarnations, driven by karma accumulated in past lives. Exploration of past lives helps in the understanding of why things happen in the present life. The process is, for all practical purposes, endless, although the goal is moksha, eventual release of the now fully formed individual into the eternal consciousness. In Hinduism, Atman, the individual soul, merges with Brahman, the universal consciousness. The Buddha is said to have achieved Nirvana upon his death and is even now drawing unto himself the Buddha consciousness inherent in every human.

Sources:
Hagen, Steve. *Buddhism Plain and Simple*. Boston: Charles E. Tuttle, 1997.

The Holy Qur'an. Trans. with a commentary by Abdullah Yusuf Ali. Beirut: Dar Al Arabia, 1968.

Lewis, James R. *The Death and Afterlife Book.* Detroit: Visible Ink Press, 2001.

May, Herbert G., and Bruce M. Metzger, eds. *The New Oxford Annotated Bible with the Apocrypha.* Rev. ed. New York: Oxford University Press, 1973.

Szulc, Tad. "Journey of Faith." *National Geographic,* December 2001, 90–129.

Tibetan Book of the Dead. New York: Oxford University Press, 1960.

ETERNITY

The Interpreter's Dictionary of the Bible defines *eternity* as an "endless span of time" and "dominion over time." This definition reflects more a religious concept of afterlife (see Eternal Life) than a scientific view of eternity. In physics, "time" is connected with "space" and is often referred to as "space/time." The two came into existence together. One cannot exist without the other. There was no time before space. One word that can be used to describe whatever it was in which space/time came into being is *eternity*. In this sense, eternity is not a long, long time. It is not time at all. It is that in which time exists.

Stephen W. Hawking's book *A Brief History of Time* grapples with the use of words such as *eternity* and *infinite*.

> When we combine quantum mechanics with general relativity, there seems to be a new possibility that did not arise before: that space and time together might form a finite, four-dimensional space without singularities or boundaries, like the surface of the earth but with more dimensions. It seems that this idea could explain many of the observed features of the universe, such as its large-scale uniformity and also the smaller-scale departures from homogeneity, like galaxies, stars, and even human beings. It could even account for the arrow of time that we observe. But if the universe is completely self-contained, with no singularities or boundaries, and is completely described by a unified theory, that has profound implications for the role of God as Creator.

> Einstein once asked the question: "How much choice did God have in constructing the universe?" If the no boundary proposal is correct, he had no freedom of choice at all to choose initial conditions. He would, of course, have the freedom to choose the laws that the universe obeyed. This, however, may not have been all that much of a choice; there may well be only one, or a small number, of complete unified theories ... that allow the existence of structures as complicated as human beings who can investigate the laws of the universe and ask about the nature of God.

What is the nature of eternity? Probably all that can be said for certain is that, for religious humans, it is envisioned as a very long time. For scientific ones, it is simply outside the scope of what can really be explained.

Ironically, perhaps a religious writer best reconciled the two points of view:

No eye has seen,
no ear has heard,
no mind has conceived
what God has prepared. (1 Cor. 2:9)

Sources:

Hawking, Stephen W. *A Brief History of Time: From the Big Bang to Black Holes*. New York: Bantam, 1988.

The Holy Bible, New International Version. Grand Rapids, MI: Zondervan, 1978.

ETHIOPIA

In the 1920s most Jamaicans of African descent lived in abject poverty in what can best be described as slum conditions. Many justly blamed white imperialism for the destruction of their culture and the absence of hope.

This is the background that incubated the Jamaica-born black nationalist Marcus Garvey's "Back to Africa" philosophy, a black self-empowerment movement that encouraged a return to the idealized African home of the ancestors, especially Ethiopia. "Look to Africa," Garvey was fond of saying, "where a black man shall be crowned king, for the day of our deliverance is at hand!" His was not a vision in the Christian apocalyptic tradition that promised the return of a messiah. It followed more in the Jewish tradition of looking for a leader who would bring about social justice in the present day. An Armageddon was not foretold as an ending to the world. The apocalypse envisioned was more along the lines of a social upheaval that would change the status quo and bring hope to the downtrodden. In this sense, the dream of Ethiopia was much the same as the Jewish yearning for Jerusalem, where a king would rule in righteousness.

In 1930, some ten years after Garvey began preaching, his prophetic vision seemed to come to pass. A black African named Ras Tafari Makonnen was crowned emperor of Ethiopia. He took the title and name Emperor Haile Selassie the First. In Jamaica the news sparked rejoicing in the streets. They called Haile Selassie the "Lion of the Tribe of Judah." He claimed direct descent from King David himself, through David's son Solomon and the queen of Sheba (thought to be an Ethiopian). When she visited Jerusalem and was swept away by Solomon's might and power (1 Kings 10), according to Haile Selassie, she came away with more than just gifts of gold and silver. Since that time, he said, the blood of Solomon, Hebrew blood, has flowed through Ethiopian veins. Ethiopia is even thought by some to be the resting place of the lost Ark of the Covenant (see Ark of the Covenant).

The people of Jamaica began to call themselves "Rastafarians," after Ras Tafari Makonnen. They saw themselves as legitimate members of the tribe of Judah, one of the twelve tribes of Israel. They began to recognize Haile Selassie as a representative, perhaps even a manifestation, of Jah (God) on earth. According to their belief, there is no afterlife, so earthly life becomes very important. The here and now is what matters. They wanted an improvement in their social condition and didn't want to wait. In this they were much like the Hebrew people of the first century who looked for a messiah to free them from the chains of Roman oppression.

Rastafarians turned to the Hebrew scriptures to guide them in their beliefs, and in the book of Daniel they found the prophecy they needed to explain the events happening in Ethiopia. In chapter 2, Daniel claimed to have had a vision. He saw a great statue. The statue, he said, had "hair like wool." Most theologians take this to mean the hair was white. Rastafarians thought it better described the hair of those with African ancestry. The statue had "feet like unto burning brass." This is generally thought to mean gold-colored, but Rastafarians saw it as a description of black skin.

It was a time of great patriotic, even messianic, excitement. The early Rastafarians despised white people. The culture of white imperialism was labeled "Babylon," after the "whore of Babylon" described in the book of Revelation. In the enigmatic words of Revelation 17, the whore of Babylon is said to be a city built on seven hills and is the personification of all that is impure, evil, wealthy, and greedy.

From 1930 until 1974, Rastafarians waited, certain the Messiah would arise and life on earth would change. But Haile Selassie died, and the Rasta world was shaken to the core. How could Jah die? Many of the elderly simply refused to believe the reports. They viewed the whole thing as a white media conspiracy. Others left the faith. Some taught that Jah went to sit on the highest point of Mount Zion with his empress, Menen.

The black nationalist Marcus Garvey in 1924. *George Grantham Bain Collection/Library of Congress.*

Today the eschatological hope that fired early Rastafarianism has largely been replaced by a movement for social justice. This new emphasis is perhaps most succinctly illustrated in the Rasta way of often saying "I and I" instead of "you and me"—a linguistic reflection of the belief that all people are truly one.

Source:
Fisher, Mary Pat. *Living Religions.* 3rd ed. Upper Saddle River, NJ: Prentice Hall, 1991.

EUROPEAN COMMON MARKET AND EUROPEAN UNION

The seventh chapter of the book of Daniel (see also Daniel) recounts a dream that is probably one of the most important blocks in the prophetic edifice constructed by biblical futurists (see Futurist School of Biblical Interpretation). It proves to their satisfaction that Armageddon is just around the corner.

The prophet Daniel claims to have had a vision of four beasts coming "up out of the sea." "The first was like a lion, and it had the wings of an eagle." The second "looked like a bear." The third "looked like a leopard.... This beast had four heads."

According to those who follow this interpretation, it is the fourth beast that commands the attention in today's world:

> After that, in my vision at night I looked, and there before me was a fourth beast—terrifying and frightening and very powerful. It had large iron teeth; it crushed and devoured its victims and tramples underfoot whatever was left. It was different from all the former beasts and it had ten horns.

> While I was thinking about the horns, there before me was another horn, a little one, which came up among them; and three of the first horns were uprooted before it. This horn had the eyes of a man and spoke boastfully.

> As I looked,

> thrones were set in place,
> and the Ancient of Days took his seat....
> The court was seated
> and the books were opened.
> Then I continued to watch because of the boastful words the horn was speaking. I kept looking until the beast was slain and its body destroyed and thrown into the blazing fire. (The other beasts had been stripped of their authority, but were allowed to live for a period of time.)

Daniel understandably confessed to great confusion at this point, but he was given a divine interpreter. The interpreter revealed that the four beasts are four nations that will arise. Many evangelical scholars claim these beasts represent Babylon, Persia, Greece, and Rome.

When asked about the fourth beast, the interpreter responded:

> The fourth beast is a fourth king that will appear on earth. It will be different from all the other kingdoms and will devour the whole earth, trampling it down and crushing it. The ten horns are ten kings who will come from this kingdom. After them another king will arise, different from the earlier ones; he will subdue three kings. He will speak against the Most High and oppress his saints and try to change the set times and the laws. The saints will be handed over to him for a time, times and half a time.

> But the court will sit, and his power will be taken away and completely destroyed forever. Then the sovereignty, power and greatness of the kingdoms under the whole heaven will be an everlasting kingdom, and all rulers will worship and obey him.

This vision, along with the one in Daniel, chapter 2, forms the basis for the futurists' belief in what they call a revived Roman Empire. According to this system of interpretation, there have been four great empires that attempted to rule the world. Babylon was the first, followed by Medo-Persia, Greece, and Rome. Babylon was the dominant force during the time of Daniel. It was overthrown, according to Daniel 5, by the Medo-Persian Empire, which in turn was conquered by the Greeks under Alexander the Great. In time, Greece fell to Rome, which was the predominant world power during the first centuries of the church's existence. It was during the days of the Roman Empire that Christianity became the official religion of the state.

When Rome fell to the barbarian hordes, there ceased to be a world empire. Futurists believe that the Roman Empire will be revived, existing on the same land it once occupied. That is the significance of the "ten horns who will come from this kingdom." The "ten horns" suggest a confederation or union of nations that will come together as one. They will occupy the same territory as ancient Rome, while being "different from the earlier ones."

When Hal Lindsey wrote *The Late Great Planet Earth* in 1970, he suggested that what was then being called the European Common Market was the fulfillment of this prophecy. There were not yet ten nations in the Common Market, but Lindsey believed that there soon would be that number. He advised people that at some point the "other king," the antichrist, would "subdue three kings" by force. He would "speak against the Most High and oppress his saints … for a time [one], times [two] and half a time"—in other words, the last three and one-half years of the Great Tribulation (see Great Tribulation). According to Lindsey, "the Common Market and the trend toward unification of Europe may well be the beginning of the ten-nation confederacy predicted by Daniel."

The problem, of course, was that as European unity continued, it soon raced past ten nations. The European Union now consists of twenty-five independent states and shows no sign of shrinking back to ten. Lindsey was not discouraged. "What happens in Europe will be very much the model for world consolidation in the 21st century," he explained in his 1997 book *Apocalypse Code*, adding that "there is no doubt in my mind that [the European Union] is the precursor to the Revived Roman Empire to which both John and Daniel refer." The belief that the "Ancient of Days" will return to judge the world during the time of this revived Roman Empire means to futurists that the end of days, Armageddon, is close.

Lindsey, of course, was hardly the first to try to fit Europe into biblical prophecy. Others have done so for centuries. Napoleon caused much worried speculation during his time. Students of biblical prophecy certainly raised the possibility of Hitler's being the antichrist in the days before and during World War II.

Does the Bible really even predict a revived Roman Empire? Past-historic students of scripture say no. Daniel, so goes their argument, was written by at least two different authors, one of whom wrote after the era of Roman rule had begun. He was not foretelling the future but describing what was even then taking place. Babylon, Persia, and Greece had already fallen into the dustbin of history. Rome was already in power, and to understand what the author meant requires study of the times in which he lived. Daniel was a code, written for the people of his day and referring to events with which they would be familiar. We may not grasp exactly what he was talking about because we have, at best, an imperfect knowledge of the history of those days. But the fact that European empires come and go doesn't mean that some "revived Roman Empire" under an antichrist will someday rule the world.

And so the debate continues.

Sources:

Borg, Marcus J. *Reading the Bible Again for the First Time: Taking the Bible Seriously but Not Literally.* San Francisco: HarperSanFrancisco, 2001.

Lindsey, Hal. *Apocalypse Code.* Palos Verdes, CA: Western Front Ltd., 1997.

Lindsey, Hal, with C. C. Carlson. *The Late Great Planet Earth.* Grand Rapids MI: Zondervan, 1970.

The Holy Bible, New International Version. Grand Rapids, MI: Zondervan, 1978.

EUROPEAN NATIONS IN PROPHECY *see* **America in Prophecy; Armstrong, Herbert W.; European Common Market and European Union**

EVANGELICALISM

Evangelicals and fundamentalists are best known for their habit of reading the Bible literally (see Futurist School of Biblical Interpretation). They understand the scriptural passages concerning Armageddon to be referring to a particular future time of trial upon the earth, after which Jesus Christ will bodily return to rule the planet from a throne room in Jerusalem. They believe this understanding to be one of the fundamentals of the faith to which Christians must intellectually agree in order to call themselves Christian.

The word *evangelical* is derived from the Greek *euangelion*, which means "good news." So does the word *gospel*. So in this sense, evangelical means "pertaining to the gospel," or the story told by the four gospels, Matthew, Mark, Luke, and John. Perhaps the apostle Paul best summarized the "evangel" in 1 Corinthians 15:1–8:

> Now brothers, I want to remind you of the gospel I preached to you, which you received and on which you have taken your stand. By this gospel you are saved, if you hold firmly to the word I preached to you. Otherwise you have believed in vain. For what I received I passed on to you as of first importance: that Christ died for our sins according to the Scriptures, that he was buried, that he was raised on the third day according to the Scriptures, and that he appeared to Peter, and then to the twelve. After that he appeared to more than five hundred of the brothers at the same time, most of whom are still living, although some have fallen asleep. Then he appeared to James, then to all the apostles, and last of all he appeared to me also, as to one abnormally born.

This is the heart of the story. The one who tells it, who brings the "good news," is an evangelist.

If it were to stop here, it would be easy. But it doesn't. So it's not.

All Christian churches use (basically) the same Bible and read the gospels at their worship services. All accept what the apostle said in 1 Corinthians. So all claim to be evangelists and all claim to be evangelical, at least in some sense of the word. But some claim to be more evangelical than others. And this is where the problem begins.

First of all, some Protestant churches began early on to differentiate between evangelical and evangelistic. *Evangelical* became a noun—something you were if you believed the gospel. But evangelism became something you did, something you lived for. Evangelistic churches purposely set out to convert souls to Christ. After a while a liturgy developed, although most evangelical churches would be mortified to admit they had a liturgy. Nonetheless, when the evangelist gave the altar call at the end of the church service and the organist struck up the familiar strains of "Just as I Am," everyone knew what to do. They came forward to "get saved." It was the whole purpose of the service. It was what the liturgy called for.

Even so, this was completely different from what had become known as "high church." If you went to "high church," the emphasis was on liturgy and worship. No one ever asked if you were "born again." That would be prying. You were a member of the church, weren't you? You were there. You were a Christian. Your name was on the rolls. In "low church," by contrast, whether you were "born again" and had "accepted Jesus Christ as your personal savior" were the only questions that really mattered.

Now there were, in effect, two different definitions of *evangelical*. Many a denomination arose that used the term in its name to advertise the idea that they were "doing" church, instead of what they often called "playing" church. "Evangelical" had become a label differentiating what is now called conservative theology from liberal theology, even though both liberal and conservative churches still used the word. It was a matter of interpretation. If your church believed in a literal interpretation of the Bible, rather than metaphorical, if your church insisted on the individual's need for a personal experience of being "saved," if your church sang the songs of John and Charles Wesley, if you preached that the Second Coming of Jesus was to be a bodily return, you were more "evangelical" than those who didn't. You might still have a formal worship service, but there was now a difference between "high church" and "low church." Everyone knew it, and many on both sides of the issue reveled in it.

The situation can be seen clearly in the formation of the Protestant Episcopal Church in the late 1700s. From the beginning, the Episcopal denomination was "high church." Methodists were "low church." Methodists considered themselves evangelical. So did Episcopalians, but not in the same sense. Style and theological substance were at odds with each other. When people "converted" from one theology to the other, they tended to lump worship style into their bag of complaints about their former church home. Low churchers declared that high churchers were only going through the motions. High churchers responded that low churchers had taken the dignity and beauty out of worship.

At this point, few people were using *evangelical* as a label, but almost everyone knew what the term meant. Anglican and Episcopal ministers might preach sermons with titles such as "We Are Evangelical." Baptists and Methodists knew better.

By the 1920s the rift had grown into a chasm. Those who were on the conservative side of what would soon be known as "evangelicalism" were suspicious of those more toward the center. With the publication of a series of pamphlets defining "The

Fundamentals" from 1910 through 1915, right-wing evangelicals began to call themselves fundamentalists. They wanted to distance themselves from what was then being called "literary" or "higher" criticism, a form of Bible study that moved away from a mere literal reading. They needed to distance themselves from those who questioned the doctrine of the virgin birth, miracles, and the Second Coming of Jesus during the battle of Armageddon. Fundamentalism united the religious right against the form of liberal Christianity then called "modernism." The Scopes "monkey trial" in Dayton, Tennessee, in 1925, pitted "modernist" Darwinism against "fundamentalist" creationism. It generated such nationwide publicity that "Fundamentalist vs. Modernist" became a national debate.

Problems arise, however, whenever something as deeply felt as religious conviction comes to the surface. Fundamentalists took great pride in what they considered to be the "purity" of their beliefs. Modernists reveled in their "educated" views and traditional worship. Eventually, the two sides simply stopped talking to each other (unless shouts of "hypocrite" and "apostate" constitute talking).

By the 1950s fundamentalism had developed something of a chip on its shoulder. Science had produced such a huge body of evidence supporting evolution that even though the fundamentalists had technically won the Scopes trial, it seemed they were losing the modernist war. Evolution, not creation, was being taught in the public schools. Men returning from World War II, bankrolled by the GI Bill, were attending liberal colleges. Having been in contact with different cultures and religions while overseas, these men were not quite so quick to condemn. Churches were booming, but many were moving to the suburbs, where Catholics, Episcopalians, Baptists, and Jews were all in the same bowling league.

The harder the fundamentalists fought, the more their image became that of the preacher with the clenched fist, unenlightened, unbending. A story from those days tells of a fundamentalist evangelist appearing at a tent meeting one night during revival week.

"I'm here to preach the good news!" he bellowed.

"What's that?" someone asked from the back row.

"You're all going to hell!" roared the preacher.

Although it is difficult to document, a good argument can be put forth that it was fundamentalist objections to Billy Graham that finally caused large numbers of Christians to disassociate themselves from the fundamentalist label. Graham himself was a fundamentalist, but he was open and inviting to everyone. He often welcomed civic leaders of various denominations and even of non-Christian faiths to sit on the dais with him at his citywide rallies. This caused some fundamentalists to draw back in horror. How could believers associate with unbelievers?

Some fundamentalists began to picket Graham. They were called "separationists." Others, called "secondary separationists," were even more extreme. They shunned not only Graham, but anyone who associated with him. Such actions were embarrassing to many who agreed with fundamentalist theology but didn't feel comfortable with fundamentalists. It became popular to declare one's theological position by announcing, "I'm a fundamentalist in theology but not in attitude."

It was Harold Ockenga, pastor of Park Street Church in Boston, who coined the phase "new evangelical." He preached a conservative theology but was greatly respected by the liberal intellectual community. When the popular religious periodical *Christianity Today* identified with the new label and the Billy Graham Evangelistic Association followed suit, the name "evangelical" stuck. It became a catchall term for people of all denominations who followed a fairly conservative brand of Christian belief but felt free to associate with those who did not. Evangelicals sought to explore their faith unencumbered by the restraints of those who were suspicious of scientific inquiry and critical biblical scholarship.

Today's evangelicals can be found in every denomination and every local church. It is almost a separate, floating denomination of its own. Evangelical members of the United Church of Christ might attend conferences with evangelical Methodists and Baptists, feeling closer to them in the faith than to more liberal people in their own church. Probably every Protestant church in America has an evangelical wing, even though it may not be specifically identified as such. Evangelicals made up the preliminary audience for the popular *Left Behind* series of novels by Tim LaHaye and Jerry B. Jenkins. What surprised the publishing industry was that the books broke through the barrier and crossed over into pop culture. This kind of popular success is what made people suspect that evangelicalism was a force to be reckoned with, especially when Presidents Carter, Reagan, Clinton, and Bush (the younger) all personally identified with the evangelical label.

Currently the labeling system is as follows: To the far right of the Christian spectrum lies the group who call themselves fundamentalists. Moving toward the center, but still on the conservative right, is the evangelical camp. In the center stand those usually called "mainstream" or "middle of the road." To the left are the liberals.

Notice that, again, it makes little difference what the denomination is. Fundamentalists of the Missouri Synod Lutherans feel more comfortable with fundamentalist Orthodox Presbyterians than they do with liberal Lutherans. And Methodist evangelicals work together with American Baptist evangelicals when the Billy Graham organization comes to town. Evangelical student organizations are found in even the most liberal of seminaries and theological schools, for evangelicals consider themselves the true heirs and modern expression of traditional fundamentalism—the essence of traditional Christianity.

Today's evangelicals are the religious group specifically awaiting Armageddon. Their battle cry is a simple one: "Gimme that old-time religion! But dress it up in a new suit!"

Sources:

Douglas, J. D., ed. *The New International Dictionary of the Christian Church.* Grand Rapids: Zondervan, 1974.

Gonzalez, Justo L. *The Story of Christianity.* 2 vols. New York: Harper & Row, 1985.

Hudson, Winthrop S. *Religion in America.* New York: Charles Scribner's Sons, 1965.

EXEGESIS

Exegesis is the science (some would call it an art) of intepreting the meaning of any particular passage of writing, including religious scripture. Scriptures of all religions were written within the context of a particular culture and belief system. No one can write without having a certain frame of reference. Words mean different things to different people. World views change. Even the meanings of words change over the years. Imagine the embarrassment a modern teenager feels when asked to stand up during a youth group meeting of her peers and read the King James version of the Ten Commandments. What will she do when she gets to the part that says not to "covet thy neighbor's ass?" She would have been on solid ground back in the seventeenth century, but the language is a bit awkward in the twenty-first.

The problem of exegesis is probably the most divisive issue facing the Christian church today. The situation becomes especially confusing when studying biblical prophecy. When a preacher appears on television to expound a particular text, people not familiar with the science of exegesis can easily be persuaded to take the speaker's point of view without realizing that they are making basic assumptions they might not fully agree with.

To understand the problem within a political context, consider the commonly held assumption that the Bible forbids, even condemns, homosexuality. There is one Bible verse that seems to do just that. It is found at Leviticus 18:22 and seems to be addressing gay men: "Do not lie with a man as one lies with a woman; that is detestable."

If we stop right there, the Bible seems to speak pretty clearly on the subject. Many TV preachers do stop there, leaving the impression that the matter is thus settled once and for all. But not everyone engaged in biblical exegesis finds the matter so cut and dried. Some liberal scholars, for example, contend that the passage pertains specifically to activities involving temple prostitutes of the era, not necessarily to the general population. And then there is Leviticus 20:13: "If a man lies with a man as one lies with a woman, both of them have done what is detestable. They must be put to death." This verse clouds the issue for many people. Many who condemn homosexuality on biblical grounds are far less outspoken when it comes to this presumed pronouncement of the death penalty on gay men.

It doesn't help that in this same group of laws there is a specific command (Lev. 19:19) never to "wear clothing of two different kinds of cloth." Even the person who wants to execute gays might feel a little nervous if he happens to be wearing a polyester/cotton-blend shirt while pronouncing that judgment.

The difficulty of interpreting even such seemingly straightforward passages as these only increases when we turn to biblical prophecy. Interpreters tend to bring their own set of cultural ideas to the text. If a person is preconditioned to believe a literal reading of the Bible, his or her understanding of a prophetic text will probably hear the words "will happen" and assume the author is talking about a yet future date (see also Futurist School of Biblical Interpretation). If, on the other hand, a person approaches the Bible with an awareness of his or her own cultural bias, he or she will be more apt to wonder if the author had a different agenda in mind.

Gabriel Fackre of Andover Newton Seminary has developed a formula that can be used by anyone who wants to do exegesis. This four-part system works especially well when dealing with the Bible but can be used by the student of mythology or any other ancient writing. In his book *Christian Basics*, written with his wife, Dorothy, Fackre sets out the steps for handling a given passage:

1. Common sense: Start with its common-sense meaning—reading it just like a newspaper story.
2. Critical sense: Next, check out the ideas of some of the other students who have studied the passage's background, original language, and literary style.
3. Canonical sense: Compare the passage with the rest of the author's writing. Is it consistent with the rest of the story?
4. Contextual sense: What does the passage mean in terms of personal and contemporary culture?

This system will save the student from arriving at conclusions that might be considered to be contemporary, even politically correct, but might also be totally at odds with what the original author really meant.

Source:
Fackre, Gabriel, and Dorothy Fackre. *Christian Basics*. Grand Rapids, MI: Eerdmans, 1991.

EZEKIEL

According to the Hebrew Bible, in 586 BCE the kingdom known as Judah was taken into captivity by Babylonians under the command of King Nebuchadnezzar. One of the captives was a prophet named Ezekiel. He is known as one of the three "major" prophets, the other two being Isaiah and Jeremiah. (Some scholars include Daniel in this list, although his book is not as long as those of the other three.) The book bearing Ezekiel's name describes the years leading up to the captivity from the point of view of a prophet who is writing a retrospective on why God allowed this catastrophe to happen. To Ezekiel there was no question that the Babylonian captivity was God's judgment on a people who had turned away from their historical religion. He believed it to be a purging, a cleansing to prepare the way for a new beginning that would take place a generation later when the Israelites returned to their land. From this perspective, the Babylonian captivity represents a Hebrew Armageddon. It was meant to pronounce judgment upon both personal sin and institutional oppression, and to provide a new start under God.

A good argument can be made that history has proved Ezekiel correct in his conclusions. The Babylonian captivity did produce a great change in Jewish religious thought. Although Judaism is often said to be the first monotheistic religion, that is not really the case. Before the sixth-century BCE captivity, Jewish writings are filled with references to "other gods." Even the Ten Commandments, purportedly given to Moses by God, stress the fact that the Jews were to "have no other gods before" YHVH (Yahveh). The text did not discount the existence of other gods. It simply placed YHVH first. Those who wrote the psalms declared many times that "YHVH was a great God" and "above all gods." The references to "all gods," "gods of the nations," and similar expressions reveal that the Hebrew theology of that time had not yet developed to the point of recognizing only one supreme being.

All this changed following the Babylonian captivity. When the Jews returned to rebuild their sacred temple and city at Jerusalem, all subsequent Hebrew writers were solidly monotheistic.

What caused this change?

Very probably it happened because the principal religion of the Persians—who, according to the Bible, defeated the Babylonians in the midst of the captivity period—was Zoroastrianism. This was the first solidly monotheistic religion (see Zoroastrianism). It was the first religion to pit a good God against an evil counterentity. It was the first religion of strict duality, of good against evil, with a final battle on judgment day. The discovery of the Dead Sea Scrolls in the twentieth century revealed Zoroastrianism's profound influence on Hebrew thought.

Ezekiel, were he to come back today and review what happened since he wrote his book, would probably agree that the Babylonian captivity produced in Jewish history that which evangelical Christians believe Armageddon will accomplish in Christianity. That is, it represented both a judgment and a new beginning.

But Christians read the book of Ezekiel, too. It is part of their Old Testament. They read it with an eye not only on the past, but on the future. Many fundamentalist and evangelical Christians believe that Ezekiel looked far beyond his own day to see a future consummation described later in the book of Revelation. They believe that in the last twelve chapters of his book Ezekiel identified the combatants of the final battle of Armageddon (see Armageddon, Battle of).

To understand all this we have to begin with the prophet himself. His writing reveals that he was twenty-five years old when captured and taken to Babylon. He began to prophecy at the age of thirty, continuing for some twenty-two years. He was married, but his wife died; he writes eloquently of his grief in chapter 24. He seems, according to chapters 3 and 8, to have had his own house, so he probably had both the opportunity and the means to live fairly well, even in captivity. Jewish tradition says he was slain by a fellow exile whose idolatries Ezekiel had rebuked. This may well be the case, because rebuking idolatry is the theme of Ezekiel's writing. That he viewed the Babylonian captivity as God's judgment is made clear when we read the words "Then they shall know that I am YHVH" seventy times over the course of forty-eight chapters.

But beginning in chapter 36, some scholars claim to see a change in emphasis. The focus, they say, is now on the future. In verse 19, Israel seems to be dispersed "among the nations," not just Babylon. The first two verses picture an enemy who has gained possession of "the ancient heights" of Israel and is gloating over the fact. Verse 24 makes a clear statement: "For I will take you out of the nations [notice again the plural]; I will gather you from all the countries and bring you back to your own land." This, say many evangelical scholars, sounds more like the Zionism of the 1940s than the return to Jerusalem in the fourth century BCE described in Ezra and Nehemiah. "I will give you a new heart and put a new spirit in you.... You will live in the land I gave your forefathers ... I will increase the fruit of the trees and the crops of the field."

The vision of Ezekiel (Ezek. 1). *Fortean Picture Library.*

With these words, according to the futurist reading of Ezekiel, the prophet moves from explaining the past to foretelling the future.

In chapters 38 and 39, according to this interpretation, the prophet begins to describe the battle of Armageddon that will occur after Israel is restored "from among the nations." Since the "restoration" took place in 1948 with the creation of a Jewish state in Palestine, many evangelical scholars suggest that the things described in these two chapters may occur any time now. Ezekiel identifies a ruler known as "Gog, of the land of Magog" (see Gog and Magog) and connects him with "the chief prince of Meshech and Tubal." "Persia, Cush and Put" (see Cush) are specifically mentioned, along with "Gomer with all its troops and Beth Togarmah from the north with all its troops" (see Togarmah). These terms are treated in greater detail in various entries throughout this volume, so it is sufficient here to identify them according to the interpretive scheme of many futurist scholars:

"Gog, of the land of Magog"—Russia
"Cush"—Ethiopia and the black African nations
"Put"—Libya and the Arabic African nations
"Gomer with all its troops"—Germany and the former iron curtain countries
"Beth Togarmah from the north with all its troops"—southern Russia and the people of the historic Cossack empires

According to this interpretation, the battle in chapter 38 takes place as follows:

Verse 7: "Get ready; be prepared, you and all the hordes gathered about you, and take command of them." (Russia gathers its allied armies.)

Verse 8a: "After many days [some translations read "the latter days"] you will be called to arms." (After the regathering of Israel, believed by many to have already occurred, the battle begins.)

Verse 8b: "In future years you will invade a land that has recovered from war, whose people were gathered from many nations to the mountains of Israel.... They had been brought out from the nations, and now all of them live in safety." (Israel is the target.)

Verses 9–16: "You and all your troops and the many nations with you will go up, advancing like a storm.... and you will devise an evil scheme. You will say, 'I will attack a peaceful and unsuspecting people—all of them living without walls and without gates and bars....' You will come from your place in the far north, you and many nations with you, all of them riding on horses, a great horde, a mighty army." (The attack begins.)

The battle itself is described in detail in chapter 39. The chapter depicts a sea of blood and devastation that will take a grand total of seven years to clean up.

The final eight chapters describe in minute detail the new temple and city that will be built (see Temple at Jerusalem) and end with the words, "And the name of the city from that time on will be: THE LORD IS THERE."

Sources:
The Holy Bible, New International Version. Grand Rapids, MI: Zondervan, 1978.
Lindsey, Hal, with C. C. Carlson. *The Late Great Planet Earth.* Grand Rapids, MI: Zondervan, 1970.

F

FAILED PROPHECY

A charismatic leader receives a message from aliens that the world will be destroyed on a particular date. A Paiute prophet preaches a new message: if the Plains Indians will dance the Ghost Dance, the buffalo will return and the whites will disappear. A Bible student discovers a scriptural code that reveals the date of Jesus' return and the battle of Armageddon.

In each case a group gathers, perhaps sell their belongings, and prepares to welcome a new beginning. Expectations run high. On THE DAY, they enter a bomb shelter, dance their dance or pray their prayers, gather on mountaintops or bunkers, and wait.

And nothing happens.

What then? What happens when prophecy fails? What happens to people who have invested both time and talents and, even more important, spiritual hopes and expectations, in a cause that seems to be utterly without merit? How do they face their taunting neighbors, let alone rebuild their entire spiritual system of belief and self-worth?

Leon Festinger's Conclusion

These are the questions the social psychologist Leon Festinger, assisted by Henry W. Riecken and Stanley Schacter, set out to answer. After studying historical records describing the plight of groups such as the Anabaptists in 1533, Jewish followers of Sabbatai Zevi in 1648, and the Great Disappointment of the Millerites in 1844 (see Millerites), Festinger chanced on a contemporary event in the 1950s that gave him an opportunity to observe and describe exactly what happens when prophecy fails. He considered this a made-to-order scientific opportunity to conduct a field test.

A "Mrs. Marian Keech"—her real name was Dorothy Martin, but Festinger used fictitious names in his account—claimed to have been told by superior beings from the planet "Clarion" that a great flood would occur on December 21, 1954, inundating North America from the Arctic Circle to the Gulf of Mexico. In order to escape the deluge, people would have to retreat to the hilltops to wait things out. Meanwhile, Mrs. Keech's enlightened followers would be whisked to safety by flying saucers (see Seekers, The).

The local newspaper carried the story in detail. Festinger was soon on the scene to observe the outcome. When the promised catastrophe didn't arrive, Keech and her disciples informed the press and everyone else who would listen that the flood had been called off. Her little group had proved so faithful and "had spread so much light that God had saved the world from destruction." They immediately began to trumpet the good news so that others could share it with them.

From this event and his other research Festinger deduced that groups respond to supposed failure by attempting to recruit new members. The dynamic was simple: If people can persuade others to follow them, the increased numbers justify the group's belief system. The more people there are who believe in something, the more peer pressure there is to affirm the belief. The majority rules.

Similar thinking can be identified in today's entertainment industry. The more famous an individual becomes, the better "artist" he or she is considered to be. If more people attend Movie A than Movie B, the implication is that Movie A is a "better" movie than Movie B. No one comes right out and says this. But it still resonates that way with many people.

Festinger identified five conditions under which he believed his thesis would prove tenable:

1. The prophetic belief must be held with great confidence and must have sufficient moral force so as to affect a person's lifestyle and ethical behavior.
2. The people holding the belief must have been moved to make a serious commitment in terms of taking some drastic action such as giving up their homes and money or leaving their families.
3. The prophecy must have real-world consequences observable by believers and nonbelievers alike.
4. Evidence that the prophecy was not fulfilled must be obvious and recognizable by all.
5. The believer must be supported by a group of like-minded believers.

Festinger concluded that when prophecy fails (the technical term he used is *disconfirmation*), it only serves to strengthen the resolve of the true believers. They will deny the obvious rather than admit to failure. Then, to strengthen their faith, they will try to persuade others they are right.

Joseph Zygmunt's Conclusion

Other social scientists pointed out numerous case studies, one as recent as 1975, that didn't confirm Festinger's conclusions at all.

The Jehovah's Witnesses have had a history of watching for the signs of the end (see Jehovah's Witnesses). June of 1966 was the focus of much expectation. It was, after all, the sixth month of the sixty-sixth year of the century. That sounds suspiciously close to 666 (see 666). During that hope-filled spring, however, the Watchtower Bible and Tract Society issued a publication entitled *Life Everlasting in Freedom of the Sons of God.* It featured a chart detailing the various ages and epochs since the creation of Adam. According to that chart, 1975 marked the end of the sixth thousand-year period since humans were created (see Bible Timelines). Many in the rank and file came to believe—some say with plenty of encouragement from the leaders—that 1975 was going to be the end of this age.

But 1975 came and went and nothing happened. The prophecy had failed.

According to Festinger's theories, this should have been the time for renewed door-to-door calls, more home Bible studies, and the placing of more tracts in laundry establishments. Instead, statistics revealed that exactly the opposite happened.

The behavioral scientist Joseph Zygmunt devoted considerable study to the Jehovah's Witnesses. An analysis of Festinger's theory concerning Mrs. Keech's group and Zygmunt's theories concerning the Witnesses suggests that the Witnesses, having a much larger resource base on which to draw, coped with the failure in ways Mrs. Keech and her followers did not have at their disposal. Keech had only a small group of disciples. The Witnesses had an organization with a capital O. They pointed fingers. They purged. They accused and they disfellowshipped. The problem, they insisted, was not within the leadership. The rank and file had overreacted. Revisionist histories were issued. Scathing orations were delivered.

From all this, Zygmunt reasoned that when groups experience failed prophecy, they tend to draw on the organizational resources available to them and react according to historical institutional habits. Zygmunt identified three "modes of adaptation":

1. Sometimes the organization acknowledges its error and restructures its belief system or expectations.
2. Sometimes the organization finds a scapegoat, either within the organization or outside of it. If the person or persons held to be at fault are members in good standing, they soon find doors slamming in their faces. With the supposedly malign influence removed, the rest of the group is free to reinterpret and tweak the divine calendar somewhat.
3. Sometimes the prophecy is spiritualized. Jehovah's Witnesses have used this method before. When Christ failed to establish a predicted "new world order" in 1914, for instance, it took a few years for the Witnesses to realize that the "new world order" did not materialize that year because, in reality, 1914 was only "the beginning of the end of Gentile times." The event had taken place. But it had happened in the realm of God, not yet in the realm of the earth. World War I and its aftermath were the earthly signs that the Gentile times were in the process of coming to an end.

Gordon Melton's Conclusion

Joseph Zygmunt's analysis of failed prophecy improved and largely superseded that of Leon Festinger in the annals of social science. It wasn't that Festinger was wrong. He merely had not accounted for enough disparate groups. But Zygmunt hadn't gone far enough either. He had failed to account sufficiently for the mindset of the typical "true believer" in prophecy. Organizations and groups can react with observable, quantifiable results. But what does it "feel" like to the individual "true believer" when prophecy fails?

The multifaceted writer J. Gordon Melton, in his 1985 essay "Spiritualization and Reaffirmation: What Really Happens When Prophecy Fails," penetrated both the mind and the heart of the "true believer" and came to a startling conclusion: Prophecy seldom fails! Building on Zygmunt's third "adaptation," he discerned that a particular prophecy is only one part of a much larger whole. It is a mistake to leap to the conclusion that a particular group exists simply because they are awaiting fulfillment of a single prophecy. Jehovah's Witnesses, like evangelical Christians, Indian Ghost Dancers, and alien cults such as Heaven's Gate, believe in a coming change. But that is not the only thing that defines them.

Melton points out: "In the face of dissonance, believers are able to rely upon the broader context of faith, on the unfalsifiable beliefs out of which religious thought-worlds are constructed." So when a prophecy fails—or, at least to an outsider, seems to fail—it is not the end of the world for the true believer. There is enough other cultural support structure in the belief system to shore up the sagging beam.

Prophecy, after all, comes from God. God cannot be wrong. So something else must have happened. Perhaps God was misunderstood. Perhaps the prophet lied or spoke falsely. Melton reminds us of the ancient safeguard in Deuteronomy 18:21 concerning prophecy: "You may ask yourselves, 'How can we know when a message has not been spoken by the Lord?' If what a prophet proclaims in the name of the Lord does not take place or come true, that is a message the Lord has not spoken. That prophet has spoken presumptuously. Do not be afraid of him."

Building on case studies drawn from the Universal Link millennial group in 1967 and the famous Great Disappointment of the Millerites in 1844, Melton comes to the inescapable conclusion that for true believers, *prophecy does not fail—it is merely misunderstood.*

It is important to note that many of the current spate of "Armageddon" books, movies, and articles seem to have learned from the past. Drawing on Jesus' words from Matthew 24:36, "No one knows about that day or hour, not even the angels in heaven, nor the Son, but only the Father," most evangelical scholars will not set dates. Some have hinted: 1975, 1986, 2000, 2006, 2012, and 2017 are among many that have been suggested. But timing for the "blessed hope" is still, officially, an unknown. The "signs of the times" seem to indicate to true believers that we are near the end. But the date for that end is still a mystery, locked in the mind of God.

Sources:

Festinger, Leon, Henry W. Riecken, and Stanley Schacter. "Unfulfilled Prophecies and Disappointed Messiahs." In *Expecting Armageddon: Essential Readings in Failed Prophecy*, ed. Jon R. Stone. New York: Routledge, 2000.

The Holy Bible, New International Version. Grand Rapids, MI: Zondervan, 1978.

Melton, J. Gordon. "Spiritualization and Reaffirmation: What Really Happens When Prophecy Fails." *American Studies* 26:2 (1985): 17–28.

Stone, Jon R., ed. *Expecting Armageddon: Essential Readings in Failed Prophecy.* New York: Routledge, 2000.

Zygmunt, Joseph F. "Prophetic Failure and Chiliastic Identity: The Case of Jehovah's Witnesses."
American Journal of Sociology 75:6 (May 1970): 926–48.

———. "When Prophecies Fail: A Theoretical Perspective on the Comparative Evidence."
American Behavioral Scientist 16:2 (November–December 1972): 245–67.

FALL, THE

The theological problem is simply stated. In Genesis 1 a "good" God creates a "good" world and even declares it to be "very good." Three chapters later everything seems to have soured. Two chapters after that God decides to destroy everything with a flood in order to start over again.

What happened?

All religions that start with a beginning face the same problem and have coped with it in similar ways. In Judaism, Christianity, and Islam, the three great worldwide monotheistic religious traditions existing today, the answer is that humankind "fell" away from God. The problem lies in humans, not in God.

But even this explanation is further elaborated upon. The fall of humankind is one step removed from the first cause of sin, or disobedience, to God. Humans fell because they were tempted by a spiritual being who himself fell away from the grace of God. The devil, Satan, or Iblis fell first (see Devil). He took a third of the angels, who became demons, with him. Disguised as a serpent in the Garden of Eden, he tempted the first woman. Then, when she disobeyed God, her husband, fully realizing what he was doing, decided to follow her into iniquity. They ate the forbidden fruit. They entered into sin.

According to those who read the Bible in a literal fashion, that historic event explains why a "good" God could create a "good" world that went "bad." God didn't do it. Our first parents did. And because sin is inherited by each generation; because each generation is "born into sin," that "original sin" taints us all. Furthermore, it will continue to infect and control us until God does something about it. Humans are incapable of "saving" themselves. God has to do it.

That is the whole purpose of the battle of Armageddon (see Armageddon, Battle of). At the end of time God will personally take on the devil. What the author of the New Testament book known as 1 John calls "the mystery of iniquity" will be forever erased.

Armageddon is the opposite of the Fall. We "fell" away from God in Eden and were denied the opportunity to live forever by eating of the tree of life. We will be "restored" to God and given permission to eat of the tree of life after Satan and his minions lose the battle of Armageddon. The tree will be placed in the New Jerusalem "for the healing of the nations.… No longer will there be any curse" (Rev. 3:1–3).

Those who read the Bible in this literal, historical fashion believe that the history of the human race is the story of what happens between the Fall in Genesis 3 and the battle of Armageddon in Revelation 22.

Adam and Eve driven from the Garden by an angel (Albrecht Dürer, 1510). *Fortean Picture Library.*

Many people, of course, do not read the Bible in this manner. For example, it might seem as though a literal reading of Genesis 1 would lead to a literal reading of the Armageddon account, and that a metaphorical reading of Genesis would lead to a metaphorical understanding of Armageddon. But such is not always the case. There are many evangelical Christians who understand the Garden of Eden story as metaphor but still look to a literal battle of Armageddon, perhaps even in the near future.

And even literalists admit the need for a little interpretation from time to time. Jerry Jenkins, coauthor of the *Left Behind* series of novels based on the book of Revelation, offers this confession: "The Bible says Jesus is going to slay his enemies with a sword that comes out of his mouth. We don't believe there's an actual sword in his mouth. The sword is his word." Jenkins also found himself stuck on the problem of hundreds of millions of people, after the battle of Armageddon, receiving personal interviews with Jesus concerning their possible redemption. If each person got thirty seconds, how long would the process of undoing the Fall take? A few minutes with a calculator so humbled Jenkins that he opted for what he calls a "pluripresence," in which "everyone has the same experience, all personal, in their own language and using their own name."

So is the Fall a literal, historical event or a metaphor? Like many other aspects of religion, it comes down to a personal choice that every individual has to make.

Sources:
Gates, David. "The Pop Prophets." *Newsweek*, May 24, 2004.
The Holy Bible, New International Version. Grand Rapids, MI: Zondervan, 1978.

FALSE PROPHET

The Lord said to me…. "I will raise up for them a prophet…. I will put my words in his mouth, and he will tell them everything I command him. If anyone does not listen to my words that the prophet speaks in my name, I myself will call him to account. But a prophet who presumes to speak in my name anything I have not commanded him to say, or a prophet who speaks in the name of other gods, must be pout to death."

You may say to yourselves, "How can we know when a message has not been spoken by the Lord?" If what a prophet proclaims in the name of the Lord does not take place or come true, that is a message the Lord has not spoken. That prophet has spoken presumptuously. Do not be afraid of him. (Deut. 18:17–22)

Prophets have been a part of the monotheistic tradition since its inception. Besides countless references to prophets and prophecy like those just quoted from Deuteronomy, the books of the Bible from Isaiah to Malachi are all named after the prophets who purportedly wrote them. Speculation during the first century of the Christian era ran rampant that Jesus was a promised prophet (Matt. 16:14). John the Baptist was called "the prophet of the Most High" (Luke 1:76). Muhammad is still called the Prophet by his followers. Nostradamus and Edgar Cayce (see entries on each) are considered prophets in various New Age circles.

Some prophets, when held to the standard of Deuteronomy, failed to make the grade. But the term *false prophet* has a specific meaning when it is applied to Armageddon and the times of the end. Revelation 19:20 and 20:10 use this term to identify the second "beast" of Revelation 13—the "beast out of the earth" (see Beasts, The). This is the false prophet envisioned by Tim LaHaye and Jerry Jenkins in their *Left Behind* series of novels (see *Left Behind* Books) and by others who believe in a futuristic interpretation of Bible prophecy (see Futurist School of Biblical Interpretation).

Of course, this is not the only possible interpretation. For many Christians, the false prophet is a metaphor for any religious system that reinforces systemic wrongs in the political system. When Martin Luther King Jr. led his followers out into the streets of Mississippi, he had to battle entrenched racism not only extolled in the statehouse but preached from many southern pulpits as well. When religious institutions support evil—for example, when religion is used to justify oppression and unjust war—they are said to be filling the role of the metaphorical false prophet of Revelation.

Source:
The Holy Bible, New International Version. Grand Rapids, MI: Zondervan, 1978.

FAMINE

In Matthew 24, Jesus is said to have listed four major "signs of the end":

1. False religions.
2. Wars and rumors of wars.
3. Famines.
4. Earthquakes in various places.

"All these," he said, "are the beginning of birth pangs." Many Christians believe that these "birth pangs" will lead to a new world that will be born following the battle of Armageddon and the destruction of evil.

Of course, the world has always known famine. But the book of Revelation relates famine to the end in a special way. Revelation 6:5–6 depicts famine as one of the famous Four Horsemen of the Apocalypse who will ride forth to prepare the world for the final judgment.

Those who read these passages as literal future history are quite fond of pointing out that wars, ecological disasters, population explosion, and chemical tampering with the food supply are all taking place even now. Hal Lindsey, in his book *Apocalypse Code*, points out:

> The truth is, you know, that the world is headed for a major food crises [*sic*] even without the impact of a major global conflagration. With the third world's population expected to grow by 2 billion people in the next few years, developing countries will need at least 75 percent more food than they are currently producing. Yet, food production globally is growing at its slowest rate in four decades and is on the decline in 90 countries. Grain stocks, in fact, are at their lowest levels in 35 years. By the year 2030 China alone will require all the world's current exports of grain.

These words by a prominent evangelical Christian, when joined with almost daily news reports about global warming, the plight of the modern farmer, bacteria in the food chain, mad cow disease, and high gas prices translating into higher prices at the supermarket, paint a pretty gloomy picture. They offer a lot of ammunition to those inclined to make bleak warnings about the future.

Famine is one of the Four Horsemen of the Apocalypse (Rev. 6:5–6). *Getty Images.*

Sources:
The Holy Bible, New International Version. Grand Rapids, MI: Zondervan, 1978.
Lindsey, Hal. *Apocalypse Code.* Palos Verdes, CA: Western Front Ltd., 1997.

FINAL JUDGMENT

Most monotheistic religions incorporate a final judgment of some kind into their picture of the endtimes (see Eschatology, Comparative). But by far the most popularized version is that of fundamentalist/evangelical Christianity. The well-known image of a bearded man in sackcloth carrying a sign with the words "Repent! The End Is Near!" comes right out of the Bible.

In Acts 17 the apostle Paul is said to have been preaching in Athens. "He was greatly distressed to see that the city was full of idols. So he reasoned with.... a group of Epicurean and Stoic philosophers." Trying to establish a mutual point of contact, Paul cast his eyes about the square and discovered a statue with the inscribed dedication "TO AN UNKNOWN GOD." He then preached a sermon in which he tried to equate the statue with the "new" Christian God who, according to Paul, had been made manifest in Christianity. During that sermon he warned the philosophers of Greece: "For he has set a day when he will judge the world with justice by the man he has appointed. He has given proof of this to all men by raising him from the dead."

Literalist Christians read this verse and think back to the words purportedly preached by Jesus in Matthew 25:31–41:

> When the Son of Man comes in his glory, and all the angels with him, he will sit on his throne in heavenly glory. All the nations will be gathered before him, and he will separate the people from one another as a shepherd separates the sheep from the goats. He will put the sheep on his right hand and the goats on his left.

> Then the King will say to those on his right, "Come, you who are blessed by my father; take your inheritance, the kingdom prepared for you since the creation of the world. For I was hungry and you gave me something to eat, I was thirsty and you gave me something to drink, I was a stranger and you invited me in, I needed clothes and you clothed me, I was sick and you looked after me, I was in prison and you came to visit me."

When the righteous folk hear these words, Jesus went on to say, they will ask, "When did we do all these things?" And the King will answer, "Whatever you did for one of the least of these brothers of mine, you did for me." These actions will earn the righteous "sheep" the reward of "eternal life."

The scenario is repeated, this time cast in the negative mode, for the "goats." They didn't help the weak and afflicted, so they didn't do anything for Jesus. As a result, "they will go away to eternal punishment."

Revelation 20:11–15 echoes the scene:

> Then I saw a great white throne and him who was seated on it. Earth and sky fled from his presence, and there was no place for them. And I saw the dead, great and small, standing before the throne, and books were opened. Another book was opened, which is the book of life. The dead were judged according to what they had done as recorded in the books. The sea gave up the dead that were in it, and death and Hades gave up the dead that were in them, and each person was judged according to what he had done. The death and Hades were thrown into the lake of fire. The lake of fire is the second death. If anyone's name was not found written in the book of life, he was throne into the lake of fire.

This is the Final Judgment.

Do Christians agree that this is a faithful picture of what will someday happen? Of course not. Christians don't agree about anything.

For one thing, the whole thrust of Protestant Christianity since the Reformation has been that human beings are not capable of getting to heaven based on their "works"—that is, what they do in life. Popular cartoons aside, "good" people don't go to heaven to sit on clouds and play harps while "bad" people go to hell and get poked by a pitch-fork-wielding devil. Protestant Christianity is based on the substitutionary atonement of Jesus Christ. Jesus became the substitute for all sinners, taking the punishment they so richly deserve. According to this view, people go to heaven because they are either predestined to go or because they choose to accept Jesus' offer of salvation.

But the passages of scripture just quoted make it rather clear that "sheep" are good folks who do good things and are rewarded with heaven while "goats" are bad folks who do not participate in what is often called "social justice" and will be punished for this failing.

To make all this fit, futurist Bible scholars have had to concoct quite a complicated formula, the gist of which is that we are "saved" by accepting Jesus on faith, but we are "rewarded" for how we act after that acceptance. They base this view of judgment partly on various writings attributed to the apostle Paul. For example, in Hebrews 9:27: "Man is destined to die once, and after that to face judgment." In 2 Corinthians 5:10: "For we must all appear before the judgment seat of Christ, that each one may receive what is due him for the things done while in the

Bad news. *Bob Ferris/Fortean Picture Library.*

body, whether good or bad." In 1 Corinthians 3:14, in an extended passage devoted to building up what he calls "good works," Paul says that although good works do not ensure salvation, they do have an influence on the state of a believer's place in heaven: "If what he had built survives, he will receive his reward. If it is burned up, he will suffer loss; he himself will be saved, but only as one escaping through the flames."

Some Christians disagree with this interpretation. They believe that such a literal way of reading scripture produces a lot of silliness and completely misses the point of what the Bible really is.

Source:
Borg, Marcus. *Reading the Bible Again for the First Time: Taking the Bible Seriously but Not Literally.* San Francisco: HarperSanFrancisco, 2001.

FUTURIST SCHOOL OF BIBLICAL INTERPRETATION

There are two competing ways of interpreting Bible prophecies. The past-historic academic school, perhaps comprising the majority of mainline theology professors in Protestant seminaries today, believes that the original authors were directing their words toward their own contemporaries, describing events and people familiar to them. Sometimes the prophetic images had to be described in code—a way of keeping outsiders, friendly or not, from discovering the message. "Babylon," for instance, was a code word for "Rome." This was no doubt for protection. Rome was then persecuting Christians, and the whereabouts of key Christian leaders needed to be kept secret. When the apostle Peter closes his first epistle with the words "she who is in Babylon … sends you her greetings," he is really writing from Rome but attempting to protect the church that gathers there, in the lair of the Roman "beast." By the same token, the person described with the number "666" was probably well known to first-century audiences (see 666).

But many Protestant theorists insist in a literal reading of prophecy. Unless a clear historic occurrence fulfills exactly the words of biblical prophecy, the event must be yet in the future. This is the view of the futurist school of biblical interpretation. Among other things, futurists believe that the bulk of the events described in Revelation have not yet occurred. They await a future fulfillment, perhaps even in the lifetimes of those now living. This is called the "blessed hope," a phrase taken from Paul's epistle to Titus (2:13) referring to the return of Jesus Christ and the attendant events described prominently in Matthew 24, some of the epistles of Paul, and the book of Revelation.

For a practical application of how these terms relate to specific scripture verses, see the entries Abomination of Desolation and Revelation.

Source:

Borg, Marcus. *Reading the Bible Again for the First Time: Taking the Bible Seriously but Not Literally.* San Francisco: HarperSanFrancisco, 2001.

G

GHOST DANCE

In 1881 the great Sioux chief Sitting Bull surrendered, ending a way of life that had existed, in the minds of his people, forever. Forced onto reservations, criticized because they either could not or would not learn to be farmers on worthless land even white homesteaders didn't want, living off government subsidies that Congress reduced every year and that were often depleted by dishonest Indian agents, the proud people had, within a few short years, been defeated, slaughtered, ridiculed, and demeaned. The buffalo, central to their religion and economy, were destroyed not because the whites needed the food but because of an intentional governmental policy based on the knowledge that the destruction of the great herds meant the destruction of the people.

Seen in these terms, the Plains Indians were the victims of a jihad, a religious war deliberately meant to destroy their heart and soul. It was sacrilege in the worst sense of the word—a war of aggression baptized under the rubric of Manifest Destiny. The Sioux had been called idolaters and devils—religious terms deliberately chosen to brainwash the Christian population, many of whom considered it the work of God to kill Indians. It is a matter of public record that many sermons and newspapers of the time printed, in supposed justification of the slaughter, the Old Testament passages urging the destruction of women, children, and livestock that God is quoted as ordering from time to time against the enemies of Israel: "Now go, attack the Amalekites [Indians] and totally destroy everything that belongs to them. Do not spare them; put to death men and women, children and infants, cattle [buffalo] and sheep, camels [horses] and donkeys" (1 Sam. 15:3). When newspaper reporters were asked about the slaughter of Indian children, it became an editorial staple to repeat the words of the Colorado militia colonel John M. Chivington, who in 1864 commanded at the Sand Creek massacre: "Nits make lice."

In the midst of the destruction an Indian fundamentalist movement began when a Paiute prophet named Wovoka had a vision in the Nevada desert. He saw a

Sitting Bull holding peace pipe, ca. 1884. *Library of Congress.*

new age, marked by the return of the buffalo, the disappearance of the whites, and the resurrection of Indian ancestors. All this would be brought about if the People danced the Ghost Dance and dared to believe. It was a simple dance, marked by religious frenzy no different from that seen in Pentecostal Holiness traditions, Sufi Dervish cults, or Jewish Kabbalah mysticism. People would fall to the ground, perhaps speaking in tongues, and describe visions of a better tomorrow. The prophet didn't call the people to fight. There were certainly antiwhite feelings expressed, but this was not a war dance. Indeed, the cult forbade the use of weapons, even against the white man. Instead, dancers wore sacred shirts they thought would protect them against bullets if they were attacked.

The Ghost Dance beliefs and rituals made newspaper reporters think the Indians were going to rise up against the settlements. Reservation officials felt their authority threatened as word of the new religious movement spread like wildfire. By 1890, Pine Ridge Reservation agent D. E. Royer called for troops. Right next door, James McLaughlin, the agent at Standing Rock Reservation, ordered the arrest of his most famous ward, Sitting Bull, whom he mistakenly thought was the looked-for messiah figure.

On the morning of December 15, forty-three Indian police surrounded the old man's cabin and arrested him when he came outside. Although exactly what happened next is in dispute, fourteen people, including Sitting Bull, were killed. In fear of reprisals that were immediately ordered, hundreds of Indians fled the reservation to seek the shelter of Big Foot, chief of the People camped at the Cheyenne River Reservation.

In the fear-shrouded days that followed, the People eventually surrendered and camped at a place called Wounded Knee. On December 28, they were ordered to turn in their weapons. For a number of reasons, among them the need to hunt and the fear of what might happen next, some of the People refused. When a single shot was fired, probably by a frightened soldier, the army troops began to pour fire into the village. The cavalry, many of whom remembered what had by then become known as "Custer's Last Stand," went berserk. Twenty-five soldiers were killed and thirty-nine wounded, most of them hit by their own crossfire. The dead were buried with full military honors. Between 153 and 300 Indians, mostly women trying in vain to shield their babies, were killed and dumped in a common pit grave. Many of the bodies were mutilated by soldiers seeking grisly "souvenirs."

The Ghost Dance and hopes for renewal were massacred at Wounded Knee. Armageddon had come to the plains.

Not all whites were sympathetic to the "official" version reported to Washington and displayed across the country in newspaper headlines. A former Indian agent with the delightful name of Valentine McGillycuddy had issued an unheeded warning: "If the Seventh Day Adventists prepare for the coming of the Savior, the army is not put in motion. Why should not the Indians have the same privilege?" It was a question asked by many in private. The public at large, seeking easy answers to difficult questions, soon forgot.

Perhaps the best epitaph to the Ghost Dance's messianic dream was written by a civilian worker called in to help with the horrible task of burying the slaughtered Indians in their mass grave, who later recalled his thoughts: "It was a thing to melt the heart of a man, if it was made of stone, to see those little children, with their bodies shot to pieces, thrown naked into the pit."

Sources:
America's Fascinating Indian Heritage. Pleasantville, NY: Reader's Digest Association, 1978.
Neihardt, John G. *Black Elk Speaks*. Lincoln: University of Nebraska Press, 1961.

GLOBAL WARMING

Carbon Dioxide Levels Rise – Mercury Climbs – Oceans Warm – Glaciers Melt – Sea Level Rises – Sea Ice Thins – Permafrost Thaws – Wildfires Increase – Lakes Shrink – Lakes Freeze Up Later – Ice Shelves Collapse – Droughts Linger – Precipitation Increases – Mountain Streams Run Dry – Winter Loses Its Bite – Spring Arrives Earlier – Autumn Comes Later – Plants Flower Sooner – Migration Times Vary – Habitats Change – Birds Nest Earlier – Diseases Spread – Coral Reefs Bleach – Snowpacks Decline – Exotic Species Invade – Amphibians Disappear – Coastlines Erode – Cloud Forests Dry – Temperatures Spike at High Latitudes

What in the world is going on?

So begins a series of articles in the September 2004 edition of *National Geographic* magazine that summarize the latest research on global warming and its effects for the future. Quoting Daniel Fagre, a research scientist from the U.S. Geological Survey Global Change Research program, the article entitled "The Big Thaw," written by Daniel Glick, conveys the essence of Glick's research: "Things that normally happen in geologic time are happening during the span of a human lifetime.... It's like watching the Statue of Liberty melt."

The *New York Times* seems equally concerned about global warming. On January 25, 2005, Larry Rohter wrote an article entitled "Antarctica, Warming, Looks Ever More Vulnerable." After documenting what he calls "the profound and potentially troubling changes that are taking place" as a result of glaciers melting, he concludes with the words of Eric Rignot, a glaciologist at the Jet Propulsion Laboratory in Pasadena: "If Antarctica collapses, it will have an effect on the whole globe." A February 10, 2005, *Times* article by Andrew C. Revkin noted that

2004 was the fourth-warmest year recorded since systematic temperature measurements began around the world in the nineteenth century, with 1998, 2002, and 2003 holding the top three positions. Quoting James E. Hansen, director of NASA's Goddard Institute for Space Studies, Revkin reported that "a weak Niño pattern was likely to make 2005 at least the second warmest year and could push it beyond 1998 and set a record."

In 1997 the Pulitzer Prize–winning journalist Ross Gelbspan wrote *The Heat Is On*. The book examines the alleged duplicity of the coal and oil industries in funding a small group of scientists who have virtually made careers out of claiming before worldwide media that global warming is a hoax. Gelbspan accuses this group of, in his words, "stealing our reality." He believes that these scientists literally have been hired to support the views of those people, including some government officials, who when confronted by evidence that humans may be dangerously affecting the earth's climate simply refuse to consider it. The arguments advanced by these scientists have become familiar in recent years: The climate has fluctuated in the past. Grapes used to grow in a balmy European climate. A thousand years ago a green Greenland greeted the Vikings. Four hundred years ago the Thames River often froze. Climate is a fickle beast. Besides all that, even if the earth warms a bit, for people in Michigan and Montana is that such a bad thing? Why should we give up our way of life for an uncertainty? Science has been wrong before.

This is the kind of thinking that some experts believe caused the United States government to back out of the Kyoto Protocol, an international agreement that would have been a first attempt, many say an insignificant attempt, to limit the emissions believed to cause global warming. It would have, according to U.S. officials, cost too much. But Jerry Mahlman, a representative of the National Center for Atmospheric Research, believes that Kyoto would have been too little too late. He thinks it "would take 40 successful Kyotos" to do the job.

Some specialists believe that the relative shortness of human life makes it hard for us to appreciate the severity of the problem. Over the course of one human lifetime, climate changes might appear insignificant. People in power now won't have to face the consequences of what we have done. Over the course of the next ten years, and certainly not within the short terms of elected officials, things won't change that much. But what used to take thousands of years now takes a hundred years. And climate changes that took a hundred years now take only a few.

The earth's atmosphere both protects us from harmful radiation and acts like a blanket, holding in heat that would otherwise escape into space. Measured levels of CO_2 gas, released when fossil fuels are burned, in the atmosphere have increased so much that the effect is much like that of adding several blankets to a bed on a cold winter night. The effect is cumulative. In other words, things are heating up more quickly than ever before in history. A one-degree jump now will grow into a two-degree jump tomorrow. Than four degrees, than eight, and so on.

A few degrees might not sound like much of a difference. But to see how quickly these numbers can indicate real significance in world climate, it may be helpful to point out that at the height of the last glacial age, when glaciers covered much of North America and Europe, the average global temperature was only seven degrees lower than it is right now.

Some of the effects can even now be seen and measured. For example, when President William Howard Taft created Glacier National Park in 1910, it was crowned by at least 150 glaciers. Now there are fewer than 30. Thirty years from now, maybe sooner, people will wonder how the park got its name. The glaciers will all be gone.

When glacial ice melts, the water has to go somewhere. It eventually flows to the sea. This causes the sea to rise. For every inch of rise in the sea level, an average of eight horizontal feet of shoreline erodes. The problem is that more than a hundred million people in this world live within three feet of sea level.

Other human activities can make the situation worse. In Louisiana, for instance, drilling for fossil fuels removes vast quantities of subsurface water, causing the land to sink. This surface land is then flooded by seawater. Louisiana is currently losing twenty-five square miles of coastal wetlands every single year.

In the United States more and more people every year flock to the arid Southwest in the winter. People need water. In the desert, water comes primarily from rivers and dams. The largest single source of water in the region is Lake Powell, formed by damming the Colorado River. Lake Powell is now holding less water than ever in its brief history. An ugly "bathtub ring" is clearly visible to those who boat on its usually placid surface. Will there be enough water for the grandchildren of these boaters to find recreation there? No one knows.

The problems mount up. Earlier springs and later autumns have affected the migration patterns of many species of animals, often disrupting their access to seasonal food sources. Does this mean extinction? For some, almost certainly. It seems probable that future generations will look back upon their ancestors and curse them for their shortsightedness. But descendants don't vote in elections for their ancestors. So the downward spiral of upward temperatures continues.

There are those, of course, who disagree with the whole idea that humans are bringing about global warming. In Michael Crichton's novel *State of Fear*, the villains are not evil megalomaniacs fashioned after those who plot to take over the world in James Bond movies. They are tree-hugging environmentalists who are proponents of the Kyoto Protocol and use the "liberal media" to advance their goals of world domination. Crichton comments: "It was very difficult to get my head around the idea that this widely held belief [global warming] may not be true, and I thought, 'If I'm going to do a book, how would I structure it so that someone could even hear it a little bit?'"

Sources:
Appenzeller, Tim, and Dennis R. Dimick. "Signs from Earth." *National Geographic*, September 2004, 10–11.

Glick, Daniel. "The Big Thaw." *National Geographic*, September 2004, 12–33.

Gray, Kevin. "Hot Times in 2004: Year One of the Warmest to Date." *Daytona Beach News-Journal*, December 16, 2004.

Kakutani, Michiko. "Beware! Tree-Huggers Plot Evil to Save World." *New York Times*, December 13, 2004.

Revkin, Andrew C. "New Climate Thriller: Scary, but Is It Science?" *New York Times*, December 13, 2004.

———. "2004 Was Fourth_warmest Year Ever Recorded." *New York Times*, February 10, 2005.

Rohter, Larry. "Antarctica, Warming, Looks Ever More Vulnerable." *New York Times*, January 25, 2005.

GOD

"God is the eschatological hope."

Theologians have employed this statement ever since the nineteenth century to describe the deity who, according to traditional monotheistic religions, will bring about Armageddon. God is the force behind Armageddon. God is predicted to be the final victor of the battle. The war between God and the devil is what first prompted the term *Armageddon* to be used (see Armageddon). A climactic battle between good and evil was the principal theological reason-for-being of the world's first monotheistic religion (see Zoroastrianism). In other words, without a conception of an Armageddon, monotheism might not even have arisen.

But who, or what, is God?

Most human beings define God by using one of five conceptual categories. Each of these categories pictures a God who has a distinctly different role to play in bringing about the end of the world. One's conception of divinity determines one's view of how the world will end. It is revealing to see how different these conceptions can be.

God as Revealed Personality

This is the God of monotheistic religion, the God who exists outside of time and space but will step through the veil at the end of time to reveal himself to humankind. (The masculine pronoun is used here because in this tradition God has historically been pictured and referred to as male.)

In spite of the great separation that monotheists believe exists between Creator and creation, they hold that God has "appeared" to human beings in the past and will "appear" again at the end of time.

In Judaism, God used various mediums to shade his appearance. Sometimes he spoke through angels, theophanies, or prophets. He spoke to Moses through a burning bush. Often he communicated to priests at the Tent of Meeting when they "cast the Urim and Thummim," which appear to have been some sort of sacred dice. Once he spoke through Balaam's donkey.

These intermediaries were not used because God was playing hard-to-get or being mysterious. There was a very practical reason God had to "filter" himself. In Exodus 33 Moses pleaded with God, "Now show me your glory." God's reply was simple: "No one may see me and live." Moses was hidden in the cleft of a rock and allowed to see only God's back (or "back parts," as the King James Version has it). Even at that, Moses wore a veil after he came from meetings with the Almighty because "his face was radiant."

According to Jewish teaching, God will appear at the end of time in the human form of a messiah who will restore earth to its intended form and bring peace and pros-

The Eternal Father (Guercino, ca. 1630). *The Bridgeman Art Library/Getty Images.*

perity to all (see Eschatology, Comparative). In Christianity, God revealed himself by "taking the form of a servant, being born in the likeness of men" (Phil. 2:7). "The Word was made flesh and lived for a while among us" (John 1:14). "The Son is the radiance of God's glory and the exact representation of his being" (Heb. 1:3).

The primary revelation of Jesus Christ was followed by another revelation through the written word. "All Scripture is God-breathed, and is useful" (2 Tim. 3:16). According to this view, at the end of time, God, through the person of Jesus Christ, will return to restore all things after the battle of Armageddon.

Islam recognizes both these revelations, even calling Jews and Christians "people of the book." The Qur'an reminds us, "We believe in ... what was revealed to Abraham, Isma'il, Isaac, Jacob, and the Tribes, and in (the Books) given to Moses, Jesus, and the prophets, from their Lord" (3:84). But Muhammad taught that both Jews and Christians rejected the revealed God. Islam teaches that a final revelation was given, that revelation being the Holy Qur'an, dictated to Muhammad, who legend says could neither read nor write, by an angel and obtaining its final form over a period of only eighteen years after the prophet's death. Allah, "the God," has made his final revelation, has called for the world to submit to his will (*Muslim* means "one who submits" to the will of Allah), and awaits the world's response.

Other world religions, to a lesser degree, contain elements of revelation. The "33 million gods" of Hinduism are all revelations of the face of the Unknowable. In Zoroastrianism, Ahura Mazda spoke through the prophet Zarathustra. Indigenous religions often communicate with God through animal spirits.

The common denominator of most conceptions of God as revealed personality is that such a great gulf exists between Creator and creation that intermediaries are necessary, but that God will complete his work and restore the world at the final, climactic battle of history. This is the principal idea of God that has led to the modern, popular conception of Armageddon as the final battle between good and evil.

God as First Cause

This definition, often referred to as Deism, was popular among the "founding fathers" of the United States. Although they are usually thought of as men of "Christian" convictions, Thomas Jefferson and many others among them thought of God more in terms of what came to be called the "watchmaker analogy."

If you are walking down a lane and find a watch keeping perfect time, you have to assume someone made that watch, wound it up, and then, for whatever reason, walked away. It's simply too big a leap to think the watch was made by accident or somehow pulled itself together out of raw materials. The only conclusion any logical person can reach is that somewhere, hidden from view, is a watchmaker who made the watch and set it to working. Perhaps he is hiding and watching to see what you do with his masterpiece. But since you can't see him anywhere, it could be that he simply left his creation behind and went away to another task. You don't know anything about him except that he makes good watches. Even his existence is pure deduction. There is no evidence except for the watch he left behind. It is a logical deduction. There seems to be no better way of explaining the watch you hold in your hand. But the watchmaker is revealed only by his craftsmanship.

This metaphor illustrates the belief that God must be the first cause, the One before and behind the "Big Bang" of creation. "The heavens reveal the glory of God," says the psalmist. "The skies proclaim the work of his hands" (Ps. 19:1). Those who hold this position believe that the universe is simply too big and too complex not to have been planned by a Mind or to have come into existence without a Creator. There may not be evidence that God is in communication with us—after all, we have only the word of prophets and preachers for that. But any logical person has to deduce that if a simple thing like a watch can't pull itself together out of nothing, the universe didn't either.

People who hold this conception of God generally believe that—again like a watch—the universe will someday run down. It will gradually slow down, cool down, and stop working. Before that cosmic event takes place, something will have to happen to the people of planet Earth. Either humans will evolve into spiritual beings or God will somehow bring about a spiritual Armageddon, a crisis in which the jump from material to spiritual happens suddenly, perhaps supernaturally. This is the position taken by many so-called New Age groups who see human development as an expression of divinity growing up into ultimate spirituality.

God as Cultural Phenomenon

"Man makes religion; religion does not make man.... Religion is the sigh of the oppressed creature, the sentiment of a heartless world, and the soul of soulless conditions. It is the opium of the people." These words, written by Karl Marx, represent the view that God is a human invention, cast in different shapes by different cultures, usually to buttress social power hierarchies. Sigmund Freud wrote that belief in God was a "universal obsessional neurosis." He considered God to be a cosmic projection of our love-hate relationship with our parents.

Certainly many cultures have enlisted religion in support of established and often oppressive authority. In India religious belief produced a caste system that kept people "in their place" socially. The same thing happened in pre–Civil War America when many plantation owners—and many other white people—believed that God had ordained slavery. Today it is not uncommon to hear the argument that Judaism, Christianity, and Islam alike "invented" a male God at least in part to subjugate women. Because almost every culture has produced a God created in its own image, it's easy to come to the conclusion that God is a cultural invention. Those who hold to this belief generally refer to themselves as atheists, declaring, like Marx, that God is an invention of humankind, a cultural phenomenon. In this view Armageddon often becomes a metaphor for class warfare. If God is created in the image of humanity, perfect "divinity" will not be reached until a perfect society is created. The image of God projected by the elite of society is really the devil who seeks to rule and subjugate the working class. The humble and downtrodden masses who represent what early Christian writers referred to as "gentle Jesus, meek and mild" must revolt in order to overthrow the devil. Armageddon represents the class warfare that will someday restore the "image of God" to humanity. Jesus said, in Matthew 10:34,

> Do not suppose that I have come to bring peace to the earth. I did not
> come to bring peace, but a sword. For I have come to turn
>
> "a man against his father,
> a daughter against her mother,
> a daughter-in-law against her mother-in-law—
>   a man's enemies will be the members of his
>   own household."

To those who follow the secular religion of Karl Marx, these words are a clarion call to social action.

God as Myth

Myths are guidepaths into human experience left by those who have gone before. They are stories illustrating truths, often richly layered. Adults often read children's stories on quite another level than that of the surface narrative. Like poetry, myths sometimes express the inexpressible.

Western society's math-and-science craze has produced a group of very literal-minded readers whose common conception is that myths are really nothing more than entertaining lies. We insist, for example, that those who wrote scripture must have been recording what they considered to be history, even though the original authors lived in a radically different culture from ours and there is ample evidence that, for example, the author or authors of Genesis did not think God really created the world in six days.

An Eskimo shaman used to begin his creation stories by saying, with a twinkle in his eye, "It may not have happened just like this, but this is a true story!" Jesus used to teach with great insight when he began his parable-myths, "A certain man went out to …" He didn't warn his listeners that he was making up the story. They knew that. What he and his audience were interested in was the deeper truth the story conveyed.

So all this doesn't mean that myths are not "true." They can be more "true" than literal fact. Myths can convey more insight through an "Aha!" experience than a straight telling of the facts because facts do not always convey the essence of the underlying reality. Poets and artists understand this. But many others do not.

Such is the case, some believe, with the idea of God. Calling God a myth does not mean that God does not exist. It just means that God exists in a form that mere facts cannot convey. In Hindu thought, for instance, Brahman is completely inde-scribable. "No tongue can spoil it," is how the sages put it. Brahman is not even a god. Brahman is more a principle. Brahman came before language, so how can words pin him/her/it down? (Even pronouns fail because Brahman is not just a noun.) The 33 million gods of India are merely faces of the indescribable.

Those who claim that God is a myth are not necessarily saying God doesn't exist. They are saying God exists in a form we are completely unable to understand and describe, because God comes before language and patterns of thought. The only way to see God is to come at God obliquely through mythology.

According to this view of God, Armageddon is a myth—a bookend to the Genesis story. Genesis, while purporting to tell us how we got here, reveals a lot of truth about what we are like. Armageddon tells a story about the end of the world but reveals truths about ethical behavior and immoral actions. Armageddon becomes "the moral of the story." It is what will happen if we don't straighten up and fly right. It is also an assurance that despite the difficulties we see around us, in the end, we will "all live happily ever after."

God as Expression of the Unknown

Historically, unanswered questions have been left to God. What caused a mountain to rise from a plain? Manitou. How did we get fire? Agni. What force was responsible for the disappearance of strange animals? Noah's flood. Who causes light-ning? Thor.

Religions form along the borders of the unknown. The whole science-vs.-reli-gion argument often has at its core the unstated assumption that as science pushes back the boundary of human knowledge, there is less and less need for God. People who hold this view generally believe that God is the historical answer to questions better answered by scientific research. The place to find truth, they imply, is not in the church, synagogue, or mosque, but in the laboratory.

But there is another category of folk who see God as an expression of the unknown. There exists in the cosmos that which cannot be analyzed under a microscope. What is love? Why are some poems "better" than others? What is quality? Why, in spite of everything, do some people believe they actually talk to God? And, wonder of wonders, that God talks back? They aren't all crazy. How can it be explained?

These questions point to answers existing in the realm of the spiritual, not the material. This leads some people to the conclusion that there must be something out there bigger than our physical existence. To these people, "God" becomes a term to explain the unexplainable. Miracles, answered prayers, and coincidences compel us, according to this view, to believe we are not alone. God is not to be explained under this way of thinking. God's existence is simply to be accepted.

Many who belong to organized religions hold this belief, even when confronted by the elaborately explained systems of theologians and orthodox teachers. Both for those who don't like to think too deeply about things and for those who believe we can never really know God, it's a convenient way to go. Those who hold this view of God tend to think of Armageddon as another unknown. They tend to refer to comets and asteroids, global warming and ice ages, as "Armageddon events." Any potential catastrophe that could end life as we know it could turn out to be "Armageddon."

Sources:

Armstrong, Karen. *A History of God.* New York: Alfred A. Knopf, 1993.

Fisher, Mary Pat. *Living Religions.* 3rd ed. Upper Saddle River, NJ: Prentice Hall, 1991.

Hawking, Stephen W. *A Brief History of Time: From the Big Bang to Black Holes.* New York: Bantam, 1988.

Marx, Karl. "Contribution to the Critique of Hegel's Philosophy of Right." In *Karl Marx, Early Writings,* trans. and ed. T. B. Bottomore, 43–44. London: C. A. Watts, 1963.

Miles, Jack. *God: A Biography.* New York: Vintage, 1995.

Miller, Kenneth R. *Finding Darwin's God.* New York: HarperCollins, 2000.

Willis, Jim. *The Religion Book: People, Places, Saints, and Seers.* Detroit: Visible Ink Press, 2004.

GOG AND MAGOG

In the book of Ezekiel (see entry), Gog, chief prince of Meshech and Tubal, originally came from the land of Magog. The thirty-eighth chapter has him leading the forces that arise to do battle with Yahveh in the final, unnamed, climactic battle of history. In Revelation 20:8, however, Magog is no longer a country. He seems to be either a person—a companion of Gog as the two fight against Jesus at the final battle that ends the Millennium—or a symbol, along with Gog, for the nations of the world. When the thousand years are over, Satan will be released from his prison and will go out to deceive the nations in the four corners of the earth—Gog and Magog—to gather them for battle.

The problem is further complicated by the fact that the Hebrew word *gog* means "chief." In other words, the verse in Ezekiel might mean that "Gog" is not a name, but a title, the "chief" of a country called Magog.

Whatever the original authors of both the Old and New Testaments meant, Gog and Magog are names prominently associated with the final battle of world history.

Gog and Magog depicted as warrior giants, Guildhall, London. *Fortean Picture Library.*

Source:

Buttrick, George A., ed. *The Interpreter's Dictionary of the Bible.* 4 vols. New York: Abingdon Press, 1962.

GRAHAM, BILLY

Billy Graham is possibly the best-known religious leader in America. His "congregation" stretches across the whole planet. From humble farm beginnings in Charlotte, North Carolina, as a quiet boy who could often be found reading in the hayloft, Graham went on to become the world's foremost preacher, a pastor even to presidents.

Born in 1918, Graham made what he would describe as a "personal commitment to God" in 1934 in the tent of a traveling evangelist named Mordecai Ham. In 1939 he was ordained in the Southern Baptist Convention. From his family's farm he went to Florida Bible Institute (now Trinity College) and on to Wheaton College in Illinois. While at Wheaton he met and married Ruth McCue Bell. For a short time he was pastor of the First Baptist Church in Western Springs, Illinois, but as soon as World War II ended, he was preaching to service members both at home and in

Europe. Thus began his ministry to the world. He has been traveling ever since.

In 1950 he founded the Billy Graham Evangelistic Association in Minneapolis. He moved the organization to his hometown of Charlotte in 2003. Graham has ministered in person, on TV and radio, through a syndicated newspaper column called *My Answer*, and in books and films to a worldwide audience. Among the many awards he has won for his work are the Congressional Gold Medal and the National Conference of Christians and Jews award for his efforts to foster better understanding between the two faiths.

Given his media presence and appeal, it is no accident that Graham's premillennial, pretribulational views about the Second Coming of Jesus and the battle of Armageddon had a tremendous impact on American society. Many people unfamiliar with the theological fine points of biblical interpretation simply assumed that Graham's position was *the* Christian position. With so many of his crusades broadcast on television, each typically featuring a sermon on the Second Coming, he was probably the most respected and listened-to preacher on the subject.

Billy Graham in 1966. *Warren K. Leffler/Library of Congress.*

Because of numerous trips to the White House to act as spiritual adviser to several presidents, many assumed that Graham was talking about biblical prophecy with those in power. But Graham has been a paragon of trust, and always, true to his strict ministerial ethics, he has kept confidential the substance of his discussions with political leaders. It is that very trust, which he has gone to great lengths to protect and maintain, that has made him such a beloved figure of American religion.

Sources:
"Billy Graham." http://www.billygraham.org/mediaRelations/bios.asp.
Hudson, Winthrop S. *Religion in America.* New York: Charles Scribner's Sons, 1965.

GREAT DISAPPOINTMENT OF 1844 *see* Failed Prophecy; Millerites

GREAT TRIBULATION

For then there will be great distress, unequaled from the beginning of the world until now—and never to be equaled again. If those days had not been cut short, no one would survive, but for the sake of the elect those days will be shortened. At that time, if anyone says to you,

"Look, here is the Christ!" or, "There he is!" do not believe it. For false Christs and false prophets will appear and perform great signs and miracles to deceive even the elect—if that were possible. See, I have told you ahead of time.

So if anyone tells you, "There he is, out in the desert," do not go out; or, "Here he is, in the inner rooms," do not believe it. For as the lightning comes from the east and flashes to the west, so will be the coming of the Son of Man. Wherever there is a carcass, there the vultures will gather.

Immediately after the distress of those days

"the sun will be darkened,
and the moon will not give its light;
the stars will fall from the sky,
and the heavenly bodies will be shaken."

At that time the sign of the Son of Man will appear in the sky, and all the nations of the earth will mourn. They will see the Son of Man coming on the clouds of the sky, with power and great glory. (Matt. 24:21–29)

These words are attributed to Jesus of Nazareth and are part of the sermon often called the Olivet Discourse, so named because he delivered it on the Mount of Olives outside Jerusalem. Jesus uses the word *distress* twice, the first time prefacing it with *great*. This, however, is the New International Version's translation. The King James Version uses the word *tribulation* instead, as do most evangelical and fundamentalist Christians, who designate the "Tribulation" and the "Great Tribulation" as the last years of human history before the battle of Armageddon. The Tribulation refers to a seven-year period. The Great Tribulation will be the last three and one-half years of that period.

To understand where the "seven years" came from, it is necessary to begin in the book of Daniel, chapter 9, and the prophecy of the "seventy sevens." This is an extremely difficult passage to translate, and its exegesis can vary considerably depending on what translation of the Bible the scholar prefers. (See the entry Seventy Sevens for a full treatment of this passage.)

Daniel, living in Babylon as a result of the Babylonian captivity described in the book of 2 Chronicles, among others, claimed that he was visited by the angel Gabriel, who told him that "seventy sevens," or "seventy weeks," were to be allowed the nation of Israel. This period was to begin when a future command was issued to begin the rebuilding of Jerusalem. Most interpreters teach that these "seventy sevens" or "seventy weeks" are weeks of years—in other words, 490 years, or seventy times seven.

Then follows a very difficult verse to translate. Most versions of the Bible render it something like this:

"Know and understand this: From the issuing of the decree to restore and rebuild Jerusalem until the Anointed One, the ruler, comes, there will be seven 'sevens' and sixty-two 'sevens.' ... the Anointed One will be cut off.... The people of the ruler who will come will destroy the city and sanctuary.... He [the ruler who "will come"] will confirm a covenant with many for one 'seven.' In the middle of the 'seven' he will put an end to sacrifice and offering."

After doing the math involved, some scholars have come to believe that if the "Anointed One" refers to Jesus, the passage becomes a specific historical prophecy. It says that from the time of the command to rebuild Jerusalem a period of 483 years (7 "sevens," or 49 years, added to 62 "sevens," or 434 years) will pass before Jesus, the Anointed One, comes and is "cut off," or crucified.

Sir Robert Anderson, writing in the nineteenth century, located the command to restore Jerusalem in the book of Nehemiah, chapter 2. In this passage, Artaxerxes, king of Persia, ordered Nehemiah, his royal cup-bearer, to return to Jerusalem and restore it to its former glory. Anderson concluded from his study of history that this command was issued in March of 445 BCE. Consulting tables and charts obtained from London's Royal Observatory and doing the calculations he felt necessary to superimpose the Jewish lunar calendar with its thirty-day months over Western solar timekeeping, and then taking into account leap years and recorded changes in the Western calendar, he determined that the 483 years ended on April 6 in the year 33 CE. Anderson believed this to be the date of Jesus' triumphal entry to Jerusalem, traditionally celebrated on Palm Sunday. Anderson's "proof" of the connection was that on this day Jesus finally announced who he really was. Usually, after performing a miracle or healing, it was Jesus' habit to try to keep it quiet. He often told the recipients of his healing not to tell anyone. On the first Palm Sunday, however, when, according to Luke 19, the people of Jerusalem began to shout and sing verses from Psalm 118, the Coronation Psalm, the religious leaders told him to quiet the mobs. Jesus' reply led to his execution five days later: "If they keep quiet, the stones will cry out." A few minutes later he wept over the city, saying, "If you, even you, had only known on this day what will bring you peace—but now it is hidden from your eyes."

Anderson believed that this was the day prophesied by Gabriel to Daniel. But most of the people of Jerusalem didn't know it, and they rejected the "Anointed One." He was "cut off," or crucified. As a result, God's clock stopped seven years short of fulfilling history. Those seven years, Anderson theorized, would come later. A divine parenthesis was dropped into the time between the first 483 years and the last seven needed to reach 490. This parenthesis, he said, is the Church Age. It began when the Holy Spirit came down and filled believers on the day of Pentecost, the birthday of the Church (Acts 2). It will end when the Holy Spirit is withdrawn at the Rapture (see Rapture). When the Rapture occurs, God's clock will start again. The last seven years of history will take place. This period is called the Tribulation.

Daniel said that "the ruler who is to come" will "confirm a covenant with many for one 'seven'"—a seven-year period. Most conservative scholars interpret this to mean that the "ruler who is to come," the antichrist, will cause a treaty to be signed that will bring peace to the Middle East. This feat, seemingly impossible in today's political climate, will springboard the antichrist into a position of leadership in the world.

In Daniel 12 the prophet returns to his end-of-the-world theme, but this time, in two different places, he refers to the very end of history, called the Great Tribulation by many, describing it as being a "time, times, and half a time," in length. If "time" equals one, "times" equals two, and "half a time" equals one half, this might be a veiled reference to three and one-half years. This period is referenced again in the eleventh verse, where it is referred to as "1,290 days." Assuming a Jewish calendar of twelve thirty-day months, three and one-half years equals 1,260 days, very close the 1,290 Daniel uses.

The eleventh chapter of the book of Revelation, building on Daniel's theme, refers to a period of "42 months," which is three and one-half years, and a period of "1,260 days," again, about three and one-half years, during which two witnesses will be stationed in Jerusalem, preaching during the last, tumultuous days of history. Many conservative scholars believe that this is a New Testament echo of an Old Testament theme.

To summarize, the typical evangelical scheme of the endtimes is that the Jews were given 483 years to repent, failed to do so, and instead spurned God's offer of salvation through Jesus, the Messiah. The Church Age was instituted to give the world a second chance. After the church is removed from earth at the time of the Rapture, the last seven years of history, called the Tribulation, will begin when the antichrist signs a peace treaty in the Middle East and is hailed as a conquering hero. He will break the peace treaty halfway into the Tribulation, declare himself to be God, and attempt to rule the world from Jerusalem. When he does so, announcing his divinity from the steps of the rebuilt temple (see Abomination of Desolation; Temple at Jerusalem), the last three and one-half years of history, called the Great Tribulation, will begin, setting the stage for the battle of Armageddon (see Armageddon, Battle of) and the return of Jesus Christ.

Sources:

Anderson, Sir Robert. *The Coming Prince: The Last Great Monarch of Christendom*. London: Hodder and Stoughton, 1881.

Holy Bible, New International Version. Grand Rapids, MI: Zondervan, 1978.

Lindsey, Hal, with C. C. Carlson. *The Late Great Planet Earth*. Grand Rapids, MI: Zondervan, 1970.

H

HAWKING, STEPHEN

The theoretical physicist Stephen Hawking is sometimes compared to no less a luminary than Albert Einstein. Although for many years Hawking has been confined to a wheelchair, a victim of Lou Gehrig's disease, his mind has soared where few can follow. Through mathematics and physics he has probed essential questions concerning the birth and death of the universe: Was there a beginning to time? Will there be an end? Is the universe infinite or does it have boundaries? What are "black holes"? Do they really exist? Can anything escape from them?

In his book *A Brief History of Time*, Hawking asks questions about the beginning of the universe that, if answered, might very well lead to an understanding of its end. He admits that, until recently, there were only two ways to describe the existence of the cosmos. It either began at a point in time and space or it is infinite, with no beginning and no end. By using the complex concept of "imaginary time," however, an almost infinite number of theories can be postulated: "Time is imaginary and is indistinguishable from directions in space. To calculate the probability of finding a real space-time with some certain property, such as looking the same at every point and in every direction, one adds up the waves associated with all the histories that have that property.... If we knew the initial state of our universe, we would then know its entire history."

Hawking proposed a radical suggestion at a conference on cosmology held at the Vatican in 1981. Perhaps, he said, "space and time together form a surface that is finite in size but does not have any boundary or edge." It's certainly hard for a layperson to conceive of an object that has a finite size and no edges. But Hawking would argue that our perceiving things to be a certain way doesn't mean that's the way they really are. In our experience, squares or circles have edges. But maybe our experiences can't be trusted. We can't make a square circle. But maybe God can—if there is a God:

> The idea that space and time may form a closed surface without boundary also had profound implications for the role of God in the affairs of the universe. With the success of scientific theories in describing events, most people have come to believe that God allows the universe to evolve according to a set of laws and does not intervene in the universe to break these laws. However, the laws do not tell us what the universe should have looked like when it started—it would still be up to God to wind up the clockwork and choose how to start it off. So long as the universe had a beginning, we could suppose it had a creator. But if the universe is really completely self-contained, having no boundary or edge, it would have neither beginning nor end: it would simply be. What place, then, for a creator?

Like the universe itself, questions about its end are left, according to Hawking, open-ended. Quoting the anthropic principle (see Big Crunch, Big Chill, and Big Rip), he asks, "Why did the big bang [see Big Bang] occur about ten thousand million years ago?" He answers his own question: "Because it takes that long for intelligent beings to evolve." It takes that long for things to cool down long enough for complicated organisms to have a chance for survival. Then the slow process of biology has to be given enough time to work. Then a species needs time to develop the experiences needed to learn how to ask the proper questions. One of those questions concerns how they got here in the first place. Another is, "Where are we going?" And a third is, "Why does the universe exist?"

Perhaps someday we will have answers to the first two questions, difficult as they are, but the third may forever elude us. As Hawking puts it, "If we find the answer to that, it would be the ultimate triumph of human reason—for then we would know the mind of God."

Source:
Hawking, Stephen W. *A Brief History of Time: From the Big Bang to Black Holes.* New York: Bantam, 1988.

HEAVEN *see* Eternal Life

HEAVEN'S GATE

In 66 CE, the appearance of Halley's comet in the skies above Palestine caused people to wonder if God was sending some kind of warning. Four years later, Titus and his Roman legions destroyed Jerusalem.

The same comet was seen prior to the battle of Hastings in 1066. Its return in 1456 was thought by some to show God's approval of the successful invasion of Constantinople by the Turks. After Halley's showed up in 1835, it was blamed for everything from a fire that destroyed much of downtown New York City in December to the fall of the Alamo early the next year. It was also accused of causing wars all over

Latin America. When, on its return in 1910, astronomers predicted that the earth would actually pass through the comet's tail, "comet pills" were sold to protect people from the poisonous gases they might encounter. The pills worked. No one who took them died. No one who didn't take them died, either.

In 79 CE, just before the eruption of Vesuvius that destroyed both Pompeii and Herculaneum, a comet appeared night after night, causing widespread fear that something terrible was about to happen. A comet seen in 1665 received the blame for a subsequent plague epidemic that claimed ninety thousand lives in London.

In the spring of 1997, many people throughout the world thrilled to the sight of the comet Hale-Bopp hanging overhead, its long tail lighting up the night sky. For some it brought delight and awe. For others, death.

The comet was discovered by two independent observers, Alan Hale of New Mexico and Thomas Bopp in Arizona, on the night of July 23, 1995. As news of the sighting flashed around the world via the Internet, some people claimed to have detected an object accompanying the comet's progress.

A group of Web page designers who called themselves Heaven's Gate, founded and led by a man named Marshall Applewhite, decided they needed to shed their "earthly containers" in order to be "beamed up" aboard a spacecraft following in the comet's wake. Over the course of three days ending on March 26, 1997, they acted on this belief. Web page designers are an organized, tidy lot. They apparently died in orderly shifts, some helping others to drink a mixture of phenobarbital and vodka. A few, it was later discovered, had undergone voluntary castration in the months before the suicide.

Some of the thirty-nine bodies of Heaven's Gate cult members found in Rancho Sante Fe, California, after their carefully planned and executed mass suicide. *Nick Ut, Associated Press/San Diego Sheriff's Department.*

What is heaven's gate? It is the portal through which people of this earth may enter the sphere where inhabitants of the "next level" dwell. The name comes from Genesis 28:17. Jacob, grandson of Abraham, fell asleep at the place he subsequently called Beth-El ("house of God"). He dreamed he saw a ladder reaching up to heaven. Angels, messengers of God, climbed up and down to carry out their ministry on earth. Perhaps inspired by the ziggurats of the Babylonians, Jacob raised a standing stone, the pillow on which he had slept, and exclaimed, "This is the gate of heaven!"

The thirty-nine members of the Heaven's Gate cult who died together obviously believed in the existence of this newest return, or opening, of the gate of heaven. They believed that Jacob's experience was probably a contact with members of the higher sphere. Their days consisted of getting up in the morning, praying, dressing in black with severe GI haircuts, doing their work, forgoing sex, drugs, and alcohol, and staring at the heavens through a telescope, trying to spot the spaceship that was coming for them.

Sources:

Kronk, Gary W. "Comet Hysteria and the Millennium: A Commentary." http://cometography. com/hysteria.html.

"One Year Later, Heaven's Gate Suicide Leaves Only a Faint Trail." http://www.cnn.com/US/ 9803/25/heavens.gate/.

HELL *see* Eternal Life

HERMENEUTICS

How does one interpret a document? Specifically as it relates to Armageddon, how does one interpret the Bible? And within that category, how does one interpret biblical prophecy? Were the prophets foretelling the future when they described events such as those found in Daniel, Ezekiel, and Revelation? (See entries on each.) Or were they merely using familiar conventions of apocalyptic writing (see Apocalyptic Writing) while speaking to their contemporaries? (See Futurist School of Biblical Interpretation.)

Hermeneutics is the art and science of interpretation, including biblical interpretation, not merely from one language to another but in terms of what a given passage really means. It is art because it calls for nuance and craft, science because it demands technique and skill. There are accepted academic rules to follow that protect students from falling into the subjective trap of simply saying, "It seems to me …"

The Bible was written within a contextual and social tradition. It is easy to forget that fact and, for example, to buttress present-day prejudices by taking verses out of their textual and historical context and applying them to present-day situations of which the original authors could have had no conception. A consistent hermeneutic position guards against this very common problem.

To illustrate the use of hermeneutics as it relates to biblical issues, consider the famous commandment "Thou shalt not kill." That seems very straightforward and easy to understand. But only a few pages later, the same God who delivered this commandment instructs his people to enter the Promised Land and kill all the Canaanites. If the word *kill* has the same meaning in both passages, God appears to be either fickle or schizophrenic.

This is precisely the problem that many encounter when they read about the bloody battle of Armageddon. How, they ask, can a loving, forgiving God send unbelievers to a tormented eternity in hell? How can a compassionate God torture the damned forever and offer them no chance of pardon? How could anyone be happy in heaven knowing that loved ones who died without asking for God's forgiveness are suffering without hope or respite?

As an example of efforts to reconcile a loving God with a vengeful one, return for a moment to the seemingly conflicting instructions about killing. In order to retain a consistent view of God, it is argued, one must look at the context of the two passages. The commandment not to kill is given within the framework of a social contract dealing with neighbors, family, and community. The order to kill the Canaanites is issued within the context of national war and political conquest. So perhaps it would be best to translate the commandment as "Thou shalt not murder." That leaves loopholes for such things as self-defense, police work, and warfare. If a contemporary Jewish or Christian soldier goes into battle with the idea that he is breaking one of the Ten Commandments, he might never pull a trigger. Soldiers are, after all, trained to kill. But they are not trained to murder.

In an attempt to produce a consistent hermeneutic concerning the battle of Armageddon, one must make a conscious choice. The text can be taken literally or metaphorically. If literally, then all we can do is accept the words as we read them from the Bible, on the basis that God has the right to do anything God wants because God is God. If metaphorically, then the role of the author or authors unknown comes into play. The text no longer necessarily means that God will do exactly what the text says, but merely that this is what a writer thought God would do—or even that the writer was using poetic license to make a point about ethical or moral behavior.

Hermeneutics is currently the principal battleground for the forces of liberal and conservative Christianity. Every argument essentially boils down to a debate about how to interpret the Bible—in short, to hermeneutics.

Source:
Fackre, Dorothy, and Gabriel Fackre. *Christian Basics*. Grand Rapids, MI: Eerdmans, 1991.

HINDU VIEWS OF THE END

Within the framework of philosophical Hinduism, time is circular. It is the ever-spinning wheel of samsara. It has no beginning and no end. So there really can never be an Armageddon in the sense that linear monotheistic religions envision it (see Eschatology, Comparative).

To understand how the Hindu view differs from the traditional Western religious conception, we must begin with the Hindu understanding of reality. Hinduism teaches that everything we see and experience is real, but because it is in constant flux and change, it is ultimately an illusion (*maya*). The book you hold in your hand seems very solid and permanent, but in fact it is made up of atoms, constantly in motion and never at rest. All is motion. Nothing is solid. It only appears that way. Leave the book out in the rain for a few years and you will see a different reality. Bury it in the earth and come back a thousand years from now and you will discover that what it appears to be now is only one stage of appearance on a journey that lasts forever. And on a totally different level, does the reality of the book consist of material elements at all? Is it paper and ink, or the essence of ideas that are written on the paper with the ink? In other words, does the book continue long after it is destroyed? Are the paper and ink simply one incarnation of eternal ideas

Detail of painting at entrance to prayer hall, Pemayangste monastery, Sikkim, India. *Richard I'Anson/Getty Images.*

that may someday take the form of governments or corporations that the words of the book define?

Scientists state that energy cannot be manufactured or destroyed. It just changes form. The Hindu has no problem with that concept. The book was once an acorn and then a tree. It might someday become soil that nurtures a flower that produces energy for a honeybee to transform into nourishment for a reader who will someday hold a book in her hand. The process continues forever. This is the wheel of samsara, the unending wheel of life.

In this sense, Hinduism has a lot in common with some of the new ways physicists are viewing the world (see Barbour, Julian). But within Hinduism there is also a certain progression of ages, each with a beginning and an end.

Brahman is the Creator. Although he is very respected in India, there are only about a half-dozen temples built in his honor. The reason he is not more universally memorialized is that he worked himself out of a job a long time ago and is no longer present on earth because creation is finished. Now he meditates on the lotus blossom growing from the navel of Vishnu, who sleeps on the cosmic ocean made up of the remains of the last universe before this one. When Brahman opens his eyes to look around, a world comes into existence. One day in the life of Brahman is four billion three hundred and twenty years, or one world cycle. Then he closes his eyes and the world disappears. When he opens them again, another cycle begins. All this goes on forever.

This is the mythology, but it is important to understand that few Hindus have ever accepted the myth as being literally true. It is a metaphor for a concept that cannot be grasped with the human mind.

If a definition of Hinduism could be reduced to fit on a bumper sticker, it might read something like, "The Universe Is Profoundly One." This overarching unity can best be understood by exploring the concepts of Brahman and Atman.

The Upanishads speak of Brahman as "Him the eye does not see, nor the tongue express, nor the mind grasp." Brahman is not God or even a god, but rather the ultimate, unexplainable principle encompassing all of creation. Because creation preceded language, words cannot grasp the totality of Brahman. Any and every definition falls short. Brahman can be called a "macro" metaphysical principle.

There is also a "micro" metaphysical principle. The subtle presence intuited within, identified as "soul" or "self" by other traditions, is called Atman by Hindus. Atman perceives Brahman. Moreover, this perception leads to a central meditation discovered by the Hindu *rishis*, or sages, described in the Chandogya Upanishad: "In the beginning there was Existence alone—One only, without a second. He, the One [Brahman], thought to himself: Let me be many, let me grow forth. Thus out of himself he projected the universe, and having projected out of himself the universe, he entered into every being. All that is has its self in him alone. Of all things he is the subtle essence. He is the truth. He is the Self. And that … THAT ART THOU!"

When one discovers that Atman, the inner self, and Brahman, the essence of the universe, are indeed one, the experienced result is one of immense peace and harmony, of coming home. The human perception of life is often that of a small, fragile being gazing out into an infinite, unknowable space. The intuitive leap of realizing "THAT ART THOU" tells us we belong. We have a place. We are one with the stars and the consciousness that brought them into being.

This awareness leaves little room for such a concept as "the end of the world." How can the world end when the individual is one with all that is? The cosmos, including all those who contemplate it, is an expression of Brahman. Such a cosmos can never end.

Sources:
Fisher, Mary Pat, and Lee W. Bailey, eds. *An Anthology of Living Religions*. Upper Saddle River, NJ: Prentice Hall, 2000.
The Upanishads: Breath of the Eternal. Trans. Swami Prabhavananda and Frederick Manchester. New York: Mentor, 1957.

HOLLYWOOD ENVISIONS THE END

The movie industry is in business to make money. No one makes a movie unless it seems at least reasonably likely that significant numbers of people will pay money to see it. Hollywood obviously believes that our culture is interested in how the world will end, or there would not be so many films on the topic. Most of them set forth scenarios that have at one time or another been presented by the scientific community as plausible causes for the end of all things.

What follows is only a sample:

Asteroids Colliding with the Earth

In the 1998 movie *Armageddon*, starring Bruce Willis (directed by Michael Bay for Touchstone Pictures), an asteroid is about to destroy the earth (see Asteroids). A group of wildcat oil drillers must be transported to the asteroid, where they will attempt to plant an atomic bomb deep beneath the surface in order to splinter the giant, menacing rock and divert it from a collision course.

Nuclear War

Many movies have been made depicting life after a nuclear holocaust, but *Dr. Strangelove; or, How I Learned to Stop Worrying and Love the Bomb* was undoubtedly the most darkly humorous view of the unthinkable to be shown on the big screen in front of a cold war–skittish public. Starring Peter Sellers, George C. Scott, Slim Pickens, and James Earl Jones, among others, Stanley Kubrick's 1964 hit tapped a rich vein of American phobias, as when the character General Jack D. Ripper (Sterling Hayden), who engineers the nuclear attack that ends the movie (and the world), utters the words, "I can no longer sit back and allow Communist infiltration, Communist indoctrination, Communist subversion, and the international Communist conspiracy to sap and impurify all our precious bodily fluids."

It was absurd, of course, but it touched a real nerve in the America of the sixties.

Life after Armageddon

Assuming that any humans survive an Armageddon event, what will life be like? Kevin Costner presents two different scenarios. In *Waterworld* (Universal, 1995), global warming has melted the ice caps and covered the earth with oceans for such a long time that some people have begun to evolve gills. In *The Postman* (Warner, 1997), post–World War III humanity has reverted to survivalist tribalism. Humans face the difficulty of remembering and deliberately choosing to preserve the best of what was once considered to be ethical, moral humanity. A similar situation is examined in Mel Gibson's portrayal of *Mad Max* (Image Entertainment, 1979).

Humans in *Planet of the Apes* (20th Century Fox, 1968) didn't have that opportunity. This movie poses a fascinating question. Sixty-five million years ago a collision with an asteroid may very well have eliminated the dinosaurs, clearing the stage for mammalian evolution. If a similar catastrophe, perhaps caused by nuclear warfare, eliminated the human race, would another species (in this case, apes) evolve to planetary supremacy in a similar fashion? That is the world astronaut Charlton Heston faces when, after a long absence in space, he returns to an earth now controlled by another species.

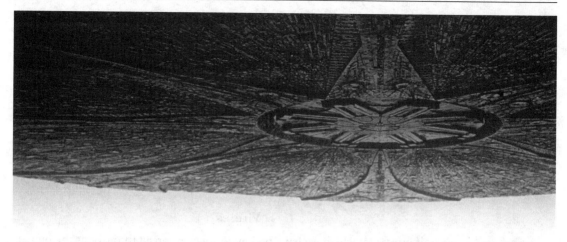

In the 1996 movie *Independence Day*, a gigantic spaceship overshadows Manhattan. *20th Century Fox/The Kobal Collection.*

Technology Run Amok

In 1984, producer James Cameron introduced a series of movies for MGM/UA that starred the man who would later become governor of the state of California. When Arnold Schwarzenegger first uttered the now-famous line "I'll be back," little did he know that he would fulfill his own prophecy in two more *Terminator* movies.

The premise of the movies is that in the future, machines will have taken over the human race. When the few remaining humans fight back, the machine culture sends a practically indestructible killing machine in human form back into the past, to our present day, to terminate the mother of the human who is leading the rebellion. Filled with special effects and car crashes, the story nevertheless asks an important question. Will our technology ever become sophisticated enough to become, for all intents and purposes, capable of independent thought and motive?

The same question is asked in a series of films starring, among others, Keanu Reeves and Laurence Fishburne. In 1999 Warner Studios launched *The Matrix*, directed by Larry and Andy Wachioski. This vision of the future presents the idea that the current perception of human reality is really an illusion. It is a computer-driven matrix that has evolved the ability to act independently of its human inventors. The technology now needs people only to fuel itself. Computers rule the world by keeping their identity and presence hidden and by generating a "normal" reality for human consumption. But once in a while something happens that reveals the presence behind the illusion. Déjà vu is one example. When we feel as if we have experienced something before, we really have. A "glitch" in the Matrix has occurred.

A future free from the destructive power of technology is contemplated in the movie *Star Trek: Insurrection* (Paramount, 1998), which posits a race from another planet who faced the frightening scenario of technology run amok, left the technology behind, and were rewarded with eternal youth in a backwater corner of a faraway galaxy. They kept their knowledge and scientific understanding. They just chose not to employ it.

Viruses

If viruses for which we have no immunity ever spread throughout the human race, humankind could well die off (see Plagues). *Outbreak*, starring Dustin Hoffman (Warner Studios, 1995), and Tom Cruise's *Mission Impossible II* (Paramount, 2000) examine this very possible and frightening scenario.

Biology and Conspiracy

Was the blood of Jesus Christ different from all other human blood? After all, he reportedly received the male half of his genetic material from a divine source, even though his mother was human. If some of his DNA were discovered (on blood taken from the preserved nails from his crucifixion, for example), could modern technology clone a superhuman being from it? An antichrist, perhaps?

Now let's stir the mix some more. What if, at the same time the false child is born, it becomes known that Jesus' bloodline really did survive, implying that he married or at least had children? Further, what if his genes had been passed on down through the human race until an actual descendant of Jesus appears on the scene at the same as the cloned antichrist?

This is the basic plot line of *Revelation* (Ange/Art, 2001). It's full of twists and turns involving Masons, the Knights Templar, pentagrams, and sacred geometry. Alchemists work in the shadow of planetary conjunctions and feminist sacred signs. Even Isaac Newton takes part, as science and religion are depicted as playing out a long secret history of which most of humankind is completely unaware.

Ecological Shortsightedness

Leonard Nimoy (Mr. Spock of *Star Trek* fame) is concerned about species becoming extinct through human neglect and shortsightedness. In *Star Trek IV: The Voyage Home* (Paramount, 1986), Nimoy, as the film's director, proposes that the world could have been visited by aliens in the far distant past, before humans evolved. Whales, of course, were here, in abundance and at the top of the food chain. When the movie begins, in the twenty-third century, the aliens have sent back a probe to ask what happened to their friends, the whales. The answer is not a pleasant one: They have been hunted to extinction.

Massive tornadoes were merely a symptom of the main problem in *The Day after Tomorrow* (2004), which envisioned ecological neglect as spinning the climate out of control. *20th Century Fox/The Kobal Collection.*

The intrepid crew of the starship *Enterprise*, although forced by circumstances beyond their control to use a captured Klingon spaceship, immediately deduce that their only hope is to travel back in time to the twentieth century, capture two humpbacked whales named George and Gracie, and then transport them back to the twenty-third century, where the whales can call off the alien threat and repopulate their species.

The plot sounds fantastic, but it's a wonderful romp and examines very important issues. What if we could go back in time to correct yesterday's mistakes? Failing that, can we stop those mistakes from happening in the first place?

A different form of ecological disaster strikes in *The Day after Tomorrow*, directed by Roland Emmerich (who also threatened the world with destruction via an alien invasion in *Independence Day*), Emmerich visualizes global warming as producing, ironically, an almost-instant ice age that makes Western Europe virtually uninhabitable and buries New York City beneath a glacier. His purpose in making this movie was, he admits, tainted by feelings that were "a little subversive." He wanted to wake people up to what he considers the danger of the greenhouse effect.

Biblical Scenarios

Tim LaHaye and Jerry B. Jenkins have written a best-selling series of novels (see *Left Behind* Books) based on the evangelical Christian futurist interpretation of the book of Revelation (see Revelation). The first two books of the series have been made into movies, *Left Behind* (Cloud Ten Pictures, 2000) and *Tribulation Force* (Cloud Ten Pictures, 2004).

Interestingly, the producers chose a different marketing path from that of most movies. Usually a film hits the big screen and then is distributed in video for home use. In this case, the movies were first produced as videos. The idea was that evangelical Christians who saw the videos would build a large fan base, use the films as tools of evangelism, and then invite their friends to go with them to the theaters when the films hit the commercial markets.

The movies take place during the last seven years before the return of Jesus Christ, the time Christian futurists call the "Tribulation." Antichrist sets out to rule the world, and believers, converted after the Rapture, organize to oppose him. (See Antichrist; Futurist School of Biblical Interpretation; Great Tribulation; Rapture.)

Alien Invasion

In the October 1953 edition of *Space Review* magazine, editor Albert K. Bender announced that he had discovered information that would completely explain the mystery behind the flying saucer craze then sweeping the nation. Unfortunately, he said, he had encountered some difficulty: Three men in dark suits had come to his door and ordered him not to publish any more information about flying saucers. After warning other UFO researchers to be extremely careful, Bender signed off and never published another edition of his magazine. He did, however, write a book called *Flying Saucers and the Three Men in Black*.

The incident eventually sparked a comic book series, written by Lowell Cunningham, about the mysterious Men in Black. After that it was only a matter of time before the story hit the big screen. The result was Hollywood's 1997 version of a secret organization that works behind the scenes to protect the planet from alien invasion. Tommy Lee Jones, Will Smith, and Rip Torn represent MIB, the *Men in Black* (directed by Barry Sonnenfeld for Sony Pictures), who are well aware that at any given moment there may be at least a few thousand aliens on earth, most of whom just want to go about their business. Many of them work for the Postal Service, but a few, including Elvis, Oprah, and Michael Jackson, have attained a fair amount of success in their respective careers.

The Battle between Good and Evil

The idea of humankind being pawns in a cosmic game of chess between God and the devil has been around since the book of Job. Both television and the movies have recently offered variations on this theme.

In 2004, HBO introduced a television series called *Carnivàle* that went on to win five Emmy Awards. Following a cliff-hanging ending on the final program, season two picked up where the award-winning first season left off. Ben Hawkins, played by

Nick Stahl, is teenage fugitive working for a traveling carnival during the Great Depression in the area of the United States that historians call the "Dust Bowl." He has the gift of healing and represents the power of good in a world slowly falling into evil. His antagonist is Brother Justin, played by Clancy Brown. Justin is a Methodist minister who has his own radio show. Both are searching for Ben's father, Hank Scudder, played by John Savage. The carnival is filled with tarot card readers, snake charmers, bearded ladies, and assorted other personalities, all oblivious to the fact that the world is heading toward a final showdown between good and evil that will determine the fate of the planet. At risk is the human potential to trade wonder for reason. The two main characters gradually come to realize that the familiar world they thought they understood is, in reality, a great game being waged between the powers of light and darkness, and that they are the key players in the game.

The special-effects-driven movie *Constantine* features Keanu Reeves, whose character, John Constantine, has the unique ability to recognize angels and demons who inhabit the earth disguised as human beings. As a teenager, Constantine was so troubled by his ability that he attempted suicide, only to be brought back to life against his will. It was only then that he fully realized his hidden talents that might save the world from destruction. The story is based on the DC Comics/Vertigo Graphic Novel *Hellblazer* series, and takes place in and around Los Angeles, where the battle between good and evil is being fought as demon half-breeds attempt to take over the world.

In this take on the eternal struggle the central character is more of an antihero than hero. He drinks and swears and lives a bitter, dark life. He'll save you from eternal darkness, but he doesn't need any thanks and certainly doesn't want you to feel sorry for him.

Hollywood may sometimes be a bit confused as to alien intentions, sometimes portraying them as relatively benign or even godlike, sometimes as hostile if not downright murderous. In 1951, during a spate of flying saucer films, one of the granddaddy classics of sci-fi thrillers seemed to combine these themes. *The Day the Earth Stood Still*, which has since become a cult favorite, sounded a warning that has continued right down to the present *Star Trek* series: the inhabitants of the earth must learn to live peacefully or they will be destroyed before they can pose a threat to other planets. Religious imagery abounds, as the hero (Michael Rennie) is named Carpenter, dies, and is resurrected. Mimicking the benevolent alien Klaatu's now-famous message for the robot Gort, canceling the order that would destroy the earth, generations of fans have learned to say the words, "Gort, Klaatu barada nikto!"

Sources:
"Carnivàle." http://www.hbo.com/carnivale/about/index.shtml.
"Constantine." http://constantinemovie.warnerbros.com/.
Craddock, Jim, ed. *VideoHound's Golden Movie Retriever 2005*. Detroit: Thomson Gale, 2004.
"The Day the Earth Stood Still." http://www.imdb.com/title/tt0043456.
"Men in Black." http://www.crystalinks.com/mib.html.

HOLY SPIRIT *see* **Church, Role of**

ICE

(See also Global Warming)

When many people hear the words *ice age*, they tend to think of great glaciers cover-ing the northern latitudes with sheets of ice a mile thick for several thousand years. This mental picture is only partially correct. For climatologists, an ice age is a much longer period—tens of millions of years—of generally cold conditions. During these long periods of cold, however, glaciation increases and decreases again and again over much shorter cycles of time. The most recent of these glaciation cycles began about 115,000 years ago and ended some 12,000 to 14,000 years ago. This period is what most people who are not climatologists have in mind when we talk about *the* Ice Age.

No one really knows why ice ages—both the long ones and the shorter ones within them—wax and wane. There are currently about four good guesses. According to specialists at the Illinois State Museum in their exhibit entitled "Why Were There Ice Ages?" the current thinking is that the answer may lie in any of them or, more probably, in a combination of some or all.

CHANGING CONTINENTAL POSITIONS. The land masses of the earth "float," as it were, on plates. The change is much too slow for us to see in one lifetime, but over mil-lions of years, when more land mass is located at higher latitudes, the concentration causes ice buildup at the poles. As more and more ice forms, it pushes out vast glaciers across land that may be thousands of miles from the poles. (See also Earth Shift).

UPLIFT OF CONTINENTAL BLOCKS. As land masses rise and fall, global ocean cur-rents are affected. Warm ocean temperatures no longer reach land or are diverted to new locations. Cold currents cause colder temperatures. Glaciers begin to form and move south. The result is a long, slow buildup to another ice age. As the ice locks up more and more of the ocean's water, temperatures vary again until equilibrium is reached and the pendulum begins to swing back again.

REDUCTION OF ATMOSPHERIC CO_2. Carbon dioxide (CO_2) is an important greenhouse gas. Its presence in the atmosphere helps strike a balance between cold and hot temperatures by trapping heat, preventing it from escaping into outer space. Too much CO_2 in the atmosphere and the world gets warmer. Not enough and things cool down. Some scientists believe there may be a periodic atmospheric reduction of CO_2 that, over the course of millions of years, causes global freezing and ice ages.

CHANGES IN EARTH'S ORBIT. The earth revolves around the sun in an elliptical orbit that has a great effect on temperatures. Besides the shape of the orbit, earth tilt—the angle of the planet's axis in relation to the sun—produces both seasonal and long-term weather patterns. Some scientists believe that slight variations in both orbit and tilt over time might be connected with long-term climate change. There might be a very slow rhythm that is not yet fully understood but that shifts the climate back and forth from heat to cold, from ice age to ice melt.

All this raises a significant question: When will the next deep freeze hit? Jon Erickson, writing in *Ice Ages: Past and Future*, says: "The next ice age is already overdue. Its onset depends on how man alters the climate by adding to the greenhouse effect. Perhaps global warming, with man's assistance, might be able to hold off the next ice age for a little while longer."

Current thinking in circles of anthropology is that it was the most recent ice age that made possible the peopling of the Americas. Although some recent research suggests there may have been several routes, including sea routes, that led to America from both east and west, traditional theory still holds that the last ice age locked up so much water in polar ice caps and glaciers that a land bridge connected Alaska with Siberia for thousands of years. It was over this land bridge that humans, following game animals, first walked onto the North American continent. As the glaciers melted, a corridor opened up between the Laurentide ice sheet, covering Canada and much of northeast America, and the Cordilleran ice sheet border on the Pacific Ocean to the west. This corridor between the mammoth walls of ice allowed penetration into what must have seemed a paradise for early hunters. They discovered animals that had no built-in fear of humans. Mastodons, mammoths, moose, and other huge game animals offered a food source more secure than our ancestors had ever known. Traveling farther and farther south into warmer climes, they didn't care that the melting glaciers effectively closed the door behind them and inundated the land bridge that had been their highway into a new world.

Perhaps even the mythology of the people reveals the truth about early North American history. Michael and Kathleen O'Neal Gear are archeologists who open up their field to laypeople by writing fiction. Their sagas of early North American history have captivated audiences worldwide while revealing an intimate knowledge of the present state of archeological discovery. In *People of the Wolf*, they comment on the fact that many indigenous people of the Americas have legends about entering this world after being forced to leave an earlier one. A common motif is that the people came to this land through a hole in the earth (see Indigenous Peoples of the Americas).

Illecillewaet Glacier, Selkirk Mountains, British Columbia. *Library of Congress.*

Could it be, ask the Gears, that the stories recall real history? Although highly speculative, their theory is that as people from the west crossed the land bridge and began to move south, their route would have, for many years, been blocked by a gigantic wall of ice. But as the climate gradually changed, the ice would have begun to melt. Very possibly, seasonal rivers flowed under the glaciers, carving out great tunnels that, during the summer, would have carried huge amounts of water. But in winter these rivers would freeze. Then the tunnels would offer passages under the glacier. It would have been terribly dangerous and probably very frightening to early travelers. But a terrifying walk through the bowels of a glacier followed by the discovery of a new land filled with easy food, warm climates, and no other humans to have to share the bounty with—now that's an experience worth remembering around the fire at night for many, many generations. Of such experiences, mythology is born.

If our world is going to end with an icy Armageddon, probably no one reading this book will be around to see it. Ice ages don't arrive overnight. By the same token, however, our climate balances on a very thin line. A small wobble in the earth's elliptical orbit or its axial tilt could cool things down very quickly. We dance very precariously on the head of a small cosmic pin. Who can say what it might take to make us lose our equilibrium?

Sources:

Erickson, Jon. "Ice Ages: Past and Future." http://oceanworld.tamu.edu/students/iceage/.

Gear, W. Michael, and Kathleen O'Neal Gear. *People of the Wolf*. New York: Tor, 1990.

Illinois State Museum. "Why Were There Ice Ages?" http://www.museum.state.il.us/exhibits/ice_ages/why_4_cool_periods.html.

Maasch, Kirk A. "The Big Chill: Cracking the Ice Age." www.pbs.org/wgbh/nova/ice/chill.html.

INDIGENOUS PEOPLES OF THE AMERICAS— END OF THE WORLD BELIEFS

Many North American Indian cultures share a belief that there have been other worlds before the one in which we now live. Some say we are living in the fourth world. The first ended in fire, the second in flood, the third in ice. A few add a fifth world that ended when the gods took all of the air out of the atmosphere. Many traditionalists teach that this present world will end and a few chosen people will survive to emerge into the next. Especially since 1994, many have come to believe this transformation will take place in the early years of the twenty-first century.

We cannot talk about Indian culture as if it were a unified whole. There are many Indian nations, each with its own unique mythology and culture. Even within nations there are disagreements concerning how to understand and interpret tribal mythology.

This is only to be expected. The very same types of disagreements are found within every world religion. When a Christian from the religious right writes a book describing how the end of the world will take place, a Christian from the religious left will write one claiming the first author is wrong and doesn't speak for real Christians. When a non-Indian writes about Hopi mythology, some Hopis will say he got it right. Others will disagree, claiming he is simply exploiting Hopi mythology. When scientists discover DNA samples that seem to prove Siberian ancestry for Zuni people, some Zunis will agree. Others will say such a thing cannot be because their people have always been in the Southwest. There are Indians who have fully adopted European American culture and have a worldview similar to that of any white Harvard graduate who was born in Boston. There are others who are traditionalists, maintaining views similar to those held by their ancestors centuries ago.

One example will suffice to illustrate the situation.

People of the Apache, Blackfoot, Caddo, Hidatsa, Comanche, Cheyenne, Arapaho, Cherokee, Chippewa, Mandan, and Sioux nations have long shared a prophecy that the birth of a white buffalo calf would mark the beginning of the changing of days on Mother Earth. Since 1933, the year the last white buffalo was born, they awaited this birth. Many Indians came to believe the prophecy was simply a superstition, and they openly scoffed at those who still embraced the hope of a major change. They taught that the day of the Indian was over. The Indian wars had ended in defeat, and it was time for the people to fully adopt white American ways. Others held on, enduring the ridicule of younger generations who either moved into mainstream American and Canadian culture or succumbed to the poverty and despair of reservation life. Others attempted to stay within the tribal structure but exploit whatever commercial avenues seemed available.

Kukulkan Pyramid, built by the Mayas, Chichen Itza, Mexico. *Klaus Aarsleff/Fortean Picture Library.*

Then on August 20, 1994, at the Heider farm in Janesville, Wisconsin, a white buffalo calf was born. The calf was not an albino. It was simply a pure white color. The Heider family, who are not Indians themselves, named the calf Miracle and opened their farm to all who wanted to come to view the young calf. Many tribal elders began to reconsider earlier views. Some tribal secret societies that had been closed to all but the initiated now began to send teaching elders out to reveal a small portion of the mythologies and legends long kept hidden from the ears of white American culture. They felt the time had come to establish a dialogue that might open paths leading to better understanding. Outsiders heard shortened versions of creation stories for the very first time. And views about the time of change were openly discussed.

Chief Arvol Looking Horse, a nineteenth-generation keeper of the sacred buffalo calf pipe of the Sioux people, announced, "We have a prophecy which I've heard since my early years of the age of twelve that someday the spirit of the White Buffalo Calf Woman would stand upon Mother Earth. At that time, great changes would happen to Mother Earth. In 1994, Miracle was the first white buffalo to be born. Now, eight have been born, signifying a great urgency!"

It is only natural that people who have been treated as badly as the Indians of North America are suspicious when outsiders, even well-meaning ones, take up their cause. During the 1960s, when many of the so-called hippie youth culture championed traditional Indian values, many Indians felt they were being exploited. Some of them retreated even further into the secrets of their tradition. Others published books and tracts completely disowning authors such as Frank Waters, with his *Book of the Hopi*, and Carlos Castaneda, with his series of books beginning with *The Teachings of Don Juan*.

This makes it very difficult for a non-Indian, even a well-meaning one, to talk about the end-of-the-world beliefs of the indigenous peoples of the Americas. Just as there are many Jewish opinions and many Christian opinions, there are many Indian opinions. Literally every Indian myth will be accepted by some and scoffed at by others. Indian mythology is so rich and widespread we can, at best, offer only a representative sample from different regions. We must keep in mind that any of these stories will be accepted by some, rejected by others. But they offer a mosaic—a window into a heritage and a worldview different from the experience of many modern Americans.

Hopi

The Hopi Indians of the Southwest are probably descendants of the Ancestral Puebloans, the people who in the past were often called "cliff dwellers." More recently they were given the name Anasazi, or "enemy ancestors," by the Navajo who came to live in their territory centuries after the Ancestral Puebloans migrated south and east to establish a new way of life better suited to changing climate and cultural patterns (see also Ecological Exploitation). The Hopi believe that their ancient gods, the thlatsinas (also called katsinas or kachinas), who came from the stars, will come again and dance in the plazas of the Hopi villages. Some legends say that only Sasquasohuh, the Blue Star Kachina, will come from his blue, invisible star. According to prophecy, the blue star is due to make its appearance in 2012. This will be a signal that a great war will begin. It is also the signal for the traditional katsina dancers to take off their masks and reveal themselves to the children of the villages as the uncles and familiar adults they are, not real gods. In the war, the United States will be destroyed, with only the Hopi people surviving in the village of Old Oraibi, on Third Mesa in central Arizona, where their culture will be rejuvenated along with its beliefs and ceremonies.

Hopi prophecy tells of two paths open to humankind. One is the sacred way of Taiowa, the Creator; the other is the zigzag way of those who don't pray. There is a connection between the two paths, so that humans who are on the troubled path can choose to switch to the path of peace and balance, or those on the path of prayer can chose the seemingly easier path. This time of choosing is said to be a time of confusion and purification. It is a time of great upheaval in which we are being asked by Taiowa to choose the path of the sacred way of the Purifier who will come after a worldwide conflagration. This prophecy was given to the Hopi people on the stone slab called Prophecy Rock in the old village of Oraibi.

Maya

The Maya of Central America believed they were descended from the mythical Atlanteans, whose technology had been taught them by visitors from other planets. Although they did not originally use the name Atlantis, their descriptions fit Plato's story so well that their modern descendants, when first hearing the Greek myth, adopted it as their own. Interestingly, Edgar Cayce (see entry) later predicted that Atlantis would arise from the Caribbean, disagreeing with Plato's description of an island outside the Strait of Gibraltar.

The visitors from space purportedly taught the Maya sacred geometry and astronomy. Buildings in the jungles of Central America are technological wonders similar to the pyramids in Egypt. Many Mayan descendants believe that we have had, and are still having, visitors from the stars to help and guide us in this life. They believe that the ancient buildings are time/space portals and landing places for starcraft. According to their cultural stories, these visitors will come back to oversee the end of this time and the emergence of the next.

Some interpreters believe that the Mayan calendar, which is based on planetary movements, tells us that with the appearance of the Hale-Bopp comet in 1997, we entered into the new calendar cycle of Great Cosmic Change. The calendar ends in 2012. It was created over two thousand years ago. According to these interpreters' astronomical calculations, the ecliptic of the sun will conjunct with the crossing point of the galactic equator, causing great distress and the possible end of the world.

Mi'kMaq

The Mi'kMaq people have lived in what is now Maine and Nova Scotia for thousands of years. They have many stories of Little People, believed to come from the stars, who are their guides in life. The Little People appear in visions telling the vision-seekers that they will be returning soon. There have been alien sightings for generations among the Mi'kMaq, and there are ancient songs about the Little People sitting on the shore, singing to others on the other side, who will be coming across. According to their prophecies, this is a time of preparation for the changes to come and for the Little People to return.

The Canadian writer Farley Mowat, in his book *The Farfarers*, raises the interesting possibility that the Little People might have come from Europe, not outer space. He proposes that a group of small-statured people he calls "Albans," precursors to the Celts, might have been chased out of their Scandinavian homelands and forced to flee westward. Linguistic, mythological, and artifactual evidence, from Scotland to Iceland and from Greenland to Nova Scotia, suggests that these people had boats and knowledge of sea routes. Although no one knows what they called themselves or what language they spoke, their cultural Armageddon seems to have come at the hands of a people the world would later call Vikings.

Iroquois

In the creation myth of the Iroquois of what is now the northeastern United States, the Woman Who Fell to Earth is the mother of all humans. Once again we discover in Indian mythology a visitor from the skies. But the Iroquois do not think in terms of linear time. They believe that the Creator, like the Sky-World and the spirit of humans, is eternal. The reason for human existence on earth is that only here can people experience the inequities of life. Pain and suffering, sorrow and greed, death and intolerance are not to be found in the eternal world. The elders believe that religions are created by people, not God. The earth is the great stage upon which humans play out the great drama. It will continue until the Creator decides the play has ended.

Shawnee

One of the greatest, most beloved leaders of all time was the Shawnee war chief Tecumseh. He tirelessly worked to unite the Indian peoples east of the Mississippi into a force that would drive the white settlers, led by such men as Daniel Boone, out of the sacred hunting grounds of what is now Kentucky. Tecumseh promised a sign that would mark the hour of the universal revolution. Although he didn't predict a specific date, legend has it that he prophesied that the earth would shake. Not long afterward, on December 16, 1811, the first of several very powerful earthquakes struck along the New Madrid (Missouri) fault.

Like many claimed prophecies, Tecumseh's was suspect among those who wondered if it was just a coincidence. The earthquakes, among the mightiest in American recorded history, happened. The revolt never really materialized. Tecumseh died in 1813, but it was predicted that he would arise, becoming an Indian messiah who would lead his people into a new world, free of white encroachment.

The Shawnee believed that Moneto, the supreme being who rules the universe, gave them what Christians called the "Golden Rule": "Do not kill or injure your neighbor, for it is not him that you injure, you injure yourself. But do good to him, therefore add to his days of happiness as you add to you own. Do not wrong or hate your neighbor, for it is not him that you wrong, you wrong yourself. But love him, for Moneto loves him as he loves you."

According to Shawnee eschatology, the Great Spirit is a grandmother who rules the destinies of all people. She weaves, for eternity, a great net which, when finished, will be dropped over the world. Someday she will draw her net up into the heavens. Those who have been found worthy will be caught up and taken to a better life. Those guilty of petty behavior will fall through the mesh and suffer an unbearable fate as the world comes to an end.

White River Sioux

Somewhere in the Badlands of the Dakotas, called "Maka Sicha" by the Lakota people, an old woman is said to live in a cave undiscovered even now, after all the highways, explorers, hikers, and hunters have crisscrossed this sacred territory. Her face is shriveled like a walnut, and she is dressed in rawhide, as the Lakota used to dress. She is working to prepare a buffalo robe, threading it with thousands upon thousands of porcupine quills. Her teeth are worn almost to nubs because she flattens the quills by biting them. This task has occupied her for more than a thousand years.

Beside her on the ground to her right lies her great black dog, Shunka Sapa, who watches her constantly as she works. On her left bubbles a steaming kettle of *wojapi*, a thick red stew. From time to time she turns to stir it, checking its progress. Whenever she does so, Shunka Sapa quickly and secretly pulls out the quills she has managed to thread into her robe, thus undoing her work.

As yet, the woman has not discovered what is going on. But if she ever finishes her robe, on the very day, perhaps the very minute she inserts the last porcupine quill and stands to admire her craft, the world will end.

Early Archaic People of Eastern Florida

No one can ever fix a date for precisely when a particular oral history began or who first told the stories. But archeologists can sometimes piece together evidence from grave burials and other artifacts that might indicate a rough time period during which stories passed down to the present day were part of a culture's oral tradition. Much can be revealed through carvings and designs left behind. Such is the case with a story that has continued down to the present day that might have been told around the campfires of a people who lived more than seven thousand years ago near an Archaic cemetery plot discovered at Windover Pond, near Titusville on Florida's east coast, not far from Cape Canaveral. The story forms the plot of the novel *People of the Lightning*, by Kathleen and W. Michael Gear.

Hurricane Breather and the Lightning Birds existed in the time before the world. One day, the female Lightning Bird laid a thunder egg in Hurricane Breather's eye. She and her husband then hid at the edge of the great winds to see what would happen next. When the egg hatched, a beautiful blue world came out. It frightened Hurricane Breather, who tried to destroy it. The Lightning Birds thought it would be a good idea to save this new world, so they created four shining eagles and ordered them to hold Hurricane Breather down and keep him from his destructive ways. Once in a while he manages to squirm free enough to send fierce storms that blast the coast, destroy forests, and kill people, but by and large the eagles do their job well.

The time will come, however, when the eagles grow old and weak. Their feathers will fall out, and they will no longer have the strength to hold down the powerful Hurricane Breather. When the last eagle falls, Sister Moon will bury her face in the clouds and weep falling stars. Sun Mother will grow black. Hurricane Breather will suck up the sea and blast the earth with water and wind. And all will then be as it was in the beginning, before the earth hatched from his eye.

Navajo

Tony Hillerman, a mystery author who has popularized Navajo culture through a series of books featuring the characters Joe Leaphorn and Jim Chee, Navajo police officers on the big reservation of the Four Corners region of the Southwest, believes that "in their own migrations out of Mongolia and over the icy Bering Strait, the Navajos brought with them a much older Asian philosophy. Thoughts, and words that spring from them, bend the individual's reality. To speak of death is to invite it. To think of sorrow is to produce it." So the Navajo don't often speak of endings, at least to outsiders. To talk about the reality is to speak it into existence. Traditional Navajos are far more concerned with finding *hozhro*, the natural way of "living in beauty," in harmony, with the world as it is. This is the path that has helped the people adapt to changing cultural patterns. As Hillerman puts it in *Listening Woman*, "While the Kiowas were crushed, the Utes reduced to hopeless poverty, and the Hopis withdrawn into the secret of their kivas, the eternal Navajo adapted and endured."

But Navajo mythology reveals that the ancients did recognize that this world, the fourth world, will someday end. The story is told that the secret of the time of the end survived the great persecution by American military forces led by Kit Carson. Navajo villages, located with the help of Ute scouts, ancient enemies of the Navajo, were destroyed. Women and children were massacred, sheep destroyed, and crops burned. Gathered up into "herds" of people, the Navajo were forced to undergo the "Long Walk" to the reservation at Bosque Redondo, wheresickness further decimated their ranks.

But through all this, somewhere, hidden in the recesses of their sacred mountains and passed on from generation to generation, was the knowledge, according to Hillerman, "that Changing Woman and the Talking God taught the people to use when the Fourth World ends." Hillerman explains:

> The Fourth World isn't supposed to end like the Third World did, with Water Monster making a flood. This time the evil is supposed to cause the Sun Father to make it cold, and the Dinee (the People, the Navajo) are supposed to hole up somewhere in the Chuska [mountain] range.... Beautiful Mountain opens up for them. Then, when the time is right, they do Sun Way [a ceremony] and call back the light and warmth, and they start the Fifth World.

Just as in the Christian biblical story, the Navajo Armageddon signals not an end, but a new beginning.

Sources:

Boissiere, Robert. *Meditations with the Hopi*. Santa Fe, NM: Bear, 1986.

Erods, Richard, and Alfonso Ortiz, eds. *American Indian Myths and Legends*. New York: Pantheon, 1984.

Gear, Kathleen O'Neal, and W. Michael Gear. *People of the Lightning*. New York: Tor, 1995.

Hillerman, Tony. *Listening Woman*. New York: Harper & Row, 1978.

Milanich, Jerald T. *Florida's Indians from Ancient Times to the Present*. Gainesville: University Press of Florida, 1998.

Mowat, Farley. *The Farfarers: Before the Norse*. South Royalton, VT: Steerforth Press, 2000.

Red Star, Nancy. *Star Ancestors: Indian Wisdomkeepers Share the Teachings of the Extraterrestrials*. Rochester, VT: Destiny, 2000.

Waters, Frank. *Book of the Hopi*. New York: Penguin, 1963.

ISAIAH

(See also Books of the Bible and Their Relation to Prophecy)

Jews and Christians read the book of Isaiah quite differently, although the book is claimed by both traditions. Jews consider Isaiah a great patriotic prophet who tried to call Israel back to its traditions. Christians believe that he predicted the birth of Jesus. Jews hear his words as a comforting assurance that God has not and will not forget God's people. Christians believe Isaiah predicts the coming Millennium.

Consider just one passage:

> Come, let us go up to the mountain of the Lord,
> to the house of the God of Jacob.

He will teach us of his ways,
  so that we may walk in his paths.
The law will go out from Zion,
  the word of the Lord from Jerusalem.
He will judge between the nations
  and will settle disputes for many peoples.
They will beat their swords into plowshares
  and their spears into pruning hooks.
Nation will not take up sword against nation,
  nor will they train for war anymore. (Isa. 2:3, 4)

To Jewish ears, this is a ringing song of hope. It affirms that God cares about his chosen people. It offers a reason to continue battling in the face of adversity.

To conservative Christians, these same words are a prediction that Jesus will someday rule from Jerusalem during a thousand years of peace on earth. It will be a *pax divina*, a divine peace, in which Jesus will wield a rod of iron. But there will be no corruption of justice.

To liberal Christians, Isaiah presents an alternative to war. Pruning hooks are better than spears, plowshares better than weapons of mass destruction.

As in many cases, scholars are divided about authorship of the book. Some say that one man who went by the name of Isaiah wrote the first thirty-nine chapters. Another man, using the same name, contributed chapters 40–66. Some scholars postulate a third author, bringing him in for the last few chapters.

An interesting Christian schematic theory even uses Isaiah as a metaphor for the entire Bible. The first thirty-nine chapters are full of judgment and condemnation, warnings and pleadings. This, says the theory, corresponds to the thirty-nine books of the Old Testament, which attempt to call the Hebrew people back to repentance through law and judgment. But beginning with chapter 40 the mood changes, just as the New Testament begins with the fortieth book of the Bible. Isaiah says in the first verses of chapter 40:

Comfort, comfort my people,
  says your God.
Speak tenderly to Jerusalem,
  and proclaim to her
that her hard service has been completed,
  that her sin has been paid for;
that she has received from the Lord's hand
  double for all her sins.
A voice of one calling;
  "In the desert prepare
  the way for the Lord;
make straight in the wilderness
  a highway for our God.
Every valley shall be raised up,
  every mountain and hill made low;

the rough ground shall become level,
  the rugged places a plane.
And the glory of the Lord will be revealed,
  and all mankind together will see it." (Isa. 40:1–5)

To Christians these words express the very essence of the New Testament. And there are exactly as many chapters from Isaiah 40 to the end of the book as there are books of the New Testament. Jewish scholars, of course, as well as many liberal Christian scholars, see this as coincidence.

Isaiah enters the field of Armageddon because Christian millennialists claim to find in his writing many passages that they say describe the thousand-year reign of Christ following his triumphal return:

Here is my servant, whom I uphold,
  my chosen one in whom I delight;
I will put my spirit on him
  and he will bring justice to the nations.
He will not shout or cry out,
  or raise his voice in the streets.
A bruised reed he will not break
  and a smoldering wick he will not snuff out.
In faithfulness he will bring justice;
  he will not falter or be discouraged
till he establishes justice on earth.
  in his law the islands will put their hope. (Isaiah 42:1–4)

A shoot will come up from the stump of Jesse;
  from his roots a branch will bear fruit.
The Spirit of the Lord will rest upon him....
He will not judge by what he sees with his eyes,
  or decide by what he hears with his ears;
but with righteousness he will judge the needy,
  with justice he will give decisions
  for the poor of the earth....
The wolf will live with the lamb,
  the leopard will lie down with the goat,
the calf and the yearling together;
  and a little child will lead them.
The cow will feed with the bear,
  their young will lie down together,
  and the lion will eat straw like the ox.
The infant will play near the hole of the cobra,
  and the young child put his hand into the viper's nest.
They will neither hurt nor destroy
  on all my holy mountain,
for the earth will be full of the knowledge of the Lord
  as the waters cover the sea. (Isaiah 11:1–9)

The calling of Isaiah (Benjamin West, 1780s). *Fortean Picture Library.*

Isaiah also offers a clue about the fall of Lucifer and the subsequent necessity for the battle of Armageddon (see Devil). But his words, while providing hope for Jews and Christians alike, don't give much solace to those who are defeated in the final battle:

"As the new heavens and the new earth that I make will endure before me," declares the Lord, "so will [my] name and descendants endure. From one New Moon to another and from one Sabbath to another, all mankind will come and bow before me," says the Lord. "And they will go out and look upon the dead bodies of those who rebelled against me; their worms will not die, nor will their fire be quenched, and they will be loathsome to all mankind." (Isaiah 66:22–24)

It is certainly a depressing end to a book by the most poetic, prolific, and at times artistic of all the Hebrew prophets.

Source:
The Holy Bible, New International Version. Grand Rapids, MI: Zondervan, 1978.

ISLAMIC VIEWS OF THE END *see* **Eschatology, Comparative**

ISRAEL

Whenever people find themselves in conversation about Armageddon, no matter whether they are religious or secular, Israel invariably comes up. From a monotheistic view, Israel is important to such a discussion for three main reasons:

1. Although the Hebrew religion didn't invent linear time ending with a duel between good and evil (that honor goes to Zoroastrianism—see entry), the Hebrew prophets certainly popularized it (see Books of the Bible and Their Relation to Prophecy). The "father" of Judaism (see Abraham and Monotheism; Abrahamic Covenant), as well as Christianity and Islam, by making his journey to this geographic spot of ground, seemed to ensure its importance in the future of the world.

2. The early Hebrew writers saw themselves as a unique people—chosen by God to be the ones through whom he was to be revealed to the world. Therefore, when God finally wraps things up, God's people, Israel, will have to be at the center of things.

3. The early Christian writers considered Israel to be a type or symbol of the church. Many evangelical scholars today consider Israel to be a significant player in the final battle of Armageddon, and this view has certainly gained a wide popular following in recent decades (see *Left Behind* Books; Lindsey, Hal).

From a secular standpoint, Israel is central to any potential Middle Eastern spark that might set off nuclear Armageddon. The longstanding Israeli-Palestinian conflict is a great cause for concern, has already led to open warfare, and continues to grab headlines as the twenty-first century unfolds.

(See also the following significant religious entries involving Israel: Abomination of Desolation; Abraham and Monotheism; Abrahamic Covenant; Adam and Eve; Antichrist; Apocalypse; Apocalyptic Writing; Ark of the Covenant; Armageddon; Armageddon, Battle of; Bible Timelines; Books of the Bible and Their Relation to Prophecy; Daniel; European Common Market and European Union; Ezekiel; Isaiah; Kabbalah; Moses and Elijah; New Heaven, New Earth, and the New Jerusalem; Temple at Jerusalem; Zionism; and these secular entries involving Israel: Carter, Jimmy; Reagan, Ronald)

Source:
Renard, John. *The Handy Religion Answer Book*. Detroit: Visible Ink Press, 2002.

JEHOVAH'S WITNESSES

Charles Taze Russell was born on February 16, 1852. Raised as a strict Presbyterian in Pittsburgh, he nevertheless became interested in views held by the Seventh-day Adventists, who were outspoken in their theories concerning the Advent, or Second Coming, of Jesus Christ. Russell began to attend their meetings regularly in 1870. After leaving an especially inspiring service one night, he is said to have remarked, "Is it possible that the handful of people in the room tonight are correct in their judgment and the rest of the world is wrong?" Members of the movement he soon formed are now called Jehovah's Witnesses.

In Luke 9, Jesus sends his disciples out into every town to preach the gospel and be witnesses of the power of God. The order was never rescinded, so Jehovah's Witnesses believe they are simply doing what Jesus asked of his followers. They are witnesses of Jehovah. "Ye are my witnesses, saith Jehovah" (Isa. 43:10). Hence, the name.

The Witnesses have been called by many other labels through the years. For a while they were known as Millennial Dawnists, then International Bible Students, members of the Watchtower Bible and Tract Society, Russellites, and sometimes Rutherfordites.

It all began when Russell, in 1879, published his first book, *Food for Thinking Christians*. By 1884 his adherents had formed a movement called the Zion's Watchtower Society. The name came from the third chapter of the book of Ezekiel. God warns the prophet to act "as on a watchtower." If the enemy comes and the watcher doesn't warn the people, their blood is on his hands. If the watcher warns the people and they don't listen, at least the fault doesn't lie with him.

Russell traveled incessantly while publishing a number of pamphlets to help his followers. Like many before him, he tried to figure out dates for the return of

Christ. He eventually determined that 1914 would be the year when "the full establishment of the Kingdom of God would be accomplished." Unfortunately, the year came and went and Christ was nowhere to be seen. After further review, Russell concluded that the date was right; it was only his interpretation of how the kingdom would arrive that was wrong. Christ did come in 1914, but only "in Spirit." It was a prelude to his physical return. Armageddon would still take place, but not before those who responded to the call of the Spirit became the "watchers" on the wall, warning the people of earth what was to come. (Here he may have been on to something. Many secular historians say the world hasn't been the same since 1914, the year World War I began. In Matthew 18, Jesus warned of "wars and rumors of wars" that would come "before the time of the end.")

Russell died in 1917. After a severe struggle among the upper echelons of the fledgling movement, which now numbered some 15,000, Joseph Franklin "Judge" Rutherford assumed command. Marketing the soon-to-be-popular slogan "Millions now living will never die," the society rebounded from what had been a scandal. Russell, it was learned, had been divorced. Besides that, he had attempted to raise money through the sale of what he called "miracle wheat."

In 1931 Rutherford coined the name Jehovah's Witnesses. Utilizing the latest technology, he provided his faithful followers with portable phonographs to enable them to play records of his comments while they made door-to-door house calls. In 1942, the year Rutherford died, a board of directors was appointed to lead the organization. The cult of personality disappeared, along with the phonographs. Now the Witnesses entered their greatest period of growth.

Their original message was very definitely aimed at those who were considered to be "culturally deprived"—the lower class. Satan was said to wield his power through the "religious, commercial and political combine." Those were the forces that oppressed society. One power structure did the bidding of the other. It was an evil conspiracy to defeat the righteous. Churches and religious organizations were called "tools of Satan." Some ministers were probably well meaning, but duped. Others, backed by entrenched political forces, were simply out to steal the cash of their innocent congregations.

Jehovah's Witnesses became famous for a few of the doctrines they espoused. For instance, Genesis 9:3 warns people not to eat "meat that has life blood in it." Many Witnesses choose to become vegetarians because of that verse. Leviticus 17:14 goes even further: "The life of any creature is in the blood." So Witnesses refuse blood transfusions. They are also forbidden to take part in ecumenical dialogues or gatherings and are often criticized for believing their religion is the only correct one. They don't dispute it, even on their official Web site.

The Witnesses believe that Jesus Christ is God's son, the "first created" of all things. As such he is inferior to God. But he will soon return to earth to rule. So the Witnesses are issuing the warning. People are hearing the message, and it won't be long until Christ returns and the world will be restored. Whereas 144,000 Witnesses (the number comes from Revelation 14) will someday go to heaven, the vast majority of the faithful, "a great multitude," will remain on earth to live life the way it's supposed to be.

More than ninety thousand Jehovah's Witnesses gathered in Yankee Stadium, New York City, at the conclusion of their national convention in 1953. *Associated Press.*

Until then, Jehovah has his Witnesses. They hand out their magazine, the *Watchtower*. They offer books and lessons free of charge. They are dedicated, polite, and motivated. And if they haven't already, they will soon ring your doorbell.

Sources:
Bombardieri, Marcella. "Street Smart." *Boston Globe*, June 23, 2002.
Hudson, Winthrop S. *Religion in America*. New York: Charles Scribner's Sons, 1965.

JEREMIAH *see* **Books of the Bible and Their Relation to Prophecy**

JERUSALEM *see* **Temple at Jerusalem**

JEWISH VIEWS OF THE END *see* **Eschatology, Comparative**

JUDGMENT *see* **Final Judgment**

K

KABBALAH

Kabbalah is a rendering in the Latin alphabet of the Hebrew word formed by the letters *qof, bet, lamed*. It means "to accept" or "to receive." But it is usually translated as "tradition."

In the fourteenth century a Spanish author named Moses de Leon privately began to teach a religious philosophy that he claimed was based on the writings of a second-century rabbi named Simeon ben Yochai. De Leon described a mystical Jewish tradition that supposedly traces its roots to the very beginnings of Creation but was not committed to writing, in books such as the Zohar, until the Middle Ages. The Zohar is a commentary on the Pentateuch, the first five books of the Bible, and is believed by Kabbalists to be equal in holiness to the Bible and the Talmud. Its underlying precept is that the very text of the Bible is a code from G(o)d to humanity. (Kabbalists, like many Orthodox Jews, do not permit the use of vowels in writing the sacred names of the deity, which must never be soiled by human speech or writing. In English they always use "Gd" or "G-d." In Hebrew, they prefer "YHVH.") They believe the Bible is filled with layers and layers of messages only now beginning to be understood. Indeed, new computer studies seem to reveal hidden meanings never before discovered. Kabbalists who study Bible codes find predictions of historical events described by some to be uncanny. Others consider them completely coincidental (see also Bible Code).

According to Kabbalah, the assassinations of the Kennedy brothers and Martin Luther King Jr. are found in sacred text. The Holocaust, both World Wars, the birth and rise to world power of America, many names of famous rabbis—all these and more are revealed as computers make the search easier. There are some who believe the twin towers tragedy of 9/11 was prophesied. Even more startling are alleged indications that the date of the end of the world may be somehow tied to events beginning in the year 2004.

Kabbalists represent only a very small minority of the Jewish community, and many other Jews are extremely skeptical about them. On the other hand, Tracey R. Rich, on his *Judaism 101* Web site, quotes an Orthodox Jewish scholar on the subject of Jewish mysticism: "It's nonsense, but it's Jewish nonsense, and the study of anything Jewish, even nonsense, is worthwhile."

Kabbalah teaches that every existing thing emanates from Gd. Humans must connect with the divine by obeying the commandments and participating righteously within the framework of the Creator's intention. The Hebrew people were given the law for that very reason. It was not just a law for Jews. It is The Law for everyone. Jews were simply the ones chosen to both demonstrate and preserve this universal law, which illustrates the very nature of the Creator. The world is even now being judged on the basis of how human beings respond to divine intention.

Since the Creator knows all things, Gd has limited the time humans will have. Before they doom themselves to a final holocaust, the end will come. The date for that ending has already been determined. And although 2004 passed without a final catastrophe, it doesn't mean the Bible is wrong. It simply means we haven't yet figured out the right time. If the code were fully understood, humans would fully understand Gd's intention. Interpretations are legion. (A favorite is that in the year 2004 the United States would elect a president who will somehow trigger the battle of Armageddon.)

Meanwhile, Kabbalists continue to study because they believe humans can yet change their ways and alter the divine plan. Of course, if they do, it won't catch Gd by surprise. The change of plans will be hidden somewhere in the sacred text.

Sources:
Bridger, David, ed. *The New Jewish Encyclopedia*. New York: Behrman House, 1962.
Drosnin, Michael. *The Bible Code*. New York: Simon and Schuster, 1997.
Rich, Tracey R. "Kabbalah and Jewish Mysticism." http://JewFAQ.org/kabbalah.htm.

KATRINA, HURRICANE

When psychologists use the word *overdetermined*, they mean that symptoms have more than one cause.

Hurricane Katrina, which devastated the coastal regions of Louisiana, Mississippi, and Alabama in late August 2005, caused more than 1,000 deaths, and displaced more than one million people, can be considered an overdetermined environmental disaster. The hurricane's severity may have been affected by global warming. Politics, economics, and bureaucracy played a part in determining who was rescued first. Socioeconomic factors such as class distinction, housing costs, and access to transportation determined how many people lived in the area, who they were, and whether they were able to evacuate. Religion was moved to the front burner when people asked for prayers and began to speculate why "God" would "allow" such an event. In some foreign capitals, people danced in the streets because they thought the storm represented God's wrath upon America, the "Great Satan." Soldiers who could have been called upon to help were busy fighting in the Iraq War, halfway around the world. That war's original justification was said to have been the threat of weapons of

ARMAGEDDON NOW: THE END OF THE WORLD A TO Z

mass destruction. It may, in fact, have been instigated because of the desire to preserve an oil supply.

Ecology, politics, economics, class distinction, religion, war, and oil. The reasons for the disaster and its aftermath were overdetermined.

The Mississippi Delta disaster can serve as an important metaphor for the fate of the world. Early Christian writers labeled the end of the present age "Armageddon." Jesus is said to have specified overdetermined "signs of the end" (see Olivet Discourse). The aftermath of Hurricane Katrina is a reminder to pay attention to a broad range of symptoms to determine what is happening to the planet. Probably no single reason will contribute to "the end." The impact of Armageddon lies in the confluence of many different streams, merging into what can sometimes feel like an overdetermined tidal wave of terror.

Sources:
Bumiller, Elisabeth and Richard W. Stevenson. "President Says He's Responsible in Storm Lapses." *New York Times*, September 14, 2005.

KENNEDY, JOHN F.

In April 1961, events took place that some believe could easily have led to a nuclear Armageddon. The president of the United States, John F. Kennedy, allowed his CIA director to organize a group of expatriate anti-Castro Cubans to invade their homeland. The subsequent armed landing at Cuba's Bay of Pigs was a miserable failure. In retaliation, the Cuban dictator Fidel Castro invited the Russian government to install nuclear missiles in his country and point them directly at key cities in the United States. By October, U.S. reconnaissance planes had spotted the weapons. President Kennedy imposed a naval blockade on Cuba to prevent any more weapons from being delivered. Russian premier Nikita Khrushchev ordered his commanders to launch tactical weapons if the U.S. attacked Cuba or any of his vessels. For seven days in May 1962, Khrushchev and Kennedy dared each other to move. The world lived with the imminent threat of nuclear war for the whole week. Nuclear weapons of the time were certainly capable of destroying enormous areas and would have produced enough radioactive fallout to kill millions, if not billions, of people throughout the world. Eventually, Khrushchev backed down and removed all the nuclear weapons he had placed in Cuba. The world was safe again to bungle its way to its next crisis.

In his book *Our Final Hour*, Martin Rees describes the times:

The Cuban missile standoff in 1962 was the event that brought us closest to premeditated nuclear exchange. According to historian Arthur Schlesinger Jr., one of Kennedy's aides at the time, "This was not only the most dangerous moment of the Cold War, it was the most dangerous moment in human history. Never before had two contending powers possessed between them the technical capacity to blow up the world. Fortunately, Kennedy and Khrushchev were leaders of restraint and sobriety; otherwise, we probably wouldn't be here today."

Robert McNamara was the U.S. secretary of defense during the crisis, as he was during the escalation of the Vietnam War. He later wrote:

> Even a low probability of catastrophe is a high risk, and I don't think we should continue to accept it.... I believe that was the best-managed cold war crisis of any, but we came within a hairbreadth of nuclear war without realizing it. It's no credit to us that we missed nuclear war—at least, we had to be lucky as well as wise.... It became very clear to me as a result of the Cuban missile crisis that the indefinite combination of human fallibility (which we can never get rid of) and nuclear weapons carries the very high probability of the destruction of nations.

Source:
Rees, Martin. *Our Final Hour.* New York: Basic, 2003.

KINGDOM

Whenever Christians gather to pray the prayer called the "Our Father" by Catholics and the "Lord's Prayer" by Protestants, they say the words, "Thy kingdom come, on earth as it is in heaven." This prayer, taken from Jesus' Sermon on the Mount in the gospel according to Matthew and his Sermon on the Plain in the gospel according to Luke, in effect looks forward toward the battle of Armageddon. The central idea is that a separation exists between heaven and earth. God rules in heaven, while the devil is free to rule on earth, within limits set by God. The battle of Armageddon, according to one interpretation of the prayer, will effectively end the reign of Satan, bringing earth completely within the realm of God's rule.

This interpretation is foreshadowed in the book of Job, which delineates Satan's present sphere of influence. In the first chapter the angels "come to present themselves before the Lord." Apparently Satan (literally "the Satan," or "the accuser") is one of these angels because he, too, is forced to come before the Ruler of all that is. God asks him, "Where have you come from?" Satan's answer is that he has been "roaming through the earth and going back and forth on it."

God brings up the subject of an especially righteous man named Job, whose life appears to show how little influence Satan has over someone who holds firm to the worship of God, even in a realm Satan seems to call his own. Satan replies that God has placed a "hedge" around Job; in essence he complains that he can't really work his evil on Job because Job is a kind of divine teacher's pet. God agrees to a test and offers to remove the limitations. Job soon loses his property, his family, his wealth, and his health. Still, he remains faithful, even when his wife urges him to "curse God and die."

The effect of this morality play is to portray the situation on earth as being radically different from what is experienced in the realm of God, where perfect justice and perfect righteousness are the rule. This is the mindset of those who pray for God's kingdom to be "on earth as it is in heaven." Apparently, for this peaceable kingdom to come about, only the destruction of Satan at a final battle between good and evil will do the trick. This is the battle of Armageddon. Until that battle, however, there are two different theological opinions concerning the status of the present world age.

In the sixteenth chapter of Matthew's gospel, Jesus is pictured sitting at a campfire with his disciples somewhere in the region of Caesarea Philippi, perhaps even at the small lake that is the source of the Jordan River. He asks them, "Who do people say the Son of Man is?" They recite many of the current opinions of the day. But when Jesus specifies that he wants to know what *they* think, Peter, speaking for the group, announces his belief that Jesus is "the Christ, the Son of the living God."

Jesus replies that because of his answer Peter will be given "the keys of the kingdom of heaven." Jesus goes even further: "Upon this rock [Peter] I will build my church. And the gates of Hell will not prevail against it." Roman Catholic theologians teach that Peter thus became the first pope. As the leader of the church, he and his successors would be assured that whatever they "bind on earth will be bound in heaven, and whatever [they] loose on earth will be loosed in heaven." According to this view, the church has the power on earth to "bind" Satan. The church is now in the process of doing just that. The kingdom is not only in the future. It is already here. Slowly, "line upon line and precept upon precept," to use the words of the prophet Isaiah, the church is going about the business of bringing the kingdom of heaven to the earth, thus fulfilling the petition of the Lord's Prayer.

Jesus, in one of his many references to "the kingdom," told the disciples that "the kingdom of God is near [or within] you" (Luke 10:9). But at his trial he also told Pilate, the Roman governor, "My kingdom is not of this world" (John 18:36). This seeming discrepancy has led some theologians to apply the ambiguous phrase "already but not yet" to the realm of God. Those who wrestle with these contradictory claims tend to believe that the church itself will bring about the results that the book of Revelation says will follow the battle of Armageddon. According to this view, the antichrist is not necessarily a single person. There may be many antichrists. "Who is the liar? It is the man who denies that Jesus is the Christ. Such a man is the antichrist" (1 John 2:22).

Some Protestant theologians agree in part with this interpretation, placing the power to redeem earth within the church but stopping short of conceding that Peter, or anyone else except Jesus, was to be the head of the church. Others think that the transfer of power was merely symbolic—that the church will never, without the divine intervention of an Armageddon, be able to bring the kingdom of heaven to earth.

Those outside the Christian faith understandably question both the Catholic and the Protestant viewpoints. Even the word *kingdom* seems to imply an outdated point of view. Not many nations in the twenty-first century are real kingdoms, and those that are often are held in disdain. For this reason, many modern theologians use the word *realm* instead of *kingdom*. The Lord's Prayer is changed to read, "May your realm come to earth as it now exists in heaven."

Whatever the shades of meaning attached to the prayer, the overall message is still the same. Things are not right on earth. Our history of warfare, inhumanity, and bigotry has not managed to accomplish much in terms of human righteousness and goodness. But even though we have never experienced real righteousness and goodness, we still have an idea of what those attributes are. They must exist somewhere "out there" in a heaven beyond the shores of earth.

This kind of thinking goes back to Socrates, the Greek philosopher. He proposed that a horse is a representation of something he called pure "horse-ness." Somewhere there must exist the perfect reality of what we can see or conceive on earth. Otherwise, we would not be able to imagine it. If we accept this premise, it is not too great a step to say that a perfect "realm," a perfect "kingdom," must also exist. That is the kingdom Christians pray for when they petition God to send the kingdom of heaven their way.

The purpose of Armageddon, either literally or metaphorically, is to produce that kingdom of perfection here. One reading makes Armageddon a philosophical concept; the other, a real war between the powers of good and evil. Although most Christians probably don't consider these rather esoteric concepts when they pray, they still manage to say, following the religious custom, "Thy kingdom come, on earth as it is in heaven."

Source:
The Holy Bible, New International Version. Grand Rapids, MI: Zondervan, 1978.

KINGS FROM THE EAST

The sixth angel poured out his bowl on the great river Euphrates, and its water was dried up to prepare the way for the kings from the East.... Then they gathered the kings together to the place that in Hebrew is called Armageddon. (Rev. 16:12, 16)

The kings from the East, introduced in Revelation 16:12, are apparently leaders of the forces of evil that will be arrayed against the heavenly army of Jesus Christ at the time of the Second Coming and the battle of Armageddon. Although they are not further identified, most conservative interpreters associate them with an immense Asian army of at least 200 million soldiers (Rev. 9:16) who will cross the Euphrates River, arriving on the scene at Megiddo just in time to participate in the final battle of history (see Armageddon, Battle of). Their defeat marks the end of the present world age.

Source:
The Holy Bible, New International Version. Grand Rapids, MI: Zondervan, 1978.

LEFT BEHIND BOOKS

Tim LaHaye is the author of more than forty books with subjects ranging from biblical prophecy to *The Act of Marriage* and *The Act of Marriage after 40*. For twenty-five years he was the pastor of a well-known evangelical church in San Diego that held services in three locations. He founded two Christian high schools, a California Christian school system consisting of ten schools, and the Christian Heritage College. Known within evangelical circles as a conservative, pretribulational (see Pre-, Post-, and Midtribulationalism) teacher of Bible prophecy, he still might never have gained a reputation in the secular world were it not for the fact that one day he found himself on an airplane wondering what would happen if the pilot were a Christian and was caught up in the Rapture (see Rapture) while the plane was still in the air.

From such random thoughts publishing history is made.

Jerry B. Jenkins is a full-time author who has worked with such notable Christians as Billy Graham, Bill Gaither, and Luis Palau, as well as with sports figures Hank Aaron, Walter Payton, Orel Hershiser, and Nolan Ryan. A former vice-president for publishing at *Moody* magazine, long a flagship publication for fundamentalist Christianity, he joined LaHaye in writing a book that became the first of a series called *Left Behind* that soon made publishing history by crossing over into the secular world and establishing numbers that caught literally everyone, including the authors, by surprise. Twelve volumes and 62 million copies later, LaHaye and Jenkins found themselves on the cover of *Newsweek*, the short LaHaye standing on an off-camera box to make him appear as tall as Jenkins.

The coauthors' working relationship consists of LaHaye, the teacher, providing the scriptural framework from which Jenkins weaves a storyline. The result is a fictionalized version of LaHaye's conception of what will happen on earth when the book of Revelation (see Revelation) unfolds:

1. *Left Behind*: Based on Revelation 4:1. The Rapture occurs on earth. Millions of people, including all children, even those still in the womb, disappear.

2. *Tribulation Force*: Based on Revelation 6:1 and 2. The antichrist arises, and a small remnant of new believers, converted after the Rapture, gather to become God's undercover agents on earth.

3. *Nicolae*: Based on the opening of the seven seals described in Revelation 6–8.

4. *Soul Harvest*: Based on Revelation 8. The first three trumpets sound, and the world begins to choose sides between God and the antichrist.

5. *Apollyon*: Based on the fourth and fifth trumpet judgments in Revelation 8 and 9. The sun, moon, and stars darken and a plague of locusts (see Locusts) strikes the earth as the destroyer Apollyon (Rev. 9:11) is unleashed.

6. *Assassins*: The scene shifts between heaven and earth as God's two witnesses in Jerusalem are killed and then rise from death after three days. Meanwhile, mimicking the miracle, the antichrist is assassinated and rises from the dead.

7. *The Indwelling*: The beast of Revelation 13 comes to earth.

8. *The Mark*: The beast issues the famous "mark of the beast" (see Mark of the Beast) and begins to take control of earth's economy.

9. *Desecration*: The beast, holding the antichrist in his power, ascends the throne.

10. *The Remnant*: The faithful on earth are mysteriously pulled toward the Middle East as the world prepares for the final battle.

11. *Armageddon*: The final battle for earth ensues.

12. *Glorious Appearing*: Jesus Christ returns and the Millennium (see entry) begins.

To illustrate how a scriptural text gets translated into a work of fiction, here are some verses from Revelation followed by related text from *Glorious Appearing*:

Revelation 19:11–19

I saw heaven standing open and there before me was a white horse, whose rider is called Faithful and True. With justice he judges and makes war. His eyes are like a blazing fire, and on his head are many crowns. He has a name written on him that no one but himself knows. He is dressed in a robe dipped in blood, and his name is the Word of God. The armies of heaven were following him, riding on white horses and dressed in fine linen, white and clean. Out of his mouth comes a sharp sword with which to strike down the nations. "He will rule them

Tim LaHaye (left) and Jerry B. Jenkins at a launch party for *Glorious Appearing,* the closing volume of their
Left Behind series. *Mary Ann Chastain/Associated Press.*

with an iron scepter." He treads the winepress of the fury of the wrath
of God Almighty. On his robe and on his thigh he has this name written: KING OF KINGS AND LORD OF LORDS.

And I saw an angel standing in the sun, who cried out with a loud
voice to all the birds flying in midair, "Come, gather together for the
great supper of God, so that you may eat the flesh of kings, generals,
and mighty men, of horses and their riders, and the flesh of all people,
free and slave, small and great."

Then I saw the beast and the kings of the earth and their armies gathered together to make war against the rider on the horse and his army.

Glorious Appearing

And then, as if God had thrown the switch in Heaven, light.

But that wasn't enough of a word for it. This was not light from above
that cast shadows. This was a brightness that invaded every crevasse

and cranny. Rayford had to shield his eyes, but it did no good, as the light came from everywhere.

It exposed a Unity Army in chaos. On the plains, horses bucked and reared, whinnying and throwing riders. On the hillsides leading to Petra, soldiers examined weapons that did not work. On the border of the city, Carpathia stood exposed atop his personnel carrier, sword at his side, stared at by saints standing side by side.

"You can see them now! Charge! Attack! Kill them!"

But as his petrified, lethargic soldiers slowly turned back to the matter at hand, the brilliant multi-colored cloud cover parted and rolled back like a scroll from horizon to horizon. Rayford found himself on his knees on the ground, hands and head lifted.

Heaven opened and there, on a white horse, sat Jesus, the Christ, the Son of the Living God.

Revelation 19:21

The rest of them were killed with the sword that came out of the mouth of the rider on the horse, and all the birds gorged themselves on their flesh.

Glorious Appearing

Rayford watched through the binocs as men and women soldiers and horses seemed to explode where they stood. It was as if the very words of the Lord had superheated their blood, causing it to burst through their veins and skin ... tens of thousands of foot soldiers dropped their weapons, grabbed their heads or their chests, fell to their knees, and writhed as they were invisibly sliced asunder. Their innards and entrails gushed to the desert floor, and as those around them turned to run, they too were slain, their blood pooling and rising in the unforgiving brightness of the glory of Christ....

It was as if Antichrist's army had become the sacrificial beasts for the Lord's slaughter.

Revelation 16:13, 14

Then I saw three evil spirits that looked like frogs; they came out of the mouth of the dragon, out of the mouth of the beast and out of the mouth of the false prophet. They are spirits of demons performing miraculous signs, and they go out to the kings of the whole world, to gather them for the battle on the great day of God Almighty.

Glorious Appearing

Jesus leaned forward and rested his elbows on his knees, the three [demonic creatures who had been sent out to deceive the nations] kept their faces to the ground, not looking at Him. "'As I live,' says the Lord, 'I have no pleasure in the death of the wicked, but that the wicked turn from his way and live.'"

"We repent! We will turn! We will turn! We worship You, oh Jesus, Son of God. You are Lord!"

"But for you it is too late," Jesus said, and Mac was hit anew by the sorrow in His tone. "You were once angelic beings, in heaven with God. Yet you were cast down because of your own prideful decisions. Rather than resist the evil one, you chose to serve him."

"We were wrong! Wrong! We acknowledge You as Lord!"

"Like My Father, with whom I am one, I have no pleasure in the death of the wicked, but that is justice, and that is your sentence."

And as the three shrieked, their reptilian bodies burst from their clothes and exploded, leaving a mess of blood and scales and skin that soon burst into flames and was carried away by the wind.

This style of biblical interpretive writing is not appreciated by everyone. Nicholas D. Kristof, writing in the *New York Times* on July 17, 2004, commented:

> If a Muslim were to write an Islamic version of "Glorious Appearing" and publish it in Saudi Arabia, jubilantly describing a massacre of millions of non-Muslims by God, we would have a fit. We have quite properly linked the fundamentalist tracts of Islam with the intolerance they nurture, and it's time to remove the motes from our own eyes....

> These scenes also raise an eschatological problem: Could devout fundamentalists really enjoy paradise as their friends, relatives and neighbors were heaved into hell?

> Each form of fundamentalism creates a stark moral division between decent, pious types like oneself—and infidels headed for hell....

> We should be embarrassed when our best-selling books gleefully celebrate religious intolerance and violence against infidels. That's not what America stands for, and I doubt that it's what God stands for.

Kristof's opinion piece was immediately criticized in a number of other newspapers across the country. Once again, the great divide of biblical interpretation, literal versus metaphorical, had split well-meaning Christians into bitterly opposed camps. It is safe that to say that, in the near future at least, the issue will not be settled once and for all.

Sources:
Gates, David. "The Pop Prophets." *Newsweek*, May 24, 2004.
The Holy Bible, New International Version. Grand Rapids, MI: Zondervan, 1978.
Kristof, Nicholas D. "'Left Behind' Series Is Un-American." *New York Times*, July 17, 2004.
LaHaye, Tim, and Jerry B. Jenkins. *Glorious Appearing.* Carol Stream, IL: Tyndale House, 2004.
———. *A Visual Guide to the "Left Behind" Series.* Eugene, OR: Harvest House, 2001.

LINDSEY, HAL

Hal Lindsey's *Late Great Planet Earth* was published in 1970. It was a popular book, not a scholarly one. It presented ideas that had been bubbling about in the Christian church for a hundred years, ever since John Nelson Darby (see Dispensationalism). It was dispensationalism for the masses, written in modern slang but given a unique twist. Lindsey tied Darby's scheme for Armageddon into current events. Where Darby saw a general economic upheaval, Lindsey saw the European Common Market. Darby foresaw the coming of a "man of sin." Lindsey called him the antichrist and said he was alive somewhere in Europe. Darby saw a great conflict with much shedding of blood. Lindsey saw tanks and ICBMs.

The book made publishing history, stayed atop the *New York Times* book lists for a decade, and was far and away the best-selling book of that period. It was followed by sequels that continued the theme: *Satan Is Alive and Well on Planet Earth; There's a New World Coming; The Final Battle; The Terminal Generation; Rapture;* and *Apocalypse Code.* It seemed the world was ready for popular, easily digested books on biblical prophecy.

With publishing success came success in other arenas. There were television interviews and radio talk shows. During the 1980s, rumors of adultery, followed by divorce, pushed Lindsey out of the limelight for a time. But the door was open, and plenty of other biblical prophecy teachers walked through into the Promised Land of fame and fortune offered by what seemed to be an insatiable public appetite for more of the same.

The second coming of Hal Lindsey occurred in the 1990s. He was back on television, writing more books, hosting a prophecy Web site, speaking at conferences, and assuring the world that if the Second Coming of Jesus looked probable in the seventies, it was even closer now.

In 1970, Lindsey touched a nerve that even experienced publishers had not yet recognized. Biblical prophecy was interesting not only to the conservative, typically Protestant, churchgoing public. It had crossed over into the mainstream.

But it all started with one book, one graduate of Dallas Theological Seminary, and an idea. The idea was simple: Prophecy had never previously been interpreted correctly because the prophets of long ago had seen into the future, viewing technologies they didn't understand. Until the technologies were invented to bring their words into life, no one could have possibly understood them. But when the technologies caught up and merged with the prophets' visions, the last days were upon planet Earth. According to Lindsey, the prophet Daniel (see entry) had foreseen this centuries before the birth of Jesus: "Close up and seal the words of the scroll until the time of the end," Daniel is told, with the explanation that at that time, "Many will go here and there to increase knowledge" (Dan. 12:4).

To see Lindsey's interpretive methods at work, consider Daniel 11:40–42:

"At the time of the end the king of the South will engage him [the king of the North] in battle, and the king of the North will storm out against him with chariots and cavalry and a great fleet of ships. He will invade many countries and sweep through them like a flood. He will invade the Beautiful Land. Many countries will fall, but Edom, Moab and the leaders of Ammon will be delivered from his hand. He will extend his power over many countries; Egypt will not escape."

Lindsey explained the text this way in *The Late Great Planet Earth*:

When the Russians invade the Middle East with amphibious and mechanized land forces, they will make a "blitzkrieg" type of offensive through the area....

The current build-up of Russian ships in the Mediterranean serves as another significant sign of the possible nearness of Armageddon. They now have more ships in the Mediterranean than the United States, according to several recent news releases. The amphibious landings will facilitate a rapid encirclement of the middle section of "the land bridge."

Or consider a sentence from the prophet Ezekiel (see entry): "I will send fire on Magog and on those who live in safety on the coastlands, and they will know that I am the Lord" (Ezek. 39:6). Lindsey's interpretation: "According to this, Russia, as well as many countries who thought they were secure under the Antichrist's protection, will have fire fall upon them. Once again, this could be a direct judgment from God, or God could allow the various countries to launch a nuclear exchange of ballistic missiles upon each other."

When enigmatic scriptural verses are thus linked with supposedly factual statements about current events, it is easy for a layperson to confuse the two. But sales of Lindsey's books indicate that a chord was struck somewhere deep in the American psyche. As Paul Boyer, in an interview for the PBS show *Frontline*, said:

What we see in contemporary American mass culture really is that apocalyptic belief has become big business.... The significance of Hal Lindsey, I think, is he represents another one of those moments of breakthrough, when interest in Bible prophecy spills out beyond the ranks of true believers and becomes a broader cultural phenomenon. And people who have never paid much attention to prophecy at all hear about this book. They pick up the paperback. They see the way Lindsey weaves together current events, and they say, "Wow, this is amazing. There must really be something to this." So Lindsey's a very important transitional figure, I think.

If the phenomenon had been just another fad, it might not have had much cultural staying power. But it went deeper—much deeper. Boyer continues:

Lindsey seems to have had a considerable influence not just on the part of the public as a whole, but at the highest levels of government. He's a somewhat boastful person, and it's not entirely clear how much to trust all of his stories, but he does tell of giving seminars at the Pentagon, seminars at the National War College, that were crowded with people. So there does seem to have been in the 1970s a considerable interest in prophetic interpretations, particularly as they related to Russia and the Cold War, at some of the highest levels of government.

Lindsey's backers view his influence on government officials as God's final warning to the powers that now exist at the end of time. His detractors see a fatal breakdown of the church-state border. Can governments trust an interpretive scheme of the Bible? Can they base policies on such a scheme? Obviously not—at least as far as the Constitution allows. But policies are written by people. And people have religious opinions that can, and sometimes do, influence them.

When dealing with a foreign power—the old Soviet Union, for instance— subliminal feelings induced by studies in the scriptures might influence even a president's decisions. If those studies caused him to be led by verses that say, in effect, "God is love," he might find himself leaning toward peaceful diplomacy. But if his religious background caused him to think mainly in terms of "godless Communism," his reaction might be totally different.

Lindsey's opponents worry that too much access to the powerful might lead to self-fulfilled prophecy. Was President Carter so convinced that a Middle East peace treaty was prophesied in the Bible that he actually brought one about at Camp David (see Carter, Jimmy)? Carter says no. Was President Reagan so convinced of the dangers inherent in the "king of the North," whom he associated with the USSR, that he pushed himself to bring about their destruction (see Reagan, Ronald)? Reagan continually swore that his motives were political, not religious. But in both cases, Lindsey's followers watched the newspapers every day for events that might demonstrate that Armageddon was at hand.

Religious opinions are deeply felt. Christian scholars who oppose Lindsey's approach carry on a constant and bitter debate with those who don't. Whether the issue will actually, or has already, spilled over into secular power politics is still hotly contested.

Sources:

Boyer, Paul. "America's Doom Industry." http://www.pbs.org/wgbh/pages/frontline/shows/apocalypse/explanation/doomindustry.html.

The Holy Bible, New International Version. Grand Rapids, MI: Zondervan, 1978.

Lindsey, Hal, with C. C. Carlson. *The Late Great Planet Earth.* Grand Rapids, MI: Zondervan, 1970.

LOCUSTS

And out of the smoke locusts came down upon the earth and were given power like that of scorpions of the earth. They were told not to harm the grass of the earth or any plant or tree, but only those people who did not have the seal of God.... The locusts looked like horses prepared for battle. On their heads they wore something like crowns of

According to Revelation, a swarm of particularly nasty locusts will be the first woe visited upon the ungodly in the endtimes. *Fortean Picture Library.*

gold, and their faces resembled human faces. Their hair was like women's hair, and their teeth were like lion's teeth. They had breastplates of iron, and the sound of their wings was like the thundering of many chariots and horses rushing into battle. They had tails and stings like scorpions, and in their tails they had the power to torment people for five months. They had as king over them the angel of the Abyss. (Rev. 9:3–11)

Like so many passages of scriptural prophecy, these verses from Revelation cause great debate among scholars from different ends of the theological spectrum. Liberal scholars are most apt to read them symbolically. They balance out the account from the book of Exodus, for instance. When Moses and Pharaoh squared off for the great duel of the gods before the Exodus, locusts were released as one of the great plagues (Exod. 10) that, culminating in the death of the firstborn of Egypt, finally convinced Pharaoh to, in the words of Moses, "let my people go."

According to this view, locusts represent the judgment of God upon a people familiar with actual locust swarms that could devastate an agrarian society. Contrasted with devastation, God's people triumph in the face of adversity. John the Baptist, for instance, made locusts a vital part of his diet—Matthew 3:4 says that John's food was "locusts and wild honey." In other words, locusts may represent plagues and judgments to those outside the will of God, but God's representatives thrive on adversity. They eat it up. That which destroys sinners nourishes saints.

Conservative scholars may approve of the symbolism, but they insist that it can't stop with spiritual morality lessons. When Exodus talks about a plague of locusts, it means there was a plague of literal locusts that temporarily destroyed the economy of ancient Egypt. When Revelation talks about a plague of locusts sent to torment the people of earth, the verses must await a literal fulfillment. Interestingly, "literal fulfillment" does not necessarily mean that the locusts will be actual insects. Many conservatives follow interpreters like Hal Lindsey (see entry) and teach that the author of Revelation was using locusts as a way of explaining a technology he couldn't comprehend. Looking into the future, he was really seeing "attack helicopters with a tail-mounted sprayer for chemical/biological weapons." At least that's how Lindsey explains it in his book *Apocalypse Code*.

In prophetic discussions, locusts have become yet another point of contention between liberals and conservatives.

Sources:
The Holy Bible, New International Version. Grand Rapids, MI: Zondervan, 1978.
Lindsey, Hal. *Apocalypse Code.* Palos Verdes, CA: Western Front Ltd., 1997.

LORD OF THE RINGS, THE

"The time of men has come to an end!" declares an orc commander in the movie version of J. R. R. Tolkien's trilogy *The Lord of the Rings*. The novels upon which the movie was based were written over a period of some sixteen years beginning in the late 1930s and published in 1954–55. After modest early sales, they suddenly became virtually required reading for many young people in the alternate-culture days of the late 1960s. The movies, directed by Peter Jackson, appeared beginning in 2001 after four years of filming.

The action takes place in a fantasy world with fantasy beings, except for the humans who share their existence. There are elves—tall, immortal, very wise forest dwellers; hobbits—small, round humanoids with furry feet who live in homes built into the ground; dwarves—tough, passionate beings who inhabit deep mountain caverns; ents—sentient trees who can move, albeit very slowly; wizards—the good and bad magicians; and orcs, ogres, and Uruk-hai who are the armies of evil itself. All the characters are developed very carefully to exhibit, full-blown and fully developed, human traits found in all of us.

Ever since the books were first published, there has been a debate as to whether Professor Tolkien was presenting a secular version of Christian themes inherent in the book of Revelation. Tolkien always claimed that such was not his intention. He merely wanted to try his hand at writing a long story and used themes and imaginary characters he had created in his childhood. But when you are a well-known, devout Catholic layman who happens to be a close friend of C. S. Lewis, the most famous Christian apologist of his generation, it's hard to quell such speculation.

Assuming Tolkien can be taken at his word, the fact that Christian themes seem to be readily identifiable in *The Lord of the Rings* opens up at least two interesting possibilities regarding its inspiration: Either Tolkien was subconsciously influenced by his Christian upbringing or, perhaps even more intriguing, he drew from the well of what has since been popularized as the "collective unconscious." In other words, the same muse that inspired the author of Revelation, be he/she/it divine or psychological in nature, caused another author to present the same themes in a different way.

The first book, *The Fellowship of the Ring*, is the story of the gathering of the hero and his entourage who will see him through his mythological ordeal to destroy a ring of power and overcome an evil that is growing in the world. In this book (and in the first movie), the journey begins with the group being beset by dangers and becoming separated. The leader of the fellowship, the mysterious wizard Gandalf the Grey, dies and travels to the world of the dead.

The second book, *The Two Towers*, takes up the journey and follows the fellowship of the ring through various adventures. Evil is spreading upon the world. The War of the Ring, pitting the armies of evil against the armies of men (assisted by elves, a dwarf, ents, and a good wizard), begins. The ring bearer is Frodo Baggins, a young hobbit, who is accompanied by his faithful companion Samwise Gamgee. While the battles rage, the two continue a solitary journey in another direction, determined to destroy the ring that holds the power of evil. Gandalf returns from the dead as the luminous Gandalf the White, who rides a white horse into battle.

In the third book, *The Return of the King*, similarities to the biblical book of Revelation become more apparent. An Armageddon-like battle takes place on the plains of Gondor (the realm of men). The King of Men, who is the scion of the ancient kings, returns from years in exile to lead the forces of good. In the triumphal ending, evil is vanquished when the powerful ring drops into volcanic fire to be destroyed. The war is won, the White Tree, or tree of life, blooms again, and the hobbits go home to the peace and quiet of their land. The elves and the remaining good wizard, Gandalf, are no longer needed in this new world. They board a ship that takes them away into the west to everlasting life. They are called in a Rapture-like fashion (see Rapture) to live in eternity. The world where evil has been a constant threat has ended. The world of men has truly begun.

One of Tolkien's central themes, inherent in the monotheistic idea of the arrow of time that points to Armageddon, is that of the conflict between the doctrines of free will and predestination (see Calvinism). Throughout the story the characters, like the characters in the Bible, all seem to work under the principle of free will. They make their individual choices and their end is by no means certain. But Gandalf, the mysterious wizard who is sent from another world into the world of men—who dies and is buried in the depths of the earth but returns in a transcendent form, who looks like a man but has mysterious powers used only for good, who battles the Dark Lord and is finally victorious—hints throughout the narrative that another power may be at work. He reminds his followers that Frodo has the ring because he "is meant to have the ring." Gandalf believes that Gollum, the fallen creature who plays an almost demonic role, must be spared "because he may yet have a part to play."

In the end, Frodo arrives at the crucial place where the ring must be thrown into the fire. The fate of the human race and all creation is at stake. Frodo succumbs to temptation and chooses to keep the ring. That is, he chooses to attempt to control evil rather than destroy it—and thereby preserves it. Here Gollum plays his part. In a desperate fight with Frodo, he wins possession of the ring. But even as Gollum claims it for his own, he falls into the abyss, destroying both the ring and himself.

Were both Frodo and Gollum led by destiny, a power greater than themselves? Were they allowed free choice but only within the parameters of divine will? In the end, was the ring predestined to be destroyed by One greater than the fallen, evil, satanic figure who, in his rebellion and quest for power, created it? Tolkien, like the biblical authors, is silent.

There are other themes in this massive work that suggest a source in common with the ideas of the biblical writers. The king of the race of humans, who has almost as many names as the biblical Emmanuel, is revealed as a mixture of human being and mysterious elf. Spending his formative years in the wilderness like Jesus of old, he takes center stage in the battle against evil, wielding a great sword while riding a white horse. Descending into the depths of the earth he frees those trapped by their sin, forms them into a mighty army, and arrives just in time to win a crucial battle held outside the gates of Minas Tirith, the principal holy city on earth—the place where, like Jerusalem, ancient kings once ruled.

The battle of good and evil begins when a central created being falls from grace due to his lust for personal power. Like Lucifer of old, he says in his heart, "I will be like God!" (see Devil).

If Tolkien did indeed get his inspiration from common mythological motifs, it raises questions about how the Bible should be interpreted. Are Revelation and Daniel, for instance, woven from threads that form the fabric of essential, universal human experience? Is the end of the world as these writers describe it an actual future event or simply an expression of a primal human fear?

Is their a destiny so far above human experience that, like Tolkien's characters, we are unaware of its existence even though, like Gandalf the wizard, we may be allowed glimpses of its intent?

Our approach to these kinds of questions determines how we read and interpret biblical prophecy.

Source:
Tolkien, J. R. R. *The Lord of the Rings.* 3 vols. 2nd ed. Boston: Houghton Mifflin, 1965.

M

MAD MAX *see* Hollywood Envisions THE END

MAGOG *see* Gog and Magog

MALACHY, SAINT (O'MORE)

Malachy O'More (or O'Morgair) was born in Armagh, Ireland, in 1094 and ordained a priest by his mentor, Saint Cellach, in 1119. He soon became the abbot of Bangor and was consecrated bishop of Connor, then appointed to the primacy of Armagh in 1132. During his long career he instituted celibacy regulations and other disciplines upon Irish clergy while introducing the use of prayers and chants at the traditional canonical hours. He practiced the laying on of hands, and many supernatural healings were attributed to him. He was the first Irish saint to be canonized by Rome.

On a trip to Rome to visit Pope Innocent II, Malachy had a vision in which he saw a list giving the names of the 112 popes who would rule between then and the end of time. The prophecy was allegedly written down but then lost for four hundred years. It supposedly became buried in the Vatican archives until found and published in 1590 by Arnold de Wyon. Since it had been missing for so long, its validity was questioned even at the time of its discovery. But those who have worked with the original manuscript claim to have discovered very accurate traits attributed to the popes on the list.

The last entry on the list reads: "In the final persecution of the Holy Roman Church there will reign Peter the Roman, who will feed his flock amid many tribulations, after which the seven-hilled city will be destroyed and the dreadful Judge will judge the people. The End." Some historians who have studied Saint Malachy's list believe that it names only two popes following John Paul II, who died in 2005. Malachy labeled the first of these *Gloria Olivae* ("glory of the Olives"). He labeled the second Peter of Rome.

The day the new pope, Benedict XVI, was named, the Internet was abuzz with a new theory. The Olivetans were an early branch of the white monks of the Benedictine order, founded in 1319. After a rather rocky start they eventually established the center of their order on a mountain covered with olive groves. They called their hermitage "Monte Oliveto" and dedicated themselves, through penance and fasting, to remembering Christ's agony in the garden on the Mount of Olives on the night before he was crucified.

Cardinal Joseph Ratzinger, now Pope Benedict XVI, took the name of the Benedictine order's founder upon his election to the papacy. Through historical association he is thus connected with the Olivetans. Because he was seventy-eight years old, the oldest pope elected in more than two centuries, within hours of his announcement speculation began to center on his successor. Was this a fulfillment of Malachy's prophecy that the next-to-the-last pope will be identified with the olive—*Gloria Olivae*? Will there be only one more pope named before the return of Jesus Christ? Will the next pope be "Peter of Rome," the last of the line to be called Vicar of Christ? Pope watchers are waiting to see.

Source:
Devine, Arthur. "Prophecies of St. Malachy." http://www.newadvent.org/cathen/12473a.htm#malachy.

MARANATHA

The apostle Paul was fond of using a familiar Aramaic phrase in his letters. It could be translated as "Our Lord has come" (1 Cor. 16:22), "the Lord is at hand" (Phil. 4:5), or more often, "Our Lord, come!" Somehow the phrase got connected to the Greek words that close the book of Revelation, "Come, Lord Jesus."

However it happened, by the early second century a Christian text called the Didache forever cemented the meaning of both the Greek and Aramaic by giving them a strong eschatological flavor and translating them both as "Come, Lord Jesus." Today the word is used in Christian traditions as both a cry of exaltation and a prayer for the return of Jesus Christ. Many Christian congregations close each worship service with the words, "Maranatha! Come, Lord Jesus."

Source:
Buttrick, George A., ed. *The Interpreter's Dictionary of the Bible*. 4 vols. New York: Abingdon Press, 1962.

MARK OF THE BEAST

He ordered them to set up an image in honor of the beast who was wounded by the sword and yet lived. He was given power to give breath to the image of the first beast, so that it could speak and cause all who refused to worship the image to be killed. He also forced everyone, small and great, rich and poor, free and slave, to receive a mark on his right hand or on his forehead, so that no one could buy or sell unless he had the mark, which is the name of the beast or the number of his name.

This calls for wisdom. If anyone has insight, let him calculate the number of the beast, for it is a man's number. His number is 666. (Rev. 13:14–18)

These are among the most puzzling and intriguing words in the Bible. As yet, no one really understands what the original author meant to say. Many Bible scholars, Hal Lindsey and Tim LaHaye among them, say they have cracked the code. They go into specific detail about the secret message of these verses. That is the whole point of LaHaye's *Left Behind* books. But there are so many conflicting theories that it is hard to believe any one of them.

Revelation 13 describes two "beasts" (see Beasts, The). One comes "out of the sea" (verse 1) and the other "out of the earth" (verse 11). The first seems to be in charge, because the "dragon" of Revelation 12, revealed in verse 9 to be "that ancient serpent called the devil, or Satan," gives this first beast "his power and his throne and great authority." "Men worshiped the dragon [the devil] because he had given authority to the beast, and they also worshiped the beast and asked, 'Who is like the beast? Who can make war against him?'" (verse 4). This first beast "seemed to have had a fatal wound, but the fatal wound had been healed. The whole world was astonished" (verse 3).

The second beast, who seems to be a kind of PR agent for the first beast (see False Prophet), "had two horns like a lamb, but he spoke like a dragon" (verse 11). He puts on display an image of the first beast and orders the people of the world to worship it. He even manages to "give breath to the image of the first beast, so that it could speak." This, of course, is a rather obvious invitation to break the first two commandments given by Moses to the Jews:

I am the Lord your God:
  You shall have no other gods before me.
  You shall not worship idols.

In order to put some teeth behind his order, the second beast orders economic reprisals against anyone who refuses to worship the beast. All the citizens of the world are ordered to receive a mark on their hand or forehead. Without this mark, no one can "buy or sell." This is the infamous "mark of the beast." It seems to consist of the number 666 (see 666).

That's all the Bible says about the matter. But where the Bible leaves off, the questions begin:

1. *Who receives the mark?* Apparently everyone in the whole world. That's what Revelation 13 seems to say. But that leaves open another question. A few chapters later the world seems to be at war as 200 million soldiers "from the East" line up against the "king of the South" and his allies. Do these people, supposedly from nations east and south of Israel, have to receive the mark of the beast when they are obviously not a part of the kingdom of the antichrist, which seems to exist on the same land Rome once occupied? The Bible is silent. Strangely, so are the conservative evangelical scholars.

2. *Why is the mark placed on "the hand or forehead"?* Some literalist scholars speculate that the mark is conspicuously placed to make it easy to scan at checkout counters. It is not revealed who gets the mark on the forehead and who gets it on the

hand. Maybe the option will be left open for the recipient so that he/she can make a personal fashion statement. Again, the author is silent. Of course, he probably never even heard of cash registers.

3. *What's the point of all this?* Hal Lindsey thinks he knows the answer to this one. He says the first beast is the antichrist and the second is a "false prophet":

> The False Prophet will perfect a way to expose everyone who believes in Jesus Christ. All beast-worshipers will receive a distinguishing mark on their right hand or forehead. Everyone who refuses the mark will be cut off from economic survival. They will be forbidden to buy or sell anything. Now, how could that have happened in the first century? The answer is, "It couldn't." Before the advent of computer technology and other high-tech gimmickry, it would not have been possible for the government to number all people on earth, let alone whether they buy and sell without a valid number. Of course, today this is an easy task for modern computers. (*Apocalypse Code*)

As if the mark of the beast needed further comment, the very next chapter of the Bible, Revelation 14, issues another warning. An angel appears to emphasize its importance. Flying in "midair," the angel says "in a loud voice ":

> If anyone worships the beast and his image and receives his mark on their forehead or on their hand, he, too, will drink of the wine of God's fury, which has been poured full strength into the cup of his wrath. He will be tormented with burning sulfur in the presence of the holy angels and of the Lamb. And the smoke of their torment rises forever and ever. There is no rest day or night for those who worship the beast and his image, or for anyone who receives the mark of his name. This calls for patient endurance on the part of the saints who obey God's commandments and remain faithful to Jesus. (Rev. 14:9–12)

How do less literal-minded scholars respond to all this? Well, at least when it comes to confronting literalists, with great difficulty. To liberal scholars, the whole concept of a ruling antichrist and marketing-expert false prophet seems rather far-fetched and provokes more questions than answers. God changes from a tender, forgiving, grace-filled "father in heaven" to a mean-spirited tyrant who takes great delight in torturing helpless victims in consuming fire that lasts forever. The images of Revelation 14:10–11 are horrible in the extreme and are probably responsible for more nightmares that any other written words in history.

Jonathan Edwards, the Massachusetts minister who, beginning in the 1730s, played a principal role in what has since been called America's Great Awakening, kept congregants glued to their seats by metaphorically dangling them like spiders over an eternal flame in his famous sermon "Sinners in the Hands of an Angry God." How does imagery such as this fit with the rest of the New Testament? It doesn't, say most liberal scholars. Besides, a worldwide economic system of retaliation against Christians, derived from only a few verses of the Bible, all of which are disputed even by scholars from differing conservative camps, seems so impossibly silly that most liberal scholars refrain from even getting involved. If they don't know exactly what the author of Revelation was driving at, neither, they claim, do the conservative commentators. So rather than debate what they consider to be nonsensical points of speculation, most remain quiet, convinced that this is one scriptural enigma that will never be solved.

Some scholars, however, think that they have found answers outside the typical liberal/conservative debate. One is Tom Harpur, an Anglican priest and writer from Toronto. Building on the work of historical scholars such as Alvin Boyd Kuhn, Godfrey Higgins, and Gerald Massey, Harpur has broken completely from the literalist position—as well as, according to him, that of the liberal theologians. Moving beyond even those who have discovered a historical, but very human, "Jesus of history," Harpur suggests that not only Revelation but also the gospels and the stories from virtually the whole Bible are retellings of ancient myths and spiritual legends found in Egypt thousands of years before they were ever written on parchment. Revelation presents many of the same images recorded on Egyptian tombs dating from before the time even of Moses, let alone Jesus. That is why, according to Harpur, both testaments take such pains to bring the Jews and, later, the holy family, to Egypt. In his view, Christianity will find its roots in the mystery religions of the ancients. There is no use looking into the future to discover the meaning of esoteric signs presented as prophecy. They come from the past. They are part of the eternal story, told by every religion, about the spiritual struggle faced by all who try to find what Christians call "the Christ within."

Harpur identifies symbol after symbol that first appeared in Egyptian mythology and later found its way into Christian thought, especially into the book of Revelation. Like Alvin Boyd Kuhn before him, he insists that the reason Christians don't understand their own religion, the religion of the original authors of the Bible, is that the fourth-century church, after it became the official state religion of Rome under the Emperor Constantine, "literalized" the mythology, ousted the Gnostics who clung to it, and produced a religion for the masses based on supposedly "historical" people and events rather than spiritual, mythological, eternal truths. The way to read Revelation, according to Harpur, is not to "demythologize" the Bible, but to "remythologize" it. Only then will passages about the mark of the beast begin to make sense.

Sources:

Buttrick, George A., ed. *The Interpreter's Dictionary of the Bible.* 4 vols. New York: Abingdon Press, 1962.

Harpur, Tom. *The Pagan Christ.* Toronto: Thomas Allen, 2004.

The Holy Bible, New International Version. Grand Rapids, MI: Zondervan, 1978.

Lindsey, Hal. *Apocalypse Code.* Palos Verdes, CA: Western Front Ltd., 1997.

MATRIX, THE *see* Hollywood Envisions THE END

MAYAN VIEW OF HISTORY *see* Indigenous Peoples of the Americas

MEGIDDO *see* Armageddon

MESSIAH/MESSIANIC PROPHECY
(See also Books of the Bible and Their Relation to Prophecy)

A messianic prophecy, sometimes called a "messianic hope," is one relating to an eschatological belief that the Messiah, anointed by God, will someday come to set things straight on earth. Those who hold such hopes are said to be awaiting the coming of the Messiah. Found first in Zoroastrianism, then in Judaism, the belief was later adopted by Christians.

Jews believe that the Messiah is yet to come. One of the "Thirteen Articles of the Creed" of Maimonides (1135–1204), considered by Jews to be the greatest philosopher, theologian, and codifier of Jewish law and thought during the Middle Ages, taught a daily ritual prayer for the coming of the one who, descended from King David, would at "the end of days" be king over the world, "when peace will be established among the nations and the Law of the Lord will come from Jerusalem to all peoples."

The Hebrew word *messiah* means "anointed one." It is related to the word found at the root of the name Moses, who is said to have led the Jewish people out of their captivity in Egypt. Its Greek equivalent is *christos*, which is the word Jewish scholars used, as in Daniel 9:5, when they translated their scriptures into a Greek version known as the Septuagint.

Christians believe that the Messiah came once, was crucified, and will come again. "Christ" was the title given by early Christians to Jesus of Nazareth ("Jesus, from the town of Nazareth"), who would have been known to his contemporaries as Yeshua ben Yosef (Joshua, son of Joseph). If Jesus' given name had been transliterated directly from Hebrew into English, he would be known to the world today as Joshua. But because the only known documents written about Jesus, the biblical gospels, were originally in Greek, the Hebrew "Yeshua" became the Greek transliteration "Iesous." Iesous, transliterated much later, became the Latin "Jesu" and then the English "Jesus."

In other words, "Jesus Christ" could as accurately be rendered as "Joshua Moses," "Joshua, the Anointed One," or "Joshua, the Messiah."

When many Christians read their Old Testament, they believe that two Jewish heroes prefigure the One who will arrive just in time to defeat evil at the battle of Armageddon. One led the Jewish people out of slavery and guided them to the borders of the Promised Land. The other led them into that land and fought the battles that gave them victory over the Canaanites. Moses stood before Pharaoh and said, "Let my people go!" Christians believe him to be a type, or figure, of Jesus Christ, who will come to free the inhabitants of earth from the clutches of what some regard as the current satanic system. Joshua (Yeshua, or "Jesus"), who served as Moses' aide-de-camp during the forty-year wilderness sojourn, was the one who led the Jewish people across the Jordan River into the Promised Land. With this deed, according to Christians, he prefigured the act that will be accomplished when Jesus returns to lead the people of earth into a Promised Land of peace and prosperity.

This is the messianic hope of those who await the coming of the Messiah, the Anointed One, at the end of the present world age. With his victory at the battle of Armageddon, history as we know it will be finished.

Sources:

Bridger, David, ed. *The New Jewish Encyclopedia*. New York: Behrman House, 1962.

Buttrick, George A., ed. *The Interpreter's Dictionary of the Bible*. 4 vols. New York: Abingdon Press, 1962.

The Holy Bible, New International Version. Grand Rapids, MI: Zondervan, 1978.

METEORS, METEOROIDS, AND METEORITES
(See also Asteroids; Comets)

Every November many people make it a habit to go outside in the dark of night, lie down in a comfortable position, let their eyes adjust to the darkness, and prepare to see a fantastic sight. Some fifty or sixty times a minute a shooting star will flash across the night sky. The viewers are witnessing the Leonid meteor shower. Once every decade or two they will see a meteor storm, with some 100,000 shooting stars an hour visible on a clear night. These meteors were spawned by the comet Tempel-Tuttle, which orbits the sun every thirty-three years.

What are they seeing, really?

Because the correct scientific meaning of the word *meteor* is often misunderstood, a few definitions are in order:

Meteoroid: Meteoroids range in size from interplanetary dust (about 0.1 millimeter) to the smallest asteroids that can be observed with a telescope (5 to 10 meters in diameter). They are thought to be composed of rock, freed from a cocoon of ice, methane, and ammonia when solar heating evaporates those substances.

Meteorite: If a meteoroid survives entry through the atmosphere and actually strikes the earth, it is called a meteorite. Since the meteoroid is heavily eroded by the heat of friction as it passes through the earth's atmosphere, only a small fraction of its original mass actually hits the ground. If it arrives at a relatively low speed (less than 15 kilometers a second) or has very shallow angle of entry, it may retain more of its original material because it won't heat up as much.

Meteorites might seem very rare, but about one out of every thousand dust particles swept up by a vacuum cleaner in an average house is a meteorite, although those this small are called "micrometeorites." (Most of the rest of the "dust" picked up be the vacuum is probably dead skin sloughed off by the human body—if that provides any comfort.)

Most meteorites that reach the surface of the earth are composed of nickel-iron, but a few are made up of carbonaceous material—organic chemicals resembling coal that seem to be connected with the same chemicals necessary to produce life as we know it. These meteorites may even hold clues to the formation of the universe because they are the oldest unaltered objects that we know about. Unfortunately, most disintegrate before they reach the ground.

Meteor: Technically speaking, there is no actual object that can be called a "meteor." A meteor is an event caused by an object, not the object itself. When a meteoroid hits Earth's atmosphere at speeds ranging from 11 to 75 kilometers a second, the resulting friction produces a streak of light called a "trail." (If it lasts for a few seconds it is called a "train.") This streak of light is a "meteor." When meteors appear fifty to sixty times an hour, the event is called a meteor "shower." When more meteors than that are spotted, it becomes a meteor "storm."

There is some archeological speculation that the observation of meteor showers had something to do with the building of both Stonehenge and the Pyramids. Astro-

Meteor Crater, Arizona, formed about fifty thousand years ago by a relatively slow-moving meteorite perhaps a few hundred feet in diameter. *Associated Press/Wide World Photo.*

nomical and historical arguments can be presented that major renovations were undertaken at both sites at times when meteor storms were visible in the night sky. Perhaps the ancient builders believed the lights in the heavens were messages from the gods.

Should the people of Earth fear catastrophic damage from meteor showers? Until recently, most scientists thought that the planet's atmosphere offered sufficient protection. Unlike the airless moon, where many more meteorites reach the surface and produce the now familiar pockmarked effect, the earth disposes of most meteorites simply by burning them up on the way down. But recently some scientists have begun to speculate on the possibility of thousands of meteorites, all the size of the Tunguska atmospheric event (see Asteroids), striking the planet almost simultaneously. Some suggest that mythology from previous cultures offers clues that this has happened before in the not-so-distant past. Duncan Steel, in his book *Rogue Asteroids and Doomsday Comets*, writes:

> In scientific publications I have pointed out that Australian Aborigines and New Zealand Maoris have oral traditions of strange rocks falling from the sky, causing awful fires and many deaths, and this sce-

nario is common in the myths of other peoples. On the one hand, astronomers have prided themselves on instructing geologists that impact catastrophes were responsible in part for the reshaping of the planet, but on the other hand, they have been blind to the fact that they have made a uniformitarian assumption when it comes to their own science: That the sky as it is now is as it ever was, at least while humans have walked the Earth. There is also ample evidence from historical records of various forms, but also from the analysis of data from this century … that around 5,000 years ago the sky did not appear as quiescent as it does now, and that since that time there have been other disruptions of the heavens, producing conflagrations here below.

If Steel is right, meteor showers, though pretty to look at, might hold more danger for the future of the planet than we previously thought.

Source:
Steel, Duncan. *Rogue Asteroids and Doomsday Comets: The Search for the Million Megaton Menace That Threatens Life on Earth.* New York: John Wiley and Sons, 1995.

METHUSELAH

According to the Bible, Methuselah was the oldest man who ever lived, reportedly surviving for 969 years before dying the very year Noah's flood occurred. Enoch, Methuselah's father, was the man many Christians believe was taken in an Old Testament rapture before the coming judgment (see Rapture). Rabbis have long taught that the reason Methuselah lived for so long was that he was God's sign: the earth would not be destroyed as long as the righteous Methuselah was alive. Every morning that his neighbors could glance out their windows and see him alive was another morning they didn't have to worry about the end of the world.

The apostle Peter referred to both the Flood and to the prophesied future destruction of the world by fire:

> First of all, you must understand that in the last days scoffers will come, scoffing and following their own evil desires. They will say, "Where is this 'coming' he promised? Ever since our fathers died, everything goes on as it has since the beginning of creation." But they deliberately forget that long ago the earth was formed out of water and with water. By water also the world of that time was deluged and destroyed. By the same word the present heavens and earth are reserved for fire, being kept for the day of judgment and destruction of ungodly men.

> But do not forget this one thing, dear friends: With the Lord a day is like a thousand years and a thousand years are like a day. The Lord is not slow in keeping his promise, as some understand slowness. He is patient with you, not wanting anyone to perish, but everyone to come to repentance.

> But the day of the Lord will come as a thief. The heavens will disappear with a roar; the earth will be destroyed by fire, and the earth and everything in it will be laid bare. (2 Pet. 3:3–10)

Those who believe Enoch to be a metaphysical type, or symbol, of the Rapture of the church have long speculated on what Methuselah might represent during the present age. Is there an agent on earth that has existed for a long time and, by its death, might signal the Lord's coming? Many candidates have been presented, but no idea or institution has yet been discovered that can claim any sort of universal appeal. Some say Methuselah represents the church. But no real scheme has ever been put forth that recognizes any real significance in the age of 969 years. Besides, if Enoch represents the church and the Rapture, where does that leave Methuselah? Some have speculated that Methuselah is represented by the Jewish nation. It is old, still around, and waiting for the Messiah. The problem with this idea, however, is that Judaism (Methuselah) gave birth to Christianity (Enoch), not the other way around.

Some wonder if Methuselah represents, in a general way, the grace and patience of God. But no other earthly institution of monotheism except the church, synagogue, or mosque seems to correspond to those attributes.

The mystery has so consumed some scholars that they suggest the Lord will not come back until we figure out this last enigma. Until then, there is still plenty of room for speculation.

Sources:
Bridger, David, ed. *The New Jewish Encyclopedia.* New York: Behrman House, 1962.
The Holy Bible, New International Version. Grand Rapids, MI: Zondervan, 1978.

MIDDLE EAST IN PROPHECY *see* **Armageddon, Battle of; Lindsey, Hal**

MIDTRIBULATIONALISM *see* **Pre-, Post-, and Midtribulationalism**

MILLENNIALISM

And I saw an angel coming down out of heaven, having a key to the Abyss and holding in his hand a great chain. He seized the dragon, that ancient serpent, who is the devil, or Satan, and bound him for a thousand years. He threw him into the Abyss, and locked and sealed it over him, to keep him from deceiving the nations anymore until the thousand years were ended. After that, he must be set free for a short time.

I saw thrones on which were seated those who had been given authority to judge. And I saw the souls of those who had been beheaded because of their testimony for Jesus and because of the word of God. They had not worshiped the beast or his image and had not received his mark on their foreheads or their hands. They came to life and reigned with Christ a thousand years. (The rest of the dead did not come to life until the thousand years were ended.) This is the first resurrection. Blessed and holy are those who have part in the first resurrection. The second death has no part over them, but they will be priests of God and of Christ and will reign with him for a thousand years.

When the thousand years are over, Satan will be released from his prison and will go out to deceive the nations—God and Magog—to gather them for battle. In number they are like the sand on the seashore. They marched across the breadth of the earth and surrounded the camp of God's people, the city he loves. But fire came down from heaven and devoured them. And the devil, who deceived them, was thrown into the lake of burning sulfur, where the beast and the false prophet had been thrown. They will be tormented day and night forever. (Rev. 20:1–10)

This passage from the book of Revelation, found in the closing pages of the Bible, is the central "proof" text for those who, interpreting it literally, believe in a thousand-year reign of Christ on earth. This reign is called the "Millennium," from the Latin words *mille*, thousand, and *annus*, year.

Once conservative scholars, following the futurist method of literal Bible interpretation (see Revelation), discovered a thousand-year reign of Christ on earth, it wasn't long before descriptions of this period were "found" in other parts of the Bible, especially the Old Testament.

Millennialism is the predominant belief and future hope of the vast majority of fundamentalist/evangelical theologians, not to mention the preachers who dominate daytime Christian TV and radio. But there are differences of opinion, of course, concerning when, and if, the Millennium will come at the end of the age. Three camps have developed, each interpreting the same biblical passages in its own way. These are the amillennial, premillennial, and postmillennial schools of thought. Because of the technical nature of their explanations, they are treated under a separate entries (see Amillennialism; Pre- and Postmillenialism).

Sources:

Bock, Darrell L., ed. *Three Views of the Millennium and Beyond.* Grand Rapids, MI: Zondervan, 1999.

Douglas, J. D., ed. *The New International Dictionary of the Christian Church.* Grand Rapids, MI: Zondervan, 1974.

The Holy Bible, New International Version. Grand Rapids, MI: Zondervan, 1978.

MILLERITES

Mid-nineteenth-century America experienced a flurry of religious activity that many historians refer to as the Second Great Awakening. Groups arose overnight, flourished within a local context, and then largely disappeared. A few had greater success: this same period saw the beginnings of such movements as the Mormons and Jehovah's Witnesses.

In the midst of this activity and interest, a New England farmer named William Miller came to believe that a literal interpretation of the Bible would reveal the time of Armageddon. He was one of many who were caught up in anticipation of the Second Coming, but unlike most others, he set out to determine for himself just what the Bible had to say about it. He studied for two years and finally concluded that the world would end in 1843.

Francis D. Nichol, who has written extensively about the early history of the Seventh-day Adventist Church, describes Miller's moment of revelation:

Specifically, he put his first and greatest emphasis on the prophetic declaration, "Unto two thousand and three hundred days; then shall the sanctuary be cleansed." Daniel 8:14. Believing that the "cleansing" of the sanctuary involved the purging of the earth by fire, the "days" in symbolic prophecy stand for years, and that this time of prophecy began about 457 BCE, he reached this final conclusion: "I was thus brought, in 1818, at the close of my two years' study of the Scriptures, to the solemn conclusion that in about twenty-five years from that time all the affairs of our present state would be wound up."

Miller spent another five years studying and cross-checking Bible passages before he worked up the courage to share his findings with anyone, but when he did open up, the results fell far short of what he had hoped for. No one paid him much attention. He remained convinced and gradually gathered a small group of like-minded people about him. By 1831 he was starting to receive invitations to preach to other groups. In 1839 he converted a man named Joshua V. Himes, who turned out to be the organizer Miller needed. What had been an informal group of believers became known as the Millerites. Three years before the scheduled Second Coming they started a Boston newspaper, *Signs of the Times*. By 1842 they had sufficient numbers to organize a general conference, also in Boston. The conference passed a resolution published in *Signs of the Times* on June 1, 1842: "*Resolved*, that in the opinion of this conference, there are most serious and important reasons for believing that God has revealed the time of the end of the world, and that that time is 1843."

The conference soon adopted the phrase "the midnight cry" to describe their warning and began a second newspaper, this time in Philadelphia, by that name. A series of outdoor camp meetings was planned for the summer before the Second Coming. Although opposition grew from traditional Christian denominations, the Millerites spread their message at a fever pitch as the day drew closer. It became difficult to rent halls big enough to hold meetings. Traditional churches wouldn't allow the use of their buildings, and secular institutions refused entrance for religious organizations. Finally the Millerites decided to build a tabernacle in Boston. A capacity crowd of 3,500 attended the dedication.

On January 1, 1843, Miller published his views without equivocation: "I believe the time can be known by all who desire to understand and to be ready for His coming. And I am fully convinced that sometime between March 21st, 1843, and March 21st, 1844, according to the Jewish mode of computation of time, Christ will come, and bring all His saints with Him; and that then he will reward every man as his work shall be." Notice that delineated a time period but set no specific date. Most of his followers overlooked this fact. Although the leaders of the movement never suggested such a thing, many Millerites somehow decided that April 23, 1843, was the last day that anyone would need a calendar. Only when that date passed without event were the followers reined in and reminded of the correct interpretation of Brother Miller's remarks.

When the rest of 1843 also passed without incident, only the far end of the prophecy's time frame, the early months of 1844, remained. Seeds of doubt were

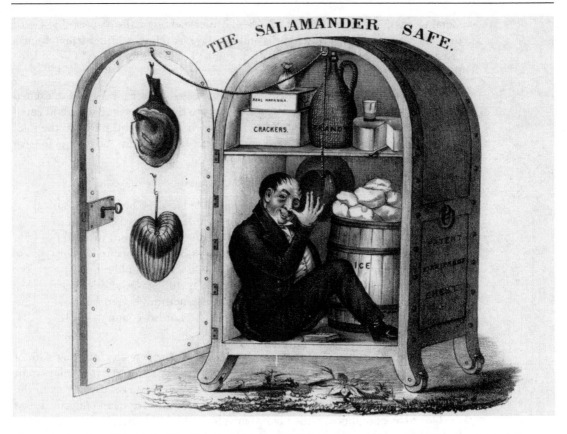

Cartoon printed in early 1843 ridiculing the Millerites' belief that the world would end on April 23 of that year. The man sits in a "fireproof" safe with food, a fan, ice, and other supplies. *Library of Congress.*

beginning to sprout, but even though they had been burned once, the followers remained generally positive.

Then came disaster. March 21, 1844, came and went. Jesus did not return.

Newspapers all over the country lambasted the Millerites with ridicule. What had happened? Miller had been so sure. He could not imagine what had gone wrong. He returned to his Bible, determined to rethink his position.

Strangely, through all this, even though the heralded year ended, Millerism did not. If anything, the movement attracted even more believers. By July, Miller and Himes were traveling all the way to Ohio to speak to new converts. Himes even wrote that, if time permitted before the Second Coming, he would voyage to London to convey Miller's amazing message to the folk there.

Then new hope appeared. A recent convert, the Reverend Samuel S. Snow, may have been new to the movement, but he was an old hand at interpreting the Bible. By tweaking a few of Miller's original estimates and factoring in various obscure Bible passages, he and Miller discovered that the actual date of the Second

Coming was going to be October 22, 1844. Miller had originally neglected to factor in a "tarrying time" of seven months and ten days. A relieved Miller triumphantly cried, "Thank the Lord, O my soul! I am almost home. Glory! Glory! Glory! I see that the time is correct."

The faithful went wild. Their numbers increased daily. Farmers were so excited they left their crops standing in the fields so as to have more time to attend camp meetings and hear the newest findings. Backsliders returned sheepishly to the fold. Although the leaders still declined to set a specific date officially, the faithful forgave them their lack of faith.

As the day approached, the *Midnight Cry* published a final editorial:

> Think for eternity! Thousands may be lulled to sleep by hearing your actions say, "This world is worth my whole energies. The world to come is vain shadow." O, reverse this practical sermon, instantly! Break loose from the world as much as possible. If indispensable duty calls you into the world for a moment, go as a man would run to do a piece of work in the rain. Run and hasten through it, and let it be known that you leave with alacrity for something better. Let your actions preach in the clearest tones: "The Lord is coming"—"This world passeth away"—"Prepare to meet thy God."

Finally October 22 came. And went. Nothing happened except that a lot of disappointed Millerites slunk back to their homes. That is, those who had homes went back to them; many had chosen to sell their possessions and give the money to the poor or use it to further the cause of the movement. Humiliation ran rampant. It was the Great Disappointment—the final straw. The faithful Millerites had survived similar letdowns over the past eighteen months, but this was the fatal one. The movement collapsed. Its members picked up the pieces of their broken dreams and returned to the world. Some drifted into bitter atheism. A few became Shakers, a Christian sect that from its beginnings in the eighteenth century demanded strict celibacy. Since the only way to become a Shaker was thus by conversion, the disillusioned Millerites propped up that faith with some much-needed new blood.

Miller died in 1849, a discredited, largely despised, and humiliated man. But a few of the faithful refused to believe they had been so wrong. They met in conference in Albany, New York, in 1845. Unable to reach consensus, the group splintered into three factions, one of which became the Seventh-day Adventist Church. The prophet of that church, Ellen Gould White (1827–1915), was able to persuade her followers that the calculated dates had been correct, but that wrongful action by the church itself has forestalled the Second Coming. People had neglected to keep God's seventh-day Sabbath commandment. They had somehow switched over to Sunday worship, and God was angry. Though only a young woman at the time of the Great Disappointment, after much study and prayer White began to refine her message. Yes, October 22, 1844, was the correct date. Miller and Snow hadn't miscalculated. They had just not interpreted correctly what was supposed to happen. Christ obviously didn't come back to earth at that time. Instead, he entered the Heavenly Sanctuary to begin the second and last phase of his atoning ministry. Because the church had neglected proper observance of the Sabbath, just as the Jews had done before the time of the Babylonian captivity, Christ was "tarrying, not willing that any should perish." The world still had time. But there was a lot of work to do. Jesus would return shortly. But first people needed to know what was happening.

So the Millerite movement lived on. It transformed itself, adapted to new information, and continued to provide hope for those who believe God will not, in the end, disappoint his faithful.

Sources:

Festinger, Leon, Henry W. Riecken, and Stanley Schacter. "Unfulfilled Prophecies and Disappointed Messiahs." In *Expecting Armageddon: Essential Readings in Failed Prophecy*, ed. Jon R. Stone. New York: Routledge, 2000.

Hudson, Winthrop S. *Religion in America*. New York: Charles Scribner's Sons, 1965.

Nichol, Francis D. *The Midnight Cry*. Washington, DC: Review and Herald, 1944.

MISSION IMPOSSIBLE II *see* Hollywood Envisions THE END

MOVEMENT FOR THE RESTORATION OF THE TEN COMMANDMENTS OF GOD

In the 1980s an excommunicated Roman Catholic priest named Joseph Kibwetere, living in Uganda, gathered a following who listened to him relate messages he claimed to have heard in visions. He said he received conversations between the Virgin Mary and God. The messages instructed his followers to live in submissive poverty, to give all of their earthly goods to Kibwetere's organization, and to follow the Ten Commandments to the letter.

In the late 1990s Kibwetere joined forces with Credonia Mwerinde, a middle-aged woman who had owned a bar but had given up the business when it failed. Mwerinde too claimed to be getting messages from the Virgin Mary. The pair's following eventually grew to at least five thousand members.

Mwerinde's messages became the dominant force in the cult. She said the Virgin Mary and God were very upset that humankind was not following the Ten Commandments, and they were going to cause the end of the world at the end of December 1999. People gave up their belongings, lived in poverty, and submitted to the wills of Mwerinde and Kibwetere.

When the prophecy failed, many in the cult demanded their money back. A bloodbath ensued. So far almost fifteen hundred bodies have been found. What began the investigation by authorities was the murder by fire of five hundred people on March 17, 2000, in what had been the cult's main chapel. Kibwetere is believed to have perished in that fire. Later, in mass graves, more than nine hundred more bodies were found. Mwerinde has disappeared.

Source:

Ross, Rick. "Credonia Mwerinde and Her Ugandan Cult." www.rickross.com/reference/tencommand ments/tencommandments110.html.

MOSES AND ELIJAH

Some biblical figures achieve such fame that their names become familiar even to those who have never studied, or even read, the Bible. Two such figures are Moses and Elijah. They are listed even by New Testament authors as being among the great heroes of Jewish history.

Moses is credited as being the great law-giver. So great was his influence that some claim he invented the Jewish religion. The people, they say, may have descended from Abraham, but the religion came from Moses. He is respected by all three monotheistic traditions, equally revered by Christians, Muslims, and Jews. The final words of the book of Deuteronomy, purported to be Moses' farewell address to his people, declare: "Since then no prophet has risen in Israel like Moses, whom the Lord knew face to face, who did all those miraculous signs and wonders the Lord sent him to do in Egypt" (Deut. 34:10).

Elijah is likewise referred to as one of the greatest prophets of Jewish history. His epic battle with polytheism was set to music in Felix Mendelssohn's great oratorio *Elijah*. He has become the stuff of legend and myth.

Moses with the Ten Commandments (Henry Schile, ca. 1874). *Library of Congress.*

The lives of both Elijah and Moses ended under suspicious circumstances. We don't know what happened to Moses, only that he was buried secretly "by the hand of God" and "no one to this day" knows where (Deut. 34). Later, the New Testament book of Jude reveals that the angel Michael, for some reason, "disputed with the devil about the body of Moses." Why did Satan want the body? We are not told.

Elijah's demise was even more spectacular. He never really died. He just went up to heaven in a fiery chariot (2 Kings 2). It was said of him that either he or a prophet from his mold would return to announce the advent of the Messiah. So prevailing was this notion that Jesus even declared that John the Baptist fulfilled the prophecy, although some of the disciples voiced the popular opinion that Jesus himself might have filled the role (Matt. 16).

But both Moses and Elijah refuse to stay buried in the pages of the Old Testament. They resurface once, and probably twice, in the pages of the New Testament, both times connected with events pointing to Armageddon. The first time we read about them, aside from quotations, is in the biblical passage describing the Transfiguration: "After six days Jesus took with him Peter, James and John the brother of James, and led them up a high mountain by themselves. There he was transfigured before them. His face shone like the sun, and his clothes became as white as the light. Just then there appeared before them Moses and Elijah, talking with Jesus…. Jesus instructed them, 'Don't tell anyone what you have seen, until the Son of Man has been raised from the dead'" (Matt. 17:1–13).

The apostle Peter was certainly impressed. Showing his typical pattern of speech before thought, he blurted out, "Lord, this is wonderful! Let us make three tents; one for you, one for Moses and one for Elijah"—as if the Old Testament duo had shown up just to go camping with Jesus!

No real explanation is ever given about why this meeting took place. Given that Jesus, from that point on, began preparations for his crucifixion, it has been surmised that Moses and Elijah came to talk to him about death.

Next the scene changes to the final days of history. The eleventh chapter of the book of Revelation presents two witnesses who come down to earth to preach about Jesus. Although they are not named, their modus operandi seems to give them away. They have the power to "turn the waters into blood." This is what Moses did in Egypt when he confronted Pharaoh. They also "shut up the sky so it will not rain." Elijah famously accomplished precisely such a feat. Could these two great leaders who died suspicious deaths have been moved out of time, so to speak, until they could return at the end of the age to finish the jobs they were originally given?

For those who approach passages like this with skepticism, the question usually becomes, "What is the author trying to tell us? What's the meaning behind the myth?" Early Christian writers liked to link both Testaments together, so maybe this was a device used to pull Moses and Elijah, both Hebrew heroes, into the new Christian movement. There are prophecies in the Old Testament that say "Elijah must come" before the Messiah appears. Matthew seems to say that John the Baptist was a sort of reincarnated Elijah, a type or symbol of the prophet himself. Perhaps that was what the author had in mind. Or perhaps Moses and Elijah were chosen because they represent "the law" (Moses) and "the prophets" (Elijah).

But Jesus spoke some enigmatic words preceding the trip up the Mount of Transfiguration: "Some of you will not taste death before you see the Son of Man coming in his kingdom." The gospels, written after most of those who knew Jesus had themselves died, must have troubled believers who couldn't understand why Jesus, after predicting his return before the death of the disciples, had still not returned. Had he been mistaken? Perhaps Matthew was trying to clarify Jesus' promise by suggesting that at least three apostles had *already* experienced the eternal kingdom by meeting with three of its most distinguished residents high atop the Mount of Transfiguration.

In the end, no one really knows the part these two heroes of old will take in the events concerning Armageddon described in Revelation 11. But they continue to tantalize those who study such things.

Source:
The Holy Bible, New International Version. Grand Rapids, MI: Zondervan, 1978.

MOVIES *see* **Hollywood Envisions** THE END

Π

NEO-PURITANISM *see* **Christian Reconstructionism**

NEW AGE VIEWS OF THE END

Robert Ellwood and Barbara McGraw, in their book *Many Peoples, Many Faiths*, identify New Age religions by using categories they label Reactive Movements, Accommodationist Movements, Spirit Movements, New Revelation Sects, Import Religions, and Hybrid Movements. They summarize these movements as follows:

> Basic features of new religious movements are likely to be: a different
> but recognizable doctrine; a practice centered on a single, simple, sure
> technique or a creative group process and practice; a charismatic found-
> ing and leadership and/or an intense, highly demanding group. On the
> other hand, they may involve a diffuse type of influence that is not
> directly competitive with mainstream religion. In every case, though, a
> new religious movement must offer inner rewards sufficiently effective
> and convincing to compensate for a break with conventional faith.

New Age religions consist of everything from a belief in "channeling" extraterrestrial entities to Western adaptations of ancient Eastern religions. There are New
Age UFO cults (see Unidentified Flying Objects) and so called "Golden Age" groups
(see Cayce, Edgar). Because the categories are so broad and the groups so divergent, it
is impossible to describe a single New Age theology concerning the end of the world.
But it is safe to say that the majority of what are called New Age religions today have
a rather optimistic view of the end. Almost universally there is found a belief that the
present world is headed for a makeover. Humankind is evolving toward something
greater than mere material existence.

One widely held New Age tenet is that the human race is being guided. Sometimes beings outside of time, either very ancient or living very far away, are described in

detail. Whether these spiritual entities were once human or never even existed on earth, they have messages for the human race. They care about us and want us to succeed. Unable to physically put pen to paper, they must find receptive conduits through whom they are able to funnel their message. Because there are more and more entities channeling books nowadays, many New Agers believer that a cosmic shift of emphasis is upon us and that the time of our particular mode of human understanding is getting short. Jane Roberts, for instance, in an immensely popular and profitable series of books, claims to channel an entity who calls himself "Seth." He offers this advice:

> If you believe firmly that your consciousness is locked up somewhere inside your skull and is powerless to escape it, if you feel that your consciousness ends at the boundaries of your body, then you sell yourself short, and you will think I am only a delusion. I am no more a delusion than you are.
>
> I can say this to each of my readers honestly: I am older than you are, at least in terms of age as you think of it.
>
> If a writer can qualify as any kind of authority on the basis of age, therefore, then I should get a medal. I am an energy personality essence, no longer focused in physical matter. As such, I am aware of some truths that many of you seem to have forgotten.

Seth goes on to say that humans have become misguided, but they are being cared for. All will turn out well in the end if we grow up spiritually.

Some New Age religions do not look outward for help and salvation. They turn inward—to the human spirit. Human potential, they believe, is a spiritual force, propelling us upward on the path of evolution. Helen Schucman, creator of the popular *Course in Miracles*, believed the world will not be destroyed, because the potential latent in humanity is even now being revived and uplifted:

> Through forgiveness the thinking of the world is reversed. The forgiven world becomes the gate of Heaven, because by its mercy we can at last forgive ourselves. Holding no one prisoner to guilt, we become free. Acknowledging Christ in all our brothers, we recognize His Presence in ourselves. Forgetting all our misperceptions, and with nothing from the past to hold us back, we can remember God. Beyond this, learning cannot go. When we are ready, God Himself will take the first step in our return to Him.

According to this way of thinking, the earth and all its human population will not end so much as it will be engulfed. Earth is a staging area, so to speak, wherein humans learn to realize their potential in the divine.

What is called New Age today is often just a modern expression of apocalyptic expectation. It is as old as the world and as new as contemporary anxiety that things look pretty gloomy. On the other side of disaster, it is hoped, lies a new beginning.

Sources:
Ellwood, Robert S., and Barbara A. McGraw. *Many Peoples, Many Faiths: Women and Men in the World Religions.* 6th ed. Upper Saddle River, NJ: Prentice Hall, 1999.

Fisher, Mary Pat, and Lee W. Bailey, eds. *An Anthology of Living Religions.* Upper Saddle River, NJ: Prentice Hall, 2000.

Roberts, Jane. *Seth Speaks.* San Rafael, CA: Amber-Allen Publishing and New World Library, 1994.

NEW HEAVEN, NEW EARTH, AND THE NEW JERUSALEM

Then I saw a new heaven and a new earth, for the first heaven and first earth had passed away, and there was no longer any sea. I saw the Holy City, the new Jerusalem, coming out of heaven from God, prepared as a bride beautifully dressed for her husband…. He who was seated on the throne said, "I am making everything new!" (Rev. 21:1–5)

It cannot be emphasized enough that when the biblical writers wrote of Armageddon, they were talking about new beginnings, not old endings. This theme is repeated throughout the Bible. Noah's flood marked the end of an old world and a fresh start for a new one. Early Christian writers saw the Old Testament as laying the groundwork for the New Testament. Jesus Christ was pictured as being a new Adam, sent to undo the problems the old Adam brought upon the human race. The church was considered to be the new Israel. The destruction of the old temple foreshadowed the building of the new temple.

Armageddon may mark the end of this world, the world with which we are familiar, but in the opinion of the ancient writers there's a new world coming after the last blow is struck. They view the future with hope, not dread. Out of death comes life. After winter comes spring. Out of the ashes of destruction will arise a new Jerusalem, a new heaven, and a new earth.

Source:
The Holy Bible, New International Version. Grand Rapids, MI: Zondervan, 1978.

NICENE CREED

In 325 CE the church held its first great ecumenical, or universal, council. Meeting in Nicaea, a city in Asia Minor, the council (some records indicate it consisted of 318 bishops) met to draft a statement that could decide once and for all what the church believed to be true concerning some controversial doctrines. As a result of its debate, it published the famous Nicene Creed, still used regularly as a statement of faith in many churches. It sounds stilted to modern ears but is a very exactly worded creed that has stood the test of time. A portion of it reads:

We believe in one God, the Father, the Almighty, maker of heaven and earth, of all that is, seen and unseen…. We believe in one Lord, Jesus Christ, the only Son of God, begotten of the Father from all time: God from God, Light from Light, very God from very God, begotten, not made, one in being with the Father. Through Him all things were made…. He was crucified for us…. He suffered, died and was buried…. He descended into hell…. He arose on the third day…. He entered into heaven and is seated on the right hand of the Father.... From thence He shall come to judge the quick and the dead, and his kingdom shall have no end.

Here is proof that even as far back as the early fourth century the Christian church considered it an act of faith to declare publicly that Jesus Christ would someday return to judge the world. Because the creed was written to be read at baptisms, no one could join the church without confessing that he or she was awaiting the return of Jesus Christ at the battle of Armageddon. Although many denominations, specifically some Protestant churches, now consider the reading of the creed to be a mere formality, it is still a prevalent custom to confess agreement with its doctrinal content when joining a church.

Source:
Gonzalez, Justo L. *The Story of Christianity.* 2 vols. New York: Harper & Row, 1985.

NOAH'S FLOOD IN PROPHECY *see* **Days of Noah**

Noah's Flood

Noah is probably the best-known sea captain in history. Millions of Jewish, Christian, and Muslim children have grown up learning the story of the great Genesis flood. "Now the earth was corrupt in God's sight and was full of violence.... In the six hundredth year of Noah's life ... all the springs of the great deep burst forth, and the floodgates of the heavens were opened. And rain fell on the earth forty days and forty nights" (Genesis 6:11 and 7:11–12).

But Genesis is not the only ancient text that tells the story of great floods. Stories from ancient Babylon recount how Enlil, the Sumerian god of the air, was offended by the noise rising from overpopulated cities. He sent a great flood to destroy civilization. A righteous man named Utnapishtim had been noticed by Ea, the water god, and was warned in time to build a great boat in which to weather the storm. When the flood subsided, Utnapishtim sent out a dove and a swallow to spy out the landscape. Both soon returned because they could not find a dry place to land. When a raven was released and didn't come back, the intrepid sea captain assumed there was dry land somewhere and led his family to safety from their refuge on Mount Nisir. His audacious act so impressed Enlil that Utnapishtim was granted eternal life.

Despite the claims made by some fundamentalist monotheists, modern geologists claim there is no credible evidence that a worldwide flood ever occurred. When confronted with scriptural "evidence" and accused of calling the ancient writers frauds, they are apt to reply that the problem lies with modern interpreters, not biblical authors. The ancients did not write factual accounts that came to be considered myth. Instead, modern readers have read ancient myths as though they were meant to be factual.

Concerning floods of "biblical" proportions, there exists a boatload of evidence that many cultures, from Mesopotamia to the Americas, recounted their localized experience with Armageddon-like language. Their way of life had ended. They had to begin life over again. They might not use the word "Armageddon," but the experience they remember had that kind of effect on them.

Still, the old biblical myth leaves the world with hope. The rainbow is said to be God's sign that floods will never again destroy the earth. Even if the ice caps were to melt there is simply not enough water to encompass the entire earth. The deep, from time to time, may swallow an occasional Atlantis. But some survivors will most certainly escape to higher ground.

Sources:

Bullfinch, Thomas. *Bullfinch's Mythology*. New York, NY: Gramercy Books by arrangement with T. Y. Crowell Co., distributed by Random House Value Publishing, Inc., 1979.

NORDIC MYTHOLOGY OF THE ENDTIMES

Norse mythology concerning the end of the world presents a very stark, destructive vision. The preordained end of the gods is called Ragnarok, perhaps better known as the German Götterdämmerung, "twilight of the gods," used in many poems and musical works. (*Ragnarok* actually means "doom of the powers" or "doom of the gods," not "twilight.") The ancient Norse believed that the seeds for this doom were sown at the very beginning of time, when the world's first creatures emerged from a violent cosmic stew consisting of the extremes of fire and ice. The universe is inherently fragile, existing between forces of destruction. It was doomed from the very beginning because Loki, the god who is always associated with evil, created three fearsome monsters or giants (Jormungand, Fenrir, and Hel) against which the earth was powerless.

Before the end comes, the earth will experience Fimbulvetr, three destructive winters with no summers separating them. Human morality will disappear. Conflicts and feuds will break out between the peoples of the earth. Skoll, the wolf, will devour the sun, and Hati, his brother, will eat the moon. The earth will be plunged into darkness. Then three cocks will crow, signaling the beginning of the end. The first will crow to announce the giants. The second will alert the gods. The final cock's crow will raise the dead. Earthquakes will rock the earth and evil will escape from any form of fetter that now contains it. The sea will rear up and the first monster, Jormungand, will rise from his resting place. The rising tide will hurry the ship *Naglfar*, commanded by the giant Hymir, toward the final battle of the world. A second ship, commanded by Loki himself, will carry the inhabitants of hell against the gods. A third ship will sail from the south captained by Surt, a fire giant identified most closely with Loki, carrying a sword that blazes like the sun itself. He will fling fire in all directions and set the cosmos alight.

To meet this threat, Odin, who foresaw the whole thing in the beginning when Loki antagonized the gods by crashing the first party they ever threw, will lead the army of the gods and ancient heroes into the fray. From every corner of the world, assorted gods, dwarves, demons, elves, and monsters will converge upon the plain of Vigrid, the Norse equivalent of Armageddon. The Valkyries, Odin's female warrior shield-masters, have been busy throughout the time of creation gathering up fallen heroes and transporting them to Valhalla, where they were kept in fighting trim specifically for this battle. But even their prowess will not prove sufficient. In the end, the world will be destroyed.

The whole affair of life is painted with a very dark brush in Norse mythology. Ragnarok casts its shadow over many a Norse myth, ending even some happy stories with a dark cast that says, in effect, "You may think this story has a happy ending. But just wait!" Hope, however, is offered in one telling of the myth. In this version a few gods manage to survive the last holocaust and the earth emerges fresh and green, giving birth to a new spring. The gods live happily ever after with humans.

This version may, however, be a late addition to the mythology. Some scholars suggest it may have been brought north with Christian missionaries as they recounted the biblical tale of Armageddon and the subsequent rebirth of the new earth.

Sources:

Cotterell, Arthur, and Rachel Storm. *The Ultimate Encyclopedia of Mythology*. New York: Hermes House, 1999.

Lindemans, Micha F. "Ragnarok." *Encyclopedia Mythica*. http://www.pantheon.org/articles/r/ragnarok.html.

NOSTRADAMUS

Michel de Nostredame is certainly the best known and arguably the most extraordinary Christian prophet since the completion of the Bible in the first century of the Christian era. His final prophecies, published two years after his death, have been widely studied and are the source of many controversial interpretations. They were written as quatrains—four-line poems. These quatrains, full of double entendre and symbols, are often obscure. But Nostradamus scholars claim that many name specific historic people and events. They believe that although quite a few of his predictions have come to pass, others are so obscure that no one has yet interpreted them correctly. Perhaps they refer to events still in the future.

Nostradamus was born into a Jewish family in 1503 in Saint-Rémy-de-Provence. Since this was the time of the French Inquisition, which labeled non-Christian beliefs heretical and severely punished those who held them, his family felt forced to convert to Roman Catholicism. Most Jewish families of that time practiced their traditions quietly at home while publicly following the Christian faith. During his lifetime the new Protestant movement was gaining momentum, so Nostradamus was probably influenced by both Protestant and Roman Catholic Christianity as well as Judaism. Erika Cheetham, in her book *The Final Prophecies of Nostradamus*, claims that he particularly disliked Protestants, believing their movement caused too much of an uproar. The printing press had been invented in the mid-fifteenth century, making the Bible available to everyone who could read, and Nostradamus probably had read it not only in Latin but also in the original Greek and Hebrew by the time he was a teenager.

As a boy he was sent to his maternal grandfather to be educated. Besides learning to read Latin, Greek, and Hebrew and studying mathematics, he was also steeped in astrology. It became a passion he held all his life. His parents, however, disapproved: astrology was not on the accepted academic curriculum of the Inquisition. After the death of his mother's father, they sent the boy off to his paternal grandfather's home to complete his education. He then entered the university at Avignon, where he studied grammar, philosophy, and rhetoric. There he became known as *le petit astrologue* because of his interest in astronomy and astrology. He went on to the University of Montpellier to study medicine. He turned out to be a very good doctor, curing many people of the bubonic plague by advocating cleanliness, running water (as opposed to well water), and fresh air. Most important, defying tradition, he refused to bleed his patients, thus alienating himself from his more traditional colleagues. He traveled all over France, becoming quite popular, and was sought after by many people who were ill. Fame, however, did nothing to improve his standing with jealous fellow medical practitioners.

Nostradamus settled down long enough to marry and have two children but lost his young family to the scourge of the plague. The pain of their deaths sent him off traveling again, but he had lost the trust of many of his patients, who felt that if he could not save his own family, he probably could not cure others.

Nostradamus. *Fortean Picture Library.*

To make matters worse, he began to gather an audience by publicly prophesying as he traveled. One famous story tells of his coming upon a young shepherd and kneeling before him. When the astonished young man asked why, Nostradamus told him that he would one day be crowned pope. In 1585, almost twenty years after Nostradamus' death, the young man did indeed become Pope Sixtus V.

Nostradamus eventually came to the attention of the queen, Catherine de' Medici. He spent a lot of time with her, giving her prophecies concerning the fates of her husband, King Henry II, and six children. He was well paid, and most of these predictions seem to have worked out as he described them.

Eventually Nostradamus settled in Salon-de-Provence and remarried. In his new home he designated the attic as his study and declared it off-limits to everyone else. There he spent many hours staring trancelike into a bronze bowl set on a tripod, then writing down the visions he saw in the water. These became the basis of his *Almanachs*, published in 1550. Though many of his predictions didn't come to pass in his lifetime, the books were successful enough to encourage him to write his *Prognostications*, which was also very well received.

In one of his quatrains Nostradamus, as translated by Erika Cheetham in her collection *The Final Prophecies of Nostradamus*, described his solitary nighttime vigils:

Sitting alone at night in secret study, it
rests solitary on the brass tripod. A slight
flame comes out of the emptiness, making
successful that which would have been in vain.

It was not until after his death that Nostradamus's wife and his protégé Jean-Aymes de Chavigny published his last volume of prophecies. Nostradamus intended to publish one thousand predictions, divided into ten books of one hundred "centuries" (*centaines*)—sets of one hundred four-line quatrains—each. When the visions were published in 1568, century 7 had only forty-two quatrains and centuries 8, 9, and 10 were missing. It is probable that he died before reaching his goal of a thousand.

Nostradamus not only saw visions in the bowl of water, he heard sounds and voices as well, making him a clairaudient as well as a clairvoyant. He seemed to see wars being fought with weapons he did not comprehend. He described famine and drought. He saw things happening to people he neither knew nor had heard about:

Pau, Verona, Vicenza, Saragossa, swords
dripping with blood from distant lands. A
very great plague will come in the great shell, relief near, but the
remedies far away. (Cheetham, *Final Prophecies of Nostradamus*)

Pau, Verona, Vicenza, and Saragossa are names of European cities Nostradamus would have recognized. But some interpreters ask if the "great plague" refers to HIV/AIDS. Could the "great shell" be a vehicle delivering a virus during some kind of germ warfare? Whatever it was that he saw, claim his interpreters, it was not of his time. Others see no reason to look beyond Nostradamus's time. The bubonic plague was widespread in his day, and it often began with the arrival of ships (great shells?) in port cities. And even earlier, the Bible mentions plagues in Matthew, Mark, Luke, and Revelation. Perhaps that was what inspired him to write these words.

Many quatrains appear to touch on either aerial or submarine warfare. For example:

Through lightning in the ship gold and
silver are melted, the two captives will
devour each other. The greatest one of the
city is stretched when the fleet travels under water. (Cheetham, *Final Prophecies*)

Could Nostradamus have seen and not understood the reactor in a nuclear submarine? He had to interpret his visions through the lens of his own time, and many things from our present day would have made little or no sense to him.

Following are two of Nostradamus' most controversial "Armageddon" prophecies. Nostradamus believed there would be three antichrists, followed by twenty-seven years of war. In the first quatrain, translated by Erika Cheetham in *Final Prophecies*, he seems to be predicting a global war:

> The third Antichrist soon annihilates everything,
> twenty-seven years of blood his war will last.
> The unbelievers dead, captive, exiled with blood,
> human bodies, water and red hail covering the earth.

The second, translated by the Nostradamus enthusiast David S. Montaigne, actually mentions a date:

> The year 1999, seventh month,
> From the sky will come great king of terror.
> To revive the great king of the Angolmois,
> Before and after Mars reigns by good luck.

Although many of the seer's devotees entered the year 1999 with great trepidation, nothing much happened. Two years later, however, many of these same disciples quickly decided that this quatrain actually describes the 9/11 attacks on the World Trade Center in New York. The "seventh month" is not September, and the year is wrong, but most believers in Nostradamus would argue that these are not large errors for a prophecy written more than four hundred years before the event. Of course, these are hardly the only interpretations possible for such a cloudy piece of writing. Some of the faithful, for example, point out that the word *Angolmois* is an anagram for "Mongolias." David Montaigne believes that the quatrain predicts the rise of the Middle East and China, areas he thinks will challenge a coalition of the United States, Europe, and Russia, bringing about a global war that will end the world as we know it. (Montaigne, however, titled his Web page discussing these events "Nostradamus World War III 2002"; the date suggests that perhaps his calculations needed further work.)

As a Christian scholar and doctor, Nostradamus probably grew up steeped in biblical lore. He would have been aware of the biblical prophecies concerning the end of time and the Second Coming. These were important issues in his day. The book of Revelation in the New Testament probably played a very big part in his thinking. With this in mind it is easy imagine that he believed he was seeing the end of time in his visions. But the images of his quatrains remain tantalizingly out of reach. Clarity and obscurity meet in utterances that might mean almost anything. It makes for a fascinating, if controversial, field of study.

Sources:

Cheetham, Erika. *The Final Prophecies of Nostradamus*. New York: Perigee, 1989.

Montaigne, David S. "Nostradamus World War III 2002." www.dazzled.com/nost2002/.

Nostradamus. *Prophecies on World Events*. Trans. and interp. Stewart Robb. New York: Liveright, 2002.

NUCLEAR PROLIFERATION

With the advent of the nuclear age, the human race, for the first time in its history on the planet, gained the power to suddenly and with very little warning destroy itself (see Kennedy, John F.; Oppenheimer, J. Robert). The doctrine of "deterrent force" led nation after nation to develop its own nuclear capability, justifying the terrible risk under the rubric of national defense. No single nation wanted to be without the power to strike back if threatened. The much-publicized arms race between the Soviet Union and the United States led to more and more nuclear proliferation, causing many U.S. citizens to remember the cold war years as a time of air raid drills and back-yard fallout shelters.

In 1968 the few nations recognized as having obtained nuclear weapon status banded together to sign a Non-Proliferation Treaty (NPT). The idea behind the treaty was to limit the number of nations that could become nuclear-weapon states to those who had "manufactured and exploded a nuclear weapon or other explosive device prior to 1 January 1967." Those nations were China, France, the Soviet Union (today, Russia), the United Kingdom, and the United States. By April 2005, these five nations' nuclear weapons stockpiles were as follows:

China: more than 100 warheads.
France: approximately 350 warheads.
Russia: 4,978 strategic warheads and approximately 3,500 operational tactical warheads; more than 11,000 stockpiled strategic and tactical warheads. (The breakup of the Soviet Union has led to many questions concerning the where-abouts of a great deal of the nuclear material the former nation once stockpiled.)
United Kingdom: fewer than 200 strategic warheads.
United States: 5,968 strategic warheads, more than 1,000 operational tactical weapons, and approximately 3,000 reserve strategic and tactical warheads.

Additionally, three nations that did not sign the NPT are generally regarded as nuclear powers:

India: 45 to 95 nuclear warheads.
Israel: Although it has never officially acknowledged having such weapons, Israel is widely regarded as possessing 75 to 200 nuclear warheads.
Pakistan: 30 to 50 nuclear warheads.

Two nations currently represent nuclear question marks:

Iran: Although it has no known weapons or sufficient fissile material stock-piles to build them, and despite assertions from its government that it intends only peaceful nuclear uses, Iran is generally perceived as secretly trying to acquire a nuclear weapons capability.
North Korea: A signator of the NPT, North Korea in 2003 withdrew from the treaty and declared itself a nuclear power. The CIA estimates that North Korea possesses one or two nuclear weapons and enough fissile material to make perhaps six. As of this writing, however, North Korea was not known to have conducted a test detonation of such a weapon.

Several states, although they apparently never had actual nuclear weapons, are known to have had, at one time or another, programs aimed at developing them but have abandoned these efforts:

Argentina, Brazil, South Korea, Taiwan: All had nuclear-weapons programs that they subsequently shelved.
Libya: Voluntarily renounced its secret nuclear weapons efforts in December 2003.

Iraq: Had an active nuclear weapons program before the 1991 Persian Gulf War but was forced to dismantle it under the supervision of UN inspectors after that war. In 2003 the United States invaded Iraq. One reason given for the attack was that American and British officials believed Iraq to be hiding weapons of mass destruction. After the invasion and occupation of the country, no such weapons were found.

Finally, a handful of nations known to have possessed actual nuclear weapons no longer do:

Belarus, Kazakhstan, Ukraine: With the breakup of the Soviet Union, these three states suddenly found themselves to be both independent and in control of a large supply of nuclear material left over from the old Soviet Union. They have since returned this material to Russia—although some of it is still unaccounted for.

South Africa: Has the distinction of being the only nation to build a nuclear program, assemble weapons of mass destruction, and then voluntarily turn over their completed weapons (there were six of them), dismantling their entire program.

Source:

Arms Control Association. "Nuclear Weapons: Who Has What at a Glance." http://www.armscontrol.org/factsheets/Nuclearweaponswhohaswhat.asp.

NUMEROLOGY

Numerology is the study of the occult significance of numbers. People sometimes go to great extremes to find numbers in combinations that might foretell the future. A few examples will shed some light on how some numerologists have predicted the date for the end of the world by finding hidden meaning in the famous 666 of the book of Revelation (see Revelation; 666).

The Visa Card Antichrist One-World Conspiracy

He [the "beast out of the earth"] also forced everyone, small and great, rich and poor, free and slave, to receive a mark on his right hand or on his forehead, so that no one could buy or sell unless he had the mark, which is the name of the beast or the number of his name.

This calls for wisdom. If anyone has insight, let him calculate the number of the beast, for it is a man's number. His number is 666. (Rev. 13:16–18)

Conspiracy buffs have long speculated that deciphering these enigmatic verses will somehow reveal the answer to when the world will end. One theory, put forth with tongue firmly in cheek, is that Visa credit cards are the first step toward promoting a world where no one will be able to "buy or sell" without being registered with the company that is really a front for the antichrist—the Visa credit organization.

Here is the "proof." In order to spell out the name of the "beast" who will someday control all commerce on earth, we first have to convert the numbers into a word. A simple chart will accomplish this:

ARMAGEDDON NOW: THE END OF THE WORLD A TO Z

1	2	3	4	5	6	7	8	9
A	B	C	D	E	F	G	H	I
J	K	L	M	N	O	P	Q	R
S	T	U	V	W	X	Y	Z	

Here the letters A, J, and S are each designated by the number 1, while B, K, and T equal 2, and so on.

Now transfer the letters V, I, S, and A to their numerical equivalents. They are: 4 + 9 + 1 + 1. Those numbers, when added together, equal 15. At this point, the casual observer might ask, So what? But the to the initiated, it is obvious that the numbers 1 and 5, when added together, equal 6.

The Bible is full of sevenfold descriptions of God (see Revelation). God created the world in seven days, creating humans on the sixth day of creation. So God's perfect number must be 7, with humans coming in just short of perfection at 6.

But God is also represented by the number 3. God, according to this way of thinking, is a trinity, after all, consisting of the Father, Son, and Holy Spirit. So sinful humanity, originally made in God's image (3) but fallen from grace, must be represented by a threefold number 6, or 666—thrice short of perfection.

Thus the Visa company, made in the image of fallen humanity, must be represented by 6 three times, or 666. The fact that so many people use Visa cards to "buy or sell" means that credit cards are the method by which antichrist, for whom Visa is a front, is even now laying the groundwork to take over the world's economy.

The Date of the Birth of the Antichrist

This is a far simpler equation. Since 666 is the number of the "beast," or the antichrist, and 3 is the number of the Trinity, the number of God, whom the antichrist tries to imitate, all we have to do is multiply: 666 × 3 = 1998. Obviously, 1998 CE must be the year of the antichrist's birth. If this is the case, then in 2005, the year this book was published, the antichrist, living anonymously somewhere in the world, celebrated his eighth birthday.

He will no doubt try to imitate Jesus in other ways. When Jesus "was about thirty years old," according to Luke 3:23, he began his public ministry. So we can expect the antichrist to go public sometime around the year 2028, when he, too, turns thirty.

These are only two of literally hundreds of theories equating numbers in the Bible to alleged endtimes events. An Internet search will reveal new theories arriving almost daily.

Source:
Callahan, Tim. "The End of the World and the New World Order: Black Helicopters, Hong Kong Gurkhas, Global Conspiracies, and The Mark of the Beast." http://www.skeptic.com/04.3.callahan-end.html.

OLD TESTAMENT *see* **Books of the Bible and Their Relation to Prophecy**

OLIVET DISCOURSE

(See also Abomination of Desolation; Seventy Sevens)

Jesus left the temple and was walking away when his disciples came up to him to call his attention to its buildings. "Do you see all these things?" he asked. "I tell you the truth, not one stone will be left standing on another; every one will be thrown down."

> As Jesus was sitting on the Mount of Olives, the disciples came to him privately. "Tell us," they said, "when will this happen, and what will be the sign of your coming and of the end of the age?" (Matt. 24:1–3)

With this introduction, Jesus began what is often called the Olivet Discourse (for the Mount of Olives, where it supposedly was delivered), in which he talked about the events that would precede his Second Coming at the battle of Armageddon. Many modern scholars have come to believe that he didn't actually say these words as they are presented in Matthew's gospel. Instead, they suggest, the discourse is a first-century, possibly even early-second-century Christian compilation based on events familiar to the audience of that day. They point to the fact that many verses in Matthew are similar to, in some cases identical with, verses in Mark 13 and Luke 21. Perhaps, goes the argument, Matthew, Mark, and Luke all had before them another document, often called "Q" (from the German word *Quell*, "source"), from which they copied the material they used in their own gospel accounts.

In this way, interpreters of the Olivet Discourse are divided along lines similar to those who write about the book of Revelation. (See Revelation for a more thorough treatment of the two interpretive positions.) Some believe that we are reading the actual words of Jesus, others that the Olivet Discourse is, in fact, merely what early Christians believed would happen in their current times.

The arguments put forth are legion. All theological camps have their own shades of meanings. But for those who believe Jesus foretold the end of the world when he delivered the discourse, the argument follows these lines: The sermon was prompted by three questions the disciples asked of Jesus. He had stated unequivocally that the temple would be torn down. (This statement is one reason that less-literalist scholars believe the gospel was written after 70 CE, the year the temple was destroyed.) The disciples were obviously shocked. In their day, the temple looked like a very substantial edifice. So they asked:

1. When will this happen?
2. What will be the sign of your coming?
3. What will be the sign of the end of the age?

Jesus didn't answer the first question. He simply left that one hanging. But his answer to the second question has covered about two thousand years of history, so far:

> Watch out that no one deceives you. For many will come in my name claiming, "I am the Christ," and will deceive many. You will hear of wars and rumors of wars, but see to it that your are not alarmed. Such things must happen, but the end is yet to come. Nation will rise against nation, and kingdom against kingdom. There will be famines and earthquakes in various places. All these are the beginnings of birth pains.

This, according to literalists, is a description of the Church Age, the last two thousand years of history, condensed into five short verses.

The answer to the third question fills the rest of chapter 24—forty-three verses—and all forty-six verses of chapter 25.

The first subject is martyrdom. True followers will be persecuted, and false prophets, or false religions, will arise and deceive many. But the "gospel of the kingdom will be preached in the whole world as a testimony to all the nations, and then the end will come." This, according to a conservative interpretation, is precisely what has happened in world history ever since these words were spoken.

Next, Jesus foretell the Rapture (see Rapture) and the signs of its coming. The "abomination that causes desolation" (see Abomination of Desolation) will be set up. The antichrist and false prophet (see entries) will take center stage. Jesus quotes from the Hebrew prophet Isaiah:

> The sun will be darkened,
>   and the moon will not give its light;
> the stars will fall from the sky,
>   and the heavenly bodies will be shaken.

And then:

> At that time the sign of the Son of Man will appear in the sky, and all the nations of the earth will mourn. They will see the Son of Man coming on the clouds of the sky, with power and great glory. And he will send his angels with a loud trumpet call, and they will gather his elect from the four winds, from one end of the heavens to the other.

Christ praying in Gethsemane on the Mount of Olives, perhaps near the scene of the Olivet Discourse (Martin Schongauer, fifteenth century). *Library of Congress.*

Following this apocalyptic vision Jesus warns his disciples:

Learn this lesson from the fig tree: As soon as its twigs get tender and its leaves come out, you know that summer is near. Even so, when you see all these things, you know that it is near, right at the door. I tell you the truth, this generation will certainly not pass away until all these things have happened. Heaven and earth will pass away, but my words will never pass away.

This last verse has sparked many, many bitter conversations and arguments. What did Jesus mean when he said, "This generation will certainly not pass away"? In context he appears to have meant the generation that heard him say the words. But that generation passed away a long time ago, and the apocalyptic events that Jesus prophesied still have not occurred.

Given this obvious fact, many conservative theologians argue that "this generation" must mean the future generation that will actually see the promised signs. If the fig tree, for instance, refers to Israel, its autumn was occurring even as Jesus spoke, and its winter began in 70 CE with the destruction of the temple and beginning of the long Diaspora. But Israel regained its nation status in 1948. Was that the beginning of the "generation" that would "see all these things?" So goes the argument. The problem is that the generation that was alive in 1948 is now growing old. People have long calculated a biblical generation as forty years. Thus there was much speculation in the 1970s that the time of the end was near, since 1988 would mark the fortieth year after 1948. But 1988 came and went. Either Jesus will have to return soon or this interpretation of the passage will have to be abandoned.

The rest of the Olivet Discourse is given over to parables or small teaching stories. Most of them concern morality lessons about being ready when the time for an appointed task arrives. They tell of wise and foolish virgins awaiting a bridegroom, of men who wisely or unwisely invest their master's money in his absence—and, of course, the famous story of the "sheep" and the "goats" who will be divided at the end of time when "the Son of Man comes in his glory." These last are divided according to their ethical behavior. The sheep are rewarded. The goats are sent away "to eternal punishment, but the righteous to eternal life."

According to Matthew's gospel, when Jesus finished this sermon, he went forth to die, beginning the path that led straight to Calvary.

Source:
The Holy Bible, New International Version. Grand Rapids, MI: Zondervan, 1978.

OPPENHEIMER, J. ROBERT

In 1939 President Franklin D. Roosevelt was informed that German scientists were working to develop atomic weapons. In 1942 he appointed J. Robert Oppenheimer to lead a secret government team, giving them the mission of winning the race whose finish would mark the beginning of the atomic age. On July 16, 1945, the first atomic bomb was exploded in the desert outside of Los Alamos, New Mexico. The United States had won. The effort was called the Manhattan Project. Ever since that moment in New Mexico, human beings have had the power to eradicate their species from planet Earth.

Oppenheimer was born into a fairly well-to-do Jewish immigrant family in Brooklyn, New York, in 1904. He attended the Ethical School in New York City and excelled in math and science as well as languages. He graduated from Harvard and studied physics at Cambridge in England and Göttingen in Germany. In 1929 he returned to the United States. He did research and taught physics at Berkeley and Cal Tech. After his appointment as director of the Manhattan Project, he set up shop in the desert near Los Alamos. There he managed more than three thousand people who did the work that paved the way for a possible nuclear Armageddon.

Oppenheimer is reported to have said after the explosion, "We knew the world would not be the same." He was right. Japan surrendered on August 10, 1945, after American atomic bombs incinerated the cities of Hiroshima and Nagasaki. World War II was over. But the age of nuclear weapons was only beginning.

After the war Oppenheimer chaired the Atomic Energy Commission. There was much pressure to continue research and develop a far more powerful bomb—the hydrogen bomb—but having seen the destructive force of the atom bomb, Oppenheimer opposed creating a weapon still more horrific. He continued his campaign against further research and was labeled a Communist sympathizer in the early 1950s for his outlook. He then left government service and

J. Robert Oppenheimer, often called the father of the atomic bomb, 1958. *Associated Press.*

went back to the academic world, teaching at the Institute for Advanced Study at Princeton. In 1967 he died of throat cancer.

Oppenheimer has since come to be known as the "father" of the atomic bomb. His work and research into atomic weaponry opened the door to the possibility that humankind is now, for the first time in its long evolution, standing on the brink of self-extinction. On one hand the fruit of his work, the atomic bomb, brought about the end of a terrible war. On the other, this same work led to even more powerful and destructive weapons. His research into splitting the atom laid the groundwork for enormous advances in physical science. Although it has been very valuable in other ways, will we use his work in a destructive or productive way? As an anonymous wag is supposed to have said, with tongue only partially in cheek, "Was the splitting of the atom a wise crack?"

Oppenheimer's views were undoubtedly mixed on the subject. He obviously felt strongly that he had opened a Pandora's box, and he was willing to risk political persecution for saying so. But he will also be remembered for something else he said: "Science is not everything, but science is very beautiful."

Sources:

"J. Robert Oppenheimer, 1904–1967." http://www.pbs.org/wgbh/aso/databank/entries/baoppe. html.

The History of Computing Project. "Robert J. [*sic*] Oppenheimer." http://www.thocp.net/biogra phies/oppenheimer_robert.htm.

P

PARABLES OF THE KINGDOM

Matthew 13 describes a scene wherein Jesus relates seven parables, often referred to as the Parables of the Kingdom. A parable is a teaching device consisting of a short story containing a lesson or moral. One conservative reading of these parables insists that, when read in their proper order, they provide a chronological description of the age of the church from its inception to the present. (See Bible Timelines for a brief discussion of each parable that also correlates them with another seven-staged interpretive scheme found in Revelation, chapters 2 and 3.)

PAROUSIA *see* Second Coming

PAST-HISTORIC SCHOOL OF BIBLICAL INTERPRETATION *see* Abomination of Desolation; Revelation

PAUL, APOSTLE

Saul of Tarsus was a Jewish teacher with a Gentile education and Roman citizenship who converted to Christianity and literally changed the course of Roman, as well as religious, history. While traveling to Damascus to arrest members of the new Christian religion that was upsetting the status quo in and around Jerusalem, he had a vision of the resurrected Christ. He changed his name to Paul, which means "little" or "tiny." After an intense period of study he became the first and most famous missionary of the religion he had once persecuted. He undertook three great missionary journeys before being placed under house arrest in Rome, awaiting a trial that apparently never took place because of the lack of accusers. Although his final days are lost to history and subject to much speculation, he managed to write almost a third of what Christians call the New Testament of the Bible.

Paul's method of operation was to enter a town and preach the new Christian gospel at the local synagogue. Most often this resulted in his being thrown out on the street, beaten, put in jail, or stoned. But in each city a small group of believers would gather around him and a new church cell was formed. Paul would then move on, but his epistles, or letters of instructions, written back to these churches were eventually included in the scriptures and form the basis for much of current Christian theology.

The people of the early church believed that Jesus would return during their lifetimes. There is a lot of evidence that Paul believed this to be true and constantly warned the new believers to be ready to receive the Lord at any moment. To the church in Corinth, for instance, he wrote:

> Now about virgins: I have no command from the Lord, but I give a judgment as one who by the Lord's mercy is trustworthy. Because of the present crisis, I think that it is good for you to remain as you are. Are you married? Do not seek a divorce. Are you unmarried? Do not look for a wife. But if you do marry, you have not sinned; and if a virgin marries, she has not sinned. But those who marry will face many troubles in this life, and I want to spare you this.

> What I mean, brothers, is that the time is short. (1 Cor. 7:25–29)

Such advice seems to indicate that Paul expected the Lord to come back at any moment. He believed that what he called "the last days" were upon humanity:

> But mark this: There will be terrible times in the last days. People will be lovers of themselves, lovers of money, boastful, proud, abusive, disobedient to their parents, ungrateful, unholy, without love, unforgiving, slanderous, without self-control, brutal, not lovers of the good, treacherous, rash, conceited, lovers of pleasure rather than lovers of God—having a form of godliness but denying its power. Have nothing to do with them. They are the kind who worm their way into homes and gain control over weak-willed women, who are loaded down with sins and are swayed by all kinds of evil desires. (2 Tim. 3:1–7)

There was a period following the death of Jesus in which the new Christian believers fully expected to hear, at any moment, the herald trumpets announcing his return. But time dragged on. The first-generation faithful got older and began to die out. Paul had laid down a basic theology, however, that comforted them: "For as in Adam all die, so in Christ shall all be made alive.… The body that is sown is perishable, it is raised imperishable; it is sown in dishonor, it is raised in glory; it is sown in weakness, it is raised in power; it is sown a natural body, it is raised a spiritual body" (1 Cor. 15: 22, 42–44).

This theology covers all believers who die—but what about those who are still alive when Jesus returns? Do they have to die as well? Paul responded to this question in both 1 Corinthians and 1 Thessalonians:

> I declare to you, brothers, that flesh and blood cannot inherit the kingdom of God, nor does the perishable inherit the imperishable. Listen, I tell you a mystery: We will not all sleep, but we will all be changed—in a flash, in the twinkling of an eye at the last trumpet. For the trumpet will sound, the dead will be raised imperishable, and we will all be changed.… Therefore, my dear brothers, stand firm. Let nothing move

The conversion of Paul, from a painting by Ercole de Ferrara. *Fortean Picture Library.*

you. Always give yourselves fully to the work of the Lord, because you know that your labor in the Lord is not in vain. (1 Cor. 15:50–58)

According to the Lord's own word, we tell you that we who are alive, who are left till the coming of the Lord, will certainly not precede those who have fallen asleep. For the Lord himself will come down from heaven, with a loud command, with the voice of the archangel and with the trumpet call of God, and the dead in Christ will rise first. After that, we who are still alive and are left will be caught up with them in the clouds to meet the Lord in the air. And so we will be with the Lord forever. (1 Thess. 4:15–17)

These critical verses have been interpreted since the late eighteenth century as expressing Paul's insight that a generation will someday see the return of Jesus Christ and that those of them who are believers will be transformed from material to spiritual in the "twinkling of an eye" (see Rapture). Paul went on to say that no one knows when all this will take place: "Now brothers, about times and dates we do not need to write to you, for you know very well that the day of the Lord will come like a thief in the night."

Many among today's religious right regard Paul's writings as inerrant revelation and certain prophecy concerning the Second Coming of Jesus. Many other Christians believe that Paul was simply a product of his time and wrote what seemed logical to him, perhaps infusing his "divine insight" with some wishful thinking. Certainly his description of the Second Coming, accompanied by trumpets and loud shouts of command while believers are "caught up in the air," is outside normal life experience.

But the very extravagance of the scenario inspires some Rapture enthusiasts to believe. What better way to wrap up history then with a final burst of something extraordinary?

Paul left only a few tantalizing verses. If he was correct in labeling his ideas as being "the Lord's own word," why isn't there more information, in a single extended treatment? Why must we stitch together fragments from so many different places in the Bible in order to produce a full-blown picture about something this important? Why does God seem to make the whole idea of the endtimes a puzzle? Is God playing games with us?

Scholars still are not in agreement about what Paul really meant, much less about whether it represents some future reality. It seems likely that this disagreement will continue unless and until the endtimes themselves actually arrive.

Source:
The Holy Bible, New International Version. Grand Rapids, MI: Zondervan, 1978.

PEAK OIL

"Gas is running low ..." (Amelia Earhart, July 2, 1937)

The famous aviator's report from somewhere over the Pacific concerning her situation just before she disappeared might very well foreshadow things to come for planet Earth.

In 1956 Marion King Hubbert, a geophysicist for the Shell Oil Company, predicted that oil production in the United States would peak somewhere around the year 1970. That is exactly what happened. He also predicted that world oil production would peak somewhere around 1995. Were it not for the great jumps in the cost of oil that took place in the 1970s, that would have happened, too. But even those price increases staved off the inevitable by only a decade. Estimates vary, but the best guesses now are that oil production will peak between somewhere between the years 2004 and 2010. Indeed, we may have already passed the time of peak oil production possible on the planet. Hubbert's prediction, highly influential in top government circles, is called "Peak Oil" or "Hubbert's Peak." Its implications are frightening. Even within the oil industry, calls of alarm are beginning to be heard. Mike Bowlin, chair of the board of directors of Arco Oil in 1999, flatly stated in February of that year, "The last days of the age of oil have begun."

What does this mean in terms of modern civilization?

Simply put, in the twenty-first century we exist on oil. It's not just a matter of how much gas we put in our cars. Every item in the grocery store is there because of oil. Fertilizers that nourish our food and insecticides that protect it are oil-based. Machinery that plows and harvests our fields and trucks that take produce to market run on oil. Electricity that keeps food refrigerated depends heavily on oil. Even the water we drink comes to our taps by means of oil. The modern household simply cannot exist without it.

It's not that oil will simply disappear, although that will inevitably happen someday. It's cheap oil that is running out. When oil begins to sell for prices ranging from $150 to $185 dollars a barrel, prices at the gas pump will be in the $7-per-gallon range. That will drastically raise the price of every item transported by truck, as well the cost of heating the average house.

Population growth confounds the problem. Biologists know that when a food supply is readily available (for the human species, that means cheap), the population increases. This is true for every species, including humans. The experts remind us that oil production equals food production. Recent population growth has been, to a large degree, based on cheap food. But if oil production has peaked and is on the way down, we face a crisis. If the year 2000 was the peak oil production year, for instance, then production in the year 2025, twenty-five years after peak, will roughly equal production in the year 1975, twenty-five years before peak. But the population in 1975 was about 4 billion people. In 2025 it will be closer to 8 billion. That means the same amount of oil will have to go twice as far. The greater the demand for oil and what it delivers, the higher the price goes.

The mathematics are sobering. According to most estimates, the earth held about 2,000 billion barrels of oil when its importance was first discovered and exploited. We have used about half of that already. In 2003 we were using 28 billion barrels a year. Simple division reveals that we have, at best, 35.7 years of oil left. But that doesn't take into account increased demand due to population growth and economics. Twenty-five years is probably a better guess.

And the problem gets even worse the more you study it. Every step in the process of finding oil, drilling for it, extracting it, and delivering it depends on expending oil that has already been processed into fuel. This ratio is expressed in the phrase "energy return on energy invested." That ratio used to be about 30 to 1. By the 1990s it had dropped to 5 to 1. Within a few years, many experts believe, it will drop to 1 to 1. In other words, it will take a barrel of oil to produce a barrel of oil. At that point the age of oil will be, for all practical purposes, finished.

But what will happen before we come to that point? In any biological species, including humans, competition for resources results in strife and warfare. The stronger individuals of a species fight the weaker and dominate the resource. Some experts wonder if that is already happening among humans. Were recent wars in the Middle East really fought over political and sociological factors, or were they about protecting oil supplies? And what will happen when those supplies dwindle? Although no one can say for sure, it seems reasonable to assume that the balance will tip even farther against the teeming millions of people who are even now starving to death. Some experts even go so far as to use phrases like "post-oil die-off." That means exactly what it says. Some estimates foresee the world's population dropping to 500 million people within the next fifty to one hundred years through starvation, illnesses caused by mal-nutrition, and wars over resources. That's a drop of 90 percent. These figures, although admittedly a worst-case scenario, aren't just creations of fantasy. They reflect what has happened and does happen to other species, from bacteria to buffalo, when population outstrips food supply.

Those who argue with the theory of Peak Oil generally follow two strategies. First, they point to unknown or untapped reserves; the recent U.S. decision to drill in the Arctic wilderness is one example. Second, they theorize that by the time oil sup-plies run out, we will have invented a new source of power. The first argument, how-ever, merely prolongs the inevitable. The second, depending on market-driven inventions, has a long way to go before offering cheap, dependable replacements for the oil-based systems already in use.

Meanwhile, the people of the earth stand on the edge of what seems to be an abyss. Whatever happens will take place in uncharted territory.

Sources:
Economides, Michael J. "Is There an Impending World Oil Shortage?" *World Energy* 7:4 (2004): 126–29.
Savinar, Matthew David. "Peak Oil: Life after the Oil Crash." http://www.lifeaftertheoilcrash. net/.

PENTECOST *see* **Bible Timelines**

PERSIA *see* **Zoroastrianism**

PETRA

Sixty miles north of Aqaba, Jordan, and reachable only by ascending the Wadi Musa ("Valley of Moses") and then passing through a narrow gorge called the Siq lie the ruins called Petra. Temples and houses are carved out of a massive cliff of red and var-iegated sandstone. A Roman basilica and amphitheater once stood here. It is certainly one of the most impressive ruins in the Near East and was featured in the movie *Indiana Jones and the Last Crusade.*

Petra is not mentioned in the Bible. Some scholars have tried to link it with the biblical Sela, pointing out that both Petra and Sela mean "rock," and that 2 Chronicles 25:12, coupled with 2 Kings 14:7, talks about a battle in the place of the "rock" in which Amaziah, king of Judah, "killed ten thousand Edomites." But despite these efforts—perhaps stemming at least partly from the perception that such an impressive place *ought* to be referred to in scripture—no positive connection has been established.

More recently, however, some with an evangelical bent have hinted at a future role for Petra—in the battle of Armageddon. Revelation 12 presents a kind of divine pageant. A woman who is about to give birth is threatened by a dragon (see Revela-tion). The dragon has been thrown out of heaven and goes forth to devour the baby. But "the woman was given the two wings of a great eagle, so that she might fly to the place prepared for her in the desert where she would be taken care of for a time, times and half a time, out of the serpent's reach."

Lithograph of Petra, from a drawing made by David Roberts in 1839. *Library of Congress.*

If the "time, times and half a time" refer to the last three and a half years of the Tribulation (see Great Tribulation), perhaps, it is argued, the woman represents a remnant of the believers converted after the Rapture of the church (see Rapture). The dragon obviously represents the antichrist. Perhaps God plans to find an easily defensible place for some believers to hang out while the rest of the world suffers the agony of evil. Could that place be Petra? The psalmist prayed, "Lead me to the rock that is higher than I." Maybe that rock is the rock fortress of Petra.

Some Christians who believe this scenario have begun to flock to Petra and prepare for a long siege. Like divinely appointed fallout shelters, some of Petra's secret caves are being filled with food, water, guns, and ammunition by Christian survivalists who regard such measures as practical in the face of impending doom. Even though it's a long shot, without one piece of biblical evidence to support it, they feel they would rather be safe than sorry.

Sources:
Buttrick, George A., ed. *The Interpreter's Dictionary of the Bible.* 4 vols. New York: Abingdon Press, 1962.
Rogerson, John. *Atlas of the Bible.* New York: Facts on File Publications, 1985.

PIT

Revelation 9, 11, 17, and 20 all refer to the "bottomless pit" that is to be the final abode of Satan where, along with "the beast and the false prophet," he "will be tormented day and night for ever and ever" (Rev. 20:10).

Although many religions have similar ideas concerning a place of punishment for the wicked, there is no doubt that the conservative Christian concept, wherein a God of love tortures the damned forever with unquenchable fire, is a particularly gruesome one. It envisions a place of torment for those who fail to attain the ethical righteousness God demands. Either a fiery hell or a nebulous place of darkness awaits the unworthy who fail to accept the substitution of Jesus' righteousness for their sin. In some traditions the pit is coupled with a "waiting room," or purgatory, where choices need to be made concerning eternity.

Some biblical scholars hypothesize that the idea of unquenchable fire came from the ancient practice of burning, outside the city wall, corpses that, for whatever reason, could not be buried. They suggest that the idea of eternal torture might also have roots in the excruciating physical punishments meted out to wrongdoers, as opposed to more modern concepts of rehabilitation.

Whatever the genesis of the image, there is no doubt that the book of Revelation paints a pretty dim picture of the eternal bottomless pit. It raises an interesting question that has consumed centuries of debate: Is human sin and willfulness more powerful than God's forgiveness? In other words, is a person's power to reject God stronger than God's power to forgive that person for his or her rejection? For those who answer yes, the pit awaits those who, after the battle of Armageddon, will be forced to agree with them.

Source:
The Holy Bible, New International Version. Grand Rapids, MI: Zondervan, 1978.

PLAGUES

There is nothing new about human beings' suffering sickness and death due to viruses and bacteria. Europeans, familiar with their own history of battling the bubonic plague, may even have used biological warfare against the indigenous native population of the Americas, in some cases reportedly providing blankets contaminated with smallpox to Indians, who had no natural immunity. Some estimates are that by the time the Pilgrims landed at Plymouth Rock, as much as three-fourths of the local native population had died of infectious diseases that had arrived in the Americas with earlier European explorers.

The identical story was enacted when the people of Florida came into contact with Spanish explorers and missionaries. Within one generation, populations were depleted by bubonic plague, chicken pox, dysentery, diphtheria, influenza, malaria, measles, scarlet fever, smallpox, typhoid, typhus, yellow fever, and secondary infections such as pneumonia—not to mention mistreatment through forced labor and slave raids. The effect was devastating. The Apalachee people alone, only one of

The Pestilence upon Israel, engraving by F. Lightfoot depicting the plague described in 2 Samuel 24. *Fortean Picture Library.*

many Florida tribes, declined from an estimated 50,000 to 8,500 in a matter of only a few years.

The European invasion was, to say the least, not kind to the indigenous people of America.

Humans have fought harmful bacteria and viruses ever since we discovered their role in the sicknesses we experience. What is so frightening today is the scope of a problem that, only a few decades ago, some doctors were beginning to think they had almost solved. The statistics are troubling, especially when such respected news organizations as the BBC use words like "pandemic potential" to describe the possibilities of viruses spreading rapidly throughout human populations. Although it seems unlikely that such viruses could completely eliminate the human race, the "Spanish flu" of 1918 killed up to 50 million people. In February 2005, health officials began to raise concerns that a new strain of Avian flu called H5N1, which had killed forty-two people in Asia since 1997, had the potential to mutate into a form that could cause a deadly pandemic (a concern, in fact, with almost all disease-causing organisms). This kind of outbreak easily leads to speculation concerning even more deadly viruses and bacteria. What is so frightening today is that people travel so freely that contagious diseases spread more rapidly than ever before.

No one knows where or when the next great plague will strike or what its cause will be. But a quick look at three existing diseases of varying prevalence and deadliness may convey some idea of the challenge faced by researchers and medical workers:

HIV/AIDS. Human immunodeficiency virus (HIV) is the virus most specialists believe leads to acquired immunodeficiency syndrome (AIDS). Although modern treatment has made great strides in helping HIV-infected people to live normal lives, more than 37 million people are believed to be carriers of the virus. HIV is spread through contact with bodily fluids of infected people, usually through sexual contact. It was first thought to be a "homosexual" disease because that community received heavy media attention when HIV began to spread among the male gay population of San Francisco. At least one prominent Christian fundamentalist said that he believed AIDS was "God's judgment upon homosexuals." He has since retracted his statement. HIV/AIDS is now growing by leaps and bounds in the community everyone once thought least likely to be in danger: *Modern Maturity*, the magazine of the American Association of Retired People, reports an alarming increase of HIV infection among senior citizens, spread through heterosexual contact.

In 2001 the United Nations declared a worldwide offensive against this deadly virus. The United States pledged $15 billion for AIDS treatment in small and poor countries. But in March 2004 the World Health Organization reported that it was losing the battle. Of the six million people in the world's poorest countries who needed HIV-fighting drugs, only three hundred thousand were actually getting them. At the close of 2003, donations to the Global Fund to Fight AIDS were coming in at about the rate of $1.6 billion a year, barely 20 percent of what was needed. The situation was so critical that it brought together politicians as far apart as a Democratic senator from Massachusetts (Edward Kennedy) and a Republican senator from Arizona (John McCain), who wrote a joint letter to the White House urging action.

SARS. In February of 2003 an outbreak of severe acute respiratory syndrome (SARS) closed down airports in Asia and soon spread to other ports around the Far East. In no time at all it was reported in two dozen countries throughout North America and Europe. In less than a month it was officially declared a global outbreak. Infected people reported a high fever, headache, body aches, and a general feeling of discomfort similar to a severe case of the flu. Within a few days patients developed a dry cough. Most of them developed pneumonia.

SARS is spread by close contact with an infected person, similar to the way colds spread each year. The frightening thing about SARS was how fast it spread from country to country. In these days of widespread travel it offered a clinical study demonstrating how rapidly a virus can be carried across oceans, infecting widely separated populations. Containment, often the only preventive option, is extremely difficult in today's world. The 2003 tourist season in Canada was devastated by the disease after more than forty people in the Toronto area died. Although the National Institute of Allergy and Infectious Diseases is working to develop a gene-based therapy, they believe testing in humans to be a long way off, much too late to come to the aid of the more than eight thousand people worldwide who are infected each year, with more than eight hundred deaths already recorded.

EBOLA. Ebola hemorrhagic fever was first documented in 1976. It is caused by the Ebola virus, named after a river in the region of the Democratic Republic of the Congo where it seems to have originated. Its exact genesis is unknown, but the current best guess is that it transferred to humans from an animal host, probably a monkey. Ebola hemorrhagic fever causes severe flulike symptoms and, depending on which strain of the virus is involved, has a fatality rate of from 50 to 90 percent in humans. It also appears to have a number of deadly cousins, related strains that have similar effect. In early 2005 an Ebola-like virus known as Marburg killed hundreds in Angola. The death rate for those known to be infected exceeded 90 percent.

Diseases and the Endtimes

Why are illnesses such as AIDS and Ebola still so threatening in today's scientific environment, which has at its disposal a host of life-saving medical miracles?

Predictably, some in the religious community, such as Dennis L. Finnan, host of the weekly radio broadcast *The World, the Word, and You*, say the answer is that we are living in the "last days" predicted by Jesus, when "pestilences in various places" (Luke 21:11) will be one of the signs of the end.

Others think population explosion is a large part of the communicable-disease problem: there are simply too many of us living too close together. "Elevator syndrome" is the experience we have when we get on a crowded elevator. Blood pressure and anxiety rise when we are hemmed in by people. If the situation continues too long, psychological symptoms such as nervous disorders develop. These eventually translate into physical symptoms. Spaceship Earth, according to this theory, is quickly turning into a very crowded elevator, and we are beginning to see the results in outbreaks of illnesses and diseases.

Still other observers believe that the problem of disease is simply one of too much information being broadcast. We are more aware of sicknesses because we detect them faster due to better medical science and because we then tell everyone about them on the six o'clock news.

Whatever the case, plagues have been with us for a long time, and according to many news sources, some of the current ones seem to be getting worse, possibly threatening, in time, our very existence as a species.

Sources:
Web sites on specific diseases:
> Ebola—www.cdc.gov/ncidad/durd/spb/mnpages/dispages/ebola.htm.
> HIV/AIDS—www.unaids.org.
> SARS—www.cdc.gov/ncidad/sars/factsheet.htm.
McNeil, Donald G., Jr. "Plan to Battle AIDS Is Falling Short." *New York Times*, March 28, 2004.
Roberts, Michelle. "Bird Flu 'Has Pandemic Potential.'" http://news.bbc.co.uk/2/hi/health/4280817.stm.

PLANET OF THE APES *see* **Hollywood Envisions** THE END

POLAR SHIFT

Whenever clay is heated to very high temperatures, any iron particles it contains align with the earth's magnetic field, recording the field's condition at that particular moment. Since clay pots have been fired from prehistoric times right down to the present, fragments of which are readily available for study, paleomagnetists—the name for scientists who study such things—possess a detailed record of the direction and strength of the magnetic field. What they are discovering is disturbing. The earth's magnetic field is growing weaker.

The north and south magnetic poles are formed by the action of forces deep within the earth. A rotating liquid metallic core creates a magnetic force field that shelters us from harmful radiation emanating from the sun. The effects of that radiation are visible in the phenomena known to those in the Northern Hemisphere as aurora borealis, or northern lights, the light show that is the result of electronic particles being magnetically rerouted to the poles as they strike earth. Without the magnetic force field that directs harmful radiation around the earth, we would be vulnerable.

Any compass reveals the normal orientation of our magnetic force field. North is "up." South is "down." But such has not always been the case. There have been times when normal polarity would have been exactly the opposite, had there been humans around to witness the phenomena. Even the sun's magnetic shield reverses itself. It happens much more rapidly. Approximately every 11 years the field reverses. Our galaxy, the Milky Way, has a magnetic field that seems to be prone to reversal from time to time. But from the standpoint of human history, earth reversals are rarer than ice ages. They occur every 250,000 years or so and take hundreds of years to complete. Given that time frame, modern humans could adjust. It might even be a beautiful experience. The idea of northern lights painting the skies of London virtually every night of the year is a beautiful thing to contemplate.

It's not just the reversal of the poles that has some scientists worried, however. Questions of a much more serious nature abound.

First of all, scientists really don't know what causes reversals, and there doesn't seem to be any consensus of opinion about why, during the last 160 million years, the reversal rate appears to have peaked about 12 million years ago. What has them concerned is that recent discoveries concerning the magnetic field of the planet Mars indicate that Mars had some kind of magnetic field collapse about four billion years ago. It hasn't had a sheltering field since and that could well have been the event that caused it to lose its atmosphere as well. Some scientists suggest that the planet was on its way to producing primitive life, and may have even done so, before the collapse of its magnetic field snuffed it out.

The implications are chilling. Could the same thing happen on Earth?

There seems to be a consensus of opinion that the earth's field is weakening. Evidence is piling up through the study of prehistoric ceramics that even in the relatively short geologic time frame covered by the human invention of pottery, the earth's magnetic field has weakened considerably. That might not be a problem. It seems to have done so in the past and then rebounded. We might be in such a period now. The field might restore itself, or it might even flip north to south and then come back as strong as ever. But if it doesn't rebound, given the current rate of decline, it will be gone in a few centuries.

Are we going the way of Mars? No one knows. Ron Merrill, a specialist in the field who plies his trade at the University of Washington, probably has the best answer any scientist can give right now. Speaking to a research team from the PBS television presentation *NOVA*, he said, "Ask me in 10,000 years. I'll give you a better answer."

All we know for sure is that something is happening that the human race has never experienced. What that means remains to be seen.

Sources:
"Magnetic Storm." PBS, November 18, 2003.
Tyson, Peter. "When Compasses Point South." http://www.pbs.org/wgbh/nova/magnetic/timeline. html.

POPULATION CLOCK

According to the U.S. Census Bureau's World Population Clock, on January 1, 2005, at 12:00 A.M. GMT, there were exactly 6,409,765,942 people on the planet ready to welcome the new year.

No one, of course, counted noses for this occasion. Even the U.S. Census Bureau is quick to point out that "the populations displayed on the clock are not intended to imply that the population of the world is known to the last person. Rather, the clock is our estimate of the world population size and an indication of how fast it is growing."

It's growing very, very fast. Humanity had reached the 6 billion mark only a bit more than five years earlier—on June 11, 1999, according to U.S. figures or on October 12, 1999, according to the United Nations. Which estimate is closer really doesn't matter a great deal. The end result is the same. The question is how many people the planet can support.

According to United Nations estimates, we will reach the 9.1 billion mark by the year 2050. Hania Zlotnik, director of the UN's Population Division, comments that this figure "will be a strain on the world." Richly developed countries will remain mostly unchanged (although their populations will become, on average, older), but less-developed countries will see their numbers swell from the current 5.3 billion to 7.8 billion if present trends continue. Although the birth-death ratio in the United States is almost even and not projected to result in much natural population growth, current immigration patterns are expected to produce an increase from the present size of 298 million to some 394 million by 2050. Eight countries—India, Pakistan, Nigeria, Congo, Bangladesh, Uganda, the United States, Ethiopia, and China—are likely to make up half the world's total increase.

Although some experts believe that the world population needs to level off at about 10 billion in order to prevent catastrophic overload, others admit they simply don't know what will happen. It's not enough to simply plot resource production. Getting those resources to where they are needed is a staggering problem. A relatively small portion of the world's surface could probably produce enough food to feed even 10 billion people, *if* all usable land is kept under cultivation and *if* the food can be delivered and *if* economic markets can support those who are growing the food.

For many theorists, those are simply too many *ifs*.

Population growth is similar to compound interest. More people tends to mean more babies, even if some of those people practice realistic birth control. Most experts agree that, barring massive disasters, the population will continue to expand. But some specialists point out that Mother Earth tends to whittle down species' populations when they get out of control. She knows exactly how many people, dinosaurs, passenger pigeons, mastodons, and so on she can feed. When that number is surpassed, any number of things can happen to reduce the excess. Disease, war, natural catastrophes, and starvation are only a few documented techniques she has used in the past.

Is there a limit to growth? Only time will tell.

Sources:
Lederer, Edith M. "U.N.: World Population to Hit 9B in 2050." Associated Press, February 25, 2005.
U.S. Census Bureau. "World POPClock Projection." http://www.census.gov/cgi-bin/ipc/pop clockw.

POSTMAN, THE *see* Hollywood Envisions THE END

PRE- AND POSTMILLENNIALISM
(See also Christian Views of the End)

Millennialism is the belief, based on a literal interpretation of Revelation 20:1–10, that Jesus Christ will return to earth and reign for a thousand years, during which time Satan will be "bound" and unable to deceive the nations. This reign will be marked by peace and contentment (see Millennialism).

Amillennialists do not believe that the words "a thousand years" should be interpreted literally. They believe the thousand-year figure is symbolic. There will be no literal Millennium. (See Amillennialism.)

The millennialist school is itself divided into two camps. Those who believe the Second Coming of Jesus Christ will take place before the thousand years begin are called "premillennialists" (*pre-* meaning "before"). Those who believe that Jesus' return will occur after the Millennium are called "postmillennialists" (*post-* meaning "after").

Premillennialists make up the majority of the millennialist school. The prime biblical proof text for their position comes from the book of Revelation. Although they use passages from other books of the Bible to buttress their argument, these texts are all only supporting actors in the main play of events described in Revelation 19:11–20:10.

The scenes are portrayed in vivid detail. As the curtain opens in the first ten verses of chapter 19, a heavenly choir sings the overture:

"Hallelujah!
Salvation and glory and power belong to our God,
   for true and just are his judgments.
He has condemned the great prostitute
   who has corrupted the earth by her adulteries.
He has avenged on her the blood of his servants."

Various groups join the chorus until finally "a great multitude, like the roar of rushing waters and like loud peals of thunder" joins in the climax of the heavenly symphony:

"Hallelujah!
   For our Lord God Almighty reigns.
Let us rejoice and be glad
   and give him glory!
For the wedding of the Lamb has come,
   and his bride has made herself ready.
Fine linen, bright and clean,
   was given her to wear."

("Fine linen" stands for the righteous acts of the saints.)

At the height of the overture the curtain opens and a white horse appears "whose rider is called Faithful and True." He has a name written on his robe and thigh: "KING OF KINGS AND LORD OF LORDS."

Premillennialists believe this to be a description of an actual event that will one day take place in human history—the Second Coming of Jesus Christ. It will end the battle of Armageddon:

Then I saw the beast and the kings of the earth and their armies gathered together to make war against the rider on the horse and his army. But the beast was captured, and with him the false prophet who had performed the miraculous signs on his behalf. With these signs he had deluded those who had received the mark of the beast and worshiped his image. The two of them were thrown alive into the lake of burning sulfur. The rest of them were killed with the sword that came out of the mouth of the rider on the white horse, and all the birds gorged themselves on their flesh.

Following this carnage, an angel comes down from heaven,

having the key to the Abyss and holding in his hand a great chain. He seized the dragon, that ancient serpent, who is the devil, or Satan, and bound him for a thousand years. He threw him into the Abyss, and locked and sealed it over him, to keep him from deceiving the nations anymore until the thousand years were ended. After that, he must be set free for a short time.

Following this, those who had died during the last tumultuous years of the time of tribulation "came to life and reigned with Christ a thousand years." It is emphasized a second time that "they will be priests of God and of Christ and will reign with him for a thousand years."

As the play continues in Revelation 20, the action quickly skips over the Millennium itself. As the curtain opens on Act 2, the thousand years have passed. Satan is released, without explanation as to why, and he quickly

goes out to deceive the nations in the four corners of the earth—Gog and Magog—to gather them for battle. In number they are like the sands on the seashore. They marched across the breadth of the earth and surrounded the camp of God's people, the city he loves. But fire came down from heaven and devoured them. And the devil, who deceived them, was thrown into the lake of burning sulfur, where the beast and the false prophet had been thrown. They will be tormented day and night for ever and ever.

In the final scene of Act 2, a great judgment takes place. Earth and sea give up their dead and "each person was judged according to what he had done. Then death and Hades were thrown into the lake of fire. The lake of fire is the second death. If anyone's name was not found written in the book of life, he was thrown into the lake of fire."

As the play closes, the narrator describes a new beginning. A new heaven and a new earth are pictured, along with a full description of the "new Jerusalem, coming down from God as a bride adorned for her husband."

To premillennialists, who read these passages literally, this play is pretty straightforward and complete. Christ returns, winning the battle of Armageddon, a thousand years of peace, the Millennium, goes by, and then heaven and earth enter into eternity. It's a simple timeline without any room for interpretation.

Postmillennialists disagree. It's not that they don't take the words of scripture seriously. It's that they don't take them literally. Even a literal reading of the words of the Revelation demands a certain amount of metaphorical interpretation. Does a "sword" really come out of Jesus' mouth? Obviously that sounds far-fetched. The "sword" must refer to what Paul, in Ephesians 6, called the "sword of the spirit," or the word of God.

Postmillennialists argue that once you start interpreting a few phrases as metaphors you have started down a slippery slope. Who is to say what is meant to be taken literally and what is to be interpreted as metaphor? To some postmillennialists, beginning with Augustine in the fourth century, the whole passage is meant to be interpreted spiritually rather than literally. In the words of Kenneth L. Gentry Jr., a prominent postmillennialist theologian: "Postmillennialism expects the proclaiming of the Spirit-blessed gospel of Jesus Christ to win the vast majority of human beings to salvation in the present age. Increasing gospel success will gradually produce a time in history prior to Christ's return in which faith, righteousness, peace, and prosperity will prevail in the affairs of people and nations. After an extensive era of such conditions the Lord will return visibly, bodily, and in great glory, ending history with the general resurrection and the great judgment of all humankind."

Pre- and postmillennialists, then, agree that Jesus Christ will literally return to earth at some future date. Premillennialists believe that he will return to straighten things out personally. Postmillennialists believe that the Holy Spirit will do that first, through the workings of Christ's body on earth—the Church. Then, when the way is prepared and humans are straightened out spiritually, Christ will return and a new beginning will take place.

Both camps take the Bible seriously, differing only in their hermeneutics, or method of interpretation. Both believe in a physical return of Jesus Christ to earth. He will have a real body, albeit a spiritual one not subject to the decay of age.

The arguments used to buttress each position are long and complex, involving many, many biblical passages and historical positions of church theologians going back almost two thousand years. In his concluding essay written for the book *Three Views on the Millennium and Beyond*, Darrell L. Bock sums up the feelings many seminary students of millennialism have no doubt experienced:

> In the midst of all this complexity, some students will surely despair about the possibility of determining what Scripture says. But debate, complexity, and nuance, which Scripture contains in many areas, are not adequate reasons to avoid the responsibility of coming to an attempted understanding of what it teaches.... We know in part now, and we make our case recognizing that we are trying our best to understand Scripture within the limitations we now possess. One day we will know fully—and more importantly—be fully known. All of us look forward to that wonderful eternity in the beyond when we can rejoice together in a unity about which now we can only dream.

Sources:

Blaising, Craig A. "Premillennialism"; Bock, Darrell L., "Summary Essay"; Gentry, Kenneth L., Jr. "Postmillennialism"; Strimple, Robert B. "Amillennialism." All in *Three Views on the Millennium and Beyond*, ed. Darrell L. Bock. Grand Rapids, MI: Zondervan, 1999.
The Holy Bible, New International Version. Grand Rapids, MI: Zondervan, 1978.

PRE-, POST-, AND MIDTRIBULATIONALISM

The terms *Tribulation* and *Great Tribulation* are now used by evangelical Christians to describe the last years of human history (see Great Tribulation). The Tribulation, in this view, will occupy the seven-year period immediately before the battle of Armageddon. The Great Tribulation will cover the last three and one-half years of that period.

A question of great interest and not a little debate concerns the scheduling of the events surrounding the return of Jesus Christ. Specifically, the argument swirls around the timing of the Rapture (see Rapture). Will it take place before the Tribulation (pretribulationalism), before the Great Tribulation but in the midst of the Tribulation period (midtribulationalism), or after the Tribulation is over (posttribulationalism)?

Those who hold to one of the three schools of thought (fundamentalists and evangelicals all) argue, often vociferously, about which interpretive scheme is correct. From time to time the passions run so deep that those in one camp accuse the others of not even being Christians. All use scriptural texts to justify their belief. All claim that the scriptures are "clear" in favoring their own particular view. All have been known to question how any other view but their own is possible as long as the Bible is read in a simple, straightforward, literal fashion.

The key to understanding the debate is to notice which scriptural texts are emphasized and which are placed in a supporting role. We might as well start with the central doctrines all three schools hold in common:

1. All three positions are premillennial; that is, they all believe that Jesus Christ will return before the Millennium (see Pre- and Postmillennialism).
2. All three believe that before Jesus returns, the Rapture will occur.
3. All three believe that the Bible is to be interpreted literally.

After that, however, the three positions diverge.

Pretribulationalism

Pretribulationalists, by far in the majority today, believe that the Rapture will take place before the Tribulation occurs. As a matter of fact, the Rapture will mark the beginning of the times of trials the earth will sustain. As a result of millions of people suddenly disappearing, the billions left behind will be plunged into confusion and despair. This is the situation that will catapult the antichrist into a position of power. He will use the confusion to attain his own political ends. By causing the powers of the Middle East to come together and sign a treaty bringing peace to the volatile region, he will win the approval of the rest of the world. The signing of that treaty will mark the beginning of the Tribulation.

The scriptural passages that "pretribs," as they are often called, use to justify their viewpoint are the ones most commonly used by those who believe in the Rapture. But 1 Corinthians 15, 1 Thessalonians 4, and 2 Thessalonians 2 are cited by all three schools. The question is this: Given the fact that Revelation, according to all three groups, is to be read literally, where does the Rapture fit into the stream of history described in its pages?

According to pretribs, the exact verse is found at Revelation 4:1. After describing the Church Age in chapters 2 and 3 (see Bible Timelines), the author says, "After this I looked, and there before me was a door standing open in heaven. And the voice … said, 'Come up here.'" This, according to the pretribulational school, describes the Rapture of the church.

Having grasped this basic truth, a lot of other verses can now be seen as buttressing the argument. In Matthew 24, for instance, while talking about the fact that "two men will be in the field; one will be taken and the other left" and "two women will be grinding with a hand mill; one will be taken and the other left," Jesus states unequivocally that "no one knows about that day or hour, not even the angels in heaven, nor the Son, but only the Father."

According to these verses, the time of the Rapture is obviously going to come as a complete surprise to everyone, even Jesus. So it must happen, goes the pretrib argument, before any of the other signs of the end. It has to be the next big event. It marks the end of the current age. All other endtime events have to follow it or it will not be unexpected.

Viewed in that way, the Rapture becomes the central event that marks the beginning of the time of the end.

Midtribulationalism

Midtribs, the small minority of the three schools, are not convinced by this argument. Revelation 4:1 just doesn't sound to them like a Rapture. The apostle Paul, for instance, spoke in 1 Corinthians 15 about "the sound of the trumpet" accompanying the Rapture. Although Revelation 4:1 mentions a "loud voice," it doesn't talk about a trumpet.

The book of Revelation does, however, describe a series of seven trumpets. When each is blown, something happens on the earth. The seventh trumpet could possibly be the "last trumpet." In this sense, it is the "last" in a series, not "last" as in "final," as it is usually referred to at funerals. And it just so happens that when this "last" trumpet is blown in Revelation 11:15, lo and behold, the heavenly choir begins to sing the Hallelujah chorus! Could this be a description of the Rapture? If so, it happens right at the midpoint of the Tribulation. The first three and one-half years, it is to be remembered, are known by peace and prosperity on the earth. The Great Tribulation marks the end of peace and the beginning of war. Perhaps the saints are left on earth to be witnesses to the machinations of the antichrist. Then, when no one pays any more attention to the warning, the church is removed and all hell breaks loose for the last three and a half years of turmoil and strife.

Pretribs counter that the moment the Middle East peace treaty is signed, anyone with a watch and a calendar will be able to count three and one-half years and know the exact moment of the Rapture. What happens to the part about "no man knows the day or the hour?" That refers to sinners, not saints, say the midtribs. God will not keep his people in the dark. Noah was warned in time to prepare an ark. In the same manner, God will warn his people to prepare by giving them the signing of the treaty.

Posttribulationalism

Posttribs don't buy any of this. They think pre- and midtribulationalists simply are hoping to miss all the bad stuff that will happen on earth. God never promised to keep us out of hard times. God just promised to keep us safe through them. Noah, after all, wasn't spared the Flood. He had to endure it. So will we have to endure the trials of the endtimes.

Pretribs counter that Noah represented the future believers who will be converted after the Rapture, during the Tribulation. Enoch represented the true believers and he was taken before the Flood (see Days of Noah).

Posttribs aren't swayed by this argument. To them, the "last trumpet" means just that—it marks the end of everything. Jesus will return to earth with his people who have died, pausing only long enough within the atmosphere of the planet to quickly swoop up those who were converted during the Tribulation period. Otherwise, they say, there would have to be two Raptures, one at the beginning of the

The Reign of Antichrist (after an engraving by Michael Volgemuth in *Liber Chronicarum*, 1493). *Fortean Picture Library.*

Tribulation and another at the end, at the battle of Armageddon. The apostle Paul says very clearly in 2 Thessalonians that "that day will not come until the rebellion occurs and the man of lawlessness is revealed." First antichrist is revealed, then the Rapture.

And so the arguments continue. To follow them all requires a breadth of knowledge of scripture in both testaments. Many, many more passages are brought to bear. In order to defend one's own position one must understand the arguments of the other sides. It is safe to say most believers in the Rapture today are pretribulationalist premillennialists. This is the position taught by popular writers from Hal Lindsey to Tim LaHaye. But some serious scholars disagree, and they are still selling books and preaching sermons.

Source:
The Holy Bible, New International Version. Grand Rapids, MI: Zondervan, 1978.

PRETERIST THEOLOGY

Many evangelical Christians believe that the prophecies of the Bible will be fulfilled at a future date. These belong to the futurist school of biblical interpretation (see Futurist School of Biblical Interpretation). Others, however, believe the authors of scripture were writing about events that would happen in their own time. These belong to the past-historic school. This second theological position is also known as preterist theology. Preterists believe that most of the book of Revelation can be interpreted as having occurred in the events surrounding the destruction of the Temple of Jerusalem in 70 CE and the persecution of the early Christian church, followed by its eventual triumph during the time of Constantine, when it became the state religion of Rome.

Recently, however, a group of people calling themselves "recontructionists" (see Christian Reconstructionism) have taken the idea even further. In its most extreme form their belief is called the "consistent preterist" position or even, by some of its detractors, "hyperpreterism."

What this view puts forth is that every prophecy of the Bible, including the return of Jesus Christ and the battle of Armageddon, has already taken place. Armageddon happened in 70 CE with the destruction of Jerusalem. The "body" of Jesus Christ came back to earth in the form of his true church, the "real" believers. The Millennium is simply the long period since then. We are now living in it. Our bodies are to be considered resurrection bodies because they are filled with the Holy Spirit. Christ, in the form of the church, is gradually transforming the world through the restoration of God's laws and mandates. But Revelation warns that at the end of the Millennium, at the end of this age, Satan will be released "for a short time" (Rev. 21:3). The current world condition proves to consistent preterists that the time of Satan's release may indeed be imminent. They are not waiting, in other words, for the battle of Armageddon. That has already happened. Instead they await the beginning of eternity on earth, that time when the Millennium has already ended.

Source:
Gentry, Kenneth L., Jr. "A Brief Theological Analysis of Hyper-Preterism." http://www. reformed.org/eschaton/gentry_preterism.html.

PROPHECY *see* **Books of the Bible and Their Relation to Prophecy;**
Futurist School of Biblical Interpretation

QUANTUM THEORY

The old standard "As Time Goes By" earned a prominent place in the American song-book due to its popularity following the movie *Casablanca*. The verse is well known, but the chorus, which was not sung in the movie, is less familiar:

> This day and age we're living in
> Gives cause for apprehension
> With speed and new invention
> And things like fourth dimension.
> Yet we get a trifle weary
> With Mr. Einstein's theory.
> So we must get down to earth at times,
> Relax, relieve the tension....
> The fundamental things apply
> As time goes by.
> —"As Time Goes By," words and music by Herman Hupfeld

From the human perspective, it appears as if time is a flowing stream. Each year, season, day, hour, and minute moves on to the next. The perceived "arrow" of time makes it almost inevitable that humans ask questions about when time began and when it will end. Even more difficult to answer are questions of purpose. One of the most difficult inquiries for both scientists and philosophers to handle is the question, "Why is there something rather than nothing?" Such questions are usually left to the theologians. "When" and "how" fall into the arena of the scientist, not "why."

In the field of science, two of the greatest contributions of the early twentieth century—some might even say they are the most important cosmological concepts of all time—were theories attempting to explain the nature of the universe. Implied in both are questions relating to how the universe will end. One is the theory of relativity. The other is the theory of quantum mechanics. The problem is that the two theories, at some points, contradict each other.

The physicist Stephen Hawking, in his book *A Brief History of Time*, makes the claim that "the principal goal of science is to provide a single theory that describes the whole universe." This elusive theory is sometimes called "GUT," for Grand Unification Theory. Such a theory, if it is ever proposed, will have to combine the theory of relativity and quantum mechanics. So far, the general approach has been to divide the search into two areas of study.

The first area involves how the universe changes with time. The assumption is that if changes can be measured in the present, those changes are probably following consistent patterns that will also be in effect in the future. By the same token, those patterns must have been in effect in the past. Thus scientists seek to understand what came before us and what will come after us. The second area of study concerns, in Hawking's words,

> the initial state of the universe. Some people feel that science should be concerned with only the first part; they regard the question of the initial situation as a matter for metaphysics and religion. They would say that God, being omnipotent, could have started the universe off any way he wanted. That may be so, but in that case he also could have made it develop in a completely arbitrary way. Yet it appears that he chose to make it evolve in a very regular way according to certain laws. It therefore seems equally reasonable to suppose that there are also laws governing the initial state.

To study the "initial state" leads naturally to questions about the final conclusion.

Einstein's theory of general relativity, like Newton's theory of gravity before it, describes how the universe operates on a macro scale. But to attempt to describe the very small, the micro scale of the universe, is to enter the strange world of quantum mechanics. Here we encounter a very fundamental problem. Simply stated, it is that we cannot measure and observe at this level without affecting the very thing we are measuring. We can study the sun and the moon and their gravitational effects upon us without changing them at all. They are too big for our small efforts to have any effect. The moon isn't going to alter its orbit because we look at it through a telescope. But what happens when we move to the area of the very small? We can't see anything unless it reflects or emits light. If the thing we are trying to study is itself smaller than the basic component of light, that something will be affected—its activity and position will be changed—by any means we use in an attempt to determine those qualities. The famous Uncertainty Principle first stated by the German physicist Werner Heisenberg sums up the dilemma we face: We cannot accurately determine both the position and the velocity of an object at this level. The more we know about its position, the less certain we can be of its velocity, and vice versa.

Think about light itself. Is it a wave or a particle? The answer depends on how we go about trying to find out. Under some experimental conditions, light behaves exactly like a stream of particles. Under others, it acts just the same as a wave of any other kind. In other words, light is either a wave or a particle depending on how we choose to study it. Our act of selecting a method determines the result of our study. Is light a wave or a particle? It depends on us.

This kind of uncertainty is at the heart of quantum theory. For example, since particles cannot be said to have both a specific position and a specific velocity at the same time, they are said to have a "quantum state." This term might sound comfortably definite, as if it were a single measurable characteristic, but it isn't. The quantum state of a particle or anything else is a matter of probability and possibility. If we are talking only about a particle's position and velocity, its quantum state amounts to all the possible combinations of position and velocity it might possess, as well as the probability for each of these combinations.

Quantum theory puts several new twists on our understanding of the very nature of matter. On one level, everything, including ourselves, appears to consist of solid material moving through space/time. This is the level on which the theories of gravity and relativity operate. It is the level of things we can fairly readily observe and measure. But as we look into the world of the very small, we discover that the very book we are holding in our hands is not solid at all. It is a swirl of protons, electrons, neutrons, and much smaller particles, all in constant motion through what we might think of as nothing, or empty space. In other words, "everything" consists primarily of "nothing," through which the component parts of "something" constantly whirl in endless motion. This is the world of classical atomic thought. Quantum theory takes things a bit farther. At the quantum level, there is really no such thing as empty space. There is only the probability that something exists in a given space. Furthermore, matter can come into existence out of "nothing." (If all this leaves you scratching your head, it may be comforting to remember the words of the physicist Richard Feynman: "If you think you understand quantum mechanics, you don't understand quantum mechanics.")

Armageddon meets quantum mechanics when it comes time to project the method by which the cosmos, at least as we know it, will come to an end. Understanding how things work now on the level of the very small might shed light on how things will eventually end.

Here the theories become curiouser and curiouser.

One possibility is that the constant expansion of the universe will eventually, through the force of gravity, be forced to cave in on itself (see Big Crunch, Big Chill, and Big Rip). This could lead to a strange phenomenon something like the "black holes" that scientists already feel certain exist. A black hole forms when a star collapses in on itself. The forces of gravity are so strong that, for all practical purposes, nothing can escape, not even light. This characteristic makes black holes invisible to the human eye. All scientists can do is deduce their presence by the action of matter being sucked into them. What would happen if such a thing happened on a cosmic scale? It is thought that the speed of contraction of all the matter of the universe would become so great that the momentum of the mass would continue to collapse past the point of nothing and travel through that "nothing" into … what? No one knows. Perhaps, according to some theories, another universe.

Quantum theory opens up even stranger areas of thought than this. For example, the physicist Hugh Everett proposed what is now know as the "many worlds interpretation": "Every time there is a quantum indeterminacy in an atom, the universe splits into multiple branches, in each of which one of the potential outcomes is actualized." This interpretation of quantum theory involves a mind-boggling multiplicity of universes, since each universe would have to split again into many branches during each of the uncountable atomic and subatomic events throughout time and space.

In other words, some physicists believe that quantum mechanics allows the mathematical possibility of there being an infinite number of universes, each with its own beginning and its own ending. This is the thinking that coined the term *multiverse* (*multi* meaning many) as opposed to *universe* (*uni* meaning "one"). It even suggests that the entity we call "I" or "me" exists simultaneously in worlds or dimensions completely beyond our ability to experience.

Or can we experience it? Some people wonder if such phenomena as déjà vu, the feeling of having already experienced something, is evidence of other, parallel universes. We experience something "here," and it feels familiar because we have already experienced it "there." And what about the now-familiar after-death description of seeing "light at the end of the tunnel"? Could this be an actual physical experience of viewing that place where the energy of the mind or consciousness has both its genesis and its conclusion?

Science-fiction writers were quick to jump on the multiverse bandwagon. As Carl Sagan, made famous by his PBS series and book *Cosmos*, pointed out, the possibility of traveling through black holes to other places in space and time opened wonderful areas of speculation. Until recently, such writers could point out that no less an authority than Stephen Hawking, often acknowledged to be among the greatest physicists since Albert Einstein, supported the notion that such multiversal jaunts might be possible.

But in July 2004, Hawking shocked the world of science by reversing a theory he had held for twenty-eight years. Speaking at the 17th International Conference on General Relativity and Gravitation, Hawking said, "I'm sorry to disappoint science fiction fans, but if information is preserved [after entering a black hole], there is no possibility of using black holes to travel to other universes. If you jump into a black hole, your mass energy will be returned to our universe, but in a mangled form, which contains the information about what you were like, but in an unrecognizable state." According to Dr. Hawking, there are no baby universes branching off from our own inside a black hole.

Does this mean that our present universe contains information from previous universes that have succumbed to past cosmic Armageddons? Such speculation begins to move from the realm of science into the realm of religion. At the quantum level it is impossible, given the current state of human knowledge, for us to peer into the strange and mysterious world of forces at the smallest levels of everything we know about. Perhaps this is what the Nobel Prize–winning astronomer Robert Jastrow had in mind when he said, "At this moment it seems as though science will never be able to raise the curtain on the mystery of creation. For the scientist who has lived by his faith in the power of reason, the story ends like a bad dream. He has scaled the mountains of ignorance; he is about to conquer the highest peak; as he pulls himself over the final rock, he is greeted by a band of theologians who have been sitting there for centuries."

Sources:

Barbour, Ian G. *When Science Meets Religion: Enemies, Strangers, or Partners?* New York: Harper-Collins, 2000.

Feynman, Richard, quoted at http://www.darwin.ws/RationallySpeaking/rationally_speaking% 20N1.htm.

Hawking, Stephen W. *A Brief History of Time: From the Big Bang to Black Holes.* New York: Bantam, 1988.

Hogan, Craig J. *The Little Book of the Big Bang: A Cosmic Primer.* New York: Copernicus, 1998.

Jastrow, Robert, quoted at http://www.godandscience.org/love/sld014.html.

Overbye, Dennis. "About Those Fearsome Black Holes? Never Mind." *New York Times,* July 22, 2004.

Sagan, Carl. *Cosmos.* New York: Random House, 1980.

QUETZALCOATL

The story is a popular one, often quoted by both traditional academic historians and New Age philosophers. Jonah Blank, writing in *U.S. News and World Report*, relates a typical version:

> Thirteen years before the millennium, an unusual man appeared on the shores of Mexico's Yucatán Peninsula. He had fair skin, wore his hair exuberantly untrimmed, and (most remarkable to the bare-chinned populace) sported a flowing black beard. In his homeland, legend had it, he had been a prince of peace. He was said to be fully man, yet fully god. His people believed he had died in an act of supreme self-sacrifice and that someday he would come again.
>
> The Maya called the newcomer Kukulkan. The Toltecs, whom he ruled before fate drove him into exile, knew him as Quetzalcoatl. Some of his story is myth, some is history, but what's certain is that the coming of this stranger marked the end of a glorious era for all of Mesoamerica and the beginning of a new world.

The story goes on to tell of how the Maya and Toltec peoples came to disagree and fight with each other. One of the issues of warfare was that Quetzalcoatl abhorred human sacrifice, whereas his enemies made it a staple of their religion. Eventually the final battle was fought. Quetzalcoatl's forces were vanquished.

> [Quetzalcoatl] decreed his own banishment. He set sail across the eastern ocean on a raft made of serpents, vowing that one day he would return....
>
> In a particular year—1519 by the Gregorian calendar—a band of strangers beached their ships after an arduous voyage across the wide ocean. Their leader had fair skin, exuberantly long hair, and (most remarkably to the bare-chinned populace) a flowing black beard. Motecuhzoma Xocoyotzin, later known as Montezuma II, king of the mightiest empire on two continents, reverently opened the doors of his

palace to the conquistador Hernando Cortés. How blessed, he thought, to welcome [Quetzalcoatl] home again at last.

There's only one thing wrong with all this: Almost certainly, it didn't happen that way. It makes for a good story, but the record is not nearly as clear as the tale's familiarity might seem to suggest. As the historian Marcelino Peñuelas writes, "rather than explain the myth, the more or less solid explanations of those who may be called mythophiles, mythophobes, and mythomaniacs add fuel to the fire which produces the halo of its mystery."

In stories such as that of Quetzalcoatl, it is important to remember that history is almost always written by the victors. It is usually edited in such a way so as to ensure that those who triumph will be remembered as heroes who had truth on their side. Numerous written accounts quote the speech Montezuma supposedly gave when he met Cortés and assumed that he was greeting the long-lost Quetzalcoatl. But that speech—the explanation usually given for how a small Spanish army could defeat so great an empire—was not written down until at least a century had passed. It goes without saying that a word-for-word rendition would have been, at best, difficult to remember that long.

As with most myths, however, there may be a kernel of truth beneath the layers of mythology. Quetzalcoatl appears in Toltec legend in so many different divine forms and wrapped in so much arcane religious imagery that it is difficult to separate a historical man, if he ever existed at all, from a mythological god. But many have tried.

Most authorities today agree that *Quetzalcoatl* means "feathered serpent" or "plumed serpent," although Friar Manuel Duarte, writing about 1640, claimed that the word meant "precious twin." His justification was that quetzal feathers (the "plumes" usually pictured as part of Quetzalcoatl's headdress) were valuable, hence, "precious." And *coatl*, in the original language of Nahuatl, is sometimes translated as "twin." Apparently Friar Duarte's reason for translating *Quetzalcoatl* in this fashion was to attempt to tie Christianity to the beginnings of Aztec religion. One of the original twelve apostles of Jesus Christ was a man named Thomas, who in the New Testament gospel accounts is called Thomas Didymus. *Didymus* means "twin" in Greek. Duarte might very well have been trying to imply that the original Quetzalcoatl, supposedly a bearded white man, was one of the twelve disciples.

The idea of the disciples fulfilling their Great Commission to take the gospel into all the world, including Central America, is an entertaining theory. But the evidence for it is, to say the least, rather weak.

As far back as the sixteenth century, some Spanish writers noticed similarities between Aztec religion and biblical traditions. Both traditions have a flood story. They have similar legends concerning a set of original parents. Images of crosses and serpents are frequently found on both sides of the Atlantic. There are even stories, written by Spanish authors and highly suspect because of the tendency for myths to accumulate interpretive additions over the years, of priests wearing white robes who taught the Aztecs a Middle Eastern sense of modesty (this in spite of the fact that the people of Central America preferred to dress according to the dictates of equatorial weather, not Jewish tradition).

Other writers have identified Quetzalcoatl with Europe and the Middle East. The "bearded white man" legend seems to have solid support in terms of sheer volume of references, if not historicity. Account after account makes the claim that the Aztecs, like their Hopi neighbors to the north, were awaiting a white savior from the east. But did these accounts, almost all of which were written by later Spanish scribes, retell actual Aztec myths, or did they merely convey what the Spanish wanted to believe?

The Church of Jesus Christ of Latter-day Saints teaches that Jesus came to the Central America region after the Resurrection. Mormons assert that the people of the Americas were the "sheep of another fold" that Jesus mentioned in John 10:16.

Thor Heyerdahl, the Norwegian leader of the *Kon-Tiki* expedition of 1947, was positive that the Quetzalcoatl legend proved pre-Columbian contact between Europe and Central America. He believed that the legendary white man had sailed west from Europe, then continued his journey across the Pacific after being defeated in battle on the shores of Lake Titicaca. When Heyerdahl sailed west from South America toward Polynesia, he did so with confidence because he believed that Quetzalcoatl had done the same thing centuries before.

Quetzalcoatl, Toltec and Aztec god. *The Bridgeman Art Library/Getty Images.*

All well and good, but what does all this have to do with the end of the world? The problem with the Quetzalcoatl myth is that, as with many other traditions, so much has been added to it over the centuries that it is hard to separate historical truth from myth. One thing is certain: The coming of Cortés marked an Armageddon event for Aztec culture. It signified a new beginning as well. The people of Central America, like many North American Indians (see Indigenous Peoples of the Americas), believed that theirs was one of a cyclical series of worlds, each marked at the end by an Armageddon-like event. Their calendar, still a marvel of accuracy, appears to indicate that this present world will end on the winter solstice of the year 2012. Undoubtedly this will become a point of interest as the date approaches.

Sources:

Berdan, Frances F., ed. *The Aztecs of Central Mexico: An Imperial Society.* New York: Holt, Rinehart & Winston, 1982.

Blank, Jonah. "Myths and Conquests." http://www.keepmedia.com/jsp/article_detail_print.jsp.

Brundage, Burr Cartwright. *The Fifth Sun.* Austin: University of Texas Press, 1979.

Peñuelas, Marcelino. "El Mito, especulaciones sobre su origen e interpretación." *Cuadernos Americanos* 133 (March–April 1964): 89.

R

RAPTURE

Two men will be in the field; one will be taken and the other left. Two women will be grinding with a hand mill; one will be taken and the other left.

    —attributed to Jesus of Nazareth (Matt. 24:40, 41)

Listen, I tell you a mystery: We will not all sleep, but we will all be changed—in a flash, in the twinkling of an eye, at the last trumpet. For the trumpet will sound, the dead will be raised imperishable, and we will be changed.

    —attributed to the apostle Paul (1 Cor. 15:51–52)

For the Lord himself will come down from heaven, with a loud command, with the voice of the archangel and with the trumpet call of God, and the dead in Christ will rise first. After that, we who are still alive and are left will be caught up with them in the clouds to meet the Lord in the air.

    —attributed to the apostle Paul (1 Thess. 4:16–17)

The word *rapture* (from the Latin *rapere*, "to seize forcibly") is not found in the Bible. But during the past century or so, many fundamentalist/evangelical Christians have come to use the term to denote Christ's carrying off his true church from earth to heaven as the endtimes approach.

The early church believed that its founder, Jesus of Nazareth, would return at any moment. But this belief posed a logistical problem. The concepts of death and afterlife were easy enough to understand, but what would happen to the believers who were still alive at Christ's return? Would they have to die before entering the afterlife?

According to the author of Matthew's gospel, Jesus answered that question. He described a situation wherein two people, one apparently a believer and the other not, would be going about their normal business of working in the field. One would suddenly "be taken," while the other was left behind. Two women would be working together grinding wheat. One would "be taken," and the other would not. He followed up this rather startling revelation with a warning that his followers must always be ready. They should not act like an incautious householder who, failing to be on watch, allows a thief to break in and steal his possessions (Matt. 24:42–44). Jesus' casting himself in the guise of a thief in the night (verse 43) must have been shocking to his listeners.

The Physical Problem

The notion of a sudden "taking" of believers has led to all sorts of speculation about the physical details of what will happen if the Rapture occurs. Will a "saved" Christian airplane pilot suddenly disappear, leaving his "unsaved" passengers to perish in a fiery crash? Will utilities go unattended? A popular bumper sticker reads, "WARNING: IN CASE OF RAPTURE, DRIVER WILL DISAPPEAR." Will God allow traffic accidents when drivers suddenly are transported to heaven?

Apparently so—at least according to the fundamentalist pastor and cofounder of the Moral Majority Jerry Falwell:

> What is going to happen on this earth when the rapture occurs? You'll be riding along in an automobile. You'll be the driver, perhaps. You're a Christian. There will be several people in the automobile with you, maybe someone who is not a Christian. When the trumpet sounds, you and the other born-again believers in that automobile will be instantly called away—you will disappear, leaving behind only your clothing, and physical things that cannot inherit eternal life. That unsaved person or persons in the automobile will suddenly be startled to find that the car is moving along without a driver and somewhere crashes. These saved people in the car have disappeared. Other cars on the highway driven by believers will be out of control, and stark pandemonium will occur on that highway and every highway in the world where Christians are called away from the driver's wheel.

A minor but interesting side question arises here. What happens to the clothes a person is wearing? Will they be transformed too? Or, as Falwell thinks, will they be left behind on the ground like so much dirty laundry? This is the scenario pictured in *Left Behind: The Movie*, based on the book *Left Behind*, by Tim LaHaye, the other cofounder of the Moral Majority, and Jerry Jenkins. In the movie and the novel, millions of people simply vanish, leaving piles of clothes as their only epitaph.

Aside from the enigmatic words of Jesus and Paul concerning people disappearing, however, the Bible is silent as to details.

The Theological Problem

There is also a theological problem surrounding the issue of exactly who will be taken. The Christian church has long contained at least two opinions concerning the requirements for entrance into heaven. Those denominations historically influenced by the theology of John Calvin (Presbyterians and early New England Congregationalists, for example) tend to espouse predestination. That is, God decided before the beginning of time who will and who will not enter heaven. Some say that this is simply an arbitrary choice by God. Others say that it is based on whether a person would have chosen to believe had they not been under the influence of original sin. The end result is the same. For whatever reason, those who were chosen have already been determined.

Other denominations (Methodists and most Baptists among them) tend to believe in free will. The individual, upon reaching an age of maturity, makes his or her choice to believe in Jesus Christ. This conscious choice to be "born again" determines the individual's eternity. (What about children who have not yet attained this age of maturity? Clear biblical guidance on the question is notably lacking, but the movie *Tribulation Force*, based on the second book of the *Left Behind* series, reveals its producer's free-will bias by having every child on earth, born into Christian and non-Christian families alike, taken at the time of the Rapture.)

When the doctrine of the Rapture was first expounded in the late nineteenth century, a story began to circulate in some church bulletins that an English clergyman, hearing the pertinent passages interpreted in this literal way rather than in the traditional metaphorical manner, remarked indignantly, "What? My Lord come and *kidnap* someone? Never!"

Jesus followed his story about the unwary householder with a parable about a servant who was put in charge of guarding his master's goods while the master went on a trip. If the servant did well by the rest of the hired help, he would be rewarded when the master returned. But if the servant took advantage of his position to lord it over the rest of the staff, he would be punished by being imprisoned with other hypocrites in a place of "weeping and gnashing of teeth" (Matt. 24:45–51). This story emphasizes a Christian's obligation in the present, balanced by an accounting for his or her actions. It illustrates a moral, ethical approach to religion. When the idea of the Rapture began to be preached in earnest, some traditionalists thought it presented a "hold on till I come" mentality—a kind of victimhood. This didn't set well with them.

The Nature of Resurrected Bodies

The writings attributed to the apostle Paul developed the theological underpinnings of the physical Rapture even further. In response to questions about the resurrection asked by the members of a new church in Corinth, Paul devoted a whole section of a letter to the subject. His explanation was that "flesh and blood" bodies cannot enter heaven. They must be changed into spiritual bodies. The bodies we inhabit on earth are "perishable bodies." The bodies we will inherit in order to live in heaven are "imperishable bodies" (1 Cor. 15:35–44).

To reinforce his case, he stated his doctrine of the first and second Adam. The first Adam, the Adam we read about in Genesis 1 and 2, had a physical body. That was the way things were supposed to be, said Paul. God created humans and declared them to be "very good." But Adam disobeyed God. As the first spelling primer printed in New England had it, "'A' is for Adam. In Adam's fall, we sinned all." Therefore, in the course of time, God sent his son, Jesus, the "second Adam." Born of a woman, his physical body was the same as that of Adam. But Jesus obeyed God's word and was sinless. Thus he fulfilled what the first Adam failed to accomplish (1 Cor. 15:44–49).

After Jesus died and was buried, he was said to have appeared again to his followers. At that time, according to the gospels, his body was different. He seems to have shed the earthly "flesh and blood" body and taken on something different—a spiritual body. This body could appear in different places seemingly instantaneously (Luke 24:13–36). It could walk through walls and appear to disciples who had locked themselves in a closed room (John 20:19–31). This, said Paul, is the kind of body awaiting believers. All those who have died already have such a body and will come back to earth with Jesus when he returns. But the "mystery"—never before revealed until, according to Paul, he wrote it down in 1 Corinthians 15:51—is that believers who are still living when Jesus returns will instantaneously be changed from physical to spiritual without first experiencing death. Since spiritual bodies are apparently not made out of physical atoms, these people's physical bodies will suddenly seem to disappear.

Because of the ambiguous words Paul used about the dead being raised first and the living then being "caught up," Christians have long been divided over the condition or state of those who have died. Some denominations, most notably the Seventh-day Adventists, believe in what they call "soul sleep." According to this view, when people die they simply rest in sleep until resurrection morning. On that future day a trumpet will sound from heaven and all, living and dead alike, will receive new bodies at the same time.

Other denominations, including most of the Baptist traditions, teach that to be "absent from the body is to be present with the Lord," a phrase borrowed from 2 Corinthians 5:8. Imperishable bodies, they say, are given to us shortly after or simultaneous with death. This view pictures Jesus coming back to earth at the front of the multitude of believers who have died. He will pause in the air only long enough to "change," or snatch up, those who are still living to join the throng, and then will reign on earth for a thousand years.

The Old Testament Rapture

If the idea of a rapture were to be found only in the Christian New Testament, it might be considered simply a new teaching by the early church. But the root of the concept first appears in an enigmatic verse in Genesis, the first book of the Hebrew Bible.

Matthew 24:37 has Jesus alluding to this verse when he says, "As it was in the days of Noah, so shall it be at the coming of the Son of Man." He goes on to explain that before the event known today as Noah's flood, people were going about their business, "eating and drinking, marrying and giving in marriage," right up until the floodwaters destroyed all humanity except for Noah and his family, who had prudently built a boat (see Days of Noah). But in Genesis 5, right in the middle of an extended passage recording who of Noah's ancestors begot whom, we come across a man named Enoch. Everyone else in the chapter is said to have lived a certain amount of years, begotten "sons and daughters," and then died. But Enoch is described as being a man who "walked with God" (Gen. 5:22). And then, instead of dying, he "was no more, because God took him away" (Gen. 5:24).

Although we know little about Enoch except that he appeared to be a righteous man and, according to the Bible, was the father of the oldest human being who every lived (his son Methuselah is reported to have lived for 969 years and died the year of Noah's flood), we are left with a strange verse telling us that one day he simply was "taken" by God. He didn't die, as is the case with all the rest of the men listed in this chapter. He "was taken." And this event occurred just before the flood destroyed the rest of humanity.

Evangelical Christian scholars believe that this is an Old Testament foreshadowing of what will happen when God again judges the earth, this time at the end of time. Jesus said that his Second Coming will be *just as* it was "in the days of Noah." In the "days of Noah" the righteous Enoch was "raptured," removed from earth before the judgment. So it will be with the modern "Enochs," the ones who "walk with God" at the time of the end.

The New Testament Rapture

There is another argument that many evangelical Christians offer for the necessity of the Rapture. This view is steeped in the tradition of the doctrine of the third person of the Trinity.

The church began, according to the second chapter of the New Testament book of Acts, on the day of Pentecost, a Jewish holiday (see Bible Timelines). The Holy Spirit came with "a sound like the blowing of a violent wind" (verse 2), entering into the disciples and giving them miraculous gifts of ministry. From that time on, they were able to speak in other tongues, heal the sick, minister grace, and do all the things the church has supposedly been doing ever since. The "Church Age" had begun.

Someday the Church Age will have to end, signifying the end of time. Jesus, however, promised that he would be with his church forever, "even unto the end of the age" (Matt. 28:20). God can't very well withdraw the Spirit from believers who have received him, because that would break Jesus' promise. So if the Spirit is recalled, those whom the Spirit indwells have to go as well. If the sending of the Holy Spirit marked the beginning of the age of the Christian church, the recall of the Holy Spirit marks its end. The age of Christianity thus becomes a giant parenthesis in history, beginning with Pentecost, ending with the Rapture.

The Timing of the Rapture

One problem still remains for evangelicals. It is the subject of considerable debate and even rancor among them. When will all this take place? When in human history will the Rapture occur? Where does it fit in to the pattern of events that will occur at the time of the end?

Three schools of thought have developed. Because of their complexities of argument, they are treated in separate entries. (See Pre-, Post-, and Midtribulationism; Rapture.)

Sources:

LaHaye, Tim, and Jerry B. Jenkins. *Left Behind* series. 12 vols. Carol Stream, IL: Tyndale House, 1995–2004.

Lindsey, Hal. *Apocalypse Code.* Palos Verdes, CA: Western Front Ltd., 1997.

Lindsey, Hal, with C. C. Carlson. *The Late Great Planet Earth.* Grand Rapids, MI: Zondervan, 1970.

The Holy Bible, New International Version. Grand Rapids, MI: Zondervan Bible Publishers, 1978.

RAPTURE INDEX

How close are we to the Rapture (see Rapture)? Is there a systematic way of determining the "signs of the times?"

Todd Strandberg and Terry James seem to think there is. They have created a Web site called *Rapture Ready* that attempts to give numerical values to current events. Oil prices, activities in Russia, droughts and famines, arms proliferation, cult activities, and about forty other topics are monitored and given scores from 1 to 5, depending on how prevalent they are in the media. Then the scores are added up to determine where we are according to their interpretation of the prophetic calendar. A score of 85 or less indicates slow prophetic activity, 85 to 110 is considered moderate, and 110 to 145 is heavy. Anything over 145 falls into the category they call "Fasten your seat belts."

So far the highest score, 182, occurred on September 24, 2001. The record low was back in 1993. The year 2004 ranged from 135 to 157.

All this quantifying and numbers crunching might have remained innocent fun known to relatively few people had not Bill Moyers of PBS fame brought it to the attention of the world in an acceptance speech he delivered during ceremonies held at Harvard University when he was awarded the Harvard Medical School's Global Environment Citizen Award. Moyers pointed out that when political ideology is married to religious theology in a powerful way within the halls of Washington, D.C., "their offspring are not always bad but they are always blind. And there is the danger: voters and politicians alike, oblivious to the facts."

He reminded his audience of the words of James Watt, President Reagan's first secretary of the interior: "After the last tree is felled, Christ will come back."

Remembering those words, Moyers went on to say: "In the past election several million good and decent citizens went to the polls believing in the rapture index. That's right—the rapture index." After explaining the index and where to find it on the Internet, Moyers said: "I'm not making this up…. I've read the literature. I've reported on these people, following some of them from Texas to the West Bank. They are sincere, serious, and polite…the invasion of Iraq was for them a warm-up act, predicted in the Book of Revelation…a war with Islam in the Middle East is not something to be feared but welcomed—an essential conflagration on the road to redemption."

Moyers pointed out that Democrats as well as Republicans had their share of Christian believers who followed the rapture index. Senator Zell Miller of Georgia, for instance, received a 100-percent rating from the Christian Coalition and, from the Senate floor, quoted the following words from the prophet Amos: "The days will come, sayeth the Lord God, that I will send a famine in the land."

According to Moyers, "He seemed to be relishing the thought."

Sources:
Moyers, Bill. "On Receiving the Harvard Medical School's Global Environment Citizen Award." http://www.commondreams.org/views04/1206-10htm.
Strandberg, Todd. "The Rapture Index." http://www.raptureready.com/rap2.html.

REAGAN, RONALD

There are many prophecies made in ancient times in the Bible which speak of the kind of destruction that will be wrought upon the earth in the last great war before Jesus comes back. And they are perfect descriptions of a nuclear war.
—Hal Lindsey, *The Late Great Planet Earth*

When these words were published in 1970, many fundamentalist/evangelical Christians voiced a hearty "Amen!" The book climbed to the top of best-seller lists and remained there for months.

One influential American who read the book, discussed it with friends, and quoted it at length on numerous public occasions was an actor who went on to become the governor of California and then president of the United States. His name was Ronald Reagan.

President Reagan shared close friendships with some of the most prominent fundamentalist/evangelical leaders in the nation. All of them offered praise for *The Late Great Planet Earth*, some going so far as to offer it for sale through their various ministries and media outlets. Soon questions began to circulate among political leaders and liberal Christian theologians concerning the influence this book might have on world events. Lindsey claimed that the Soviet Union would play a major role in the final battle of Armageddon (see Armageddon, Battle of). He was convinced that the word *Rosh* (see Rosh) in Ezekiel 38 and 39 (see Ezekiel) refers to Russia and describes a nuclear exchange that will take place just before the final war and the return of Jesus Christ.

Apparently Reagan concurred. During an interview with Thomas Dine, then executive director of the American Israel Public Affairs Committee, Reagan said, "I turn back to your prophets in the Old Testament and the signs foretelling Armageddon, and I find myself wondering if we are not the generation that is going to see that come about. I don't know if you have noted any of the prophets lately, but, believe me, they describe the times we are going through."

According to Reagan's biography *Reagan Inside Out*, issued during his 1984 campaign, Herbert Ellingwood, a longtime confidant and legal adviser to Reagan, discussed the Bible at prayer meeting with the chairman of the Joint Chiefs of Staff and the chief of naval operations. Ellingwood was quoted as saying that Reagan "was familiar with some of the books that were in this area; for example, *The Late Great Planet Earth*, by Hal Lindsey, which was a book that he had read. I've given him a lot of books and *The Late Great Planet Earth* was one which has been repeatedly discussed."

Ronald Reagan during his presidency. *Library of Congress.*

James Robison, a fundamentalist minister, opened the 1984 Republican National Convention with prayer. In a sermon distributed through his national ministry, Robison wrote, "There will be no peace until Jesus comes! That is what the Anti-Christ promises. Any teaching of peace prior to his return is heresy. It is against the word of God—it is anti-Christ!"

In March 1981 Reagan arranged for Jerry Falwell, a leading fundamentalist spokesman and co-chair of the Moral Majority, to meet with the National Security Council in order to discuss the Soviet Union.

In 1980 George Otis, the honorary chairman of Christians for Reagan and a longtime friend of Reagan's, said that the president-to-be "does recognize the fact that this nation has a unique opportunity to have an influence upon the coming of the Kingdom Age. It is clear that this is in the forefront of his mind." Otis added, "Ronald Reagan indeed is very conscious of the fact that the Bible speaks of Armageddon. Ronald Reagan seems to be very cognizant of the Scriptures particularly as contained in Ezekiel: 38 and 39, involving that group of nations such as Persia and modern Iran, and Libya, and of course Israel, and Assyria (what had been Assyria then) and the linkage somewhere downstream to Russia." The political operative Doug Wead quotes Reagan as saying, "We may be the generation that sees Armageddon." According to the reporter Bob Scheer, Reagan told Jerry Falwell, "Jerry, we are heading very fast for Armageddon right now." In an address to students at Harvard University, Reagan's secretary of defense Caspar Weinberger said, "I have read the book of Revelation, and, yes, I believe the world is going to end—by an act of God, I hope—and every day I think that time is running out."

There is no direct evidence that Ronald Reagan pursued the downfall of the Soviet Union because of his religious beliefs. There is no direct evidence that he sought to change world history because of his reading of biblical prophecy. But questions arising from anecdotal evidence and conversations, even casual ones, deserve to be raised and answered. Can world leaders be influenced by their theology to seek what they see as a predetermined path, thus bringing about self-fulfilled prophecy? People, including liberal Christians, who do not accept the Bible as a divine road map of future events feel that they have a right to know—especially when the leader in question has his finger on the nuclear trigger.

In 1960 the theology of president-elect John F. Kennedy was called into question regarding his church's teachings concerning abortion and birth control. Because the Roman Catholic Church, of which Kennedy was a communicant member, opposed both of these things as a matter of church doctrine, some people asked if Kennedy would be influenced to appoint Supreme Court justices who agreed with his church. They also wondered if it would be proper for a sitting president to acknowledge the supremacy of a foreign religious leader whose rule often extended into the political realm.

In the same vein, Presidents Carter, Clinton, and George W. Bush all claim the label "evangelical." All have read *The Late Great Planet Earth* and are no doubt familiar with Lindsey's theories concerning modern nations in prophecy. Was President Reagan's pursuit of the downfall of the Soviet Union in part due to his understanding of the part Russia might play in the final days of history? How big a role did biblical prophecy play in his world view and vision for the future?

The question remains unanswered.

Sources:
"Armageddon Theology and Presidential Decision-Making: Religious Leaders' Concern." Transcript of a Press Conference for Religious Issues '84, in Association with Conference on the Fate of the Earth and Washington Research Center. San Francisco, 1984. http://www.rumormillnews.com/ARMAGEDDON%20THEOLOGY.htm.
Fackre, Gabriel. *The Religious Right and Christian Faith*. Grand Rapids, MI: Eerdmans, 1982.

RED SHIFT

As a train moves rapidly past an observer and then away, the sound of its whistle lowers in pitch. This familiar phenomenon, called the "Doppler effect," has long been known to result from the lengthening of sound waves as their source recedes.

The same phenomenon exists in the world of light waves. When a light source is rapidly receding from an observer, the light shifts toward the red end—the longer-wave end—of the spectrum. Logically enough, this phenomenon is called the "red shift."

In the early twentieth century, the American astronomer Vesto Slipher established that stellar objects then known as "nebulae" exhibited red shift, indicating that they were moving away from the earth. At the time, nebulae were thought to be part of the Milky Way, since that was the only galaxy known to exist. In the 1920s another American, Edwin Hubble (for whom the Hubble Space Telescope was named), demonstrated that the so-called nebulae were in fact separate galaxies. Hubble soon showed that these galaxies' red shifts indicated that they were receding not only from our own galaxy, but also from one another. Perhaps just as surprising, the more distant they were, the faster they were receding. (The principal exception is the nearby Andromeda Galaxy, which is actually coming nearer to the Milky Way because of mutual gravitational attraction.) In other words, the universe seemed to be expanding outward, much like a balloon being filled with air.

In 1948 the Russian-born physicist George Gamow made the next logical conclusion. If the universe was expanding, he reasoned, with all galaxies moving away from one another, it follows that the process, when played backward, so to speak, would inevitably lead to the conclusion that the whole thing was once concentrated at a single point in time and space.

The renowned American astronomer Fred Hoyle, when confronted by this idea, derisively dubbed it the "Big Bang" theory (see Big Bang). The term caught on and is still used today.

In the 1960s, Arno Penzias and Robert Wilson were plagued by noise in an AT&T Bell Laboratory antenna. Assuming that they were hearing local interference, perhaps even birds nesting in the wires, they tried everything they could think of to get rid of it, but to no avail. As a last resort they called an astrophysicist at Princeton University. Unknown to Penzias and Wilson, he and his colleagues had been having the same problem with their equipment. He was able to tell them what he thought was causing the problem, but after hanging up the phone he turned to his associates and said, "We've been scooped!" Penzias and Wilson quickly discovered they had been tuning in to the background radiation left over from the initial Big Bang at the beginning of space/time. They were awarded the Nobel Prize for their discovery.

Knowing what happened at the birth of the cosmos inevitably leads to wondering what will happen at its end. If the universe is expanding, the two most logical explanations as to what will bring down its final curtain are that it will either continue to expand into nothingness or will someday contract and collapse inward upon itself (see Big Crunch, Big Chill, and Big Rip). Either scenario sends a chilling conclusion. Will there be a cosmic Armageddon? Is the universe destined eventually to come to an end?

The discoveries and theories of Slipher, Hubble, and Gamow opened a scientific debate that will no doubt continue long into the future.

Sources:
Hawking, Stephen W. *A Brief History of Time: From the Big Bang to Black Holes*. New York: Bantam, 1988.
Hogan, Craig J. *The Little Book of the Big Bang: A Cosmic Primer*. New York: Copernicus, 1998.

REFORMATION, PROTESTANT

Modern evangelical views of millennialism, including the futurist school of biblical interpretation (see Millennialism; Futurist School of Biblical Interpretation), are a product of relatively recent conservative Protestant Christianity.

Traditional Catholic belief is that the Millennium is simply the long period of time bracketed by the first and second advents of Jesus Christ. The church is considered to be an expression of the body of Christ on earth during this time. In other words, we now live in the Millennium. The final judgment awaits, but not in the form predicted by conservative Protestants (see Roman Catholic View of History).

The story of how modern Protestant millennialism came about is a complex one, arising from a series of theological disputes.

During the final centuries of Rome's existence, Christianity became the state religion of most of the Western world. Perhaps Edward Gibbon, in his monumental *His-*

tory of the *Decline and Fall of the Roman Empire*, said it best: "While that great body [Rome] was invaded by open violence, or undermined by slow decay, a pure and humble religion gently insinuated itself into the minds of men, grew up in silence and obscurity, derived new vigour from opposition, and finally erected the triumphant banner of the Cross on the ruins of the Capitol."

With Saxons, Vikings, Visigoths, and Franks nibbling away at the borders and Attila the Hun, the "Scourge of God," eyeing Rome itself, the empire fell apart. But the church, for all its faults and power struggles, served as glue to hold together at least a semblance of order. Schools existed within the arms of the church. The church provided education and a social framework of common thought that brought some sense of meaning to the collapse of what was considered to be God's handiwork—the empire that had blessed the church and made it a world power. Faulty, fallible, and flawed though it was, the church was still there when the lights, one by one, began to come on again as the Middle Ages, the "Dark Ages," finally came to a close.

By the end of the fifteenth century, reform movements were abroad. Columbus had "sailed the ocean blue" and discovered new worlds. The feudal system was coming to an end. Gutenberg's printing press was spewing forth

Martin Luther (1483–1546), who ignited the Protestant Reformation. *Library of Congress.*

ideas brought to the West by Byzantine scholars fleeing the Muslim invasion of Constantinople. The wisdom of ancient Greece had been rediscovered. People were chafing at the bit and felt that the institutional church needed reforming from its traditional ways. Sometimes there were two popes, even three, claiming power. Intrigue ran amok at the highest levels of church hierarchy. Souls were up for sale to the highest bidder. The Dominican friar Johann Tetzel would ride into town to raise money for a new cathedral singing, "As soon as a coin in the coffer rings, a soul from Purgatory springs!"

The religious, intellectual forest was dry and ready to burn. Only a spark was needed. That spark fell into dry tinder on October 31, 1517. An obscure German monk named Martin Luther had been struggling with the idea of what the apostle Paul called "justification by faith." How does justification take place? Although he had been taught that the phrase meant that God delivers justice to sinners by punishing them, Luther came to the conclusion that the righteousness he sought was a gift, given freely not only to those who had faith enough to receive it, but to all those upon whom God wished to bestow it. Luther was later moved to write that when he first had this idea, "I felt that I had been born anew and that the gates of heaven had been opened. The whole of Scripture gained a new meaning. And from that point on the phrase 'the justice of God' no longer filled me with hatred, but rather became unspeakably sweet by virtue of a great love."

Compiling a list of ninety-five theses about which he wanted to debate the established church, Luther nailed it to the door of the castle church in Wittenberg, Germany. Little did he understand what commotion he would cause. The world has never recovered. Challenge followed challenge, debate followed debate. The levels of both heat and light rose as Luther's ideas caught the public's attention.

Things came to a head at a church meeting called a "Diet of the Empire," held in the town of Worms in 1521. Luther wasn't the only item on the menu. There was plenty of backstage political maneuvering going on. But at least the world will forever be treated to the wonderful thought that Protestantism began with a "Diet of Worms." For there, when confronted and told he was challenging the entire established order of the universe and all conceivable suburbs, Luther stood alone and cried, "My conscience is a prisoner of God's Word. I cannot and will not recant, for to disobey one's conscience is neither just nor safe. Here I stand. God help me. Amen."

He left the assembly, never to return. His followers formed their own church. And others left them to start others. Disagreements caused still others to do the same. Anabaptists and Mennonites broke fellowship with Lutherans and Calvinists. And on … and on … and on. They weren't called "Protesters" for nothing.

It is intriguing to study Luther's ninety-five theses because, considering the amount of reform the Catholic Church has undergone in the last few hundred years, it is conceivable that if Martin Luther were alive today, he would still be Catholic. His ideas concerning the last days, however, would not be accepted by most fundamentalist/evangelical Christians today, even the ones who call themselves Lutherans. (For example, by the end of Luther's life he was referring to the pope as the antichrist.) He believed that the duty of those who protested the Catholic Church was to bring the church back to its original intent. In that regard, his theology was Augustinian (see Roman Catholic View of History), much the same as that of traditional Catholicism.

What changed millennial belief in America and helped polarize Protestant Christianity into fundamentalists and liberals was a jury trial held in Tennessee in the spring of 1925.

John Scopes was a high school science teacher accused of breaking a new state law forbidding the teaching of evolution. Clarence Darrow, who faced the flamboyant prosecutor William Jennings Bryan, defended him. Scopes lost and was fined one hundred dollars (although the conviction was later overturned on technical grounds). Biblical creationism, not evolution, was thenceforth to be taught in the Tennessee school system. But the trial polarized Americans, many of whom thought the fundamentalist witnesses looked old-fashioned and foolish. As far as public education was concerned, the liberals lost the battle but eventually won the war. The fundamentalist/modernist controversy, however, is still with us.

At issue is biblical interpretation. Is the Bible to be read literally or metaphorically? Does prophecy foretell the future or offer a window into the times of the original author? This is the central issue polarizing Christianity.

Fundamentalists have developed an entire tradition of preaching, teaching, and singing based on a historical, literal interpretation. The "old-time religion" of conservative Christianity, updated and redefined as evangelicalism (see Evangelicalism), is the fastest-growing religion in the world today, with television stations featuring *The 700 Club, The PTL [Praise the Lord] Club*, and the numerous preachers showcased on TBN (Trinity Broadcasting Network). The popular Bill Gaither "Homecoming" gospel music concert series, held in big-venue halls and stadiums, attracts thousands of people to each show. Conservatives have organized politically into groups such as the Christian Coalition, with enough clout to field presidential candidates such as Pat Robertson. Tim LaHaye's *Left Behind* series of novels tops the fiction charts at booksellers' conventions.

Conservative Christians belong to every denomination. They may be called evangelicals, charismatics, pentecostals, or fundamentalists. But there are traditional, or conservative, Lutherans, Presbyterians, Methodists, and Catholics as well as Baptists and Seventh-day Adventists. The hymns may be different and worship traditions vary, but generally, within the framework of their tradition, conservatives read much of the Bible as they would a historical textbook (see Futurist School of Biblical Interpretation).

Liberals belong to every denomination as well. Although they read the same Bible, they see it through totally different eyes.

The Protestant Reformation was not a unified movement resulting in a homogenous blend of uniform thought concerning Armageddon, differing from the Catholic position. In the beginning, little changed at all. But contemporary debate over the meaning of Armageddon may almost be called a second Protestant Reformation. It is that divisive. Liberal and conservative Protestants disagree with each other as much as the Protestants and Catholics of the sixteenth century. Name-calling abounds.

Now, as then, arguments often generate more heat than light.

Sources:
Gonzalez, Justo L. *The Story of Christianity*. 2 vols. New York: Harper & Row, 1985.
Willis, Jim. *The Religion Book: Places, Prophets, Saints, and Seers*. Detroit: Visible Ink Press, 2004.

RESURRECTION, THE

The five largest religions existing today, Hinduism, Buddhism, Judaism, Christianity, and Islam, are often referred to as "world" religions. Four of them are also called "founder" religions because they trace their beginnings to a single founder—Buddha, Abraham (or Moses), Jesus, and Muhammad. Of these four, only one, Christianity, makes the claim that its founder was divine. A central component of most Christian doctrine is that the historic Jesus Christ of Nazareth was somehow God. He was born to reconcile humans with divinity and was crucified for his convictions and to atone for sin. His death was not in vain, because he rose from the grave.

On this last point, however, Christianity is deeply divided. Some say that the Resurrection was a bodily resurrection. Others regard it as spiritual. In either case, historic Christianity tends to view the Resurrection in terms of "Coming Events." In other words, what happened to Jesus will happen to all who believe in him (see Christian Resurrection).

The Resurrection of Christ; woodcut after an image from a sixteenth-century ballad sheet. *Fortean Picture Library.*

But the resurrection of Jesus was in one great sense different from the general resurrection of all believers. After his resurrection Jesus commanded his followers, "Go and make disciples of all nations" (Matt. 28:19). They were to keep a commemorative meal called Communion, the Lord's Supper, the Last Supper, or Holy Eucharist "until he comes again" (1 Cor. 11:26). The words "until he comes again" are the key. According to traditional Christian doctrine, Jesus will return "in the same way you have seen him go into Heaven" (Acts 1:11). The events surrounding that return are interpreted in many different ways, and these differing interpretations constitute the various schools of thought concerning Armageddon and the end of days.

Source:
The Holy Bible, New International Version. Grand Rapids, MI: Zondervan, 1978.

REVELATION
(See also Apocalyptic Writing)

The last book of the Bible gets its name from its opening words: "The revelation of Jesus Christ, which God gave him to show his servants what must soon take place." It is an example of apocalyptic writing that has intrigued, mystified, and baffled readers right from the start. More than nineteen centuries after its creation, it remains the most famous single source of popular speculation concerning the end of the world.

The author of the Revelation introduced terms such as *Armageddon, antichrist, Millennium,* and *Four Horsemen of the Apocalypse* into modern vocabulary. He was the first to link the serpent of the Garden of Eden (Gen. 3) with "that ancient serpent called the devil, or Satan, who leads the whole world astray" (Rev. 12:9). He is the biblical writer who most fully describes events that are today called the battle of Armageddon and the Second Coming (see Armageddon, Battle of; Second Coming).

When the committee that put the Bible together in 200 CE gathered to decide what books would pass muster, they were divided over whether Revelation should be included. Not until 393 at the Council of Hippo did the book finally get a majority vote. Still, not everyone was persuaded. A fourth-century church father known as Cyril of Jerusalem decreed that Revelation was not to be read in public or studied in private, and he completely left it out of his version of the Bible. The book was also at the center of a debate between the Roman Catholic Church and the Eastern Orthodox Church, which didn't accept it into the Bible until 810 CE, and then only reluctantly. As late as the sixteenth century, Martin Luther, the man who was at the forefront of the Protestant Reformation, wondered whether Revelation should be considered inspired scripture. In a story from his time that may or may not be factual, he is supposed to have emerged from his study after a lengthy session with the book and complained in exasperation to a student, "A revelation is supposed to *reveal* something!" He finally consented to include it in his own German translation of scripture, but only after remarking that he would rather have seen it tossed into the Elbe River. His contemporaries in the new Protestant movement had similar views. Ulrich Zwingli threw it out, and John Calvin simply ignored it, although he wrote commentaries on every other New Testament book.

So from the very beginning, the final book of the Bible has caused controversy. It still does. Today it is at the heart of a disagreement dividing the Christian church. Christians no longer argue about whether it should be included in the Bible. That issue has been long settled. The central problem today is one of interpretation. Should Revelation be read as yet-unfulfilled prophecy? Does it tell the future? Or should it be read as the coded words of people concerned with talking about their own times in language the authorities wouldn't be able to use against them?

Interpretation Systems

The modern controversy, which had been simmering in the Christian kettle for centuries, caught the public's attention in 1970 with the publication of Hal Lindsey's *Late Great Planet Earth*. He took the view that the Revelation was written by a first-century fisherman, the apostle John, who also wrote the gospel of John and the letters called First, Second, and Third John in the New Testament. In 1997 Lindsey's book *Apocalypse Code* expanded his thesis. In this account John the Apostle was transported from his time into the future. According to Lindsey, that future was the present day, or at least the early twenty-first century, and John saw things that he didn't have the vocabulary to describe:

> Supersonic jet aircraft with missiles, hyperspeed cannons, guided bombs, advanced attack helicopters, modern battle tanks, intercontinental ballistic missiles with Multiple Independently Targeted Reentry Vehicles tipped with thermonuclear warheads (ICBMs that are MIRVed), battlefield artillery and missiles with neutron-nuclear warheads, biological and chemical weapons, aircraft carriers, missile cruisers, nuclear submarines, laser weapons, space stations and satellites, the new HAARP weapon system (High-frequency Active Auroral Research Program) that can change weather patterns over whole continents, jam global communications systems, disrupt mental processes, manipulate the earth's upper atmosphere, etc.

Now, this is only a partial list.

In short, Revelation is difficult to understand because its first-century author simply had no words to describe twenty-first century technology. This explanation is representative of the view sometimes called "millennialist" because it places the events of Revelation before the final millennial reign of Jesus Christ (see Millennialism). Most scholars prefer to call this school of interpretation "futurist" because of its belief that the events described in the book will happen in the future. This position has been so popularized by Lindsey, Tim LaHaye and Jerry Jenkins, and others of the religious right that people can be forgiven if they think that it is *the* Christian position concerning Revelation.

In fact there is another view accepted by a large number, probably even a majority, of mainline Christian scholars teaching in seminaries today. It is the view that Revelation was written for those Christians who were contemporaries of its author. When Revelation talks about Rome, for instance, or more properly the "woman" who sits "on seven hills" (17:9), followers of this interpretation say that it is not talking about a "Rome" (the city that even today is said to "sit on seven hills") that will arise at the end of time. It is talking about the very real Rome that was back then persecuting Christians. When the author talks about the Messiah coming back

The Four Horsemen of the Apocalypse. *Fortean Picture Library.*

to earth on a white horse (19:11), he doesn't mean that Jesus will someday arrive like a modern-day Wyatt Earp riding in to clean up Dodge City. He is using metaphorical language to give hope to a suffering community.

Similarly, at the time Revelation was written, it was a rather common practice to use gematria, a kind of code based on assigning a number to each letter of the alphabet. Using rules current at the time of the writing, and sticking to the Greek language in which Revelation was written, the number 666 decodes into "Caesar Nero." Nero was the first caesar to persecute Christians. So there is no reason to search around today for antichrists with associations to this supposedly mystical number (see Antichrist; 666); the author was simply referring to Nero.

Raymond Brown, writing in his *Introduction to the New Testament*, comments that "Revelation is widely popular for the wrong reasons.… A great number of people read it as a guide to how the world will end, assuming that the author was given by Christ detailed knowledge of the future that he communicated in coded symbolism." Marcus Borg, author of *Reading the Bible Again for the First Time: Taking the Bible Seriously but Not Literally*, would agree with Brown's dismissal of futurist assumptions. Borg summarizes the past-historic alternative:

The past-historical reading, which grows out of the belief that we understand the message of Revelation only by setting the text in the *historical context* in which it was written, emphasizes what Revelation would have meant *in the past*. In this reading, Revelation tells us what the author believed would happen in his time. This approach takes seriously that the visions of Revelation are found in a letter addressed to specific Christian communities in Asia Minor late in the first century. As such, the text was meant to be a message to *them*, not a message to people thousands of years later.

The past-historic position held by Borg and many other scholars makes a significant point. If the futurist position is correct, then (in Borg's words), "Though John wrote the … apocalypse to a specific audience, its message could not have been intended for them." To write a letter that has no hope of being understood by its recipients seems a strange thing for God to do.

Followers of the past-historic school believe that Revelation is a retelling of the ancient "myth of cosmic combat" told by every culture from the Egyptians and Hebrews to the Zoroastrians and Hopi. It's good against evil, God and the devil, Ahura Mazda versus Ahriman. It's the myth reenacted in modern "good guy/bad guy" made-for-television wrestling matches. It tells a story meant to answer the eternal human question of why bad things happen to good people, so that good people, while experiencing bad things, can have hope that good will triumph in the end. The rider on the white horse (or Clint Eastwood on a pale horse), the tenth avatar of Vishnu, or the *Return of the King* will eventually set things straight.

Keeping these two interpretations in mind, we can proceed to a summary of what Revelation actually says.

Content

The first chapter of Revelation is a prologue. John, the author, claims to have been "in the Spirit" on "the Lord's Day" (1:10) when he heard a voice telling him, "Write on a scroll what you see and send it to the seven churches" (1:11). (See Bible Timelines for a detailed account of the seven churches.) He claims that what he saw is a vision "which God gave him to show his servants what must soon take place" (1:1).

The chapter is a study in significant numbers. It talks about "the seven spirits before [God's] throne" in verse 4. It describes Jesus Christ with a threefold description in verse 5 and "someone 'like a son of man'" with a sevenfold description in verses 14–16. The message of the book is summarized in another threefold phrase. John is told to write "what you have seen, what is now, and what will take place later" (verse 19).

This pattern of threes and sevens is repeated throughout the book.

The second and third chapters contain the text of letters written to seven churches, situated roughly in the geographic pattern of a circle. (An analysis of the content of these letters is treated in depth in the entry called Bible Timelines.) Each letter consists of an introduction, an evaluation of the particular church, either a condemnation or an encouragement, and a promise.

The Opening of the Sixth Seal (Francis Danby, 1855). *Fortean Picture Library.*

In chapters 4 and 5, John claims to have been taken to heaven and placed in a position where he could look down upon the earth in order to see the events that next transpire there. This material forms the bulk of the modern interpretive controversy and is found in chapters 6 through 22.

Three visions, or judgments, each containing seven sections, are described in typical apocalyptic language (see Apocalyptic Writing). The first vision is of seven seals fastened upon a scroll that seems to contain judgments about to be released upon the earth. As each seal is opened in heaven, something happens on earth. The second vision concerns the blowing of seven trumpets. Again, at the sound of each trumpet, events happen on earth. The final vision is of seven "bowls of God's wrath" emptied unto the earth. In each series—after the sixth seal, the sixth trumpet and the sixth bowl—a "meanwhile, back at the ranch" segment returns the reader to heaven to see what is happening there while judgments are being unleashed on the earth.

An overview of these chapters looks like this:

The Seven Seals (6:1–8:5)

1. A white horse appears whose rider carries a bow (but with no mention of an arrow). He wears a crown and rides as "a conqueror bent on conquest."

2. A red horse appears whose rider has "power to take peace from the earth."

3. A black rider appears whose rider holds "a pair of scales in his hand." A voice cries out, "A quart of wheat for a day's wages, and three quarts of barley for a day's wages, and do not damage the oil and the wine!"

4. A pale horse appears whose rider is named "Death, and Hades was following close behind him."

(These are the famous Four Horsemen of the Apocalypse.)

5. At the opening of this seal, those who have died as a result of the "testimony they had maintained" are heard to call out, "How long, Sovereign Lord … until you judge the inhabitants of the earth and avenge our blood?" They are given "white robes" and "told to wait a little longer."

6. A "great earthquake" takes place, the sun turns black, and the moon turns blood red. The sky rolls up "like a scroll" and mountains and islands are "removed from [their] place."

(*Parenthesis in heaven*: 144,000 Jews are "sealed," 12,000 from each of the twelve tribes of Israel. A "great multitude that no one could count, from every nation, tribe, people and language" appear in heaven, "holding palm branches in their hands." They sing a great hymn of praise to God and are joined by "all the angels standing around the throne.")

7. As the seventh seal is opened, there is "a great silence in heaven."

The Seven Trumpets (8:6–11:9)

1. Hail and fire rain down upon the earth.

2. "Something like a great mountain, all ablaze, " is "thrown into the sea."

3. "A great star, blazing like a torch," falls from the sky, and "a third of the waters" turn bitter. "The name of the star is Wormwood."

4. A third of the light from the sun, moon, and stars turns dark.

(Trumpets 5–7 are described by a flying angel as "woes" about to befall the inhabitants of earth.)

5. A "star" falls from heaven and is given "the key to the shaft of the Abyss." When he (it is usually assumed the "star" is a fallen angel) opens the Abyss, smoke pours out and an army looking like "locusts" comes forth. They have "hair like women's hair," "teeth like lion's teeth," and "breastplates of iron." The sound of their wings is "like the thundering of many horses." They have "tails and stings like scorpions," and they torment people "for five months." They are led by a king "whose name in Hebrew is Abaddon, and in Greek, Apollyon."

6. Four angels are released who have been "bound at the great river Euphrates" and "kept ready for this very hour and day and month and year to kill a third of mankind." An army of 200 million "mounted troops" materializes to help carry out this task. These troops are riding on horses whose heads "resembled the heads of lions, and out of their mouths came fire, smoke and sulfur."

Although a "third of mankind" is killed, the survivors still do not "repent of their murders, their magic arts, their sexual immorality or their thefts."

(*Parenthesis*: An angel comes down from heaven, places one foot on the sea and the other on the land, and shouts with the sound of "seven thunders." The content of his message is "sealed up." John is told "not to write it down." Instead, he is to "eat" a scroll the angel holds in his hand. It tastes "as sweet as honey" but turns his stomach sour. Two "witnesses" then appear on earth who "have power to shut up the sky so that it will not rain during the time they are prophesying; and they have power to turn the waters into blood and to strike the earth with every kind of plague as often as they want." "If anyone tries to harm them, fire comes from their mouths and devours their enemies." They prophesy for "1,260 days, clothed in sackcloth" to the "Gentiles," who "trample on the holy city for 42 months." The witnesses are finally killed and lie in the streets for "three and a half days" but then come to life and are transported to heaven.)

7. The seventh trumpet sounds, and the angelic choir breaks forth into the song immortalized by George Frederick Handel in his chorus "Hallelujah!" from his oratorio *Messiah*: "The kingdom of the world is become the kingdom of our Lord and of his Christ, and he will reign for ever and ever."

Before the final set of seven "bowl judgments," a pageant takes place in heaven. Chapters 12 through 14 tell the story of a woman who appears "clothed with the sun and with the moon" and is about to give birth. A "red dragon with seven heads and ten horns" stands in front of her waiting to devour her child. A son is born to her but is "snatched up to God and to his throne" before the dragon can pounce. The woman then "flees to the desert to a place prepared for her by God, where she might be taken care of for 1,260 days."

War then breaks out in heaven. The archangel "Michael and his angels" fight "the dragon and his angels." The dragon—"that ancient serpent called the devil, or Satan, who leads the whole world astray"—is "hurled down."

Then, in chapter 13, John sees "a beast coming out of the sea" with "ten horns and seven heads, with ten crowns on his horns." The dragon gives this beast "his power and his throne and a great authority." "Men worshiped the dragon because he had given authority to the beast, and they also worshiped the beast." This beast is given "authority for forty-two months."

Finally in the pageant, John sees another beast who has "two horns like a lamb" but speaks "like a dragon." He performs miracles, "causing fire to come down from heaven." He sets up an image of the first beast and orders humanity to worship it. He also forces "everyone, small and great, rich and poor, free and slave, to receive a mark on his right hand or on his forehead," and no one can "buy or sell" unless he has this mark, "which is the number of his name. This calls for wisdom. If anyone has insight, let him calculate the number of the beast, for it is a man's number. His number is 666."

John again sees the 144,000 Jews from chapter 7, but this time they are in heaven. They are described as "those who did not defile themselves with women, for they kept themselves pure" and as having been "purchased from among men and offered as firstfruits to God and the Lamb." Three angels then fly in the heavens warning humankind not to worship the beast or receive his mark. One "'like a son of man'" appears in the heavens, carrying a "sharp sickle." He is told to gather in his harvest, for "the time to reap is come … the harvest of the earth is ripe." There follows the image that inspired the well-known words "He is trampling out the vintage where the grapes of wrath are stored," from the "Battle Hymn of the Republic": "The angel swung his sickle on the earth, gathered its grapes and threw them into the winepress of God's wrath. They were trampled in the winepress outside the city."

The stage is now set for the seven last plagues.

The Seven Bowls of God's Wrath (Chap. 16)

1. Those who had received the mark of the beast (see Mark of the Beast) are inflicted with "painful sores."
2. The sea turns to blood.
3. Fresh water turns to blood.
4. The sun scorches the earth with "intense heat."
5. Darkness covers the earth, and the sick fester in agony.
6. The Euphrates River dries up, preparing the way for "the kings from the East."

(*Parenthesis*: The armies of the earth gather for battle in a place that "in Hebrew is called Armageddon" [see Armageddon, Battle of].)

7. Tumultuous earthquakes, fires, explosions, and floods break out on the earth.

The Final Battle (Chaps. 17–20)

In chapter 17, John is shown the "punishment of the great prostitute, who sits on many waters." The woman is "sitting on a scarlet beast" that has "seven heads and ten horns." A title written on her forehead reads: "MYSTERY, BABYLON THE GREAT, THE MOTHER OF PROSTITUTES AND OF THE ABOMINATIONS OF THE EARTH." When John wonders about all this, the angel "explains" things in a way that has only introduced more mystery over the past two thousand years:

1. "The beast," according to the angelic interpreter, "once was, now is not, and will come up out of the Abyss and go to his destruction."
2. As for the "seven heads and ten horns," the angel says:

This calls for a mind with wisdom. The seven heads are seven hills on which the woman sits. They are also seven kings. Five have fallen, one is, the other has not yet come; but when he does come, he must remain for a little while. The beast who once was, and now is, is an eighth king. He belongs to the seven and is going to his destruction. The ten horns you saw are ten kings who have not yet received a kingdom, but who for one hour will receive authority as kings along with the beast. They have one purpose and will give their power and authority to the beast. They will make war against the Lamb, but the Lamb will overcome them because he is Lord of lords and King of kings.

Then, having cleared up that mystery, the angel goes on to tackle the third part of the vision.

3. The prostitute is sitting "on many waters." According to the angel, "The waters you saw, where the prostitute sits, are peoples, multitudes, nations and languages."

To sum up the whole vision, the angel recaps: "The beast and the ten horns you saw will hate the prostitute. They will bring her to ruin and leave her naked; they will eat her flesh and burn her with fire.... The woman you saw is the great city that rules over the kings of the earth."

Chapter 18 describes the fall of "Babylon the Great," which seems to be a center of commerce. Merchants despair because their markets have disappeared. Ships stay at sea, afraid to enter port. Music is silenced in the streets, and workmen and tradesmen are no more. There is no light to be found in the city, and "the voice of the bridegroom and bride will never be heard in you again." By the "magic spell" of this great center of commerce and trade "all the nations were led astray."

In chapter 19 the rider on a white horse comes to earth. "With justice he judges and makes war." This rider is called "Faithful and True" but also "has a name written on him that no one but he himself knows," besides which "on his robe and on his thigh he has this name written: KING OF KINGS AND LORD OF LORDS."

The beast and the false prophet are captured and thrown alive "into the fiery lake of burning sulfur."

Chapter 20 sees the imprisonment of Satan "for a thousand years." He is thrown into "the Abyss." Christ reigns on earth during this time, but at the end of the thousand years Satan is released, gathers up an army, and is quickly defeated. He is, at last, "thrown into the lake of burning sulfur, where the beast and false prophet had been thrown. They will be tormented day and night for ever and ever."

Then comes the final judgment from the "great white throne," when the "book of life" is opened and "the dead were judged according to what they had done as recorded in the books. The sea gave up the dead that were in it, and death and Hades gave up the dead that were in them, and each person was judged according to what he had done.... If anyone's name was not found written in the book of life, he was thrown into the lake of fire."

The End (Chaps. 21 and 22)

The final chapters paint a picture of life on a recycled earth. There is "a new heaven and a new earth ... and there was no longer any sea." The "new Jerusalem" comes down from heaven "prepared as a bride beautifully dressed for her husband." Here "God himself" will live with men: "They will be his people, and God himself will be with them and be their God. He will wipe every tear from their eyes. There will be no more death or mourning or crying or pain, for the old order of things has passed away." He who calls himself the "Alpha and Omega," the "Beginning and the End," declares, "It is done."

The "tree of life," denied to Adam and Eve in the book of Genesis, now stands in the center of a restored Jerusalem. The "river of the water of life" brings it sustenance. And "the leaves of the tree are for the healing of the nations. No longer will there be any curse."

Blessing and Warning

Revelation ends with both a blessing and a warning.

Blessing: "Blessed is he who keeps the words of the prophecy of this book.... Blessed are those who wash their robes, that they may have the right to the tree of life and may go through the gates into the city."

Warning: "Do not seal up the words of the prophecy of this book because the time is near.... I warn everyone who hears the words of the prophecy of this book: If anyone adds anything to them, God will add to him the plagues described in this book. And if anyone takes words away from this book of prophecy, God will take away from him his share in the tree of life and in the holy city, which are described in this book."

The final words seek to offer hope to all who read the book, whatever their interpretive scheme:

He who testifies to these things says, "Yes, I am coming soon."

Amen. Come Lord Jesus.

The grace of the Lord Jesus Christ be with God's people. Amen.

Conclusions

Largely based on a futurist reading of the final book of the Bible, there is a widespread feeling in Western cultures, especially in the United States, that Jesus is coming soon. Gallup polls dating back to 1980 indicate that 62 percent of Americans (note: "Americans"—not "American Christians") have "no doubts" that Jesus will someday return. During the weeks preceding Easter it has become the custom for many news magazines to run articles citing polls indicating many people believe the return will be sooner rather than later. Obviously Revelation has influenced many people, whether or not they have actually read the book. But the message it conveys is debatable.

Still, in the words of Marcus Borg, "It is difficult to imagine a more powerful ending to the Bible."

Sources:
Borg, Marcus J. *Reading the Bible Again for the First Time: Taking the Bible Seriously but Not Literally.* San Francisco: HarperSanFrancisco, 2001.
Brown, Raymond. *An Introduction to the New Testament.* New York: Doubleday, 1997.
LaHaye, Tim, and Jerry B. Jenkins. *Left Behind* series. 12 vols. Carol Stream, IL: Tyndale House, 1995–2004.
Lindsey, Hal. *Apocalypse Code.* Palos Verdes, CA: Western Front Ltd., 1997.
Lindsey, Hal, with C. C. Carlson. *The Late Great Planet Earth.* Grand Rapids, MI: Zondervan, 1970.

REVIVAL

In its general sense the word *revival* means a renewed interest in something. It is often applied specifically to religion to indicate such a renewed interest, whether on a relatively local scale or in terms of a widespread religious awakening. There have been several periods of broad religious revival throughout American history. The Great Awakening of the eighteenth century is only one example.

On the smaller scale, many conservative Protestant churches, especially Baptist churches in the southern Bible Belt, have made it a tradition to hold annual "revivals." Usually in the fall of the year, a visiting preacher or "revivalist" comes to town, sometimes setting up a tent, and seeks to inspire the faithful to repent and be "born again." Billy Graham is probably the best known of the revivalists who carry on the tradition. His fame is such that stadiums are needed to seat all the faithful.

A staple in the arsenal of revival preachers is a sermon on the Second Coming of Jesus. It is always a highlight of the week's meetings. The thinking is that people need a reason to decide now, rather than later, to "accept Christ." The fear that Jesus may return at any minute gives great motivation to a person who is on the fence. "Don't get left behind" may well be the most frequently used expression of all time when it comes to persuading people to "walk the sawdust trail," a reference to the sawdust traditionally poured on the floor of the revival tent.

Source:
Gonzalez, Justo L. *The Story of Christianity*. 2 vols. New York: Harper & Row, 1985.

ROMAN CATHOLIC VIEW OF HISTORY

In the first half of the second century CE, a Christian bishop named Irenaeus of Lyons began to conceive a grand idea of history as being the process whereby God is joined with the human race. In his two surviving works, *Demonstration of Apostolic Faith* and *Refutation of the So-Called Gnosis*, Irenaeus taught that God's original intent was to create two beings, Adam and Eve, place them in the Garden of Eden "like children," and then let them develop into spiritually mature adults. God's idea was that human beings would grow in communion with the divine. Eventually they would surpass even the angels, whose function was to care for humanity much as a caretaker cares for a young prince, until the prince grows to become a king. But sin entered the picture. God had to introduce plan B. In the words of the historian Justo L. Gonzalez, "Although the actual course of history is the result of sin, the fact that there is history is not. God always had the purpose that there would be history. The situation in paradise, as described in Genesis, was not the goal of history, but its beginning."

Irenaeus came to believe that history was the unfolding of a process he called "divinization." By this he meant that God is making humans more like the divine. The process will never be complete. Humans will never become God. God is, after all, the ultimate being, infinitely above humanity. But humans will continue to grow toward that objective.

Saint Augustine. *Library of Congress.*

When the original sin occurred in Genesis 3, it necessitated the incarnation, the coming of God in the form of a human, which became the focal point of history. God had always planned on being one with the human race, so incarnation didn't really represent a new plan; it was simply a response to a new situation. From this perspective, the incarnation was not the result of sin. Instead, it incorporated the new reality that sin brought about. Its significance grew to that of offering a remedy for the climate and culture of sin brought about by Satan's temptation and the fall of Adam and Eve.

Irenaeus taught that the Millennium (see entry), the thousand-year reign of Christ, was to be the last of a series of workdays that imitated the original seven days of creation (see Bible Timelines). It was to be a day of rest. In this sense, his teachings are close to the conservative Protestant eschatology of today. This theology of the Millennium has become so popular that many think of it as "Christian" theology, and many conservative Protestant scholars point to Irenaeus as evidence that they are teaching the "historic" belief of the Christian church.

The Roman Catholic Church, by far the largest segment of Christianity and the largest Christian denomination in the United States, did not adopt the teachings of Irenaeus as official doctrine. Today's Roman Catholic doctrine was not adopted until the fifth century. It was brought into focus and systematized by one of the greatest theologians, Catholic or Protestant, who ever lived.

Augustine of Hippo was a professor of rhetoric, born in the little town of Tagaste, North Africa, in 354 CE. The purpose of rhetoric, as practiced in those days, was not necessarily to present truth. That was left to the philosophers. Students of rhetoric aimed simply to present clear and forceful arguments for whatever they were called on to defend. In this respect they resembled modern-day lawyers. In fact, professional rhetoricians often spoke for one side or another in legal cases.

As a teacher of rhetoric, Augustine was deeply familiar with the works of Cicero, the famous orator of classical Rome. But Cicero was a philosopher who very much cared about truth, and while studying his works, Augustine came to the conviction that style was worthless without substance.

That belief led him to the study of Manicheism. Mani, its third-century founder, was convinced that the Zoroastrian concept of "light" battling "darkness" was basically true (see Eschatology, Comparative; Zoroastrianism), but he interpreted the struggle as taking place between spirit and matter. Manichean teaching explained that light and darkness had somehow mingled within each individual. Salvation consisted of separating the two so as to prepare the human spirit for its return to pure light. Mani believed that this principle had been revealed to Buddha, Zoroaster, and Jesus.

Augustine responded to Manicheism for two reasons. First, any teacher of rhetoric probably considers the language of the Bible to be inelegant at best, and to a professor like Augustine, some of it must have appeared positively barbaric. Second, Augustine had a real problem accepting the Christian concept of evil. How did a "good" God allow evil into the universe, especially after pronouncing his creation "very good?" If evil came from God, God couldn't be good. If it didn't, God couldn't be all-powerful. It was as simple, and as complex, as that.

But Augustine was simply too intelligent for his Manichean teachers to handle. Their explanations didn't help him in his quest. He turned to Neoplatonism, a philosophy that was very popular at the time. It had religious overtones that appealed to him. Neoplatonism sought to reach the One, the Source of all being. Neoplatonists taught that all reality derived from one principle that was totally good. The more one understood the good, the farther one moved from evil. Moral evil consists of looking away from the One and living in the world of contradictions and inferior ideas. Augustine became convinced that evil was not a "thing," but rather a direction—away from the One and the good. This idea became the first great block of his eschatology.

For a while Augustine was satisfied. Then he went to a series of sermons preached by Ambrose, who was at that time the most famous Christian preacher in Milan. Although Augustine attended at first just to listen to Ambrose's rhetoric, he was soon captivated by his message. According to Ambrose, the Bible should be interpreted allegorically, not literally. This insight became the second building block of Augustine's biblical eschatology. It was what he needed to hear. It meant that he didn't need to check his great intellect at the door of the church. He decided to become a Christian.

After years of intellectual and emotional struggle, Augustine decided that biblical prophecy could not be tied to specific historic events. The word *millennium* was to be interpreted allegorically. The Millennium was the time during which God was engaged in the process of bringing about that which Irenaeus had called "divinization." The church, God's children on earth, was even now living in the Millennium.

Even while Augustine watched from afar the destruction of Rome in 410, he refused to believe the end of the world was at hand. Instead, he taught that the prophecies of the Bible could apply metaphorically to a wide range of historical events. The fall of Rome was only one of them. In his book *The City of God*, he contrasted two cities. A city built by humans can only fall. The City of God, "not made with human hands," will last forever.

The Roman Catholic catechism adopted after Vatican II recognized Augustine's influence. Paraphrasing his words from the *City of God*: "Since the Ascension God's plan has entered into its fulfillment. We are already at 'the last hour.' Already the final stage of the world is with us, and the renewal of the world is irrevocably under way; it is now anticipated in a real way, for the Church is endowed already with a sanctity that is real but imperfect. Christ's kingdom already manifests its presence through the miraculous signs that attend its proclamation by the church."

The Roman Catholic Church eventually adopted Augustine's views as doctrine. Sometimes Roman Catholicism is called amillennialist or even postmillennialist (see Amillennialism; Pre- and Postmillennialism), but it is really antimillennialist. The church does not view the end of history as a climactic battle between good and evil. Instead, history is the process of fulfilling God's original intention to bring the human race into the divine family. The phrase often used to describe this process is, "already—but not yet." In other words, "divinization" has already taken place in the mind of God but is still working its way out through the historical process.

All this does not mean that there have not been Catholic mystics who claimed to see glimpses of the end. Nostradamus (see entry) is a prime example. Or consider the furor over the sightings of the Virgin Mary at Fatima, Portugal, in 1917. There, three young children claimed to have had visions of and received messages from the Virgin on the thirteenth of every month, beginning in May and ending in October. The third of these messages allegedly concerned the end of the world. It has never been published. One of the children, by then a nun, wrote it down in 1944, and it was delivered to the pope, but beyond that even its existence was never revealed until 1960. When Pope John XXIII died in 1963, rumors were rampant that the message of the Fatima children was so terrible that it killed him when he read it.

In the 1980s Cardinal Joseph Ratzinger (now Pope Benedict XVI), prefect of the Congregation for the Doctrine of the Faith, implied that the message was nothing more than a restatement of Revelation 13. This was confirmed a few years later when Pope John Paul II decided to publish the third message. In the introduction of then-cardinal Ratzinger's theological commentary on the message, he was even moved to write, "It will probably prove disappointing or surprising after all the speculation it has stirred." Such was indeed the case. There was no great prophecy concerning the end of days. The only thing remotely approaching a prophetic announcement was the message: "If my requests are heeded, Russia will be converted, and there will be peace; if not, she will spread her errors throughout the world."

Some have heard in a few of Pope John Paul's sermons a revival of interest in the third message of Fatima. When he called for prayers for Russia and the Soviet Union subsequently collapsed, it was widely regarded as a partial fulfillment of the children's prophecy. But because the world did not enter a period of unprecedented peace after the collapse, hope died down.

Augustine might have had much the same feelings when Rome fell. He probably would have claimed again that prophecy is for all ages and all cultures. It will fulfill its allegorical function until the end of time.

Sources:
Gonzalez, Justo L. *The Story of Christianity*. 2 vols. New York: Harper & Row, 1985.
Martin, Malachy. *The Keys of This Blood: The Struggle for World Dominion between Pope John Paul II, Mikhail Gorbachev, and the Capitalist West*. New York: Simon and Schuster, 1990.
Reilly, John J. "The Millennium and the Roman Catholic Church." http://pages.prodigy.net/aesir/catmil.htm.

ROME, SEVEN HILLS OF *see* **Revelation**

ROSH

The word *rosh* in Hebrew means "top" or "head." Perhaps its most familiar use is in the name of the Jewish holiday Rosh Hashanah, meaning "head of the year." In Ezekiel 38:2 and 3, it is translated "chief": "Son of Man, set your face against Gog, of the land of Magog, the chief [*rosh*] prince of Meshech and Tubal."

The nineteenth-century German linguist Wilhelm Gesenius wrote a Hebrew lexicon in which he claimed that "Rosh was a designation for the tribes then north of the Taurus Mountains, dwelling in the neighborhood of the Volga." He believed that Ezekiel's use of the term is the first historic reference to the people now called *Rus* or "Russian." Carl Friedrich Keil, a German scholar of the Old Testament, also argues that *rosh* should be translated as a proper name. His theory is that "the Byzantine and Arabic writers frequently mention a people called Ros and Rus, dwelling in the country of Taurus and reckoned among the Scythian tribes." This means the text could be translated, "Son of Man, set your face against Gog, of the land of Magog, the 'Russian' prince of Meshech and Tubal."

Whatever the meaning of this obscure term, Christians who believe that Ezekiel 38 and 39 literally describe the final battle of the world and the last seven years of human history have also become firmly convinced that somehow Ezekiel foresaw Russia as having a major role to play in the conflict (see Armageddon, Battle of; Reagan, Ronald).

Source:
Bridger, David, ed. *The New Jewish Encyclopedia.* New York: Behrman House, 1962.

RUSSIA IN PROPHECY *see* **Armageddon, Battle of**

RYRIE, CHARLES C.

Before Hal Lindsey and his book *The Late Great Planet Earth*, published in 1970, there was Lindsey's teacher at Dallas Theological Seminary, Charles C. Ryrie. Ryrie has written more than twenty books and is perhaps best known in evangelical circles for his *Ryrie Study Bible*, a Bible version containing notes and reflections based on his years of experience as a Bible scholar and teacher.

In 1996 Ryrie wrote *Come Quickly, Lord Jesus*, an overview of the evangelical pretribulational Rapture interpretation of the Second Coming of Jesus Christ (see Armageddon, Battle of; Pre-, Post-, and Midtribulationalism). It is, for all practical purposes, a summary of the endtime schedule adhered to by Tim LaHaye and Jerry Jenkins in their *Left Behind* series of novels and the same sequence of events followed by Lindsey in *The Late Great Planet Earth* and subsequent books.

According to Ryrie, the events preceding the Second Coming of Christ will take place in this order:

1. The Rapture of the church.

2. The Day of the Lord, marking the beginning of the Tribulation, a seven-year period of judgment. During this time:

God's wrath is poured out on planet earth in a series of judgments.

144,000 Jews are redeemed and serve as God's witnesses on earth.
A great multitude of believing gentile "witnesses," who testify to the saving grace of Jesus Christ, are separated out of the general population of earth.
The antichrist begins to rule the earth, but the earth sees him as a savior, not a tyrant. World peace reigns for the first half of the tribulation.

3. Three and one-half years into the Tribulation, two witnesses appear in Jerusalem. They testify about Jesus Christ and are martyred. Their death marks the end of world peace and begins the Great Tribulation, the period of judgment on the earth.

4. The Great Tribulation ends with the Second Coming of Christ to earth.

5. The Millennium begins, during which:

Satan is chained for a thousand years.

Peace covers the earth as Jesus rules. The "wolf will live with the lamb … and a little child will lead them" (Isaiah 11:6).

6. At the end of the thousand years, Satan is released, gathers an army, and is finally destroyed.

7. The final judgment of all humankind takes place, after which eternity begins.

Sources:

Ryrie, Charles C. *Come Quickly, Lord Jesus: What You Need to Know about the Rapture.* Rev. ed. New York: Harvest House, 1999.
———. "The Seven Bowls." www.sumnerwemp.com/ryrie/.

Sagan, Carl

Carl Sagan was the founder and first president of the Planetary Society, a prolific writer, and a consultant to NASA ever since the 1950s. He was chosen to brief the Apollo astronauts before they went to the moon. He lent his expertise to experiments carried out on the Mariner, Viking, Voyager, and Galileo planetary expeditions. He wrote and served as host of the award-winning PBS series *Cosmos*. He won more awards than probably even he could easily count, and his circle of colleagues encompassed experts in the fields of teaching, astronomy, literature, education, environmental studies, entertainment, and many overlapping science specialties.

On top of all this, Sagan made an important contribution to end-of-the-world hypotheses with his work on the study that coined the term *nuclear winter*. In 1983 a few select scientists began to examine the possible worldwide effects of a massive exchange of nuclear weapons. Taking into account such factors as smoke resulting from forest fires, fossil fuels suddenly released into the atmosphere, and other forms of pollution, the authors of the study painted an alarming picture of devastation that would, even apart from blast damage and nuclear fallout, wreck the climate of the planet. R. P. Turco, O. B. Toon, T. P. Ackerman, J. B. Pollack, and Sagan combined their initials to name the results of their study the TTAPS Report. It predicts uncontrollable firestorms over any city or forest remotely near the scene of a nuclear blast. The smoke and dust thrown into the atmosphere could obliterate sunshine for weeks and perhaps for years. Several hundred million tons of smoke and soot would be carried to high altitudes, there to be spread by winds around the entire earth between the latitudes of 30 and 60 degrees north. Average surface temperatures would drop by 20 to 40 degrees. Killing frosts and high doses of radiation would follow. Photosynthesis would, for all practical purposes, cease. The human population would be reduced to a fraction of its current numbers, assuming any survived.

Carl Sagan in 1986. Sagan's books and television appearances made him perhaps the most widely known astronomer in history. *Lennox McLendon/Associated Press.*

Ever since the TTAPS Report was published, the term *nuclear winter* has carried with it echoes of Armageddon and the destruction of life as we know it. The authors agree that some people would probably survive in places far removed from present-day areas of civilization. But whether they would survive in sustainable populations is anybody's guess.

Carl Sagan died in 1996, but his work remains compulsory reading for anyone who considers the impact this generation of human beings can have on the future of life on planet Earth.

Sources:
Sagan, Carl L. *Cosmos.* New York: Random House, 1980.
———. *The Demon-Haunted World: Science as a Candle in the Dark.* New York: Random House, 1996.
———. *The Dragons of Eden.* New York: Ballantine, 1977.
Turco, R. P., et al. "Nuclear Winter: Global Consequences of Multiple Nuclear Explosions." *Science* 222 (1983): 1283–97.

SATAN *see* **Devil**

SCIENTIFIC "GOD" LANGUAGE

When the ancient Greeks confronted lightning, they saw it as emanating from the strong right arm of Zeus. The sun rose and set because Apollo pulled it through the heavens each day on the back of his chariot. The Norse heard thunder rolling from the hammer and anvil of Thor.

From the beginning we have taken refuge in religious terminology to explain the unexplainable. When facing horror or fear, it is second nature to resort to calling on God, and even atheists, when angry enough, will "damn" someone to a hell they do not believe exists. Scientists, too, with a long tradition of very technical and specialized vocabulary, sometimes retreat to using "God talk" when faced with the inexpressible.

When Albert Einstein first confronted the strange conclusions of quantum theory that seem to defy logic, he shook his head and proclaimed, "God does not play dice with the universe." Stephen Hawking, concluding his popular book *A Brief History of Time*, tried to sum up his thoughts about discovering the elusive Grand Unification Theory: "However, if we do discover a complete theory, it should in time be understood in broad principle by everyone, not just a few scientists. Then we shall all, philosophers, scientists, and just ordinary people, be able to take part in the discussion of the question of why we and universe exist. If we find the answer to that, it would be the ultimate triumph of human reason—for then we would know the mind of God."

Thus it is probably inevitable that when the human race has been forced throughout history to face up to extinction, its greatest fear, it has chosen to use "God talk" and a word right out of its best-known religious text: *Armageddon*.

Source:
Hawking, Stephen W. *A Brief History of Time: From the Big Bang to Black Holes*. New York: Bantam, 1988.

SCIENTIFIC VIEWS OF THE END

The unkempt religious zealot marching down the street with a sandwich board proclaiming that the end of the world is near has been the subject of many a cartoon. But given the technological power humanity has taken into its hands, coupled with catastrophic natural events such as the Asian tsunami of December 2004, it is not just the religious community that has questioned the future of life on our planet. Throughout this book we have examined many end-of-the-world scenarios that scientists have begun to consider. Following is a list of covered topics divided into broad categories:

Natural Disasters: Big Bang; Big Crunch, Big Chill, and Big Rip; Cosmos, Fate of; Earth Shift; Plagues; Polar Shift; Quantum Theory; Sun, Death of; Water.

Disasters from Outer Space: Aliens; Asteroids; Comets; Meteors, Meteoroids, and Meteorites; Red Shift; Unidentified Fly Objects.

Human-created Disasters: Atomic Age; Doomsday Argument; Ecological Exploitation; Einstein, Albert; Global Warming; Nuclear Proliferation; Oppenheimer, J. Robert; Population Clock; Y2K.

SCOFIELD, CYRUS INGERSON

(See also Chafer, Lewis Sperry)

There is no doubt that the *Scofield Reference Bible*, first published in 1909, was the single most influential source for the spread in America of dispensational theology and the doctrine of the pretribulational Rapture of the church (see Dispensationalism; Rapture). The current evangelical trend of waiting for Armageddon is based to a great extent on the work of Cyrus Ingerson Scofield (1843–1921).

Born in Michigan, Scofield moved to Tennessee in the late 1850s. He served a year's enlistment in the Confederate army during the Civil War. Heading west, he was admitted to the Kansas bar in 1869 and won election to the legislature in the 1870s before his career went into decline, apparently partly because of alcoholism. Following a religious conversion, he turned to the ministry in 1880. He was a Congregationalist pastor in Dallas, Texas, from the early 1880s until 1895, when he answered the call of the famed evangelist Dwight L. Moody to move to Moody's church in East Northfield, Massachusetts. By the time he moved back to a Dallas church in 1903, he had conceived of the idea of publishing an edition of the Bible that contained his own notes and study guides. In 1907 he left the parish ministry to begin work in the new Bible Conference movement. Two years later the *Scofield Reference Bible* was born. Its dispensational, premillennial position concerning the Second Coming of Christ became the standard of the conservative Christian movement during the fundamentalist-versus-modernist controversy that was a household debate during the early years of the twentieth century.

The popularity of the Scofield Bible was no doubt helped along because of an early editorial decision by the Oxford University Press to keep the pages of every new edition exactly the same as in every other edition. A person from Philadelphia could replace a Bible or buy a different-sized Bible in Dallas and be confidant that the page numbers would be exactly the same as in his or her old Bible. It soon became normal for entire congregations to carry their Scofield Bibles with them to church so as to follow along with the preacher's text. When the minister turned the pages in his Bible during the scripture reading, the entire congregation could be heard to turn the pages in their personal Bibles. In some communities, the notes in the margins and Scofield's diagrams concerning the events of the Second Coming were considered to be just as sacred as the words of Holy Writ.

So prevalent was the feeling that the Scofield Bible was the final Bible God intended for use in the church that when the publisher finally brought out an updated edition, revised from the wording of the King James translation used in previous editions, there were those who actually preached that the new Scofield Bible was the work of the devil. "True" Christians shunned it. But the diagrams and charts were not changed. They remained the same, and the *Scofield Reference Bible* remains the staple of worship for many fundamentalist and evangelical Christian students of prophecy who await the coming of Jesus Christ with bated breath.

Sources:

Douglas, J. D., ed. *The New International Dictionary of the Christian Church.* Grand Rapids, MI: Zondervan, 1974.

The Scofield Reference Bible. New York: Oxford University Press, 1945.

SCRIPTURES *see* Books of the Bible and Their Relation to Prophecy

SECOND ADAM

(See also Adam and Eve)

In 1 Corinthians the apostle Paul wrote that one of the reasons Jesus Christ was born was to undo the sin Adam and Eve committed in the Garden of Eden. Whereas Adam chose to sin, Jesus, equipped with the same human resources, chose not to sin. In this sense he became the second Adam—the Adam who "got it right." According to this view, if Adam had not sinned, there would never have been the need for an Armageddon. Humans would have remained innocent. But as soon as the sin occurred, the road to Armageddon began and could have only one result—"the last enemy to be destroyed is death." In the apostle's words: "For as in Adam all die, so in Christ all will be made alive. But each in his own term: Christ, the firstfruits; then, when he comes, those who belong to him. Then the end will come, when he hands over the kingdom to God the Father after he has destroyed all dominion, authority and power. For he must reign until he has put all his enemies under his feet. The last enemy to be destroyed is death" (1 Cor. 15:21–26).

Source:
The Holy Bible, New International Version. Grand Rapids, MI: Zondervan, 1978.

SECOND COMING

The Greek word *parousia* is used in the New Testament to refer to the expected arrival of someone. In 2 Corinthians 7:6, for instance, the apostle Paul refers to the *parousia*, or arrival, of his colleague Titus, who brought Paul solace and comfort during a time of affliction. But the word is most often used as a technical term relating to the Second Coming of Jesus Christ at the battle of Armageddon.

In the apocalyptic writing of the book of Revelation, the Second Coming is linked to what some scholars call the myth of the Divine Warrior. This designation refers to the universal body of mythological stories concerning the leader of an army of truth and justice who will someday come to earth to set things right by destroying evil. The concept is found everywhere from Hinduism's tenth triumphant avatar of Vishnu to Judaism's belief in a coming messiah to some Native Americans' belief in the return of Tecumseh (see Tecumseh).

The apostle Paul, in his body of letters and specifically in 2 Thessalonians, teaches that God is allowing something or someone—namely, the presence of evil—to work until the return of Christ. Paul sees the Second Coming as a new beginning at which the inner workings of what he calls the "mystery" of lawlessness will be laid bare for all to see.

In the Christian gospels, as in Jewish eschatology, the writers seem more concerned with events leading up to the Second Coming than those that follow the return of the Messiah. All, however, to at least some degree, see the Second Coming as an object of hope. This hope of an all-encompassing future rectification of wrongs and curing of ills is often offered as comfort to those who are suffering in the here and now. Although some belittle it as a "pie in the sky by and by" doctrine, there is no doubt that many people since the time of the disciples have taken refuge in the hope that someday Jesus will return to set things right. Meanwhile, they follow the words attributed to him—"Hold fast till I come" (Rev. 2:25).

Sources:
The Holy Bible, New International Version. Grand Rapids, MI: Zondervan, 1978.
Rowland, Christopher. "Parousia." In *The Anchor Bible*, vol. 5. New York: Doubleday, 1992.

SECOND DEATH

The term *second death* comes from Revelation 20:11–15; it is also referenced in 20:6 and 21:8. In all cases it refers to the final judgment of the world following the battle of Armageddon:

> Then I saw a great white throne and him who was seated on it. Earth and sky fled from his presence, and there was no place for them. And I saw the dead, great and small, standing before the throne, and books were opened. Another book was opened, which is the book of life. The dead were judged according to what they had done as recorded in the books. The sea gave up the dead that were in it, and death and Hades gave up the dead that were in them, and each person was judged according to what he had done. Then death and Hades were thrown into the lake of fire. The lake of fire is the second death. If anyone's name was not found written in the book of life, he was thrown into the lake of fire. (Rev. 21:11–15)

Source:
The Holy Bible, New International Version. Grand Rapids, MI: Zondervan, 1978.

SEEKERS, THE
(See also Failed Prophecy)

During the closing years of the 1940s a woman named Dorothy Martin believed that she had been contacted by higher beings. She voiced their messages through a technique she called "spirit-writing" and began to teach a small group of followers that her spiritual contact was a "Guardian" that she called "Elder Brother." His name was Sananda, and in his earthly form he had been the historical Jesus.

Sananda confided that a new age had begun. The Guardians were reaching across the spiritual divide to bring light into the world. They had first tried two thousand years earlier, when Jesus was born on earth. But because his message was largely rejected, humanity had again been enveloped by the Prince of Darkness. "It is ignorance of the Universal Laws that makes all the misery of the Earth," the Guardians supposedly told Martin. "We see and know that you struggle in darkness and want to bring real light, for yours is the only planet that has war and hatred." They planned to use Martin, a willing conduit, to bring light into the world. They assured her that flying saucers would soon appear in all the major cities of the earth.

The small group of followers who believed Martin's message called themselves "the Seekers" and waited patiently for the spacecraft to arrive. The event was scheduled to precede a worldwide flood that would destroy much of Western Europe and North America on December 21, 1954. But the flood never came. Neither did the flying saucers.

Through the first weeks of December 1954, the Seekers waited. But when the appointed day came and went, bringing intense disappointment, they were comforted with good news: The prophecy had not come about because the Seekers themselves had evidenced so much faith. They had saved the world and given it another chance. The Guardians were emphatic: "Not since the beginning of time upon this earth has there been such a force of Good and light as now floods this room and that which has been loosed within this room now floods the entire Earth."

The Seekers became even more fervent in their faith and resolve. They had rescued the world and could write triumphant letters to the press: "The cataclysm has been called off. The little group, sitting all night long, had spread so much light that God saved the world from destruction."

Although most of the Seekers are gone now, they died secure in the knowledge that they had saved the world from Armageddon.

Source:

Stone, Jon R., ed. *Expecting Armageddon: Essential Readings in Failed Prophecy.* New York: Routledge, 2000.

SEVENFOLD SEQUENCES *see* **Bible Timelines**

SEVENTH-DAY ADVENTISTS

(See also Millerites)

Seventh-day Adventists derive their name from two important tenets of their faith. "Seventh day" refers to their belief that Saturday, the seventh day of the week, is still the day that God commands people to observe as the Sabbath. "Adventist" comes from the fact that a central doctrine of the church is that the Second Advent of Jesus Christ is even now coming to pass.

Drawing heavily on the book of Daniel, Adventists teach that the Second Coming will occur in stages. In stage 1, Jesus Christ entered into the "Heavenly Sanctuary" to "cleanse" it by reviewing the sins of humans and judging them accordingly. When this work is done, he will return to earth. Daniel 8:14 allows 2,300 days for this task of "cleansing the sanctuary." The work actually began, according to Adventist interpretation, when Artaxerxes gave the command to "rebuild and restore the temple" at Jerusalem (Nehemiah 2). Although many evangelical Christians place this command in 445 BCE, Adventists believe it was given in 457 BCE, the year they believe was the seventh year of Artaxerxes' reign. Without going into all the mathematical and scriptural complications (see Seventy Sevens for some of them), suffice it to say that Adventists believe the end of the prophecy came in 1844. In that year (specifically, October 22, 1844) Christ came to the Ancient of Days and began the final phase of his ministry, filling the role typified by the actions of the priests who worked in the earthly sanctuary in Jerusalem. When this work is done, Jesus will return to earth and the events described in the book of Revelation will take place. No one knows when this return will take place. Adventists, having learned their lesson in 1844, when they believed Jesus would return all the way to earth (see Millerites), are now much more cautious about setting dates.

Source:

Damsteegt, P. G., ed. *Seventh-day Adventists Believe … : A Biblical Exposition of Fundamental Doctrines*. Washington, DC: Ministerial Association of the General Conference of Seventh-day Adventists, 1989.

SEVENTY SEVENS

Daniel 9, verses 20–27, contains some of the most disputed passages of the Bible. Translations differ at key points, making it very difficult to decide exactly what the author is saying. The reason the translations differ is that the ancient manuscripts from which the translators work are not in agreement with one another. To further complicate the problem, the Western calendar was not in use when Daniel was written and has been adjusted a few times in the centuries since, clouding the calculation of the numerous dates involved.

But those who say that the Bible's prophecies await future fulfillment (see Futurist School of Biblical Interpretation) agree that this is a key passage of scripture and reveals dates concerning the endtimes.

To put it mildly, interpretive controversy prevails more often than not.

Although we cannot outline the technical details of every position, which get very involved and demand a lot of biblical familiarity, what follows is the position held by probably the majority of futurist evangelical scholars today.

As the chapter opens, Daniel is studying the book of Jeremiah. There he reads that Jerusalem will lie desolate for seventy years as a punishment for her sins. Daniel was a young man when Jerusalem was torn down by Nebuchadnezzar and the Babylonian army. He was taken in that captivity to his present place of residence in what he now knows as Persia. It takes only a quick calculation to discover that the time of punishment is almost over. But he can't discover anywhere in his Bible what is scheduled to happen next. So he prays for nineteen verses and is interrupted in the middle of his heartfelt exhortation by no less a heavenly messenger than the angel Gabriel.

In Gabriel's words: "Daniel, I have now come to give you insight and understanding. As soon as you began to pray, an answer was given, which I have come to tell you, for you are highly esteemed. Therefore, consider the message and understand the vision: Seventy sevens are decreed for your people and your holy city."

First of all, what does "seventy sevens" mean?

Some translations use seventy "weeks." It is generally explained that Gabriel was referring to "weeks of years," or seventy periods of seven years. In other words, 70×7, or 490 years.

Some interpreters stop right there and insist that already we have made a pretty big interpretive leap. But that doesn't deter those who are bound to move forward where even the angel Gabriel fears to tread. So we continue.

The purpose of these 490 years, according to Gabriel, was to allow time for the completion of seven items on God's priority list. Again, in the words of Gabriel, this time was "decreed for your people and your holy city " (notice the two separate entities—Daniel's "people," the Jews, and the "holy city," Jerusalem) "to finish transgression, to put an end to sin, to atone for wickedness, to bring in everlasting righteousness, to seal up vision and prophecy, and to anoint the most holy " (or "the most holy place" or "the most holy one"—translators differ).

Again, we run into problems with translations and interpretations. But at least a pattern seems to be developing. God is devoting a certain period—490 years is as good a guess as any—to accomplishing a set of objectives. If we can figure out when that period starts we can then figure out when it will end.

Gabriel now becomes even more enigmatic: "Know and understand this: From the issuing of the decree to restore and rebuild Jerusalem until the [or 'an'] Anointed One, the ruler, comes, there will be seven 'sevens' [or 'weeks'] and sixty-two 'sevens' [or 'weeks']."

The "decree to restore and rebuild Jerusalem" is generally thought to be the one given by Artaxerxes in Nehemiah 2. The British theologian and Bible scholar Sir Robert Anderson, in his book *The Coming Prince*, asserted that this chapter refers to a decree issued in 445 BCE. This is the date most evangelical scholars use when marking the beginning of God's clock for the 490 years. Because Nehemiah claims the command was given during the month of Nissan in the Hebrew calendar, it is generally thought that the prophecy period began during the month of March, 445 BCE.

It marked, according to Gabriel, the beginning of a period of "seven sevens" and "sixty-two sevens." Do the math and you'll come up with 483. In other words, according to this interpretation, 483 years after the command to restore Jerusalem was given in 445 BCE, the Anointed One would come. But these, according to Sir Robert, were Hebrew years, which were based on a lunar calendar rather than our solar one. Each month of the ancient Hebrew calendar consisted of only thirty days. Consulting charts, graphs, and astronomical data, Anderson finally deduced that the 483 years ended on, according to our calendar, Palm Sunday, April 6, 33 CE. His thesis was that when Jesus entered the city on that day, he offered the people a kingdom. If they had received him, the final seven years of the prophecy would have unfolded. (The prophecy, remember, was for 490 years, but only 483 had transpired before the coming of the Anointed One.) The people began to sing the psalm reserved for the coronation of the Messiah, Psalm 118: "Hosanna in the Highest! Blessed is he who comes in the name of the Lord!" Anderson believed that Jesus knew very well this was the promised day because, when the Pharisees told him to "rebuke his disciples," his reply was, "If they keep quiet, the stones will cry out" (Luke 19:37–40). Jesus even went on to say to the people of Jerusalem, "If you, even you, had only known *on this day* [emphasis added] what would bring you piece—but now it is hidden from your eyes."

Gabriel had spoken the truth, according to this interpretation. God allowed a period of 490 years to redeem the earth. The clock began to tick when the Jews came back from the Babylonian captivity. With seven years left to play in the game, Jesus rode into Jerusalem to offer the people a kingdom. They refused and he was crucified. At that point the Heavenly Referee stopped the clock but let the teams go on playing. Like a great parenthesis, the Church Age was dropped into the slot between the first 483 years of the prophecy and the last seven. But the time will come when the Church Age will end (see Rapture).

When that happens, the clock will begin again. The Jews will be back in Jerusalem. The European emperor, this time called antichrist, will again be in control. The final years are called years of Tribulation. They are begun with a peace treaty (a "covenant with many"). In the middle of the Tribulation the antichrist will "put an end to sacrifice and offering." Desolation (the Great Tribulation) will continue until the battle of Armageddon brings the whole game to a screeching halt and time runs out.

Is this the correct interpretation of Daniel 9? Probably not. It is simply the most popular right now. Many liberal Hebrew and Christian scholars believe the whole concept is out of bounds. They believe Daniel was writing about events that happened during his own time (see Abomination of Desolation). Others, while believing in the future fulfillment of prophecy, disagree over this particular interpretation because they have different views on what the "sevens" mean and when the prophecy began to unfold in history.

This passage, however, does offer a case study in biblical interpretation. Personal prejudice and already-formed opinions make a difference. We tend to find in the Bible what we hope to find there. And arguments to the contrary seldom make a difference.

Source:
The Holy Bible, New International Version. Grand Rapids, MI: Zondervan, 1978.

666

The [false prophet] also forced everyone, small and great, rich and poor, free and slave, to receive a mark on his right hand or on his forehead, so that no one could buy or sell unless he had the mark, which is the name of the beast or the number of his name.

This calls for wisdom. If anyone has insight, let him calculate the number of the beast, for it is man's number. His number is 666. (Rev. 13:16–18)

These may very well be the most enigmatic verses in the Bible. They are certainly at the core of many a conspiracy theory, and private speculations, especially those published on the Internet, run rampant. The numbers have caused so many fears that some people refuse to use any check numbered 666. Highways in both Arizona and Texas have had their official numbers changed due to complaints from fundamentalists. Urban legends spread like wildfire, usually through people who claim they know people who are related to people who have had Social Security checks snatched mysteriously out of their hands by bank tellers who report that these checks were not yet supposed to be issued.

It is entertaining to speculate on the possibility that all this sound and fury might have been expended on the wrong number. A papyrus manuscript fragment discovered in Egypt sheds a different light on the issue of the number. It is purported to be a very early copy of a portion of the book of Revelation that lists the number as 616, not 666. If 616 is indeed the original number used by the author of Revelation, it would change much of the numerological speculation surrounding the interpretation of this passage.

Whether or not the findings support the traditional text, what do the numbers really mean? Do they point to a yet-to-be-revealed antichrist, an ancient figure known to the original author of the book of Revelation, or a metaphysical power lurking behind the scenes of world history?

The many theories about the number 666 generally fall into one of three categories.

Past-Historic School of Biblical Interpretation

(Authors espousing this view include such New Testament scholars as Marcus Borg and Dominic Crossan. It is discussed in detail in various entries. See, for instance, Abomination of Desolation; Revelation.)

This is the interpretive scheme that insists the original authors of Holy Writ must have been writing in terms their readers could have understood. If 666 refers to a man, it must have been a coded reference to someone who was alive at the time. Perhaps Nero or one of the other caesars might fit the bill. After all, it was a time of persecution for the early church. Maybe the antichrist from "Babylon" was really Caesar from Rome (see Revelation).

Futurist School of Biblical Interpretation

(Those espousing this view include popular authors such as Tim LaHaye and Jerry B. Jenkins. Their theories are presented in detail in other entries. See, for instance, Antichrist; *Left Behind* Books; Lindsey, Hal; Revelation.)

This school of thinking, followed by most modern evangelical Christian writers, believes that even if the prophecy has a meaning grounded in the past, it awaits an even greater fulfillment in the future. They insist that the number refers to a man and a system of economic control that will someday, just before the Second Coming of Jesus and the battle of Armageddon, engulf the whole earth (see Numerology for one example of this kind of theory).

New 666 candidates are introduced every year, but so far no one person or bureaucratic system has been positively identified.

Intuitive/Metaphysical School of Biblical Interpretation

(The author credited with popularizing this kind of theology is Walter Wink, professor of biblical interpretation at Auburn Theological School in New York City.)

This approach is more difficult to understand. Some background in both biblical interpretation and history is required to fully grasp the ideas these theologians espouse.

Biblical Background. In 1984 Walter Wink published the first volume of what eventually became a trilogy examining the language of power in the New Testament. His thesis was that the first-century writers intuitively understood realities they couldn't fully explain, at least in language familiar to our modern academic culture. They understood, for instance, that human organizations such as governments seem to operate under forces quite beyond their own control, taking on a personality that is bigger than any individual. In the United States, for example, it often doesn't seem to matter much whether Democrats or Republicans are at the helm. Policies may vary somewhat, but the Washington mindset grinds on. "Pork" projects, filibusters, back-room deals, and heavy spending continue unabated. Similarly, in the private sector, the entire board of directors of General Motors can be replaced, but the company will continue on. And, of course, the military will lumber on in their familiar fashion long after their inefficiency is proved beyond a shadow of a doubt. Change can be effected, but it requires a herculean effort. Even smaller institutions manifest this syndrome. Churches, for instance, or universities develop "personalities" that seem to last for generation after generation.

Wink believes that the New Testament writers recognized this fact and labeled the "powers" that control these forces "angels" or "principalities," among other descriptive terms. He quotes from the book of Revelation, for instance, when Jesus addresses comments not to the "church of Laodicea" but to "*the angel of* the church of Laodicea." By this Wink doesn't mean that some fallen angel fluttered by and took control of the organization. Instead he argues that human organizations actually develop traditions and customs that are so strong they almost take on a metaphysical life of their own. In order to change the institution, the "angel," or spirit of tradition, the metaphysical reality of the institution, has to be changed. Whether the original authors understood all this modern psychology doesn't make any difference. They intuitively recognized the reality of it and gave it a name.

How does this kind of thinking relate to the battle of Armageddon and the number 666?

The author of Revelation does not say that the number 666 refers to "a" man. He says that "it is man's number." In other words, it symbolizes humanity, not one distinct individual. Six is one short of seven, the number of perfection assigned to God throughout the Bible; thus 666 represents either fallen humanity or humans striving to become more than they are. As such, 666 represents a system, not a man.

But what system? It must represent an economic system because the number is associated with "buying and selling." "No one could buy or sell unless he had the mark" (Rev. 13:17). Perhaps the early writers intuitively understood, even two thousand years ago, that whoever controlled the economy controlled the population.

Historical Background. The current economic system of Western civilization that has now spread to the entire planet began some six thousand years ago, probably in Mesopotamia. It began with the Agricultural Revolution, that evolutionary leap that brought us writing, cities, specialization of jobs, warfare over territory, male-dominated society, and gods and religions. The time before the Agricultural Revolution is called prehistory. The time after the invention of writing, originating as a result of this revolution, is called history.

Title page of *An Interpretation of the Number 666*, by Francis Potter (1642). *Fortean Picture Library.*

In other words, "history," and the "buying and selling" economy that so marks modern life, began about six to eight thousand years ago. This is also approximately when the Bible says the world began. Perhaps the biblical writers really referred to the beginning of "our" world, not "the" world. This is when Adam and Eve walked out of the Garden of Eden and began to earn their bread by toiling at agriculture. "By the sweat of your brow you will eat your food" (Gen. 3:19), God cautioned Adam. Ever since the Agricultural Revolution humanity has lived by trade. Civilizations rise and fall, but commerce is at the root of everything. Economic systems have been put in place. They all revolve around who controls the means of production—who can "buy or sell." But they all have one other thing in common: in each civilization the rich tend to get richer and the poor tend to get poorer, until, eventually and inevitably, the civilization falls and something new replaces it. A spiritual or metaphysical "economic power" is in place. It demands of each one of us that we participate. No one can really go it alone anymore. We all have Social Security numbers. We all carry credit cards. We have numbers, fingerprints, files, and computer databases. We cannot "buy or sell" without them.

As Walter Wink might well ask, is this what the biblical writer intuitively recognized, even two thousand years ago? Do we all wear the "mark of the beast"? As such, does Armageddon really refer to the demise of a six-thousand-year-old social system that carried, at its root, the seeds of its own destruction? When the Agricultural Revolution began its long ascendance, did fallen humanity, who unknowingly invented it, place on their hand and forehead the mark of antichrist?

What, after all, does "antichrist" really mean? According to the author of 1 John, everyone who denies Jesus the Christ is an antichrist: "Who is the liar? It is the man who denies that Jesus is the Christ. Such a man is the antichrist" (1 John 2:22).

In other words, those who subscribe to the intuitive/metaphysical school of biblical interpretation believe that an Armageddon will mark the destruction of the economic system that has been in effect for six thousand years. It is contrary to the commands of Jesus. He ordered us to "give a cup of cold water" in his name, to "turn the other cheek" and "walk the second mile." Jesus insisted that true religion meant giving, not hoarding. He never suggested anyone ever save for a rainy day.

To people who read the Bible this way, Armageddon represents spiritual warfare against the "prince of this world" who has held sway ever since the Agricultural Revolution. We "fight not against flesh and blood," says Paul in Ephesians 6:10, "but against the rulers, against the authorities, against the powers of the dark world and against the spiritual forces of evil in the heavenly realms." These powers are not beings who were created by God and subsequently fell from grace. They are metaphysical powers inherent in a human invention called modern human economics. Fed by greed and avarice, sins that are contrary to Christ ("antichrist"), they have now grown so big as to take over our very lives. So great has their power become that we now take such powers for granted. But in the end, they will destroy us.

This is a totally different way of interpreting the book of Revelation and its depiction of the battle of Armageddon than those offered by biblical systems advanced before Wink's work in the 1980s.

Sources:

Borg, Marcus J. *The God We Never Knew: Beyond Dogmatic Religion to a More Authentic Contemporary Faith.* San Francisco: HarperSanFrancisco, 1997.

———. *Reading the Bible Again for the First Time: Taking the Bible Seriously but Not Literally.* San Francisco: HarperSanFrancisco, 2001.

LaHaye, Tim, and Jerry B. Jenkins. *Left Behind* series. 12 vols. Carol Stream, IL: Tyndale House, 1995–2004.

Lindsey, Hal. *Apocalypse Code.* Palos Verdes, CA: Western Front Ltd., 1997.

Wink, Walter. *Engaging the Powers.* Minneapolis: Fortress Press, 1992.

———. *Naming the Powers.* Philadelphia: Fortress Press, 1984.

———. *The Powers That Be: Theology for a New Millennium.* New York: Doubleday, 1999.

———. *Unmasking the Powers.* Philadelphia: Fortress Press, 1986.

SPACE/TIME CONTINUUM *see* **Hawking, Stephen**

SUN, DEATH OF

Poets of many times and places have written in awe of the "eternal stars." But astronomers know that stars are not eternal. A star is an ongoing thermonuclear reaction. As such, it burns fuel. When the fuel runs out, the star dies.

Our sun is a fairly ordinary star and will undergo a fairly ordinary death. Roughly 5 billion years old, it is now entering middle age. But eventually it will achieve the stellar equivalent of codgerhood. And that will be, to put it mildly, very bad news for any living thing still occupying planet Earth, including any of our descendants.

As the aging sun consumes its hydrogen fuel and loses mass, it will paradoxically become larger and more luminous, swelling into a fiery ball known as a "red giant." It will grow two thousand times more luminous and a hundred times larger than today's familiar yellow globe. At some point its outer edges will enclose the earth. The entire planet will be, in effect, cremated. Of course, life here will have ended long before this, as the oceans boil away and the land becomes barren, red-hot rock.

The good news is that this scenario gives us quite a bit of time to escape—or at least to put our affairs in order. Most astronomers estimate that the red-giant stage will not arrive for another 4 to 7 billion years. The bad news is that procrastinators should not take too much comfort from this timetable. The sun is even now growing steadily brighter. Those who study such things suggest that in a mere billion years (some say as little as half a billion), it will be 11 percent brighter than today, heating our planet to a level inhospitable to life. And 3.5 billion years from now, it will be 40 percent brighter, probably broiling everything on the earth's surface.

In short, it may be later than we think.

Sources:

Britt, Robert Roy. "Freeze, Fry or Dry: How Long Has the Earth Got?" http://www.space.com/scienceastronomy/solarsystem/death_of_earth_000224.html.

———. "Recipe for Saving Earth: Move It." http://www.space.com/scienceastronomy/planet earth/earth_move_010207.html.

"The Evolution of a Sun-like Star." http://astronomy.nju.edu.cn/astron/AT3/AT32002.HTM.

SUPERNOVA THREAT

The subject of Armageddon is not an inherently cheerful one. Even those who see the end of the world as generally desirable from a religious point of view perhaps have a few pangs of regret when they contemplate the elimination of all life on planet Earth. And as this book illustrates, there is no shortage of endtime scenarios.

But once in a while good news appears on the doomsday front. Such seems to be the case with the threat of extinction by way of a nearby supernova event.

Many stars, including our sun, will go to their demise in gradual, predictable stages (see Sun, Death of). But some, including stars more massive than the sun and, at the other end of the size scale, those known as white dwarfs, tend to exit more spectacularly. They explode. Picture the detonation of a star-sized hydrogen bomb. That is roughly what happens in a supernova event. Such an occurrence naturally does little to improve property values in the immediate neighborhood—including on the planets of other stars nearby.

From the 1970s until fairly recently, many astronomers thought that a supernova explosion within about 55 light years of the sun would strip the earth of its ozone layer and much of its atmosphere. Massive extinctions would be certain. In the worst case, life on earth would end completely.

But now researchers believe that such an explosion would need to occur much closer to us in order to cause major damage. Scientists at NASA and Kansas University suggest that a supernova would have to be within 26 light years of earth to damage the ozone layer and, in turn, allow cancer-causing ultraviolet radiation to flood the planet's surface.

The difference might not seem great at first glance. But a cosmic sphere surrounding the earth with a 26-light-year radius is very much smaller than one with a 55-light-year radius. Thus it contains far fewer stars that are candidates to go supernova. According to Dr. Neil Gehrels of NASA's Goddard Space Flight Center, a supernova explosion within 26 light years of us is likely to take place only once in every 670 million years.

Given that such an event has probably taken place at least once during the existence of multicellular life on our planet, scientists are also reexamining the probable consequences. Some suggest that the effects might be considerably shorter-lived and less dire than those predicted only a few years ago. Mass extinction is still a possibility, especially with a very nearby supernova, but a more likely outcome is the stripping of perhaps half of the ozone layer. Although this would mean serious trouble for us and many other living things, it would not bring about a planetary Armageddon.

As comforting as this scientific reevaluation may be, a distinctly spooky side of the supernova threat remains: If it ever happens, it will strike without advance notice. The first and worst effect of a supernova is the storm of deadly gamma radiation generated by the explosion. Gamma rays travel at the speed of light. So the effects of the event arrive simultaneously with the news of its occurrence. If a star within a few light years of earth ever goes supernova, we will probably never know what hit us.

Source:
"Earth Likely Spared from One Form of Cosmic Doom." http://www.spacedaily.com/news/supernova_
   03b.html.

TECUMSEH

Without historical perspective it is easy to assume that the return of Jesus Christ at the end of time is a unique story that burst full-blown upon the human eschatological consciousness. A deeply religious figure preaches about the need to overthrow the present social system and gathers a group of followers who come to share his vision. He is killed before his dream is fulfilled, but before his death he promises that he will someday return, accompanied by signs in the heavens and natural disasters on earth, and bring to fruition his vision of a new society. Until then, his disciples are told to hold on in faith.

But the story of the returning messiah figure is not unique to Christianity. Indeed, slightly before the formation of the Christian church, then overlapping it while sharing the same years of history in the same culture, Mithraism told a strikingly similar story. It shared so many points of common mythology that some scholars think Christianity was modeled upon the ancient Roman "soldier's religion." In the same way, both King Arthur and Merlin of old are rumored to be awaiting a return to history when the time is right.

But we needn't go that far back to find a similar story told by another culture. In America, one of the most striking messiah-figure legends grew up around Tecumseh, hero of the Shawnee Indians and one of their greatest leaders. His story is strikingly similar to that of Jesus, especially as it impacted later generations of Shawnees.

Tecumseh means "shooting star." He earned the name because his birth was marked by an unusual event in the nighttime heavens, perhaps something as unusual as the star that supposedly inspired wise men from the East to journey to Bethlehem. Tecumseh and his brother Tenskwatawa, "the Prophet," formed a political-religious duo that bears striking resemblance to the political leader and false prophet who share center stage at the battle of Armageddon. Tecumseh was a Shawnee fundamentalist.

Tecumseh. *Library of Congress.*

He urged his people to reject white European inventions, believing that only by a return to their own "old-time religion" could the Shawnee ever be free to live on the land God had given them. He became a political and war leader—a far-seeing politician who sought to unite all Indians. His brother became the mystical voice of the Shawnee religion.

Believing that strength lay in unity, Tecumseh traveled to virtually every Indian tribe between Ohio and Florida. His message was always the same. Holding up a single arrow to represent a single tribe, he easily broke it. But when many arrows were held together, even the strongest man could not break them. Likewise, if the tribes banded together, they would become an unbreakable, invincible force to withstand the European invasion.

Tecumseh urged all tribes to unite and strike the whites on a single day. The signal that the time had come—at least according to legend—was to be a miraculous earthquake that would cause the Mississippi River to flow backward. Tragically for the Shawnee, Tecumseh's brother proved to be a false prophet. Ignoring Tecumseh's strict order not to attack the whites while Tecumseh was traveling, building his political coalition, Tenskwatawa claimed that the Master of Life, the primary god of the Shawnee, had personally visited him with instructions to strike before the divine sign was given. The results were disastrous. The battle of Tippecanoe in November 1811 decimated the Prophet's people. Tecumseh's leadership, along with his alliance, fell apart.

Less than a month later, on December 16, the Mississippi River Valley experienced the first of a series of magnitude-8 earthquakes that were among the most powerful in American history. So great was the upheaval that the waters of the Mississippi River actually flowed backward for a time.

Though by now it was too late to mount an effective campaign, there were still those who believed. In 1813, at the battle of the Thames, a combined British and Indian army, including Tecumseh and his warriors, met American forces under the command of William Henry Harrison. The British fled the field, leaving the Indians all alone.

Tecumseh, it is said, had previously given instructions that if he fell in battle, someone had only to strike his body three times with a rifle ramrod and he would rise from the dead. The whites would be defeated and forced to leave the continent. Indian religion would be restored, and old values would return. So strong were his words that when he fell in the fight one of his trusted lieutenants did, indeed, try to reach him, brandishing a ramrod. But the man was shot and killed before the deed could be accomplished.

After the battle, Tecumseh's body could not be found. Many historians suggest that the scout Simon Kenton (a.k.a. Simon Butler), who had developed great respect for Tecumseh, either hid the body or deliberately failed to identify it so as to prevent mutilation by American troops, and that Tecumseh's followers returned by night to take the body away. Whatever happened, the missing body caused rumors to fly and legends to grow. To this day there are those who believe Tecumseh will return to restore the fortunes of his people. The legend persists that a great battle is yet to be fought. An Indian army will defeat the whites and restore the land to what it was originally intended by the Creator.

The Indian Armageddon, in other words, might yet come.

Meanwhile the legend serves as a reminder that the biblical prophets are not alone in believing that their savior will return. They are mining a rich source of human mythological history.

Sources:
Eckert, Alan. *The Frontiersman: A Narrative.* Ashland, KY: Jesse Stuart Foundation, 2001.
"Simon Kenton." www.ohiohistorycentral.org/ohc/h/peo/kentons.shtml.

TEMPLE AT JERUSALEM

Many evangelical Christians believe that we are living in the last days of human history. That belief hinges, at least in part, on events that they believe have transpired or will transpire in one particular location—the center of Jewish-Christian sacred history. It is important to Islam as well, because this spot of ground is now occupied by a Muslim mosque popularly referred to as the Dome of the Rock. It was formerly the location of the Great Temple at Jerusalem. Every photograph of the skyline of Jerusalem prominently displays the golden roof of the mosque that is the destination of many a contemporary tourist, whether Christian, Jew, or Muslim.

It is perhaps inevitable that controversy should swirl around this particular piece of real estate. Following their scriptures, Jews believe that a Jewish temple will again stand on this site. In a passage dealing with a future time, the Hebrew prophet Isaiah wrote, "This is what the Lord says.... he will say of Jerusalem, 'Let it be rebuilt,' and of the temple, 'Let its foundations be laid'" (Isa. 44:24, 28). Needless to say, Muslims resent the idea that their sacred mosque is only temporary. Meanwhile, many evangelical Christians believe that a physical temple must be rebuilt on this site before Jesus returns.

A good case can be made that the entire Bible revolves around this small spot of ground. Biblical history starts here in Genesis and ends here in Revelation. At the end of time, according to the author of Revelation, we will know that the plan of God concerning humans is complete because, after Satan is cast into the "lake of fire," we will see "the Holy City, the New Jerusalem, coming down from God, prepared as a bride beautifully dressed for her husband"; the writer adds, "I did not see a temple in the city, because the Lord God Almighty and the Lamb are its temple" (Rev. 21:2, 22).

The place is mentioned first in Genesis 14. Abraham, father of the Jewish people, is returning victorious from a tribal war called the battle of the Five Kings. On his way home he stops off at the city of Salem (now called Jerusalem, which means "City of Peace"). Here he encounters a mystery man named Melchizedek, who is both a king and a priest. Melchizedek offers Abraham a gift of bread and wine. Abraham, for reasons left unexplained, immediately offers Melchizedek a tithe, or tenth, of his spoils from the war. Melchizedek then returns to Salem, and nothing more is written about him until an obscure reference in the New Testament: Hebrews 7, written more than two thousand years after this incident supposedly took place, presents Melchizedek as a type, or symbol, of Jesus Christ. He was both priest and king of the City of Peace, offered bread and wine, and received tithes and offerings. The similarities between the two men's religious actions had been noticed very early in the Christian tradition.

When Genesis takes up the history of this site, it tells the story that has become the foundational theological treatise of three religions. In Genesis 22, Abraham offers his son Isaac as a sacrifice to God in the mountains of Moriah, near Salem. Both Jewish and Christian tradition claim that this incident took place on the very spot of ground where the Dome of the Rock now stands, in the center of today's Jerusalem. God provided an animal substitute for the human sacrifice, and religion in the Middle East took an evolutionary step forward.

This sacrifice forms the basis for the religious traditions that followed. The Jewish sacrificial system came to insist that sacrifices could be offered only here, at this place. When the Jews no longer controlled the location, the sacrificial system ceased. Until they get it back, that system cannot be resurrected. Christians go a step farther. According to their theology, it was here, in the mountains of Moriah and the city of Jerusalem, that Jesus was offered as a sacrifice for the sins of the world.

But that was all still in the future when, somewhere around 2000 BCE, according to tradition, Abraham walked down from the mountains of Moriah and began his journey into history. Much more would happen here over the next two millennia.

The scene now moves forward in time and across the Sinai Peninsula. Moses has led the Jewish people out of Egypt and is in the process of forging the religion that would become known as Judaism. Part of that religion consisted of building a portable tabernacle in the wilderness (Exod. 35–40). The tabernacle became the central gathering place for worship. It housed the Ark of the Covenant (see entry), which contained the Ten Commandments, and it was the only place where sacrifices could be offered for sin. The people would approach the great bronze altar standing before the door of the Holy Place, the inner sanctuary, and confess their sin while placing their hands upon a sacrificial lamb. A spiritual substitution would occur. The lamb received their sin, they received the lamb's innocence, and the lamb suffered the penalty in their place. This transaction is now called "substitutionary atonement."

The Building and Destruction of the First Temple

This practice persisted for five hundred years. But about 1000 BCE, King David decided that he must build a permanent center of Jewish worship. Through divine intervention—a complicated story described in 1 Chronicles 21—the place for the temple was

The Dedication of the Temple (reproduction, ca. 1925, of a painting by William Hole). *Library of Congress.*

revealed: the spot in Jerusalem where the Dome of the Rock now stands. That's why the Hebrew rabbis still refer to this hill as the Temple Mount, not the Dome of the Rock.

David's son Solomon built the first temple (2 Chron. 3–5), and it stood as the center of Jewish worship until 586 BCE. According to Masonic tradition, its construction was carried out by the members of the first order of Masons, sent by King Hiram of Tyre to accomplish the project. Many people who have studied temples around the world believe that the Masonic order knew of mystical measurements and construction dimensions, "divine geometry," that they secretly passed on through their order down through the years. According to this belief, mathematical proportions revealing spiritual mysteries are to be found in sacred buildings as far apart as the Pyramids, the cathedrals of the Middle Ages, and the temples of Central America.

The temple at Jerusalem was so magnificent that the queen of Sheba, visiting from afar, was moved to declare that Solomon was the greatest living king. But it was not to last forever. The prophet Ezekiel, writing in the sixth century BCE, detected what he considered to be a weakening of Jewish spirituality. In a vision recorded in Ezekiel 10, he saw "the glory depart from Israel." In 586 BCE Nebuchadnezzar, king of Babylon, besieged the city and destroyed it, carrying off the cream of its population and ushering in the great Jewish dispersion that became known as the Babylonian captivity.

The Building and Destruction of the Second Temple

For a century the temple lay in ruins, even while Babylon was in turn conquered by the Persians. But a Jewish remnant returned to the site when Cyrus the Great of Persia had a change of heart (Ezra 1) and sent the Jewish priest Ezra back to rebuild the temple. Cyrus's successor, Artaxerxes, went even further. He sent a band of workmen under Nehemiah to rebuild the wall around the old city of Jerusalem (Neh. 2). The ancient city of Melchizedek, the place where Abraham sacrificed his son, the magnificent center of Solomon's empire, now experienced urban renewal. It stood for another five hundred years.

At the time of Jesus, the city was experiencing yet another renovation. King Herod Antipas, demonstrating patriotic pride, was in the midst of beautifying the place when Jesus and his disciples rode into town on what is now called Palm Sunday. The disciples were quite impressed with the whole building project, exclaiming how magnificent everything looked. But Jesus, like Ezekiel of old, was not impressed with the outward trappings. He looked inward to the spirituality of the people around him. After lashing out against what he considered to be religious corruption, he is said to have cried out:

> "O Jerusalem, Jerusalem, you who kill the prophets and stone those sent to you, how often I have longed to gather your children together, as a hen gathers her chicks under her wings, but you were not willing. Look, your house is left to you desolate. For I tell you, you will not see me again until you say, 'Blessed is he who comes in the name of the Lord.'" Jesus left the temple and was walking away when his disciples came up to him to call his attention to its buildings. "Do you see all these things?" he asked. "I tell you the truth, not one stone will be left on another; every one will be thrown down." (Matt. 23)

Forty years after Jesus reportedly made his final statement concerning the temple at Jerusalem, Titus and the Roman legions destroyed it all. Rome was tired of constant religious bickering and the refusal of the Jewish rabbis to allow a statue of the caesar to be placed in what the Jews called their Holy City. Jewish leaders considered such a thing to be a graven idol, forbidden by the Ten Commandments. So Rome acted with a vengeance and destroyed the place, carrying the population off in yet another great diaspora. Not one stone was left standing on another. All that remains today of that original magnificence are a few courses of the original wall around the city, now commonly called the Wailing Wall, after the vocal Jewish manner of praying. The courtyard is daily filled with worshipers, Jew and Gentile alike, who make pilgrimages to this sacred spot. It is arguably the spiritual center of Judaism today.

But from an evangelical Christian and conservative Jewish viewpoint, the history does not end here. More will transpire and is occurring even now.

A Third Temple

On May 21, 1967, an advertisement appeared in the *Washington Post*, author unknown:

> To persons of the Jewish Faith all over the world: The project to rebuild the Temple of God in Israel is now being started. With divine guidance and hope the Temple will now be completed. It will signal a new era in Judaism. Jews will be inspired to conduct themselves in such a moral way that our Maker will see fit to pay us a visit here on earth. Imagine the warm feeling that will be ours when this happy event takes place.... God will place in the minds of many persons in all walks of Jewish life the desire to participate in this work. Executive talents, administrators and workers in all levels are needed. All efforts will be anonymous. God will know those desiring to participate. God's will shall prevail.

Two weeks after this ad appeared, Old Jerusalem was conquered by Israeli troops in the 1967 Six-Day War. It is said that when the young soldiers ran through the streets toward the site of the old temple and the Wailing Wall, they threw down their weapons, pulled out their yarmulkes, and fell to the ground in prayer even while bullets continued to fly around them. So great was the religious/patriotic response to this emotional moment that the Israeli government issued a stamp to commemorate the occasion. On the stamp was a fig tree, the national symbol of Israel. Underneath were the Hebrew words—the very ones uttered by Jesus in Matthew 23—*Baruch haba*, "Blessed is he [who comes])."

Both Jewish prophets and Christian evangelists insist that a third temple must be built before the Messiah comes or Jesus returns. Hal Lindsey, author of *The Late Great Planet Earth*, writes: "There remains but one more event to completely set the stage for Israel's part in the last great act of her historical drama. That is to rebuild the ancient Temple of worship upon its old site."

Is it any wonder that tempers flare in Jerusalem when it comes to the politics of ownership of this spot of ground? To Muslims this is a sacred mosque. To Christians it is the scene of the triumphal return of Jesus Christ. To Jews it is their religious heritage and the place the long-awaited Messiah will come to earth.

Evangelical Christians received a jolt of prophetic adrenaline during the tumultuous six days of the 1967 war. In Matthew 24, Jesus is reported to have listed a long series of events that have since been labeled "the signs of the times" or "the signs of the end" (see Endtimes). One of the keys to that prophecy involves the "abomination that is desolation" (see Abomination of Desolation), a profanation of the holy center of worship that can only occur at the site of the final temple. He then warns that "this generation will certainly not pass away until all these things have happened" (Matt. 24:34). What "generation" was he talking about? The answer, according to many evangelical scholars, is the generation that will see "all these things" happening. Figuring a biblical generation to be about forty years, the capture of the temple site in 1967 is considered to be a possible beginning to the countdown. For those who think in these terms, Jesus will return during the first decade of the twenty-first century. Others warn that we must not begin counting until the temple is rebuilt. Still others, appearing on Christian television shows such as Pat Robertson's *700 Club* speaking in "endtimes" chat rooms on the Internet, and hosting Web sites dealing with various conspiracy theories, claim the building is going on in secret even now.

Other Interpretations

Alternative viewpoints about the temple exist within Christianity (see Revelation). Evangelical Christianity has traditionally been known for a literal reading of the Bible and for linking passages scattered throughout both Testaments, even though the authors of those passages may have been separated in time by thousands of years. The evangelical justification for this interpretive technique is that the Bible really has only one author. The individuals who wrote the various books were merely God's instruments. Prophecies, according to this view, are cumulative, foretelling events yet in the future.

Other branches of Christianity and Judaism counter that the authors did not intend their words to be used in this way but were writing about contemporary events that would have been recognized by people of their day (see also Abomination of Desolation). According to this view, the temple site is important because of its history and emotional impact upon people today. What will yet happen there is anyone's guess.

Sources:

The Holy Bible, New International Version. Grand Rapids, MI: Zondervan, 1978.

Lindsey, Hal, with C. C. Carlson. *The Late Great Planet Earth.* Grand Rapids, MI: Zondervan, 1970.

Willis, Jim. *The Religion Book: Places, Prophets, Saints, and Seers.* Detroit: Visible Ink Press, 2004.

TEN-NATION CONFEDERACY *see* **European Common Market and European Union**

TERMINATOR, THE *see* **Hollywood Envisions THE END**

THEONOMIC POSTMILLENNIALISM
(See also Christian Reconstructionism)

This delightful if rather intimidating label describing the end of history becomes more understandable after breaking it down to its component parts.

First of all, *theonomy* means "God's law." The word can best be understood as denoting the concept that human society should be founded upon divine decree, specifically the law as it is found first in the Ten Commandments and later in the fully developed 613 laws in the Pentateuch. Theonomists believe that these laws have never been rescinded and so are still in effect.

"Postmillennialism" is the belief that the Millennium (see entry) is not a specific thousand years, but rather a long period of time during which God will bring about God's will on earth. At the end of this period Jesus Christ will return to rule over a unified and restored people.

Theonomic postmillennialism, then, a feature of Christian reconstructionism, is the belief that the time between the first and second advents of Jesus Christ is to be spent gradually returning to Old Testament social and legal norms. This result will be achieved through a slow, widespread acceptance of the gospel through the success of preaching, teaching, evangelism, and ministry. When the world has thus proved that it deserves the honor, Jesus Christ will return and rule from Jerusalem, the new capital city of planet Earth. Armageddon will be the final battle to eliminate the last of those who will not follow God's laws.

Source:
Bock, Darrell L., ed. *Three Views on the Millennium and Beyond.* Grand Rapids, MI: Zondervan, 1999.

THEORIES OF THE END

A theology or religious philosophy of the end of time directly stems from a conception of how things began and how things are being sustained. Preliminary belief structures led to the differing schools of thought popular today. Whether reading about a scientific theory or a religious doctrine, it is helpful to sort out the writer's underlying point of view concerning the force or consciousness behind the cosmos.

Determining an author's train of thought begins with a critical question: Does the universe demonstrate purpose or is it an accident? The answer leads down one of two philosophical paths that arrive at quite different theories about how the world will end.

If the universe happened naturally and life arose out of normal forces still at work today, without divine consciousness, then theories about how it will end usually involve natural forces as well. For example, an asteroid that struck the earth 65 million years ago very probably destroyed the dinosaurs that had been the planet's dominant vertebrates for millions of years. What happened once will very probably happen again. If the universe arose from the Big Bang (see entry), then there is a good chance it will collapse in on itself or run out of energy and cool down (see Big Crunch, Big Chill, and Big Rip). Perhaps this is only one of many universes. On and on the possibilities continue. Each is valid. Each consists of taking natural, testable processes now at work to their logical conclusions. This kind of thinking concludes with an Armageddon event recognizable by today's level of scientific knowledge.

Another branch down this same path, but running parallel to it, leads to what has been called the "anthropic principle." In its simplest form, this is the idea that the universe seems fine-tuned to produce a conscious, carbon-based life form that will eventually evolve to the point where it can begin to wonder whether it exists "in the image of God" or not. This line of reasoning leads to an understanding of Armageddon consisting of the possibility that life can destroy itself by its own actions as soon as it reaches a sufficient rung on the technological ladder. No "higher power" will intervene.

These two paths are generally labeled "scientific" viewpoints.

The philosophical path that begins with the premise that life seems to have been arranged by a higher power leads to quite a different end. This is the so-called religious viewpoint. One often-stated side argument of this belief system is that a creative consciousness would not create life only to see it destroyed. This path accepts the axiom of purpose, not chance. In other words, a heavenly parent is watching his/her children at play and will step in if needed to prevent catastrophe.

When following the doctrines of those who travel this path, one discovers inevitable signposts along the way. The signposts are written in the distinctive language of the various religious traditions. They are usually warning signs: Don't do this or that or else! Ten well-known examples hang on the walls of many a religion's place of worship: the Ten Commandments.

One common variation on this theme is that the earth and human beings are somehow special. Earth was created so life would have a place to live. It wasn't an accident. Many people with a religious point of view feel comfortable with this way of thinking because it seems to embrace both a scientific and a religious philosophy. Earth might have arisen through natural processes, but those processes were guided, or at least begun, by a higher power. Earth is a natural home for human beings because the cosmos was designed to be that way. The time spans of geologic and cosmic history were designed to produce life as we know it. Many who hold this view take the further step of deducing that the universe must have an end, and that Armageddon, in one form or another, is the inevitable result of a divine mind that projected the arrow of time toward a conclusion point.

How do the scientific and religious viewpoints progress toward the full-blown end-of-the-world theories discussed in this book? Generally through one of four basic patterns of thought.

Process

In this view, life is gradually unfolding. There is no sudden eschatological upheaval as is pictured in the book of Revelation. Armageddon is a metaphor, not a historical event. Christianity evolved from Judaism. Islam evolved from both. Buddhism evolved from Hinduism, as did Jainism. Both Confucianism and Daoism evolved in response to cultural stimuli. Science builds upon a base of evidence for or against various hypotheses. It is all cumulative knowledge.

Many who adhere to this viewpoint believe that a spiritual process or a body of knowledge is continually pulling us toward something that is usually defined as either spiritual completion or full knowledge of everything. The end result is something akin to a biblical battle of Armageddon or a scientific Theory of Everything.

Relationship

Ever since Einstein (see Einstein, Albert) people have tended to view the cosmos in term of relationships. Einstein hypothesized the interconnectedness of space and time. Matter curves space by gravitational attraction, but the curvature of space-time affects the path of matter. Quantum theory (see entry) suggests that subatomic particles remain entangled in unending relationship despite their location. Theology is about relationship, too. People exist in relationship with their Creator, the creation, and each other. A central doctrine of all monotheistic religions is to love both God and other human beings.

This view of the cosmos tends to lead to endings consisting of perfected relationships. In the religious world that usually means the relationship between Creator and created or a final resting place in perfect consciousness. In the scientific world it is in relationship itself that all things exist. Armageddon will come when those relationships, especially those that are gravitational in nature, will either exert enough force to collapse everything into a perfect unity or lose their power to hold things together.

Information

Science seeks to understand. Religions are all about the renewal of the mind. Knowledge is the basis for each. The old-time religious euphemism for sexual intercourse (as in, "Adam knew his wife and she conceived") even expresses a basic biological imperative in terms of knowledge.

Science seeks to understand completely. The apostle Paul expressed the yearning of all theologians when he said, "Now I know in part; then I shall know fully, even as I am fully known" (1 Cor. 13:12).

In this point of view, Armageddon represents either the end of knowledge by destruction of the questioners (if you are a scientist) or a beginning of true knowledge in the spirit (if you are a religious person).

Language

A mathematician will say that prime numbers have "always been there." But where were they? It's difficult to say. Mathematics is a scientific, universal language expressing universal cosmic reality. Religions also develop a language to express metaphorical and social reality. Both fields must use language to convey their particular versions of truth.

In a note to Einstein's widow after the great physicist's death, his colleague Michele Besso wrote, "Now he has departed a little ahead of me from this quaint world. This means nothing. For us faithful physicists, the separation between past, present and future has only the meaning of an illusion, though a persistent one." Notice the scientist's use of "religious" language to convey a universal expression of the end of life. Language crosses over boundaries between fields, perhaps because the fields are dealing with similar concepts of truth (see Scientific "God" Language).

All this is to say that when confronted by myriad theories of the end, it sometimes helps to trace the final result back down the corridor to its starting point. The writers and spokespeople may not be revealing as much about ending differences as beginning similarities.

Adolf Hitler in 1923. *Library of Congress.*

Sources:
Jammer, M. *Einstein and Religion.* Princeton, NJ: Princeton University Press, 1999.
Polkinghorne, John. *The God of Hope and the End of the World.* New Haven: Yale University Press, 2002.

THESSALONIANS *see* **Books of the Bible and Their Relation to Prophecy**

THOUSAND-YEAR REICH

Adolf Hitler and his propaganda machine regularly and loudly plumped their grand scheme of building a Third Reich upon the legacy of the Holy Roman Empire (the First Reich) and the German Empire beginning in 1871 (the Second Reich). Hitler swore that the Third Reich would last for a thousand years. It lasted for twelve.

There is considerable debate about where Hitler's idea of a thousand years came from. Some believe he got it from the Bible. He was mimicking the book of Revelation's claim that Jesus Christ will return to earth and reign for a thousand years. Others suggest that "a thousand years," as used by both Hitler and the author of Revelation, is simply a metaphor for "a very long time" (see Millennialism; Revelation).

During World War II, many saw in Hitler's actions and heard in his words the echo of an antichrist who desired to imitate the actions of God. They believed the war that soon engulfed the whole world was a sign of the endtimes. Many a sermon was preached that attempted to link biblical passages with current events. The swastika, for instance, was a symbol often used on ancient Hebrew synagogues and models of the Ark of the Covenant (see entry). Some preachers saw in Hitler's use of the symbol, given the fact of the Holocaust and the slaughter of ten million people, six million of them Jews, an act of apostasy and blasphemy aimed directly at God. In this way, Hitler became a personal epitome of all that was evil, not just because of his inhumanity, but because of his challenge to the very authority of the Christian God. Those who held this view saw World War II as a holy war—perhaps even, before history proved them mistaken, the prophesied battle of Armageddon.

Source:
Gonzalez, Justo L. *The Story of Christianity.* 2 vols. New York: Harper & Row, 1985.

THOUSAND YEARS *see* **Millennium**

TIME THEORIES *see* **Barbour, Julian**

TOGARMAH

According to the prophet Ezekiel (see entry), Togarmah is the region in Asia Minor that will supply most of the horses and horsemen who will fight in the final battle of the world (Ezek. 27:14). They will sweep down from the north upon a land of unprotected cities and wreak havoc upon unsuspecting people (Ezek. 38:9–16).

Because this is the same region historically identified with the Cossacks, many evangelical Christian theologians believe Togarmah to be a code name for Russia. During the evangelical awakening of the 1970s it was common for conspiracy buffs to declare that the USSR was secretly buying and hoarding bridles. Their theory was that the terrain between Russia and Israel favored the use of horses.

Although a few recent literary treatments of the endtimes go so far as to picture the principals in the battle of Armageddon riding horses, it is getting harder these days to find theologians, even in conservative camps, who view the Russian horsemen of Revelation as being anything but metaphorical.

Source:
Buttrick, George A., ed. *The Interpreter's Dictionary of the Bible.* 4 vols. New York: Abingdon Press, 1962.

TOYNBEE, ARNOLD

No one has a better reputation for understanding the rise and fall of civilizations than the British historian Arnold Joseph Toynbee (1889–1975). His best-known work, *A Study of History*, follows the course of virtually every major civilization known on earth, and many minor ones. He identified a total of twenty-six of them, five of which he labeled "arrested civilizations."

But his work was subject to criticism from some quarters because he chose to follow a novel approach. Rather than analyze civilizations by the traditional method of studying national criteria, he chose to identify them by cultural patterns, especially religious tendencies. In his words: "An intelligible field of historical study is not to be found within a national framework." He believed civilizations are founded as a direct response to challenges that arise when "creative minorities inspire unprecedented effort to solve the problems faced by the society." He determined that all civilizations follow two distinct stages. The first sees a civilization arise in response to a time of troubles. The Roman Empire and Western Christianity are two examples. The second stage is the age of decline, for which Toynbee identifies three phases of eventual breakdown:

1. The vision of the initial creative minority begins to decay.
2. The majority of the civilization's people gradually withdraw their allegiance.
3. Social decay follows.

In this regard Toynbee followed the lead of Edward Gibbon, whose eighteenth-century work *The History of the Decline and Fall of the Roman Empire* listed five reasons for the fall of Rome:

1. Sports and entertainment received more and more money while the plight of the poor was neglected.
2. Money went to the military rather than public infrastructure.
3. Violence became increasingly prevalent.
4. People's faith in government became undermined, and justly so.
5. Religious roots fragmented and became cause for dissension.

If Toynbee's assessment is correct, his ideas have profound implications for modern civilizations. His description of society in decay is precisely the vision put forth by popular Hollywood movies such as *The Postman* and the *Mad Max* series (see Hollywood Envisions THE END). Toward the end of his life Toynbee became increasingly troubled by the impact of technology and what was beginning to be called the "global village." In 1976 his *Mankind and Mother Earth*, published posthumously, warned that "a man-made catastrophe could wreck the biosphere and would eventually destroy mankind together with all other forms of life." The only way to prevent such devastation—in Toynbee's words, "murdering Mother Earth"—was for humankind to "redeem her [Mother Earth] by overcoming the suicidal, aggressive greed that, in all living creatures, including Man himself, has been the price of the Great Mother's gift of life."

Sources:

Toynbee, Arnold. *Civilization on Trial*. New York: Oxford University Press, 1948.
———. *Mankind and Mother Earth*. New York: Oxford University Press, 1976.
———. *A Study of History*. Reprint ed. New York: Oxford University Press, 1987.

TREE OF LIFE *see* **Cross, The**

TRIBULATION *see* **Great Tribulation**

TRILATERAL COMMISSION

It has somehow become almost an axiom that the Bible foretells a "one-world government." In fact, it doesn't. There are veiled references to a "ten-nation confederacy" of European nations (see European Common Market and European Union) led by an antichrist (see Antichrist) who causes everyone to wear a "mark of the beast" (see Mark of the Beast). But no scholars, even very conservative ones, teach that the whole world will one day be united under a single government. Indeed, if that were the case, who would fight the final battle of Armageddon? The whole point of the battle is that the antichrist is trying to unite the world under his power. If he had already done so, there would be no reason for the battle to take place.

Nevertheless, the popular idea somehow arose that a secret society that is "anti-Christ," contrary to the will of God, is attempting to rule the world. In the evangelical frenzy of the 1970s, in part spurred by the author Hal Lindsey's condemnation of the Trilateral Commission in his speeches throughout the country, a candidate for one-world government was identified that united the evangelical world with the fundamentalists and the John Birch Society. All three groups featured outspoken leaders who thundered that the Trilateral Commission was the secret, world-ruling, devil-inspired organization destined to become the tool of the antichrist.

Founded in 1973 by international financier David Rockefeller, the Trilateral Commission certainly seemed a likely candidate. Rockefeller had been inspired by a book, *Between Two Ages*, written by Zbigniew Brzezinski, a political scientist who advised several U.S. presidents. The book proposed an alliance among the United States, Western Europe, and Japan. Hence the name Trilateral, meaning "three-sided." Brzezinski believed that "the American system is compelled to accommodate itself to this emerging international context." In time, social forces would compel the economic elite to unite in order to protect their interests in the world.

When the commission discovered a relatively unknown but sympathetic southern governor, deemed him an appropriate presidential candidate, helped to finance his campaign, and worked hard to get him elected to the highest office in the land, it seemed they were well on their way to accomplishing their goals. When their candidate became President Jimmy Carter, Brzezinski even found himself in a position to further their cause from the hallowed sanctuary of the Oval Office as Carter's national security adviser.

Although critics like Senator Barry Goldwater of Arizona declared that the Trilateral Commission was simply a surrogate of the Rockefeller family—Goldwater claimed that "every individual who was invited to participate" was "screened and selected" by David Rockefeller—such complaints fell mostly on deaf ears. Those who did listen were primarily evangelical Christians who eventually turned on the most solidly evangelical president ever elected. They fought to replace the Baptist Sunday-school teacher Jimmy Carter with an Episcopalian actor, Ronald Reagan. Their revolt mystified many national media pundits and reporters. How could such high-profile members of the religious right as Jerry Falwell and Pat Robertson abandon one of their own? Most news sources were simply not yet aware of the underground goings-on and philosophical musings of the Christian right. In the 1970s it was still a force running largely under the radar of the mainstream media. They would soon learn.

The simple fact was that a great many evangelicals had become convinced that the end of the world was at hand. Their preachers had discovered in the Bible the sure and certain verses from the Creator himself proving that the last days would soon be upon us. And in this context of apocalyptic ferment the Trilateral Commission, sounding for all the world like the architects of a "one-world government," became a catalyst of change that helped propel a religious-political movement into power.

That movement is still growing and has become a force to be reckoned with in American politics. Its members still believe that the world will soon see the return of Jesus Christ. They still search the headlines for evidence of that return. Anything smacking of a one-world government that might control whether they can "buy or sell" (Rev. 13:17) justifies their belief.

It is a supreme irony that even the leading proponents of endtimes prophecy claim the Bible teaches no such thing.

Sources:
Fackre, Gabriel. *The Religious Right and Christian Faith*. Grand Rapids, MI: Eerdmans, 1982.
"Trilateral Commission: World Shadow Government." http://www.afgen.com/trilateral.html.

UNIDENTIFIED FLYING OBJECTS

(See also Aliens)

> The UFO phenomenon burst onto the world scene in the wake of a
> sighting made over the Cascade Mountains on June 24, 1947, when
> private pilot Kenneth Arnold spotted nine shiny disks moving in for-
> mation at a speed of more than 1,200 mph. The sighting, and those
> that immediately followed it, in the Pacific Northwest and elsewhere,
> inspired an anonymous headline writer to coin the phrase "flying
> saucers." The more sober, Air Force–concocted term "unidentified fly-
> ing objects" did not come into popular usage until the mid-1950s.

With these words in *The UFO Book: Encyclopedia of the Extraterrestrial*, Jerome
Clark introduces readers to a popular, psychological, emotional, scientific, and yet
strangely religious field—the field of flying saucers, or UFOs. Clark's book contains
example after example of reported unidentified flying objects and possible extraterrestrial visitations.

The UFO phenomenon took hold in the popular imagination only a few years
after the explosions over targets in Japan of the world's most horrific weapons to date.
It was only natural that some people began to suspect that mysterious lights in the
evening sky might be associated with extraplanetary beings who, recognizing the
nuclear technological display for what it was, decided that they had better watch us in
case we either became dangerous to others or threatened to destroy ourselves.

After the UFO genie was out of the bottle, it wasn't long before people began
to recognize in earlier writings the supposed fingerprints of beings from outer space.
Even the Bible yielded some interesting evidence:

> I saw a windstorm coming out of the north—an immense cloud with
> flashing lightning and surrounded by brilliant light. The center of the

fire looked like glowing metal, and in the fire was what looked like four living creatures. In appearance their form was like that of a man.... I saw a wheel on the ground beside each creature [that] sparkled like chrysolite.... Their rims were high and awesome ... spread above their heads was what looked like an expanse, sparkling like ice and awesome. Above the expanse over their heads was what looked like a throne of sapphire, and high above on the throne was a figure like that of a man ... and I heard a voice speaking. (Ezek. 1)

Speculation arose that the pyramids of Egypt, the mysterious lines crossing the landscape of Peru, the seemingly far-advanced cosmology of the ancient Maya, even England's Stonehenge were evidence of very foreign influences. Erich von Däniken's book *Chariots of the Gods*, in which he found human history littered with evidence of UFOs, was snapped up at bookstores from coast to coast. Roswell, New Mexico, became a home away from home for those who believed that a UFO had crashed there. (They claimed that the evidence had been carefully hidden by the U.S. government.) Project Blue Book, a governmental investigative program, looked into all reported UFO sightings. But the fact that it usually seemed to find evidence of terrestrial, rather than extraterrestrial, origins only fanned the flames of true believers' distrust in government agencies.

As late as 1997, flying saucers made the front-page headlines. By March of that year the members of the Heaven's Gate cult had come to believe that a spaceship sent to transport them to a higher sphere was arriving in the wake of the comet Hale-Bopp. They all committed suicide in preparation for leaving this plane of existence. Later, Daniel Smith, a leader in the Unarius Society, a large UFO group, claimed that Heaven's Gate had made a terrible mistake: they got the date wrong. The spaceship actually was coming in 2001. But 2001 came and went. The ship has still not made its arrival.

Still the reports come in. Some say we are being watched so that older, more experienced civilizations from space can keep us from creating our own Armageddon of nuclear disaster. Others warn that beings from outer space covet the natural resources of our planet. The plot of the movie *2001: A Space Odyssey* revolves around extraterrestrials providing us the means to evolve as humans in the first place. That is the position taken by the Raëlian movement, who claim we began to evolve when people from outer space tampered with our DNA at the dawn of humanity.

There are, of course, scientists who believe space is simply too big for any UFOs to cross. The time and distance problems are literally astronomical. Physics being what it is, they say, it is simply impossible for any beings similar to us and subject to our biology and life span to travel from some faraway solar system to earth.

So the discussion continues. Are there beings from "out there" who care enough about us to keep us from a human-triggered Armageddon? Have they found a way to cross the vast distances required to spy on us? Are we being watched? At this point, the scientific community voices an almost unanimous no. But that doesn't stop those who think they have seen UFOs and perhaps even been abducted by them. They claim human history is full of evidence if we only open our eyes and minds to see it.

This truth was exemplified on February 24, 2005, when the ABC television network, a media giant, featured one of its biggest hard-news readers, Peter Jennings, hosting a two-hour program entitled "UFOs: Seeing Is Believing." This overview of the subject of aliens among us sought to present both sides of the story. On the one hand, a witness was heard to say, "I have seen alien vehicles on eight occasions." Then, after Jennings warned that UFOs were "real to some, fiction to others," another speaker, said to be representing the scientific community, presented his opinion that, considering the body of eyewitness accounts on record, "none of it passes the rigorous test of scientific inquiry." In the end, no conclusions were drawn. But such a serious treatment by a major network at least bears witness to popular interest in the subject. Jennings reminded his viewers that 50 million Americans believe we have been visited by intelligent beings from other planets.

Many have speculated that the only way our divided planet will ever be united in time to prevent its demise is by either a threat or a helpful contact from outside. They still look to the heavens in hope.

Photograph, allegedly of UFOs, taken by fifteen-year-old Stephen Pratt near Doncaster, England, in 1966. *Stephen C. Pratt/Fortean Picture Library.*

Sources:

Clark, Jerome. *The UFO Book: Encyclopedia of the Extraterrestrial.* Detroit: Visible Ink Press, 1998.

Cohen, Daniel. *Prophets of Doom: The Millennium Edition.* Brookfield, CT: Millbrook Press, 1999.

UNIVERSE, FATE OF *see* **Big Bang; Big Crunch, Big Chill, and Big Rip; Quantum Theory; Red Shift**

Visions and Dreams

In the last days, God says,
I will pour out my spirit on all people.
Your sons and daughters will prophesy,
 your young men will see visions,
 your old men will dream dreams. (Acts 2:17)

These verses are from the Christian church's first recorded sermon, preached by the apostle Peter on the Day of Pentecost, the birthday of the church. He quotes from Joel 2:28–32, specifically linking the final days of history to an increase of visions and dreams. He seems to be saying that visions and dreams will be a prominent means of God's declaration that the end is near. Over the years many cults formed, affirming their existence because God supposedly gave a charismatic leader a "vision" that the time is near for the advent of the last days of history (see Failed Prophecy).

The idea of gods communicating through visions and dreams is not a Christian invention. The belief seems to have been almost universal. Ancient Greek and Roman histories are full of interpretations of dreams, as is the Old Testament. In New Testament times no one raised an eyebrow when the Magi, "being warned in a dream not to return to Herod, returned to their country by another way" (Matt. 2:12) or when an "angel of the Lord, who appeared to him in a dream" guided Joseph, husband of the mother of Jesus (Matt. 1:20, 2:19). The urbane, educated apostle Paul describes a vision wherein a man who seems to have been Luke, the physician, appeared to him and called him to Macedonia (Acts 16:9). It was the custom in ancient Britain, when a guest retired for the evening, for the host to bestow a blessing: "May the gods send you a dream." The idea was that dreams were messages sent from the spirit world. In as remote a place as Australia, the Aborigine's whole concept of "Dreamtime" postulates a spiritual plane accessible through dreaming (see Dreamtime). In sixteenth-century

Painting in the Church of the Nativity, Bethlehem, Israel, depicting Joseph's dream that warned him to flee to Egypt with Mary and the infant Jesus. *Library of Congress.*

France, Nostradamus claimed to have seen visions of the end, and in twentieth-century America, Edgar Cayce, the "sleeping prophet," caused many of his endtimes dreams to be recorded (see Cayce, Edgar; Nostradamus).

Even after Sigmund Freud's research paved the way for modern dream interpretation, many people still believe that God communicates with us through our dreams, revealing the future or interpreting current events. It can be argued that this makes both psychological and mythological sense if modern dream research is correct. Some popular theories tell us that dreams come from our subconscious. When people surrender their conscious thought to sleep, their subconscious is free to make known to them what they have experienced without conscious realization. Much more information comes to people each day than they can possibly process, so dreams originate in the intuitive, nonverbal portions of the mind. Viewing symbolic images thrown up on the screen of relaxed consciousness, people can often discover in dreams that which they already know but don't yet comprehend in a conscious manner. Inventions have come into being when a dream supplies the clue necessary to discovering the key ingredient of a new technology. Personal relationships come into focus when people suddenly discover something about an acquaintance that they saw but didn't quite process.

When this happens, some draw the conclusion that the dream came from the spirit within—that spiritual fire or divine spark that some people call "God." In this way they superimpose new dream research terminology over old—some might say superstitious—beliefs. But perhaps, they argue, the reverse is true. Maybe the ancients were intuitively describing a process that we are only now learning to express with scientific terminology. If "God" is defined as being the universal spiritual component found in every human, who is to say that this spiritual component—"God"—does not speak through dreams and visions when the brain is quieted in sleep?

Visions were important to biblical prophets (see Daniel). Consider the vision John described while on the Greek isle of Patmos. Filled with obscure images, strange beasts, and supernatural events of nature, it has come down to us as the book of Revelation (see Revelation). One way of explaining the battle of Armageddon that John depicted is that he was trying to convey something he intuitively grasped but couldn't quite find words to describe. He might have come to believe that the human race is capable of destroying itself. Its only hope is to be found in a rescue by that which is both "without" and "within." John calls it "God." Others might use the words *love* or *spirit*. This is the view Freud would probably have used. Revelation is typical of a dream (perhaps *nightmare* is a better word). It seems to be fantastic and impossible. But that is the case with many dreams. Its interpretation can be found by understanding the symbolism and applying it to reality. The interpretation, according to this view, will be found in the overlying message, not the details. In this sense, Revelation might tell us more about the personality of a first-century dreamer than the predestined history of the human race.

This avenue of inquiry opens up yet another way to interpret prophetic literature. It implies that visions and dreams of the end are mythological expressions of universal archetypes dealing with questions humans ask about a future that is always unknown, and therefore always mysterious.

Sources:
Delaney, Gayle. *All about Dreams*. San Francisco: HarperSanFrancisco, 1998.
The Holy Bible, New International Version. Grand Rapids, MI: Zondervan, 1978.

WATER

All living things, including humans, of course, depend on water. If something were to happen to the planet's supply of water, life would cease to exist. When NASA scientists sent a probe to Mars to look for signs of life, they looked for evidence of water. Water means life. No water, no chance of life. It's that simple.

So it became a subject of extreme concern when the United Nations Environment Program issued a report on March 29, 2004, announcing that there exist "dead zones" in the world's oceans. These zones are completely devoid of any living thing. There are no fish, no plankton, and most important, very little oxygen. Even more disturbing, according to the report, is the fact that these areas are growing. There are now 150 dead zones around the world. In 1990 there were half that many. Some are measured in thousands of square miles. Scientists believe that they are caused by runoff from farm fertilizers, sewage, and industrial pollutants. In other words, dead zones are caused by human negligence. It's not just the zones already in existence that frighten the scientific world. It's the fact that they are growing so rapidly.

And not only the oceans are affected. Many species of amphibians around the world, spending so much of their life cycle in water, are becoming extinct. Frogs and newts, especially, are disappearing in frightening numbers. Many that survive are grotesquely deformed. Some are missing legs. Some have two heads. There are currently 435 species undergoing rapid decline. Some of these species have been so depleted that it may already be too late for them.

Simon N. Stuart of the World Conservation Union describes the decline as "outside our normal experience." He wonders if it is an early warning signal that animals farther up the food chain, such as human beings, will soon follow.

Amphibians have porous skins. They are subject to whatever contaminant enters their watery world. In the words of Trevor Beebee, a professor in biochemistry at the University of Sussex in England, "In my view, this assessment of amphibian declines is very important, because it quantifies an extremely worrying set of observations. Amphibians are declining in many places all over the world, often in areas where we might expect human effects to be minimal." He goes on to explain that just because humans don't live near some of these areas doesn't mean they are not at fault. In fact, he believes the opposite to be true. Human pollution has invaded far-flung places of the globe where no humans live. Even well-protected havens such as state preserves, national parks, and remote, hard-to-reach areas are not safe, so pervasive is the heavy hand of human harm.

Global water shortages are expected to increase. Dust storms and sandstorms will become more frequent and occur in places they have never before been seen. United Nations environmental studies indicate that chronic water shortages will affect more than a third of the earth's population within the next few decades.

The prognosis is bleak. Even conservative studies predict that by the year 2015 the problem will be critical. And many are voicing the quiet concerns of many scientists. Is it already too late?

Sources:
Associated Press. "Amphibians in Jeopardy Worldwide, Report Says." *Arizona Daily Star*, October 15, 2004.

Greimel, Hans. "U.N. Warns about Ocean 'Dead Zones.'" http://www.flmnh.ufl.edu/fish/InNews/deadzones22004.html.

WATERWORLD *see* **Hollywood Envisions** THE END

WESTMINSTER CONFESSION *see* **Calvinism**

WHITE THRONE JUDGMENT *see* **Day of Judgment**

WHORE OF BABYLON

In Revelation 17, John, the author of the book, claims to see in a vision a harlot, or prostitute, "sitting on a scarlet beast that was covered with blasphemous names and seven heads and ten horns." She was dressed in magnificent attire and had "a title written on her forehead: MYSTERY, BABYLON THE GREAT, THE MOTHER OF PROSTITUTES AND OF THE ABOMINATIONS OF THE EARTH."

She was "drunk with the blood of the saints, the blood of those who bore testimony to Jesus" (see also Revelation).

When John evidenced astonishment at all this and asked for an explanation, an angelic guide gave him an interpretation that, for the last two thousand years, has only muddied the prophetic waters:

> This calls for a mind with wisdom. The seven heads are seven hills on which the woman sits. They are also seven kings. Five have fallen, one is, the other has not come; but when he does come, he must remain for a little while. The beast who once was, and now is not, is an eighth king. He belongs to the seven and is going to his destruction.

The Whore of Babylon astride the seven-headed beast of Revelation. *Fortean Picture Library.*

The ten horns you saw are ten kings, who have not received a kingdom, but who for one hour will receive authority as kings along with the beast. They have one purpose and will give their power and authority to the beast. They will make war against the Lamb, but the Lamb will overcome them because he is Lord of lords and King of kings—and with him will be his called, chosen and faithful followers.

Then the angel said to me, "The waters you saw where the prostitute sits, are peoples, multitudes, nations and languages. The beast and the ten horns you saw will hate the prostitute. They will bring her to ruin and leave her naked; they will eat her flesh and burn her with fire. For God has put it into their hearts to accomplish his purpose by agreeing to give the beast their power to rule, until God's words are fulfilled. The woman you saw is the great city that rules over the kings of the earth." (Rev. 17:9–18)

What does all this mean? No one really knows, although many claim they have cracked the prophetic code. For every explanation there are a dozen countertheories.

ARMAGEDDON NOW: THE END OF THE WORLD A TO Z

Most biblical scholars agree that the city on the seven hills probably represents Rome, for which "Babylon" was a common code name in the first century. But is it the Rome of the that time or a revived Roman Empire of the future? Those who believe that Revelation is coded apocalyptic literature written for people who lived in the first century also think that the references pertain to that historical period. Although some details seem mysterious today, people who read them back then would have understood them clearly.

Those who believe that Revelation is about the future, on the other hand, contend that the references are obscure because the events they depict haven't happened yet. The familiar motif of the "ten horns" (see Daniel) seems to refer both to ten kings and ten nations. But who the kings are remains a mystery. Some explanations link them to ten different caesars or ten waves of first- and second-century persecutions. Others believe that they represent ten nations that will someday form a European union. These ideas are, at best, speculation.

Especially mysterious is the beast "who once was, now is not, and yet will come." The motif of the "once and future king" is a popular mythological formula. But how it applies in this case is, again, a matter of speculation.

The identity of the harlot is likewise up for grabs. The term is often used, throughout both testaments, to represent those who have left their "marriage" with God to sell themselves to "the world" and its ways. The opposite relationship is used when the church, for instance, is called the "bride of Christ" (2 Cor. 11:2). But why "the beast and the ten horns ... will hate the prostitute" is anyone's guess. One would think that nations who have "committed fornication" with "Babylon the Great" would have exactly the opposite feeling.

This is, without doubt, a very difficult passage to interpret. Whether a historian or a futurist definitively cracks the code and identifies the harlot remains to be seen.

Source:
The Holy Bible, New International Version. Grand Rapids, MI: Zondervan, 1978.

WORLD WAR III *see* **Armageddon, Battle of**

Y2K

As the final months and weeks of the twentieth century drew to a close, much of the world was inundated by a quiet panic. There were the usual religious predictions. Some Christian writers, especially, saw a divine symmetry at work (see Bible Time-lines). Many books were written concerning prospective heavenly or natural disasters. (A quick check of the publishing dates for many references used in this volume shows a definite shift toward the late 1990s.)

But as the century—and the millennium—ticked toward its end, perhaps the most highly publicized single fear centered on what came to be called the "Y2K bug."

Y2K is an abbreviation for "year two thousand." The Y2K "bug" had nothing to do with pest control or insect manifestations. Instead it involved a potential problem with computers. In the 1950s, the infancy of the computer industry, programmers badly needed to conserve storage space on their primitive machines. They decided, among other things, to express dates with only six digits—two for the month, two for the day and two for the year. "December 31, 1999," for instance, became 12/31/99. This worked just fine during the twentieth century and saved a lot of room on early-generation computers.

But in 1971 Bob Bremer, a pioneer in developing the early computer language known as COBOL, warned of a potential problem looming over the horizon. What would happen when computers moved out of the twentieth century and had to cope with the twenty-first? Would they recognize that when "00" succeeded "99" in six-digit dates, the "00" referred to the year 2000? Or would they revert to 1900 and start the twentieth century all over again?

Bremer was largely ignored. Given the human tendency to operate in the here and now, the busy programmers of the 1970s figured that by the time 2000 rolled

Instant nostalgia: employees manning the Hewlett Packard Company's Y2K Command Center on December 31, 1999. *Associated Press.*

around, it would be somebody else's problem. But by the end of the 1990s the warnings, unheeded up to now, made their way into big business and governments. Everything, it seemed, ran by computers. What would happen if banks could no longer keep track of money and investments? What if weapon-systems computers got confused? What if the programs that kept the world's electric grids up and running suddenly figured that they had a hundred years to kick in? Would worldwide panic ensue? Would New Year's Day 2000 mark the end of civilization as we know it?

The truth was, no one had any answers. This was a possible case of human technology running amok and turning on its inventors. Everyone's worst nightmare, a huge technological glitch that could mean the end of life, might be right around the corner.

The experts didn't know what to do. A delightful (in hindsight) quote from that time sums it all up. Ted Ulusoy knew as much about the Y2K bug as anybody. He was president of one of the many consulting firms that sprang up overnight to help governments and industry sort out the problem. As such, he was the most knowledgeable expert available at the time to advise presidents and kings. What was his opinion? "Nobody knows what's going to happen. But my guess is that everything will happen, but not one thing will happen everywhere."

Not very much there on which to build corporate or Defense Department policies.

When advice like that began to spread around the world on the Internet, thanks to computers that might stop functioning at midnight on December 31, many people panicked. Dehydrated food, generators, and wood-burning stoves flew out of shops and stores. Survivalists held seminars. Gun manufacturers hired extra shifts. Propane and gasoline shortages occurred in diverse places.

Even though, toward the very end, people began to be reassured that things were probably under control, the plain truth was that no one really knew what would happen. On December 31, 1999, people went out to party, to bring in the New Year, and to celebrate the coming of a new century.

When the clocks ticked over, the lights stayed on. The world didn't end. No nuclear explosions were triggered. Computers had no problem with the change. The world went on as before.

And Y2K became an amusing, some might say nostalgic, memory.

Source:

Christenson, John. "Gearing Up for the Gold Rush." http://www.cnn.com/TECH/specials/y2k/ stories/y2kgoldrush/.

ZECHARIAH *see* Books of the Bible and Their Relation to Prophecy

ZION AND ZIONISM

"Sing, O barren woman,
  you who never bore a child....
The Lord will call you back
  as if you were a wife deserted and distressed in spirit....
For a brief moment I abandoned you,
  but with deep compassion I will bring you back....
To me this is like the days of Noah,
  when I swore that the waters of Noah would never again cover the earth....
My covenant of peace will [not be] removed,"
  says the Lord, who has compassion on you. (Isa. 54:1, 6–10)

These words, like many in the Hebrew scriptures, offer a promise Jewish rabbis have for generations read to congregations who often were persecuted and forced to live far from what they considered to be their divinely mandated homeland. Judaism teaches that Israel is a gift from YHVH (Yahveh) to his people. At the end of time, the Messiah will rule the whole earth from Jerusalem.

Many Hebrew prophets taught that whenever Jews were scattered all around the world, victims of persecution, their return to Jerusalem would signal the last days of history, the last days of the present age: "In that day the Lord will reach out his hand a second time to reclaim the remnant that is left of his people.... he will assemble the scattered people of Judah from the four quarters of the earth" (Isa. 11:11, 12).

Christians have also claimed these verses. Many conservative theologians believe that the creation of a Jewish state fulfills the last prophetic requirement for the

Second Coming of Jesus. The first gathering of the Lord's people occurred at the end of the Babylonian captivity during the time of Ezra and Nehemiah. The second gathering began in 1948.

Nathan Birnbaum, who founded the first organization of Jewish nationalist students in the West, first used the word *Zionism* in 1893. Jewish families end every *seder* meal with the words "Next year in Jerusalem!" Eastern European Jews especially, having experienced centuries of persecution, began to take the words literally. The early years of the twentieth century saw a heartfelt passion awake. Not even Hitler could drive that passion down.

Zion is the traditional name for one of the hills in the city that was to become known as Jerusalem, "City of Peace." It is the spiritual center of the Jewish universe, the Holy Land given to Abraham and his descendants forever. Ever since the destruction of their beloved temple in 70 CE, Jews had longed to return to establish *Eretz Israel*, the "Land of Israel."

In the late nineteenth century this land was still known as Palestine. Jews had migrated there to live, work, and study. It was the destination of many a pilgrimage. But it wasn't home.

The first Zionist Congress was held in 1897, convened by the man who has come to be known as the father of political Zionism, Theodor Herzl. That first congress adopted the Basel Program, named after the Swiss town in which the representatives met. Their purpose was to establish in Palestine, then under Turkish rule, a permanent home for the Jewish people. They formed the World Zionist Organization, whose mission was to win approval for their cause by appealing to the leading world powers. It was an uphill battle all the way. The Balfour Declaration, issued by the British government in 1917, began the process. The next year, after Britain received a League of Nations mandate to settle the area, saw an influx of Jewish migration. By the time World War II broke out, Jewish residents in Palestine numbered about 500,000.

The aftermath of the war brought Nazi atrocities to the attention of the world. With the news of the Holocaust fresh in the public mind, the newly formed United Nations in 1947 overwhelmingly approved the establishment of a Jewish state in part of Palestine. The birth of the state of Israel was proclaimed on May 14, 1948 (the fifth day of the month of Iyar, 5708, by the Jewish calendar).

Seven Arab nations promptly invaded the new state. For most practical purposes, the war that started then continues to this day.

Not all Jews are pro-Zionist. A very vocal faction of Orthodox Jews, calling themselves "anti-Zionists," are happy that Israel exists—it offers, after all, a safe haven for oppressed Jews to study Torah. But they believe very strongly that God pulls rank over the United Nations. Israel must be divinely established and protected or it will not last. As a result, some Orthodox Jews living in Israel today are exempted from serving in the army and receive other political benefits not extended to everyone. This infuriates many other Israelis, some of whom fight for political rather than religious reasons. They wonder why they should fight, and perhaps die, while protecting the "freeloading" Orthodox community from Palestinian "terrorists."

Mount Zion, Jerusalem, photographed in the late nineteenth or early twentieth century. *Library of Congress.*

But the anti-Zionists stick to their spiritual guns. They point out that the Torah lists three oaths Israel took when it began its second exile, back in the first century:

1. Israel would not "go up like a wall." That is, massive force would not be used to restore the nation.
2. Gd (Torah does not permit vowels to be printed in the sacred name of God) made Israel swear they would not rebel against the nations of the world.
3. Gd made non-Jews promise not to oppress Israel "too much." Persecution is Gd's way of strengthening his people.

So for anti-Zionists it's far more productive to study Torah and remain faithful. Gd will handle the details.

Palestinians, meanwhile, rightly claim they are being pushed out of their homes. Americans debate which side they should support. Have Israeli Jews become the oppressors, rather than the oppressed? Will this emotional powder keg lead to the explosion of the battle of Armageddon? This, after all, is where the Bible says the battle will take place. Are we seeing the beginning maneuvers in that war? Hundreds of Christians have moved to Israel to be in the front-row seats. They are called "Christian Zionists."

Zionism is an important part, some say the most important part, of the prophetic puzzle called the battle of Armageddon.

Sources:
Bridger, David, ed. *The New Jewish Encyclopedia.* New York: Behrman House, 1962.

ZOROASTRIANISM

The world's first true monotheistic religion probably began about six centuries BCE. Zoroastrianism was the first religion to teach that history would end in a great, climactic battle between good and evil. Zoroastrianism gave the world the concept of Armageddon.

In Persia, Zarathustra—or Zoroaster, as he was later called by the Greeks—began to preach that a battle between good and evil, between the high god Ahura Mazda and the evil Ahriman, was being carried out on earth. Ahriman had been lured into the earth's realm so he could be weakened and eventually destroyed at the end of time. This marked the first time that history was portrayed in a straightforward, linear fashion. History, said Zoroaster, would someday come to an end. After the destruction of Ahriman, the earth would be recycled and purified. Humans would be rewarded with paradise, an ideal heavenly realm featuring a divine court abiding over the blessed. Hell awaited the wicked. It was not eternal, but its fires would purify the earth of evildoers.

Just before that final day, Zoroaster would return. A virgin impregnated with Zoroaster's own seed, which had been preserved in Lake Hamun, a mountain lake, would conceive him. Until then, every thousand years a prophet would appear until the final restoration of the world. This final restoration would occur three thousand years in the future, or about the year 2500 CE, according to modern calendars.

We simply cannot overestimate the influence Zoroastrianism has had upon the world. The Jews first experienced it during the Babylonian captivity in the sixth century BCE. When they returned to their homeland in present-day Israel, their religion had completely changed. Christianity, and later, Islam, would follow. Both religions grew out of Judaism. The result was monotheism, the religion that totally transformed Western civilization. The concept of a final Armageddon is a direct result of monotheism.

Before the Babylonian captivity, Jewish religion was full of references to "other gods." After they returned, there were none. Now there was only one God. The "gods" of the other nations were merely idols, figments of the human imagination. The Dead Sea Scrolls are full of references to a "battle between light and dark," the Zoroastrian dualism that has so captured Western thinking today (see Abraham and Monotheism).

Zoroastrian priests were called *magi.* From them we get the word *magic.* Magi were among the first to formally institutionalize the idea of astrology. They studied the skies for signs and portents. From their *ziggurat* towers they nightly scanned the stars and constellations. (The biblical gospel of Matthew has some of them journeying to Bethlehem at the time of the birth of Jesus, following a star that signified to them that "the King of the Jews" had been born.) Astrology became, among other things, a method of determining when and how the world would end.

The Resurrection of Zoroaster (Austin Osman Spare, 1905). *Fortean Picture Library.*

There is no doubt about Zoroastrian religion and its influence. But there are those who question the existence of Zoroaster himself. Was he a product of Persian mythology? Those who claim that he was a real person vary in their estimates of when he lived. Some say as late as the sixth century BCE. Others speculate he may have lived as long as six thousand years ago. But aside from his religious legacy we have no proof of his actual existence. The same can be said, of course, for figures such as Moses, Abraham, and Jesus. For many people, such a strong legacy is proof in itself that he must have existed. As is the case with other religious founders, he may not have performed all the feats that accompany his legend. But where there is so much smoke, there must have been at least a small fire, and probably a big one, for Zoroastrianism became the official religion of Persia. Without it, we might not even be contemplating the idea of an Armageddon.

Sources:

Ellwood, Robert S., and Barbara A. McGraw. *Many Peoples, Many Faiths: Women and Men in the World Religions.* 6th ed. Upper Saddle River, NJ: Prentice Hall, 1999.

Ludwig, Theodore M. *The Sacred Paths: Understanding the Religions of the World.* 2d ed. Upper Saddle River, NJ: Prentice Hall, 1996.

BIBLIOGRAPHY

Alschuler, William A. *The Science of UFOs*. New York: St. Martin's Press, 2001.

America's Fascinating Indian Heritage. Pleasantville, NY: Reader's Digest Association, 1978.

Anderson, Sir Robert. *The Coming Prince: The Last Great Monarch of Christendom*. London: Hodder and Stoughton, 1881.

Appenzeller, Tim, and Dennis R. Dimick. "Signs from Earth." *National Geographic*, September 2004, 10–11.

Ár nDraiocht Féin: A Druid Fellowship. Web site: www.adf.org.

"Armageddon Theology and Presidential Decision-Making: Religious Leaders' Concern." Transcript of a Press Conference for Religious Issues '84, in Association with Conference on the Fate of the Earth and Washington Research Center. San Francisco, 1984. http://www.rumormillnews.com/ARMAGEDDON%20THEOLOGY.htm.

Armstrong, Herbert W. *The United States and British Commonwealth in Prophecy*. Pasadena, CA: Ambassador College Press, 1967.

Armstrong, Karen. *A History of God*. New York: Alfred A. Knopf, 1993.

Associated Press. "Amphibians in Jeopardy Worldwide, Report Says." *Arizona Daily Star*, October 15, 2004.

Augustine of Hippo. *The City of God*. Chicago: Encyclopedia Britannica, 1952.

"Aum Shinri Kyo." http://www.gbs.sha.bw.schule.te/tsld026.htm.

"AUM~Sparky's Cayce Readings on Earth Changes." http://all-ez.com/earth.htm.

Ayer, Eleanor. *A Guide to the Anasazi and Other Ancient Southwest Indians*. Frederick, CO: Renaissance House, 1991.

Bakker, Jim. *I Was Wrong*. Nashville: Thomas Nelson, 1996.

———. *Prosperity and the Coming Apocalypse*. Nashville: Thomas Nelson, 1998.

———. *The Refuge: The Joy of Christian Community in a Torn-Apart World*. Nashville: Thomas Nelson, 2000.

Barbour, Ian G. *When Science Meets Religion: Enemies, Strangers, or Partners?* New York: HarperCollins, 2000.

Barbour, Julian. Julian Barbour Web site. http://216.92.126.230.

Barzak, Ibrahim. "Hamas Founder Killed in Israeli Airstrike." Associated Press, March 22, 2004.

Bell, Art, and Brad Steiger. *The Source: Journey through the Unexplained*. New Orleans: Paper Chase Press, 1999.

Berdan, Frances F., ed. *The Aztecs of Central Mexico: An Imperial Society*. New York: Holt, Rinehart & Winston, 1982.

Berkhof, Louis. *Systematic Theology*. Grand Rapids, MI: Eerdmans, 1962.

"Billy Graham." http://www.billygraham.org/mediaRelations/bios.asp.

Blaising, Craig A. "Premillennialism." In *Three Views on the Millennium and Beyond*, ed. Darrell L. Bock. Grand Rapids, MI: Zondervan, 1999.

Blank, Jonah. "Myths and Conquests." http://www.keepmedia.com/jsp/article_detail_print.jsp.

Bock, Darrell L., ed. *Three Views on the Millennium and Beyond*. Grand Rapids, MI: Zondervan, 1999.

Boissiere, Robert. *Meditations with the Hopi*. Santa Fe, NM: Bear, 1986.

Bombardieri, Marcella. "Street Smart." *Boston Globe*, June 23, 2002.

Borg, Marcus J. *The God We Never Knew: Beyond Dogmatic Religion to a More Authentic Contemporary Faith*. San Francisco: HarperSanFrancisco, 1997.

———. *Reading the Bible Again for the First Time: Taking the Bible Seriously but Not Literally*. San Francisco: HarperSanFrancisco, 2001.

Boslough, John. *Stephen Hawking's Universe*. New York: Avon, 1980.

Bostrom, Nick. *Anthropic Bias: Observation Selection Effects in Science and Philosophy*. New York: Routledge, 2002.

Boyer, Paul. "America's Doom Industry." http://www.pbs.org/wgbh/pages/frontline/shows/apocalypse/explanation/doomindustry.html.

Bridger, David, ed. *The New Jewish Encyclopedia*. New York: Behrman House, 1962.

Bright, Bill. *Come Help Change the World*. Old Tappan, NJ: Fleming H. Revell, 1970.

———. *The Coming Revival: America's Call to Fast, Pray, and Seek God's Face*. Nashville: Thomas Nelson, 1995.

Britt, Robert Roy. "The Big Rip: New Theory Ends Universe by Shredding Everything." http://www.space.com/scienceastronomy/big_rip_030306.html.

———. "Freeze, Fry or Dry: How Long Has the Earth Got?" http://www.space.com/scienceastronomy/solarsystem/death_of_earth_000224.html.

———. "Recipe for Saving Earth: Move It." http://www.space.com/scienceastronomy/planetearth/earth_move_010207.html.

Brockman, John. "The End of Time: A Talk with Julian Barbour." http://www.edge.org/documents/archives/edge60.html.

Brown, Raymond. *An Introduction to the New Testament*. New York: Doubleday, 1997.

Brundage, Burr Cartwright. *The Fifth Sun*. Austin: University of Texas Press, 1979.

Bunds, David, and Mark Swett. "History of the Branch Davidians." http://www.fountain. btinternet.co.uk/koresh/history.html.

Buttrick, George A., ed. *The Interpreter's Dictionary of the Bible*. 4 vols. New York: Abingdon Press, 1962.

Callahan, Tim. "The End of the World and the New World Order: Black Helicopters, Hong Kong Gurkhas, Global Conspiracies, and The Mark of the Beast." http://www.skeptic.com/04.3.callahan-end.html.

Campbell, Joseph. *The Inner Reaches of Outer Space: Metaphor as Myth and as Religion*. New York: Harper & Row, 1986.

Campbell, Joseph, with Bill Moyers. *The Power of Myth*. New York: Doubleday, 1988.

Chase, T. "Revelation 13: Prophecy Calendar, Recent Past Dates (1998–2002)." http://wwwangelfire.com/zine2/Number666/calendar1.html.

Cheetham, Erika. *The Final Prophecies of Nostradamus*. New York: Perigee, 1989.

Christenson, John. "Gearing Up for the Gold Rush." http://www.cnn.com/TECH/ specials/y2k/stories/y2kgoldrush/.

"Christian Reconstructionism, Dominion Theology, and Theonomy." http://www. religioustolerance.org/reconstr.htm.

"Christian Zionism: Misguided Millennialism." http://www.christchurch-virginiawater. co.uk/articles/coloradohistory.htm.

Clark, Jerome. *The UFO Book: Encyclopedia of the Extraterrestrial*. Detroit: Visible Ink Press, 1998.

Cohen, Daniel. *Prophets of Doom: The Millennium Edition*. Brookfield, CT: Millbrook Press, 1999.

"Concerned Christians." http://www.apologeticsindex.org/c35.html.

"The 'Concerned Christians' Cult—Originally of Denver CO." http://www.religious tolerance.org/dc_conc.htm.

Cotterell, Arthur, and Rachel Storm. *The Ultimate Encyclopedia of Mythology*. New York: Hermes House, 1999.

Craddock, Jim, ed. *VideoHound's Golden Movie Retriever 2005*. Detroit: Thomson Gale, 2004.

Damsteegt, P. G., ed. *Seventh-day Adventists Believe…: A Biblical Exposition of Fundamental Doctrines*. Washington, DC: Ministerial Association of the General Conference of Seventh-day Adventists, 1989.

Delaney, Gayle. *All about Dreams*. San Francisco: HarperSanFrancisco, 1998.

Devine, Arthur. "Prophecies of St. Malachy." http://www.newadvent.org/cathen/ 12473a.htm#malachy.

Diamond, Jared. *Collapse: How Societies Choose to Fail or Succeed*. New York: Viking Adult, 2004.

Dixon, Jeane. *The Call to Glory*. New York: William Morrow, 1972.

Douglas, J. D., ed. *The New International Dictionary of the Christian Church*. Grand Rapids, MI: Zondervan, 1974.

"Dr. Tim LaHaye: Premillennial Dispensationalist." http://www.preteristarchive.com/StudyArchive/l/lahaye-tim.html.

"The Dreamtime." *Aboriginal Art and Culture Centre*. http://aboriginalart.com.au/culture/dreamtime.html.

Drosnin, Michael. *The Bible Code*. New York: Simon & Schuster, 1997.

———. *Bible Code II: The Countdown*. New York: Viking Penguin, 2002.

Eckert, Alan. *The Frontiersman: A Narrative*. Ashland, KY: Jesse Stuart Foundation, 2001.

Economides, Michael J. "Is There an Impending World Oil Shortage?" *World Energy* 7:4 (2004): 126–29.

EdgarCayce.org: The Official Site of A.R.E. [Association for Research and Enlightenment]. http://www.edgarcayce.org.

Ellwood, Robert S., and Barbara A. McGraw. *Many Peoples, Many Faiths: Women and Men in the World Religions*. Upper Saddle River, NJ: Prentice Hall, 1999 [6th ed.], 2002 [7th ed.].

"Endtimes, Millennium, Rapture." http://www.ewtn.com/expert/answers/endtimes.htm.

Erickson, Jon. "Ice Ages: Past and Future." http://oceanworld.tamu.edu/students/iceage/.

Erods, Richard, and Alfonso Ortiz, eds. *American Indian Myths and Legends*. New York: Pantheon, 1984.

Fackre, Dorothy, and Gabriel Fackre. *Christian Basics*. Grand Rapids, MI: Eerdmans, 1991.

Fackre, Gabriel. *The Religious Right and Christian Faith*. Grand Rapids, MI: Eerdmans, 1982.

Feiler, Bruce. *Abraham: A Journey to the Heart of Three Faiths*. New York: William Morrow, 2002.

Festinger, Leon, Henry W. Riecken, and Stanley Schacter. "Unfulfilled Prophecies and Disappointed Messiahs." In *Expecting Armageddon: Essential Readings in Failed Prophecy*, ed. Jon R. Stone. New York: Routledge, 2000.

Fisher, Mary Pat. *Living Religions*, 3rd ed. Upper Saddle River, NJ: Prentice Hall, 1991.

Fisher, Mary Pat, and Lee W. Bailey, eds. *An Anthology of Living Religions*. Upper Saddle River, NJ: Prentice Hall, 2000.

Focht, Doug. "The Age of Aquarius?" *Bible Search*. http://www.biblesearch.com/articles/articl14.htm.

Gates, David. "The Pop Prophets." *Newsweek*, May 24, 2004.

Gear, Kathleen O'Neal, and W. Michael Gear. *People of the Lightning*. New York: Tor, 1995.

Gear, W. Michael, and Kathleen O'Neal Gear. *People of the Wolf*. New York: Tor, 1990.

Gentry, Kenneth L., Jr. "A Brief Theological Analysis of Hyper-Preterism." http://www.reformed.org/eschaton/gentry_preterism.html.

———. "Postmillennialism." In *Three Views on the Millennium and Beyond*, ed. Darrell L. Bock. Grand Rapids, MI: Zondervan, 1999.

Gerner, Alice: "The Atomic Age Opens: Selections from the Browne Popular Culture Library." http://www.bgsu.edu/colleges/library/pcl/pcl36.html.

Gibbon, Edward. *The Decline and Fall of the Roman Empire*. 2 vols. Chicago: Encyclopaedia Britannica, 1952.

Glanz, James. "New Data on 2 Doomsday Ideas, Big Rip vs. Big Crunch." *New York Times*, February 21, 2004.

Glick, Daniel. "The Big Thaw." *National Geographic*, September 2004, 12–33.

Gonzalez, Justo L. *The Story of Christianity*. 2 vols. New York: Harper & Row, 1985.

Gould, Stephen Jay. *Rocks of Ages: Science and Religion in the Fullness of Life*. New York: Ballantine, 1999.

Gray, Kevin. "Hot Times in 2004: Year One of the Warmest to Date." *Daytona Beach News-Journal*, December 16, 2004.

Greimel, Hans. "U.N. Warns about Ocean 'Dead Zones.'" http://www.flmnh.ufl.edu/fish/InNews/deadzones22004.html.

Hagen, Steve. *Buddhism Plain and Simple*. Boston: Charles E. Tuttle, 1997.

Hannaford, Alex. "Return to Waco." *Guardian/UK*, October 28, 2003.

Hapgood, Charles. *The Earth's Shifting Crust*. Foreword by Albert Einstein. New York: Pantheon, 1958.

Harpur, Tom. *The Pagan Christ*. Toronto: Thomas Allen, 2004.

Hauptman, Laurence M., and James D. Wherry, eds. *The Pequots in Southern New England*. Norman: University of Oklahoma Press, 1990.

Hawking, Stephen W. *A Brief History of Time: From the Big Bang to Black Holes*. New York: Bantam, 1988.

Hillerman, Tony. *Listening Woman*. New York: Harper & Row, 1978.

Hitching, Francis. *Earth Magic*. New York: William Morrow, 1977.

Hogan, Craig J. *The Little Book of the Big Bang: A Cosmic Primer*. New York: Copernicus, 1998.

The Holy Bible, New International Version. Grand Rapids, MI: Zondervan, 1978.

The Holy Qur'an. Trans. with a commentary by Abdullah Yusuf Ali. Beirut: Dar Al Arabia, 1968.

Hudson, Winthrop S. *Religion in America*. New York: Charles Scribner's Sons, 1965.

Hymns for the Living Church. Carol Stream, IL: Hope, 1978.

Illinois State Museum. "Why Were There Ice Ages?" http://www.museum.state.il.us/exhibits/ice_ages/why_4_cool_periods.html.

"J. Robert Oppenheimer, 1904–1967." http://www.pbs.org/wgbh/aso/databank/entries/baoppe.html.

James, Simon. *The World of the Celts*. New York: Thames and Hudson, 1993.

Jammer, M. *Einstein and Religion*. Princeton, NJ: Princeton University Press, 1999.

Jawer, Jeff. "From Pisces to Aquarius: The Epochal Shift That Is Shaking Our World." *StarIQ.com.* http://www.stariq.com/Main/Articles/P0003036.htm.

Johnson, Carolyn Y. "Were the Dinosaurs Done In by Fungus?" http://www.boston.com/news/globe/health_science/articles/2005/02/22/were_the_dinosaurs_done_in_by_fungus/.

Jones, Prudence, and Nigel Pennick. *A History of Pagan Europe.* New York: Routledge, 1995.

Josephus, Flavius. *The Works of Flavius Josephus.* Trans. William Whiston. London: T. Nelson and Sons, 1873.

Kakutani, Michiko. "State of Fear: Crichton Questions Global Warming in Thriller." *New York Times,* January 9, 2005.

Kirkpatrick, Sidney D. *Edgar Cayce: An American Prophet.* New York: Riverhead, 2000.

Kristof, Nicholas D. "'Left Behind' Series Is Un-American." *New York Times,* July 17, 2004.

Kronk, Gary W. "Comet Hysteria and the Millennium: A Commentary." http://cometography.com/hysteria.html.

LaHaye, Tim, and Greg Dinallo. *Babylon Rising.* New York: Bantam, 2003.

LaHaye, Tim, and Jerry B. Jenkins. *Left Behind* series. 12 vols. Carol Stream, IL: Tyndale House, 1995–2004.

———. *A Visual Guide to the "Left Behind" Series.* Eugene, OR: Harvest House, 2001.

LaSor, William Sanford. *The Dead Sea Scrolls and the Christian Faith.* Chicago: Moody Press, 1956.

Lederer, Edith M. "U.N.: World Population to Hit 9B in 2050." Associated Press, February 25, 2005.

Lewis, James R. *The Death and Afterlife Book.* Detroit: Visible Ink Press, 2001.

Lightner, Robert. "Covenantism and Dispensationalism." [Dallas Theological Seminary] *Journal of Ministry and Theology* (fall 1999).

Lin, Kevin. "The Doomsday Argument." http://www.greylabyrinth.com/puzzles/puzzle.php?puzzle_id=puzzle106.

Lindemans, Micha F. "Ragnarok." *Encyclopedia Mythica.* http://www.pantheon.org/articles/r/ragnarok.html.

Lindsey, Hal. *Apocalypse Code.* Palos Verdes, CA: Western Front Ltd., 1997.

Lindsey, Hal, with C. C. Carlson. *The Late Great Planet Earth.* Grand Rapids, MI: Zondervan, 1970.

Ludwig, Theodore M. *The Sacred Paths: Understanding the Religions of the World.* 2d ed. Upper Saddle River, NJ: Prentice Hall, 1996.

Maasch, Kirk A. "The Big Chill: Cracking the Ice Age." http://www.pbs.org/wgbh/nova/ice/chill.html.

"Magnetic Storm." PBS, November 18, 2003.

Mann, James. *Rise of the Vulcans: The History of Bush's War Cabinet.* New York: Penguin Group, 2004.

Martin, Malachy. *The Keys of This Blood: The Struggle for World Dominion between Pope John Paul II, Mikhail Gorbachev, and the Capitalist West.* New York: Simon and Schuster, 1990.

Marx, Karl. "Contribution to the Critique of Hegel's Philosophy of Right." In *Karl Marx, Early Writings*, trans. and ed. T. B. Bottomore, 43–44. London: C. A. Watts, 1963.

May, Herbert G., and Bruce M. Metzger, eds. *The New Oxford Annotated Bible with the Apocrypha.* Rev. ed. New York: Oxford University Press, 1973.

McKay, Brendan. "Assassinations Foretold in Moby Dick!" http://cs.anu.edu.au/~bdm/dilugim/moby.html.

McKay, Brendan, and Friends. "Scientific Refutation of the Bible Codes." http://cs.anu.edu.au/~bdm/dilugim/torah.html.

McNeil, Donald G., Jr. "Plan to Battle AIDS Is Falling Short." *New York Times*, March 28, 2004.

Melton, J. Gordon. "Spiritualization and Reaffirmation: What Really Happens When Prophecy Fails." *American Studies* 26:2 (1985): 17–28.

Milanich, Jerald T. *Florida's Indians from Ancient Times to the Present.* Gainesville: University Press of Florida, 1998.

Miles, Jack. *God: A Biography.* New York: Vintage, 1995.

Miller, Kenneth R. *Finding Darwin's God.* New York: HarperCollins, 2000.

Miller, Kim. "Unconcerned Christians." http://www.kimmillerconcernedchristians.com.

"Minutes to Midnight: The History of the Doomsday Clock." *Bulletin of the Atomic Scientists.* http://www.bullatomicsci.org/clock/doomsdayclock.html.

Monbiot, George. "Their Beliefs Are Bonkers, but They Are at the Heart of Power." *Guardian/UK*, April 20, 2004. http://www.commondreams.org/cgi-bin/print.cgi?file=/views04/0420-03.htm.

Montaigne, David S. "Nostradamus World War III 2002." http://www.dazzled.com/nost2002/.

Mowat, Farley. *The Farfarers: Before the Norse.* South Royalton, VT: Steerforth Press, 2000.

Moyers, Bill. "On Receiving the Harvard Medical School's Global Environment Citizen Award." http://www.commondreams.org/views04/1206-10htm.

Myre, Greg. "Hamas Leader Calls Bush Foe of Muslims." *New York Times*, March 29, 2004.

Neihardt, John G. *Black Elk Speaks.* Lincoln: University of Nebraska Press, 1961.

Nichol, Francis D. *The Midnight Cry.* Washington, DC: Review and Herald, 1944.

North, Gary. *The Sinai Strategy: Economics and the Ten Commandments.* Tyler, TX: Institute for Christian Economics, 1986.

Nostradamus. *Prophecies on World Events.* Trans. Stewart Robb. New York: Liveright, 2002.

Oderberg, I. M. "Religion in the Age of Aquarius." *Theosophy Northwest.* http://www.theosophy-nw.org/theosnw/world/general/rel-imo.htm.

"One Year Later, Heaven's Gate Suicide Leaves Only a Faint Trail." http://www.cnn.com/US/9803/25/heavens.gate/.

Origen. "On First Principles." In *Readings in Christian Thought*, ed. Hugh T. Kerr. Nashville: Abingdon Press, 1966.

Overbye, Dennis. "About Those Fearsome Black Holes? Never Mind." *New York Times*, July 22, 2004.

Peñuelas, Marcelino. "El Mito, especulaciones sobre su origen e interpretación." *Cuadernos Americanos* 133 (March–April 1964): 89.

Plant, David. "The Copernican Revolution." http://www.skyscript.co.uk/copernicus.html.

Polkinghorne, John. *The God of Hope and the End of the World*. New Haven: Yale University Press, 2002.

Posner, Richard A. *Catastrophe: Risk and Response*. New York: Oxford University Press, 2005.

Red Star, Nancy. *Star Ancestors: Indian Wisdomkeepers Share the Teachings of the Extraterrestrials*. Rochester, VT: Destiny, 2000.

Rees, Martin. *Our Final Hour*. New York: Basic, 2003.

Reilly, John J. "The Millennium and the Roman Catholic Church." http://pages.prodigy.net/aesir/catmil.htm.

Renard, John. *The Handy Religion Answer Book*. Detroit: Visible Ink Press, 2002.

Revkin, Andrew C. "State of Fear: Some Scientists Say Best Seller Distorts Science." *New York Times*, January 9, 2005.

———. "2004 Was Fourth-warmest Year Ever Recorded." *New York Times*, February 10, 2005.

Rich, Tracey R. "Kabbalah and Jewish Mysticism." http://JewFAQ.org/kabbalah.htm.

Roberts, Jane. *Seth Speaks*. San Rafael, CA: Amber-Allen Publishing and New World Library, 1994.

Roberts, Michelle. "Bird Flu 'Has Pandemic Potential.'" http://news.bbc.co.uk/2/hi/health/4280817.stm.

Robinson, B. A. "Aum Shinri Kyo (Supreme Truth)." http://www.religioustolerance.org/dc_aumsh.htm.

Rogerson, John. *Atlas of the Bible*. New York: Facts on File Publications, 1985.

Rohter, Larry. "Antarctica, Warming, Looks Ever More Vulnerable." *New York Times*, January 25, 2005.

Ross, Rick. "Credonia Mwerinde and Her Ugandan Cult." http://www.rickross.com/reference/tencommandments/tencommandments110.html.

Rowland, Christopher. "Parousia." In *The Anchor Bible*, vol. 5. New York: Doubleday, 1992.

Rushdoony, R. J. *The Institute of Biblical Law*. Nutley, NJ: Craig Press, 1973.

Ryrie, Charles C. *Come Quickly, Lord Jesus: What You Need to Know about the Rapture*. Rev. ed. New York: Harvest House, 1999.

———. "The Seven Bowls." http://www.sumnerwemp.com/ryrie.

Sacks, Jonathan. "What Was God Thinking?" *Times* (London), January 1, 2005.

Sagan, Carl. *Cosmos*. New York: Random House, 1980.

———. *The Demon-Haunted World: Science as a Candle in the Dark*. New York: Random House, 1996.

———. *The Dragons of Eden*. New York: Ballantine, 1977.

Savinar, Matthew David. "Peak Oil: Life after the Oil Crash." http://www.lifeaftertheoilcrash.net/.

The Scofield Reference Bible. Grand Rapids, MI: Zondervan, 1971.

"Simon Kenton." http://www.ohiohistorycentral.org/ohc/h/peo/kentons.shtml.

Stedl, Todd. "Intro to Quantum Mechanics." http://www_theory.chem.washington.edu/~trstedl/quantum/quantum.html.

Steel, Duncan. *Rogue Asteroids and Doomsday Comets: The Search for the Million Megaton Menace That Threatens Life on Earth*. New York: John Wiley & Sons, 1995.

Stone, Jon R., ed. *Expecting Armageddon: Essential Readings in Failed Prophecy*. New York: Routledge, 2000.

Strandberg, Todd. "The Rapture Index." http://www.raptureready.com/rap2.html.

Strimple, Robert B. "Amillennialism." In *Three Views on the Millennium and Beyond*, ed. Darrell L. Bock. Grand Rapids, MI: Zondervan, 1999.

Strong, James. *The Exhaustive Concordance of the Bible*. New York: Abingdon Press, 1890.

Szulc, Tad. "Journey of Faith." *National Geographic*, December 2001, 90–129.

Teepen, Tom. "No Fairy Dust for the Biosphere if It Collapses." *Daytona Beach News-Journal*, April 2, 2005.

Tenn, Joe. "The Copernican Revolution." http://www.phys-astro.sonoma.edu/people/faculty/tenn/CopernicanRevolution.html.

Tibetan Book of the Dead. New York: Oxford University Press, 1960.

Tolkien, J. R. R. *The Lord of the Rings*. 3 vols. 2nd ed. Boston: Houghton Mifflin, 1965.

Toynbee, Arnold. *Civilization on Trial*. New York: Oxford University Press, 1948.

———. *Mankind and Mother Earth*. New York: Oxford University Press, 1976.

———. *A Study of History*. Reprint ed. New York: Oxford University Press, 1987.

"Trilateral Commission: World Shadow Government." http://www.afgen.com/trilateral.html.

Turco, R. P., A. B. Toon, T. P. Ackerman, J. B. Pollack, and C. Sagan. "Nuclear Winter: Global Consequences of Multiple Nuclear Explosions." *Science* 222 (1983): 1283–97.

Tyson, Peter. "When Compasses Point South." http://www.pbs.org/wgbh/nova/magnetic/timeline.html.

The Upanishads: Breath of the Eternal. Trans. Prabhavananda, Swami, and Frederick Manchester. New York: Mentor, 1957.

U.S. Census Bureau. "World POPClock Projection." http://www.census.gov/cgi-bin/ipc/popclockw.

Velikovsky, Immanuel. *Earth in Upheaval.* Garden City, NY: Doubleday, 1955.

Visiting Hopi. Second Mesa, AZ: Hopi Cultural Center, 2004.

Walnut Canyon. U.S. Department of the Interior: National Park Service, 2003.

Waters, Frank. *Book of the Hopi.* New York: Penguin, 1963.

Whitcomb, John C., and Henry Madison Morris. *The Genesis Flood: The Biblical Record and Its Scientific Implications.* Nashua, NH: P&R Press, 1989.

Willis, Jim. *The Religion Book: Places, Prophets, Saints, and Seers.* Detroit: Visible Ink Press, 2004.

Wilson, Colin, and Damon Wilson. *The Mammoth Encyclopedia of the Unsolved.* New York: Carroll and Graf, 2000.

Wink, Walter. *Engaging the Powers.* Minneapolis: Fortress Press, 1992.

———. *Naming the Powers.* Philadelphia: Fortress Press, 1984.

———. *The Powers That Be: Theology for a New Millennium.* New York: Doubleday, 1999.

———. *Unmasking the Powers.* Philadelphia: Fortress Press, 1986.

Zygmunt, Joseph F. "Prophetic Failure and Chiliastic Identity: The Case of Jehovah's Witnesses." *American Journal of Sociology* 75:6 (May 1970): 926–48.

———. "When Prophecies Fail: A Theoretical Perspective on the Comparative Evidence." *American Behavioral Scientist* 16:2 (November–December 1972): 245–67.

INDEX

Boldface refers to page numbers on which main entries appear.